THEORETICAL SOCIOLOGY

THEORETICAL SOCIOLOGY

• RANDALL COLLINS •

University of California, Riverside

HARCOURT BRACE JOVANOVICH, PUBLISHERS

San Diego   New York   Chicago   Austin   Washington, D.C.
London   Sydney   Tokyo   Toronto

PREFACE

This is a book with an immodest ambition. It is an attempt to set forth the core of what we know about how to explain the social world. It is theoretical knowledge, not description; it does not tell how many people at various times and places have acted and thought in particular ways and what social structures they have formed; it does tell us why these kinds of things in general happen as they do. The theories may not all be correct, and none is as strongly validated by empirical evidence as one might wish. But sociologists have been at the business of theory and research for more than a century now, and we have learned some significant things over that time. I have attempted to assess the state of our sociological knowledge: in addition to presenting theoretical models, to judge how likely these theories are to be true, where their weaknesses lie, and in what directions they need to be developed. Inevitably, there are many theoretical points that have been left out. My only hope is that I have captured many of the most important theoretical principles that we have so far developed.

Thanks are owed to many scholars who have provided me with inspiration, information, stimulation, and concrete help over the past twenty-five years. These include my teachers, Talcott Parsons, Winston White, Reinhard Bendix, Erving Goffman, Harold Wilensky, Joseph Ben-David, Kingsley Davis, and Herbert Blumer; colleagues, such as Arthur Stinchcombe, Jonathan Turner, Robert Hanneman, Norbert Wiley, Samuel Kaplan, Stanford Lyman, Harold Garfinkel, Emanuel Schegloff, Aaron Cicourel, Jeffrey Alexander, Albert Bergesen, Robert Hamblin, Marshall Meyer, Carol Warren, Rae Lesser Blumberg, Edward Laumann, Mark Granovetter, David Heise, Richard Hilbert, Ronald Burt, Barry Markovsky, Theodore Kemper, Alan Sica, and P. K. Saha; and reviewers, Richard Appelbaum, University of California, Santa Barbara; Fred Block, University of Pennsylvania; Karen S. Cook, University of Washington; Neil Fligstein, University of Arizona; Richard Madsen, University of California, San Diego; David McCaffery, State University of New York, Albany; Michael Powell, University of North Carolina, Chapel Hill; Ino Rossi, St. John's University; Paul Sites, Kent State University; and Walter L. Wallace, Princeton University. The cultural capital accumulated here was obviously produced as a collective enterprise.

Randall Collins

CONTENTS

Preface   v

Introduction   1

PART I

MACRO THEORIES   9

Chapter 1

EVOLUTIONISM   11

The Variety of Evolutionary Theories   12
Stage Theories   14
Organic Differentiation Theories   22
Natural Selection Theories   29
Idealist Evolution   36
Conclusion: The Dream of Progress   38
Summary   41

Chapter 2

SYSTEM THEORIES   45

General Systems Theory   47
Functionalism   54
Talcott Parsons' Functionalist Action System   57
Jeffrey Alexander's Defense of Multidimensional Action Theory   72
The Analytical and the Concrete   74
Summary   75

Chapter 3

POLITICAL ECONOMY   77

The Basic Marxian Model   79
Criticisms and Revisions of the Marxian System   91

The World System   93
Marxism as Philosophy   101
Marxian Theories of the State   107
Summary   114

Chapter 4

CONFLICT AND SOCIAL CHANGE   117

General Principles of Conflict   119
Conflict Theory of Social Change   130

Chapter 5

MULTIDIMENSIONAL CONFLICT THEORY AND STRATIFICATION   149

Explaining Inequality: Lenski's and Turner's Theories   153
Sex and Gender Stratification   163
Educational Credential Stratification   174

PART II

MICRO THEORIES   185

Chapter 6

INTERACTION RITUAL   187

Durkheimian Theory of Moral Solidarity   188
Goffman and Interaction Ritual   203
Ritual Theory of Class Cultures   208
Conclusion   226
Summary   227

Chapter 7

SELF, MIND, AND SOCIAL ROLE   229

The Social Self   230
The "Me" Side: Role Theory   234
Expectation States Theory   239
The Sociology of Thinking: Mead and Peirce   243
Self as a Sacred Object   250
Multiple or Unitary Self?   255
Summary   259

Chapter 8

DEFINITION OF THE SITUATION AND THE SOCIAL CONSTRUCTION OF REALITY   263

Definition of the Situation   265
Ethnomethodology   273

Implications of Ethnomethodology   286
Goffman's Frame Analysis as a Reconciliation of Relativism and Objectivity   291
Conclusion: Idealism and Relativism in the Current Intellectual World   297
Summary   298

Chapter 9

STRUCTURALISM AND SOCIOLINGUISTICS   301

French Structuralism: The Language-Model of Reality   302
Chomsky's Generative Grammar   311
Goffman's Social Ecology of Language   320
Toward a General Theory of Language   330
Summary   335

Chapter 10

SOCIAL EXCHANGE AND RELATED THEORIES   337

Homans: Basic Principles of Exchange Theory   339
Exchange Theory and Power: Blau and Emerson   343
From Social Behaviorism to Rational Choice   350
Interaction Ritual Chains   357
Heise's Affect Control Chains   366
Summary   370

PART III

MESO THEORIES   373

Chapter 11

THE MICRO-MACRO CONNECTION   375

History of the Micro-Macro Question   376
The Nature of Micro and Macro   385
Reductionism   389
Theories of Micro-Macro Linkages   398
Conclusion   407
Summary   408

Chapter 12

NETWORK THEORIES   411

Network Analysis   412
Network Effects on Individual Action and Belief   416
Network Theories of Social Ties   418
Network Theories and Economics   429
Network Theories of Power   435
Summary   447

Chapter 13

ORGANIZATIONS 449

Organizations in Sociological Theory   450
Control Theory   451
Motivation, Class Conflict, Organizational Culture, and Decision Making   464
Organizational Structure   467
Organizations and Environments   480
Summary   489

Appendix

THEORY AND METHODOLOGY 493

Introduction   494
A. What Is Statistics: Method or Theory?   496
B. Developing Sociological Theory by Computer Simulation   511

References   519

Index   545

INTRODUCTION

The focus of this book is knowledge. I will review what sociological theory claims to know in the late twentieth century—100 years into the development of the discipline. I have chosen not to stress the distinctness of our various schools of thought, but to bring them into dialogue, to show what they have to contribute on the major questions of the field. Hence this textbook is organized by areas of knowledge rather than by intellectual personalities or schools of thought. Inevitably, some theorists and schools of thought have concentrated on particular topics, and hence they will be located in few places in the book; others were interested in a number of different issues and they will turn up in many places.

I hope sociological theory can be turned toward this knowledge-oriented way of looking at the field. Our current habit of dividing up the territory—by schools, each supporting a different theory, and by hero-figures of the past, whose ideas and lives are excavated in growing detail—threatens to institutionalize this fragmentation of knowledge into a permanent condition. This style of scholarship looks backward; it implies that everything of importance has already been done, and all we can do is study its separate lines of development. This approach also deepens the split between the sociologists engaged in research in substantive fields and those concerned with theory, as if each group has nothing to do with the other. But if we can see that both theory and research have a concern with knowledge in various topic areas, it becomes easier to bring them together. The dividing lines among parts of sociology then run right through both the theoretical and the empirical sides.

It is not my intention to ignore the classic sociologists. On the contrary, I think we make best use of them if we treat them as our intellectual contemporaries and see what they still have to say to us. That means bringing them into the theoretical dialogue on various issues, rather than treating their intellectual personalities as the subject of our attention. Moreover, I would argue that this is consistent with the spirit of the classic theorists themselves. Weber, Durkheim, and Mead in their day were not especially concerned with their predecessors, but with substantive issues of theory building. They did not try to create a particular school of thought, but worked on the solution to topics that they thought were crucial, making use of whatever intellectual and empirical tools they found useful for the job. This is true, too, of theorists of more recent generations, whom we are now enshrining in our textbooks: Parsons, Homans, Garfinkel, Goffman, and others. Some of them, it is true, did a good deal of commentary on their predecessors (especially Talcott Parsons' treatment of Weber, Durkheim, Pareto and other predecessors in his 1937 classic *The Structure of Social Action*). But even then, the classic theorists were constructors, building upon past theories with an eye toward the knowledge that could be advanced. It is that kind of spirit that we need to recapture from our predecessors.

ORGANIZATION OF THE BOOK

Having decided that this text would be knowledge-oriented, I was then faced with the question: what topics should it include? How is the terrain to be divided?

As the table of contents shows, the major divisions I decided on are the macro and micro levels of analysis, with a third section focused on the meso level in between them. Inevitably there are some rough edges. Any classification is a matter of convenience, and no set of categories is likely to catch most of the important lines of difference in a complex world. But as a practical matter, we cannot think about everything at once, and chapter divisions are necessary in order to have some coherence to the material. The only criteria are whether the chapters group topics that are usefully treated together; and whether they are put in a sequence that makes it easiest for us to understand what has come so far without having to rely on what will come later.

Yet macro and micro levels are implied in each other, and it is a tricky task even to set forth the issues of how this is so. There have been vigorous arguments as to which is more fundamental, and how one might be constructed from the other. But, although such issues are "basic," in an abstract sense, they are not the topics which are easiest to understand. Hence I have put them near the end of the book, since an appreciation of them depends on knowing a good deal about other aspects of the field beforehand.

MACRO THEORIES

For the same kind of reason, I have chosen to lead off with macro theory, and, within that section, to move from the largest-scale theories toward more sharply focused ones. Macro topics are those concerned with long sweeps of time and space and with large numbers of persons. I begin with evolutionary theories, not because I am convinced that this is a crucial explanation, but because it introduces us to the most macro-level phenomena: the way societies change over extremely long periods of time, and the extent to which these patterns of change have something in common with the rest of life during the history of our planet. System theory, which comes next, is very general in a different way: it concerns the most abstract models of social (or for that matter, any kind of) organization, anything that has parts with relationships among them. Again, we may find that not everything which theorists have done here is a useful contribution to knowledge; here we encounter debates over functionalism, and over Parsons' analytical system, for example. But we also learn that systems in general do not have to be in equilibrium, nor do they need closed boundaries or self-maintaining characteristics; and the concept of systems as generative structures gives us a means to see our way through controversies that will be treated later in the book.

From here on, the macro chapters become more specific. Political economy is the Marxian tradition. Its classic version can be seen as a type of system theory, which gives a central role to the economy in the dynamics of change. We also examine the various kinds of revisions in Marxism, which have deemphasized some elements of the original model and built up other parts of the system. The next two chapters take macro processes apart into smaller pieces, following the strategy of conflict theory to see the world as fragmented into various interests, pulling and hauling against one another across multiple dimensions. Here we consider theories of conflict itself, and conflict-driven theories of political change, both within states and among them. The "conflict theory" side of society, I would suggest, has come a long way since its debates against functionalism 20 to 30 years ago. There is no longer much self-conscious argument about the merits of approaches, and researchers have split up to build theories across a broad front: theories of resource mobilization; of revolution; of the distribution of wealth, power, and other inequalities; of sex and gender stratification; of educational credentialism and modern status systems.

This macro section of the book proceeds from more general issues toward more specific ones, and from grander sweeps of space and time toward partial and fragmentary phenomena within societies. From the point of view of a fundamental theory of society, it may be the case that much of this macro analysis implies micro processes, and may even be reducible to the micro level. But as a practical matter, it has not been necessary to refer to most of these micro issues while we were becoming acquainted with the patterns that exist on the macro level.

THE LOOSE BOUNDARIES OF MICRO THEORY

When we arrive at the section on micro theories, even the practical situation of exposition becomes less simple. We can of course go ahead and deal with various issues in micro theory as they come along. But microsociology overflows its boundaries into macrosociology, much more than vice versa. Micro theory is less autonomous, as a purely practical matter in the doing of sociology. I don't mean that micro theories cannot be pursued as specialities in their own right, since they obviously are. But micro theory finds it less easy to ignore macro theory than vice versa. The very dispute between micro and macro theory, the issue of which is more fundamental and whether one can be reduced to the other, was set off by micro theorists, and it has generally been microsociologists who have been most interested in pursuing this debate. Micro theory seems to feel it is implicated in macro theory, but that the relationship is formulated in an unsatisfactory manner.

Why should this be so? As a crude approximation, we can define microsociology as dealing with relatively small slices of space, time, and numbers of persons: with the individual and the interaction, with behavior and consciousness. But this micro unit has unclear bounds. The very meaning of "social" is that the individual exists in a context of other people: and these other people have a context of still other people, stretching further out into the reaches of the larger society, and further back into a past of interactions which have happened before. Hence, when we examine an individual, or situation, or thought process, in however micro detail, we tend to encounter elements which lead outward toward the wider society. Some theories formulate this as "normative" constraints on interaction, or rules by which they are constituted; but even theories which try to focus on the hardheaded manuevering for self-interest usually end up being concerned with macro outcomes in the form of exchange links and power relationships. Micro theories, even when they are militantly opposed to macro theories, and even when they doubt the reality of macro phenomena, seem to be drawn toward their own borders in a way that macro theories are not. This is one reason why it is easier to treat micro theories after the macro theories have been described first.

There is another, more serious way in which the topics of the micro section overflow their bounds. The micro implies the small scale, the individual. But examining the individual human being brings us face to face with the phenomenon of consciousness—the realm of the mental, and hence the cultural. But if we take this seriously, we find ourselves in a realm which is not individual at all—language, symbolism, the very media of our thoughts. Hence there is a version of microsociology which leads right back into an extreme version of macrosociology. In positions like French structuralism (and implicit to some extent in social phenomenology and ethnomethodology), there is a strong argument that individuals are not at all ultimate, that we are only the transmitters of a set of cultural elements that exist over and above us.

This leaves the organization of the book in a dilemma. Should we then transfer French structuralism, sociolinguistics, and other theories back into the macro side, whenever they have this kind of implication of processes existing beyond the individual? Once we start on this track, though, there is hardly a place to stop, and virtually the whole section would end up being transferred. Furthermore, once we had moved all this material back into the macro section, it would be necessary to fit it into some useful sequence of presentation, and that means deciding what is distinctive about it as compared to the macro theories which we have already dealt with. We could adopt Wallace's (1983) solution, in which all social phenomena are divided into physical or mental, and each of these in turn is split between micro and macro levels. But this kind of symmetry is artificial. For the most part, we would like to be able to examine the physical side of social interaction—the assembly of human bodies across a real landscape in relation to real material goods and interests—to see how this connects with mental processes and see how they affect each other, or run in parallel or in opposition.

Despite the fact that positions like French structuralism are anti-individual and hence sound "macro," I think there is a good reason to treat them in relation to other micro theories. That is: most of the macro theories are either materialist or multidimensional, including both mental and physical dimensions. The world of microtheories, on the other hand, has tended to be much more polemical on this point: though some (rather few) have a materialist emphasis, most micro theories give a central place to human consciousness. Thus, even though language and culture generally transcend the individual, there is something crucial about human consciousness even here, since it is the *location* in which language manifests itself. There is a "family resemblance," in Wittgenstein's famous words, between symbolic interactionism, ethnomethodology, frame analysis, sociolinguistics, and French structuralism, even though there is a strong antagonism between the most extreme points within this spectrum on some issues, especially the issue of the individual and situational versus the transcendent elements. This "family resemblance" is not there if we put structuralism (or any of these other positions) into the group of macro theories.

The theories of Part I are explicitly concerned with the kinds of variations which occur across historical time and space: why there are certain kinds of stratification systems in some societies but not in others, when and how revolutions take place, what are the mechanisms of long-term stability and change. Structuralism, sociolinguistics, and other culture-oriented positions do not operate on that level of analysis. Even when they posit structures or cultures existing over and above the individual, they do not produce theories of what causes variations or changes in these structures, but focus instead on the general characteristics of consciousness, language, and culture, in a way that ties them closely to the concerns of other microsociologies. We might say they are involved in the microsociological debates, even when their arguments take an anti-individual stance.

Another way of putting it is that most of the theoretical positions in Part II are on the "idealist" side, in the sense of being connected to positions in philosophy related to Kant, Hegel, and their descendents (including Dilthey, Husserl, and others). The paradox of idealism is that it starts out from being extremely empirical. It focuses on the individual mind and asks what the world really *is* as seen from the point of view of one's self. One's own consciousness is more immediate and real than physical objects, which one is merely perceiving or inferring; this is the classic idealist strategy for undermining belief in the primacy of the material world. But if we push the idealist analysis further, a second paradox emerges: if we examine the self, then the individual disappears too. The self does not appear as a "thing": it too is a construct, something which we infer, separate out, while the more primary reality appears to be a flux of ideas in which we happen to exist. Thus idealism in philosophy has often gone beyond the individual and become Platonic or "transcendental."

The same thing can happen in the realm of sociology. Microsociologies often stake their claim to primacy upon the fact that everything else we want to study is experienced first and foremost through one's self. This is the line, for example, of symbolic interactionism. But if we push on the nature of the self, the second shift takes place: instead of a solid "thing," we find language, ideas, perhaps norms. The individual becomes a repository of culture. This is what makes micro analysis such a fruitful site for theoretical controversies. It is as if we go down through a narrow tube into the details of micro analysis, until, like Alice in Wonderland, we come out the other side into the realm of macro subjectivity. But we have gotten there via a different route than the more conventional kind of macro theories, which started out with large patterns across time and space. I think that is the best justification for treating structuralism and similar positions within the context of other micro theories.

As we will see, micro theories are not all idealist, nor do they all lead equally strongly into a macrocultural realm. Some attempt to pick out exactly what is the local, situational, micro mechanism in society. These positions are compatible with the view that there is a macro structure; but there are principles in their own right of how phenomena take place within this local, small-scale compass, which it is the business of micro theory to discover. Part II is organized, roughly, around different topics or mechanisms within the local, micro realm. We begin with interaction ritual theory. This position does not have a very prominent identity in the way sociologists have traditionally divided up their schools of thought; but it is an important theoretical lineage, going back to Durkheim's classic analysis of how religious rituals hold society together. It explains how both symbols and moral sentiments of group membership are created, and it gives a mechanism by which various conditions of interaction create various degrees and intensities of connection between individuals and groups. This model has been extended by Goffman to include a wide range of implicit or "natural rituals" in everyday life and by various researchers and theorists, including myself, as a basis for the micro foundations of stratification.

Next we take up the topic of the self, as analyzed by various theories: Mead's analysis of the internal component of the self, including his important theory of the mind as social role-taking and internalized conversation; theories which derive the self from the surrounding structure of social roles; as well as multilevel theories (such as Goffman's) which question the reality of the self except as a series of transient situational selves. The following topic moves away from the individual and out into the interaction itself: here we encounter the line of thought which makes up "symbolic interactionism," with its stress of the fluid and self-defining nature of situations, and the development of a more formal model in expectation states theory. A more radical version of this emphasis on social construction of reality is ethnomethodology. I will suggest, in that same chapter, that Goffman's frame analysis is a way of mediating between the extremes of straightforward realism and the more reflexively relativistic schemes.

Following this, we deal with theories which take language as its central phenomenon: French structuralism, with its claim that society itself is a kind of language and that linguistic theory is the code for unlocking everything else. Taking up this claim, we examine various theories of language, ending up with the distinctive contribution that sociologists have been making to this realm. Part of the implications of this work, we will see, is that any future success in creating a computer artificial intelligence that is genuinely similar to human thinking will have to build upon sociological models.

Finally, we deal with exchange theories and their intellectual relatives. Here we are rather explicitly dealing with the border between micro and macro phenomena; since exchanges lead into chains connecting individuals with others, exchange theorists have often been concerned with the nature of these patterns. I discuss the various slants here, both those which push in the direction of social behaviorism, of rational choice, and also of emotional/symbolic exchanges. These issues link together some of the models from other parts of microsociology.

MESO THEORIES: BETWEEN MICRO AND MACRO

Part III, "Meso Theories," raises the question of the relationship between micro and macro as an issue in its own right. The first chapter here reviews the micro/macro controversy and theories which have been proposed to link the two levels. The next two chapters introduce topics which have not conventionally been treated in sociological theory, but which have a strategic importance in the field today: networks and organizations. Network analysis began as a research specialty with a merely descriptive focus. But it has grown in theoretical importance, both as it has developed a theoretical apparatus of its own, and as it has gotten involved in controversies with older theoretical schools. Exchange theory in particular leads directly into a network model at the larger level of analysis; network theories, though, challenge the open-market models which exchange theories have often assumed. On the macro level, network theories have begun to provide a sociological alternative to economics itself. Network theory has connections both "downward" to micro theories (especially ones that emphasize situation and structure rather than individual characteristics) and "upward" to macro issues of political economy, stratification, and politics.

Another area of meso theory which occupies a strategic place in sociology today is organizations. Theory here developed to a large extent indigenously, as several generations of researchers have accumulated findings and converged on explanatory models of how individuals behave in organizations, as well as the factors which determine organizational structure. Since so much of social life takes place in organizations, a good theory in this area potentially has very wide applications. Much of what we study in sociology under other labels is also an organizational phenomenon. Here again I attempt to show how organizational analysis meshes with micro theories that we have met earlier in the book and how organizations are concrete examples of solving the micro/macro problem. Much of the larger macro structure of society consists of relationships among organizations, which we can analyze using the models of organization theory itself.

The Appendix, finally, attempts to mend some other fences in sociology. It tries to bring out into the open the dispute that goes on between theory and methods, between general verbal formulations versus statistical and mathematical techniques. The issues are deep-grained in our field by now, but by distinguishing between mathematics as a device for modeling and statistics as a research method, we can see some ways that there are important theoretical elements on all sides. Mathematical sociology is fundamentally a type of theorizing; statistical methods, although connected basically with empirical research, have their theoretical implications as well. I also suggest that mathematics is embedded in words and that verbal theory will always be with us, as the most basic frame of our science. There is also an introduction to computer simulation as a new device for working with theory.

THE MAIN THRUST

Throughout this book, my main concern is to look forward. I bring in the intellectual strategies and the grand thinkers of the past because of what they have contributed to our development of knowledge today. For the same reason, I have organized the textbook around substantive topics, so that we can see what knowledge we have acquired about them, or at least what considerations there are between competing positions on them. Our knowledge is certainly not complete, but I do think we know some patterns with a reasonable degree of confidence that our theories are on the right track. I would like this book to be an encouragement to everyone, practitioners of sociology and students as well, to think about what we have accomplished, what remains to be done, and how it can be achieved.

Sociology has been created by a community of theorists and researchers, stretching by now across more than a century. For all its conflicts and divisions (and often because of them) it has been a creative community. We are a part of that community right now. Theory is our collective memory, the brain center in which we store the basic elements of what we have learned and the strategies we have available to carry us into the future.

PART I

MACRO THEORIES

Chapter 1

EVOLUTIONISM

THE VARIETY OF EVOLUTIONARY THEORIES
  Progress
  Stages
  Two Biological Analogies
  Idealist Evolution

STAGE THEORIES
  Similarity of Stages
  Number of Stages
  Does Every Society Go Through Every Stage?
  Alternative Stages
  Single-factor vs. Multi-factor Patterns
  How Much Explanatory Power Do Stage Theories Have?
  Are There Any Modern Applications of Stage Theories?

ORGANIC DIFFERENTIATION THEORIES
  Differentiation and Specialization
  Functional Upgrading
  The Need for Integration
  Strains and Lags
  Criticisms

NATURAL SELECTION THEORIES
  Natural Selection as an Umbrella for Causal Theories
  Sociobiology: Evolution at the Level of the Gene
  The Challenge of the Punctuated Equilibrium Model in Biology
  Is Natural Selection Directional?

IDEALIST EVOLUTION

CONCLUSION: THE DREAM OF PROGRESS

SUMMARY

Evolutionism is the oldest part of sociology. It dominated the first century or more of sociological thinking. Auguste Comte, writing in the 1830s and 1840s, coined the term *sociology*, and the laws he proposed for his new science of society were laws of the succession of historical stages—laws of evolution. Throughout the late nineteenth century, evolutionism was in the ascendent in sociology; Spencer and Maine in England, Sumner and Ward in the United States, Lillienfeld in Germany, and Novikov and Kropotkin in Russia were among its leading figures. Evolutionism also touched Durkheim in France and Toennies in Germany in some respects, although we shall see that both of them criticized certain assumptions of the evolutionary tradition. In the first half of the twentieth century, however, the tide began to turn against evolutionism in sociology. Other points of view were put forward, and strong opponents of evolutionism appeared, such as Weber, Simmel, and Pareto. By 1937 Talcott Parsons could begin his major work, *The Structure of Social Action,* by quoting a historian who declared:

> Who now reads Spencer? It is difficult for us to realize how great a stir he made
> in the world. . . . He was the intimate confidant of a strange and rather unsat-
> isfactory God, whom he called the principle of Evolution. His God has betrayed
> him. We have evolved beyond Spencer. (Parsons, 1937: 3)

Yet in the last two decades, there has been a revival of evolutionary thinking. Parsons himself, 30 years after his put-down of Spencer, produced an evolutionary model of world history (Parsons, 1966). And in recent German sociology, theorists have made efforts to turn Weber's work into an evolutionary scheme. Other evolutionary models have come from importing biology and genetics into sociology under the title of *sociobiology,* while in more circumscribed areas, models of biological evolution have been applied by sociologists to such topics as the population of ecology organizations.

THE VARIETY OF EVOLUTIONARY THEORIES

There are a number of different forms of evolutionary theories in sociology. It is important to distinguish among them, because what may be valid in one particular type of theory may not be valid in another and vice versa. Some of the following features overlap among theories; that is, they characterize models put forward by more than one theorist.

PROGRESS

Most evolutionary theorists believe that societies undergo progress or improvement over long periods of time. This was perhaps the basic tenet of nineteenth century evolutionists, as well as their eighteenth century predecessors, the French *philosophes*. Taken as a blanket pronouncement, however, this is one of the more dubious of evolutionary beliefs, as we shall see in examining the evidence below. We should also bear in mind that it is possible for theories to be evolutionary without affirming a belief in progress; that is, they may describe evolutionary mechanisms or stages without attaching value judgments to them. Some evolutionary theories also allow for the possibility of degeneration.

STAGES

Many evolutionary theories (and most of the earlier ones) represent change as a series of stages through which societies pass. Questions arise, however, as to whether societies can skip stages, and whether there may not be alternative routes to change. An evolutionary theory need not be a stage theory, however, since it may suggest evolutionary mechanisms without implying that the product moves through a series of stages. As we shall see, biological evolution itself is best characterized as a non-stage theory.

TWO BIOLOGICAL ANALOGIES

ORGANIC DIFFERENTIATION   Many evolutionary theories see the principles of social evolution as analogous to the principles operating in biology. But there are two different analogies that may be pursued. One takes embryology as the model and represents society as growing like an organism, becoming not only larger but differentiating into specialized organs and functions. Such theories see society as a harmonious, functional unit (and hence overlapping with functional/systems theories, treated in Chapter 2). The main characteristic of change is thus an increase in the division of labor, and a subsequent integration of society's parts.

NATURAL SELECTION   A second biological analogy is to the Darwinian theory of how species evolve through the variation and natural selection of those forms best adapted to their environments. There are several differences between this model and the organic differentiation model. Differentiation sees societies as analogous to single organisms, growing during their own lifetime; natural selection sees societies as analogous to the variety of species (populations of organisms), some of which are selected as favorable adaptations, and some of which are not. Moreover, there are different mechanisms of change in the two analogies: differentiation models may assume that change is purely natural, like "growth," or they may cite various pressures towards increasing the division of labor; whereas the natural selection model focuses on a mechanism of change itself. Differentiation models are almost inevitably stage theories (as well as progress theories); natural selection models are not necessarily either. There is a wide variety of natural selection models, including sociobiology, technological evolution, and population ecology of organizations.

IDEALIST EVOLUTION

Finally, it should be recognized that not all evolutionary theories are necessarily based on biological analogies. There is a tradition going back to the philosophy of Hegel which emphasizes progressive historical change, but which sees the prime mover in the realm of ideal rather than material factors. Such theories are usually hostile to any reduction of humanity's rational and mental characteristics to principles of biology. Recent Idealist evolutionisms have been put forward by German sociologists, Habermas, Schluchter, and Tenbruck, for example.

STAGE THEORIES

Figure 1-1 indicates the evolutionary stages proposed by a number of different theorists. The comparison immediately raises questions. Since the theories give different numbers of stages and different names to them, can they all be valid? If not, how does one decide among them?

SIMILARITY OF STAGES

Quite a few of the theories distinguish only two stages; others discern three, five, or describe even messier structures with side branches. Are the more elaborate models merely extensions of the simpler ones? To some extent this may be so. Maine, Toennies, Durkheim, and Linton all suggest two categories, which may be regarded as polar ends of a continuum. The concepts around which they are built, however, are different. Maine (1861/1963) based his generalization (the shift from *status* to *contract*) on the history of law; Linton (1936) based his on a contrast between tribal societies in which behavior is "ascribed" according to kinship position, and modern societies in which positions are "achieved." Toennies (1887/1963), drawing upon a German philosophical tradition, described the traditional rural community *(Gemeinschaft)* as reflecting an emotional, particularizing kind of human will *(Wesenwille)*, whereas modern, impersonal society *(Gesellschaft)* is based on a human will which reduces everything to abstract calculations *(Kürwille)*. Durkheim (1893/1964) is more structural; his *mechanical solidarity* refers to the intense moral bonds generated by a small, homogeneous group, whereas *organic solidarity* refers to a more abstract and universalistic kind of morality generated in a large society with a complex division of labor.

There are family resemblances among these dichotomies. *Status, custom,* and *ascription* all emphasize the treatment of individuals according to their traditional positions; while *Gemeinschaft* stresses that type of society's emotional tone, and Durkheim's *mechanical solidarity* points to its structural basis. Similarly, *contract, law, achievement,* and *Gesellschaft* depict an ideal type of impersonal, rule-bound society, while Durkheim's *organic solidarity* again emphasizes the structural form of the group. We should note, though, that there are explanatory differences among the theories. Maine and Linton are essentially descriptive and lack an explanatory mechanism for change. And while Durkheim saw organic solidarity as produced by competitive pressures brought about by sheer growth in size, which in turn increased the division of labor, Toennies saw the shift to *Gesellschaft* as caused by capitalism. Thus, for Toennies—unlike most other theorists—the shift to the modern type is *not* considered to be progress but a loss of the personal relationships found in *Gemeinschaft* as a result of the pressures of an exploitative and impersonal economic system.

FIGURE 1-1

EVOLUTIONARY STAGE THEORIES

COMTE	MAINE	BAGEHOT	TOENNIES	DURKHEIM	LINTON
Military	Status	Custom	Gemeinschaft (community)	Mechanical Solidarity	Ascription
Legalistic					
Industrial	Contract	Law	Gesellschaft (society)	Organic Solidarity	Achievement

MARX AND ENGELS	SPENCER	PARSONS	LENSKI
Primitive Communism	Simple: Headless (no chief)	Primitive	Hunting and Gathering → Fishing
	Headed (permanent chief)	Advanced Primitive	Simple Horticulture → Herding
Ancient (slave-owning) / Oriental Despotism	Compound (hierarchy of chiefs)	Archaic (Egypt, Mesopotamia)	Advanced Horticulture
Feudal	Doubly Compound (political state)	Historical Intermediate (China, India, Rome, Islamic Empires) Seed-bed Societies (Israel, Greece)	Agrarian → Maritime
Capitalist	Triply Compound (modern)	Modern	Industrial
Socialist-Communist			

NUMBER OF STAGES

What about the more complex forms? A mere two categories, such as the pairs given above, are unlikely to capture all of world history. Comte's (1830–42/1898) three stages *(Military, Legalistic, Industrial)* are not much improvement, since they amount to little more than a contemporary political argument of the 1830s, which claimed that the new industrial society of the nineteenth century was superior to the absolutist states of the Old Regime (the *Legalistic* stage), just as those states were superior to the warring medieval states which preceded them (the *Military* stage). Spencer's (1874–96) five-level scheme is much more generalized, reaching back to the simplest tribal societies from which all others have historically evolved. Spencer's scheme is also more formally derived from theoretical principles, since it envisions societies as moving from the simple to the complex through a series of differentiations of their parts (Thus, Spencer's scheme is not only a stage model but also a differentiation model.) Durkheim's structural dichotomy—small undifferentiated groups vs. large-scale divisions of labor—is in a sense an abstract summary of the end points of Spencer's continuum. As Turner (1985a) has argued, Spencer's model of evolutionary structure is without doubt the most formally complete of all the abstract stage models—at least, those produced by the classic theorists. This, however, does not mean Spencer's model is an accurate one.

DOES EVERY SOCIETY GO THROUGH EVERY STAGE?

Does world history consist merely of societies becoming larger and more complex and developing a more elaborate political hierarchy? All of these models imply a unilineal development, in which all societies go through the same stages in the same order—at least, that is all evolutionary theory is capable of dealing with. For while a particular theorist may recognize that not all societies go through the same sequences, evolutionary theory has no way to deal with that except by putting it aside as a kind of accident. The fact that tribes whose territory is taken over by a colonial state move directly into an industrial society is not accounted for by stage theories, nor do instances such as the replacement of the urban civilization of the Roman Empire by the tribal war coalitions of the barbarian Germans fit very well.

Stage theories thus lack predictive power. They cannot claim that every society goes through a predictable series of stages, but only that *world history in general shows the successive appearance of certain types of societies, in a given order*. They observe that more complex forms come later than simpler ones, although not every simpler form is immediately followed by a more complex one.

ALTERNATIVE STAGES

Some theories attempt to be more definitive about what actually happens at various points in history. For example, I have included Marx and Engels' stages in Figure 1-1; although their model is rather different from most evolutionary theories, it has a formal similarity as a stage model, and in some respects is parallel to models such as Spencer's. Marx and Engels' *Primitive Communism* refers to tribal societies of the sort that Spencer called *Simple* (lacking in permanent authority structures).

With the crude condition of anthropological knowledge in their day, Marx and Engels had little information about the variety of tribal societies, and provide little insight into the fact that such tribes can be highly complex and have their own histories. What is worth noticing here is that at the levels between this beginning-point and *Capitalism* Marx and Engels describe two stages, *Ancient slave-owning societies* (the Greek and Roman states of Mediterranean antiquity), and the *Feudal societies* of the European Middle Ages. By itself, the scheme is somewhat ethnocentric, since massive slave-based economies do not succeed tribal societies in the history of the Orient (Patterson, 1982); nor are feudal societies, in the European sense, found everywhere in the medieval world. Marx and Engels provide some recognition of these facts by introducing an alternative concept, *Oriental Despotism,* to refer to societies such as the Chinese empire, in which the state organized the economy through public works, such as irrigation systems. In fact, the concept of *Oriental Despotism* is not a completely accurate one, either; it is introduced here merely in order to show that stage theories may provide for alternate stages at the same "level." Nor should it be taken for granted that Marxism is necessarily wedded to an evolutionary stage model. As we shall see in Chapter 3, modern world-system theory replaces the Marxian stage model with a theory in which different types of societies are always *simultaneously* present, and determined by each other.

Another version of alternative stages is found in Parsons (1966). In general, his stages are equivalent to those of Spencer, but under different names. As we shall see, Parsons makes more provision for explicitly considering different types of societies at the same "stage" or "level." He also somewhat arbitrarily adds a stage of *Archaic* societies (ancient Egypt and Mesopotamia) to the *Historic Intermediate Empires* (China, India, Rome, and the Islamic world). This is a concession to history, in that the Egyptian and Mesopotamian empires were several thousand years earlier; but theoretically, it is not clear that the latter represent a distinctly different evolutionary "stage" from the former. Of greatest interest for our purposes is the fact that Parsons feels he has to step outside the linear sequence to introduce two "seed-bed societies"—ancient Israel and Greece. Structurally, these were quite different from the large-scale empires listed as contemporary with them. If one strictly followed a Spencer-type theory of evolutionary complexity advancing as a function of size and political centralization of the stage, then neither of these would qualify as advanced types at that point in history. But Parsons sees them as the basis for cultural (intellectual and religious) developments that later brought about the modern type of society. Greece produced the basis of modern science and philosophy, as well as modern political ideals; while Israel, together with the Hellenistic milieu, produced Christianity, which Parsons (along with Weber) saw as crucial in the distinctive history of the West. Hence, Parsons grants ancient Greece and Israel a special status as alternative evolutionary developments, off at the side of the "main line" of growth. This, however, is another admission that a stage model does not capture all the important things about history—even in an evolutionary scheme.

Lenski's stages (1966, 1974) are the most empirically defensible version of an evolutionary stage model. Lenski does not make any moral claims about the quality of interaction in various of these stages (unlike, say, Toennies or Linton), nor does he make the sequence depend upon the size and resulting structural differentiation of the society (as in Spencer, Durkheim, and Parsons). Instead, Lenski proposes a *sequence of technologies*. It is a sequence in the sense that the later technologies cannot develop until the earlier ones do. He also proposes that technologies have a major effect in determining the rest of the structure of society. Thus, hunting-and-gathering techniques dictate a small population size, and (because of little or no economic surplus) minimal stratification hierarchy; the digging-sticks and pottery of simple horticulture, on the other hand, result in a different economic productivity and a different social structure. Lenski's model is appealing because it explicitly allows for other causal factors to enter the determination of social structures along with the technological type. Also, it does not assume that members of society are necessarily "better off" with each technological change (for instance, inequality and oppression become worse with a shift towards agrarian technology).

Lenski's model, too, has to make provision for alternative stages. Both hunting-and-gathering and simple horticultural societies may coexist with a different type of society which makes its living by *fishing* technologies. And since it has a different technology and a different ecological situation, such a society could have a social structure quite different from its contemporaries. *Herding societies,* for example, branch off from and coexist with both horticultural and agrarian societies; as did the Mongols and other nomads, who lived outside the bounds of the ancient and medieval empires, and were capable of threatening them militarily. Also contemporary with agrarian societies have been *maritime societies* (such as ancient Phoenicia and Carthage, or medieval Venice), which again have provided an alternative social form. Lenski's conception of these alternatives is an advance over previous stage models, since it does not leave them as inexplicable accidents but systematically derives them from particular kinds of technologies emerging for specialized ecological situations. Lenski's model thus shows a useful shift away from a theory of stages per se towards a formulation of the general mechanisms which produce particular types.

SINGLE-FACTOR VS. MULTI-FACTOR PATTERNS

One major weakness of stage models is that they imply that all aspects of society change together. In most such theories, primitive societies are characterized as small and undifferentiated; they are seen as lacking any political structure, their people guided by custom and hereditary status (kinship position) rather than by formal laws or personal achievement, while their behavior is seen as deriving from emotional solidarity and religious beliefs rather than from scientific calculation and self-interest. At the opposite extreme, modern society is characterized as large, differentiated, impersonal, achievement-oriented, calculating, and all the rest. At first glance, this seems like a reasonable generalization, but in fact in many empirical instances it is incorrect. Anthropologists have found that small tribal societies vary a great deal and that some of them place much greater emphasis upon the ascription of kinship position than others. Very simple hunting-and-gathering tribes, for example, often have a shifting structure of personnel, with very little determined by kinship and a great deal by individual achievement in such matters as successful hunting or food gathering. Again, the mentality of tribal peoples is not simply one of complete subservience to ritual and custom. Malinowski (1948) pointed out that tribal people are capable of rational calculation in practical situations and tend to fall back on ritual only when there is an insurmountable difficulty. Mary Douglas (1973) shows that there are many other variations *within* tribal societies. Lévi-Strauss (1962/1966) has attempted to show that tribal mythologies, too, are not mere indications of irrationality and "primitive mentality," but are ways of categorizing the relationships between significant objects in the environment—in fact, a kind of science. (See Chapter 9.)

If small and simple societies have mixtures of traits which the stage theories have assigned to the "modern" end of the typology, the reverse is also true. Custom, emotional identification with a community, and religious beliefs do not disappear in our own societies. Emile Durkheim (1893/1964), although sharing many evolutionist conceptions, began to separate *what evolves* from *what remains constant* as societies change. He criticized Spencer, for example, as well as theorists such as Maine and Toennies, for assuming that modern society ends up in a totally impersonal form in which the sentiments, customs, and moral feelings that characterized smaller societies have been replaced by self-interested calculation. Durkheim devoted a great deal of theoretical and empirical analysis to showing that rationality itself cannot exist except on the basis of a nonrational foundation; that contracts always rest upon a precontractual solidarity, a moral obligation to fulfill the contract; and hence that some form of moral solidarity must always exist beneath the surface of modern society (see Chapter 2). No matter how scientific, rational, businesslike and calculating we become, something like the mechanisms which produce moral solidarity in small tribal communities must nevertheless continue to exist. Beneath the surface, modern society still shows many traits of traditional societies.

Durkheim is in fact quite correct on this. Whereas Comte once believed that in industrial society religions would be replaced by science, it is clear that religions continue to play an important role today, especially in modern politics. Spencer believed that customs and ceremonies would become unimportant and wither away, whereas Erving Goffman has shown how they continue to exist in new forms in modern everyday life (see Chapter 6 and 7). Toennies, along with many other critics of modern society, saw the community disappearing into a mass society of purely market relationships; instead, we find that small groups continue to exist and provide solidarity for their members, even in the most massive cities (Fischer 1982), and that social classes and status groups themselves make up little clusters of "tribes" inside the complex division of labor (see Chapter 6).

One reason why evolutionary theory began to lose its popularity after about 1900 was just this sort of recognition. Evolutionary stage models were too simple-minded to capture the complex dimensions that underlie any society. Multi-factor theory began to replace single-factor theory. Durkheim, though he remained in some ways an evolutionist, nevertheless gave impetus to the turn against evolutionism.[1]

---

[1] Durkheim (1912/1954) thought he could find the basis of religious ritual by examining the evolutionarily "most primitive" society, the Australian aborigines. But in fact the aborigines turn out to have unusually complicated kinship systems, and are not at all typical of most "early" hunting-and-gathering societies in other ways as well. Durkheim was misled by the fact that the aborigines have almost no possessions (houses, clothes, implements) into thinking they were extremely primitive; but their pared-down technology, as well as other rather complex *social* features of their lives, appear to be, rather, an adaptation to the extremely barren environment of the Australian desert (see Elkin 1979). What Durkheim really showed was a general mechanism of social ritual and solidarity which operates in societies at any level. It was this side of Durkheim's theory, rather than the evolutionism, that was developed by the British school of social anthropologists (Radcliffe-Brown, Lloyd Warner, Evans-Pritchard, Mary Douglas) and was brought into sociology by Parsons, Goffman, and others.

Using Durkheim's ideas (as well as others), Parsons proposed that the dimensions of the earlier evolutionary theories should be taken, not as stages, but as *analytical dimensions,* capable of varying independently with each other. Thus, for example, a society is not necessarily characterized by either *ascription* or *achievement,* but can have some amount of both of them. All societies have to carry out certain universal functions; hence, all of them—not just small tribal societies—must have some component of *latent pattern maintenance* (unquestioned ceremonial or cultural custom which maintains the basic beliefs) and of *integration* (sources of common moralities beneath the level of *instrumental* techniques for achieving practical ends). During this phase of his work, Parsons (1951) was critical of evolutionary models; it was what all societies had in common, if in different amounts, that counted.

HOW MUCH EXPLANATORY POWER DO STAGE MODELS HAVE?

Another weakness of stage models is that they do not give much insight into the workings of any particular type of society. Some of the evolutionary stages, as we have seen, are mere dichotomies. In effect, they just draw the distinction between "modern" and "premodern" societies, but lump everything together within those categories. Even more refined sets of stages do not tell us very much. Neither Spencer's *Simple Societies* nor Marx and Engels' *Primitive Communism* take account of the considerable variety of kinship systems, cultural forms, and other variations found among small tribal societies. And theories of "industrial" societies fail to tell us why communist and capitalist societies differ from each other—still less explain the many other differences among societies which exist today.

Similarly, those theories which add "intermediate" stages tend to be rather weak in explaining them. It soon becomes apparent that the intermediate stages are either overly abstract—mere intermediate points along a continuum—or else, little more than concrete historical instances dressed up as if they were generalizations. Spencer's intermediate forms are an illustration of the first problem. He abstractly proposes that societies gradually grow bigger, with more specialized institutions and more elaborate political hierarchies. Thus, empires and kingdoms like those of China, Rome, Persia, India, the Islamic world, Japan, and medieval Europe all fall into this category. But if one knows much about the actual history of these societies, the generalizations fall flat. China's extensive periods of highly centralized dynasties (which were nevertheless punctuated by periods of dissolution) contrast sharply with the political fragmentation of India. Rome's long phase of republican institutions is very different from the theocratic government of Islam and the feudalism of medieval Europe. Spencer's theory ultimately makes size and differentiation the criteria of an evolutionary stage. But it is clearly not size that distinguishes among stages, and the differentiation model is far too vague to tell us why these specific forms exist. Moreover, there are other theories (nonevolutionary ones) which propose that it was precisely these variations that were crucial for subsequent history: Weber (1916/1951, 1916–17/1958, 1917–19/1952, 1923/1961) attempted to show why capitalism emerged upon the basis of the Judeo-Christian societies of the West rather than the Oriental religions; Perry Anderson (1974) has proposed that the Roman Empire was the crucial background for the rise of the "modern" European state; and I have suggested (Collins, 1986) that late medieval China, in fact, led in the early development of capitalism.

We can try the other tack, then, and try to get as much historical detail as possible into the model. Parsons' model of evolution is ultimately an extension of the same stages of differentiation theory that Spencer had initiated; Parsons (1966) distinguishes various subtypes and adds more historical description. This is realistic, but is it theoretical? That is to say, Parsons can use historical hindsight to declare that Israel and Greece were "seed-beds" for modern developments; but he has no theoretical reason for supposing that such societies would come into existence in the first place. An evolutionary stage scheme would find these "seed-bed societies" to be inevitable, but they clearly do not follow the neat sequence of stages and appear more like historical accidents.

It is the same with Marx and Engels. Because they knew some of the facts of world history, such as that the Roman Empire existed and was followed by feudalism in northern Europe, they put these into their general model of stages. But there is no real theoretical base for supposing that propertyless tribal societies should be followed by societies based on slavery, and these in turn followed by societies based on serfdom, which in turn would be overthrown by capitalism. Marx's admission of *Oriental Despotism* as an alternative pathway shows that the scheme is *ad hoc*, merely a sketching of world history as he knew it, rather than the derivation of a theoretical explanation which made these stages inevitable. To grasp the difference, consider the following: if you found other planets inhabited by people elsewhere in the universe, would you expect that they too would go through the sequence of propertyless tribes, slaveownership, serfdom, capitalism, socialism? Marx and Engels' scheme gives no confidence that any such sequence would be followed, because it offers nothing but *ad hoc* reasons or mere historical descriptions for most of the stages. The only part of their scheme that is theoretically derived, in fact, is the part dealing with capitalism, its emergence and downfall. Their theory thus actually becomes reduced to one stage, plus a predecessor (of whatever sort) and a successor (which still remains problematic).

ARE THERE ANY MODERN APPLICATIONS OF STAGE THEORIES?

Perhaps the biggest weakness of stage theories is that they do not tell us very much about our own societies. All stage theories include a "modern" stage, whatever else they may contrast it with. But stage theories concentrate entirely on describing the difference between modern societies and premodern ones. They tell us we are larger, more differentiated, have more specialized institutions, more impersonal attitudes and relationships, more scientific rationality, and so on. But having said this (and if the theory is sophisticated, it will have hedged its bets by saying that all these processes are not so extreme as to rule out the persistence of more traditional traits), what does it predict specifically about what will happen? It is essentially a theory of the transition, a theory of "modernization," not a theory of what happens once the modern stage is reached. Evolutionary stage theories offer no means of predicting what will happen once we are within the final stage. For example, Lenski's stage theory manages to show empirically (which is better than most stage theories do) that inequality reaches its peak in agrarian societies, then declines to a moderate level in industrial societies. But can we assume that once industrial societies are reached, inequality will go on declining continuously? We can make no such inference, since the stage model itself says nothing about what happens *within* the stage itself. And since this is the last stage delineated, there is no way of predicting what will happen in the future.

There is one exception to this weakness, however. In Figure 1-1 there is a theory which includes a stage beyond the "modern." This is the theory of Marx and Engels, which includes a further stage, or rather, a set of stages: socialism, which is a transition, followed by full fledged communism. This is one of the *theoretical* strengths of the Marxian position; it does not hesitate to make predictions based on theoretical judgments where other theories shy away. After all, knowledge of the future, if valid, is of greater importance to us than knowledge of the past. The problem here, however, is that widespread doubts have arisen about the empirical capabilities of the Marxian theoretical scheme to predict the conditions for the shift to the socialist-communist stage. (As we shall see in Chapter 3, this is one part of Marxian theory that virtually all contemporary Marxists have tended to jettison.) Moreover, when societies have reached that stage, how do we know this is the *final* stage, not subject to further changes?

ORGANIC DIFFERENTIATION THEORIES

Theories which see the evolution of societies as analogous to the growth of organisms are always stage theories. Of the theorists we have discussed, Spencer, Durkheim, and Parsons all make use of organic differentiation models. Of course, not all stage theorists use organic differentiation models; Marx and Engels, Toennies, and Lenski for example, do not. There are also organic differentiation models which have not been mentioned, such as Niklas Luhman's (which will be discussed in the next chapter under System Theories). For the purposes of discussion, however, we will focus on Parsons' theory, which is sociologically the most sophisticated.

The guiding principle of organic differentiation theories is the analogy between society and a growing organism. In an embryo, the germ plasm begins with a cell (or cells) containing DNA, the genetic blueprints for the mature plant or animal. Growth is then a process of cell division and multiplication. The result is not only greater size, but the development of specialized organs. Moreover, it can be seen that over the entire period of biological evolution organisms themselves have become successively more differentiated. Simple one-celled animals were followed by multicelled colonies, and these in turn were followed by various more complex species of plants and animals. Specialized systems emerged for locomotion, digestion, and reproduction, and along with these, nerve and endocrine systems for internal communication and coordination of the various parts of the organism.

Applying the organic analogy to human societies, Parsons and others pick out the following characteristics:

DIFFERENTIATION AND SPECIALIZATION

The primary tendency is for specialized functions to split off and be performed by specialized institutions. In small tribal societies, the family is virtually the only organized institution, and it carries out all functions: economic, political, religious, as well as child-rearing, and so forth. The only specialization takes place within the family, according to age and sex. As the society evolves, various specialized roles appear: first, a magician or shaman who performs rituals and medical cures, then temporary military and political leaders. Eventually the political structure becomes permanently organized, and society begins to split into a class of full-time warriors and an underclass of economic producers. The ruling class then subdivides within itself, with priests separated from the secular aristocracy, and warriors separated from bureaucratic administrators. Similarly, the nonruling class subdivides as an economic division of labor grows up and various specialized crafts emerge. Somewhere in this process, the family is separated from economic and political functions, and becomes a private institution specializing in domestic comforts and child rearing.

In this model, a society's transition to "modernity" is its arrival at a high level of differentiation among its various structural parts. The industrial economy is simply an economy with a very high division of labor. Numerous factories and workshops produce specialized products, and the number of different forms of work increases, both in manual labor and in technical and professional areas. Educational institutions become independent of the family in order to train the numerous technical specialists demanded by this economic system. The older religious system differentiates, splitting off into secular intellectuals, scientists, scholars, and entertainers. In short, in all institutional areas there is further subdifferentiation.

FUNCTIONAL UPGRADING

The differentiation model had already been outlined in the nineteenth century by both Spencer and Durkheim. What Parsons added was its application to a further set of differentiations in the twentieth century, as well as a more abstract definition of the functional areas that were being differentiated (more of this in Chapter 3). Parsons also added the theoretical hypothesis of *upgrading of system performance*. That is, as a system becomes more differentiated, it becomes better able to perform its various functions. When a doctor had to be both a magician and a tribal priest, for example, his (almost certainly his, not her) ability to do any of these was limited, compared to what a modern doctor who specializes in medicine alone can do. Similarly, the family which grew all its own food, saw to its own defense, and made all its own clothes and utensils did none of these things particularly well. Specialized soldiers, specialized farmers, and specialized manufacturers all improved the performance of their activity. Thus, differentiation improved the output of each of society's parts, and the performance of the system as a whole.

Parsons and his followers have thus been strong advocates of the merits of specialization. Where critics have lamented the loss of various functions in modern society, the Parsonians have declared that these alleged losses are actually gains (for example, White, 1961). Marxians have described as "alienation" the disappearance of the all-around crafts worker, capable of fulfilling himself (again, the "him" is deliberate—these are very male-oriented theories) by his variety of skills in turning out his own products. In contradiction, Parsons sees the capacity of the whole system increasing by such specialization, with (theoretically) greater skill levels for the individual as well. Where critics have seen the modern family as losing its functions to the school, the mass media, and the separate workplace, Parsons counters that the specialized family is now better able to concentrate on its core function, the emotional care of children and spouses.

THE NEED FOR INTEGRATION

As a system becomes more differentiated, the greater becomes its need for a means of integrating its diverse parts into one whole. The specialized units need to be coordinated by an over-arching control system. According to evolutionary theorists, it is the state which emerges in order to provide this necessary integration as societies grow more complex. This is analogous to the emergence of the brain and the central nervous system in the evolution of biological organisms. Early cellular organisms at first simply clumped together in symbiotic colonies, but further evolution depended upon these colonies becoming specialized and coordinated around a nervous system. Similarly, early tribal societies had to acquire a specialized state in order to regulate a more extensive division of labor. In modern societies, where the division of labor among various specialized institutions is extreme, the state itself has to provide a large number of regulatory agencies to control the stock market, to provide welfare for those not fitting current occupations, and so forth in every area. According to the evolutionary view, the state cannot be dispensed with without going against the whole trend of evolution. And despite idealistic longings for a stateless society by both right-wing (laissez-faire) or left-wing (anarchist, pure communist) thinkers, any society with a complex division of labor will inevitably have a correspondingly complex state to regulate it.

STRAINS AND LAGS

Integration does not always come about when it is needed, however. Evolutionary theory thus uses the concept of lags and strains to account for social problems which occur as the result of social change. Smelser (1959), for instance, argued that the abuses of child labor in the factories of the early industrial revolution were due to the differentiation of a new occupational structure before the traditional family structure had changed. Because children had assisted their parents when work was located in the home, it seemed natural for parents to bring children with them to help them when they worked in factories. Once the children were there, they quickly became seized upon by employers as the most exploitable source of labor. To solve this problem, children had to be removed from the workplace, and this required a new integrating institution to be developed—public schools—which would take care of the children while their parents were working.

This type of explanation is most frequently used to account for political and social movements. The organic differentiation model sees society as a smoothly operating system in the normal course of events, whose parts fit together harmoniously into a working whole. However, change can occur unevenly, especially as differentiation takes place before a corresponding integration catches up with it. This results in *strains of transition* between one state of the system and another. One particular type of theory, for example (Lipset, Parsons) argues that democratic government is a structural concomitant of the advanced differentiation of modern society. Put more simply, industrial societies tend to become democracies. However, some societies make an abrupt transition to modernity, which puts a special strain on their populations. Parsons (1949) thus explained the Nazi government in Germany in the 1930s through World War II as the result of a strain of transition. Germany had become differentiated industrially, but its government lagged in a traditional form. When democracy was finally established, the initial adjustment of a population used to traditional authoritarian control was shaky, and the result was a backlash in the form of a mass movement for fascism. Lipset (1960) similarly explains authoritarian governments in the so-called developing nations as the response to the strains of transition; and the authoritarian dictatorships of the communist bloc have similarly been explained as the result of a too rapid transition to modernity.

We can see that in general strain theories are optimistic. In the long run, societies are moving in a favorable direction, and it is only the rapidity of change which brings about temporary problems. The preference is for an image of societies which are "normally" harmonious. Any social movement, then, is the result of some strain—usually due to an imbalance between expectations and reality—as the result of uneven patterns of differentiation. Smelser's theory of social movements (1962) uses this conception as a premise; the severity of a social movement, ranging from mild fads to violent uprisings, depends on the level at which the strain occurs in the social system, with more fundamental strains giving rise to more powerful movements. Parsons and Platt (1973) interpreted the student movements of the 1960s and early 1970s in similar fashion. According to their argument, the increasing specialization of modern society requires that a longer period be spent in school as training. But this sets up a strain between traditional expectations that education will quickly lead into an adult job, and the new reality of lengthening years spent in the student community without a fixed social identity. Parsons and Platt regard this, too, as transitional; as new role definitions become established, the status of the long-term student is no longer a matter of strain, and student politics should disappear. Thus, Parsons, as well as Marx, implies a prediction for the future of society: continuous differentiation and functional upgrading.

CRITICISMS

DOES THE ORGANIC ANALOGY HOLD?   Society, of course, is not really an organism. It is not alive, it does not have a consciousness in any literal sense, and so on. These criticisms were raised in the late nineteenth century in response to the early organicist models, such as that of Durkheim. Durkheim in particular was severely attacked for his doctrine that society is a reality *sui generis* (of its own kind), not reducible to individual psychological states, and for his concept of the *collective consciousness*. Where, it was asked, is consciousness to be found empirically, except in real human beings? The individual is a distinct biological organism, but to say that society as a whole is an organism is an error.

Nevertheless, such judgment may be too hasty. The question is not one of deciding what a society "really" is, but of what kinds of explanatory principle might be applied to it. Durkheim, Parsons, and others who have used the organic analogy have usually been aware that society is not literally an organism, but they have claimed that it is similar in ways which make it possible to apply the same theory to both. Society as a whole may be a set of relationships over and above the individuals who make it up, and in that sense it is *sui generis* and not reducible to psychology. Consciousness may be *located* in individuals, but it can still be "collective" in the sense that it is the configuration of the group that is the source of ideas, and therefore this must be the focus of our theory rather than the individual. It has even been argued that society as an "organic" unit can legitimately be goal-directed rather than blind, if it is provided with feedback loops (see the discussion of systems theory in Chapter 2).

In general, then, the issue is not whether one is free to use organicist imagery to suggest what a society is like; such analogies suggest explanatory principles. The crucial question is whether the laws that apply to biology actually turn out to be valid for societies as well.

IS THERE ANY CAUSALITY IN THE MODEL?   One question that arises immediately is, what causes a society to go through a sequence of differentiation? In the case of plant and animal embryos, the answer is usually taken for granted: biological organisms naturally grow because of built-in growth timetables in their genes. But this is plainly inadequate to explain human societies. Historically, many have stayed small and undifferentiated over thousands of years. We cannot assume that growth is merely natural and automatic (any more than we can assume, as the organic analogy would also suggest, that there is a natural timetable for the death of societies—an aspect of the analogy that differentiation models have *not* picked up). This considerably weakens the theory's explanatory power, since it does not tell us *when and why* growth occurs, but only that *if* growth occurs, it will result in differentiation.

Durkheim, who, as we shall see, had reservations about other aspects of the evolutionary theory (such as belief in progress), is one of the few theorists to explicitly add a theory of the causal mechanism producing differentiation in societies. (Parsons added a natural selection mechanism to account for differentiation—see page 31.) Durkheim proposed that the sheer growth of population results in increased competition over ecological resources, and it is this competition which results in a specialized division of labor. Hence, if societies do not grow in size (because population stays low, or there is plenty of space for excess numbers to migrate, and so forth), they do not differentiate. This model has much to recommend it as a first approximation to an explanatory generalization.

However, Durkheim's theory does have some drawbacks. Not all big societies are highly differentiated. For instance, the large population of medieval China or India did not result in a society more differentiated than many of the smaller European states of today. Size may be one condition for differentiation, but it isn't necessarily the only one. (In the biological realm as well, sheer size is not the only criterion of organic differentiation; the largest organisms—whales, huge trees—do not necessarily have the most specialized organs.) It is also possible that a society may remain constant in size and still undergo continued specialization of its social roles. Our own society, the United States, has in the last few decades had relatively little population growth, but the number of occupational and organizational specializations has continued to grow (for reasons indicated in Collins, 1979; see also Chapter 5). A reasonable conclusion, then, would be that Durkheim's theory that size causes differentiation may be true in some instances, but a full theory of the differentiation of social specializations requires some additional conditions.

It is often assumed that differentiation (increased division of labor) grows because of its greater efficiency. Rueschemeyer (1986), however, questions whether this assumption holds up under careful examination. An increasing division of labor, either within an organization or in the whole society, can increase productivity if it leads to higher skills in the specialized roles, or if it saves time that would have been spent by a worker shifting back and forth between tasks. But specialization can also be inefficient if work is bureaucratically subdivided for purely formal reasons; moreover, fragmented jobs can result in alienation and problems of morale and motivation. Rueschemeyer adds that efficiency and productivity are contested goods, and raises the question: for whom is a system efficient? If some persons benefit from its output more than others, then it cannot be simply the needs of the system as a whole which explain its direction of change. Rueschemeyer concludes that it is power, more than efficiency, which is the cause of the division of labor. And power can work in two ways: it can cause an increasing differentiation—even if it is not efficient—or it can prevent differentiation from occurring, even if factors such as size push in that direction.

IS THERE A SEQUENCE OF HISTORICAL DIFFERENTIATION? Once the trend towards specialization gets under way (for whatever reason), does it follow a particular sequence? This is analogous to the question of whether society passes through a set of evolutionary stages. Differentiation models simply state that each stage will be more differentiated than previous ones. For more detail, such theories usually fill in with specific historical data. Thus, Spencer and Parsons note that the homogeneity of early tribal societies was first broken by the specialized role of the shaman (medicine man, magician); and that later the first specialized organization to break off and assume some of the functions of the family was the state. But is there any theoretical reason why this should be so? What is so distinctive about a tribal magician that this should become the first differentiated role? Why couldn't it have been, say, the role of the metal worker, or the midwife? Similarly, why should the state be the first separate organization, rather than, say, an economic organization, or a cultural one? These questions cannot be answered in the framework of differentiation theory, which predicts only that some differentiation will occur, not what kind. To explain the unique significance of the state in transforming society, one would have to leave the differentiation model entirely and use some other theory—such as a conflict theory.

DOES DIFFERENTIATION PRECEDE INTEGRATION? The assumption that differentiation takes place first, and then in turn gives rise to a need for integration is also questionable. The argument sounds logical in the abstract, but it does not seem to fit the historical facts. Units which produce "integration," in the sense of social control, often precede the development of differentiation in the rest of the social roles. A state has often arisen first, whether by conquest, alliance, or expansion from a previous state nucleus, and then has been followed by differentiation of economic roles, and so forth. Weber's theory of capitalism (1923/1961; see Collins, 1986) shows that the elaborate division of labor in the capitalist economy depended upon the prior development of a bureaucratic state; and the differentiation of the private family household from the prior undifferentiated family was due as well to political developments of the state. Thus, there are many instances in which "integration" precedes, and is a necessary condition for, differentiation.

Nor can we assume that integration will "naturally" follow in cases where differentiation results in social problems. A highly differentiated set of economic roles may give rise to problems of unemployment, job dissatisfaction, and other issues; but it is not inevitable that society will always "find a solution." (Chronic levels of unemployment and poverty in advanced societies are one example.) In general, the organic differentiation model uses the analogy of biological organisms as a way of *assuring* us that change is natural and all works out for the best.

THE PROBLEM OF INEQUALITY   Most of the theoretical flaws in the differentiation model boil down to the same source: its inability to deal with issues of inequality and conflict in society. Social conflicts are assumed to be "unnatural" in the same sense that a biological organism does not have conflict among its parts. Similarly, the state is primarily an agency of power and hence of potential coercion and inequality; we cannot assume that it is simply an agency of "integration," or one unit among many which differentiates. Even the question of whether growth in size is the main trend/cause of differentiation is tangled up with the issue of inequality. In recent years, there has been a tendency for large business corporations to grow larger, but not because they are simply moving towards greater functional upgrading and efficiency. On the contrary, they have grown primarily as the result of takeover maneuvers in the financial world, and the resulting conglomerates are often unwieldly and less efficient than the earlier units had been. The prime movement here is not an organic trend, but a struggle for financial domination.

If societies often move toward a greater differentiation and specialization of positions, what effect should this have on inequality? The organicist model does not recognize inequalities as real; each part of society is somehow on the same "level," all contributing equally to the functioning of the whole. In this sense, the organicist model has often been an ideological cloak for real inequalities. The organicist model, when applied to the mid-twentieth century family, argued that male and female roles were simply functional specializations, and that no gender inequality was implied in the fact that women were not supposed to hold any significant jobs or earn any money. The differentiation model has often carried with it the optimistic *assumption* that as societies upgrade their functional capacity, they must place a greater emphasis on "achievement," since they can no longer afford to discriminate according to "ascribed" characteristics. But this does not follow from the logic of the model. All the model shows is that the evolutionary trend is likely to be in the direction of more specialized positions. If in reality—as seems to be the case—specialization gives more scope for monopolizing different resources, then this could just as well result in greater real inequality. It is perfectly in keeping with the logic of organicist theory that societies should be completely male-dominated, for example. To understand the conditions under which inequality is actually challenged or reduced, it is necessary to go to a different kind of theory.

NATURAL SELECTION THEORIES

Natural selection is another biological theory applied by analogy to society. In this case, society is not compared to the development of a single organism, but to whole species or populations of living organisms.

Evolutionist models of this sort include the following elements:

1. *Long-term change.* Neither societies nor biological species are static, but constantly change over long periods of time.

2. *Descent of later forms from earlier forms.* There is a kinship of all species as a "family tree": plants and animals alike descended from microbes, just as mammals descended from earlier chordates (animals with dorsal nerve cords or spinal cords). Similarly, more recent societies have descended from earlier societies.

3. *Natural selection as the mechanism of change.* This includes:

   a. Some basic "genetic" elements from which the other features of societies (or of biological structures) unfold.

   b. Variation in these genetic elements.

   c. The selection of certain variations which survive and propagate, and the extinction of other varieties, which do not survive.

At one time the phrase "survival of the fittest" was used to describe this process (for instance, by Herbert Spencer and his followers). This implied that what is naturally selected is better, more efficient, more fit, and that evolution is a record of progress. This optimistic conclusion is no longer so widely accepted, even by theorists of biological evolution itself. We might ask: what does "fittest" mean? It means no more than whatever is fit to survive under the circumstances in which it exists. Sometimes this is described as "adaptation to the environment." Whatever is best adapted to the environment around it will survive, while whatever is less well adapted will be selected out, and made extinct. But even this notion of "adaptation" is undercut by the technical definition of natural selection: *differential capacity for reproduction.* In the biological history of the earth, a species does not have to be "fittest" or "adaptive" in every possible respect; it merely has to be able to reproduce itself across the generations. Any species that can reproduce itself to some degree will survive, since it is extinguished only when it cannot reproduce itself at all. In this sense, the theory of natural selection is rather abstract and empty: all it says is that whatever is able to continue to survive from one generation to the next will be evolutionarily "selected." The theory itself does not tell us exactly why one characteristic rather than another will be selected.

One of the reasons why evolution is generally unpredictable is that species are constantly adapting to their environments, finding favorable niches in which they can reproduce themselves. But in the biological sphere, these environmental niches are largely *the other species themselves*. The birds could not have evolved until the insects appeared, since these are their major source of food; similarly, most insect species depended upon the appearance of the flowering plants. The mutual connections of biological ecology are complex and include the very composition of the atmosphere which animals breathe and plants feed on—which is itself an evolutionary product of earlier forms of life. The environment is a complex web of causes. A variation which enables one species to prosper may result in the extinction of some other species, and the rise of a host of ancillary species living off the first.

The same may well apply to the natural selection of societies. Different types of societies may all exist at the same time, precisely because some types provide the "environment" which supports other types. Militaristic societies of the past (like many nomadic tribes) existed in a "niche" made possible by the existence of sedentary peasant societies which they could plunder. Modern Marxian world-systems theory (Chapter 3) proposes that the dominant "core" societies of world capitalism live by economically exploiting the "peripheral" societies which provide crude labor and raw materials. If we see "natural selection" as a process of reproduction of certain forms in an ecological network, then we cannot say simply that all societies will be selected in a certain form, but rather that each of them is "selected" by its own particular conditions, including its relationship to the other societies (and the other biological species and conditions of its location).

NATURAL SELECTION AS AN UMBRELLA
FOR CAUSAL THEORIES

Natural selection by itself does not "do" anything; it is simply a way of characterizing a dynamic process by which various functionally important characteristics in each given context contribute to different levels of survival and reproduction. Hence, it is not a cause in itself, but an umbrella of various specific causes that is responsible for what is formed in each particular case. Evolution is multicausal and multileveled, with genes, cells, organisms, populations, and societies all having feedback loops upon each other and in various directions (Corning, 1983, Chapter 2). Even in biological ecology, the prevailing approach to "communities" of living species in an environment does not regard them as naturally evolving in any particular direction. "Each Darwinian species finds its own range, jostling its neighbors, living in its own individual niche. Communities come and go, mere temporary alliances of plants thrown together by fate and history" (Colinvaux, 1978: 72). Equilibrium among different species of plants and animals in a particular place is only temporary, depending upon the climate and physical setting, as well as on the complicated interrelationships of mutual predation and migration from outside. Thus, there is no biological basis for assuming that a community as a whole is a unit of natural selection, or that it changes in any general pattern found in all communities. How much equilibrium or fluctuation there is in the numbers of members of different species found together, and how long any particular combination will exist in a particular place, cannot be assumed by a general theory, but must be established empirically in each case.

The natural selection model, although probably an accurate representation, turns out to be a relatively weak theory. It is a kind of umbrella under which we can put specific theories about how societies change and survive in various conditions. Sociological theories differ on what are the core "genetic elements" that determine the rest of society, on why these elements vary, and why some of them turn out to survive better than others. Natural selection theory is merely a set of "black boxes" in which we can insert various elements and theories.

For instance, Lenski's (1966, 1974) theory (included in Figure 1-1) proposes that the core elements are technologies. Societies whose basic technology is centered on hunting wild animals and gathering food and materials from wild plants will necessarily be rather small in size, and they will have a relatively uncomplex social structure with little hierarchy or specialization. This is because the technology makes available no surplus, and everyone must take part in the basic food-acquiring activities. Societies with primitive horticultural technology—cultivation of plants by hoes—produce a modest surplus, and are able to support a larger, denser, and more sedentary population on a given space. Advanced horticultural technology, using metal tools, makes possible yet further extraction of surplus, larger social groupings, and more stratification and inequality. Agrarian technologies involve large-scale agriculture using metal plows drawn by animal power, irrigation systems, and long-distance transportation that make possible huge civilizations with urban centers like those of ancient Egypt, or medieval China and Europe.

For Lenski productive technology is the core "genetic element" from which most other aspects of society proceed. Productive technologies evolve by natural selection, so that over time new and more powerful technologies appear, enabling a larger and more powerful society to survive. Societies using the more "primitive" technologies may survive also, if they exist in remote environments and are not overrun or driven out by the more advanced societies; but generally there is a tendency for the more advanced forms to absorb and displace the earlier forms. We should note that Lenski has plugged a number of *specific theories* (including a conflict theory of inequality) into the larger evolutionary model: that technology is the main "genetic element," that genetic elements affect the structure of society in particular ways, and that over time the later forms expand at the expense of the earlier ones.

However, we could just as easily plug some other element into the "black box." Parsons uses a version of Max Weber's theory that Christianity (and Protestantism in particular) was crucial in setting the West on the path to capitalism, while the differing religions of the Orient (Hinduism, Buddhism, Confucianism, Taoism, and Islam) kept their societies at a pre-capitalist stage. Thus, Parsons proposes that the major genetic element is not technology, but religion. In doing so, he combines a stage theory, a differentiation theory, and a natural selection theory of evolution. As variations occur in religious beliefs, some are selected for further evolutionary development, while others become "evolutionary dead ends." This is the reason why, in Figure 1-1, Parsons' *Historical Intermediate Empires* includes both those which are presumed to be static (Rome, Egypt, China, India, and Islam) and "seed-bed societies" (ancient Israel and Greece) which became the basis of later developments. Like Lenski, Parsons has made specific theoretical choices about how to fill in the natural selection model: he assumes that religion is the basic genetic element determining the rest of society, that crucial variations are produced in religions, and that the advanced forms are so much more powerful than the others that they eventually displace them.

All these specific theories need to be examined and tested in their own right. Is technology really that powerful a determinant of the rest of society, or is religion, or something else? Is it always true that the more "advanced" form drives out the "primitive" form? The biological analogy would lead us to doubt this, since the rise of the "higher," more complex species does not usually eliminate the earlier and simpler species (see Figure 1-2). Human beings have not displaced the other mammals, nor have the more complex flowering plants displaced primitive mosses and ferns that continue to live in abundance among them. In general, animals and plants have not displaced bacteria; and viruses, which resemble the simplest forms of life to evolve several billion years ago, continue to live all around us, prospering in the benevolent environment we provide (as anyone who gets the flu is uncomfortably aware).

Hence, it does not automatically follow from natural selection theory, that "higher" forms necessarily displace "lower" ones. Social history may be different in this respect, since industrial societies (and agrarian states before them) do tend to overrun and transform the simpler tribal societies around them. But this is not an automatic, or even a rapid, process, and at any moment in history there are likely to be several types of societies existing side by side probably living off each other as predators or partners in ecological symbiosis.

But why do new technologies emerge? Or new religions, capable of transforming the rest of society? A basic weakness of all these natural selection models is their vagueness about what causes the initial variation in the core elements. Natural selection cannot operate until it has something to work on, yet natural selection theory itself says very little about why variations occur in the first place. Natural selection models leave major gaps in our understanding of social evolution, since we need to know the causes of technological change, as well as its consequences.

SOCIOBIOLOGY: EVOLUTION AT THE LEVEL OF THE GENES

One type of theory which has become prominent recently is sociobiology. Its primary advocates have not been sociologists, but biologists and geneticists, such as E. O. Wilson and Charles Lumsden. Sociobiology uses a natural selection model in which the basic genetic elements are considered to be the genes chemically encoded in each physical organism. E. O. Wilson is an entomologist, an expert on social insects, such as bees, ants, and wasps. He theorized that their social behavior must have been produced by genetic variation and selection in the ancestry of these insect species; accordingly, he has speculated that human social forms must also be due to the selection of genes which human beings have inherited. In his earlier work, Wilson (1975) argued that genetic determination affects society through the selection of general mechanisms operating in individuals—for instance, the human capacity for cooperation and symbolic communication. What emerges in each particular society is due to the application of these "tools" to specific circumstances. Sociobiological theory is a relatively weak predictor, since it is applicable to all sorts of different societies, each of which needs to be explained in its own right by additional (non-sociobiological) theories.

Subsequently, Lumsden and Wilson (1981) have produced a further theory proposing that the type of culture possessed by each different society is itself encoded in the brain as the result of a genetic selection. It should be emphasized that this model, although mathematically expressed, is purely theoretical and not based on supporting evidence. Moreover, it seems particularly difficult to reconcile with the rapidity sometimes found in cultural change; for instance, whole societies can change in a few generations or less, as do individuals who move from one culture to another. Other versions of sociobiology argue that our genes predetermine that human societies will be dominated by aggressive males, that females are biologically specialized to function primarily as mothers, and that warfare and hierarachy are inevitable (Tiger and Fox, 1972; Ardrey, 1966). These are "stronger" versions of sociobiology, in the sense that they claim the predetermination of more specific patterns of behavior than the very abstract "weak" version, which proposes only very general capacities for building social forms. It appears, however, that the "strong" versions are empirically wrong (Blumberg, 1978, 1984).

THE CHALLENGE OF THE PUNCTUATED EQUILIBRIUM MODEL IN BIOLOGY

We often hear the phrase "evolution, not revolution," meaning change which occurs gradually and by small increments, rather than rapidly and in a major upheaval. It has traditionally been assumed that biological evolution is of the former type. Recent debates in biology itself, however, have seriously weakened this assumption. Stephen Jay Gould, Elizabeth Vrba, Niles Eldridge, and others (see Gould, 1982; Raup, 1986) have argued that the evidence of the fossil record does not show that biological evolution is a continuous, smooth development of small cumulative changes. Instead, there tend to be long periods during which species remained fairly constant, punctuated by periods of relatively rapid change. One dramatic example is the theory, supported by a mass of evidence which is still being evaluated (Alvarez, 1980; Lewin, 1985) that the dinosaurs and numerous other species were made extinct when the earth was struck by a large asteroid at the end of the Cretaceous period (65 million years ago). The resultant clouds of atmospheric dust obliterated the sunlight and changed the climate. Not only did various species of animals and plants die out in these conditions, but other species, whose environmental niches depended upon eating or living off the products of these species also died. Because nature is an ecological web, a major change in one part of the environment has rippling effects which spread out to many other species. There is also a positive side, however; since the environment had now changed, the way was opened for new species to be selected—those which were capable of reproducing most rapidly in the new conditions.

A single theory about the impact of an asteroid probably will not turn out to provide a complete explanation of the Cretaceous extinctions. Other environmental changes, such as the shifts in climate which have gone on throughout the history of the earth, apparently were also bringing about a long-term decline of the dinosaurs and other species. The more general point, though, is that evolution is not necessarily continuous and gradual, but is hastened by sudden catastrophes "punctuating" long periods of relative stasis or equilibrium. There is evidence of a number of such mass extinctions in the earth's history (Lewin 1985). This theory tends to undermine the traditional biological view that changes in the genes, produced by random mutations, are what underlie natural selection. In fact, genes may be much less specific in their effects than was once believed, and may have relatively little effect in producing changes. Instead, the major source of evolutionary change shifts to the environment—whether sudden impacts, such as an ecological catastrophe, or slower changes in the world climate, together with the concomitant rippling effects throughout the web of species living off one another. Notice that this model of evolution undercuts sociobiology, since it makes genes much less important in the process of biological explanation. Not surprisingly, Stephen Jay Gould and E. O. Wilson, who are colleagues at Harvard University, are antagonists in biological theory.

Something like a punctuated equilibrium model may be especially appropriate for social evolution. Historically, major changes in societies have often occurred "catastrophically" rather than gradually. Not only revolutions but even more importantly, wars and conflict in general have played a major part in affecting the form of the state, the economy, religion and culture, the family, and other social institutions.

IS NATURAL SELECTION DIRECTIONAL?

Finally, we may ask whether evolution is moving in any particular direction. It used to be believed that there is a long-term trend. The stage theories which we have examined all propose a definite sequence towards the most "modern" type. This model specifies that the direction is towards increasingly specialized, differentiated social structures. However, we have seen that this kind of prediction is shaky. Stages do not follow one another automatically in a sequence, and there is considerable doubt that differentiation happens continually, or that it can go on endlessly, without limits.

The biological evidence offers us further grounds for doubting whether natural selection has much of a direction. It is true that traditional biologists used to argue (and to some extent still do) that there is a hierarchy of evolutionary forms, from the simple bacteria up through multicelled creatures, animals, mammals to the final culmination of *homo sapiens,* whose brain is the highest product of evolution. This theme goes back to the static, nonevolutionary hierarchies of medieval theology (such as that of Thomas Aquinas), in which human beings are categorized as standing between the animal kingdom and the angels. But it is an error to speak of biological evolution as if it did nothing more than evolve towards humans. The dominant picture is not of the replacement of lower species by higher ones, but of the coexistence of all these forms at the same time (see Figure 1-2). Plants and animals have evolved at the same time, and the later forms—such as the relatively recent phyla of insects and of angiosperms (flowering plants)—have merely added a further diversity to already existing species. It would be accurate to say that the dominant theme of

FIGURE 1-2

LINES OF BIOLOGICAL EVOLUTION

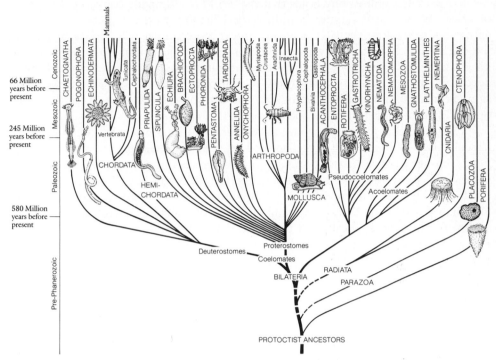

Adapted with permission from *FIVE KINGDOMS: An illustrated Guide to the Phyla on Earth* by Lynn Margolis and Karlene V. Schwartz. Copyright © 1982 W. H. Freeman and Company.

evolution is diversification, not a hierarchical sequence. If this applies to human societies too, we would have to conclude that a dominant form would not displace all other types of societies. The world is not necessarily growing more alike, and it would be unwise to predict that in the long-term future every society will resemble the United States, as Parsons seemed to think, or France, as French evolutionists like Comte have equally ethnocentrically believed.

Of course, it is possible that human social evolution may be different from biological evolution precisely because biological species maintain more diversity than human societies do. Whereas biological species seem to be able to live in symbiosis with each other, human societies seem to be more aggressive and expansionary, and actively destroy competing forms to a much greater degree. Industrial societies do seem to drive out tribal societies, and capitalism penetrates almost everywhere. Nevertheless, this may be only a passing stage; certainly it has not been a characteristic of all of world history. Even today there are major differences between capitalist and socialist societies, while we still see other variants emerging all the time, such as the militant Islamic states now prominent in the Middle East. The lesson of biological evolution leads us to expect that such diversity may well always be with us.

IDEALIST EVOLUTION

Idealism as a philosophy holds that the world is ultimately constituted by *ideas,* or *mind.* As such, it is remote from biological theories of the evolution of material entities. Nevertheless, the two positions appear more similar when idealism seeks to understand world history in terms of the progressive development or unfolding of ideas. In the early nineteenth century, the German philosophers Schelling and Hegel developed their metaphysics, according to which the forces of attraction and repulsion (Schelling), or a dialectic of logical contradictions (Hegel), results in the developing forms of the natural and social worlds.

This dialectical model of evolution was taken up by Marx, who began his intellectual career as a left-wing Hegelian, and retained the dialectical scheme of evolution even after converting the system to a materialistic base (see Chapter 3 for a more detailed exposition of his economic model). In recent years, Jürgen Habermas, a German Marxian, has modified Marx by returning to something like the original Hegelian position while also retaining elements of Schelling's position. Habermas' system is not entirely idealist, in the sense that the world is taken to be mind or ideas; Habermas is more of a dualist, but his work tends towards the idealist position because it stresses the key role that human consciousness plays in determining social evolution.

Habermas (1971) sets himself up as an opponent of positivism (the belief that all knowledge consists of hard scientific laws of cause and effect in the material world). He argues that positivism is an ideological cover for modern capitalism, which claims to make its decisions on merely objective, "technical" grounds, while actually maintaining class domination and control over the individual by an irrational economic and political system. Against this "technocratic domination," Habermas points out there are two other forms of knowledge: the social norms which guide human interaction and conscious, self-reflective thought. Habermas regards all three kinds of knowledge as "quasi-transcendental," meaning that they reach beyond the bounds of human experience toward the ultimate grounds of reality, what Immanual Kant (Schelling and Hegel's predecessor) had called the *thing-in-itself.*

Habermas' own critique of capitalism led him to move beyond Marxism. Marx had presented a vision of capitalism as essentially "instrumental," based on the objective laws of economic development. Habermas instead attempts to transform Marxism from historical materialism into an evolutionary development driven by the moral and intellectual development of human beings. From his early statement *Knowledge and Human Interests* (1971), he went on to describe the crisis of modern society not as an economic crisis but as a legitimation crisis in a work of that name (1975). Then followed *Communication and the Evolution of Society* (1979) and finally *The Theory of Communicative Action* (1984). Habermas extrapolates from psychological theories of individual cognitive development to a theory of the historical development of human minds across the centuries. Jean Piaget (Piaget and Inhelder, 1967) had proposed that the infant begins with crude, action-oriented mental schemas which go through a series of transformations until reaching highly abstract and generalized ideas; Lawrence Kohlberg (1976) proposed an analogous development in the realm of moral ideas, with human moral awareness proceeding from a crude consciousness of local group rules to an ability to reflect on the needs of a universal morality for all humanity. Taking this further, Habermas reinterprets world history as going through similar stages. In this scheme, human mental development takes precedence over Marxist materialism, since Habermas sees the progressive development of ideas as determining the forms of human interaction, and hence setting the frame within which any technical and economic development can take place.

The process is evolutionary in that Habermas proposes that communicative structures develop just like biochemical structures: in both cases, there are random mutations, of which the more effective ones are selected for survival. Like Parsons, Habermas believes that more abstract, generalized, and universal forms of communication and morality are evolutionarily more adaptive, and lead to more advanced forms of society, displacing older forms. But it is not just a matter of random "accidents" which bring about the advance of consciousness. Habermas argues that the very nature of human language presses in this direction. For language intends to communicate: its very structure aims at truth and at social consensus. Even if it becomes distorted through ideology and domination, language nevertheless always has this underlying movement towards emancipating us from these distortions. The human being, talking and thinking, is always pressing towards greater knowledge and towards a situation in which knowledge can be understood and agreed upon by all human beings without being deflected by any outside forces.

Habermas thus aims to bring modern society to an "ideal speech situation," in which everything is fully discussed and agreed upon without any coercion, whether by political or economic powers. Furthermore, he believes that the thrust of world evolution is in this direction, and he is optimistic that we will approach this ideal in the future. Human beings become emancipated by becoming self-reflective, and we have made great advances in this sphere, in part through the advance of psychological and sociological theory such as Habermas' own. In this respect, Habermas resembles Hegel, who also felt that world history was a trend towards freedom through self-recognition, and that the apex of this development was the insight achieved by his own philosophy.

There is also a practical side to this deepening human capacity for self-reflection. Psychoanalysis, invented in the early twentieth century by Freud, provides a method for self-insight.[2] Encounter groups and other forms of group therapy provide an even more social form of self-reflection and insight. It is in this that Habermas finds a practical example of the "ideal speech community," in which everything can be said without inhibition, and dialogue can go on until consensus is finally reached without any coercion. Extrapolating from this to the large scale, Habermas believes that societies evolve towards producing more and more of these "emancipated" individuals and groups, which then enable humanity to take conscious control of its own evolution.

Habermas' theory has considerable intellectual appeal, since it combines sophistication in the spheres of philosophy and linguistic and psychological theory, as well as sociology. Like Marxism, it is more than an analysis of society: it proposes a

[2] It should be borne in mind that psychoanalysis made little impact in Germany or France, but was carried on largely in Britain and the United States until the 1960s and 1970s; since that time it has become a major intellectual movement on the Continent, which is part of what Habermas is reflecting.

praxis, a way of acting to transform society. In Habermas' own terms, it is a *critical* and *emancipatory* theory. Nevertheless, the theory has its weaknesses. It goes too far in assuming that mental processes determine material ones, for as we shall see in subsequent chapters, there is considerable evidence that the reverse is often true. Habermas' theory that language has an intrinsically "emancipatory" interest built into it does not capture very well the social processes involved in language and symbolism (see Chapters 6, 8, and 9). Also, Habermas' "ideal speech situation" may be utopian, for even encounter groups and psychoanalytic sessions cannot overcome conflicts of real opposing interests among their members just by endless discussion; and in fact there are absolute limits to how much information people can process without resulting in cognitive overload (see Chapter 8). Modern researchers in organizations, economics, computer programming, as well as sociological ethnomethodology have emphasized the discovery of *bounded rationality,* or cognitive limitations, which imply severe limits on the cognitive utopia towards which Habermas believes we are evolving.

CONCLUSION: THE DREAM OF PROGRESS

The underlying theme in most evolutionary theories is a belief in progress. The general notion is that time brings improvements which then supersede earlier, inferior forms. Yet we have seen that this is not an accurate view of biological evolution, which is multidirectional, and in which adaptation occurs episodically to whatever environments happen to exist. In fact, the idea of progress has come primarily from social evolutionists and seems to have been borrowed by the biologists.

Not all social evolutionists have been entirely optimistic. For Marx and Engels, there is a long-term progress, but one proceeding through a series of economic and political crises, so that improvements occur only after periods of strife and suffering. Herbert Spencer was more equivocal about whether the long-term trend was favorable, since societies might become more militaristic rather than peacefully industrial. Durkheim (1893/1964: 233–55) explicitly argued that although societies evolve structurally towards an increasing division of labor, there is no increase in either happiness or rationality. Happiness is always relative to people's values and aspirations, and these are set by their own society; hence, people could be just as happy in a primitive tribal society as in an industrial society—possibly more so, since there is more chance for *anomie* in the latter (gaps between individual desires and social regulation). Nor did Durkheim believe that societies become steadily more rational, for (as we shall see in Chapter 2) the basis of social order always remains nonrational, emotional and moral sentiments. Lenski provides some empirical evidence for a qualified pessimism, since he shows that inequality and social oppression actually *increase* from one technological stage to the next, reaching their peak in agrarian societies and then declining somewhat in industrial societies, though remaining far short of the level of equality found in hunting-and-gathering societies. Recently, Lind (1983) has proposed a model of social evolution in which what is naturally selected is simply the capacity of societies for military coercion, which stamps out weaker and more pacifistic forms.

Thus, even a number of the social evolutionists deny that the trend of evolution is completely progressive. The more popular version of evolutionism, though, continues to believe in progress (for example, Boulding, 1978; Corning, 1983; and some versions of organizational theory). In Parsons' version, negative events are merely strains along the way, resulting from prior differentiation, and giving rise to further regulatory institutions which provide solutions to the strains. This optimism appears to be based more on ideological assumptions than on empirical evidence. Evolutionary theories are actually backwards-looking; they arose mainly by reflecting on the differences between the present, "modern" society and those of the past, and most such theories contain a strong note of self-congratulation. Talcott Parsons, writing in the United States in the 1950s and 1960s, felt that he was living at the apex of human civilization, just as August Comte in the 1830s believed that his own France showed the face of the future to less modern societies of his time. This stance can lead to naive predictions of the future, and an inability to understand the processes actually occurring.

For instance, Parsons (1967, 1971), Lipset (1960), and other mid-twentieth century theorists believed that democratic government is an inevitable part of the differentiated modern social structure, and societies elsewhere throughout the world were destined to undergo political "modernization" into democracies as soon as they became economically mature. (This theory was even used as a rationale for supporting dictatorial regimes, such as that of South Viet Nam in the 1960s and 1970s: if only order could be maintained until economic development took place, eventually democracy would evolve by itself.) This kind of prediction would not now be so easily accepted. Democracy seems to demand special conditions (see Chapter 4), not just the evolution of society as a whole to some "advanced" form. Democracy can occur at widely differing moments in world history—in the city-states of ancient Greece, for instance, as well as in the modern era—and there is unfortunately no guarantee that modern advanced societies will not become dictatorships.

It is true that certain features of society do show "progress" in some sense; notably, more efficient and powerful technologies tend to evolve and displace cruder technologies. You can indeed get a sharper picture on your TV set than you could 30 years ago, and that was no doubt an improvement over the prior technology, which had no TV transmission at all. But technology is a relatively limited area, and its "progress" says nothing about the human and social side of life.[3] Yet leaving aside the question of happiness and rationality, does the mere passage of time bring more democracy, tolerance, freedom, peace and nonviolence? There is no evidence for such trends. Though democracy survives in the United States and in other Western-style countries, it seems shaky elsewhere and is matched by the many dictatorial regimes in other parts of the world. On theoretical grounds, I would not even claim that our own society is exempt from the danger that its democracy might be overthrown by self-aggrandizing bureaucracies, or by a military faction in time of crisis.

---

[3] Nor can one say that technological change itself is inevitable. Lenski's theory is more about the consequences of technological change than about its causes. In general, a good theory of when technological innovation does or does not occur is lacking. But see Collins (1986: 77–116) for an effort to generalize from the comparative historical evidence on this question.

Similarly, one must doubt whether there is a long-term trend in the direction of greater tolerance among religious groups, those living different lifestyles, or even ethnic and racial groups. The upsurge of intolerant fundamentalist religious movements, both in the Christian and in the Islamic worlds, has been occurring many years after it was confidently stated that such "transitional" phenomena were becoming things of the past.

Even more alarming is the threat of nuclear war. It is precisely our advanced technology which has made it possible for human beings to destroy virtually their entire population, and perhaps also induce ecological changes which could extinguish many of the more complex species of life on the earth. The threat of nuclear war is realistic enough, yet such an event would be beyond the range of comprehension of most evolutionary theories. Such theories hedge by declaring nuclear war an "accident" outside the realm to which they apply. Yet this is an admission of considerable theoretical weakness: how good can a theory be if it cannot make room for an event whose magnitude would shape the entire history of the planet? Stage theories and differentiation theories allow no room for such a reversal, and most optimistic models of natural selection would not anticipate it. However, a more realistic and hard-nosed version of natural selection theory is capable of incorporating such a nuclear catastrophe. It would simply be seen as another cause of variation, in this case, one with major impacts throughout the ecology of life on earth, as the human species and its social evolution would abruptly be selected out—and along with it many other species locked into the ecological web with us. Nuclear catastrophe would not be the end of existence, but merely the end of certain branches of evolutionary life on earth after a few millions (or hundreds of millions) of years. Primitive microorganisms, perhaps certain plants, marine animals, and so forth, would survive, and would evolve in another direction. Perhaps in a few hundred million more years, nothing would indicate that the catastrophe had occurred, and some other species might be achieving consciousness and congratulating itself on being the apex of evolution.

My point is not that a pessimistic conclusion ought to be substituted for an optimistic one. Rather, we ought to recognize that trend theories of any sort are weak and speculative. History is complex and does not proceed simply in one direction, whether upwards or downwards. If such a movement were evident, it would imply that there is a single, basic causal factor operating, which is highly unlikely; the reality of our world seems to be resolutely multicausal. Whatever technological "stage," or degree of differentiation, we may arrive at, there are always alternative conditions which apply, and which affect whether we have war or peace, democracy or authoritarian government, cultural tolerance or militantly intolerant movements, and the like. We need specific theories to explain these phenomena, and to find them we have to move out from under the "umbrella" of an evolutionary model.

I would conclude that stage theories fail to capture the complexity of world history and tell us nothing about the future. Differentiation models assume that the process of increasing division of labor is more continuous and endless than it really is, as well as overstating the tendency toward integration. Natural selection theory is more plausible, but mainly because it makes weaker claims: it boils down to the proposal that if variations occur (by whatever mechanism, including ecological catastrophe), those most able to reproduce themselves in the conditions of the time will survive, while others may be selected out. This is realistic but vague. In some sense, human beings and their societies are part of the long-term sweep of biological life upon the earth. We don't escape from its laws, no matter what forms we create. But this is mainly because the "laws" of biological evolution are extremely general and include anything that can manage to survive on the earth. Unfortunately, we are still left with the theoretical task of explaining what actually happens to societies.

SUMMARY

1. There are several types of evolutionary theories: stage theories, organic differentiation models, natural selection theories, and idealist theories. Any particular theory may combine elements from several of these types.

2. *Stage theories* which distinguish only two stages—generally, a modern and a premodern type—are not very powerful predictors of historical change. These dichotomies are better treated analytically, as concepts which may also refer to different types within the same society.

3. Stage theories with a larger number of stages (such as theories of Comte, Marx and Engels, Spencer, Parsons, and Lenski) disagree over the major determinant of each type of structure. It is not true that every society goes through the same set of stages, since (1) it is possible to skip stages, and (2) there are often alternative or "side" stages. Moreover, societies of different types or stages are often simultaneously in existence, and determine each other's structure by external contact and domination. In general, stage theories are too simplistic to capture the variations of history, since they imply only a single causal factor or process.

4. Stage theories generally lack any power to predict what will happen in or after the "latest" stage. Only the Marxian model and the differentiation model provide a prediction of a future stage, but the Marxian prediction of the final universal transition to socialism/communism is no longer much believed, even among modern Marxist theorists.

5. *Organic differentiation theories* regard societies as developing analogously to the growth of an embryo. In the model developed by Herbet Spencer and Talcott Parsons, differentiation proceeds by the splitting off of specialized functions and institutions. For Parsons, differentiation can occur among any of the analytical elements of social systems, including culture, personality, and structure. Differentiation produces greater social efficiency in all spheres—economic, political, administrative, cultural—as well as greater individualism.

6. In the Spencer-Parsons theory, differentiation produces a need for integration, which takes place by elaborating agencies of control (for instance, political controls to regulate the economy). In Parsons' version, integration is also established by an upgrading of the culture into greater abstraction and universalism, to legitimate the variety of new activities and institutions. Strains occur when there are lags between differentiation and integration, or between differentiation and older cultural values attuned to previous evolutionary levels. Democracy is considered to be a part of the differentiated institutions of modern society, but authoritarian governments are transitional phenomena due to such strains. Social movements, including those of alienated youth as well as racist, fundamentalist, or other traditionalist movements, are also regarded as results of such transitional strains.

7. The differentiation theory does not claim society is a living organism but only that it has analogous laws of development. But differentiation is not merely a natural and inevitable trend; it requires a mechanism of change. Durkheim proposed that differentiation arises because of increased population density which gives rise to competition. But large societies are not always highly differentiated, and differentiation can occur in the absence of increases in size. Rueschemeyer argues that differentiation does not necessarily result in increased productivity, and that power rather than efficiency is the main determinant of the division of labor. Evolutionary theories of differentiation do not predict specific details of what institutions actually change; and they are often empirically wrong in assuming that "integrative institutions" (such as the state) follow rather than precede differentiation of other spheres.

8. *Natural selection models* apply the principles used to explain the development of biological species upon the earth to societies, organizations, or any other social unit. Such theories propose that change occurs over long time periods by the descent of newer societies (or species) from older ones, through a mechanism of variation and natural selection. Natural selection does not mean "survival of the fittest" in any other sense than the neutral criterion of whatever manages to reproduce itself under the environmental conditions of the time.

9. Natural selection itself does not "do" anything, but is merely an umbrella covering various particular theories of what causes variations to occur and to reproduce themselves. Such theories vary as to what are the "core" or "genetic" elements which determine the rest of society. Lenski amasses empirical evidence to show that basic productive technologies (hunting-and-gathering, horticultural, agrarian, industrial) affect major aspects of social structure, but he lacks a theory of what causes technological change in the first place. Parsons elaborates a version of Max Weber's theory, which makes religious innovations, especially Christianity, central in determining development to the higher social stages. Sociobiology hypothesizes that the core causal elements of societies are actually biochemical genes, which provide the capacities for communication and cooperation which make societies possible.

10. The punctuated equilibrium model in biology proposes that variations and changes do not occur smoothly and gradually, but often are the result of catastrophic changes in the environment. This is compatible with a pattern of revolutionary and conflictual changes in human societies, between long periods of comparative stasis. Natural selection theory in its most general form does not predict any strongly defined direction to history. In the history of biological species, old and primitive forms have often continued to coexist along with later, more complex forms. Human societies may differ from biological species in that they are more likely to destroy or take over less powerful ones militarily and economically, but a great deal of social diversity is always possible.

11. Habermas' version of evolution is idealist in that it gives special precedence to the development of abstract and self-reflective human consciousness as a determinent of the rest of social structure. Habermas' theory is aimed especially at an "emancipatory" critique of capitalism, and the development of a further stage via the agency of an "ideal speech situation" exemplified by psychoanalysis and group therapy. This model appears unrealistic in ignoring the extent to which conscious-

ness is itself determined by social conditions. Intrinsic limitations on human cognitive capabilities also make complete and open communication unrealistic.

12. Although some evolutionary theories, notably Parsons', continue the belief that the general trend of evolution is progress and the improvement of the human condition, many theories are sceptical. The natural selection model itself is compatible even with nuclear disaster, which would constitute just another extinction process resulting in new species variations and developments.

Chapter 2

SYSTEM THEORIES

GENERAL SYSTEMS THEORY
    Mechanistic or "Dumb" Systems
    Open and Closed Systems
    "Smart" or Goal-seeking Feedback
    Negative and Positive Feedback: Equilibrium or Explosion
    Self-referential Systems and Consciousness
    Is Society a "Smart" Feedback System?

FUNCTIONALISM
    Stinchcombe's Functionalist Feedback Loops

TALCOTT PARSONS' FUNCTIONALIST ACTION SYSTEM
    The Four-function Model
    The Hierarchy of Control
    Durkheim's Theory of Precontractual Solidarity
    Socialization and Deviance
    The Pattern Variables
    The Differentiation Model
    Parsons' Two Theories of Social Change
    Media and Interchange: Niklas Luhman
    Criticism of the Parsonian System

JEFFREY ALEXANDER'S DEFENSE OF MULTIDIMENSIONAL
    ACTION THEORY

THE ANALYTICAL AND THE CONCRETE

SUMMARY

What is a system? A system is anything that has parts which are connected to each other. The parts can be of any sort: metal machinery, biological organisms, molecules, information, ideas, emotions, behaviors—anything at all that can be described as being in some condition at some time. The system can be material or ideal, living or inorganic, imaginary or actual; it can also be a combination of different sorts of elements, such as an ecological system which involves both living species and geological features. Connections between parts can be physical ties or flows (pipes, electrical currents, chemicals); communications, signs, or acts of meaning; or even purely abstract mathematical or conceptual connections.

A system, in short, is a very general conception. What makes it useful is that its relationships can be represented by certain techniques. We can make a diagram of a system since it has an implicit architecture which can often be visually described. For most systems a computer program can be written, and the system can be simulated. Computerization of systems is relatively recent in sociology, and we are just beginning to see what can be done with it. Systems have been expounded in sociology since long before computers existed, and many of them do not immediately take the form that more recent system models of the computer era do. Nevertheless, there is an affinity between the older system models and the more general conception of systems which has become clearer now that computer modeling, especially by personal computer, has become relatively easy.

A system can be social, cultural, or mental; or it can exist merely as the set of elements in a computer program—in fact, this may be the common denominator of all systems. There is a system on any of these levels if there are elements which are related to each other. That having been said, a caveat is immediately in order. To say that there is such a thing as "a social system" does not specify anything about what kind of system it is. It does not mean, for instance, a functionally self-equilibrating system, or Talcott Parsons' particular theory which he called *"the* social system." These are particular kinds of theories about systems in society, and the validity of each construction has to be assessed on its own merits. The evolutionary conception of society described in the previous chapter is a type of system theory. In its strong version, as we have seen, it is very probably wrong. In its weak version, it may be accurate but it is extremely vague in what it specifies. It needs to be supplemented with other system models in order to explain what actually happens under what conditions.

There is probably no such thing as "the" social system, since there is not just one system but a series of systems defined by different theories about society. Numerous different systems can be going on at the same time: a geopolitical system among states, as well as a world economic system of global capitalism; political and organizational systems within each state, as well as systems made up of networks among them; systems of intellectual specialists and religious memberships, as well as other culture carriers which cut across national boundaries. On the micro level, a system takes place within each conversational ritual, in addition to the somewhat larger system of the interaction ritual network that links conversational encounters together. A system is an analytical device: it is a set of entities and connections that we pick out from all the possible systems to be found in the world.

Systems can be "open" or "closed"; tightly or loosely coupled; stable or unstable; rigidly deterministic or open-ended; conscious, self-conscious, or unconscious. Our theoretical problem is to find out what kind of systems exist in the world and how they operate.

GENERAL SYSTEMS THEORY

One line of inquiry has been the search for panscientific laws, for principles that apply to systems found in all areas of science. This approach is called "general systems theory." Its principal advocate, Ludwig von Bertalanffy, draws on intellectual traditions in engineering, biology, gestalt psychology, and especially cybernetics. But the basic idea that there are principles underlying all the sciences can be traced back further than these theories of the 1920s through the 1960s. Herbert Spencer, whom we have treated in the previous chapter as an evolutionist, may also be described, in Turner's words (1985a), as the first general systems theorist. Spencer's sociology was merely a late volume in his series, *Synthetic Philosophy,* which also included treatments of the astronomical cosmos, biology, and psychology. Across all of these areas, Spencer proposed that the same basic principle rules: entities evolve from "an indefinite, incoherent homogeneity to a definite, coherent heterogeneity" (Spencer 1862:396)—in other words, from a homogeneous, chaotic mass of identical particles into differentiated structures. For Spencer, this particular kind of evolutionary "law" (which we have seen is not so generally true) is the key to every kind of system.[1]

Von Bertalanffy (1968) aimed to broaden the basic principles of systems so that they would apply not merely to the physical sciences but to the social and cultural world as well. Hence, the panscientific principles must be not merely the mechanical principles of physics but should allow humanistic applications, including applications to consciousness and goal-seeking. This would be possible, he believed, by taking these basic principles from cybernetics. *Cybernetics* is the theory of control systems, first developed during World War II in research on missile guidance systems, which gave rise not only to systems engineering but also to information science and the development of computers. This approach allowed systems to be conceived as operating with information as well as with physical materials and forces, in particular, by making use of the concepts of *feedback* and *feedforward.*

MECHANISTIC OR "DUMB" SYSTEMS

Various kinds of systems can be put together out of different combinations of these elements. A mechanistic system is made out of dead matter, like the combination of gears in a clock (the old-fashioned clockworks, not the digital electronic

---

[1] In fairness to Spencer, it should be added that evolution is only one part of the overall cosmic process. There is a phase of the evolutionary development of matter, but also eventually a parallel phase of dissolution, as the universe runs down in accordance with the law of entropy, the second law of thermodynamics (see Turner, 1985a). This principle of dissolution of systems has been little applied to social systems, however.

timepieces which are popular today). Take, for example, a car engine, which may be crudely diagrammed as follows:

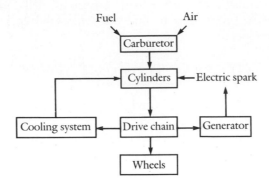

The basic system is a set of feedforwards. Fuel and air come into the system and are mixed together in a certain proportion (which is what the carburetor does); then electricity flows in from the spark plugs, setting off combustion. This results in power, which is transmitted through the gears and the drive chain to turn the wheels of the car. These physical entities and forces flow from one place to another in a chain, each part of which can be called a feedforward.

There are also some *feedbacks* in the system. Part of the motion of the drivetrain is used to turn the generator, which recharges the batteries, providing further electricity to be used in igniting combustion. Another part of the motion turns the cooling system, which keeps the temperature of the engine at a level at which the other processes will operate; another portion operates the fuel pump, and so forth. Thus, parts of the system operate in a circle; producing electricity and other necessities which are repeatedly used up as the system repeats. This is a self-reproducing system, but only in a mechanical sense. If something goes wrong, there is no way that the system itself can correct it. If any one component breaks, the car engine will simply stop. This example reminds us that *feedback by itself is not necessarily "intelligent" or "goal-directed."* We have here a case of what Hanneman (1987) calls "dumb feedback" or "mechanical feedback."

OPEN AND CLOSED SYSTEMS

The car engine is, for the most part, a "closed system." The components operate simply with reference to each other. An "open system," by contrast, interacts with the environment. The car engine is not completely closed however; fuel and air come in from outside the system, and if you neglect to fill the gas tank, the system will eventually run down and stop. One of the basic principles of physics (the second law of thermodynamics) implies that no system is completely closed, and since there are no perpetual motion machines, any system will eventually run down unless new energy is poured into it from the environment. Also, there is an output from the system into the environment in the form of exhaust from the burned fuel, as well as whatever you do with the motion of the car wheels (that is, where you drive your car). But from the point of view of systems theory, these contacts with the environment are episodic or random; once you have filled up the gas tank and turned on the engine, what happens under the hood is for the time being a closed system.

By contrast, we can conceive of such a thing as an "open systems theory," that is, a theory of systems which interact continuously with their environments so that inputs and outputs are themselves understandable and predictable as part of the system pattern. The theory of open systems, however, is not very advanced. Organizational theorists such as Katz and Kahn (1966) have proposed that organizations are really open systems; but beyond stating their general characteristics as interacting with their environments, no general "laws" have been developed. What has been done, instead, has been to broaden the scope of what are considered to be the borders of the system, so that a set of organizations are treated as a system in relation to each other. To speak of an "open system," is really to point to the areas of indeterminism, the factors which arbitrarily come into our model but which are not part of the model itself (for instance, whether you fill up the gas tank of the car). As soon as we try to include a causal connection to explain this, we have made the "closed" part of the system a little broader. For this reason, we may never have a complete theory of "open systems."

"SMART" OR GOAL-SEEKING FEEDBACK

A "higher-level" kind of feedback is one that involves flows, not of physical materials, but of information. Interestingly enough, we do not have to deal with consciousness, or even with living creatures, to find informational feedback systems. An ordinary thermostat found in most homes, for example, may be diagrammed as follows:

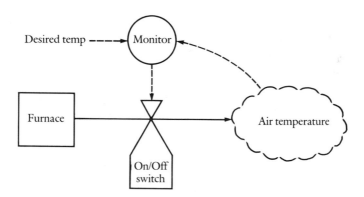

Here we have a heater connected to a monitoring device. This device consists of three parts: a reading of the actual temperature, a goal set at the temperature desired, and a control mechanism. If you set the goal at 70 degrees, whenever the actual temperature falls below that (say to 66) the heater will switch on. When the temperature rises to 70 or above, the heater will switch off. The only thing that flows between the thermostat and the heater is information: in one direction a reading, in the other direction, instructions to turn on or off.

Fundamental theory of the physiology of the human body, or of any biological organism, centers on this kind of feedback loop. The medical scientist Walter Cannon referred to the process as *homeostasis*. Any living organism has certain goal-states programmed in. When we become too hot, certain mechanisms, such as sweating or panting, are automatically turned on to bring the body temperature down. When we are too cold, other mechanisms kick into action, such as shivering, which is a mechanical action of the muscles to generate local heat. When the level of energy fuel for the body cells falls below a certain level, the organism feels hungry and goes into action to find food, which in turn will bring the body's energy "thermostat" back to the desired level and turn off the food-seeking behavior. The body's reaction to diseases is essentially the releasing of a number of these homeostatic mechanisms designed to restore health. The fever we feel when we have an infection is the body's reaction of raising the temperature in order to destroy the invading bacteria. Living organisms appear to be set at the juncture between a large number of such physiological homeostatic mechanisms working in pairs: some operate to bring a bodily process up if it is too low, while their opposites kick in at the appropriate point to bring the bodily process down if it is too high.

NEGATIVE AND POSITIVE FEEDBACK: EQUILIBRIUM OR EXPLOSION

All of the feedback mechanisms described in the preceding section are *negative* feedback. That is, they involve a process of comparison to a goal. If there is a discrepancy between the current state and the goal state (if temperature is too high, if blood sugar level is too low), a corrective action is turned on; once the goal is reached, the action is turned off. *Negative feedback, in other words, is related to establishing and re-establishing states of equilibrium*. It evokes an image of systems as essentially passive, reacting rather than acting, with their "preferred" state one in which nothing has to be done, until they are disturbed again.

Whether this is an appropriate model for a society (or even for an individual personality) has been questioned: do societies (and individuals) merely react to disturbances, rather than seek out their own goals and activities? And are such systems always seeking equilibrium? Notice that the homeostatic model does not say that systems always *are* in equilibrium, but only that they are tuned to some equilibrium point, around which they are constantly varying and being corrected by negative feedback. I will not attempt to answer these questions here. A good deal of theorizing about systems, though, has assumed that the homeostatic model is the appropriate one. Parsons' functionalism endorses this model (although it contains other elements as well); and so does von Bertalanffy and a number of other advocates of a biological systems model (for instance, J. G. Miller, 1978). Neoclassical economic theory similarly uses an equilibrium concept as a kind of centerpoint around which the elements of an economic system continually fluctuate. On the other hand, in psychology, there has been a tendency recently to reject "drive-reduction" models which assume the organism is essentially quiescent unless some equilibrium level has been disturbed.

It is possible, using the system model itself, to show that there are systems which are not equilibrating. One simple example of this is a population growth model. It has only two elements:

The population gives rise to a number of births at some constant rate, and these births feed back into and augment the population. As this system flows through its cycle again and again, the sheer number of births grows larger and larger, and so does the population as a whole. The result is a population explosion. This is because the feedback loop is positive, not negative. Whereas if negative feedback is equilibrating, *positive feedback is explosive*. If this were a completely closed system, the population would grow to infinity. In reality, there is an environment whose resources are needed to keep the population alive. Hence, when such positive feedback loops occur (and they are frequently observed in the propagation of bacteria, fruit flies, and many other organisms, as well in some social analogies, such as the growth of organizations and the spread of innovations), they usually take the shape of a so-called "S-shaped curve": a period of accelerating (or exponential) growth, followed by a slowing down as the environmental limits are asymtotically approached.

The population example does not involve informational feedback but a sheer physical flow which we have called "dumb" feedback. But the same explosive pattern occurs whenever there is a positive feedback loop, even in informational form. A good example of this is an arms race model.

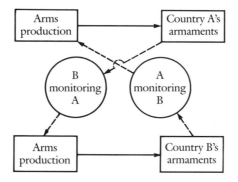

In this system, Country A, the United States, is monitoring the arms level of its opponent, the USSR; and Country B, the USSR, does the same for the arms level of its opponent, the United States. All that it takes for this to be an explosive arms race is for each to set its goal level at slightly above the level of its opponent's arms (say 101 percent, though 110 percent is probably more realistic). As the cycle runs through each repetition, each side's arms will grow exponentially. In reality, again, there are environmental constraints, such as how much of its resources a country can afford to put into arms. But taken purely as a positive feedback system, its results are not equilibrating but explosive.

SELF-REFERENTIAL SYSTEMS AND CONSCIOUSNESS

We have now seen examples of systems which are lifeless machines (car engines or Newton's system of planets revolving around the sun), living organisms (the homeostatic mechanisms of physiological functioning, hunger, and response to disease), as well as social entities (populations or arms races). None of these, properly speaking, can be said to include consciousness—at least, not in its higher forms. Although the actors in the arms race might be said to be operating via conscious goals of keeping their armaments above the level of their opponent, their behavior has a "mechanical" quality that keeps them trapped by the system. Consciousness, at least in the human forms which we value most, has the quality of being able to reflect and especially of being conscious of itself and what it is doing, so as to reset its own goals. For the arms race system to be truly conscious, it would have to include some mechanism by which it could reflect on the fact that it is locked into an explosive situation and by which it could reset its own goals. It would also involve communications by which the two opponents could point out their mutually destructive behavior and negotiate ways to control their competitive system.

How can systems theory model something of this sort? Von Bertalanffy follows a strategy which implies that consciousness emerges as informational feedback loops become more complicated. Although this model is not well worked out in any detail, the general hypothesis seems to be that the human brain itself is a kind of super-feedback loop, a place where various other goal-monitoring mechanisms are themselves monitored. The bodily organism includes various feedback systems, most of them unconscious (such as the autonomic system for regulating body temperature, breathing rate, and so forth), but some of them (such as the feedback loops involving hunger or reaction to dangerous things in the environment) involving choices of actions to make in relation to the world outside. One can imagine the brain having to decide which goals take immediate priority over others: if one is hungry and the food-seeking mechanism is set off, but one is also getting parched by the sun, and hence ready to move into the shade, and also being threatened by a snarling dog, one must set the various goals in some sequence in order to decide which action is to be taken first. The system then becomes *self-referential*, examining its own loops and goals as if they were part of the environment to be taken account of. Presumably consciousness can be explained as a higher level system that emerges to deal with this nexus among various goal-seeking loops.

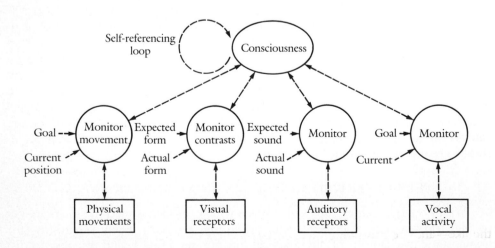

No doubt, the process is more complicated than this; consciousness presumably involves the nesting of several levels of such goal-coordinating systems, one above the other. Thus, there is no absolute dividing line between the conscious and the unconscious, but an increase in consciousness as the number of such meta-feedback loops grows.

There are some attractive parts in this model of consciousness, and we will make further uses of it in Chapters 7 and 9 as we deal with sociological theories of mind and language. At this point, however, it should be borne in mind that the model is merely a very general hypothesis, not well worked out in general systems theory. It does have the weakness, from the sociological point of view, that it derives human consciousness somewhat mysteriously from some unexplained complication which occurs in feedback loops within the individual human organism. By contrast, sociological theory explains consciousness as intrinsically social, involving language and symbols generated by interaction itself, which are then available for use inside the individual mind.

IS SOCIETY A "SMART" FEEDBACK SYSTEM?

There is a tendency to assume that systems are arranged in a hierarchy, from lifeless mechanical systems, up through living organisms, to the human mind, with society and culture as still "higher" levels (for example, von Bertalanffy, 1968: 28–29; Boulding 1978; Miller, 1978). If there is an increasing complexity of feedback, a shift from the physical to the informational and the goal-directed, as we "ascend" up to the human level, there is a natural inclination to continue the "series" to still higher levels and to portray society itself as an even "smarter," more "self-referential" system than any of these. (The neo-Parsonian Niklas Luhman, as we shall see, explicitly regards society as a self-referential system.)

But this may be a mistake. Societies are larger than individual persons, but are they thereby "higher"? And are cultures any more than abstractions, which exist only as lodged in the brains of particular individuals? Actually, I believe this question can be settled more concretely than by philosophical discussion. We can actually model societies and particular social forms (such as organizations) and see what kinds of feedback links these actually involve. We have already seen two brief social examples: a population explosion model, which is a "dumb" feedback system, and an arms race, which involves "smart" or informational, goal-seeking feedback but is nevertheless distinctly lacking an effective self-referential component—exactly the reason why arms races are so dangerous. These do not settle the question, since there are many other models of society, which we will meet throughout this book. But in fact, most of these turn out to be mechanical and "dumb" rather than displaying any higher degrees of self-referentiality. The Marxian model in Chapter 3—except for one significant, hypothetical moment (at the time of the socialist revolution)— is essentially a mechanical feedforward and feedback system. In fact, we can say that the reason why large-scale society is alienating for the human individuals who are in it is that the system itself is mechanical rather than self-referential. Individual human beings are "smart" self-referential systems, but at the size levels "beyond" the individual, the systems are mostly mechanical—population explosions, arms races, and the like—and are frustrating precisely because they are not intelligent. Even systems that include culture as one of their components, like that of Parsons which we will consider, are not necessarily conscious or intelligent *as an overall system*. One of their components may be intelligence, but they are locked into a larger, nonintelligent aggregate in much the same way that your own capacities for self-reflection do little good when you are inside your car alongside thousands of other self-reflective human beings in a freeway traffic jam.

The major problem that most prescriptive, action-oriented political philosophies face is precisely the fact that the macro world is a system that we are caught in, but it is not a goal-seeking system. Alienation may be the condition of teleological individual human beings making up a social system which is by no means as self-reflexive as themselves.[2]

FUNCTIONALISM

Functionalism is a particular subtype of system theory. Functionalist theory was prominent in sociology in the 1940s, 1950s, and early 1960s, but has subsequently been discredited as a genuine model of explanation and is now no longer widely used. The method of functionalism is to explain any particular social institution by the role it plays in maintaining the larger society. As Jonathan Turner (1985: 55) points out, functionalism is an analysis of the relationship between wholes and their parts; it explains the parts by their place in a larger system.

What causes any particular social pattern to exist—the modern family, the institution of love, the restrictive licensing and high pay of the medical profession, the democratic state, or anything else? The functionalist answer in general is that these institutions are explained by the functions that they serve for society (for example, see Merton, 1968; Davis and Moore, 1945; Parsons 1951). The typical family pattern, with the husband the breadwinner and the wife caring for home and children, is explained by the need of society to efficiently socialize children; the licensing which restricts the practice of medicine to a relatively small number of doctors is explained by the need to protect society against incompetent practitioners; and the high pay of doctors is explained by the need to attract the most competent individuals to train themselves for this specialty. Functionalism thus tends to give the most favorable interpretation to everything. One reason it has come under attack is because these explanations ignore any self-interest or advantage and any resulting inequality. Economic and sexual advantages and disadvantages between men and women would hardly enter the mind of a functionalist theorist of the family, nor would it occur to such a theorist that the reason medical doctors receive such high pay is because they have restricted or monopolized the supply of medical services relative to the demand. In the eyes of feminists, conflict theorists, and advocates of greater social equalities, functionalism looks like an ideological justification for the interests of dominant groups.

---

[2] As we shall see in examining Goffman's theory (Chapter 7), even the individual human self may be more of a "mechanical" concatenation of social episodes than we would like to believe. Modern culture glorifies the human self, but this turns out to be more like self-congratulatory ideology than a realistic social science.

However, there is a more formal criticism of functionalism as a mode of explanation. When we ask for the causes of a given phenomenon, the functionalist answer points to its consequences, the functions it serves for society. This appears to be an illogical mode of causation, since an event happening at one time is explained by consequences happening at a later time. How can causality flow backwards in time?

STINCHCOMBE'S FUNCTIONALIST FEEDBACK LOOPS

Arthur Stinchcombe (1968) has attempted to solve this problem by formally diagramming functional relationships in systems terminology. For example, the argument is sometimes made that modern societies have democratic governments because democracy is necessary for social integration (Parsons, 1971). Modern societies are highly differentiated and require a good deal of personal initiative for their roles to be carried out effectively; hence, individuals cannot be controlled in an authoritarian manner, and the state must be relatively participatory and democratic to keep up favorable motivation. Stinchcombe would diagram this argument roughly as follows:

Democratic government ⟶ Social integration of modern society

There is a feedback loop from the consequences to the cause, like the thermostat illustrated under general systems theory. Now the causal sequence can be explained by some device which monitors the level of social integration of society. If that level is too low, a corrective process is set in motion which increases the amount of democratic government, thereby increasing social integration.

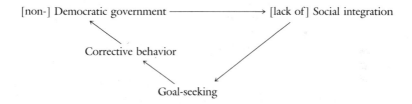

If the level of social integration is high enough, corrective behavior stops, and the existing state of affairs is merely repeated or reproduced.

In theory this seems to be an elegant solution. However, it should be borne in mind that the feedback mechanism is hypothetical and vague. What does it actually consist of in reality (if it really exists at all)? It is doubtful that there really is a "social integration thermostat" somewhere which turns on corrective processes leading to more democracy when the level gets too low. Or if such a mechanism exists, it is still to be specified. We could argue that it is purposive human beings who provide the feedback mechanism; they consciously feel a problem and seek means of achieving their goal. But this does not seem very satisfactory theoretically, since it cannot be assumed that just because people feel dissatisfied they will actually be able to change the larger system to reach their goals. One kind of solution, of course, would be to fall back on the natural selection process described under evolutionary theory (Chapter 1): governments vary, and some of them are more democratic than others; those which are more democratic contribute to greater social solidarity, and hence are selected, while nondemocratic governments and their societies are less likely to survive. But this does not specify why democracy should emerge in the first place. As we have seen in the previous chapter, natural selection models are themselves rather vague, merely "umbrellas" for causal explanations still to be supplied, rather than explanations themselves.

The major problem with functionalist theory from a strictly scientific viewpoint is that it jumps too quickly to conclusions. It tends to justify whatever exists. Since the United States, Britain, and other highly industrialized countries have had democratic governments, it is assumed that democracy is functionally needed for the social integration of modern society. But what about industrial societies which are not democracies, such as most communist states, the Union of South Africa, or Germany in the Nazi period? Here functionalist theory can go two routes. One argument simply plunges ahead with functionalist reasoning: if a society has a dictatorship, it must be because there is a functional need for it. Perhaps one could claim that South Africa functionally needs to be integrated by minority force, or that the USSR's functional need is for dictatorship (as Parsons [1951: 194] claimed by suggesting that its basic system values are collective rather than individualistic).

This kind of argument is not very satisfying. When confronted with a democracy, we are told that it exists because it is functionally necessary; when we are confronted with a dictatorship, we are told that it, too, happens to be functionally necessary. Such a theory obviously lacks predictive power. Under what conditions should we expect to find democracy, and when do we find dictatorship? Functionalism of this sort is only a speculation offered without any proof, or indeed, any evidence except for each single instance itself. Functionalism as a method generally ignores the basic method of scientific research, which is to make comparisons among different conditions in order to show which are associated with different outcomes. Part of the reason functionalism has been abandoned is that we have become better at doing comparative research and now apply more rigorous criteria to explanations before we accept them as true, or at least, plausible.

The other path open to functionalist theory is to claim that all advanced industrial societies need to be democracies; hence nondemocracies are either in societies which are not really advanced, or else they are on their way to becoming democracies. Russia, Nazi Germany, and South Africa would all thus be described as not truly modern societies. To assert this, however, seems to be a distortion of the facts. Parsons (1949: 104–41) once explained the period of Nazi government as a transitional phase resulting from Germany's relatively late industrialization; but in fact, Germany in the early twentieth century was one of the three great industrial powers of the world, on an equal footing with Britain and the United States and ahead of France. It was no more a "late industrializer" than was the United States. Another functionalist approach might argue that modern dictatorships are on their way to becoming democracies. But this seems an over optimistic conclusion. The party dictatorship in the USSR has been in place for about 70 years now and shows no major signs of change; nor would I bet any large sum of money on the assurance that South Africa will soon become democratic. To be realistic, I do not believe that it is *functionally necessary* that democracy will continue in the United States, Britain, or other countries which are now democracies. Functional theory lulls one into a sense of false security; to truly understand the conditions which support democracy or threaten it, we need to move to a stronger mode of theorizing.

TALCOTT PARSONS' FUNCTIONALIST ACTION SYSTEM

Writing principally between the 1930s and 1960s, Talcott Parsons (1949, 1951, 1967) produced a theory which claims to be extremely general and is sometimes referred to as his "Grand Theory." Whereas functionalism, especially in the "middle-range" form advocated by Robert Merton, has a tendency to produce *ad hoc* explanations of whatever happens to exist at a particular time, Parsons aimed at a general statement of how all social systems function. Parsons' theory achieved a certain amount of popularity for a while, especially in the 1950s; then it was severely attacked, by both neo-Marxism and conflict theory, and by microsociologies such as symbolic interactionism and social phenomenology. Yet while Parsonian functionalism was fading in the United States in the 1970s, it was nevertheless acquiring some popularity among German theorists, most notably, Niklas Luhman, Jürgen Habermas, and Richard Munch. And in recent years, even some American theorists, led by Jeffrey Alexander, have called for a revival of Parsonian "Grand Theory" in a revised form, eliminating Parsons' errors and ideological distortions.

THE FOUR-FUNCTION MODEL

Parsons' system is extremely abstract, since it intends to supply basic components for the analysis of any society that has ever existed or might exist, as well as any subsystem within society. We might interpret Parsons as answering the question: what are the basic functions that must be fulfilled in any social system? Presumably, if we knew these functions in advance, we could then classify any existing institution according to the functions it served, and could predict that certain institutions would come into being. Parsons answers with the following diagram:

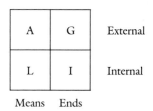

This is called the *L-I-G-A* or *A-G-I-L* scheme (depending on the direction in which we read the boxes). L stands for *latent pattern maintenance*; it refers to the necessity for any system of action to have some basic pattern. Metaphorically speaking, it is a guiding script. *I* stands for *integration*, and refers to a system's need to actively keep its parts together. *G* stands for *goal attainment*, and refers to the fact that every system has some output, or goal, that it achieves in relation to its environment. *A* stands for *adaptation*, and refers to the way the system supports itself as a physical entity in relation to the material environment.

The scheme is generated very abstractly by the two dichotomous dimensions, *Internal/External* and *Means/Ends*. Everything in a system may be regarded as operating in either internal or external directions, and can be either a means or an end. By cross-cutting these two dimensions, we create four boxes, which Parsons labels *L-I-G-A*.[3]

Parsons' scheme is easiest to understand when it is applied to the functional subsystems of society, which we can set out thus:

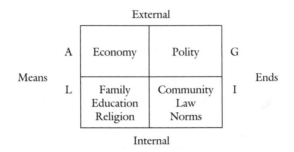

In the *L* box we find all those institutions which are regarded as producing the basic cultural pattern and inculcating it into individuals (hence, the inclusion of the family—an agency for socializing children). Under *I* we find institutions which actively promote social integration, both the actual community—the personal associations which people have with one another—and also the laws and norms which supply the rules by which members behave. These are both *internal* to the system, dealing only with inner relationships within society. In this sphere, the basic cultural patterns are laid down by the items in box *L* (hence, they are *means*), while the actual integration is worked out by the items in box *I* (hence, they are *ends*). The top row is the *external* side. The economy *(A)* is regarded as means; the system deals with the external world, adapting to it by taking material inputs and transforming them economically to serve the system's physical needs. Finally, the ends of the system, as it acts externally (either in relation to the physical world, or towards other systems) is *G* (goal attainment). Parsons regards *polity* (state) as this sector, in which all the other functional components and inputs culminate in some output or action on behalf of the whole system.

Parsons believed his *L-I-G-A* scheme gives the basic dimensions of any system of action and at one time called his whole scheme "The General Theory of Action."

---

[3] We might ask why the first box is called *latent pattern maintenance* rather than merely *pattern maintenance*. *Latent* implies that the pattern is implicitly rather than explicitly upheld, although this is not always the case in Parsons' empirical examples of what goes in this box. Personally, I believe that he avoided calling it "pattern maintenance" or *P* because he did not think *P-I-G-A* was as euphonious as *L-I-G-A*.

This was at a time when he was trying to integrate the psychology, anthropology, and sociology departments at Harvard University into a single Department of Social Relations.[4] "Action" could be in any system, including an individual personality (the province of psychology) or any collectivity (such as an organization) or society as a whole. Culture, although not precisely a system of action itself, since culture is not alive and does not act (Parsons and Shils, 1951: 7), is nevertheless yet another component level of the system, and is capable of being analyzed in the same terms as any other component. Parsons assigned culture to anthropology as a research area; the other social sciences, economics and political science, Parsons treated as merely specialties dealing with particular subsystems within the social system. He was not, however, successful in drawing them into his grand coalition of the Social Relations Department at Harvard; although he did produce a book (Parsons and Smelser, 1956) showing how economics integrated with, and was generally subordinate to, sociology.

Parsons' four-function scheme was meant to be applied *analytically,* that is, abstractly, rather than confined to any particular empirical level of analysis. Thus, the social system could be divided into four boxes, as in the preceding diagram. But each one of these boxes, in turn, could be subdivided into its own set of boxes. Treated in its own right as a system, the economy, for example, had to fulfill its own internal *L-I-G-A* functions:

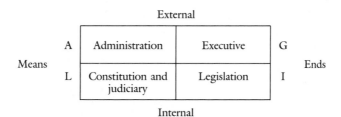

Similarly, the polity subdivides into:

External

A	Administration	Executive	G
L	Constitution and judiciary	Legislation	I

Means   Ends

Internal

---

[4] For the statement of the "committee" which legitimated this maneuver intellectually, see Parsons and Shils (1951). In his autobiography (1984: 293–307), George Homans, who was a junior member of the department at this time, reminisces critically about this maneuver, which he saw as a power ploy on Parsons' part.

In principle, the subdivision of boxes within boxes could be endless. We could take the legislative function within the polity, for example, and show that any actual legislative body would itself have to meet its own *L-I-G-A* functions.

Or we could go in the other direction, towards the larger system rather than the smaller. Thus, the social system itself is merely part of a larger complex. We have already seen that Parsons believed the General Theory of Action would include personality, society, and culture. When he comes to put this into his *L-I-G-A* boxes, however, he feels impelled to add a fourth component, which he calls the *behavioral system* (labeled *A*), alongside *personality* (labeled *G*). Personally, I think that this is an artificial distinction, introduced because of Parsons' propensity for putting things into symmetrical boxes—he could not of, course, leave a box empty! This having been done, each of these boxes *(personality, behavioral system, cultural system)* can then be further subdivided into its own functional subsectors, and so on (see Figure 2-1).

We may begin to conclude that Parsonian theory, at least this part of it, is only a kind of parlor game in which one invents puzzle-boxes and then solves them, with each solution making possible a whole further set of puzzles. I think this is often the case, although Parsons also tries to make use of these boxes for his theory of media or interchanges (see pages 67–69). In defense of Parsons, though, we could say that at least his basic claim may be right: that in fact any social organization at all will have to take care of the four basic functions if it is to survive. Any organization must have some basic culture, must have a community of personal relationships to integrate things, must take care of its economic side, and will have its own politics. All four functions are necessary: an idealistic social movement will never last if it forgets about economic resources, and a business cannot be economically successful if it does not provide enough social integration among its members. And every organization, like it or not, will have some kind of politics. Treated in this way, Parsons' model provides at least a baseline of what any organization must

FIGURE 2-1

PARSONS' GENERAL THEORY OF ACTION

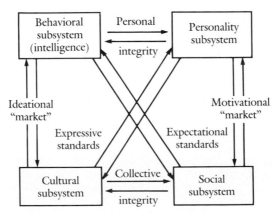

realistically have; and he stresses that "realistic" means not merely focusing on material things, since an organization can fail by ignoring the equally important side of social integration.

THE HIERARCHY OF CONTROL

What holds the system together? For Parsons the process is multidimensional, so that different aspects of the system work together to ensure that people will properly play their parts. However, he gives special emphasis to socialization, the process by which individuals learn the basic values and norms of the system.

There is a hierarchy of control within the system:

> Values
> Norms
> Roles
> Sanctions

At the most general level, the system lays down certain values. In American society, for example, one of the most basic values is supposed to be achievement. This is a basic cultural pattern (thus, belonging in the *latent pattern maintenance* square). In more specific situations of interaction *(I)* this general value is specified into particular norms—rules which state how actors should behave. In the school setting, for example, it is striving for good grades; in an athletic contest, scoring points; in business, making money; and so forth. These rules become patterned into roles, according to the individuals' "position" in an organization; for instance, the role of student or teacher, employee or manager or customer, and so forth. (This process is part of the *G* sector, considered as output of the system.) People enforce the norms for particular roles by applying sanctions *(A)*, rewarding those who conform and punishing those who violate the norms.

From an abstract point of view, all of these elements go together to ensure conformity with the system. Parsons, however, places particular emphasis upon the basic values, since these are believed to set the basis for norms and roles (which merely specify how the values will operate in particular situations and for particular persons). But what about the sanctions? Couldn't we say that people conform basically because they are externally controlled, rewarded for compliance (say, by being paid for their work) and threatened with punishment for violations (such as being fired if they don't work)? Parsons places sanctions far down on the list of control elements, however. That is part of his general rejection of a utilitarian or economic determinism of behavior.

DURKHEIM'S THEORY OF PRECONTRACTUAL SOLIDARITY

Parsons takes his argument from Durkheim's theory, which demonstrates that society could not be held together simply by rational agreement or exchange of rewards (Durkheim, 1893; Parsons, 1937: 343–50). Durkheim pointed out that society could not have been created by an original "social contract," since any agreement—say, to exchange the products of one's labor on a market—could not be undertaken without some assurance that no one would cheat or violate the contract in order to get something for nothing. Any contract, therefore, requires an enforcer. It might seem as if the state, with its police and law courts, acts as an enforcer for contracts. Yet people would first have to agree to set up the state and law courts, and there is always the possibility that someone would cheat on *that* agreement as well. Durkheim concluded that no contract or merely utilitarian exchange is possible without a prior "agreement" or understanding that the contract—the rules of the exchange—will be upheld. Any contract requires *precontractual solidarity,* a basic feeling of trust between the persons involved. Thus, economics cannot be the fundamental basis of society; economic relationships themselves are only possible on the foundation of an already existing social solidarity.

What causes this social solidarity to exist? We cannot assume that it is always there, or be certain which people it will include. Special conditions are necessary to produce it. In Durkheim's theory, the mechanism that produces social solidarity consists of what I have called *interaction rituals,* in a model presented and developed in Chapter 6. There, we will see that the Durkheimian theory of solidarity is compatible with a conflict theory in which material resources, rewards, and punishments are also important. Solidarity is a variable and characterizes particular groups in their struggle for power over each other, rather than a harmonious social system as a whole. Parsons uses Durkheim's general argument that sanctions must be based on prior social solidarity, but in a very different fashion from conflict theory.

SOCIALIZATION AND DEVIANCE

For Parsons, solidarity is produced primarily at the level of values, which are shared by more or less everyone in a society. His answer to how precontractual solidarity is produced is to say that children are socialized by their parents so that the basic values of society are "internalized" as parts of their personalities. In Parsons' terms, the need-dispositions of their personalities become shaped by the basic values of society, with the result that individuals need and want to do what society demands of them. If society places a basic value upon achievement, then children grow up with a personality need to achieve. If society's basic values emphasize group conformity, children are produced whose personality is most strongly oriented towards belonging to the group. In general, early childhood is the time at which children internalize the general social values. As they grow older, they become oriented towards particular spheres of activities and their norms, and in doing so, take on certain roles: boys learn to achieve in sports and go on to identify with the role of professional athlete or insurance salesman; girls learn to be nurturant and go on to identify with being housewives and mothers. (Some readers may find the sexist examples offensive, but this is the typical mode of analysis of Parsonian theory, which is oriented towards the most conventional version of society.)

During the 1940s and 1950s, when Parsons was formulating this model, Freudian psychoanalysis was very popular among American intellectuals. Parsons himself underwent psychoanalysis, and devoted considerable effort to integrating the Freudian theory into his own system. For Freud, the infant begins as *id,* the raw biological impulses of hunger, aggression, and sexual drives. Eventually, these impulses are controlled and partially repressed into the unconscious, while a reality-oriented conscious self, or *ego,* appears. Most importantly, the child comes to identify with his or her parent, and internalizes the parent in the form of a *superego.* This is a psychic representation of the parent, no longer in the external world but operating as an internalized conscience and ideal. The parent is no longer outside telling the child what to do, but is inside the psyche, invisibly overseeing the child's thoughts and actions, praising what is right and making the child feel guilty for wrongdoing (or even thinking of wrongdoing). This fantasy parent also serves as an ideal, holding up the image of what the child is trying to emulate.

For Parsons, the Freudian superego is the key device by which society's values are transmitted to the child. They become part of his or her personality, so that the well-socialized individual does not have to be controlled from outside; instead, he or she obeys society's rules because of an internal need to do so. Society passes along its values from generation to generation in this way; children internalize basic values from their parents and pass them along to *their* children.

Parsons regarded Freudian theory as a solution to the problem of what holds society together. His system may be described as a combination of Durkheim's and Freud's theories (or at least, of certain aspects of these theories). This is not to say that Freudian theory is necessarily very accurate as an explanation of the individual self; differing sociological approaches will be met in Chapter 7. Parsons, however, assumes that it is accurate and incorporates it into his model in a fundamental position.

Parsons thus makes use of a psychological theory to explain how values operate as the center of the social system. But his theory does not reduce society, or culture, to psychology. The values themselves are not generated by psychology but by the autonomous pattern of culture, and especially by the history of its religions. Parsons was not sympathetic to anthropologists of the "culture-and-personality" school, who tried to show that the values of a society depended upon its methods of rearing small children (the claim, for instance, that early toilet-training would result in a drive to control the environment). Parsons was more inclined to turn this the other way around: how children are brought up depends on their society's values.

For example, deviance from society's preferred pattern could occur because of strains at any level of the system. One way that deviance can occur, of course, is through faulty socialization. Because parents are not available, or otherwise fail to bring up a child properly, the child may fail to develop the value of achievement and may become a thief, a delinquent, unemployed, a drop-out, and so forth. But deviance could also be caused at some other level. Individuals may simply not have learned the norms of the particular situation they are in: perhaps they are immigrants from a different culture. Or the roles themselves may be responsible; there may be a conflict between different roles—say, between being a loyal family member looking out for relatives' economic welfare and being an employee of an organization whose property is supposed to be protected. And finally there may be a breakdown at the level of sanctions: if white-collar crime is not being controlled in an organization, individuals may be punished by fellow workers if they don't go along with it and rewarded if they do. Parsons thus leaves room for the system to become unhinged at various points. Although the central tendency of the system is towards conformity and harmonious operation, there is the possibility of deviance and conflict. In the long run, though, Parsons expects that conformity and control always reassert themselves.

THE PATTERN VARIABLES

The *L-I-G-A* model and the hierarchy of control describe what all social systems have in common. The differences among systems Parsons accounts for in two ways: (1) the pattern variables, or fundamental choices in the realm of culture and (2) the level of differentiation.

In the abstract, any actor's behavior can be seen as guided by certain basic choices. Parsons derived these dimensions by analyzing certain theories of social evolution, particularly the *dichotomous stage theories* already described in Chapter 1. Toennies had distinguished between traditional societies or *Gemeinschaft* (community) and modern commercial societies or *Gesellschaft* (society, formal association); Durkheim, between the *mechanical solidarity* of small, homogenous tribes and rural communities and the *organic solidarity* of the large-scale division of labor. Parsons elaborated these distinctions into five dimensions. As we have already seen, the distinctions are intended to be treated analytically rather than historically; that is, they should not be seen as either/or characterizations of two different phases of history, but as continuous variables, different values, both of which might be found within different parts of the same society.

Ascription vs. achievement: (This was Linton's dichotomy in Chapter 1. Are individuals born into their positions in society? Is their position "ascribed" to them by virtue of their age, sex, race, and family membership? Or must they achieve their own positions by their own merits?

Particularism vs. universalism: Does one judge people and situations by who they are in relation to oneself—for example, giving preference to one's friends and relatives over strangers—or does one apply abstract, universal standards, such as "hire the person with the highest test scores"?

Diffuseness vs. specificity: Does one make a global judgment about the kind of person one is dealing with? For instance, if dealing with a high-ranking official, does one assume that he or she is right about everything, or does one deal with him or her very specifically in terms of the task at hand ("I don't care who you are, in this office all we are concerned about is getting the job done")?

Affectivity vs. affective neutrality: Does one allow one's emotional attitude (warmth or hostility) to influence one's behavior, or does one just concentrate on "getting the job done"? Parsons has in mind the distinction between tribal societies with their pervasive religious taboos and spiritual influences that are constantly being placated, and the attitudes of detachment and cool calculation that go along with modern technology.

Collectivity orientation vs. individualism: Is one basically concerned with the group, one's place in it, and maintaining one's group loyalty, or is one concerned with following one's own path, making up one's own mind?

In general, Parsons' ethical sympathies are always with the latter of these pairs of elements. Ascription and particularism indicate lack of individual opportunity, unfairness, and prejudice; while achievement and universalism are the "modern" values of equal opportunity and equal treatment according to the rules. Looking at these as analytical elements, though, Parsons believes that no society can move completely to the poles of achievement and universalism; for families must always ascribe the status of the husband to his children and wife (at least during the time when children are young), and that always creates the inequities of personal relationships and inherited advantages. Similarly, Parsons believes that specificity and affective neutrality are better than their opposites, since they are fairer, less irrational, more scientific, and more efficient. Again, Parsons does not believe that any society can survive without some general emotions (since the core values themselves must always underlie any merely instrumental, rational calculations). But he does not agree with the criticism of modern society that it is too specialized, impersonal, and calculating. It is only because we have an *underlying commitment* to these characteristics as values that our society does have this much rationality and calculation; we have a kind of fundamental emotional commitment to being unemotional, so to speak. Apart from this analytical reason, Parsons is, as usual, a vigorous apologist for modern society, which he sees as superior to earlier forms of society.

Contrary to some of the critiques of modernity which see us as trapped in a mass society, ordered around by bureaucracies, and coerced by economic markets and governmental controls, Parsons believes that the modern trend is towards individualism, not collectivism. This, of course, is an analytical dimension, too, and not all aspects of modern society are necessarily individualistic. An entire modern society, such as the Soviet Union (or, in another sense, Japan), can be characterized as emphasizing the collectivity value rather than the individualism value stressed in the United States (Parsons, 1951: 180–200). (This is part of Parsons' solution to the need for a functional explanation of nondemocratic government, already discussed.) But in general, Parsons also believes that the long-term evolutionary trend is towards individualism rather than collectivism. He derives this from Durkheim's theory that the division of labor produces greater specialization of roles and hence greater emphasis on individuals following their own unique trajectories through the complexities of the social system.

There is a certain amount of inconsistency in the way that Parsons uses the pattern variables scheme. On one hand, they are indeed analytical variables, and presumably any combination of partial values along any continuum is possible. Thus, industrial societies can have both achievement- and individualism-oriented values, as does the United States; yet also collectivity- and universalism-oriented systems, as does the USSR; or collectivity- and achievement-oriented systems, as does Japan; as well as greater elements of ascription (allegedly) in modern Germany and England, and so on. The values in some sense are arbitrary, and since they are seen as controlling the system once they are plugged into the L box, they give different flavors to different societies. Yet another strand of Parsons' theory regards some of the values (the right hand of each pattern variable) as evolutionarily more "modern" than those on the left hand; hence, there is a trend towards these values, and societies which represent them more fully (such as the United States) are regarded as evolutionarily more advanced.

THE DIFFERENTIATION MODEL

Parsons uses the differentiation model in his understanding of social change. As we have already seen, in this type of theory change is viewed as a process of differentiation which upgrades the capacity of the system, making it more efficient. Differentiation also may cause strains, bringing about a need for integration. This integration of the system is provided in several ways: in part by the creation of new agencies of regulation (especially governmental agencies), which themselves are an additional differentiation, and also at the level of norms and values. In the latter case, the norms of interaction are widened towards greater inclusion; whereas the previous, less differentiated system operated with only specific kinds of behaviors and persons allowed (for example, the hiring of white males only), the more differentiated system widens its norms to accommodate other kinds of persons. At the level of values, Parsons sees social systems as tending towards greater universalism; for instance, early Western industrial society, which demanded adherence to doctrinal Christianity, has now (allegedly) moved towards greater tolerance, admitting all religions as long as they adhere to a general ethical code.

PARSONS' TWO THEORIES OF SOCIAL CHANGE

Again, we see Parsons as a liberal optimist, convinced that the direction of social change is toward greater equality of opportunity, greater tolerance, more universal laws, and greater efficiency of the system, to boot. It is worth noticing that two components of his theory work in opposite directions. One aspect of the theory stresses values (the pattern variables) in that it sees society's basic pattern as laid down by its values (which are instilled into individuals by the socialization process). Here Parsons follows a version of Max Weber's theory (1904–1905/1980) which suggested that the Protestant version of Christianity produced an emphasis on hard work and economic achievement, resulting in the spirit of modern capitalism. In his later works, Weber (1916/1951, 1916–17/1958, 1917–19/1952) broadened his argument from Protestantism to Christianity in general, contrasting the Christian emphasis on working out one's salvation by ethical conduct in the world, with the mystical salvation of Hindu or Buddhist religion, and the ethical adjustment to the world, without an other-worldly salvation, in Chinese Confucianism. Parsons (1966) interpreted this to mean that the great religious prophets and innovators—Jesus and Paul, Confucius, the Buddha, Mohammed, and a few others—laid down the basic religious values of their civilizations. With this explanation of change, a new value is placed in the L box of the L-I-G-A model, which in turn establishes new norms, organizational roles, and economic structures. Here change can be diagrammed as creating a causal sequence around the box from L up through A:

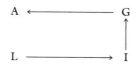

In the differentiation model, however, change generally proceeds in the opposite direction. Typically there is differentiation in the economic sphere (*A*), resulting in upgrading of system output (*G*), as well as governmental regulation (*G*), with pressures for greater inclusiveness in the normative sphere (*I*), and the final result of a greater universalism in the basic values (*L*).

In this model values are no longer autonomous determinants of the system. Differentiation itself pushes towards greater universalism, and (as we have seen) also greater emphasis on achievement, individualism, specificity, and affective neutrality.

Can the two versions of causality in Parsons' system be reconciled? Perhaps, but I doubt whether it is worth the effort. For both sides of the model are essentially speculative, and in fact, it is not clear that values really do determine the rest of the social system. Religion may well have been important in the different directions taken by Western and Eastern societies in world history, but there are other ways to interpret Weber's model than the one Parsons has chosen. We do not have to accept a model in which religious values are mysteriously given from "on high"; religious prophets themselves may be predictable, because of certain things happening in the social structure. For that matter, values themselves can be the response to certain structural forms. As we shall see in Chapter 6, the direction of causality may be from society to culture, rather than vice versa.

We have already seen some of the weaknesses of the differentiation model in Chapter 1. It is only worth noting here that the differentiation theory does not specify in which part of the system it must start. Parsons' main empirical examples of change start with the economy, giving rise to the need for government regulation, and so forth; but more abstractly, differentiation may presumably happen among any elements in the whole system or in various subsystems, with no particular way of predicting which will happen when or where. Parsons' differentiation model is more about the consequences of differentiation than about its causes; and even the theory of the consequences appears too optimistically functionalist to be realistic or predictive.

MEDIA AND INTERCHANGE: NIKLAS LUHMAN

The differentiation model and the four-fold functional boxes have yet another use in Parsonian theory. As societies differentiate, the different functions become carried out by separate organizations. In a small tribal society the family not only provided cultural pattern maintainance, it was also the locus of economic production, political organization, and social interaction. As all these activities become localized in different organizations and then are further subsplit as these organizational spheres become internally differentiated, there arises a need to coordinate the different organizations. This is done in two ways.

First, there is an actual exchange of the "products" of each sector. The political sphere needs material inputs from the economy in the form of money, weapons and other material resources to support the state and its personnel. In return, the political sector provides support for economic property, tax policies, and other governmental actions which favor economic production. There is a similar exchange between each pair of functional sectors. We might notice, incidentally, that Parsons developed this argument in a debate against C. Wright Mills, who had charged (1956) that there is a "power elite" in the United States, consisting of a structured exchange of favors between big business executives and the heads of the federal government and the military. Mills saw this as undermining democracy; Parsons, with his usual optimistic defense of the status quo, saw it merely as an instance of a much more abstract process which goes on in *all* social systems: a coordination by way of exchange between political and economic sectors. In an abstract sense, Parsons is probably right that politics cannot exist without economic resources, and vice versa. But Parsons automatically assumed that exchanges among sectors were equal and balanced, and that they benefited the whole system. The idea that private business corporations might be unduly favoring their interests by their political influence at the expense of the population at large seems never to have occurred to him.[5]

Parsons (1967) went on to analyze the interchanges between sectors in a more abstract way. That is, he observed that there are not only physical flows from one institution to another, but there are media of exchange which operate on a symbolic level. The basic analogy here is money. Money emerged to facilitate economic exchanges in a differentiated society; instead of having to barter one's goods or labor for some immediate physical substitute—grain for fish, wagon wheels for wedding dresses—the system gains much more flexibility by using money, which is acceptable for all of these things, as a token of exchange. Parsons thus points out that money actually has a moral quality; rather than being the root of all evil, it indicates a higher level of trust between people. Whereas barter implies a hard-nosed attitude—not giving up anything until one has the goods in return—money indicates an implicit promise to pay in the future. Thus, the acceptance of money (and of high-order financial instruments, such as checks, stocks, credit cards) actually indicates the spread of trust throughout society.

Money is one medium of exchange, both within and among different functional spheres. (In this sense, media of exchange are more abstract than the actual flows of output of each functional sector.) Another medium of exchange is power. Within the political sphere—or, more generally, between the leaders of the state and the members of society—power operates as a medium analogous to money. It, too, is a form of trusting future promises. Citizens vote for a leader because they expect him

---

[5] It is easy to produce a computer simulation of the abstract model of system interchanges in Figure 2-1 or any of the analogous subsystem diagrams. In doing so, we are forced to recognize how vague and abstract these models actually are. There is nothing in Parsons' theory to tell us how much of any quantity ought to be flowing from one sector to another; the general implication seems to be that the flows in each direction are proportional to each other. Parsons does not deal with the possibility that the economy might get more from the state than vice versa. He assumes the system is balanced, by theoretical fiat.

to fulfill certain purposes for them; putting this more abstractly, we can say that they are giving him power as a kind of long-term loan to be invested. Using the analogy of money, Parsons distinguishes between inflationary and deflationary periods in political power. In an inflationary period, citizens have increasing confidence in government and are willing to give general support for relatively long terms without expecting immediate payoffs. On the other hand, governments may not be very effective, or voters become more suspicious; then political deflation sets in, and voters do not trust leaders except for very short periods and only if they produce very concrete results for them.

The German theorist Niklas Luhman, who was a graduate student of Parsons' in the early 1960s, has greatly expanded this part of the theory. Luhman (1979, 1980, 1982) sees society as a system in the formal sense, which he declares is "self-referential" and has purposes of its own. Individuals are necessarily subject to the demands of the system. Nevertheless, the system must work with human materials. Luhman uses the phenomenological philosophy of Husserl and Heidegger to describe the individual human situation of ordinary life as one in which the world is merely taken for granted as natural and familiar. But because modern society is highly differentiated, the individual is always experiencing contingencies: new people that one encounters, new situations, unpredictable futures, and remote institutional sectors (when one's life is intruded upon by new bureaucratic agencies or new business ventures that are always proliferating). The modern world is depersonalized and complex, and this arouses anxiety in the individual. The way this anxiety is allayed is by the rise of "media of communication."

These media include money and power, as well as two more that Luhman adds, *love* and *truth*. These four each operate within a particular cell of Parsons' four-fold table of social subsystems. All of them provide standardized symbols which cut across situations and enable individuals to trust in the system even though it is far too complex for them to grasp all its contingencies. Money provides this trust in bringing together the far-flung exchanges of the economic sphere, just as power does in the political sphere. In personal interaction, love is a symbolic ideal which people use in order to establish favorable personal relationships with others whom they have not known all their lives: the possibility of romance, or more generally, of human charity and sympathy, is what holds together the huge number of social interactions among strangers in modern society. And in the cultural sphere, truth is a general mechanism allowing people to accept on faith that the unfamiliar institutional sectors they encounter each have their own experts and forms of knowledge, so that what happens there, too, can be regularized and normalized.

Luhman (1982, 1986) includes historical treatments of how each of these media of communication has gradually developed. One reason for his popularity in German sociology is the way in which he provides erudite histories of these various aspects of culture, enlivening the bare abstractions of Parsons' system with vignettes of the development of courtly love in post-Renaissance Europe and the development of the concept of truth, as well as the phenomena of politics and economics. A more critical observer would say that Luhman illustrates his points rather than proves them. (For instance, a conflict theory of sexual property and male/female domination would explain the history of courtly love in a different way from Luhman's purely system-function analysis.) Luhman is actually more conservative than Parsons, who comes across as an optimistic, somewhat naive, liberal. Luhman, on the other hand, makes little room for individual preferences or freedoms in modern society; rather, he observes that there is an inevitable force of differentiation at the level of social institutions, which reduces the freedom of individual choices and requires individuals simply to take the system on trust. More consistent than Parsons, he does not see culture as an autonomous source of social change; instead, culture (including such cultural phenomena as truth and love) is forced to take certain forms because of the differentiation of the system.

Luhman argues that each medium is relevant only to its own differentiated subsystem: love holds value in personal relationships (sphere of social interaction), truth in science and intellectual life (sphere of culture), while neither is appropriate for the political sphere. In the latter, politicians are necessarily guided by the bargaining and coalitions that make up the exercise of power. Luhman's theory thus has a somewhat cynical outlook. Luhman stresses the fact that social systems at the macro level are not usually very stable or well integrated. That is because individual actors can select from a huge variety of possible communications and actions, and hence there is often little real consensus among individuals. Normative order is largely a myth. Individuals are able to operate socially because they *assume* the existence of order even when it is lacking. This is what the symbolic media do for the system; they give individuals a feeling of confidence in dealing with situations beyond their personal experience, even when their assumptions are inaccurate.[6]

CRITICISM OF THE PARSONIAN SYSTEM

Perhaps the basic flaw of Parsonian theory is that it has relatively little explanatory content, and does little to identify the cause of any particular social arrangement. Functionalism in general tends to take whatever exists and explain it as serving the needs of the system; but as we have seen, even if quite different social phenomena existed, they, too, would be explained as serving system needs—or else as a strain that will be resolved by future social change. Most of this is extremely vague, and tells us nothing about whether there will be democracy or dictatorship, capitalism or socialism, traditionalist sexism or women's liberation.

We might describe this as a typically functionalist lack of vision regarding stratification. Parsons was a traditional, unconscious sexist, who described the "division of labor by age and sex" as a functional way of specializing social roles of males and females (1949: 89–103). No doubt, Parsons' system could be revised and made compatible with a more liberated, egalitarian view of women's position in society, but Parsons himself would never have cut through the ideology, nor led the way to any liberation. My main point is not an ideological one, however, but simply to point out that Parsons' scheme does not give us any leverage on these questions because it does not really contain a causal model of what happens when and under what conditions. Parsons' underlying strategy is very close to the philosophy "whatever is, is right" (that is, functional). This operates well enough at the level of op-

---

[6] In this respect, Luhman's theory is like Garfinkel's ethnomethodology, as Luhman (1984: 157–65) explicitly recognized. See also Fuchs (1986).

timistic justifications of social arrangements, but it is not very penetrating or useful as explanation.

To the extent that Parsons has explanations, they are weak or wrong: evolutionism as a theory of social change; the differentiation model (without any good causes, and with inaccurate views of its effects); and the socialization model taken over from Freud to explain individual development. Parsons' theory consists largely of a category scheme, a device for dividing everything into four boxes and then drawing arrows between them. Substantively, the most important part of the theory may concern some of the media of exchange. But even here we find vagueness and unresolved questions. Luhman regards love as a medium of exchange, but surely it is not comparable to money in all respects. We cannot collect love, or invest it for a future return. And truth seems even less like a monetary currency circulating from one situation to another. We might ask why he calls it "truth," with that word's connotation of what is accurately known, when he is really describing the mere acceptance of information from strange experts in unfamiliar situations? Even the most solidly based analogy, between money and power, tends to make power more of an equal exchange than it usually is. Power, as the ability to coerce others, may well have a symbolic and emotional side (as we shall see in conflict theory and in the interactional ritual model), but this is not well captured by declaring that it flows like a nicely equilibrating economic marketplace. Still, insofar as exchange models are now being developed in the sphere of emotions and cultural capital (Chapter 10), Parsons deserves some credit for preparing the way with his initial model, however crude.

Finally, something may be said in defense of Parsons' functionalist vision. Any social system has to include ways of overriding sheer self-interest. A purely Hobbesian conflict situation cannot exist (at least, not very extensively). As soon as there is any kind of social organization at all, no matter how coercive, there must be some elements of integration of the sort Parsons (and Durkheim) speak about. There must be honor among thieves, for instance, if they are to be successful as thieves. This is one of the reasons why there is less crime than we might imagine: even the most extreme, exploitative self-interest, if it is to survive, must make these "functional" concessions. Burglars cannot survive economically without an organizational network of "fences" (illegal businesses) to dispose of their stolen goods, and these businesses must fulfill basic organizational requirements if they are to survive. At minimum, crime becomes the rivalry of opposing "societies," each with its own morality, enforcement, and so forth. "Organized crime" is considered so dangerous, in fact, because it operates as a little private government. The same phenomena can be seen in the history of the state. Historical states (the Mongol Empire, for instance) may actually have begun as marauding conquerors; but bands of raiders or robber-barons, no matter how cruel, must create solutions to these organizational problems. Of course, this cooperation may take place only within the organization of the coercers themselves and need not extend to their victims. The conquering army or the ruling class needs internal solidarity, even as it applies brute force to controlling the lower class, and this always introduces at least a partial element of functional integration into the system.

This issue can be put in terms of a theological analogy. (Theology, according to Durkheimian theory, is actually about social issues and in fact we can use its metaphors readily.) Evil always includes an element of good insofar as there is a social element in evil. But lest we get carried away with the Pollyannaish tone common to functionalism, we should remember that the opposite is also true: good always includes an element of evil. Analytically, there is always an element of self-interest—and usually of coercion—in society, along with the elements of value integration. These combinations of what is useful and necessary with what is coercive give a dramatic and even tragic tone to many theories. Marxism, as we shall see in the next chapter, can be regarded as the functionalism of evil.

JEFFREY ALEXANDER'S DEFENSE OF MULTIDIMENSIONAL ACTION THEORY

Recently, Jeffrey Alexander (1980–83) has argued that the Parsonian system is the most important advance in fundamental sociological theory since the era of the classics—Marx, Durkheim, and Weber. According to Alexander, each of these theories was one-sided: Marx in his mature work erred on the side of materialism and economic determinism, and took account mainly of utilitarian, instrumentalist motivational factors, while Durkheim went too far in relying on subjective ideals and moral factors. Neither of these positions is seen as completely erroneous, but both need to be taken together to achieve a fully rounded theory. Although Weber attempted to be multidimensional, in Alexander's judgment, he was merely inconsistent: in some parts of his works (especially the sociology of religion) he stressed the independent power of religious ideas and values; elsewhere (especially in his politics) he dealt with mere material conditions and Machiavellian self-interest. The two sides of Weber never fitted together into a single system.

In Alexander's view, Parsons alone saw the need for full multidimensionality. We can see this in the *L-I-G-A* boxes, which include the material, cultural, political, and interactional worlds as equal components of what was truly a "general theory of action." The model also gives full scope to both individual actors and to the macro level of the social system, and yet another macro level of values. The bare outlines of Parsons' model, then, give the dimensions of a truly general sociology.

Alexander argues that the theories which criticized Parsons in the 1960s and 1970s, conflict theory and subjectivist/phenomenological theories, are actually on weaker grounds *as general theories*. Conflict theory, especially from the Marxian side, reduces society to one or two boxes of the system—economics and politics. The phenomenological theories, on the other hand, miss the entire level of macro structure, of patterned interaction above the level of the individual. For however insightful they may be about individual action and consciousness, they make the error of reducing society to portions of the bottom boxes, culture and interaction. Only on the grounds of a general action theory, such as Parsons provided, can the insights of these theories be properly integrated.

At the same time, however, Alexander is critical of Parsons for falling back from his insight into multidimensionality. Alongside Parsons' exposition of this general theory, there is a more particular Parsonianism: the side which is functionalist, all too ready to adopt Pollyannaish complacency about the working of present institutions and a facile opitimism about the future. Alexander wants to strip away the functionalism from the system; he prefers to call it the *theory of action* rather than *structural functionalism*. Further, he criticizes Parsons for stressing values and value socialization as the guiding element in the system (see "Parsons' Two Theories of Social Change," pages 66–67), rather than making values merely one element interacting on an equal par with the others. Alexander stresses the aspect of Parsons which focuses on conflict, especially as the process of differentiation produces imbalances. Alexander currently points out that a system theory does not have to be in equilibrium and criticizes Parsons for his tendency to assume that, empirically, a social system (such as the modern United States) will generally be in equilibrium, or that interchanges among the sectors will always be equal.

Alexander has been treated by unsympathetic commentators as simply an effort to revive Parsonian theory with all its idealism, its abstractions, and its conservative biases. This is inaccurate. Alexander's theory is a criticism of Parsons from the left, an effort to purify it in the light of modern postpositivist philosophy, and to introduce the insights of conflict theory and phenomenology. Alexander's massive four-volume *Theoretical Logic in Sociology* (1980–83) is patterned after Parsons' first major work, *The Structure of Social Action* (1937). Both are efforts to induct and accumulate the main theoretical accomplishments of the past. But there is a significant difference in the classics they choose to build upon. Both Parsons and Alexander select Durkheim for his major insight that common values underlie any utilitarian, self-interested social action (the nonrational or precontractual basis of solidarity). Both take Weber, although Parsons essentially assimilates him in to Durkheim, by interpreting his emphasis on religion and status groups as converging with the fundamental importance of values; Alexander, on the other hand, sees Weber as an attempt to be more fully multidimensional, especially on the materialist and conflict side.

For an economic sociology, though, Parsons used primarily the work of Vilfredo Pareto (as well as that of the economist Alfred Marshall). It was Pareto who made Parsons into a systems theorist—but of the conservative type that Alexander critiques—by being the source of the idea of an abstract analytical system whose self-equilibration might be worked in terms of simultaneous differential equations. Alexander throws out Pareto and includes instead the obviously "missing" classic: Marx. It is Marx's hard-boiled economics of conflict and domination and his dialectical drive towards human liberation that Alexander wishes to incorporate into his fully multidimensional system of action.

It must be admitted that Alexander has not worked out a full system. He has barely even sketched where the Marxian side will enter the overall model. The concluding volume of his argument is taken up with Parsons' theory itself, with demonstrating the validity of the basic multidimensional scheme and disentangling it from the more one-sided and conservative version of Parsons which has attracted most commentators. In this sense, Alexander should be regarded as a beginning, as a very general program, rather than a specific theory. His abstract multidimensional model is a challenge to other theorists to produce a system doing justice to both micro and macro; to values and ideas, as well as material resources and interests; and to solidarity as well as conflict. However, Alexander may not realize how far afield such a theory might take us from the Parsonian system he uses as his home base. I will claim in Chapters 4 and 5, for example, that a multidimensional conflict theory may in fact be closer to filling the specifications.

THE ANALYTICAL AND THE CONCRETE

One of the major lessons in both Parsons and Alexander is the distinction between the analytical elements of a theory, on one side, and the concrete empirical phenomena and lower-level explanatory principles on the other. Parsons' four-function table is conceived at the level of the most abstract theoretical concepts necessary for any system,, just as his pattern variables are abstracted from the more concrete historical models of Toennies, Durkheim, and Linton. Alexander stresses this distinction even more strongly, and polemicizes against naive "positivist" philosophies or methodologies which believe they can immediately test all theory against raw "facts." Alexander particularly needs the distinction because it enables him to separate the analytical elements of Parsons' approach—the stress on multidimensionality itself—from Parsons' more concrete theories about value integration, functionalism, and so forth, where his ideology betrays him into theoretical errors.

The distinction is valuable. It is what enables me to suggest that a version of conflict theory may fit the bill on the general multidimensional level better than Parsons' theory itself could. Both Parsons and I would agree with Durkheim's fundamental point, that there is always some "precontractual solidarity" underlying any group action. But Parsons confuses this analytical primacy of "values" with the empirical notion that it applies to the level of society as a whole, missing the point that "societies" which are well integrated may exist only at the level of local groups, and that the value solidarity they have may be fluctuating and temporary. The analytical importance of values should be to point us towards the mechanisms that produce them in each situation, so that we may examine the extent to which they are produced and see how they may fit into situations of class conflict, political domination and other less-than-ideal phenomena of real life. Seen analytically rather than concretely, values become a tool in a social conflict analysis.

The same distinction between the analytical and the concrete is characteristic of a number of other recent approaches to theory. This is particularly so of the range of theories grouped under such labels as "structuralism," "rationalism," or "new social realism." These tend to be system theories in the sense that they are structures of relationships among very general elements. Often these are opposed to positivist, empiricist theories, as well as to subjectivistic, individualistic ones. They are antipositivist because they regard the structure as a set of logical elements or possibilities transcending the merely factual level; and they oppose the interpretive, situationalist social psychologies because they see the structure as transcending the merely individual and making it possible. We will meet various versions in subsequent chapters: the Marxian form in Chapter 3 (Althusser, Bhaskar), and the French structuralist, semiotic, or linguistic versions in Chapter 9 (Lévi-Strauss, Derrida, Chomsky). Other structural theories, however, such as the network theories in Chapter 12, are anti-individualistic but not antiempiricist, stressing interactional structures rather than cultural ones. "Systems" theory is itself an analytical construct. As such, we must expect it to appear again in different guises and various locations.

SUMMARY

1. A system is anything which has parts connected by processes or relationships. A system may be open or closed, stable or unstable; there are many types of systems.

2. *Feedforward* is a flow from one part of a system to another. *Feedback* is a set of flows linking parts in a loop. "Smart," or goal-seeking, feedback regulates flows with information about whether the system is approaching or maintaining a goal state. *Negative feedback* reacts to deviations from goals and results in reestablishing equilibrium. *Positive feedback*, in which flows accumulate through a loop, is explosive and results in an unstable system.

3. Systems may be mechanical or self-referential. Consciousness in human individuals may be regarded as a complex, multilevel self-referential system. The macrostructure of a society, however, is not itself conscious, and large-scale social processes (such as arms races or population growth) are often mechanical, containing explosive positive feedback loops.

4. Functionalism is a particular type of system theory which attempts to explain the existence of parts of society by their contribution to maintaining the whole society. Functionalism has been criticized for ignoring the effects of self-interested domination of some members of society by others.

5. Another criticism of functionalism is that its models explain present structures by their future consequences. Stinchcombe proposes to solve this by postulating a negative feedback mechanism: the presence or absence of social integration feeds back to produce corrective behavior, creating or sustaining functional institutions. It remains questionable whether societies have a goal-seeking mechanism to guide this process towards equilibrium. Functionalism also lacks predictive power to explain which structures are selected in which situations.

6. Parsons theorized that any social system must satisfy four functions: *latent pattern maintenance* (a cultural blueprint), *social integration*, *goal attainment* (output towards the environment), and *adaptation* (resource inputs from the environment). The functions are *analytical* (that is, abstract) and apply to any level of analysis: the individual personality, particular organizations, institutions, communities, nations, or the entire world.

7. Parsons proposed that a social system is held together through a hierarchy of control. *Values* are the most basic element, which are specified into *norms*, patterned into *roles*, and reinforced by *sanctions*. Basic values are inculcated in the individual by socialization. Deviance is the result of strain at any level: faulty socialization of values in individuals, failure to specify norms, conflict of roles, or failure of sanctions.

8. Durkheim argued that society could not be held together fundamentally by rational agreement or exchange of rewards. Any utilitarian contract requires "precontractual solidarity," feelings of trust that other people will uphold agreements. Parsons used Durkheim's argument as a basis for his own theory that societies are rooted in common values. However, it is also possible to interpret Durkheim's theory on a micro level, which allows for conflict between solidarity groups.

9. Parsons proposes two mechanisms of change: (1) the injection of new values into the system, especially by charismatic religious leaders; (2) differentiation taking place among parts of the system, which pushes values towards universalism, achievement, individualism, specificity, and affective neutrality.

10. As societies differentiate, functions become carried out by specialized organizations. Interchanges among subunits are carried out via *media of exchange*. Parsons emphasized the importance of *symbolic* media which facilitate transactions: *money* in the economic realm, and *power* in the political realm. Luhman adds *love* as a medium of exchange in personal relations and *truth* as a generalized medium for dealing with situations in the cultural sphere which are remote from personal experience. For Luhman, societies at the macro level are usually not very well integrated; these media do not produce normative consensus but only allow individuals to act with confidence in the absence of consensus.

11. Alexander argues that the most important contribution of Parsonian theory is not its functionalism but the insight that any theory of society must be *multidimensional*. It must interpret both individual and structural levels, material conditions, self-interest, and also ideas and collective moral values. Another crucial distinction is between the *analytical level* of basic theoretical concepts and principles, and the *concrete empirical phenomena* to which they may be applied. A system model is itself analytical rather than concrete, and hence may be applied at many different levels.

Chapter 3

POLITICAL ECONOMY

THE BASIC MARXIAN MODEL
    The First Analytical Step: Economic Reproduction
    The First Complication: Profit and Growth
    The Second Complication: Labor-saving Technology and System Crisis
    The Full Model: Classes, Property, and Control of the State

CRITICISMS AND REVISIONS OF THE MARXIAN SYSTEM

THE WORLD SYSTEM
    World Economy vs. World Empire
    Core, Semiperiphery, Periphery, and External Area
    Dynamics of the World System: Cycles, Crises, and Wars
    The End of the Capitalist World System: Socialist World Government
    Criticisms of World System Theory

MARXISM AS PHILOSOPHY
    Capitalism as Alienation and Consciousness
    Lukacs and Gramsci: False Consciousness and Ideological Domination
    Lefebvre and Marcuse: Alienation in Everyday Life
    Althusser's Structuralist Marxism
    New Social Realism

MARXIAN THEORIES OF THE STATE
    Poulantzas' Structuralist Theory of the State
    O'Connor's Fiscal Crisis Theory of the State

SUMMARY

*P*olitical economy refers to the Marxian tradition in sociology. More analytically, we can say it focuses attention on two spheres of society, economics and politics, as sociology's central concerns. Here is "where the action is," according to the Marxian perspective—the major events and structures with which sociology should concern itself. Here, too, are the prime determinants of the other features of society. In terms of Parsons' multidimensional model, the *A* and *G* function boxes are singled out as crucial, with culture, social interaction, and all their forms regarded as derivative in ways that political economy theory sets out to specify.

The Marxian tradition is famous for emphasizing economics—even for a form of economic determinism. Yet this is an oversimplification. As the term *political economy* itself stresses, politics is also important. I would even say that politics is what Marxians are primarily interested in explaining. They wish to show when and why revolutions occur, which social classes will control the state, and which states will dominate others imperialistically in the world system. Since Marxism is above all a political movement, it is concerned with the conditions of its own political success and with the political resources of its enemies. Economics enters the scheme because it is the major theoretical explanation of these political phenomena. Politics, then, is what Marxism wishes to explain, the "dependent variable"; economics is the means of explanation, the "independent variable." This is the classic version of Marxism; in recent theorizing, however, there is a tendency to give the state (the political sphere) a more nearly equal role in explanation, so that its effects can be seen as playing back into the economic arena, and even having some independent role in causing major social changes.

Marxism itself is not only an intellectual analysis, but the philosophy of a militant social movement. It is not only a theory but a *praxis,* a form of action. It critiques the dehumanizing aspects of social life, and aims toward the transformation of society in a way that will liberate human potential to the highest degree. Together with its philosophy of egalitarianism, this makes Marxism extremely idealistic in its aims, perhaps even utopian. This aspect of Marxism derives ultimately from Hegelian philosophy, which sees history as the divine spirit unfolding through various contradictions until it reaches complete self-realization on earth. Marxism has secular goals which are equivalent to religious salvation in their transcendental ambitiousness, but which are worked out in the material world. These are supposed to be realized eventually in the ideal of a communist society, in the move to which, socialism is only a transitional phase. By the late twentieth century, most Marxists (except perhaps some of the official mouthpieces of socialist regimes) have become critical of the progress toward human liberation made by socialism as it actually has been practiced so far. Though little systematic theorizing (except in Wallerstein's world system theory) has been done in the Marxian tradition about the future conditions that may move beyond the current phase found in the communist regimes of the world, it appears that no one believes such societies represent a final stage of historical development.

Nevertheless, Marxism remains intellectually healthy. Though it suffered a decline in popularity earlier in the twentieth century, in the last few decades Marxism in one form or another has commanded the sympathies of a majority of intellectuals in France, Germany, and Italy. In the 1980s, there has been a turning away from Marxism in those countries, but it continues to be strong in British social thought and elsewhere in Europe and has a sizable impact on American sociology. There are several reasons for this intellectual popularity. One is that Marxism has become separated from the advocacy of communism. Having survived disillusionment about the Soviet-style regimes, Marxism as an intellectual doctrine does not have to defend them, but can act as a critical wing attacking injustice and dehumanization everywhere. Another development is that Marxism has become more scholarly, more of an academic position bent on analysis rather than praxis. I say this even though one rather prominent theme in academic Marxism is to attack "positivist" value-neutrality, and to argue that social science cannot be neutral, but must take a stand on what is right and wrong in the subjects that it analyzes. Ironically, the advocates of the "praxis" philosophy tend to couch their arguments in highly abstract philosophical terms, which obviously cannot be understood except by highly trained intellectuals. "Praxis" has become a technical philosophy, far removed from the old-fashioned image of socialist speech makers leading factory workers out on strike against the capitalist system.

Within the intellectual world, Marxism has found important roles to play. One version has become analytical as well as praxis-oriented. It has enlivened and enriched contemporary theory and research by introducing a concern with conflict, with material and economic factors, and the central role of politics. It also fosters attention to important sociological topics, such as stratification. Its vision of long-term change and the large-scale picture has encouraged dynamic and historical analysis, and led theorists to look at the entire world system rather than "social systems" in isolation. Together, these intellectual trends have helped make the last 20 years a "golden age" for historical sociology and for macrosociology generally.

Political economy in its broad theoretical form has outgrown Marxism in the more narrowly construed sense of the membership of a particular political movement. It has provided a set of intellectual tools that has become an important part of our sociological analysis, and is a source of major current theories. Contrary to Parsons and Alexander, it argues that all four function boxes are not of equal significance, and that if we are to explain society as a whole, we must look above all at the working of the economic box and its interactions with politics. We will now try to ascertain to what extent this is correct.

THE BASIC MARXIAN MODEL

Classical Marxian theory is above all a system theory. Perhaps uniquely in sociology, it provides a model which, at least on the abstract level, is complete and closed. It sets out all the elements of a social system and shows how they interrelate. Furthermore, the model is both static and dynamic. On one level of abstraction, it shows how the different parts of the "machine" mesh together so that the system reproduces itself. As we shall see, this is a "first approximation," a simple analytical model set up so that elaborations can be built upon it. An important set of elaborations makes the system dynamic, changing through its own internal processes or "contradictions." The outcome is a predictive, deterministic model of social change. More concretely: the social system which is modeled is capitalism. Marx shows how it reproduces itself, and then how it moves by its own inner necessity through a series of changes, eventually culminating in its downfall and the ushering in of socialism.

It is fashionable in certain intellectual circles these days to deny that Marx was so crassly positivist as to have a deterministic model, or even that he gave priority to the economy. These Marxists point to Marx's (1842–44/1971) early writings of the 1840s, when he was heavily influenced by Hegel, and argue that he never gave up the humanistic conceptions, even when he wrote his *Capital* (published 1867– 1894), itself part of a larger, never-completed work called "Critique of Political Economy." This is true to an extent. Marx believed he had fused Hegel with an economic model; the contradictions and dehumanizing processes in capitalism are themselves a working out of the Hegelian dialectic. Moreover, he insisted that human beings are always creating their own world through their praxis; capitalism itself is a product of human labor in exactly this sense. So are politics and the state, which are not reified entities existing in themselves (though they give such an impression through a process of ideological mystification), but are merely forms of human action, capable of being changed by human action. And the end process, the revolutionary downfall of capitalism and the ushering in of socialism and communism, is not merely an overcoming of an economic crisis and a change in material conditions, but a liberation of the human potentiality in the fullest sense.

For all this, it remains a fact that Marx's own system—especially the part on which he worked hardest—is essentially deterministic and centered on economics. Human beings make society though their own praxis; but it is precisely the problem of capitalism (and of class-divided societies generally) that though in one sense humans are active and free, in another sense they are bound by the system that they themselves have created. This is in fact the definition of *alienation*: workers are alienated from the products of their own labor, which circulate around in a larger economic market system possessing laws of its own, and oppress the workers who created it. "Men make history," Marx declared, "but not under conditions of their own choosing." The humanistic side of Marx is integrated with the deterministic, mechanistic side. Because this is so, Marx believed he had scientifically proven that capitalism would go through certain crises, and that its downfall was inevitable. When the right moment came, human actors would rise up and take action, in a sense mechanically, but also as free, liberated beings. The crisis of the mechanical system is precisely what opens up this moment of freedom.

The problem with Marx's deterministic model, I would say, is not that it is deterministic, but that it is incorrect. If, in fact, Marx's original model were correct, the revolution would have long since happened, and no one would be complaining that the theory is too deterministic. Marx's predictions have gone awry; although certain aspects of modern history bear enough resemblance to some of his processes to make many sociologists believe that the model can be patched up rather than thrown out completely. The latter part of this chapter will detail some of the efforts to modify and improve the system. But the very fact that it *is* a system, and the most comprehensive and neatly deterministic system we have in social science, is one of its great sources of intellectual appeal. Structuralist thinkers, like Claude Lévi-Strauss, have expressed their admiration of Marxist theory, not so much because they have borrowed anything concrete from it, but because they see it as an ideal, an underlying all-encompassing structure which generates all the possibilities we observe on the surface of the empirical world as historical reality.

We have already seen in Chapter 1 that Marx and Engels provided an evolutionary theory of all of world history in the form of a series of stages. Each stage is characterized by a certain economic mode of production, whose core is a particular property system. Although they believed that a dialectical materialist theory could be worked out to explain the dynamics of each stage and its transition to the next, in fact the only model that they did provide was for capitalism. It is here that the full-scale deterministic model is presented.

THE FIRST ANALYTICAL STEP: ECONOMIC REPRODUCTION

The first step, at a very high level of abstraction, is to show the basic elements of the economy. These are, of course, connected to the rest of a social system, to what Marx called the "mode of production," and to the "superstructure" of politics and culture built upon it. But for now, the task is to achieve clarity about the core of the system by abstracting away these elements. Furthermore, the economy is represented, not exactly "at rest," but in a static mode insofar as it is seen as merely reproducing itself over and over again in the same form.

Figure 3-1 sketches the basic elements of a capitalist economic system. The elements are connected in a circle. Production requires labor and capital (the latter referring to the material input in the form of shops and factories, tools, raw materials, land, and so forth). The products are sold, resulting in income. The income in turn is divided to reproduce the two factors of production, some of it going to cover the costs of capital, the rest to wages to support workers. The workers spend their wages on products they need to keep themselves alive, while the income to

FIGURE 3-1
BASIC REPRODUCTION OF CAPITALISM

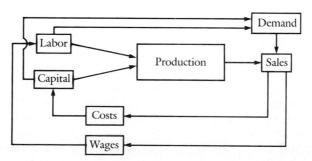

capital goes into purchasing material products needed for further production. The system is neatly balanced: all production is sold, and the resulting income goes into reproducing labor and replacing capital used up in the previous round of production. All this activity keeps up the level of demand, so that sales can continue. It can be shown by computer simulation that such a self-reproducing system is logically possible (Hanneman and Collins, 1987).

In the abstract, then, capitalism is a perfect system: nothing is produced that can't be sold or used, no one is unemployed, and no one exploits anyone else. What makes this unrealistic? For one thing, in this stripped-down model, no one ever makes any profit, nor does the system grow or change. Yet these are two of the most obvious characteristics of capitalism—perhaps even its most important facets— for they have made it a key transforming force in the modern world. Marx connects the two of them together: profit is the source of growth, since it can be ploughed back into the stock of capital, enabling the system to expand its production with each turn of the cycle.

THE FIRST COMPLICATION: PROFIT AND GROWTH

Where does profit come from? This is a key problem in the classical economic theory with which Marx worked, for the market operates by supply and demand; whenever the demand for a certain product exceeds the supply, prices go up. The manufacturer of these products then can make a profit, taking in more than it cost to make them. But if the system is operating smoothly (that is, nothing impedes competition), then other manufacturers will quickly see that prices are higher for that product, and they will shift over to producing it. Higher prices attract more production, which raises the supply relative to the demand and drives the prices back down. Thus, profit is only short term and temporary, and is always driven out. There is nothing unorthodox about Marx's argument here. Even neoclassical economics, which has dominated the economic profession for almost a century, uses a similar conception of a "general equilibrium"—the notion that economies always fluctuate around some analytical point at which all goods and services have established a balance between supply and demand. And analytically, at this point there can be no profit in the system. The law of supply and demand always forces the price down to exactly what it costs to produce a product—no more, no less. For if the price were more, competitors would come pouring in and drive prices down by increasing production; if the price were less than costs, manufacturers would have to go out of business until only enough were left to fill the demand.

In Marx's formulation, all the factors of production must be paid a return exactly proportional to what it took to produce them. If it cost X amount to buy raw materials to manufacture shoes, then shoes will be priced on the market at just such a level that it returns enough to pay X for those raw materials. There is only one factor of production, Marx concluded, that can be the basis of any profit (or as he calls it, "surplus value"), and that is human labor. For labor has a price on the market too, and the law of supply and demand guarantees that labor will be paid exactly what it took to reproduce it. If it takes $20 a day to keep a laborer alive (counting all the costs of housing, food, clothing, bringing up children to be future laborers, and so forth), then the market guarantees that laborers will be paid $20.

Any manufacturer who tried to pay workers higher wages would be driven out of business, because the products that workers produce will only bring in so much on the market; on the other hand, workers cannot be paid less, since labor will not then be able to reproduce itself, and manufacturing will not be possible without the labor. In this perfect market system, laborers can move from job to job, attracted by higher wages, just as in any other buyer-seller relationship. But as all the levels of supply and demand even out at the price that just covers costs, the price of labor, too, will even out at the cost of keeping workers alive.

How then can labor be a source of profit? The answer becomes clear, Marx argues, if we calculate not in money but in hours of labor. For money is only a veil, a unit of exchange. Even though capitalism creates a psychological glorification of money so that everyone strives after money and forgets that it is only useful in acquiring real goods, nevertheless the basis of the system is not money but the actual production that is carried out. Production can exist without money, but not vice versa. And since it is human labor which turns raw materials into capital, it is labor that is the ultimate source of all value. All other economic quantities can be expressed in terms of the number of hours of labor time it takes to produce them.[1] Hence, if it takes an hour of labor to produce a shirt, and two hours of labor to produce a pair of shoes, the price of a shirt ought to be half as much as the price of the shoes. All other prices will be similarly proportional.

The payoff is when Marx applies this analysis to the wages of labor itself. Since labor is also something that is bought and sold on the market, it too will have a price, and that price can be stated in terms of the amount of labor time it takes to produce it. If it takes six hours of labor to produce all the goods necessary to keep a laborer alive for one day, then the laborer's wages will be exactly the equivalent of six hours worth of labor products. If we calculate the monetary system in labor hours, their dollars (or British pounds, or French francs, or whatever) will translate into exactly six labor-hour units.

This provides the opening that capitalists need in order to make profit. For the market guarantees that workers will be paid exactly six labor hours' worth. But since the day is 24 hours long, the capitalist can make the worker labor for longer hours: say 8 or 10 hours a day. (Realistically, in the early 1800s when Marx was writing, the working day in British factories was between 12 and 16 hours a day; his point was not merely theoretical, but a major issue in the factory conditions of the time.) Whatever the difference is between the reproductive wage (say six hours) and the actual working day (say ten hours), the capitalist may appropriate as profit. It produces extra goods which can be sold, but whose income does not have to be passed

---

[1] In technical economic terms, Marx is making two points here, that labor is actually the source of all value, and also that hours of labor can be used as a measure of value—in the French term, as a *numeraire,* the numerical unit chosen in which to express prices. Just as American dollars can be translated into British pounds, either of these currencies could be translated into units of some other commodity. Say a pair of shoe laces sells for one dollar; we could then calculate everything in terms of shoe laces. A car which costs $9,000 would be expressed as costing 9,000 shoelaces. Marx is saying that he will calculate everything in terms of the cost of labor. But since he also believes that labor is *really* the source of all value, not just a convenient unit of measurement, he is thus demonstrating just how much everything is really worth in the economic system that produced it. If one translates all costs into so many shoelaces, one cannot say that shoe laces really are what determines the value of everything.

FIGURE 3-2

PROFIT AS EXPLOITATION OF LABOR

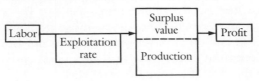

along to the worker who made them. This difference produced by the extra labor hours is *surplus value*.

If we model this in the system now (Figure 3-2), we find that production does indeed grow. In the simple model, we assume that the extra profits are all ploughed back into buying extra capital, and thus expanding the base and the output for each round of the cycle. We now have a capitalist system in which profits are made and economic growth does occur. This is a closer approximation to historical reality.

THE SECOND COMPLICATION: LABOR-SAVING TECHNOLOGY AND SYSTEM CRISIS

Our model remains unrealistic in that it takes no account of industrial crises, unemployment, or overproduction. These, too, are part of the capitalist scene and are the processes which Marx wished to show as eventually widening and leading to the downfall of the system. He demonstrated this by introducing another element which, historically, has been central to modern capitalism since the Industrial Revolution began with the English textile mills of the 1700s: technological innovation.

Technology increases production, and it does so while using less labor power. Thus, initially, any new invention—the steam engine, the power loom, factory machinery in general—lowers costs for the manufacturers who introduce it. The result is a temporary rise in profits. But this rise in profits is short lived, because technological innovations spread rapidly to competitors. Eventually the amount of production is vastly increased, even to the point of exceeding demand; hence, prices fall and profits disappear. This motivates manufacturers to seek further technological innovations, which will further cut costs and enable them to get a temporary edge on their competitors. The process repeats itself, and capitalism goes through a series of innovations—with a drastically increasing level of production—driven by the need of manufacturers to stay technologically ahead of the competition.

But there is a more serious problem. Technology itself has costs. Furthermore, according to the basic laws of supply and demand, the amount of return it will bring in market prices ultimately balances out at exactly the point where returns are equal to the costs of producing the technology in the first place. In other words, technology does not produce profit; for the technology has to be paid for, and the market will drive its products down to the level at which manufacturers get back nothing more than what it cost to introduce the new technology.

Even worse, technology affects the true source of profit in the system. Only labor can produce surplus value, by bringing in more income than it costs to repro-

FIGURE 3-3

LABOR-SAVING TECHNOLOGY, UNEMPLOYMENT, AND FALLING DEMAND

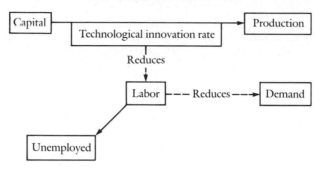

duce itself. But technology is labor-saving; this means that the proportion of the product which embodies labor is constantly being reduced by the shift to technology: in Marxian terms, by the replacement of *variable capital* (embodied labor) by *constant capital* (machinery). The rate of exploitation of labor (hours actually worked versus hours needed to reproduce labor) remains the same, but the sheer amount of labor being used is declining. Hence the rate of profit tends to fall.

This produces industrial crisis, and there are two loops in the system (Figure 3-3) by which this occurs. First, the rate of profit falls because technology is being substituted for labor, the source of profit. In concrete terms, manufacturers are losing money, and some of them are going out of business. Second, since laborers contribute to demand by spending their incomes, the declining number of workers results in less demand. The result is an overproduction crisis. Technology is turning out larger and larger amounts of goods, but there are fewer and fewer consumers who can afford to buy them. This is another reason why manufacturers go out of business.

THE FULL MODEL: CLASSES, PROPERTY, AND CONTROL OF THE STATE

The economic system is thus heading towards a breakdown (Figure 3-4). If left to go on unchecked, the end result will be that profit falls almost to zero, while unemployment rises to nearly 100 percent. Overproduction rises to a very high level, resulting in the spectacle of huge amounts of goods sitting around unsold while masses are starving, because no one can afford to buy them. (The computer simulation shows, though, that overproduction slows down after a while too, mainly because the whole system is in depression, and profits are not feeding economic growth any more. See Hanneman and Collins, 1987.)

Actually, the system moves cyclically, in a pattern of boom and bust, growth and depression. As a crisis occurs, some businesses go bankrupt. The larger and stronger capitalists can buy out their goods and equipment at a bargain, thereby making a profit. Further, the introduction of new technology can cheapen the price

FIGURE 3-4

ECONOMIC CRISIS

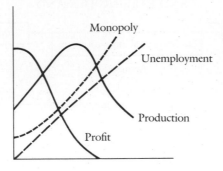

of goods, bringing them within the purchasing range of a larger group of consumers. These enlargements of the market also temporarily increase profit and get the business cycle started up again.[2] For a while there is growth; but the familiar problems take hold again, and the cycle enters a decline. According to Marx's model, each round of the business cycle is a wider swing than the last, as each time the number of businesses is reduced into a smaller and smaller monopoly, and the substitution of technology for labor reaches more and more extreme proportions. Eventually the crisis reaches a level at which the system cannot continue and a revolution occurs.

Here we can drop the last level of abstraction and recognize that the economic system does not exist in a vacuum. First and foremost, there is the fact that people occupy different places in the economic system. Some derive their income from the fact that they own capital, while others own nothing but their own labor power, which they are forced to sell on the labor market in order to stay alive. Thus, property (and the fact that some people have none) is a crucial fact of the social structure undergirding the economic system. Property classes set the economic system in motion; and with each turn of the wheel as the system reproduces itself, social classes are economically reproduced.

However, over time the system methodically changes the lineup of economic classes. The falling rate of profit drives many of the capitalists out of business and into the working class or *proletariat*. Employed workers are gradually driven into an ever-expanding pool, "the reserve army of the unemployed." The capitalist class is shrinking through the growth of monopoly, while the working class is both growing and is becoming increasingly poor.

---

[2] There is an additional complexity: the rate of exploitation can rise and thus offset the falling rate of profit. This can happen indirectly if technology reduces the amount of time necessary for labor to reproduce itself—that is, it makes it cheaper, in hours of work, to stay alive. Recall that the exploitation rate is the *difference* between the hours that workers work and the hours necessary to support them. Hence, exploitation can go up *in this sense* even if workers are not being forced to work longer hours. This increase in the exploitation rate raises profits, and contributes to the cyclical upswing as business gets going again.

This by itself is not enough to bring about revolution. Revolution requires an additional link—from the economy and the class structure to the state. Ordinarily the state, which is the organization of military force in society (including the police), operates to uphold the property system. The full links of reproduction of the system can therefore be seen as follows: the economy reproduces social classes, which in turn reproduce the economy; the dominant social class reproduces the state, which in turn upholds the property system; this in turn undergirds and reproduces the structure of the economy.

For the structure of the economy to change, the property system must be abolished or modified. This can only be done by shifting control of the state.

In *Capital,* Marx does not specify exactly how or when this revolution would occur. In general, people become increasingly aware that the economic system is in contradiction with itself, or rather, that its forces of production (the economic system in the narrower sense) is in contradiction to the social relations of production (the property system). There is the visible size of the pile of unsold goods, and an awareness of poverty in the midst of plenty. Meanwhile, capitalists are going bankrupt and falling into the proletariat, thus increasing their incentive to go over to the other side politically as well. Awareness of alienation increases, in the sense that people become increasingly conscious of the fact that they have produced the system with their own labors, but are being controlled by what is essentially an impersonal machine. Instead of production being carried out for the sake of people, it is apparent that people are being used for the sake of production, which is for the sake of nothing but the relentless cycles of the economic machine grinding out further and further production in the search for profit.[3] Eventually the dialectical contradictions of the system result in a rise in consciousness in exactly the sense that Hegel meant when he described the system becoming conscious of itself. Consciousness gives freedom to act back upon the system, to break the bonds, and thus to carry out a revolutionary transformation.

This process fits a long-term pattern. Capitalism proves to be unable to develop its own productive forces to their full extent, because its social relations—private property—are in conflict with the underlying forces of production. This makes it vulnerable to overthrow by another, more "progressive" class, whose social relations will be in tune with the forces of production and will allow their full development. Although Marx and Engels concentrated on the capitalist epoch, earlier stages of world history presumably had their own contradictions between the forces and social relations of production, and each of these, too, moved towards a crisis which transformed it into another system of production.[4]

In Marx's writings, especially those carried out in collaboration with Friedrich Engels (who was more sociologically oriented than Marx), there are sketches of how this process of consciousness and political power actually operates (Marx and Engels, 1846/1947, 1848/1959; Marx, 1852/1963; Engels, 1850/1967). At all times,

---

[3] As Marx put it: not $C \rightarrow M \rightarrow C'$ (people work for commodities to exchange for money, which they use to buy commodities for their own use); but $M \rightarrow C \rightarrow M'$ (money is used to invest in commodities, in order to acquire more money—which is in turn reinvested, and so on, without any human end-point).
[4] One of the few efforts to work this out as a systematic theory of the dynamics of the slave and feudal modes of production is that of Perry Anderson (1974).

there is a link from social classes to control of the state. The economy shapes the political activity of social classes in three ways: (1) interests, (2) ideology and means of mental production, and (3) material means of political mobilization.

1. INTERESTS   Each social class has a particular interest in the state. The property-owning class is primarily concerned that the state should uphold private property. It wishes the police to protect it from theft; to keep workers from taking over their factories; and if possible, to keep them from striking, forming labor unions, and the like. Exactly how much the capitalist class (bourgeoisie) is able to achieve these ends depends on its resources (listed under (2) and (3)). At a minimum, though, the economic system cannot exist unless the basic property laws themselves are upheld. However, individual capitalists and particular factions of capitalists may also attempt to use the state to favor their own businesses against their rivals by getting government monopolies, or by attaining a bank rate more favorable to borrowers than investors, or by obtaining regulations favoring insurance companies over the manufacturers they insure, and so on. Many conflicts of interest in economic politics, in other words, take place *within* the capitalist class rather than between it and the workers. Only when the whole system is threatened do the capitalists come together to face their common enemy.

Workers, too, have their interests shaped by the system. Fundamentally, their interest in the long run is to change the property system: in Marx's view, to do away with the private property which undergirds capitalism as a whole. In the short run, however, workers seek to use politics to distribute the fruits of production away from capitalist profit and into their own hands. This can be done by organizing locally to form trade unions in order to shorten working hours and raise wages. Marx, however, believed that this level of "trade-union consciousness" would not alleviate the crisis of the system in the long run; in fact, it would hasten the crisis, by cutting into the sources of profit and contributing to economic depression, unemployment, and eventually to the final crisis leading to revolution.

2. IDEOLOGY AND THE MEANS OF MENTAL PRODUCTION   Ideas are a political and social weapon. The group which is able to become conscious of its interests and to achieve unity as a self-conscious group will be able to act together to achieve power. Conversely, those persons who are not aware of their own interests, who falsely identify with some other group because of the way they define themselves and the world, are unable to achieve power. For example, Marx regarded religious ideas as ideologies which serve to bolster the power of ruling classes. Religion usually makes the social order seem god-given and incapable of change, while exalting the upper classes into paragons of respectability. Similarly nationalism, by making the working classes feel that being an Englishman, a Frenchman, an American, and so forth, is their fundamental identity, obscures their social class, and makes them incapable of acting in their class interests against the system.

Ideas are produced by material and social circumstances. Just as it takes factory machinery, capital, and labor to turn out manufactured goods, ideas require books, writing materials, printing presses and the like, as well as material resources to pay for intellectuals who do the thinking. Whichever social class controls the means of mental production is able to control what types of ideas are produced. Generally the dominant ideas of any social era will reflect the economic interests of the property-owning class, since they pay to have the ideas produced. Control over the material means of producing ideologies, then, is a major political weapon. It helps the capitalist class achieve consciousness within their own ranks of the need to protect their system, while it helps to keep the working class confused about their own interests. It may even make workers into supporters of the system that oppresses them economically (for instance, by making them vote for religious conservatives who are also economic conservatives).

3. MATERIAL MEANS OF POLITICAL MOBILIZATION   To participate in politics is a physical action which requires material resources. Organization rather than sheer numbers is what brings power; thus, a relatively small group of capitalists can control the state against the unorganized opposition of huge numbers of workers. Material means of mobilization include transportation; communications networks provided by writing materials, telephones, and so forth; money for political campaigns; the actual use of armed force; and the economic surplus to provide time free from work in order to pursue political activities. Generally, the economic property owners have far more of these resources than the nonpropertied classes. As a result, they do most of the participating in politics and win most of the political power.

In any social system the various political resources deriving from economic positions can be charted. Ordinarily, the circular, self-reproducing relationships will hold firm among the parts of the system: economics will reinforce political power, which will result in upholding the property system and therefore the economic structure (see Figure 3-5).

But the crisis of capitalism systematically changes these political resources. (1) The sheer number of capitalists diminishes by monopolization, while the number of workers grows. Thus, the workers' interest comes to outweigh the capitalists' interests by an increasingly larger amount. Some members of the ruling class, too, can

FIGURE 3-5

CLASS CONFLICT AND CONTROL OF THE STATE

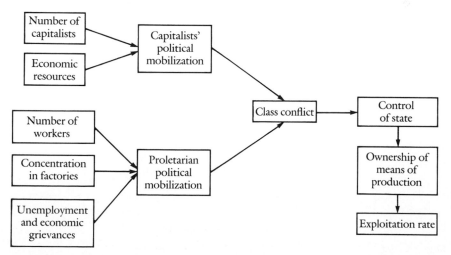

see the writing on the wall and may decide to join the other side before they are actually thrown into it. (This is Marx's explanation of how upper class intellectuals like himself came to join the revolution.)

(2) The ideology of the ruling class becomes increasingly thin as it is more and more contradicted by the reality of economic crisis. The sheer growth of productive capacity in the capitalist system, too, means that the material means of mental production are expanding. There are more printing presses, newspapers, writing materials, popular entertainment media, and so forth available; and although these are owned by the capitalist class, it becomes easier for some of them to be used to spread revolutionary ideas. Though Marx himself did not say so, we might add that the growth of educational institutions, which are massive economic investments in the production of ideas, provide fertile breeding grounds for the growth of new forms of consciousness which may act politically against the system.

(3) Above all, the material means of mobilization shifts in favor of the workers. Marx and Engels themselves pointed out that the growth of large factories brings workers together in one place, where it is easier for them to organize. Capitalist development centralizes production in large cities; the large numbers of rural workers, once separated in small villages and factory towns, now acquire political strength from urbanization. As large monopolistic businesses supplant smaller ones, they actually draw the communications and transportation networks of society more tightly together. The end result is to prepare the way organizationally for socialism.

In the computer simulation of the Marxian system, these various processes have been lumped together into a general level of mobilization for capitalists and a level of mobilization for workers. Though Marx and Engels do not spell it out, presumably the power of a social class is a combination of its sheer size and its resources for mobilization. The political opposition of the working class should tend to grow, therefore, as its level of alienation rises with economic crisis. Thus, when capitalism is operating reasonably well economically, the resources available to a moderate-sized group of capitalists keep them well in control of the state and the larger number of unmobilized workers. But as the number of capitalists shrinks and the profit rate upon which their mobilization resources depends falls, capitalist political power declines. Simultaneously the number of workers grows into a vast majority and their

FIGURE 3-6

REVOLUTION

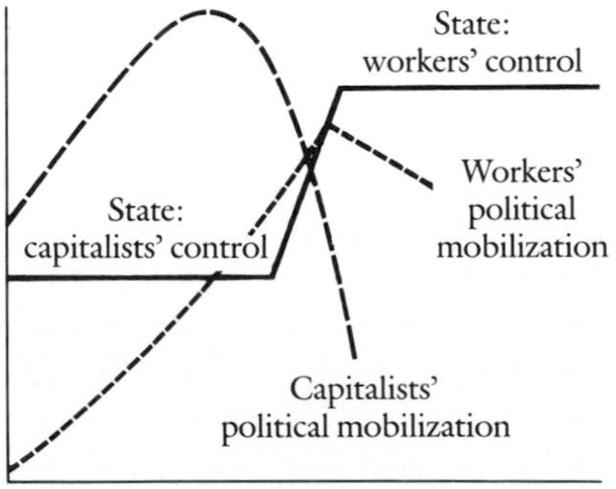

level of mobilization and alienation rises. At some point, the workers' political mobilization passes that of the capitalists (see Figure 3-6).

We might add that conflict will probably break out at the point at which the two forces are approximately equal. Perhaps it is true that workers must reach a substantial margin over capitalists to actually wrest control of the state from them (due to forces of inertia, which favor the status quo). But at some point, if the Marxian model is correct, the economic crisis gives rise to a massive shift in political power and a new set of interests take over the state. The new rulers are free to change the property system, and to abolish capitalism. Presumably they can put a new economic system in its place. In theoretical terms, however, Marx and most of his followers have been extremely vague about just what would happen after this point.

CRITICISMS AND REVISIONS OF THE MARXIAN SYSTEM

There are some obvious problems with the Marxian theoretical model. It predicts that capitalism will go through steadily worsening economic crises, culminating in socialist revolution. But although there have been economic crises, capitalism has survived them. Moderate moves towards socialism have been made in some capitalist countries, but the full-scale revolutions have occurred only in some relatively non-capitalist parts of the world, such as early twentieth-century Russia, mid-century China, and Cuba, while Eastern Europe became communist as the result of guerrilla warfare and military conquest at the end of World War II. Though unemployment has been a problem in the advanced capitalist countries, the bulk of the working class has not fallen into the "reserve army of the unemployed" (the highest unemployment rates were around 25 percent at the depth of the Great Depression of the 1930s). The economic "immiseration" of the working class in general has not happened, and instead, the standard of living for workers has generally improved under capitalism. Marx predicted growing monopolization among capitalist businesses, driving most capitalists down into the ranks of the proletariat; again, although many businesses have failed, and monopolies (more technically speaking, oligopolies; see footnote 17 on page 108) are prominent, nevertheless new businesses have formed, and the size of the capitalist class has remained fairly substantial.

So why not just forget about Marxian theory as a failed effort? This would be a mistake, I believe, for several reasons. On the more general level, Marxism points us sociologically at some important phenomena: at conflict, at stratification and social class, at the material conditions that affect group mobilization and political power, at the way ideas function as ideologies, and at the social conditions that produce ideas. All these topics lead us into conflict theory and to a good deal of empirical research. But at a more specific level, the Marxian model of political economy also has something to offer. For while there are clearly some major flaws in the model, the phenomena that it talks about *do* happen to a certain degree. Although socialist revolutions have not broken out where the theory predicts they should be, nevertheless such revolutions have happened in other parts of the world, where they remain a major challenge for sociological theory to explain. Similarly, there is a class-based, working-class politics of some form in every capitalist society, including our own, in which the liberal wing of the Democratic party has traditionally emphasized workers' interests. Also, the degree to which class legislation, such as the welfare state and Scandinavian-style socialism, has occurred remains another problem to be explained. Although capitalism has not collapsed, it does tend to go through periodic crises as if part of the Marxian model were operating, but with some additional factor stopping it from going all the way through its conclusion.

The same may be said about most of the other empirical problems with the classic Marxian predictions. Workers' incomes have often risen, but at the same time, the distribution of wealth remains rather unequal, and at times portions of the working class do fall into unemployment and economic misery. There is a steady trend towards monopolization, and most smaller capitalist businesses go bankrupt or have to sell out to a larger firm. The question then becomes one of degree: to explain the conditions that push these processes further in one direction or the other.

There have been three main ways in which Marxian theory has been modified in the twentieth century to try to correct these theoretical problems. (1) Theorists have shifted the level of analysis toward the world system. Instead of modeling capitalism as if it operated within a single state, Marxists have brought in imperialism, war, and other interactions among states to show how capitalism may prosper in the wealthy, advanced states, while its contradictions work themselves out on the international level. (2) Analysis shifts away from the economic level to a philosophical level as theorists reinterpret the model as a Hegelian dialectic in a more general sense, perhaps as a process of alienation and its overcoming; or, in a different philosophical direction, as a meta-empirical structural system in which all elements, including noneconomic ones, interact. Relatedly, the emphasis can be put upon culture and consciousness as the crucial element. Thus, ideology and ideological hegemony, false consciousness, and the social production of ideas come to be seen as the major elements holding the capitalist system together. (3) Emphasis is placed on the state as an independent or even determining force in the system. Politics is seen as having the power to react back upon the economic system and to control it, thereby preventing economic breakdowns. System crises are therefore mainly political crises.[5]

These revisions may be stated in terms of the abstract model which I have used for computer simulation of the Marxian system (Figures 3-1 to 3-6). When a set of interacting factors, connected by feedback loops, fails to match the empirical world, it is not possible to specify in advance exactly which part of the system is in error. It may be that additional factors have been left out, or that the arrows connecting them are drawn wrongly. Thus a problem may be in the economic part of the system itself (for instance, in linking the rate of profit purely to the rate of exploitation of labor); or it may be in the link between the state and the economy (for instance, in making the state merely a reflex of economic conditions); or it may be in the mobilization variables (perhaps greater autonomous input should be allowed in the

---

[5] I have omitted a fourth modification: revision of the economic model itself. For instance, Paul Sweezey (1942; Baran and Sweezey, 1966) has replaced the labor theory of value with a model which derives economic crises from an underconsumption model deriving from the work of John Maynard Keynes. Though this has been important in Marxist economics, most of the revisions sociologists have been interested in have concerned the three strategies mentioned above.

production of consciousness, or the material conditions of mobilization need to be revised). It is possible that more than one of these revisions should be made in the system.

THE WORLD SYSTEM

Marx himself mentioned imperialism, but without giving it any special priority in determining which states would first undergo socialist revolution. At the turn of the twentieth century, after several decades during which England, France, Germany, the United States, Japan, and other countries had been carving up the undeveloped parts of the world into colonies, theories of imperialism began to appear. The British economist J. A. Hobson formulated a model in which imperialism is a necessary device for propping up the internal contradictions of capitalism in the home states. The Russian revolutionist V. I. Lenin adopted Hobson's theory and predicted that wars between rival imperialist states would be the process by which socialist revolution would occur. This was politically astute insofar as the defeat of the Russian armies in World War I did open the way for Lenin and Trotsky to lead an insurrection. On the other hand, the Russian revolutionists expected a revolution to follow on their heels in Germany, a much more centralized capitalist state, and were gravely disappointed when it did not. More recently, experts on Latin America, such as Andre Gunder Frank (1967) developed *dependency theory*, which attempted to show that countries were not "underdeveloped" simply by failure to advance through the normal capitalist stages, but because they were themselves dependent upon advanced economies like Britain and the United States, which kept them structurally unable to become industrial economies in their own right. Out of this argument, a number of theories of the capitalist world system have arisen, including those of Samir Amin (1976), Arghiri Emmanuel (1972), and Giovanni Arrighi (1978). The most comprehensive and sociologically ambitious of these models is that of Immanuel Wallerstein (1974, 1980), who is in the midst of a four- or five-volume project synthesizing the historical literature on the development of the world economy since the Middle Ages.

WORLD ECONOMY VS. WORLD EMPIRE

Wallerstein distinguishes analytically between two ways in which states can be linked together into a larger "world system." They can be connected as a *world empire*, in which one state is dominant and uses its military power to extract economic tribute from the others. Or they can be connected as a *world economy*, in which there are multiple states, some of them of approximately equal power, who compete among themselves by warfare and are linked by economic trade.[6]

---

[6] It should be apparent that Wallerstein uses "world" here in an analytical sense, rather than literally meaning the entire globe. There was a "Roman world," a "Chinese world" (before it became connected to the West via European expansion), and a "Mediterranean world" (in the terms of Fernand Braudel [1949/1972], the French historian from whom Wallerstein drew much of his inspiration). Eventually, the capitalist world system does expand to include the whole physical earth, but only when this happens do the two meanings of the word *world* finally coincide.

This distinction is crucial because the two different kinds of world system have drastically different effects on economic development. The *world empire* inhibits economic growth and stifles capitalism. Since everything hinges upon military and political power, officials and soldiers are supreme, and merchants and manufacturers are subordinated. Any economic advances that are made, any economic wealth that is generated, can be immediately appropriated by sheer force. The empire responds to economic needs merely by taxing the peasants more harshly and by conquering new territories.

Such states are caught in a vicious circle. The military is the main prop of the state. A strong state requires wealth in order to support its military forces. Wealth is acquired by taxation, which requires that the ruler have a large hierarchy of officials to collect the taxes. But as such hierarchies grow, they become more difficult for the ruler to control. Officials gain increasing power for themselves and eat up most taxes in their own support. In many traditional empires, rulers resorted to selling government offices to their incumbents as a way of raising funds.[7] But this was only a temporary expedient which made matters worse in the long run; the money from sale of offices was soon used up, while expenses continued, and the government was left with less control over its taxes and fewer government offices available to sell. Governments tried to escape from this problem both by periodic reforms and purges of officials and by taxing the peasants more heavily. But putting pressure on officials or revoking their purchased offices and rights brought political trouble and threats of secession and coups, while increasing taxation led to peasant revolts. Putting down these rebellions required the expenditure of military force, which cost money. Thus, the vicious circle: military force costs money, and efforts to raise money undermine efficiency and raise resistance; putting down resistance requires escalating military force, hence more expense, more resistance and so forth. Eventually the empire falls, to be replaced by another.

This was the pattern in most states throughout world history. It was particularly noticeable in China, with its cyclical rise and fall of dynasties, but also existed in India, the Middle East, and the ancient Mediterranean.

The same vicious circle tended to exist in medieval Europe as well, with empires rising and falling because of the economic problems of supporting their own military power. But in Europe after about 1450 A.D., a second type of system gradually arose and supplanted the world empire model. This is the *world economy*.[8] Here, no state is powerful enough to dominate others. Military competition among states therefore leads to efforts to rationalize the state structure, to keep officials under

---

[7]This was known as "venality of offices," and was connected to the practice of "tax-farming." For instance, the King of France sold private individuals the rights to collect taxes. It was recognized that tax collectors always managed to keep a portion for themselves; tax-farming legitimated this practice and tried to cash in on it by selling the right to make this profit.

[8]It should be noted that Wallerstein uses the concepts *world economy* and *world empire* analytically (as Max Weber would put it, as *ideal types*). Though it is possible for a part of the globe to be either a *world economy* or a *world empire,* it is also possible for elements of both situations to exist at the same time in varying degrees. It was this combination of conditions that made up the dynamics of Western Europe in the early modern era. More generally, one might say that the "world empire" dynamics (the vicious circle of military states mentioned above) are always present in any set of states, but sometimes they are overlaid by the "world economy" dynamics.

control by bureaucratic regulation and legal rules, and to keep taxes below oppressive levels. This is done, not out of benevolence, but simply because rulers cannot afford to antagonize their own populations if they are to have maximal resources available for keeping up militarily with their neighbors. Similarly, rulers make concessions to merchants and bankers in order to make their own states economically prosperous. The long centuries of warfare in Europe between states which were unable to subjugate each other kept open the possibility of locating businesses in the place where conditions were most favorable. Warfare cost money, which the rulers borrowed from merchants and bankers and in return had to give relatively favorable terms on which to do business. The economic thus began to get some leverage over the political realm.

CORE, SEMIPERIPHERY, PERIPHERY, AND EXTERNAL AREA

A world economy includes several different types of states and areas. At its center are the *core* areas. These contain the military "Great Powers" of the time, states which achieve greatness by virtue of being the leading economies, since economic resources translate into military might. (Though Wallerstein says relatively little about culture, he expects them also to be the cultural centers of each era as well, in such matters as fine arts and literature, science, philosophy, and so on [Wallerstein, 1980: 65–67]; this is mainly because they have the wealth and prestige to support or attract the leading intellectuals and artists of the time.)

The basis of any core area's economy is its position in the world system, especially its domination over the *periphery*. The periphery consists of the "colonial" or "undeveloped" areas of the world—Latin America for the Spanish Empire, India for the British Empire, and so forth—which provide raw materials to the core areas on cheap terms because they are coerced into doing so. Before incorporation into the world system, these were *external areas,* isolated tribal (or other, less economically and military advanced) societies, available for conquest by the core states. Wallerstein also uses the concept of *semiperiphery*; these are states which are halfway between core and periphery in terms of power and economic structure: either the weaker members of an "advanced" area (like the minor states of Europe) or else the leading members of a colonial area. Semiperipheral states attempt to economically exploit still weaker states in their area. The semiperiphery is also a kind of social mobility pool through which some peripheral states might move upwards, eventually even reaching core status. Thus, North America began as an external area, inhabited only by Indian tribes; it became a periphery during the colonial period, then moved up into semiperipheral status by the time of the American Revolution. Eventually it became the core area of mid-twentieth century.

The main interaction in the system is between the core areas and the periphery. Each determines the other's internal structure. Because of the inflow of economic resources to the core, these states enjoy relatively light taxation. Labor is free and fairly well paid. (In terms of the Marxian model in Figure 3-2, there is an additional input into the system from outside, raising economic profit without increasing exploitation of domestic labor.) Thus, a core area has within itself a good consumer market which can afford to buy relatively advanced or luxurious products. In the periphery, on the other hand, labor is usually forced, in the form of slavery or peonage on the colonial plantations and mines, with living conditions for workers at an extremely low level.

DYNAMICS OF THE WORLD SYSTEM: CYCLES, CRISES, AND WARS

Although they enjoy dominance, core states remain subject to some of the same pressures as other military states which operate as world empires (see footnote 8). They fight with other core states, engaging in imperialist wars to conquer peripheral areas (such as the battles between Spain, Holland, France, and England over their colonial possessions in the 1600s and 1700s). As a result, they tend to be caught in the vicious circle of rising military and governmental expenditures, taxation pressures, and domestic revolts. The only way to get ahead of the vicious circle is to conquer more successfully, and thus bring in income and raise confidence at home faster than the rise of military expenditures and domestic resistance. The state which is best able to maintain an empire by conquering the periphery will be able to get ahead of the cycle; its enemies who fall behind in foreign conquest, fall behind at home as well.

Often, Wallerstein points out, the biggest and strongest states end up with a disadvantage in this situation. Spain, which had the great world empire of the 1500s and early 1600s, and France, which was growing into the largest land power in Europe during this time, were caught in the Great Power syndrome which made them ambitious to dominate all of Europe. Their continuous wars ruined both of them economically (Spain more so than France); eventually they neutralized each other's power, creating a vacuum into which the Dutch Empire in the 1600s, and then the British, were able to move. Thus, these semiperipheral countries from northern Europe were able to displace the former core states to the south.

All this takes place, according to the theoretical model, in a large-scale cycle, operating not within states but on the level of the entire world system. Wallerstein and his associates (Research Working Group, 1979) propose that there are pairs of cycles, each of which takes approximately 150 years. In technical economic terms, these are Kondratieff waves, or long waves, and consist of phases labeled A_1 and B_1, followed by phases labeled A_2 and B_2. The underlying cyclical process is economic. The core consists of high skill, high wage economies, producing technologically advanced manufactured goods at high prices. The periphery consists of low skill, low wage economies, producing raw materials. Thus:

In the A_1 phase, the demand for high-priced manufactured goods exceeds their supply. Business production expands and drives up the demand for raw materials. This in turn leads to a geographical expansion into external areas in order to secure those materials, that is, to imperialism.

The B_1 phase begins when a turning point is reached in this expansion. Eventually too many raw materials are produced, so that their supply exceeds demand. Foreign expansion slows down; and since fewer raw materials are being brought in, core production stagnates. The Marxian dynamic takes over at home (as in Figure 3-4). Weaker businesses go bankrupt or are taken over by competitors; monopoli-

FIGURE 3-7

CYCLES OF THE WORLD SYSTEM

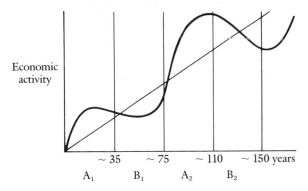

zation grows; and capital is centralized, preparing the way for new expansion. (Here we have the Marxian domestic cycle reaching the bottom, then beginning to rise again.) Additionally, the stagnation of production in the core reduces the favorable conditions once enjoyed by core workers. As unemployment grows and incomes fall, class conflict breaks out. Rulers attempt to repress it, and sometimes lose their thrones in the process. But eventually workers are given concessions in the form of some economic redistribution. This increases consumer demand once again, leading to a new economic growth. Then cycle begins again (see Figure 3-7).

On the basis of historical data on economic indicators, Wallerstein *et al.* propose that there are always two pairs of these *A-B* cycles. The second down phase, B_2, is the more severe economic crisis. It coincides with a period of all-out warfare between the core states and results in the older core state being displaced by a new hegemonic state.

So far, Wallerstein *et al.* indicate, we have gone through four such double cycles, each one dominated by a particular hegemonic state:

1450–1620/40	Spain
1600s–1750	Netherlands (France)[9]
1750–1917	Britain
1917–	United States

---

[9]Wallerstein (1980) describes this phase as dominated by the Dutch sea empire, citing in support the fact that Amsterdam had become the center of world finance in the mid-1600s; that Holland had the world's highest standard of living and level of urbanization; and that it was the center of science, art, and philosophy (Huygens, Descartes, Spinoza, Rembrandt). One could argue, though, that the Netherlands was a world military power for only about 30 years of this time, when its fleets ruled the seas; and that in many respects (above all militarily, but also economically and culturally) France was the core power. This dispute might be resolved if we look at general geographical areas rather than official state lines. The Netherlands and France are contiguous and there was little border line between them in this period. This was especially so in the southern part of the Netherlands, now called Belgium, but at the time a set of small feudal territories subject to fluctuating control by various great powers.

The end of each period was a time of showdown wars, which temporarily ruined the European economy: the Thirty Years War 1620–1650, the French Revolutionary/Napoleonic Wars 1792–1815, and World War I and II 1914–1945 (seen as an overall period of war). The last set of wars reduced Britain from hegemonic status and raised the United States to leader of the core states.[10]

THE END OF THE CAPITALIST WORLD SYSTEM: SOCIALIST WORLD GOVERNMENT

Wallerstein and his associates are not pessimistic about the future, since they do not expect the cycles and wars to repeat themselves endlessly. The *A* phase of expansion always depends upon there being some reserve of unexploited external area that can be brought into the system. By coercing new areas and tapping new raw materials and cheap labor, the core areas bolster their profits and get their economies in a privileged position. Eventually, however, the external area will be exhausted. The world system will literally take up the whole globe, and there will be no further escape valve. The whole world will gradually become capitalist, and its internal contradictions will work themselves out without possibility of any external input to save it. When that happens, the system will have to face its final crisis. Optimistically, Wallerstein *et al.* propose that the outcome will be the abolition of the military framework of the system and the existence of separate states themselves. Just as in Marx's classical model the state is finally taken over by the workers and the property system abolished, the final stage of Wallerstein's model mirrors this process on the world level. The end result is socialist world government.

This part is still rather far in the future and therefore vague. Wallerstein does make the striking point, however, that because of the dynamics of the world system, individual socialist economies are not really possible. In the twentieth century, there are states with socialist governments (Russia, China, and so forth), but their economies are tied to the world economy, and therefore they are parts of the capitalist economy. Russia has no choice but to act as part of this capitalist system whenever it has economic dealings outside its own borders; as a result, it acts just like any other would-be core state, exercising economic imperialism and bolstering its economy at the expense of others. Wallerstein is thus no advocate of Russian-style socialism. He believes that socialism in a true sense can exist only in a situation of democracy, but democracy organized on a world level. The socialist states that now exist are important, though, as part of a coalition of antisystemic forces that is expected to destroy the capitalist world system.

---

[10] By this logic, there should be no *major* showdown war between the United States and a challenger for hegemonic status until some time in the middle of the twenty-first century. The obvious candidate would be nuclear war between the United States and the USSR. Wallerstein's logic suggests that there is no structural reason in the world system why this should happen within our lifetimes, however. Presumably the world economic difficulties of the 1970s and 80s mean that we are now at the B_1 phase of economic downturn, whereas structural realignment in the world system is not due until the end of the B_2 phase, another 70 years from now.

CRITICISMS OF WORLD SYSTEM THEORY

Orthodox Marxists have often been rather critical of the world systems theory. An influential critique by Brenner (1977) argues that Wallerstein, Frank, and Amin define capitalism in terms of unequal exchange between states on the world market. But this is un-Marxist. For the fundamental Marxian principle is that economies are built upon class relationships in a mode of production, between capitalists who monopolize ownership of economic resources, and workers who must sell their labor for wages. Capitalism could not have emerged in Europe in the first place, Brenner argues, except by class struggle inside the prior mode of production which existed there, feudalism. Capitalism was created when the bourgeoisie wrested economic control from the feudal lords, and the land-bound peasants were transformed into propertyless proletarians. The fact that imperialism (the Spanish Empire, the British Empire, and so forth) took place at the same time is only a coincidence; imperialism is found for thousands of years in previous history without giving rise to capitalism. European capitalism did not depend upon imperialism; similarly, the structures of colonial societies depend essentially upon their own class relations, on the struggles between local feudal lords and local peasants (or their equivalents), and between local capitalists and local workers.[11]

The orthodox Marxian position, I think, has too much faith in the classic Marxian model's ability to explain the operations of capitalism. But as we have seen, the classic Marxian model has flaws which need repair, and the world system model provides one way to repair them. Moreover, the world system model, when viewed in a less polemical light, is actually rather close to the orthodox model. As Bergesen (1984) points out, it can be best understood as seeing the entire world as a single capitalist system instead of a set of separate systems, each with its own state and own economy. There is a political sphere (equivalent to the state in Figure 3-5) for the entire world system, which determines economic property. A crucial aspect of this property is the extraction of raw materials, and a crucial activity of this world political sphere is to coerce, or otherwise make available, cheap labor for the world owners of capital. The fact that states are divided among themselves in rivalries and wars is no more than a general representation of the political struggle that goes on most of the time between different factions of the economically most mobilized class.

At the same time, however, I would agree that there are unanswered questions about the world system theory. Wallerstein has written mostly about the origins of capitalism in the 1400s and 1500s, and its early empires of the 1600s.[12] There is

---

[11] One reason that orthodox Marxists are offended by world system theory is that it implies that workers in core countries owe their prosperity to their privileged position in the world system, and are therefore, in a sense, exploiters of workers in the periphery. They also dislike the implication that workers in Third World countries, by carrying out their struggles against the local ruling class, are nevertheless caught in a larger dynamic over which they have no control: that socialism cannot be achieved on the local level at all, but depends upon a transformation of the whole world system. World system theory tends to endorse much more loosely defined "anti-systemic movements," such as as nationalist and even religious movements (for instance, in the Arab world), rather than worker's movements per se.

[12] At this writing, only the first two volumes of *The Modern World System* have been published. Each volume corresponds approximately to one double *A-B* cycle with its hegemonic crisis.

some truth in Brenner's charge that the initial rise of capitalism in Europe depended more on indigenous developments than on overseas imperialism; Weber's model (1923/1961; see Collins, 1986: 19–44) shows a long chain of prior institutional developments within Europe necessary for its emergence. But neither Marx nor Wallerstein has his focus of attention on the origins of capitalism. Their models concern the nature of the capitalist system once it is under way, and what causes its crises and its dynamics of expansion. Wallerstein, in particular, sets out to show how the system operates in a fashion that violates Marx's predictions of revolution and class structure in advanced capitalism but is nevertheless consistent with an underlying economic logic; and he manages to do so, at least in principle. (We will have to wait for his later volumes to judge his success at the theoretical showdown point of events since Marx's time.)

There is also the problem of demonstrating by what mechanisms the core states exploit the periphery in the modern era. Wallerstein's analysis rests upon old-fashioned empires, in which Spanish conquistadors and British gunboats quite literally enforced colonial rule, and cheap labor was ensured by herding Indians onto haciendas and importing slaves from Africa. In the twentieth century, though (and even to a degree in the nineteenth), direct political rule has largely fallen away. Labor in the Third World today, and for some decades past, is free labor, not fundamentally different from workers elsewhere in the world. World system theorists argue that different mechanisms of control produce essentially the same results, that cheap labor can still be obtained in Mexico and Taiwan, for instance, and that raw materials are extracted from Chile at low world prices. They suggest that these mechanisms are, to some extent, disguised forms of military empires in that local governments depend on arms and advisors supplied from overseas, and military interventions are used to uphold antirevolutionary regimes. Other mechanisms are economic and can be found in the penetration of multinational corporations into Third World economies, and the influence of world banking, which has an unequal bargaining power, on the glutted world markets connecting producers of raw materials and capitalist buyers in the wealthy regions of the world.

But this is an area in which the mesh of theories with facts is unclear. Even Marxists disagree over the question of whether economic imperialism really works to keep raw materials cheap and local labor costs low. One version of orthodox Marxism (Szymanski, 1981) argues that despite international economic conditions, capitalist development nevertheless does take place in Third World countries (a phenomena that they greet, since it means that the working class displaces precapitalist peasantries, opening the way for classical socialist politics). We would have to distinguish between dependency theory (Frank, 1967, 1979) and Wallerstein's world system theory on this point, however. Whereas dependency theory argues that the periphery is permanently kept from developing, world system theory leaves much more flexibility. In fact, it claims that imperialism becomes exhausted as a solution to capitalism's home problems because the entire world eventually becomes penetrated by capitalism. Capital which a few years ago moved its assembly plants to Mexico or Hong Kong to take advantage of lower wages, is now moving them out again as local wages have risen; this seems to indicate that this phase of intensive world capitalism may already be well advanced.

World system theory also allows for mobility to take place in the system. Peripheries become semiperipheries; in our own day, Taiwan, Hong Kong, Singapore, and South Korea have become little industrial giants, capturing markets in the still more peripheral, less developed parts of the world (such as Africa and Arabia). Over the last century, Japan has moved rapidly from the periphery into the core, and according to some observers, now threatens to challenge the United States for hegemonic status in the entire world. On the other side, once mighty Britain is falling towards semiperipheral status in Europe, just as Spain did three hundred years before. Movement up and down seems to be characteristic of the history of the world system since its beginning. Wallerstein's model is obviously incomplete on this point, since it does not explain what conditions govern these movements. It is similarly vague about which core state wins or loses in hegemonic wars. At a minimum, the theory is in need of further additions on these points. As we will see, some of these may be provided by parts of conflict theory.

MARXISM AS PHILOSOPHY

Another way in which theorists have revised Marxist theory for the modern era has been to de-emphasize the economic model, and especially its deterministic aspects. In its place, Marxism is treated as philosophy, generally as a version of the Hegelian tradition from which it sprang. This is a retreat from Marx's own position, since Marx himself regarded his system as a science based on economics and (except in his earliest writings) was quite hostile to philosophy. But it has been a strategic retreat, since the major problem of Marxism in the mid-twentieth century has been how to keep the intellectual system going in a world of widespread economic affluence. Rebellious political movements have occurred, even in some economically prosperous periods, such as the 1960s in Europe and the United States. Thus, philosophers like Herbert Marcuse, Jürgen Habermas, and others have turned Marxism into a critique of affluence rather than of immiseration.

There have been two main themes in this philosophical revisionism, and both derive ultimately from Hegel. One wing stresses alienation as a form of subjective consciousness, while the other wing attacks this as a form of "humanism" and, instead, stresses structures existing independently of the individual. More recently, there has been an effort to reintegrate the humanist and structuralist versions of philosophical Marxism in a synthesis sometimes called "new social realism."

CAPITALISM AS ALIENATION AND CONSCIOUSNESS

Hegel was the most historically and politically oriented of the German idealist philosophers.[13] In his system, history moves through a dialectic, which is both a struggle between social groups, and an unfolding of the logic of the Idea which

---

[13] A group of philosophers who flourished in Germany during the upheavals of the French Revolution and the Napoleonic wars (1789–1815). The original "critical" philosophy of Immanuel Kant began the movement, which turned in an idealist direction with the writings of Fichte, Schelling, Hegel, and Schopenhauer.

underlies our conscious reality. Hegel's central concept is *alienation*. This means more than a merely psychological sense of unhappiness with the world as it is. Alienation is a technical term in Hegel's philosophical system. It refers to the fact that the human individual (in Hegel's view, a manifestation of the Spirit) creates the world by his or her labor, but is then alienated from it because the world, in turn, controls human beings. Alienation means the ironic relationship of being controlled by the products of one's own action. In Hegel's idealist viewpoint, this means quite literally that the whole world is really created by Mind, but that Mind is alienated from itself since it takes the world to be matter. The final stage of history is when the human mind finally recognizes that it is Mind, and hence that the "material" world is indeed under its own control. This is a quasi-religious doctrine, ultimately implying a mysticism something like Buddhism. But there is a more mundane, even materialist interpretation, which Marx seized upon: in the economic system, workers create capitalism and all its products by their own labor, but they are caught in this system and oppressed by it. The "exploitation" of labor, the extraction of "surplus value" which Marx saw as the central element in capitalism, is thus the same thing as alienation in the philosophical sense.

This aspect of Marx, as well as other elements taken from Hegel (such as dialectics, the attack on positivistic science, and an emphasis on "praxis" and transformations of consciousness), have provided the materials for twentieth-century Marxists embarrassed by the failure of Marxian economic predictions.

LUKACS AND GRAMSCI: FALSE CONSCIOUSNESS AND IDEOLOGICAL DOMINATION

Writing just after World War I, a young Marxist who had been active in the effort to establish a communist regime in Hungary used Hegelian concepts to explain the failure of workers to become sufficiently revolutionary. Georg Lukacs (1923/1971) (pronounced "Lu-kotch") pinned the problem on the production of "false consciousness" which kept people from seeing the contradictions in capitalist society. People failed to see that they themselves had created the system and were oppressed by it; they "reified" the system as if it existed on a purely external base, immune from human control. Lukacs was optimistic that this form of alienation from reality could be overcome in a revolutionary movement. He argued that the degree of false consciousness was actually highest among the dominant social class, and that the working class was closer to freedom from ideological conceptions because of its implicit alienation from the dominant society. It would take only the actions of a vanguard of intellectuals to show the workers their true class interest.

The Italian Marxist Antonio Gramsci, writing a few years later in his *Prison Notebooks* (1928/1971),[14] however, argued that the working class is most afflicted by the power of the dominant class's ideology. If not deceived by outright illusions, their minds are subject to "contradictory consciousness," with confused and fragmented judgments on the nature of the world they inhabit. This is because the ruling class is *hegemonic:* controlling not only property but—even more importantly—the means of producing beliefs about reality. These include religion, educa-

---

[14] He was imprisoned by Mussolini's Fascist movement, which took power in Italy in 1922.

tion, and more recently, the mass media. Thus the working class is severely crippled in its ability to revolt against the dominant order, or even think critically about it. (For modern examples, see Gitlin [1979] on the power of television, or the French sociologist Pierre Bourdieu's [1984] theory of the stratification produced by differences in personal taste and styles of entertainment, which he calls "cultural capital.")

However, other branches of Marxism have criticized this theme (summarized in Gottdiener, 1985). The Marxist historian E. P. Thompson (1963) has described how the British working class developed its own culture based on its own local institutions, such as evangelical religion and popular entertainment, which enabled it to uphold its own consciousness, independent of the dominant class and its culture. On the theoretical level, there may be no real debate here. Gramsci's theory of ideological hegemony is similar to the Marx-Engels model of the means of mental production.[15] Schematically, that model may be stated:

Class control ⟶ Means of mental production ⟶ Ideas

Gramsci focused on the arrow at the right side of this model, stressing the mechanisms by which culture is produced. Thompson and others focus on the left side, disputing over *who* controls which idea-producing resources at what time. Both arguments may be correct. But the *general theory* for the left side has not been well developed. It would have to provide answers to a number of questions: When (under what conditions) do the upper classes control the means of mental production? When, and to what extent, do the working class (and other subordinate classes) acquire control of their own mental-production resources? Are there conditions under which the mental production sector (for example, religion, education, mass media) become organizationally independent, and develop a dynamic of their own? (For further developments of "the dominant ideology thesis" see Abercrombie, Hill, and Turner, 1980.) These quesions suggest a bridge between Marxian-Engelsian theory and other branches of sociology.

LEFEBVRE AND MARCUSE: ALIENATION IN EVERYDAY LIFE

A different version of Hegelian Marxism focuses on the critique of modern society. Its main argument is that life in a society of material affluence is itself alienating. The French philosopher Henri Lefebvre (1971), for instance, began by arguing that the characteristic of modern life is fragmentation. Individuals confront tiny portions of the world in their own specializations at work and in the misleading focus of attention on material objects of consumption and popular entertainment. The aim of Marxism, then, is not so much overthrowing a materially depriving economic system as restoring totality in the full Hegelian sense—overcoming this alienation and fragmentation of consciousness. The bureaucratic society has ob-

[15] Marx and Engels' famous statement regarding "the means of mental production" appears in *The German Ideology,* written in 1846. It was not published, though, until 1932. Hence, Gramsci may be credited with independently discovering this idea, although he formulated it in the language of early twentieth-century Italian neo-Hegelianism, as compared to Marx and Engels's militant materialism.

scured the class struggle; it has split the working class by making a portion of it affluent consumers and merging their lifestyle with that of the middle class. Advertisements and the desire to emulate ownership of consumer goods results in a society of controlled consumption. The modern world of capitalism is made up of dull and repetitive routines. Even time and space come under capitalism's control and are reduced to commodities: time is money, space is real estate. The naturalness of peasant villages is replaced by the linear roads and factories of the modern city, and time shifts from being a cyclical consciousness of the seasons of nature to being the alienated clock-time of modern life. Workers are driven by the compulsion to sell their labor on the market; and even though this may involve affluence under today's labor conditions, the result is nevertheless alienating because they are deprived of the satisfying relationship to their work that had prevailed when they were self-employed craftsmen or peasants with a close relationship to nature.

Lefebvre, although his writings go back to the 1930s and 1940s, was the philosopher of the French radical students who attempted to overthrow the French government in an uprising in 1968. In the United States, a similar role was played by an emigré German philosopher, Herbert Marcuse. Marcuse's critique of modern society is similar to that of Lefebvre: both were Hegel scholars, using Hegelian concepts of alienation, totality, and praxis; both stressed heavily the reduction of modern life to a chase for consumer goods under the impulsion of advertisements. Marcuse added some elements of Freudian theory, in which modern life emerged as "repressive desublimation": rather than a repression of sexual drives, such as Freud found underlying the work ethic of the Victorian era, there is now an encouragement to indulge in the satisfaction of hedonistic drives. But this remains repressive in the sense that it keeps capitalism going, and reduces the person to what Marcuse (1964) called "one-dimensional man."

Lefebvre and Marcuse extend their critique to the modern intellectual world as well, attacking empiricism and scientific or causal explanations generally. Lefebvre rejected the economic version of Marx as "positivist," that is to say, a philosophical viewpoint which is deterministic, focusing on laws that exist outside the observer. Similarly, Marcuse's first book (1941) used Hegel to claim that any analysis which merely explains the world is incomplete because it accepts the world as given. The higher form of analysis is critical, showing that any concept is only partial, and that its "essence" (an Aristotelean term appropriated by Hegel) is its *potential*, what it might become. Since in Hegel's scheme every concept has dialectical contradictions, reality is never completed until everything has turned into its opposite and has then been received in a still higher synthesis. This means that any "science" of modern society is inaccurate because it does not contain a critique of society and an exposition of its potential for turning into a higher form (presumably socialism). Mere knowledge, then, (as Lefebvre argued) is a form of alienation as long as thinkers do not try to change the world but only to know it. There is an anti-intellectual implication in this doctrine, which comes out in the slogan of *praxis,* (purposeful action) which Lefrebvre popularized.

These versions of humanistic or Hegelian Marxism share certain weaknesses. There is a romanticist tone in their critique of modern society, which depicts it as a downfall from an era of happy peasants living close to nature, into a world dominated by clocks and advertisements. This is not a very realistic picture of preindustrial societies, where the level of sheer physical oppression—surveillance and abuse of the lower classes in general and of virtually all women—by the dominant aristocracy was much more severe than most people experience today. The humanistic Marxists imply that the spiritual degradation of everyday life now is far worse than any previous conditions. I suspect that this is empirically inaccurate, and that all periods of society (at least, stratified society) have their own forms of degradation. A more useful side of these doctrines would be to focus upon what kinds of society are possible in the future, and on the higher levels of human potential that might be released.

ALTHUSSER'S STRUCTURALIST MARXISM

An alternative in Marxian philosophy is structuralism. Althusser provides a strategy of backing off from rigid economic determinism, which seems to be empirically inaccurate, without going all the way to merely subjectivist forms. Althusser is an explicit enemy of the humanist approach to Marxism. In this he means also to repudiate such philosophies as the existentialism of Jean-Paul Sartre, with its emphasis on the individual human consciousness and its choices. Althusser (1971, 1972; Althusser and Balibar, 1970) declares that history is "a process without a subject," since its true subject is the relations of production. Society is above all a structure—over and above the individual human beings who fill particular places in it. This structure is not immediately visible; it is, rather, a kind of abstract grid of relationships from which concrete historical reality is always a realization of certain possibilities. Hence, history is merely a reshuffling of different combinations of these structural possibilities.

Althusser shares the French structuralist view that there is a "deep" structure beneath the surface of the empirical world. Any particular historical period, or any particular events in the lives of particular persons, are merely a selection and combination of these structurally given possibilities. For Althusser, one cannot speak of a simple causation, that *this* is the cause of *that*. Rather, any specific event is "over-determined" in much the same sense that Freud said that any particular psychic symptom, such as something that happens in a dream, can have multiple meanings, each determined by a different psychic mechanism. A particular political event—say, the outcome of an attempted revolution—has a variety of structural causes: some in the economic structure of capitalism in general; some in the specific nature of property in that particular country; some in the realm of political structures, ideologies, and so on. All together, they converge in bringing about a particular event at its particular time.

Althusser is thus not only reacting against the subjectivistic interpretations of Marxism, but is also making room in the Marxian paradigm for other levels of causation besides the economic. There are also political, ideological, and other structures, each with its own partial autonomy from the economic. The economic structure is overriding only in the sense that it determines "in the final instance" the rest of the society. One might interpret this to mean something analogous to Lenski's (1966) cross-societal comparisons of societies with different technologies. Possessing a particular technology (for example, industrial machinery or horticultural tools) does not automatically determine everything that happens in that society, but it does set the stage by shaping the basic social structures within which everything else happens. "In the final instance" means, logically, that if we looked at societies over a very long period of time, we would find that the most important thing to know about them would be their economic system (for Althusser) or their technology (for Lenski).

In practical terms, if the humanist Marxists are retreating from economics into culture and consciousness, structuralist Marxism is a rejection of economic Marxism in favor of a theory of the state. In the last instance the economy is determining; but the "last instance" is a very long time span, and in the short run in which we live, the state is where one should focus one's attention. Structuralist Marxism is thus a kind of philosophical justification for turning Marx's failed economic system into political sociology. Such a theory was developed primarily by Althusser's former student, Nicos Poulantzas.[16]

NEW SOCIAL REALISM

An effort to reunite the two wings of Marxian philosophy has taken place recently in Britain under the label *new social realism*. Its main exponents have been the philosopher Roy Bhaskar and the sociologist Anthony Giddens.

Giddens calls his version "structurationism," to emphasize that there is a continuous rollover between structures and individual action. Giddens (1981) adopts Lefebvre's position on the nature of everyday life and brings Heidegger's existentialism into the Marxian critique of capitalism. In his more general model (1976, 1984), Giddens makes use of modern microsociology (including the ethnomethodologists and Goffman) to sketch how individuals reproduce the larger system in their daily interactions. Structures now become mental categories, the "rules and resources" which individuals have handed down from prior interactions and out of which they recreate society. Giddens thus attempts to combine structures, with their objectivity and determinism, with subjective experience and action, each of the two continually flowing into the other.

Bhaskar (1978, 1979) provides a more abstract argument. He uses the structuralist notion that there is a "deep structure" which is at a different level of reality from empirical appearances. This deep structure of modern society is none other than Marx's own economic model. But this is interpreted not as a deterministic system, but as a set of relationships and abstract possibilities. In fact, appearances are usually contradictory to the underlying structure, and this contradiction is what is specifically dialectical (in the Hegelian sense). Structures are *generative*, not deterministic, in the same way that the rules of grammar generate an infinite number of different sentences we can speak, without determining which one will actually be spoken. It is impossible to find "closed systems" in the social sciences, though they may exist in some parts of physical science. Predictions are impossible, except in the most general, probabilistic sense. Statements of laws are merely statements of tendencies which may or may not be actualized. Human beings and their sense of voluntarism, of free will, are part of this arena of interacting elements; their sense

---

[16] French structuralism is treated more generally in Chapter 9.

of freedom is entirely justified, because it is their action that actualizes the possibilities that are latently there in the structure. Bhaskar and Giddens thus endorse each other's notions of how the individual and the structure are reciprocally related.

Bhaskar does not actually make any new statements of structural principles. Instead, he reiterates the basic Marxian economic model, including the notion of capitalism as the creation of surplus value, the substitution of constant for variable capital (that is, introduction of labor-saving machinery), and the falling rate of profit. How do we know, though, that these are the underlying structures of capitalism, since these are precisely the phenomena which do not fit historical reality in the twentieth century? Bhaskar declares that they are merely generative structures, a set of possibilities from which reality selects through human action, and furthermore, that empirical reality is usually at odds with the deep structure.

It is true, as we have learned from systems theory, that a complex theory cannot be simply tested and rejected on the basis of how it predicts reality. This is because we do not know which among its many interacting elements and relationships is at fault. But how do we know we have found the actual "deep structure"? It should be possible to improve our generative model, and surely empirical evidence is relevant to that in some degree. I would say that we must try to test the separate parts of the model and to see how well they cohere with theory and research in other areas of sociology. From this perspective, some of the more "surface-level" reconstructions of Marxism, (the world system model, the model of political mobilization, even conflict theory in general) appear worth salvaging, while the fundamentals of the economic model need to be seriously revised.

MARXIAN THEORIES OF THE STATE

The other major focus of modern Marxism has been on the state. The two main positions are "instrumentalist" and "structuralist." The *instrumentalist* position is closer to classical Marxism, since it holds that the capitalist class personally participate in state power and shape government policies in their class interests. The state, in other words, is an instrument of class domination. This position has been put forward largely by empirical researchers (for example, Domhoff 1967; Useem, 1986) who attempt to show that leading government officials are mostly drawn from the ranks of big business and financial executives and that political parties in capitalist democracies are heavily funded by the wealthy, and point to other signs that capital still wields political power.

The *structuralist* side, however, is impressed by the extent to which the state in the modern era has grown independent of the economy. Structuralist theorists recognize the reality that liberal and even socialist parties (in Europe) have taken power and have put into effect various reforms which constitute the "welfare state." These reforms have generally been brought about in the face of strenuous resistance from the business class, although they have had the effect, it is believed, of propping up capitalism against its own failings. Social security, unemployment benefits, direct government employment, and intervention in the economy have all operated to counteract economic depressions and to protect workers from the negative effects of the capitalist market system. To be sure, capitalism still survives; in fact, it does so apparently *because* these "liberal" reforms were carried out. This is the background of Marxist structuralism: to show how the modern state preserves capitalism, even against the overt opposition of capitalists.

POULANTZAS' STRUCTURALIST THEORY OF THE STATE

The principal structuralist theorist of the state was the French sociologist, Nicos Poulantzas. Using Althusser's structuralist concepts, he proceeded to construct a system based on a series of analytical (abstract) distinctions (Poulantzas, 1968, 1974, 1978). First of all, there are various kinds of *modes of production,* or economic systems, of which the capitalist mode of production is one. At a more concrete level, there is a particular historical *social formation,* which is "a complex unity in which a certain mode of production dominates the others which compose it" (Poulantzas, 1968: 15). That is to say, the economic system is an abstraction, and in the reality of any particular point in time, there are usually several different types of economy (feudal, laissez-faire capitalist, monopoly capitalist, socialist) which are mixed together. But one of these modes of production usually dominates, and thus becomes the main structuring principle of that society or "social formation."

But there is more to a social formation than the economy. A social formation is a complex whole, comprising various "regional structures" each of which constitute one another. The state is one such "regional structure." It is a concrete "instance" of the three "organizing matrices" of "practices, norms and rules": economic, political, and ideological. (In other words, Poulantzas incorporates Weber's tri-partitite distinction of class, status, and party into a Marxian framework.) Each of these has "relative autonomy," though the economic side—the mode of production—is determinative "in the last instance." (See the discussion of Althusser on pages 105–106.) Poulantzas wishes to avoid the reductionism of declaring that the state, or the realm of ideology, is merely "superstructure" determined by an economic "base." Instead, they are all constitutive of each other, in that none of them could exist without the other parts.

The capitalist mode of production divides owners of the means of production from the owners of labor power and thus involves relationships of class struggle. There are also struggles within the capitalist class. *Possession* is analytically distinct from *ownership,* so it is possible for possessors to be identical with owners (in which case we have traditional, nineteenth-century–style individualist capitalism), or possessors can be different from owners (in which case we have the corporations of modern "monopoly capitalism," possessed by their managers, but owned by absentee stockholders or financial institutions).[17] Poulantzas thus makes room for the complexities of empirical reality. Individual and monopoly capitalism can both exist at the same time; and there is often a political struggle between monopoly and nonmonopoly capitalists, a struggle to survive in business and a struggle over what

[17] I put "monopoly capitalism" in quotation marks because although it is a commonly used Marxist term, strictly speaking it is inaccurate. *Monopoly* means domination of a market by a single firm. This hardly exists anywhere; what we find instead is domination of markets by a small number of large corporations (for example, 15 large United States oil companies controlling 86 percent of international investments in petroleum [Szymanski, 1981]). In technical terms, this should be called "oligopoly" capitalism.

policies the state will carry out. Within the "monopoly" sector, there are further struggles between industrial and financial capitalists.

When we add to these struggles between different types of capitalists, the struggle between capitalists and workers (and of different kinds of workers), we can see that the state is a "site" for class struggle. In fact, the state itself is constituted by such class struggles, and serves to hold society together through them. At the same time, the fact that it is the location of the most explicit struggles—the manuevers of politicians of various classes to gain power—makes the state structurally autonomous (at least relatively so), and capable of intervening in the economy.

The extent to which the state intervenes is also the result of class struggle and has a certain correspondence with the economic mode of production. The "liberal state" of the nineteenth century merely upheld property and regulated the currency; the "interventionist" state of the twentieth century acts to prop up capitalism more directly. In particular, it raises profit (and thereby combats the main structural contradiction in the Marxian system—the tendency for profit to fall) by reducing the private input of constant capital: that is, it takes upon itself the provision of some of the costs of machinery by subsidizing scientific research on new technology, training workers, aiding new industries, and so forth. The "monopolistic" fraction of capitalists is especially in favor of these interventions, while the more traditional, competitive capitalists make up a conservative opposition. (Hence the split, noticeable in the Republican party in the United States, between "moderate" and "conservative" wings.)

It should be borne in mind that Poulantzas, as a Marxist politician, was also establishing the basis for a political strategy (see Hirsh, 1981). The French communist party, like those in Italy, Spain, and Greece, was winning substantial portions of seats in parliamentary elections and was on the verge of winning part of the government offices in the event of victory of a socialist/communist coalition. (This actually came about in France in 1980.) This gave rise to a new approach called "Eurocommunism," which explicitly renounced the Soviet-style model of armed revolution and "dictatorship of the proletariat" and accepted the alternation of parties in a parliamentary democracy. Poulantzas' theory provided a theoretical justification for this move. If the state was an integral part of structuring and restructuring the economy, and the state itself was the site of class struggles, then becoming primarily a parliamentary rather than a revolutionary party was justified as a way of fighting for socialism.

For our sociological search for an adequate explanatory theory, these political motives are irrelevant. Our question is, rather, whether this line of analysis advances sociological theory. My judgment would be that it does not take us much further than conventional sociological theories. Despite its innovativeness in Marxian circles, Poulantzas' introduction of the "relative autonomy" of economics, politics, and ideology reiterates a point Weber had introduced 60 years earlier, which is a mainstay of much American sociology. His structuralist analysis also bears a deep resemblance to the functionalism of Talcott Parsons, especially in the version espoused by Jeffrey Alexander (Chapter 2). In effect, by saying that the three spheres are "relatively autonomous," he is giving up on any power to predict what will actually cause what. Sometimes political action dominates, sometimes economic action: but which happens when?

Further, there is the problem that Poulantzas' theory does not identify a mechanism of social change. The various parts of the structure, though engaged in relationships of conflict, are nevertheless on the analytical level parts of a single system. They not only constitute each other, they appear to have a tendency to preserve one another; the "interventionist" welfare state acts, over the heads of the capitalists, to preserve the capitalist system. Like most other modern Marxists, Poulantzas has given up on the possibility of revolution; and in the process, he has thrown out the part of the Marxian theory which attempts to predict social change. For this reason, Poulantzas has been accused of being a Marxist version of functionalism (for instance, by Block, 1980).

Poulantzas has explicitly denied that his theory is functionalist in the sense of Parsonian theory. He states (1968) that the social formation is constituted by relations of conflict, which are certainly missing from Parsons; and that the social formation as a whole does not have needs, but is made up of contradictory needs. Nevertheless, the theory comes out as equivalent to a kind of shadow-functionalism, a system which is not good for its members as a whole—a kind of functionalism of evil. It resembles functionalism in its overriding concern to show how everything the system does (especially the modern state) acts to keep the basic structure (the capitalist mode of production) intact. It has the same weakness of failing to account for why particular structures happen to exist in terms of comparative conditions that cause them. We might add that Poulantzas theory also resembles conventional ideology in that it takes the technocratic claims of the modern state at face value, assuming that technical training of workers, the support of the educational system, and so forth are actually functionally needed by the modern economy. According to the modern conflict theory of education and of work, however, this is inaccurate (see Chapter 5).

O'CONNOR'S FISCAL CRISIS THEORY OF THE STATE

A more dynamic theory of the state has been created by American theorists willing to cut loose from the abstractions of structuralism and recognize the state as playing an independent role in the modern economy. Fred Block (1980), Poulantzas's critic, argues that the managers of the state are a distinct group, separate from the managers and owners of capitalist economic organizations. Hence, there is another dimension within modern class conflict, in which state managers come into conflict with capitalists. The state, in short, has its own interests (a position shared by Theda Skocpol, in her historical analysis of revolutions, to be treated in Chapter 4). Block thus proposes that a mechanism of social change in the future will increasingly be this conflict of state vs. capitalists.

Block's most important step has been to recognize that the state itself is an *economic* entity, and hence is part of the dynamics of the overall economy. This is developed in the theory of James O'Connor (1973). He proposes that a modern capitalist society like the United States is divided into three sectors:

1. *The "monopoly" sector* This comprises the large corporations, using the most modern technology and producing the most profitable goods. The labor force working in this sector is unionized, relatively well paid, and therefore politically rather satisfied and conservative.

2. *The competitive sector*   This comprises smaller businesses, either in areas of retail trade (restaurants, beauty shops, and other personal services) unprofitable areas of manufacturing (traditional areas of food production, and so forth), or the newest innovative businesses before they have grown large enough to be taken over by the monopoly sector. Here the labor force is generally not unionized, pay is very low, and working conditions are poor; but because these workers are disproportionately female, recent immigrants, or racial minorities subject to discrimination, they have little power to change their conditions.

3. *The state sector*   This comprises the government agencies which have grown to employ 20 percent or more of the modern labor force, including the massive educational system. Here the labor force is largely white-collar and not unionized, but moderately well paid because these employees are politically aware and active in their own interests. (In fact, they make up a major portion of the liberal vote, since they vote to provide social services, which they themselves receive paychecks for administrating).

Class conflict is structured along the lines of these sectors, rather than simply between capitalists and workers. O'Connor develops a version of the "dual economy" model, which has been used to show why minority and other disadvantaged workers receive lower incomes than similar workers in the "monopoly" (corporate) sector (summarized in Attewell, 1984). He also explains why the working class is politically split: not because of "false consciousness" imposed by ideology, but because the three sectors actually do have distinct economic interests to defend. Monopoly sector workers do best by defending the economic interests of their own capitalist corporations, provided that their unions are also given their share. It is not part of their interests to defend the un-organized workers of the competitive sector, and the white-collar workers of the state sector look out for themselves by keeping up expenditures in the state budget.

THE FISCAL CRISIS   Nevertheless, there is a Marxist-style crisis built into the system. It does not accumulate revolutionary pressure, but it is a chronic source of economic strain and unrest. The basic mechanism can be found in the fact that the state budget subsidizes economic productivity, but the profits are private and accrue to the big corporations. However, the monopoly sector capitalists have the political power to evade paying their share of taxation, and as a result there is an increasing gap between government expenditures and revenues. We are thus in the era of the permanent government deficit and an intermittent round of budgetary crises, especially afflicting local states and municipalities.

The state subsidizes industry by paying for research and development, education, and underlying business resources, such as roads, airports, and the rest of the transportation system. There is also a tax system of incentives for business investment. In addition, the state keeps peace on the labor front by paying for welfare, public recreation facilities, and urban development, as well as for the repressive force of the police. Corporations are relatively well insulated from paying for these services through taxation; but to the extent that they are taxed, they protect their profits by passing on the costs to consumers by charging oligopoly prices. They can do this because the number of corporations per market is small enough for them to effectively imitate each other's price levels, as well as using government regulation to set prices for them. The businesses in the competitive sector cannot do this because they must keep prices genuinely low in order to get their share of business from their competitors.

INFLATION   A further source of crisis comes from the effects of this process on the value of money. The monopoly sector can put all its labor costs (of its well-fed union workers) and its tax costs into prices. This results in "cost-push" inflation: higher prices lead unionized workers to demand higher wages, which lead to higher prices, and so on. From another direction, government policies also foster inflation. Government expenditures rise, under pressure both from the monopoly sector to pay its underlying costs, and from its own employees who favor budget expansion benefiting themselves. Taxation lags behind expenditures, and therefore new debts are created, producing further inflation. The government ends up having to pay even higher prices for the goods it buys to undergird the economy. The fiscal crisis thus feeds on itself.

OVERPRODUCTION AND UNDERCONSUMPTION   There is also a classic Marxian angle to this crisis. The monopoly sector, with the latest technology paid for by the state, increases production faster than its need for labor. More goods are produced, but there are fewer workers who can afford to buy them. The competitive sector, which is labor-intensive rather than technology-intensive, cannot offset this lagging demand, since it pays low wages and generates a lower level of consumer demand. The government tries to overcome this problem of underconsumption by "Keynesian" methods, including welfare to absorb surplus labor, as well as hiring workers into the government sector, paying for retraining programs (which at least keep workers out of the labor force for a while). Expanding military production also helps absorb some of the excess production. But all of these government efforts further exacerbate the fiscal crisis and the inflation crisis. In O'Connor's model, the different aspects of the crisis of advanced capitalism all reinforce each other. Though a government can muddle through by expenditures on wars, welfare, and by financial manipulations of the currency, the condition of crisis will not go away; it is chronic.

In O'Connor's assessment, the only way to solve the problem would be to abolish the three sectors by moving all the way to socialism. Although this is not regarded as inevitable (O'Connor, too, has no theory of political change, much less political revolution), it remains the logical possibility, which may some day be realized. But in the short run, the fiscal crisis splits all the classes who might be opposed to capitalism. State employees are opposed by the tax-paying public on the issue of government expenditures; monopoly sector unions are split against nonunion workers; even monopoly capitalists and managers face the ideological obfuscation coming from nonmonopoly sector capitalists, who still believe the solution is more free enterprise, even though the system is intrinsically noncompetitive at its core and undergirded by the state. In this respect, O'Connor's version of political economy gives an empirically realistic picture of the current deadlock in the class struggle.

ASSESSMENT

O'Connor's fiscal crisis theory has the advantage of building on the strength of the Marxian tradition: it is genuinely a model of political economy. It adds the economics of the state itself to the economics of the economy and points out an economic as well as a political relationship between these spheres. It is also a highly systemic model, well suited for dynamic simulation. In this respect it resembles Marx's original model and Wallerstein's world system and parts company from the vaguer structuralist models, which evade questions of causality and fail to pin down the dynamics of the system over time.

O'Connor's model contains a number of causal links and feedback loops: among monopoly sector profit, competitive sector poverty, governmental expenditure and deficit, inflation, overproduction, underconsumption, unemployment, and business crisis. All of these are elements of modern reality. But the formal systemization shows up the weaknesses of the model as well. O'Connor's model logically leads to an escalating crisis on all fronts, whereas in reality fiscal crisis often stays within manageable bounds. There have been some severe periods of inflation in the twentieth century (most recently, in the 1970s), but this has fluctuated downwards as well as upwards. Overproduction, underconsumption, and unemployment have similarly moved up and down.

Although O'Connor's model appears to have captured in part the dynamics of the modern political economy of capitalism, it is missing those factors which act to contravene the fiscal crisis. Writing in the early 1970s, O'Connor stayed too close to the historical reality of that particular period; the more generalized analytical model is yet to be written.

One point at which the system could be widened deals with the mechanisms by which the "monopoly sector" makes the government underwrite only its own expenses, while passing on its costs to the competitive sector. These must be mechanisms of political mobilization and power, similar to (or an extension of) those spelled out in the original Marx-Engels model (Figure 3-5). If these mechanisms were spelled out in the O'Connor model, it would be possible to see the process of political influence as a variable. Under some conditions they produce great advantages for the corporate sector, along with the problems (fiscal crisis, inflation, and so forth) which follow from them. Under a different configuration of these political variables, the relative power of the state or of the competitive sector would increase, thereby mitigating some of these economic problems.

There are also other analytical omissions in the O'Connor model. Not only are the factors that contravene the fiscal crisis not spelled out, neither are some of the factors which exacerbate it. In the latter category, most notably, must be military spending, especially in time of war (such as the Viet Nam war, which constituted the primary economic burden of the U.S. federal government during the time O'Connor was writing). Put in generalized form, this requires a mechanism in the model linking the internal economy and government expenditure to external geopolitical conditions. We shall see in Chapter 4 such a link is consonant both with Theda Skocpol's theory of revolutions and with the more generalized Weber/Collins model of the state.

At this point the political economy tradition in sociology explicitly meets the conflict theory tradition. The latter tradition is more generalized than the Marxian emphasis upon the economy as prime mover, more detached from political activism itself, and therefore more capable of analyzing political factors in their own right. The corresponding weakness of conflict theory is its tendency to downplay the political economy side. A successful comprehensive theory will have to draw upon both traditions of analysis.

SUMMARY

1. The classical Marxian model is a dynamic system explaining political and cultural change in terms of the economy. The economic system reproduces itself over time. In the capitalist system, profit is the source of economic growth, but the process of supply and demand eliminates profit by driving the price of every factor of production down to the level it costs to produce it. Thus, the only source of profit is labor: propertyless workers can be made to work longer hours than the time it takes to reproduce their own labor, and this difference is *surplus value*—the source of capitalist profit.

2. Competition among capitalists leads to the introduction of labor-saving technology. But this reduces the amount of labor time embodied in products, and hence reduces the rate of capitalist profits. Technology also increases the quantity of goods produced, while at the same time causing workers to become unemployed and therefore unable to buy the goods. The result is periodic economic crises. In each crisis period, the stronger capitalists buy out the weaker, who fall into the ranks of the workers, creating a trend towards monopoly. Eventually a crisis becomes so severe that the productive forces cannot be developed further under the capitalist social relations of private property, and this brings about a revolutionary transformation to socialism.

3. Marx and Engels add a theory of classes and of political and ideological mobilization. The state upholds the property system, and hence social classes have an economic interest in controlling the state. The class which owns the means of production has a political weapon to the extent that its members own the *means of mental production*—the material resources for producing ideas which define how people think about their world. The *material means of political mobilization* are resources which determine how well a class can organize itself for political action.

4. The property-owning class normally controls most of these political and ideological resources. But the development of capitalism itself shifts these resources over time, so that eventually the workers become better mobilized, as well as more numerous. The amount of class conflict is proportional to the relative mobilization of subordinate classes. When their resources for political and ideological action exceed those of the property-owning class, revolution takes place.

5. Marxian theory has been revised in several directions to take account of the failure of its predictions. World system theory shifts the level of analysis from the individual society to the larger world arena. In Wallerstein's model, the capitalist dynamic occurs only when there is a *world economy* consisting of competing states, and does not occur within a militarily centralized *world empire*. *Core* areas in the world system have the most advanced means of production, the highest paid labor, and the strongest states. *Peripheral* areas provide raw materials and cheap, coerced labor, which are the basis of the core's prosperity. *External areas* over time become incorporated into the periphery by imperialism. The *semiperiphery* mediates between core and periphery. Over time, areas of the world can move up or down between these positions within the world system.

6. The dynamics of the world system take place in a double cycle (A_1, B_1, A_2, B_2) of approximately 140–200 years. During the A_1 and B_1 phases, the world econ-

omy expands in production and widens its territories through imperialism. The contraction phases, A_2 and B_2, occur because of the economic crisis set off as foreign expansion reaches the level of unprofitability. Class conflict increases in the core, bringing about economic redistribution and, eventually, growth in a new cycle. A hegemonic state dominates the expansion phase, but a showdown war among core states occurs during the major crisis of the B_2 phase, resulting in the rise of a new hegemonic state. The cycles will continue until the external area has been exhausted, making further imperialist expansion impossible and resulting in a global crisis which can be resolved only by socialist world government.

7. Another type of revision interprets Marxism primarily as a philosophy in the Hegelian tradition. Lukacs proposed that capitalism generates *false consciousness* in which people reify their society as if it were a purely external object. Gramsci theorized that the *hegemonic* class exercises control not merely materially but ideologically. Lefebvre and Marcuse emphasize alienation in modern life as a result of capitalist commodification of everyday activities and objects, and even a commodification of space and time.

8. Althusser's structuralist Marxism opposes this emphasis upon consciousness and argues that society is a system without simple causation in which events are overdetermined by converging levels of causality. Political and cultural factors are important, but the economic structure is determining "in the last instance" (that is, in the long-term comparative perspective). New social realism proposes that capitalism is a generative structure, a set of abstract relations and possibilities of which the historical surface is a selection.

9. Recent Marxist theorists have concentrated on the state as a key factor, independent of the economy and capable of acting back upon it. In Poulantzas' structuralist theory, the state is the site of struggle both between and within classes and is constituted by struggle. The state acquires relative autonomy to intervene and prop up the system, as in the case of the modern welfare state.

10. Block proposes that a major conflict within modern capitalism is between state managers and capitalists. In O'Connor's theory, the *state sector* is a major employer and economic actor in its own right, while the private economy is divided into the profitable, high-wage–paying *monopoly sector,* and the unprofitable and low-wage *competitive sector*. The state budget provides services for the monopoly sector, but the latter has the political power to pass along taxes to the unorganized sector of business and consumers. The result is a fiscal crisis of the state, a built-in gap between its expenditures and its income.

Chapter **4**

CONFLICT AND SOCIAL CHANGE

GENERAL PRINCIPLES OF CONFLICT
    Simmel and Coser: Conflict and Social Integration
    Dahrendorf: Power Groups and Conflict Mobilization

CONFLICT THEORY OF SOCIAL CHANGE
    Weber's Theory of Politics
    Geopolitical Theory of the State
    Resource Mobilization Theory
    Revolutions

SUMMARY

Conflict theory began as a development from the Marxian tradition. On one side, there was an effort on the part of non-Marxists to develop a non-Marxian theory of conflict; on the other, revisions within Marxism led to the point where certain fundamental assumptions about the primacy of economics were replaced. Ultimately, both sides of conflict theory cut themselves adrift from the Marxian political program as well; modern conflict theory is "agnostic" on the question of socialism vs. capitalism, as it is on the desirability or necessity of revolution. It moves to a more detached level of analysis and a search for the general laws of society. Such principles, in turn, might be applied in support of various political ends, though there is a tendency for conflict theorists to support the liberal or left side of the political spectrum and to be critical of the abuses of power and property in modern society. But the basic thrust is toward understanding society as a system of conflicting interests, rather than taking sides with a particular economic class or promoting a particular kind of economic revolution.

Intellectually, this has proven to be a fruitful approach. The original strength of conflict theory is as a theory of social change, stratification, and large-scale organization. Moreover, conflict theory is perhaps the prime area in sociological theory where general theoretical principles are fairly well buttressed by empirical research. Current conflict theory is able to make contact with micro theories and micro research on interaction, cognition, and emotion in everyday life. As we shall see in Chapters 6 and 11, it has a detailed program for establishing the micro-macro connection and has a branch showing how conflicting interests also operate on the level of micro interaction.

As conflict theory has broadened, its name has become somewhat misleading. Initially it began as a theory of conflict itself, considering the causes and consequences of conflict and engaging in a polemic with functionalist theory over the question of which has primacy, conflict or social order. But conflict theory is not merely about the occasions when conflict breaks out, nor merely about social change. It is also concerned with explaining social stability because it aims to be a general theory of society. Where it differs from the traditional functionalist concerns is that it sees social order as the product of contending interests and the resources groups have for dominating one another and negotiating alliances and coalitions. Its basic focus has become, not overt conflict, but (in Dahrendorf's terms) *latent conflict;* it deals with social order as domination and negotiation. For this reason, conflict theory is not surprised by sudden upheavals and changes in times of war or revolution. It expects this pattern of movement, because it sees social order as maintained by forces of domination which cling to the status quo and attempt to legitimate it by traditional ideals; but this leaves tremendous stores of social energy locked up in latent opposition, capable of being suddenly released by a catalytic event.

This is not to say that everyone is in conflict with everyone else all the time. Society may be something of an ongoing war, but it is not a war of all against all. One reason, as we shall see, is that conflict tends to limit itself. Conflict is a form of social organization, mainly carried out by groups rather than by individuals. How then are groups organized? How do they maintain the internal solidarity which is a crucial weapon in imposing their interests on one another? The answer to this takes us into certain aspects of micro theory, and especially into the Durkheimian/Goffmanian tradition of social rituals which produce solidarity, moral sentiments and ideas. As we have seen, aspects of this Durkheimian tradition have been used by Parsons to bolster his argument for the primacy of values in society as a whole. I believe Parsons was correct to a certain extent, but that he was mistaken about the level of analysis at which the argument applies. Values are crucial for social integration, but this applies at the level of particular groups, rather than to the social system as a whole. Furthermore, value integration is a variable which can range empirically from low to high. Seen in this light, we can move forward to a stronger explanatory theory which shows the conditions and resources that actually produce moral sentiments and group symbols or ideologies.

Conflict thus becomes an *analytical* rather than a concrete category. It is part of a set of concepts, some of which come from theories for analyzing social order. The question is, how do they mesh together? Modern, multidimensional conflict theory is a strategy for building a complete and general sociological science. At the fundamental level, it does not ask whether something is good for society (which is what functionalism does) or bad for the members of society (which is the ultimate thrust of Marxism); but it asks the more fundamental questions, why are things as they are, what conditions produce them, and what conditions change them into something else? If we have such a theory, we will at last be in a position to know what we really *can* do about the shape of our society.

GENERAL PRINCIPLES OF CONFLICT

SIMMEL AND COSER: CONFLICT AND SOCIAL INTEGRATION

Modern conflict theory began early in the twentieth century with the work of Georg Simmel (1908), which was revived and systematized 50 years later by Lewis Coser (1956). Simmel's concern was to deal with conflict in abstract terms and, specifically, to show that conflict operates on a much more general level than the particular instance of Marxian class conflict. In fact, both Simmel and Coser (especially the former) were more conservative than the Marxists. They wished to show that conflict does not always (or even usually) lead to social change and that it can be the basis of social order. Coser even couched his argument in functionalist terms (the title of his book is *The Functions of Social Conflict*), as if to show that there is a functional need for conflict to support society. Let us see how much validity there is in these arguments.

Simmel's basic point is that conflict is not the opposite of social order. The opposite of order would be indifference or isolation; there would be no society only if people were in a condition of having nothing to do with one another. In other words, society does not automatically disappear because of conflicts among opposing interests. There are two alternatives, "fight or flight," and society ceases to exist only if the latter alternative is taken.

Conflict, in fact, is a rather intense form of interaction. Even in sheer physical terms, it is likely to bring people more closely together than normal, nonconflictual social order. Think of an excited crowd in the streets of a riot or revolution, or the way in which a quarrel between two persons locks them together into matching each other's gestures and angry tone of voice as they trade insult for insult. It is only because we tend to put a value judgment upon peaceful interaction that we let it monopolize the term "social order." In fact, conflict is itself a very strong form of order in the structural and behavioral sense.

Nor does the conflict have to be overt for it to constitute a social structure. The Hindu caste system, Simmel observes, is a structure based precisely on a strong principle of repulsion among members of groups. Conflicting interests thus can shape people into the repetitive, enforced behaviors that make up a structure. By implication, any stratified social order will be largely structured by conflict.

CONFLICT PROMOTES SOCIAL INTEGRATION   The Simmel/Coser theory offers a series of principles by which conflict leads to the integration of society. Such conflict can be either with external groups or within the group itself. Let us illustrate first with external conflict.

(1) Conflict sharpens the sense of group boundaries and contributes to a feeling of group identity. Members of a nation never feel more clearly that they are Germans, French, Americans, Russians, (or whatever) as when they are at war with someone else. This holds for conflicts or contests of any sort between groups. For this reason, high school and college sports are so important as a source of community identification.

(2) Conflict leads to a centralization of the internal structure of the group. In times of war, for example, the power of the government increases as people feel more willing to subordinate everything to the common effort. In smaller groups, the more external conflict there is, the more the group gathers around and gives power to a strong leader.

(3) Conflict leads to a search for allies. Modern warfare between two states immediately sets both of them on the path to bringing other countries in as their allies. In primitive tribal societies, warfare was of great importance in this respect. Since these groups were usually geographically isolated and economically self-subsistent, it was only because of conflicts that they established bonds with their neighbours, usually in the form of exchanges of marriages. Conflict thus divides two groups, but on either side of the divide it results in an extension of the network of social ties, thus promoting more social organization than had existed in times of peace.

Simmel adds the curious point that one group even has an interest in maintaining the social existence of their enemy. For if external conflict is the only thing that holds one's own group together—say it is a tribe whose centralized leadership emerges only in times of war—then a complete victory and the destruction of the enemy means the destruction of one's own group as well. The implication seems to be that group leaders might try covertly to maintain their enemies. Certainly it is true in modern times that there is a covert alliance between the most militaristic factions in enemy countries: the huge arms budgets of both the United States and the USSR depend upon both sides keeping up the conflict.

Do the same principles hold in internal conflict? Simmel and Coser do not systematically treat this as a separate question, but many of their examples refer to internal conflicts. Internally, conflict is between the group and some of its own members who serve as a scapegoat. In highly religious societies, such as those of late medieval Europe (or the American colonies), internal enemies were heretics or witches, and these societies gained a strong sense of their community identity and a rein-forcement of their defining values by gathering in the village square to watch a few lone individuals tortured or burned to death (Erikson 1966; K. Thomas 1971). In modern societies, the scapegoats tend to be ethnic and racial groups: the Jews who presumably contributed to the group identification of the anti-Semitic majority, and the blacks who held together the group boundaries of whites. Similarly, criminals and moral deviants—homosexuals, drug users, pornographers, gamblers—are func-tionally useful internal enemies, the struggle against whom contributes to the self-identity and moral solidarity of the "moral" majority. Empirical support of this re-lationship is found in our own time; for example, the scapegoating of women who have abortions is strongest among those who most closely identify themselves with society and its moral order in the traditional sense (Luker, 1983; Cavanaugh, 1986).

Thus, there does seem to be some truth in the principle that internal as well as external conflict contributes to group boundaries and social identity. In the case of internal conflict, however, the other two principles are dubious. It does not seem to be true that internal conflict necessarily leads to a centralization of social organiza-tion; much of the persecution of minorities and scapegoats is carried out at the "grass-roots" level, especially in small communities and by the lower-middle classes and below. Nor does the principle necessarily hold that internal conflict leads to an extension of networks through a search for allies. Moreover, there is a major flaw in the first principle. Simmel and Coser use examples only of small or even tiny minor-ities: a single old woman being burned as a witch, a handful of homosexuals, small minorities of Jews or blacks. Here we have got a one-sided persecution rather than a fully fledged conflict between two well-mobilized sides. Simmel and Coser avoid mention of class conflict, precisely because it is a more equal conflict among major groups. When both groups are large, it is less possible for one to monopolize the official definition of reality and to label the other as merely deviant. Empirically, too, it is doubtful whether two-sided internal conflict promotes social integration of the larger group in which it takes place. In fact, it would seem to be doing just the opposite. On this point the theory fails.[1]

[1] In their effort to play down class conflict, Simmel and Coser tend to go to the extreme of asserting nothing but functional interpretations of conflict. Thus, persecuting minorities and scapegoats emerges as a kind of normal function of society, a useful thing to keep society together. But surely this is displaying society at its most despicable. In addition to the empirical inadequacies noted above, it is worth pointing out that a more adequate theory would not merely carry the implication that this kind of persecution is an inevitable, functionally useful part of social integration, but would show the con-ditions under which this kind of persecution is most and least likely to happen. I would suggest that it depends on the level of resources different groups have to defend themselves, to turn one-sided domi-nation into two-sided conflict. Groups which are small but nevertheless begin to make gains or challenge a majority's domination are probably those which are most subject to persecution. But we must also explain why it is that particular groups are disliked in the first place. A hypothesis is that this derives from differences in cultural style which offend ritually central symbols of the dominant group (see Chapter 6).

THE SELF-LIMITATION OF CONFLICT   Simmel and Coser argue on the more general level that conflict is not inherently destructive because it tends to limit itself. If both sides are aiming at the same object (say, control of the state or the economy), they nevertheless have an interest in limiting the conflict so that their mutual object is not destroyed (Simmel 1908/1955: 27). In consequence, standards arise to restrict conflict so that it is reduced to a regular competition following rules of the contest: medieval warriors develop a code of honor, economic struggle becomes politically regulated, and the struggle for power turns into peaceful elections. Simmel even comments that a conflict group has an interest in maintaining the unity of its enemy; otherwise it would be hard to get a decisive victory. For instance, an army can win a war if it captures the enemy's capital city, but has a much harder time if it has to deal with disunified guerrillas spread out all over the countryside. The point gains some credence when we observe that business associations (such as in the auto industry) prefer to negotiate with a single union rather than deal separately with the less controllable mass of unruly local unions.

These examples show that there is some truth to the suggestion that conflicts tend to limit themselves. But it is only a partial truth. Simmel himself pointed out elsewhere in his works that a major way of winning is to "divide and conquer," to break the enemy's force by breaking his organization into mutually contending parts. Similarly, there are plenty of instances in which a conflict has gotten out of hand, and armies have ended up destroying the territory they were fighting to control. All-out nuclear war would clearly be an example of this sort. Again, the Simmel/Coser theory is not strong enough to state the conditions under which one or the other result might occur.

Subsequent research on the escalation and de-escalation of conflict helps clarify the issue (Kriesberg, 1982). Conflict escalates when the use of force or other sanctions by one side provokes a reprisal from the other, resulting in a continuously reinforcing spiral. The original issue widens to include grievances about subsequent reprisals; attitudes polarize and conflict grows. This is the opposite of the self-limitation of conflict. However, we may add that conflict does not always escalate, nor does the use of repressive force against a conflict group always lead to counterattacks. The empirical examples usually given (Kriesberg, 1982) refer to such cases as the use of violence by police against protesters in a civilian context, usually in a democracy; the result is to further outrage the protesters and to bring in allies who are similarly outraged. But extreme uses of repressive violence—for example, in an authoritarian state with a strong military—can end escalation by destroying opposition. The proper generalization would seem to be that counterforce leads to an escalation of conflict when both sides have sufficient resources for continuing to mobilize. Bombing attacks on an enemy do not usually end a war as long as the enemy still has governmental control and the resources to fight on. Similarly, merely "punitive" strikes, such as those used against terrorists, do not sufficiently destroy resources and probably enhance group solidarity in the side under attack (as follows from the principles stated above).

But even when escalating processes do occur, conflicts always come to an end. De-escalating processes often set in after a passage of time. De-escalation involves the contraction of goals from demands for all-out (but usually symbolic) destruction of the enemy to realistic compromises; the fragmentation of issues, separating out points which can be settled piecemeal; and, as the result of these steps, a reduction in polarization (Kriesberg, 1982). The emotional arousal of intense conflict mobilization eventually becomes exhausted. Behind these processes, I would suggest, is a resource factor: the material costs of conflict eventually reduce the capacity for mobilization, and it becomes less and less possible to carry on conflict. A missing part of a comprehensive sociological theory is the time-laws which are involved in this process. In the case of wars, the time limit may be several years, depending on the level of destructiveness. (This refers to all-out modern wars, which usually last four years or less; lower levels of mobilization, as in guerrilla wars, can go on much longer.) In general, I would propose, the less expensive the conflict (that is, the less violent it is, and the more it depends on regular organizational resources rather than requiring the creation of special *ad hoc* conflict organizations), the longer it is possible for conflict to go on without de-escalation. At the opposite extreme, very destructive war ends itself even without de-escalation, simply by destroying the population or social organization. Thus, a modified version of the principle of the self-limitation of conflict says that conflict must stay at moderate levels beyond which it exhausts itself increasingly rapidly.[2]

CROSS-CUTTING CONFLICTS   The major principle of self-limiting conflict is known as the *pluralist theory,* of which Coser (1956) is principal advocate. If there is more than one conflict going on at the same time, and the groups involved have cross-cutting, over-lapping boundaries, then conflict on one dimension will reduce conflict on other dimensions. For example, there is a division between workers and capitalists in modern society; but if this is cross-cut by racial divisions (some workers and some capitalists are both black and white), ethnic divisions (some of each are Anglo, Italian-America, Mexican, and so forth), religious divisions (Protestant, Catholic, Jewish), or gender division (male, female), then conflict will be reduced. We might call this the "grid-lock" model of social conflict: there is conflict in so many directions that no one dimension can become very intense. The reason is that any one individual is a member of several different conflict groups. If he is a white, Italian-American, Protestant worker, his class conflict with capitalists will be diminished by his conflict with blacks (many of whom are also workers), Catholics, women, and so forth.

The pluralist model has given rise to a great deal of controversy. This is largely because it has been taken as a political doctrine, denying that any serious class conflict is possible in the United States. However, an important distinction must be made. The *theoretical* statement is that *if* there are cross-cutting group memberships, *then* conflict will be gridlocked into a low level of intensity. Most of the controversy has centered on a second question, the *empirical* issue of whether in fact *there really are such cross-cutting groups in the modern United States.* It is pointed out, for example,

---

[2] There are other specific arenas in which the principle of the self-limitation of conflict does seem to hold. Goffman (1969) shows that on the micro level, games of mutual deception (such as espionage) cannot be carried very far, because of the difficulties of carrying out sustained deception or living at an extremely high level of suspicion and self-reflectiveness. Another instance is in intellectual competition where I have proposed that the number of intellectual factions always tends to reduce itself over a period of years to between three and six factions; larger numbers of contenders than this tend to self-destruct (Collins, 1987).

that the majority of blacks are members of the working class, and that religion may reinforce class, so that really there are only a few significant divisions, and pluralism *as a fact* may not be true.

The theoretical question is what is at issue here, however. Is the if–then relationship between cross-cutting groups and low intensity of conflict a reality? There is little research of a sufficiently comparative sort to bear on this theoretical question. But I think it can be said that the theory suffers from being framed mainly in order to show why class conflict is relatively slight in the United States. Class conflict is only one form of conflict; the if–then relationship posited in the theory says that cross-cutting groups should reduce conflict on *all* dimensions. If we look at the recent history of the United States (certainly, ethnically and religiously one of the most heterogeneous of modern societies), it is true that class conflict has been low. But the 1960s—not long after the pluralist theory was put forward—began with a period of intense and violent conflict between blacks and whites, followed by equally intense conflict between college-age youth and their elders over the Viet Nam war, followed by a very militant phase of conflict between females and males over women's rights. At a minimum, we would have to say that the pluralist theory is no use at all in predicting when and why such conflicts should break out. More abstractly, there must be a logical flaw in the theory, since it predicts a low intensity of conflict on *all* dimensions, not just in class conflict. It is also damaging to the theory that the various conflicts of the 1960s and 1970s not only did not diminish each other, but were actually linked together. The antiwar movement developed out of white activism in the Civil Rights (racial equality) movement, and the militant feminists organized out of participation in the antiwar movement. The pluralist model has not only empirical but theoretical problems, and needs considerable revision. (This is why pluralist theory has given way to resource mobilization theory and other newer models.)[3]

DAHRENDORF: POWER GROUPS AND CONFLICT MOBILIZATION

The German sociologist Ralf Dahrendorf, writing at about the same time as Coser, made a further move toward generalizing a theory of conflict. Unlike Simmel and Coser, his aim was not to downplay Marxian class conflict, but to develop a theory which would revise Marx to account for the shape of modern society. Hence the title of his major book: *Class and Class Conflict in Industrial Society* (1959). The problem is the familiar one we discussed in the last chapter, which gave rise to other modern revisionist versions of Marxism. Dahrendorf's work marks the break from Marxism into conflict theory, however, since he went over the dividing line and became a true heretic of the Marxist tradition. The central concept in Marxian sociology is *property,* and the ownership of the means of production is seen as the basis of social class. Thus, conflicts are over property; they are structured into the eco-

---

[3]I would even suggest that class conflict is likely to return to the forefront in the 1990s. If current trends continue towards displacing workers with robots and white-collar employees with computers, there will undoubtedly develop increasing conflict over economic issues of employment and the distribution of wealth, and quite possibly, a full-scale Marxian-style underconsumption crisis in capitalism.

nomic system around the capitalists' search for profit to enhance and protect their property against the workers. In turn, the workers are subject to the labor market in order to stay alive. Dahrendorf took the fatal plunge and redefined class and class conflict so that it was no longer based on property but on *power*.

CLASS DIVISIONS AS POWER DIVISIONS   The main empirical problem confronting Marxism in the twentieth century, in Dahrendorf's view, is not that class conflict disappears, but that it appears where it should not be and does not appear where it should. Strictly speaking, if we divide classes into property owners vs. non-property owners, then most white-collar employees would be members of the working class.[4] But in their voting patterns, social behavior, and personal identification, they act not as workers but as if they were members of the dominant class. Marxian theory has tended to treat this as the question of "false consciousness"; in empirical sociology, on the other hand, researchers have simply redefined class as if it were synonymous with manual vs. nonmanual employees. Empirically, this does seem to identify a main dividing line (Halle, 1984), but it is definitively contradictory to the Marxian definition of class. For that matter, even the top level managers, in so far as they do not own their companies but merely work as employees of the stockholders, should also count as workers. Why, then, do they act as if they were loyal capitalists?[5]

A related issue, especially important to a West German like Dahrendorf, is the fact that the socialist countries of Eastern Europe (such as East Germany) are themselves stratified. There have even been severe outbreaks of what looks like class conflict in these nations: a violent revolt in East Berlin in 1953, another in Hungary in 1956, the Russian invasion of Czechoslavakia to put down an insurrection in 1968, and the struggles of Polish labor unions against the socialist government in the early 1980s. It is difficult even to conceptualize such conflicts in Marxist terms, since socialist societies have no property, and hence, by definition, no classes.

Dahrendorf solves both problems regarding stratification in modern capitalist and socialist societies by redefining class. Wherever there is any organization in which some people have power, there is a division between those who give orders and those who have to take orders. Giving orders is pleasurable, and it is also the major means to acquiring wealth, prestige, material goods, and almost all other desirables. Taking orders is intrinsically unpleasurable, and the lack of power means that one will be less well off on other dimensions. Hence, power divides people into classes, order givers vs. order takers, and creates class conflict.

Marx is thus subsumed into a broader theory rather than disproven. In his day—the early 1800s—property was indeed the most visible form of power. Government agencies were virtually nonexistent, and businesses were run by their owners, who personally gave orders to their employees. Marx did not live long enough to see the

---

[4] This is using the Marxian criterion of ownership of the *means of production*. Home ownership does not make one a member of the capitalist class. It does, however, have a conservatizing effect on political attitudes (Halle, 1984).

[5] It should be pointed out that there is an empirical, as opposed to a theoretical, controversy over this issue. Considering the economy as a whole instead of individual organizations, top managers tend to be stockholders of other companies and hence are members of the capitalist class in that regard (Useem, 1986).

bureaucratic corporation or the massive growth of government bureaucracy. Modern socialism is essentially rule by government bureaucracy, so that its classes and class conflicts become entirely those of sheer organizational power.

This aspect of Dahrendorf's theory is surely correct. It brings a mass of empirical evidence back into agreement with conflict theory. The research which shows the strongest divisions between manual and white-collar workers, and between particular sectors among them, shows that these divisions take place between those who take orders and those who give orders.[6] We shall see in Chapter 6 that Goffmanian micro theory provides a solid foundation for these divisions in the processes of everyday life, and explains why order giving and order taking have very different cultural and behavioral effects. On the macro level, we shall see in Chapter 5 that there is good evidence that power is a strong predictor of many other things, including the distribution of economic wealth. And in analyzing the current world scene, Dahrendorf's model is essential for understanding why there are conflicts such as those in Poland, which are no doubt latent in the USSR and other socialist states. For the Marxists, history comes to an end once socialism appears, since their theoretical apparatus, based on property classes, no longer applies. Dahrendorf reopens that large part of the world to theoretical analysis and enables us to ask such questions as, under what conditions would a revolution actually be possible in the Soviet Union?

The weakness in Dahrendorf's redefinition of class as power is that he tends to see all modern societies as being essentially the same. Organizationally, insofar as socialist and capitalist societies are both ruled by bureaucracies, the class structure and conflicts are analytically similar in both. However, Dahrendorf fails to pay enough attention to subtypes of power. Property remains a kind of power resource different from sheer bureaucratic or political party power; for one thing, it connects property holders through banks, stock markets, the monetary system, and hence market relationships, which are quite a different sort from the organizations found among the elite in a socialist society. In a sense, the ways in which power is organized under modern capitalism are more complex than under socialism; capitalism has both the bureaucratic power form and an additional form based on property. A theory of capitalism is still necessary, even in the modern era.

OVERT CONFLICT IS ALWAYS TWO-SIDED   If order givers vs. order takers is the basis of social conflict, how many social classes are there? Potentially, there could be a very large number. For one thing, there may be several different kinds of organizations in a society, so there can be power conflicts within government and its various agencies, the military, business corporations, philanthropic organizations, clubs, sports, churches—even within the home. Furthermore, in any large-scale organization, there are several levels of hierarchy: not only are there persons at the top who give orders and those at the bottom who take them, but there are levels in between which both give and take orders. Dahrendorf's model suggests that conflict might be very complex indeed.[7]

---

[6] The neo-Marxian empiricism of Erik Olin Wright (1978, 1979) actually uses a Dahrendorfian definition of class.

[7] By contrast, the Marxian model reduces conflict analytically to the dividing line of property owners versus non–property owners, which allows for greater simplicity in prediction. In practice, though,

Dahrendorf's is a realistic view, leading to an organizational analysis in which society is made up of multiple lines of power conflict. As we shall see in Chapter 6, it fits a multidimensional theory of class cultures, grounded both in micro theory and empirical evidence. But the identification of multiple lines of conflict does lead to a question about social change, and indeed whether conflict can actually break out. For as Simmel and Coser have argued, multiple lines of conflict may negate each other, draining off energy from one conflict into one dimension after another, and thus resulting in conflict gridlock and social stability rather than change. Dahrendorf also accepts that multiple cross-cutting conflicts may have this effect. But he does not see this as the main point of a theory of conflict, but only a particular arrangement of variables.

His more generalized point is that conflict may be latent or mobilized. *Quasi-groups,* in his terminology, are persons who share a similar position in one of the many possible lines of power conflict in a society. But they only become real *conflict groups* if they are mobilized into action. This overt conflict is always two-sided. Middle managers, say, might be latently in conflict with their superiors, who give them orders, as well as with their subordinates, who take orders from them. But they cannot overtly be in conflict with both at the same time. Conflict always boils down to two sides. Once it breaks out between two parties, the other parties must either stand aside as neutrals or join one side or the other.

This appears to be a structural necessity. Wars, for example, always take this two-sided pattern, even though they often involve more than two parties. Some conflicts, however, get put aside until one conflict is over. (For instance, in World War II, Japan, the Chinese nationalists and their allies, and the Chinese communists were mutual antagonists, but the latter pair made a tacit alliance until the Japanese were defeated, whereupon their own war started again.) Sports, which are controlled forms of conflict, virtually always have this two-sided structure; to understand why, imagine the chaos that would ensue if there were three basketball teams, or three football teams, playing at once.[8]

Dahrendorf's main deduction is that if conflict is two-sided, one side (the order takers) favors change and the other side (the order givers) favors stability. This leads to his conflict-based theory of social change. He neglects the fact that changes may be imposed "from the top," as has often been the case in "modernization," which Reinhard Bendix (1967, 1978) describes as a chain of emulation of more powerful states in the world arena by less powerful ones. Further, change does not happen merely because it is intended by some group; the process of conflict itself may result in a change in the structure, different from what either side intended.

---

there are different modes of property (land owners, manufacturers, finance capitalists, petty bourgeois worker/owners); and conflicts for domination can go on within a class (for instance, in business competition) as well as among these classes. Hence, even a Marxist economic model faces the Dahrendorfian problem of explaining the effects of multiple conflicts.

[8] There are a few sports, like golf, in which there are multiple competitors. But these are more properly "contests" rather than "conflicts," since each player is trying to get the highest score, without impeding the other players. In short, there is no defense in golf, and logically speaking, no offense either. It is not a zero-sum game, whereas power, the prototype of conflict, is zero-sum: whatever one side gains the other side loses.

Of greater theoretical importance is Dahrendorf's focus on the structure of relationships among latent and overt conflict groups. It is implicit in some of the classic analyses of the manuevering among factions in revolutions (for instance, Marx's *Eighteenth Brumaire of Louis Bonaparte;* see my analysis in Collins, 1985: 76–78), and is central to theories of coalitions in parliamentary and electoral politics. To work out a fully explicit structural theory of overt conflict along these lines remains a major goal for sociology.

CONDITIONS OF CONFLICT GROUP MOBILIZATION   Dahrendorf prefers to concentrate on the conditions that turn latent quasi-groups into mobilized conflict groups. There are three kinds of conditions:

1. *Technical conditions:* the presence of a leader and an ideology.
2. *Political conditions:* sufficient political freedom in the surrounding society to allow groups to organize themselves.
3. *Social conditions:* communication among group members, geographical concentration, and similar culture.

This third category of conditions is analytically identical to the conditions of political mobilization in the Marx-Engels model (Chapter 3 pp. 89–91). The theory here has been elaborated under the rubric of "means of mental production" and "material means of mobilization," and leads to the *resource mobilization theory*.

The first and second conditions, however, are more dubious, or at least incomplete, as a general theory. In the second Dahrendorf is making the point that there will be more overt conflict in a democracy than in an authoritarian regime because political freedom allows it. But this begs a crucial question that a conflict theory must be able to face: what determines the amount of political freedom or authoritarianism in a state. A crucial type of conflict is precisely that which allows democratic revolutions to break through authoritarianism. Thus, although democracy may facilitate the mobilization of conflict groups, it cannot be necessary for any mobilization at all to occur. Marx's model seems more accurate here, stressing social conditions as more fundamental.

Similarly, technical conditions seem to be only an additional, incidental factor. I am inclined to believe, along with Marx, that leaders are produced by circumstances, not vice versa, and that sufficient social conditions for mobilization will produce both leaders and ideology.

CONSEQUENCES OF CONFLICT: INTENSITY, VIOLENCE, AND SOCIAL CHANGE
Dahrendorf proposes two sets of principles about the nature and consequences of conflict, once it occurs. He distinguishes between first the *violence* of conflict—how much actual physical destruction there is (and relatedly, how much emotional hatred)—and second the *intensity* of conflict—how strongly rooted it is, how long it goes on. One of his major points is that conflict may be intense without being violent, as well as vice versa. A democracy, in his view, fosters a good deal of conflict, but it is not generally very violent conflict; in addition, he believes that it *may* not even be very intense. The former judgment may be more accurate than the latter.

(1a) *The better organized the conflict groups, the less violent the conflict;* (1b) *absolute deprivation* (physical abuse, starvation, poverty) *leads to more violent conflict, whereas*

FIGURE 4-1

More organization $\longrightarrow$ ⎫
Relative deprivation $\rightarrow$ ⎭ Less violence $\longrightarrow$ Slow social change

Less organization $\longrightarrow$ ⎫
Absolute deprivation $\rightarrow$ ⎭ More violence $\longrightarrow$ Rapid social change

relative deprivation (having less than the higher classes) *leads to less violent conflict;* (1c) *but the more violent the conflict, the more rapid the social change.* This is summarized in Figure 4-1.

Principle (1a) is probably correct. Dahrendorf draws his evidence from the history of labor unions, which began as violent, revolutionary movements when they were illegal, underground associations; but as they achieved recognition, acquired bureaucratic organization and a full-time staff of their own, they became part of the normal condition of society. Robert Michels (1911), writing about the transformation of the German socialist labor unions from Marxist revolutionaries into part of the Establishment, enunciated the so-called "Iron Law of Oligarchy" to refer to this conservatizing of leadership by its own bureaucratization. But it should be borne in mind that this process affects the violence of conflict and the desire for a radical social change. It does not affect the intensity of conflict, since labor unions exist precisely in order to carry on their demands over wages, working conditions, and so forth. Institutionalizing conflict does not make it go away, but it does make it less violent and revolutionary. That, in fact, is Dahrendorf's advice about the extent to which conflict can be limited.

Principle (1b) does not appear to be correct. Dahrendorf offers no evidence for it, and it would seem from studies of revolutionary movements and riots (Tilly, 1978) that violent conflict does not break out where the lowest class is most oppressed, but where it has the resources to mobilize itself (compare my theory on the conditions of extreme violence, "Three Faces of Cruelty," in Collins 1981).

Principle (1c) is also dubious. Dahrendorf appears to be thinking that a violent revolution is the fastest form of social change. But many violent transfers of political power (for example, South American revolutions, or the numerous changes of emperors in the later Roman Empire) produced no real social change at all. Violent riots also may be totally without effect, especially if the rioters are severely repressed. The Paris Commune of 1871 was put down with over 20,000 dead; however, it did not result in a rapid change toward a socialist France but the opposite, the reimposition of bourgeois society. Violence, in fact, may be connected not with rapid, revolutionary change so much as with what Georges Sorel in his *Reflections on Violence* (1906) called a "myth"—the belief among the conflict group that they are fighting for a very high ideal. Sorel argued that violent conflict and its accompanying belief exist not mainly for the social changes that are actually produced, but because of the solidarity they produce within the conflict group itself.[9]

---

[9] Sorel was a contemporary of Simmel but connected with the French Left. His theory of conflict producing solidarity within the group is similar to Simmel's theory, except that Sorel adds that violence is especially likely to produce solidarity. He also points out that this solidarity consists of a feeling that

(2a) *Where membership lines among contending power groups are superimposed, conflict is more intense;* however, *where such dividing lines are dissociated or cross-cutting, conflict is less intense.* Here Dahrendorf adopts the Simmel-Coser "pluralist" or "gridlock" theory, except that he makes explicit that these conditions refer to the intensity of conflict rather than its violence. The same criticisms of the validity of this theory (page 123) apply here. (2b) *The more intense the conflict, the more radical the social change:* that is to say, where groups are mobilized for a long, hard struggle, the end result is that society will be pervasively changed. Again, the principle of social change seems dubious. Dahrendorf offers no evidence for it, but seems to be deducing logically that stronger conflict forces will change society more than weak forces.

What Dahrendorf leaves out of both his principles of social change, (1c) and (2b), is any consideration of *who wins.* He baldly states that more intense or more violent conflict will produce social change of a pervasive or rapid sort. But if the conservative side wins, there may be no change at all, or possibly a change in the direction of building more repressive structures to preserve other structures (for example, to protect the property system, or the religious Establishment). There is also the possibility that neither side will win, but that conflict will go on at great length. This is a formula in which intense conflict leads to a complete blockage of any movement in the society. I would suggest that this is a major problem of democracies, since it mobilizes classes and other power groups, but enables them to neutralize each other. In short, Dahrendorf is probably correct that conflict has, at least potentially, something to do with social change, but the process is much more complex than his principles allow. On the face of it, only principle (1a) appears to be generally correct (and even that has exceptions, such as the fact that well-organized armies can produce more violence than less-organized ones; though it may well be true that well-organized groups have to overcome more inertia to get themselves into action). Dahrendorf opened the way to a conflict theory of social change, but the theory itself has to be built from elements found elsewhere.

CONFLICT THEORY OF SOCIAL CHANGE

The conflict approach to social change analyzes social process in terms of the actors pursuing their interests and the resources they have relative to each other. This is a generalization of the Marx-Engels theory of class interests and the material conditions of political mobilization. However, interests are now broadened to include any kinds of interests and groups; and resources are broadened to include the social and symbolic resources that allow individuals to form into groups, both formal organizations and informal communities of consciousness. The theory, in other words, has become multidimensional. Ultimately, there can be a conflict theory of change in any aspect of society: economy, technology, demography, religion, intellectual life, or anything else. For brevity, we will focus here on political change.

the group is defending morality. In this respect, Sorel's theory is really a conflict version of the Durkheimian theory of rituals (Chapter 6). One might reconstruct Sorel's theory as saying conflict produces a "natural ritual" through a high focus of attention and social density, in which the build-up of emotion is based on anger and hatred.

WEBER'S THEORY OF POLITICS

What should a theory of political change explain? A comprehensive theory should explain (1) the conditions under which various kinds of state structures (democracy, dictatorship, feudalism, centralized empires, and so forth) will emerge; (2) who the actors in the political drama will be—the lineup of groups who fight over power at any given time; (3) the kind of political events that will take place; and (4) who will win what in these struggles. A truly comprehensive theory of this sort has not been built, although some pieces of it exist. Notice that explaining changes in all these features is the same thing as explaining what structures, groups, and so forth will exist statically, at any given time; the static-comparative theory is just an outcome of the dynamic theory, since it is the dynamic processes that produce the "snap-shots" that we may see if we stop the action at some point in time. We should notice, too, that a full theory of politics will overlap into many areas of sociology: the kinds of groups that take part, and the way they see the world, are the subject of stratification theory and class culture theory; while the organizational structure of the state will lead us to organization theory, and the processes of politics will lead into some versions of network theory. In a sense, the intellectual strategy of conflict theory is to look for the "political" side of everything—"organizational politics" in organizations, "family politics" in families, and so on. Hence, many of the details of a theory of politics will be found in other chapters throughout the book.

The main focus of a theory of politics is the state. Weber (1922/1968) defined the state as an organization claiming a monopoly over the legitimate use of violence upon a given territory. There are three crucial elements in his definition: violence, legitimacy, and territory.

VIOLENCE   The state has a military foundation. Most states throughout history were formed by a military coalition, by military conquest or diplomatic annexation of other territories, or by revolution or splits within an already existing state.[10] Up until 1800 in Western Europe, states consisted of little more than an army (or even just a network for raising troops), and military expenses were by far the largest part of government expenses (Mann, 1986: 416–99). The bureaucratic apparatus of the state has developed, largely in the last few centuries, to collect taxes and supply the military. Once this bureaucracy was in existence, its uses could be extended to other

---

[10] There is a controversy, however, about how the very earliest states first emerged (see Mann, 1986: 34–178). The early Mesopotamian and Egyptian states, *ca.* 2000–3000 B.C., grew up around temple storehouses; they were both economic producers and suppliers of welfare—in a sense, something like primitive socialism under a religious guise. Economic coordination seems to have come first in these instances (and perhaps others, as in the networks of economic exchange which were seen in complex tribal societies in Africa, the Pacific, and elsewhere). The military state seems to have emerged out of temporary defensive armies, whose leaders made themselves permanent and embarked on conquest abroad and despotism at home. But it appears that even the early "coordinating" aspect of the state was felt to be coercive by much of its population; Mann (1986) points out that until people became "caged" by ecological constraints and dependence on the state centers, they usually escaped from state power whenever they could, by migration or resistance. After the full military-centered state emerged, some of these ancient and medieval states continued to regulate the economy (as in the Chinese empire after about 200 B.C., which controlled public works in the form of irrigation systems and canals). But they performed this regulation by coercion, forcing peasants to contribute to the state storehouses and carrying out public works projects by coerced labor.

forms of regulation—support for the economy, the supply of welfare, the provision of education, or the regulation of civilian life. But as Mann (1986) has shown, the modern state expanded from a military core, and it exercises control, ultimately, by backing up its commands with the threat of force. What makes something legally binding, rather than merely a private understanding, is the assumption that it will be enforced by the courts, the police, and other government officials; and the fact that their authority, if challenged, is ultimately backed up by the army. The power—and indeed the very existence—of a state depends on its military organization; for when a state loses all military power, it ceases to be a real state. The disintegration or defection of an army is always the final and decisive element in any revolution.

At the core of any state, then, is its military apparatus. Weber says that a state claims a monopoly over force; that is, it attempts to be the sole military organization for that area. This is an ideal type definition, which recognizes that states do not always succeed in this monopolization. Feudalism, for example, is a coalition of self-armed lords; the official coalition, based on the loyalty of lower lords to higher ones in a hierarchy culminating with the king, is theoretically a single military unit, but in practice it tends to undermine the monopoly of the means of violence. In a sense, feudalism is only a quasi-state. This definitional problem should not mislead us into believing that a Weberian approach cannot be used for feudalism. Politics is a dynamic struggle to build or maintain states; the full-fledged, force-monopolizing state is the goal of the centralizing faction, and the theory gives the conditions under which it succeeds or fails.

LEGITIMACY   Weber adds that the state aims not just at monopolizing force, but monopolizing legitimate force. Criminal violence may exist within a state, but the state is not challenged as long as that violence is regarded as illegitimate. Legitimacy is a claim that the use of force is proper, that it is procedurally and morally justified. Weber points out that a legitimate state can rule more easily than one relying on sheer terroristic coercion. People are more likely to obey orders willingly, or at least without resistance, if the state is regarded as legal or otherwise legitimate.[11]

This introduces a cultural element into Weber's multidimensional theory. However, we should not conclude that culture is a static or transcendental intrusion into the theory. The state is not simply determined by ideals. Legitimacy is caused by social conditions and rises and falls with changes in those conditions. In a little-known part of his theory, Weber (1922/1968: 901–10; also Collins, 1986: 145–66) points out that, historically, the state acquired legitimacy by forging a coalition to fight wars. The ideal of defense against external enemies (or in early conquest states, the ideal of conquering a new land for the people) is the crucial element in state legitimacy. As long as a state is able to carry out this successfully, it will be legitimate; when it ceases to have enough military power, its legitimacy disappears. Originally, this legitimacy was felt only by the warriors themselves; in a feudal society or patrimonial empire, the conquered peasants generally did not regard the state as legitimate, but as alien oppressors (Eberhard 1965: 1–17). But since the

---

[11] Legal legitimacy is characteristic of bureaucratic states, but there are other types of legitimacy. Traditional legitimacy, as found in feudal or patrimonial states, can be based on family loyalty or the prestige of a ruling house, or on religious beliefs in the sanctity of existing authorities. Charismatic legitimacy is based on the emotional appeals and the ideals enunciated by the leader of a social movement.

peasants were unmobilized, their opinions did not count; the only feelings of legitimacy that were important were those among the nobility themselves. (And these feelings could shift from one ruling house to another in the interminable dynastic intrigues and wars of feudal-patrimonial states.) Weber traces the rise of modern mass legitimacy of the state to the creation of mass conscript armies, beginning in the 1700s and 1800s in Europe; only when all adult males were subject to fighting in their state's armies did the state acquire the modern "nationalist" sense of legitimacy.[12]

It is consistent with this theory that modern states began to create compulsory public education systems at the same time that they created modern mass armies (Collins, 1977; Ramirez and Boli–Bennett, 1982). Often it was the threat from military rivals which provided the immediate impulse to institute school reforms. Durkheim (1961), who was himself involved in building the French school system after the French had been defeated in the Franco-Prussian war of 1870–71, theorized that it would provide a secular basis for national solidarity; empirical studies on the effects of schools on childrens' political attitudes have proved him correct (Hess and Torney, 1967).

Weber's theory thus makes legitimacy into a dynamic process, rather than a static quality which all states possess. We might, in fact, define politics as the struggle for legitimacy. Politicians attempt to attach the feelings of state legitimacy to themselves while undermining the legitimacy of their opponents. There are several elements in such a theory. Weber gives us only the starting point. He argues that the legitimacy of a state (and hence of its leaders at a particular time) depends on its international power prestige. Populations of states which are strong vis-à-vis their neighbors have intense feelings of legitimacy (that is, in whatever population is actually politically mobilized). States which are weak, defeated in wars, or dramatically humiliated by their enemies lose legitimacy. There are several consequences of this. One is the importance of foreign affairs for the success or failure of politicians;[13] as a result, politicians are strongly motivated to make face-saving or prestige-enhancing gestures in foreign affairs (which is one of the dynamics producing international crises). Failure in foreign affairs reduces legitimacy; at an extreme, it is a major cause of revolution.[14]

---

[12] This theory would not account for feelings of state legitimacy among women. However, women did not acquire the vote in most places until the twentieth century. When they did, they were brought into a political system already characterized by the emotional dynamics of mass legitimacy. We may thus broaden the model to a chain-linked set of causes: military participation provides the core of the orginal state and its legitimacy; mass armies then broaden legitimacy feelings by extending them to the adult male population; and finally, additional processes of incorporation and "emotional production"—such as public schools set up by the state—extend the legitimacy feelings throughout the rest of the population.

[13] The ups and downs of American presidents, in the wake of various foreign crises, are readily accessible illustrations of this process: the Viet Nam war, the Iranian hostage crisis in 1980, the Grenada invasion in 1984, the Libya bombing raid in 1986, (and no doubt whatever else has happened by the time one reads this book).

[14] It is sometimes argued that if a world-system perspective is adopted, it is not permissible to refer to states as a unit of analysis, nor to "foreign affairs," since this would be from the perspective of a particular state. However, a world system nevertheless does have states in it, and it would put unnecessary blinders on oneself to avoid ever looking at how the world system appears from the point of view of one of these states.

International power prestige is the first and most important element in a state's legitimacy. Other sources of legitimacy can be added onto this. A state may gain or lose legitimacy, depending on how well its domestic economy is doing; ancient Chinese emperors could lose "the Mandate of Heaven" if the people were devastated by famine or flood, and modern politicians can lose office during an economic depression. Although the relative weights of these factors have not been measured, I would judge this a weaker determinant of legitimacy than sheer military strength. Traditional empires never fell merely because of natural disasters, but only if there was also a military crisis. Some types of states are more vulnerable to economic legitimacy processes than others; feudal states, which took no economic responsibility at all, were oblivious to them; the modern welfare state, in which a large proportion of the population is employed by the state itself, seems to be most vulnerable. But even in modern states, the most extreme shifts of legitimacy—revolutionary downfalls of the state—have never happened as the result of economic depressions, even severe ones, but have frequently occurred as the result of military strains or defeats.[15]

Finally, we should add that feelings of legitimacy persist for some time. A military defeat does not immediately destroy the legitimacy of the government. It may even increase it temporarily by motivating people to rally around their leaders (by actual participation in political rituals, or by an increase in the ritual density of the society; see Chapter 6. This is an application of the Simmel-Sorel principle that conflict produces solidarity, although it also adds limitations to it.) Even a conquest by alien forces may leave feelings of resistance alive, attached to the ideal of the no-longer-existing state. Though we have not measured this precisely, it appears that such lingering feelings of legitimacy for a particular state can survive for a few years, but not usually for more than a generation.[16] Eventually, success does breed legitimacy; whatever state maintains itself in power long enough will generate its own feelings of legitimacy, especially if it makes use of secondary ritual procedures (such as the indoctrination of a school system and the mass media).

TERRITORY   The third element in the Weberian definition is that the state controls a given territory. This may seem obvious, but it suggests a crucial line for the development of explanatory theory. A successful state is usually one that controls a lot of territory, especially territory rich in population and resources. States lose power by losing territory. The history of states is to a large extent the history of wars in which territory is gained or lost. Organizationally, the form of the state was initially laid down by the structures for controlling and supplying an army, including raising taxes for its support. Because power prestige is crucial for legitimacy, this same process has also determined the sense of national identity and the fate of politicians in the state. Wars account for much of the suddenness of change, for the jerky rather than smooth and evolutionary nature of human history.

---

[15] A current example: the USSR has a level of economic production and a dearth of civilian consumer goods that would be fatal for any politician's career in the United States; but the military strength of the Soviet dictatorship keeps the state not only strong but highly legitimate.

[16] The long-lived Polish nationalism of the nineteenth century, after the Polish state itself had disappeared as a result of German and Russian conquests, is an exception. A comparative study of the survival of national identity under different conditions would help refine the theory of legitimacy. See A. Smith (1986).

Putting these three factors together, we can see that a basic theory of politics must include an explanation of the power of military organizations, of the territories they can defend, conquer, or lose, and hence of the resulting ups and downs of legitimacy of politicians inside a state.

GEOPOLITICAL THEORY OF THE STATE

The following are some geopolitical principles of state power (from Collins, 1978, 1981; Stinchcombe, 1968: 218–30). They are based on an examination of historical evidence, including historical atlases, for the territories of Europe and China over the past 3,000 years.

1.0 TERRITORIAL RESOURCE ADVANTAGE. States based upon the largest and wealthiest heartlands tend to dominate the smaller and poorer ones.

    1.01 Larger and wealthier territories have greater population and production for a given territory. Hence they have larger armies, and defeat smaller states and expand at their expense.

2.0 MARCHLAND ADVANTAGE. States with enemies on fewer sides are stronger than comparably sized states with enemies on more sides.

    2.01 Therefore peripheral ("marchland") states are stronger than centrally located states. Peripheral states tend to capture territory over time, while centrally located states tend to lose territory. In a milder form, weak central states lose control of their military forces by becoming dependent "allies" of the stronger states.

3.0 STABLE BALANCES OF POWER. Large, strong states meeting on opposite sides of a natural land barrier foster a stable buffer state on the barrier.

3.1 UNSTABLE BALANCES OF POWER. Multisided balance of power among numerous states results in the long-term fragmentation of the middle states.

    3.11 The militarily weaker position of interior states (because of 2.0) results in their loss of territory [and hence, from Weber's theory of legitimacy, internal circulation of elites].

    3.12 Alliances with neighboring states split different internal factions within the interior states, fostering political fragmentation, internal struggle, or the tendency to break away and form separate, smaller states. Principles 3.1–3.12 then repeat.

4.0 CUMULATIVE RESOURCE ADVANTAGE. Larger, wealthier, and geographically peripheral states grow cumulatively larger over time, while their neighbors progressively diminish. This may also occur through the development of informal empires, in which weaker states are made to be allies of the stronger ones.

5.0 CUMULATIVE TURNING POINTS. Peripheral states (or alliance networks) grow cumulatively larger and wealthier, while their central neighbors become progressively smaller (from 4.0). Eventually all central states are swallowed up, and the large peripheral empires (or alliances) confront each other in a showdown war [unless a natural barrier exists, within which a buffer state is fostered, as in 3.0].

5.01 Major wars occur at cumulative turning points, characterized by an unusually high degree of military mobilization, ferociousness, expenses, and casualties.

5.02 The outcome of a showdown war is either destruction of one state and the establishment of a universal empire; or the mutual military and economic exhaustion of both sides, leading to the decline of both empires and the revival of smaller states.

6.0 OVEREXPANSION AND DISINTEGRATION. States disintegrate militarily when they attempt to conquer territories more than one natural heartland away from their own economic-territorial base.

6.01 Organizational and economic strain of transporting military forces increases beyond each ecologically unified heartland economy according to Stinchcombe's (1968: 221) principle:

$$V_{OA} = \Sigma_i \ (1-cd) \ kIp_i$$

where V is the military vulnerability of any point A to state O; k is a constant; I is average per capita income; p is the population of area i; d is the distance in kilometers from area i to point A; and c is the proportion of military resources used up in transporting it one kilometer. That is, vulnerability goes down the farther a point is from the home territory on which an army draws its economic resources and manpower, and as more of its resources are used up in transporting them to distant places.

6.02 Legitimacy strain increases exponentially as military conquest is extended further from home ethnic territory. [Ethnic identity is determined by the number of generations a politically and economically connected community lives on a given territory.] The strain of administering a state across two or more ethnically distinct territories is militarily very high; breakdown in control results relatively quickly.

The geopolitical approach is unusual in sociology, but it is becoming increasingly important. It is a world-system model in which causal conditions work from the outside inward. It differs from the neo-Marxian world system of Wallerstein (Chapter 3) in that it regards military-political conditions rather than economic conditions as central. But the two are connected. Wallerstein's model makes military hegemony a crucial factor in a state's ability to create an empire over the world periphery, and hence to acquire the cheap materials and labor which build its economic position. The geopolitical model fills in a crucial blank in Wallerstein's theory: namely, which state will become hegemonic and which will win the showdown wars which Wallerstein sees as occurring in periods of long-term cyclical transition from the B_2 phase to a new A phase. In the geopolitical theory, too, possession of economic resources is one of the factors influencing military strength, which in turn can bring acquisition of new territories and hence a further growth in economic resources. But the geopolitical theory adds further factors: even economic resources do not bring expansion if they are matched by an unfavorable geographical position, whereas a "marchland" position with enemies on few sides aids a state militarily.

There is also a danger of too much success: overextension of conquests too far from home base strains a state's resources and makes it vulnerable to sudden disintegration of its military apparatus. A similar process of strain can occur if a state is engaged in a deadlock war with an equally matched rival (or coalition of rivals). These weaknesses caused by wars, as we shall see, are crucial in revolutions.[17]

RESOURCE MOBILIZATION THEORY

Resource mobilization theory proposes that conflict and power are functions of the resources that particular interest groups can draw upon in order to mobilize themselves for struggle. Geopolitical theory, in a sense, is a resource mobilization theory at the level of the state vis-à-vis other states. The better known version was formulated to explain internal conflict within states. It began as a theory of social movements, especially revolutionary protest movements (Tilly, 1978; Oberschall, 1973). Resource mobilization theory may be seen as an elaboration of Dahrendorf's point regarding the social conditions for conflict group formation (page 128).

Tilly (1978) developed the resource mobilization model in reaction to theories which held that revolutionary protest is the result of deprivation and oppression. These may be factors, but they are not a sufficient explanation. Historically, most revolutionary or dissident movements have arisen not at the worst periods of deprivation, but at times of comparatively mild distress. Classically, the deprivation theory was reformulated to account for this by the hypothesis of rising expectations: protest breaks out not when things are absolutely at their lowest but when conditions are improving, and then receive a setback (Davies, 1962). However, Tilly points out that even this is not a sufficient condition for a protest movement, still less a successful one. The merely psychological conditions of discomfort are not enough to get a movement organized; there must also be actual organizational resources available. Examining peasant uprisings in agrarian societies and workers' movements in early industrialized societies, Tilly finds that the strongest movements occur where certain organizational conditions are present—for example, where peasants are settled on land in such a way that they habitually communicate with one another in their own villages—whereas mobilization is low—even with equal or worse conditions of deprivation—where the peasants are split up geographically or where the villages are controlled by government agents and priests.

In the same vein, we may add that exposure to the capitalist market is itself mobilizing. For example, Calhoun (1982) shows that the radical protest movements in England during the early industrial period (the early 1800s) were primarily among independent craftsworkers rather than machine operators in the new factories. The

---

[17] Wallerstein (1974: 133–45) argues that a state can enter a cycle of military expenditure and income. It is a vicious cycle when the state expands its military commitments faster than it conquers economic resources (including the ability to coerce more taxation out of its own domestic population). The cycle is positive when the military successes are easy or cheap, and revenues get ahead of expenditures, thus allowing further successful expansion, further revenue, and so on. Whether a state will get into a vicious or a positive cycle is left unexplained in Wallerstein's model. It appears to be the result of geopolitical advantages or disadvantages, which determine whether a state will fight easy enemies or face extensive (and hence expensive) opposition, and whether it will strain its resources by becoming geopolitically overextended.

craftsworkers were most immediately threatened by the market, since they were being driven out of business by competition from the new factories; hence their struggle developed against the capitalist system itself. The factory workers, on the other hand, were shielded from the direct effects of the market by their employers; their struggle was less revolutionary and was directed toward a local effort to build trade union strength in their own factories. We will see again the importance of markets as a mobilizing factor when we come to Barrington Moore's theory of revolutions.

Resource mobilization theory has been criticized (Skocpol, 1979) as inadequate to explain revolutions. No matter how mobilized a peasants' or workers' movement is, it does not produce a revolution unless the state itself crumbles. A revolution thus requires a crisis or breakdown of state power. Nevertheless, this objection may be reformulated as an extension of resource mobilization theory. The weakness of the current theory is that it focuses on only one side of the conflict, the protest movement from below. But the dominant elite or class also has organizational re- sources; because the rulers are more mobilized, they are able to hold power. A crisis or breakdown is important because it reduces the resource mobilization of the elite to a point below the level of the mobilization of their opponents.

There is evidence that the dominant class is better mobilized (Mann, 1970). Its resources include those which produce greater class consciousness and greater awareness of its own interests and of itself as a group. Thus, the higher social class is usually more politically interested and active than subordinate classes. One of the factors which produce this mobilization in a capitalist society is the market, just as exposure to the market tends to mobilize workers. But capitalists are themselves active in attempting to manipulate markets, rather than merely being subject to the market after the fashion of the workers and small producers; and they have some unity already through the role of financial institutions. As we shall see in Chapter 12, businesses mutually monitor one another. All this increases the mobilization and the class consciousness of capitalists and makes them better able to push their interests politically.

A full theory of political power would take into account the resources which mobilize all factions, both dominant, subordinate, and intermediate, as well as the various particular interests among them. The general hypothesis is that the most mobilized interest group wins the most power (for a version of this applied to the democratic politics of modern Sweden, see Korpi, 1983).[18]

REVOLUTIONS

Barrington Moore's seminal theory (1966) stresses the importance of revolu- tions in shaping the nature of the modern state. Moore rejects the evolutionary model which claims that all societies proceed through the same stages and that the

---

[18] A related theory (Andreski, 1968; Weber, 1923/1961: 237) explains the degree to which a state is democratic by its military participation ratio. Where the weapons used by a state foster mass military participation, it tends to be democratic. Instances of this are ancient Athenian democracy, which de- pends on maximizing the number of citizens to row in its war fleet, and the spread of the voting franchise with the creation of mass conscript infantries, beginning at the time of the Napoleonic wars and reaching its culmination with the massive armies of the twentieth century. Where weapons are restricted to a small fighting elite, such as armored knights, participation in state power is restricted to an aristocracy.

"modern" is characterized by democracy. Instead, there are at least three different types of modern state: democracy, as found in capitalist states such as Britain and the United States; state socialism of the Soviet type; and authoritarianism, of which the most extreme examples were the Fascist governments of Germany, Italy, and Japan.

The preconditions for these structures were laid down in the previous period, the beginning of commercialization and industrialization within agrarian societies. The first wave of commercialization, and hence of capitalism, occurred in the rural sector, in agricultural production. The class conflicts around this development produced various kinds of revolutions and hence modern states. Moore examines a series of case studies: England, France, the United States, China, Japan (and drawing on earlier material, Prussia and Russia). His theoretical model must be extracted from these accounts. In general form, it proposes that social groups act politically to favor their economic interests. In this sense, it is a neo-Marxian conflict theory. But it is a sophisticated interest-group model; the government that each group prefers is that which best matches its own interests, but that depends on who the opposing forces are. Thus the overall *structure* of contending interests (we might say, the relative resource mobilization of different sides) determines what a group will do. Each group has its first choice for type of government, and a second choice which it will turn to if its first choice is not possible.

According to Moore, there are five main actors in this drama: the bourgeoisie, the landowners, the government bureaucrats, the peasants, and the workers.

The *bourgeoisie* prefers democracy if possible. This is because they are best able to influence this type of government in favor of their interests. We may gloss this point by saying that if economic conditions are not interfered with, the capitalists will dominate a market system because of their superior mobilization (as indicated above). However, if capitalism itself is threatened by a strong workers' movement, or by a government bureaucracy as a form of socialism, the bourgeoisie will fall back on their second choice, authoritarian government. Usually this is done through an alliance with conservative land-owning and military classes.

The *landowners* prefer authoritarian government, to maintain their aristocratic privileges against the bourgeoisie, peasants, and workers. If these classes are weak, however, and the main threat to the landowners is the central bureaucracy itself, the landowners will favor a mild form of democracy, that is, a decentralized sharing of power among the aristocratic class. (This point was stressed not by Moore but in Montesquieu's (1748/1949) and Tocqueville's (1852/1955) classic theories, pointing to the parliamentary institutions and assemblies of nobles which balanced the power of medieval kings in Europe.)

The *government bureaucrats* favor traditional authoritarian rule as a means of keeping up their elite privileges. They are especially likely to make this choice if they are recruited from the landed aristocracy. Their second choice, perhaps surprisingly, is socialism, since it keeps the bureaucracy in power, instead of rendering it subservient to the bourgeoisie (whom the aristocracy traditionally held in contempt). This second alternative is especially likely when there is a conflict between the central bureaucracy and the landowners, or when the bureaucrats are recruited from a competitive educational system rather than via hereditary position. (Hence the number of revolutionary leaders who came from careers in the lower bureaucracy: Lenin, Mao, Robespierre.)

The *peasants* are generally unmobilized. Though they are sometimes capable of protest, they cannot take over the state themselves and are always pawns for other forces. Their revolts against absentee landlords can provide the revolutionary forces which bring down a traditional authoritarian regime and produce either democracy or socialism. But the end result of a revolution is often that the peasants expropriate the land, and thus turn themselves into small commercial farmers. This makes them the weakest members of the capitalist class and those most subject to economic pressures if the prices for agricultural products decline. Hence post-revolutionary peasants tend to turn into a conservative force and are likely to join an authoritarian (especially Fascist) movement against what they perceive as the threat of socialism in the urban sector.[19]

The *workers* are the strongest opponents of authoritarian government because of its threat of direct coercion in their own working conditions. Whether they favor democracy or socialism depends on other conditions (these are better formulated by Bendix, 1956, than in Moore). If the bourgeoisie allies with the state and the landowners in order to get control of labor (as happened in Germany during the Bismarck era or in Russia during industrialization under the czars), the workers favor socialism. If the bourgeoisie remains liberal and allows the formation of trade unions, the workers' struggle is confined to limited issues of wages and working conditions instead of establishing a "workers' state," and hence their political aim is to acquire the franchise within a democracy. (This was the path followed in England.)

The fulcrum of this system is the landowners. Which way they move depends on how they carry out the commercialization of agriculture. The landowners may go directly into the market by driving the peasants off their traditional plots, enclosing their lands to produce wool or establishing mines or factories on them, and using hired wage labor. In this case, the landowners actually eliminate themselves as a traditional aristocracy by becoming rural capitalists. Henceforward, their interests are those of capitalists, and their first choice of government is democracy. This was the English route; the English revolutions of the 1600s were those of the commercial aristocracy (led by Cromwell) with the urban bourgeoisie as a junior partner, defeating a coalition of the traditional aristocracy and the king. The process also removed the peasants from the land, which eliminated a potential source of authoritarian political support. England thus became the classic case of democratic capitalism, in which the major antidemocratic forces were weakened or eliminated.[20]

A second possibility is that the landowners become rentiers, retiring to the city and collecting rents from their peasants, who are allowed to go into the market themselves. This reduces the power of the landowners, since they are no longer directly involved in production or in controlling their peasants. It also tends to

[19] Lipset (1950) has shown that under special conditions there are rural populist movements favoring agrarian socialism. Wiley (1967) analyzes such movements in the late nineteenth-century United States as a class conflict on the credit market.

[20] Moore classifies the United States as a similar case. The American states lacked peasants or hereditary land-owning aristocracy and had little central government; U.S. agriculture was largely commercial from the outset, and its policies pro-capitalist and pro-democratic. The only threat to democracy came from the slave-owning states of the South, where the slave-owners were the closest equivalent to a conservative aristocracy, relying upon the power of the state to control their slaves. The Civil War, by eliminating slavery, was thus the equivalent of the English revolution, removing the last threat to democracy.

mobilize the peasants, since they are directly subject to the vicissitudes of the market. (This follows from the principle that markets mobilize, as noted above.) When prices fall due to a market glut, or when weather conditions cause hardships and reduce crops, the peasants nevertheless continue to owe rents to the landowners. This increases resentment against the land-owning class, who become viewed as worthless parasites (and who are no longer capable of dominating the situation of ritual deference, due to their absence from the countryside). The weakness of the aristocracy and the mobilization of the peasants tends to result in a revolution. This was the scenario of the French Revolution of 1789, and the Chinese Revolution of 1949. The structural outcomes of these revolutions differed because of the other class actors who remained on the scene. In China, the bourgeoisie was weak, and the revolution was organized into socialism by state bureaucrats. In France, the end result was a rough balance between class forces, which resulted in long-term political instability. France thus had a series of revolutionary conflicts—1830, 1848–51, 1871, the 1930s, and after World War II that tended at different times toward all three structural alternatives—authoritarian government, democracy, and state socialism.

The third possibility is that the landowners produce crops for the market, but do this by keeping the peasants on the land and attempting to squeeze more productivity out of them by tightening traditional labor controls. The aristocrats remain tied to the state since they need its support to enforce control over the peasantry, while the peasants remain unmobilized, since they are subject to traditional deference conditions and are not directly exposed to the market. This is the route followed in the commercialization of agriculture in Prussia and in the "revolution from above" by which Japan modernized after the Meiji Restoration in 1867. This was the political formula for Fascism.

Moore's theory has been extended to a number of other cases. Paige (1975) shows that the various types of commercialization of agriculture explain the kinds of politics and revolutions experienced by many twentieth-century states in Asia, Latin America, and elsewhere.

Moore's theory focuses on the political results of revolutions. One of his former students, Theda Skocpol (1979), develops the prior question of when and why revolutions break out in the first place. Skocpol takes issue with the traditional theory of revolutions, shared by both Marxists and non-Marxists, that revolutions are caused by rising social classes "bursting the bonds of the old social order." The bourgeoisie, she points out, was not historically strong before the French Revolution or the English Revolution, but developed its power after those revolutions, and largely as the result of them. Revolutions pave the way for economic transformations as much as they are caused by them, and hence revolutions give rise to new social classes. The most basic factor in revolution, rather, is a breakdown in the military power of the state. The state is no longer able to enforce control, which in turn allows rebellious forces to mobilize. Skocpol concentrates on the three great revolutions of modern times: the French Revolution (1789–99), the Russian Revolution (1917), and the Chinese Revolution (1911–49). In each case the state was weakened by war: either because of direct military defeat of its armies (Russia in World War I, and China by Western colonial incursions and then the Japanese invasion of the 1930s) or because military expenses had built up to a point where state bankruptcy threatened (as in France before 1789).

Skocpol's theory thus far resembles the geopolitical theory, which predicts state breakdown or revolution as the result of military defeat or geopolitical overextension. Skocpol adds a distinction between types of revolutions. One type is *political revolution,* which changes mainly the type of government (examples include the English revolutions of 1640 and 1688, the American Revolution of 1776–83, the Prussian reform movement of 1807–14, the Meiji Restoration in Japan in 1867, as well as numerous revolutionary coups in Latin America, Africa, and elsewhere). A second type is *social revolution,* which includes not only a political change but a transformation in the class structure of society. These are much less frequent; Skocpol confines the instances to the French, Russian, and Chinese cases.

Skocpol argues that social revolutions always involve a three-sided struggle: the state class versus the property-owning class versus the producing class. In her historical cases, these were the king (or emperor) and his bureaucracy, the rural landowners, and the peasants. These are the major classes of Moore's theory (with the workers and bourgeoisie reduced to minor roles). Notice the implication that the state itself is now treated as a social class. The bureaucrats do not merely carry out the interests of other classes, as in classic Marxian theory, nor mediate between them as in structuralist Marxism (Chapter 3), but have economic interests of their own. The bureaucrats are interested in increasing state revenue, while the landowners attempt to exempt themselves from taxation. Since the landowners are the wealthiest class, the power of the state is curtailed unless it can win concessions or gain control over the landowners. The major class struggle within the feudal-agrarian state, then, is between the two different ruling classes. A paralyzing struggle between state officials and the landed aristocracy weakens the power of the state; then a peasant rebellion sets in motion the revolution.

Skocpol's model is a version of Moore's. She adds to it an explanation of why the struggle between state bureaucracy and landowners becomes acute: it is because the state has been involved in wars which have been militarily disastrous or which have strained the resources of the state treasury. Hence, the state has been weakened vis-à-vis its principal domestic opponent, the aristocracy, and has had to make concessions to them in order to extract more wealth to support its armies. This was the pattern of France, following its long series of expensive wars in the 1700s (and just before the 1789 crisis, the costly support of the American colonies in their fight against England), as well as of the military strains of Russia and China, which resulted in a series of inconclusive reform efforts prior to their revolutions. In these cases, the reforms just enhanced the deadlock between opposing elites. This created a vacuum, into which revolutionary forces could move, especially when the army actually disintegrated because of defeat in war or lack of pay.

Skocpol, however, has focused on a limited set of Moore's conditions. All three of her revolutions are cases in which the landowners had commercialized agriculture by becoming absentee rentiers. This is the formula, as we have seen, for a weak aristocracy, as well as for a militant and rebellious peasantry. Skocpol's France, Russia, and China thus had not only a weak state (by military strain) and a weak aristocracy, but as a result, the revolutionary forces were able to get the upper hand. The English Revolution, which Skocpol does not treat because she regards it merely as a "political" rather than "social" revolution, may also be explained by extending the model. Here, too, the government was locked in a struggle over revenues with the landowners and had to make concessions to parliament. The situation grew acute because of expenditures that built up in England's foreign wars, both with Spain in the previous century and before 1640 with Scotland. This was the formula for state breakdown and revolution; but the peasant rebellion was missing because of the way English agriculture had commercialized in a capitalist direction. This is not to say that England had no social transformation; but the social change occurred separately from the political revolution, as the landowners peacefully transformed themselves into capitalists and their peasants into workers, while the revolution shifted the form of government power.

The chain of causes in Skocpol's theory can be better understood by invoking geopolitical theory: why does a state get in the position where its government is militarily strained? Notice that this is not simply a matter of being defeated in a war, since this has happened to numerous states throughout history without creating revolution. Small states are usually just swallowed up by their conquerers or become client states with puppet governments propped up from outside. Skocpol's great revolutions all occurred in large, resource-rich states; they were too large to be directly swallowed up, so that a weakened but autonomous government was left to undergo a revolution. Various conditions can contribute to this outcome: in England, the protection of being an island; in China, the fact that the Japanese invaders were themselves being driven out by defeat at the hands of the United States on another front; in Russia, the fact that victorious Germany was still occupied on the western front.

In terms of geopolitical theory, these prerevolutionary states had mixed ratings in the different geopolitical factors: all were strong in territorial resource advantages, but they were weak on the marchland position (that is, they fought in too many directions at once) or were militarily overextended by the range of their former wars. Their size and resource advantage kept them from being directly taken over by their conquerers after their defeat (in the case of Russia and China), thus allowing a revolution to take place. Putting the various parts of the theory together: revolutions tend to happen when a state has considerable size and resource advantages which have tempted it to expand too far from home base or take on too many enemies at once; when these geopolitical advantages result in military defeat or severe budgetary crisis; and when the government thereby becomes paralyzed in a struggle between revenue-seeking bureaucrats and property-owners whom they seek to tax. In this situation, efforts at reform often serve to mobilize oppositional interests, creating a liberalizing expectation which is frustrated by the continuing deadlock of opposing elites. This is a formula for political revolution. In addition, if the situation in the rural sector involves absentee rentier landlords and a commercialized peasantry, there will be a revolutionary peasant movement, resulting in a destruction of the aristocracy and the old absolutist state and its replacement with a socially revolutionary state. From the most macro perspective, we may say that revolutions are likely in a world system in which the major states are well balanced, and hence subject to a continuous probability that they will become temporarily overextended and subject to abrupt military crises.

Because Skocpol emphasizes the role of the peasants in producing a social revolution, she concludes that there will be no more great social revolutions. The peasant class is gone in the late twentieth century, and the great revolutions are merely historical events of the past. Any further great social changes, she proposes, will happen by peaceful parliamentary politics. However, this conclusion is overdrawn. It may be true that peasant revolutions are becoming increasingly unlikely, but there are parts of the world (Algeria in the 1950s and 1960s, Iran in the 1970s, and so forth) where similar conditions still exist. And more generally, the model of revolutions which stresses geopolitical conditions resulting in the breakdown or fiscal strain of the state, paralysis between different elite factions, and the mobilization of an oppositional underclass should continue to be valid. Wars, unfortunately, are still with us, and the potential for state breakdown via defeat or the strains of overextension continues. Government officials and the military, as well as capitalist interests in some societies, are capable of deadlocking among themselves in a time of budgetary crisis or military defeat; and other oppositional classes (for example, an upsurge of unemployed white-collar workers displaced by robotization and artificial intelligence; or less remotely, an urban underclass of the chronically unemployed, which has already contributed to numerous black ghetto uprisings in the 1960s) could take the place of the peasants. One state that may well experience a revolution in the next century is the USSR; its overextended geopolitical position and resulting fiscal strains provide some of the basic ingredients[21] (see Collins, 1986: 186–209).

Most work on the theory of revolutions has focused on the famous revolutions of the last few centuries. When seen more abstractly, the theory of revolutions summarized here may explain revolutions in a variety of contexts. Although "social revolutions" of the sort Skocpol focuses upon may be particularly interesting—especially for someone coming from the Marxian tradition and looking for the sources of the "bourgeois" or "socialist" eras—it should be recognized that there are many other social and political outcomes that can be produced by other arrangements of conditions. It is often of interest to understand the conditions for merely political revolutions, as well as for various social outcomes (like the "revolution from above" which followed the purely political Meiji restoration in Japan after power prestige was dashed by the incursion of U.S. warships). Revolutions are not characteristic merely of modern or early modernizing times; they also occurred in the city-states of ancient Greece, in Rome, and in the cities of medieval European. All of these involved multisided class struggles, as well as geopolitical conditions. A truly general theory, based on the elements that we now have, can be built by further comparisons.

---

[21] Recent revolutions demonstrate that the military breakdown of the state can take yet other forms. The inability of the U.S. forces to win in Viet Nam and the economic strains of fighting a long-distance war, which resulted in the pullout in 1975, not only allowed a victory of the communist forces there, but also undermined the power of other dictatorial military regimes supported by the United States. This, in turn, led to the revolutions in Iran (1979) and Nicaragua (1979). The administration of President Carter, which took office on a liberal platform after the Viet Nam defeat (which had occurred during a conservative administration), contributed to these revolutions by its own reform efforts, vacillating though they were, in withdrawing or threatening to withdraw support from dictatorial regimes. This is not an accidental feature: the replacement of a conservative by a liberal government in the United States was itself a result of the defeat in Viet Nam, illustrating the principle that the domestic legitimacy of a party declines when it is in office during a drop in international power prestige. Similarly, President Carter was defeated in his bid for reelection as the result of the Iranian hostage crisis in 1980.

SUMMARY

1. Simmel and Coser's theory proposes that conflict leads to social integration. Conflict sharpens the sense of boundaries and contributes to group identity. Conflict leads to centralization of the group, and to a search for allies. A conflict group has an interest in maintaining the existence of its enemy. Some of these principles apply to internal conflicts within a group as well as to external conflicts, but only if one side is much more powerful than the other, especially a majority attacking weak scapegoats. Where there is conflict between equally powerful factions inside a social group, the result is not integration but disintegration.

2. Simmel and Coser theorize that conflict tends to be self-limiting for three reasons: opponents have an interest in not destroying the object they are fighting over, norms develop which regulate conflict, and the victorious side has an interest in maintaining the unity of its enemy. But there are instances in which conflict does escalate beyond these limits, such as when there is a mutually reinforcing spiral of attacks and reprisals. Yet, even these escalations eventually lead to de-escalation as the goals of the conflict are reduced and issues are fragmented and settled piecemeal. How long it takes for a conflict to de-escalate depends on how expensive it is; the less expensive the conflict, the longer it can continue.

3. Coser proposed the "pluralist" theory that cross-cutting lines of group division keep conflict from becoming intense on any single dimension. There is an empirical issue, however, of whether such cross-cutting groups exist in a given case or whether different lines of group cleavage (for instance, class, race, religion) are superimposed.

4. Dahrendorf revised Marxian theory to take account of the fact that major differences among stratified groups exist not merely between property owners and non–property owners, but between white-collar and manual workers, and between similar groups, even in socialist societies. The fundamental class division is in the organization of power, between persons who give orders and those who take orders.

5. Although there may be many potential factions and conflicts, overt conflict can take place between only two sides at once. Hence, the existence of some overt conflicts inhibits other conflicts. Latent *quasi-groups* consist of persons who share similar positions within the organization of power. They can become mobilized into overt *conflict groups,* especially under social conditions of communication among group members, geographical concentration, and similar culture.

6. Dahrendorf theorized that the better organized the conflict groups, the less *violent* (physically destructive and emotionally aroused) the conflict will be. This appears to be true, but two other of his principles may not be empirically accurate: that absolute deprivation increases violent conflict, while relative deprivation lowers it; and the more violent the conflict, the more rapid the social change.

7. According to Dahrendorf's theory, conflict is most *intense* (continues for the longest time) when membership lines among power groups are superimposed rather than cross-cutting. The more intense the conflict, the more radical the social change. Dahrendorf's propositions about social change are weakened because they leave out any consideration of who wins. The victory of conservative forces, for example, or a stalemate between the sides would be very like to affect the rate of change.

8. A theory of politics should explain the conditions for various kinds of state structures, the lineup of groups who contend for power, the political events that take place, and who wins what in these struggles. Weber's theory defines the state as an organization claiming a monopoly over the legitimate use of violence within a given territory. The legitimacy of a state rises or falls depending on its level of international power prestige; one consequence is that politicians rise and fall depending on the prestige of their state in foreign affairs. There are also domestic factors which determine the legitimacy of the political leaders in office, including economic conditions and natural disasters. But the most extreme shifts in legitimacy, revolutionary downfall of the state, have been due primarily to military defeats or strains caused by military expenses.

9. Geopolitical theory proposes that the power of a state is determined by its size and wealth, and whether it has enemies on few or many sides. States in an interior position between enemies tend to fragment over long periods of time, which makes them progressively weaker; peripheral states tend to grow cumulatively larger and more powerful by acquiring formal or informal empires of weaker states. Showdown wars between major powers occur when rival empires have acquired control of the intervening territory between them; the outcome of these major wars is either the establishment of a universal empire or mutual exhaustion of both sides and the decline of both empires. States also disintegrate rapidly or undergo revolutions, when they strain themselves militarily in attempting to rule territories too far from their home economic and social base.

10. Resource mobilization theory argues that social movements of revolt do not occur when deprivation is at its worst; nor are merely psychological feelings of discomfort due to rising expectations a sufficient explanation. Organizational conditions for mobilization are necessary for a movement to arise. These include geographical patterns of residence and work which permit communication within the group and freedom from surveillance by government agents. The capitalist market itself mobilizes those groups which are most directly in contact with it. Resource mobilization theory has been criticized as inadequate to explain revolutions, because the breakdown of the state is also required. More generally, however, it can be seen that the resource mobilization of all the opposing sides determines the outcome of conflict.

11. Barrington Moore theorizes that the nature of the modern state is determined by revolutions which took place during the period when agriculture became commercialized. The outcome depended on the structural lineup among the contending classes. The *bourgeoisie* prefers democracy if it can control it, but falls back on authoritarian government if capitalism is threatened by other social classes. *Landowners* prefer authoritarian government to protect their aristocratic privileges, but will favor democracy if their main threat is from the power of government bureaucracy. *Government bureaucrats* favor traditional authoritarian rule, but will support socialism in a situation of class conflict. *Peasants* are only weakly mobilized as a class and can join revolutionary forces, but they typically attempt to expropriate their own land and become small commercial farmers, which turns them into weak members of the capitalist class. *Industrial workers* oppose authoritarian government and hence favor either democracy or socialism.

12. The landowners were the crucial determinant of political change. Where landowners established capitalist agriculture by driving the peasants off the land, the landowners themselves became a capitalist class and other pro-democratic classes were strengthened; the result was democracy (the English route). Where the landowners became absentee rentiers, the peasants were squeezed between the market and the landlords, and became revolutionary; the result is state socialism (the Chinese route). Where the landowners produced crops for the market by tightening traditional controls over the peasantry, the aristocrats remained tied to the authoritarian state, and the result was Fascism (the German and Japanese route).

13. Skocpol's theory proposes that full-scale social revolutions involve a three-sided struggle between the state bureaucracy, the property-owning class, and the producing class. Military defeat or expenses weaken the state and set it at odds with the property-owners, from whom it attempts to extract more resources; when this deadlock between the two dominant classes coincides with a revolt from below by the peasantry, the result is a major revolution. This theory combines Moore's model of the commercialization of agriculture with a geopolitical theory of state power. A more general theory of revolutions (and other transfers of state power) can be developed by extending these two types of conditions.

Chapter 5

MULTIDIMENSIONAL CONFLICT THEORY AND STRATIFICATION

EXPLAINING INEQUALITY: TURNER'S AND LENSKI'S THEORIES
   The Distribution of Wealth
   The Distribution of Power
   Status Groups and Prestige
   Turner's Overall Model of Stratification

SEX AND GENDER STRATIFICATION
   Economic-Marxian Theories
   A Theory of Sexual Politics

EDUCATIONAL CREDENTIAL STRATIFICATION
   Credential Inflation as Status Competition
   The Sinecure Society as Solution to Keynesian Economic Strains

SUMMARY

Conflict theory is not concerned only with overt conflict and social change. It is a perspective on all aspects of society and on social order in all its forms. The conflict theory of social organization is a theory of stratification. Societies are not merely differentiated; differences among individuals and groups are generally forms of inequality which are produced by differences in resources and represent the pursuit of conflicting interests. Conflict theory proposes that the various forms of social organization can be explained as parts of a theory of stratification.

Stratification, moreover, is a strategic site on which to build a sociological theory. Stratification has turned out to be empirically central to sociological research. Virtually all topics in sociology are connected with it. When sociological community studies began in the 1920s and 1930s (the *Middletown* studies of Helen and Robert Lynd and the *Yankee City* and other studies of W. Lloyd Warner and his students), their aim was simply to describe what there was to be seen; these turned into studies of stratification, because a complex modern society does not present a simple and unified cultural pattern, but a series of lifestyles and groupings arranged by social class. Survey research, too, quickly discovered the importance of stratification variables in explaining all manner of attitudes and behaviors. In general, it has turned out that hardly any area of sociology is not illuminated by understanding its connection with stratification.

The same research shows, however, that stratification cannot be seen in terms of a single dimension. Social class is not the only form of stratification; inequalities and differences among ethnic or religious groups are also important, as are stratification by sex, age, education, and other features. The economic factors in social class itself are complex rather than simple. This is not a weakness of the stratification approach, because multidimensional stratification theory reflects the various levels of society itself.

Most of the complexity of stratification can be encompassed in the three-dimensional scheme set down by Max Weber (1922/1968: 926–40). In analyzing the various kinds of groups which can take part in politics, Weber picked out the general categories: *class, status group,* and *party.* Although what Weber said about them is somewhat specific to his concern for political action, it is possible to generalize these categories into a theory of stratification. Sometimes it has been pointed out that Weber gives us three kinds of resources or abstract dimensions of social action: economic, cultural or status, and power. This is true, but we should also bear in mind that Weber has a theory of the formation of interest groups on these bases. Furthermore, these dimensions are not all on the same level; some of them are nested within others.

Class is the economic dimension. Weber defined it as a set of individuals who share a common position in a market situation. For example, there is the class of workers who sell their labor on the market and the class of employers who buy labor.[1] However, these are not the only classes in a labor market. The various

---

[1] This is similar to Marx and Engels' definition of classes in capitalist society. However, Weber explicitly defines classes in relation to a market, whereas the Marxian definition is in terms of ownership or

professions and occupations (medicine, law, governmental bureaucrats, and so forth) may separate themselves out from other forms of labor by establishing some mechanism of "closure" or "monopolisation" over their part of the labor market (Parkin, 1974; Murphy, 1984). This makes the particular profession or occupation into a separate interest group, no longer allied with workers in general, but quite possibly opposed to other workers.

Furthermore, (1) the *labor market* is only one of three kinds of markets distinguished by Weber. (2) There is also the *credit market*, which divides the interest group of people who borrow money from the group who lend money. This dimension cuts across the labor market dimension; employers or capitalists, who are a single class on the labor market, can be separated into financial debtor and creditor classes. (3) There is also the *commodity market*, separating purchasers of goods (consumers) from sellers of goods.

Class conflict can occur along any of these dimensions. Wiley (1967) points out that the United States historically had relatively little class conflict along the dimension of workers versus employers, although there were periods of labor militancy during the 1880s and again in the 1930s; and strikes, as well as union-breaking actions by employers, go on at some level all the time. This is the dimension of class conflict which Marxians focus upon, and the conclusion is sometimes drawn that there is very little class conflict in the United States. But if we focus on the other dimensions, we can see a good deal of class conflict in U.S. history. The 1800s were dominated by conflict between creditors and lenders (dimension 2), especially the battles between debt-ridden farmers and the bankers, which were the source of populist movements (an issue which has appeared again in the 1980s, with the bankruptcy of many small farmers). The commodity market (dimension 3) tends to have less overt conflict, mainly because consumers are so spread out that they are hard to organize as a militant group. Nevertheless, Wiley argues, the black ghetto uprisings of the 1960s were not merely a racial issue, but were attacks by a group of poverty-level consumers upon the stores in their neighborhoods in reprisal for their high prices. The formation of OPEC (Organization of Petroleum Exporting Countries) and the resulting battles over the price of oil in the 1970s and 1980s is another instance of class conflict in a commodity market. Weber's model of class thus gives us a more flexible and comprehensive view of economic conflicts than the narrower Marxian theory.[2]

---

nonownership of the means of production. Contemporary Marxists have made much of this distinction, arguing that the Weberian view focuses on a superficial aspect of capitalism. According to this argument, only the Marxian theory is useful, since it points to the basic alienation of workers by their exclusion from the means of production. Contemporary Weberians (Murphy, 1985) reply that market position is, in fact, an empirically more useful way to define class, and that the Marxian approach is too closely tied to the labor theory of value, a fallacious premise on which to build an economic theory.

[2] Weber (1922 / 1968; 930–32) extracted his categories from an overview of economic conflicts in world history. He pointed out that in the ancient Greek city-states, the main conflict was between debtors (the poor farmers) and creditors (the wealthy aristocracy) and that the former made up the supporters of democratic politics in those states, while the latter were the oligarchic faction. In the cities of medieval Europe, the struggle shifted to the commodity market, where the main protests and uprisings concerned the price of bread (the staple food of the time) and were mounted against hoarders and suppliers in times of shortage. Conflict over the price of labor—the characteristic trade union issue—emerges only in modern times.

Status group is on a different level of analysis from the social class. A status group is a community, a group of people who have a common lifestyle and share a sense of group identity. Hence, they exist in the realm of culture and consciousness; another term for status group could be a "consciousness community." An ethnic group[3] or religious group is a prominent example of a status group. In this way, status groups can cut across social classes.

However, I stressed that the status group is on a different level of analysis from the social class because the former is a conscious community, but the latter is a collection of individuals who happen to share the same economic interest. These are not mutually exclusive. Probably the most common form of status group is not ethnic, but a status group based on class. All that is necessary is that the members of a class recognize one another, socialize together and intermarry, and develop a similar lifestyle. In fact, there are strong empirical tendencies in this direction: class position (insofar as it involves occupation) tends to strongly influence values and lifestyle (see Chapter 6); and there are tendencies to friendship and marriage endogamy by class, although some societies are much more extreme in this than others—which is itself a variation to be explained by stratification theory.

Weber's distinction here parallels a more limited one made by Marx. Marx distinguished between a class *an sich*—"in itself"—and *für sich*—"in itself"; the former is merely a latent collection of individuals in the same class position, while the latter has acquired "class consciousness." Marx expected the working class to be able to revolt only when it arrived at the latter condition. Empirically, however, it has often been found that the working class is not very class conscious (Form 1985). The theory of the conditions under which class consciousness emerges needs to be treated separately.[4] In general, it is the upper class which is most likely to be class conscious (Mann 1970), which is one reason why it maintains its dominance. In Weberian terms, the upper class is most likely to become organized as a status group. Historically, the feudal upper class achieved a high degree of closure by making itself an "Estate" (Weber's German term is *Stand*), the "aristocracy," with privileges and lifestyle prescribed by law. Even more extreme is the Indian caste system, in which the status groups are radically separated by strict rules against intermarriage, eating together, or even sometimes touching or being seen by another caste. In modern capitalist society, distinctions are much milder, but the upper class still generally has the highest degree of status consciousness and closure, through such practices as debutantes' "coming out," "Society" balls, the Social Register, and the like.

Party. Weber's third category, on yet another level of analysis. Parties, Weber says, live "in the house of power." He means that they are specifically political groups, factions organized to struggle for power. Parties (or power groups, as we may call them) are thus a level which can emerge out of the other social groups, classes, or status groups. There can be a working-class party or a capitalist party, as well as an

---

[3] I am including "racial" groups as a version of ethnic groups. The crucial feature is not biological, but the social organization of a community which is consciously recognized as distinct.

[4] Marxian theory has taken a step in this direction with the theory of how consciousness is produced by control of the material "means of mental production" (Abercrombie, Hill, Turner 1980). A broader theory of class cultures is given in Chapter 6, which includes social rituals. These might be made compatible with the general Marxian scheme in the sense that these are produced by what may be called the "material means of emotional production."

ethnic or religious party. A party is a way that some group in the society mobilizes for political action. However, the realm of power has some autonomy. A party can also emerge within the structure of the state itself: the bureaucrats striving to maintain themselves in office, for example, or to enhance the power of the government (as in the Moore-Skocpol theory in Chapter 4). When Weber refers to "the house of power," he means a real organization; any organization (see Chapter 13) is a structure of power, and is internally divided into different power factions. For this reason, politics can be complex and is not simply reducible to the manipulation of the state by class or other outside interest groups.

This is not to say that it is impossible for classes to dominate politics. That is one empirical possibility. The relationship between classes, status groups, and power groups can be diagrammed as follows:

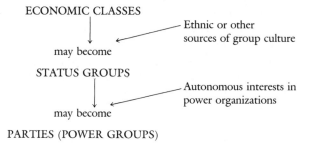

The Marxian model is a special case, or simplified version, of the general Weberian model in which economic classes (or rather, one specific version of them—workers versus employers) are translated into status groups (that is, acquire class consciousness), and these in turn are the sole basis of parties. From the Weberian perspective, a special theory is needed to explain when stratification and politics will be simplified to this form. More generally, a full theory of stratification would give the conditions under which all the possible variants in this model take place.

EXPLAINING INEQUALITY:
TURNER'S AND LENSKI'S THEORIES

A good theory of stratification should not merely categorize. It should give the conditions under which different degrees and kinds of inequality exist. A theory of stratification is not necessarily pessimistic—one of the possible variants is zero stratification, or little or no inequality on one or all dimensions. However, we need a theory of stratification comparing outcomes across the whole range to tell what conditions would reduce inequality in this way.

Unfortunately, much of the work on stratification is descriptive rather than explanatory. Some dimensions, such as the distribution of power, have barely been conceptualized as the subject for a general explanatory model until very recently. We do have the pioneering work of Gerhard Lenski (1966), however, and more recently, a fully multidimensional theory has been proposed by Jonathan Turner (1984).

Turner's comprehensive model proposes that there are six different aspects of stratification to be explained: (1) the concentration of material wealth, (2) the concentration of power, (3) the distribution of prestige, (4) the formation of culturally homogenous groups, (5) the status ranking among cultural groups, and (6) social mobility. These dimensions may be seen as an elaboration of Weber's three-dimensional model: class, status, and power.

Why does Turner have six dimensions rather than Weber's three? Turner's first two dimensions, the concentration of *wealth* and *power*, are distributional aspects of Weber's economic class and political power group dimensions. Recall that Weber was concerned not with stratification but with naming the interest groups which take part in political conflict. Turner shifts the analysis to the possession of resources of which these dimensions themselves are composed: the degree of equality or inequality in the distribution of wealth (which results from economic action) and of power (the structure of political action).

Another three of Turner's dimensions are an elaboration of Weber's category of *status group*. Why is this broken into three? The distribution of *prestige* (dimension 3) has been a topic conventionally studied by empirical sociologists (Treiman 1977). However, this has been conceptualized as the distribution of prestige among the occupations. (Thus it turns out that judges and doctors have high prestige, shoe shiners low prestige, and so forth.) This is an analysis of the ranking of individuals in their occupational roles. This is not the same thing as Weber's status groups, which are communities rather than individuals. Hence, Turner adds two more categories: (4) the formation of groups themselves and (5) the status ranking among them. He breaks this into two separate theories because it is possible for such groups to form without any status hierarchy existing. Two different ethnic or religious groups might inhabit the same society, without one being ranked above the other, even if they have cultural homogeneity and strong group boundaries against outsiders. (This is likely the case with many of the "lifestyle" communities of contemporary American society: different kinds of age-based communities with different recreational lifestyles—"swinging singles" communities, middle-aged family neighbourhoods, retirement communities, and so on.) Hence we need a theory to explain when a society will be divided into many such groups and when it is culturally homogeneous and without "horizontal" boundaries among groups.

Additionally, we need a theory (5) to explain the conditions under which these cultural communities actually become ranked among themselves.[5]

Turner has yet a sixth category, *social mobility*. This is on a different level of analysis from the others. Mobility is the movement of individuals (or the rate of movement of the total population) from one category to another. But mobility theory itself does not specify the categories; these must be taken from some other distribution. There can be many kinds of mobility: movement of individuals up or

---

[5] An interesting implication is that a given society could be higher on the conditions that produce group ranking (5) than on the conditions that produce distinctions or boundaries among groups themselves (4). That is to say, cultural differences are ranked, and people are status conscious; but the groups they belong to are amorphous and not tightly closed. This would be the case of a society in which there is a good deal of movement between groups, friendship circles overlap, and cultures fade into each other at the boundaries (how status groups tend to be in the United States today, with the exception of the black-white distinction) yet at the same time there is much concern for status superiority and for status mobility—"moving into the right circles."

down in terms of wealth, power, and occupational prestige (this being the form that most empirical research has concentrated upon), as well as in their membership of status groups (which may be either unranked—horizontal group movement—or ranked, which is what is usually referred to as "social climbing"). This is one reason that social mobility requires a rather complicated theory, and why sociologists have not yet been very successful in producing a good theory of mobility. In general, we may say that mobility refers to a different kind of inequality from that of the other distributions, these, (that is, 1, 2, 3, and 5) deal with *inequality of distribution,* while mobility refers to *inequality of opportunity.*

A full theory of stratification would have to explain the conditions for variations on all of these. Since the dimensions of stratification implicate most of the institutions of society and involve most forms of individual behavior, if we could arrive at a satisfactory theory of stratification or even a good approximation, we would have a major part of a general explanation of the subject matter of sociology. For that reason, the effort to build such models is important, even if they are crude and need further development in many respects.

THE DISTRIBUTION OF WEALTH

Lenski (1966) provided the first breakthrough to a conflict theory which actually explains the variations in inequality. The main focus of his theory is explaining the distribution of wealth. Using evidence from the range of societies which have existed throughout world history, Lenski constructed the following general model: wealth is divided into two portions, that which is necessary to keep the population alive and the surplus beyond this amount. The wealth necessary for reproduction is distributed by need; if it were not, then some proportion of the population would die. Hence, they would no longer exist and no longer make up part of the society. We can infer from this that societies with very low levels of economic production, which have no surplus, cannot have any stratification in wealth. On the other hand, surplus wealth, where it exists, is appropriated by power: whoever can enforce control of it gets it. Thus, Lenski's comparative model proposes inequality in the distribution of wealth is determined by two factors: the size of the economic surplus and the concentration of power.

Empirically, Lenski finds that inequality in wealth follows a bell-shaped curve in relation to the major forms of production which have existed across human history (see Figure 5-1). Inequality is lowest in hunting-and-gathering societies, then rises though primitive and advanced horticultural societies, and reaches its peak in agrarian societies (the feudal-patrimonial empires of the Middle Ages). Then the curve declines to industrial societies, although to a moderate rather than low level. Why does the curve take this shape? The surplus rises from zero in hunting-and-gathering tribes, to a steadily higher level in each succeeding form of production. Inequality must be low in hunting-and-gathering and can *potentially* become greater in each successive form as productivity goes up. However, the distribution of power follows a bell-shaped curve also. Horticultural societies begin to differentiate into powerful versus weak kinship groups, and agrarian societies have fully fledged military states in which the means of violence are monopolized by a warrior aristocracy. Hence, the extreme inequality of power in agrarian empires (medieval China or France, or

FIGURE 5-1

LENSKI'S THEORY OF WEALTH AND POWER

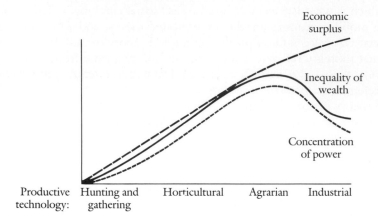

the ancient Roman Empire) produces extreme inequality in wealth. However, industrial societies reverse the curve, mainly because the distribution of power has shifted. The democratic or bureaucratic state shifts the concentration of power, and the inequality of wealth is moderated. It does not disappear, since power is not distributed equally; but it settles at a moderate level.

Lenski's model provides the skeleton of a theory of wealth, which can be elaborated in various ways. If we knew more about the distribution of power, we could predict more details about variations in wealth. Lenski's model can be applied in various ways, not only by comparison among societies of different historical types, but among different industrial societies. In general, political factors affect the distribution of economic wealth, but the ways in which this may happen are complicated.[6]

One caveat is in order. The shape of Lenski's curve should not be interpreted to mean that history flows directly in that order. Horticultural societies are more productive than hunting-and-gathering societies, industrial more than agrarian societies, and so forth; but this is not a necessary historical sequence. Some tribal societies are directly incorporated into industrial or agrarian empires (by mechanisms such as those described in Wallerstein's theory described in Chapter 3), resulting in a hybrid of mixed forms; and some societies may skip directly from one type to another, omitting the other types. Moreover, just because the figure shows

---

[6] Studies of the effect which the degree of democracy in a country has on its level of income inequality have yielded inconsistent results; the bulk of the evidence may favor the view that democracy does not reduce inequality (Bollen and Jackman, 1985). This may happen because the groups which are most mobilized to participate in a democracy do not favor redistributive policies or because policies do not have the effects which are anticipated. Levine (1983) thus shows that government expenditures in the United States have under some conditions favored capital and under other conditions favored labor; thus political intervention can be turned toward increasing either inequality or equality. Stack (1978a) argues that it is the strength of socialist party movements, rather than democracy or participation in general, which reduces inequality; and more generally, that the degree of government intervention in the economy, especially in the form of socialist states, is the crucial correlate of differences in inequality (Stack, 1978b, 1980; this is controverted by Jackman, 1980, and Firebaugh, 1980).

a downward curve from agrarian to industrial societies, this does not mean that industrial societies continue towards ever greater equality. The evidence indicates that this is not so (at least, not so far); once a typical industrial level is reached, it remains more or less stable or fluctuates around that level.[7] It is apparent that we are not evolving towards an egalitarian utopia. Even socialist societies, although they eliminate some sources of economic inequality, nevertheless may have substantial inequality insofar as power is highly concentrated in an official communist party or government bureaucracy. Moves toward further equality are not impossible, but it would require, according to Lenski's theory, major changes or revolutions in the distribution of power.

Turner builds his theory of the concentration of material wealth upon Lenski's model. Turner wishes to state his theory precisely, and to show what happens to the various factors across their entire range of variation. Hence, he uses a quasi-mathematical form of statement. In the interests of readability, however, he eliminates unnecessary mathematical detail. For example, cause-and-effect relationships can take various forms (see Figure 5-2). Linear relationships rise or fall in a straight line, and therefore the concentration of wealth might be proposed to be exactly proportional to the concentration of power. In reality, however, things are usually not this simple. Some relationships are logarithmic; that is, the curve begins to "bend over" or "flatten out" as it reaches a high level. For example (and this is the way Turner actually proposes wealth is related to power in Proposition 1), the concentration of wealth goes up sharply at first as power concentration increases. But as power concentration reaches high levels, its effects "slow down": inequality in wealth is already quite high, and further increases in power do not do much more to it. This type of asymptotic curve is quite common, as most relationships weaken as they near a ceiling.

A third type of relationship is exponential. Here, the process may start slowly, but it accelerates as it reaches a high level. Turner proposes that internal conflict has this kind of relationship with power (Proposition 2, page 160): low levels of conflict do very little to increase the concentration of power, but as conflict becomes severe, the result is a great strengthening of the power of the state to deal with it. All these relationships can be positive or negative. A negative logarithmic curve goes downward, gradually reaching a "floor" rather than a ceiling. A negative exponential curve accelerates downward. In Proposition 1, Turner proposes that inequality in wealth has this relationship with the number of power hierarchies. When there is only one power hierarchy, wealth inequality is extreme; but when the number of power hierarchies begins to increase, the concentration of wealth declines slowly at first, and then more and more rapidly later.[8]

---

[7] See Pilcher (1976) for data on trends within industrial societies. Agrarian societies are also variable over time; for example, economic inequality became more severe in the ancient Mediterranean societies during the Hellenistic period and the Roman Empire (Ste. Croix, 1981). There are variations within any of Lenski's categories. Tribal societies generally have low degrees of inequality; however, those tribes which inhabit lush environments tend to have more inequality (Blumberg, 1978: 15–19). This is in keeping with Lenski's principle of the potential rise in inequality with the rise in the surplus. The more we know about the conditions for variations in power within any type of society, the more closely the theory can be applied.

[8] Turner's model, to be realistic, should include a final stopping point, or floor, for the concentration of wealth, since it cannot fall below zero.

FIGURE 5-2

TYPES OF RELATIONSHIPS BETWEEN VARIABLES

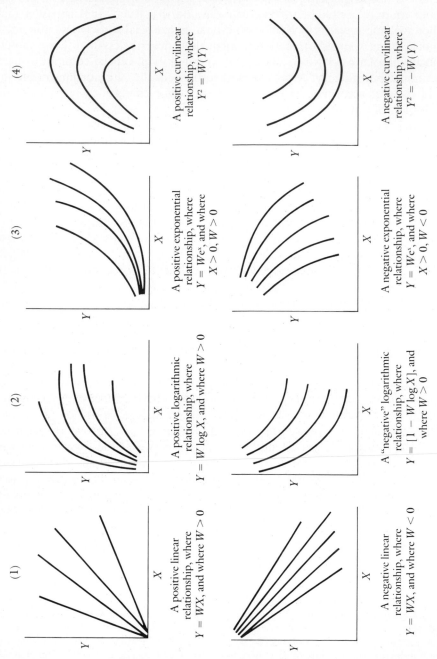

(1) A positive linear relationship, where $Y = WX$, and where $W > 0$

A negative linear relationship, where $Y = WX$, and where $W < 0$

(2) A positive logarithmic relationship, where $Y = W \log X$, and where $W > 0$

A "negative" logarithmic relationship, where $Y = [1 - W \log X]$, and where $W > 0$

(3) A positive exponential relationship, where $Y = We^x$, and where $X > 0, W > 0$

A negative exponential relationship, where $Y = We^x$, and where $X > 0, W < 0$

(4) A positive curvilinear relationship, where $Y^2 = W(Y)$

A negative curvilinear relationship, where $Y^2 = -W(Y)$

From Jonathan Turner, *Societal Stratifiction: A Theoretical Analysis*, p. 24. Columbia University Press, 1984.

Mathematical statements conventionally turn all variables into letters or other symbols. This places a burden on the reader's memory, since he or she must keep in mind, or constantly look up, what these symbols refer to. A mathematical equation can actually be read as a verbal sentence, however, and Turner attempts to replace the cryptic *A*'s and *B*'s, *x*'s and *y*'s, Greek letters and so forth, with abbreviations which are closer to the actual concepts being referred to. I have taken his equations one step further in this direction and have translated some of his abbreviations into fuller words. (This is in keeping with the method of computer simulation, spelled out in Appendix B.)

Turner's Proposition 1 (1984: 203) thus looks as follows:

$$(1) \qquad \text{WEALTH} = W_1(\text{PROD}^{\text{exp}}) + [W_2(\text{NUM.HIER.}^{-\text{exp}}) \times W_3(\text{SUBUNITS}^{-\text{exp}})]$$

In words, this says that the concentration of wealth is determined by the level of economic production in a society, plus the combined effect of the number of power hierarchies times the number of subunits that organize people's activities. The *exp* and − *exp* superscripts add detail about these relationships: the effects of productivity accelerate as productivity becomes larger, while the number of power hierarchies and number of subunits accelerate in a negative direction. As these become greater (power is more dispersed and society becomes more complex), the distribution of wealth diminishes, slowly at first, then more rapidly.

Turner uses *W* with various subscripts (W_1, W_2, W_3) to indicate the weight given to various factors. In Proposition 1, he is proposing that productivity is the strongest determinant of wealth inequality, followed by the number of power hierarchies as the second strongest determinant, and the number of subunits as the weakest determinant.

We can recognize that this is a version of Lenski's model. The first factor, productivity, is a surrogate for Lenski's economic surplus; presumably, the lowest level of productivity any society can have is that at which there is no surplus; from then on, the higher the productivity, the higher the surplus. Lenski's concentration of power here becomes *NUM.HIER*, the number of organizational hierarchies that link people together. Turner makes this part of the theory more complicated by multiplying this by *SUBUNITS*, the number of differentiated subunits in the society. This is saying that a more differentiated society (more complex organizational structure in which people work) multiplies the dispersion of power, making it harder for a single power group to control everyone. This is a realistic addition to Lenski's model. The number of hierarchies *(NUM.HIER)* gets at the vertical or political dimension of society, while the differentiation of subunits *(SUBUNITS)* tells us that the sheer complexity of the modern economy will also tend to disperse the distribution of wealth. In other words, it is not just modern governmental structure which gives us less wealth concentration than medieval agrarian societies, but the complexity of the private economy as well.[9]

---

[9]Turner multiplies the last two factors by each other, assuming that a differentiated society will not just add to the dispersion of power, but will actually enhance the dispersion of every unit of power. I am not convinced this is entirely correct; a computer simulation indicates that multiplying variables by each other results in very strong trends, even if the initial values of the variables are quite low. A more

THE DISTRIBUTION OF POWER

Turner's theory of the concentration of power, Proposition 2, is as follows:

(2)
$$\text{POWER} = W_1[\log(\text{EXTHREAT})] + [W_2(\text{PROD}^{exp}) \times W_3(\text{CONFLICT}^{exp}) \times W_4(\text{TRANSACT}^{exp})]$$

This says that the concentration of power is determined first and most heavily by the degree of perceived threat from outside the society, and then by an interaction among (in descending order of importance) the level of economic production, the amount of internal conflict, and the amount of internal transactions among the sub-units of the society. The first part of the theory, external threat *(EXTHREAT)*, incorporates the familiar idea that societies threatened by external enemies tend to pull together around a strong government. In slightly different terms, we could say that societies involved in wars (or threatening to become so) tend to have concentrated governmental power. Put in this way, we find Turner's model is related to part of the Weberian geopolitical theory spelled out in Chapter 4: the legitimacy of power holders depends on their international power prestige.

The latter part of the equation says that power increases as the society's economic level goes up, as the amount of conflict inside the society goes up, and with the number of transactions between the society's subunits. All these processes are supposed to be multiplicative—mutually enhancing—so that conflict in a rich society presumably increases the concentration more than in a poor society. Also, if there are more internal transactions[10]—the differentiated subunits do more dealing with one another, rather than remaining isolated—this should enhance the effects of economic productivity upon the concentration of power.

The theory is a valiant effort toward establishing a truly general theory about the distribution of power. I am not certain, though, that it specifies all the most important factors, or gets the relationships among them correct. The general picture is that power is determined by three factors: the amount of external conflict, the amount of internal conflict, and the extent to which a society is economically productive and well integrated. The two conflict factors seem to be on the right track, since historically, we could say that state power is built up when there is a centralized military apparatus and that this results from involvement in conflicts, both external and internal. Turner proposes that the relationship between power and external threat is logarithmic: that is, as threat reaches high levels, power reaches a ceiling and fails to grow any more. I would say that the result is more extreme: very high threat results in the defeat or destruction of the state, and thus in a decline of power. This relationship is not merely logarithmic but curvilinear, reversing itself after a certain point.[11]

The same could be said about internal conflict, although Turner here proposes that the relationship is exponential: power centralizes slowly through low levels of

realistic model might be to replace the multiplication sign before W_3 in Propostion 1 with an addition sign.

[10]This could also be called *level of communications,* or *level of market activity.*

[11]A more complex and accurate theory could perhaps be built by filling in external threat with a full geopolitical theory like that in Chapter 4, which predicts the rises and falls in the military power of a state.

internal conflict, then builds up as conflict becomes severe. But surely this depends on who wins; if the government loses, power may crumble rather than build. Also, even if the government wins and centralizes power, this could result in stifling all internal conflict (modern totalitarian dictatorships come to mind) so that the correlation between conflict and power would disappear over time.

Finally, Turner suggests that power concentrates as the society grows richer and better integrated. This has some appeal historically, but only for the period up through medieval agrarian societies, when power was actually growing. It is difficult to explain the modest decline in the concentration of power that happened with the transition to industrial societies. Turner's model would seem to imply that power should become more concentrated (because of vastly increased production and internal transactions). The only alternative is that the other factors—external threat and internal conflict—have decreased, but I do not believe this is so. The level of warfare (and certainly of military threat) has been high in both historical periods, and it may well be the case that there is more internal conflict now, since the population is more mobilized. I would suggest, in fact, that the internal conflict factor probably works in the opposite direction from that which Turner proposes. Modern society does mobilize more people for political conflicts than medieval agrarian societies, and for that reason power has become more dispersed. But since there are factors moving in the opposite direction, namely higher productivity and continuously high external threat, the modern power distribution tends to occupy a middle level rather than becoming either extremely high or extremely low.[12]

STATUS GROUPS AND PRESTIGE

I will omit Turner's theory of the distribution of prestige, since the equation is quite complex. Its basic outlines may be gathered from Figure 5-3: the distribution of prestige is generally affected by the distribution of power and wealth (as also proposed in Lenski, 1966: 45), plus cultural and ideological factors determining the way people perceive and evaluate the skill and importance of various positions.

Turner's Proposition 3 on the formation of cultural groups may be stated as follows:

(3) $\text{CULTGROUPS} = \{W_1\,[\log\,(\text{POP})] \times W_4\,(\text{DIFF.OCCUP}^{\exp}) \times W_5\,(\text{MOBIL}^{-\exp})\}$
$+ \{W_2\,(\text{INEQUAL}^{\exp}) \times W_3\,[\log\,(\text{DISCRIM})]\}$

This means that the number of culturally distinct groups *(CULTGROUPS)* is determined by the size of the population *(POP)* multiplied by the differentiation of occupational specialties *(DIFF.OCCUP)* multiplied by the amount of intergroup mobility *(MOBIL);* plus the overall degree of inequality of rewards *(INEQUAL—the distri-*

---

[12] Totalitarian states in time of war, however, such as Nazi Germany or Stalin's Russia, had extremely high concentrations of power, and the United States during an actual nuclear-war mobilization would probably be similar. That is to say, very high levels of external threat can push concentration of power near the ceiling; but when this falls off, the tendency of a complex industrial society toward moderate levels of decentralization and multiple-group mobilization counteracts this somewhat.

   Efforts to actually measure the distribution of power are virtually nonexistent. One proposed measure (Blau, 1977: 225–234) calculates power as the cumulative number of persons in organizational hierarchies who take orders from levels above.

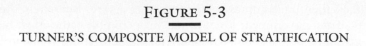

FIGURE 5-3

TURNER'S COMPOSITE MODEL OF STRATIFICATION

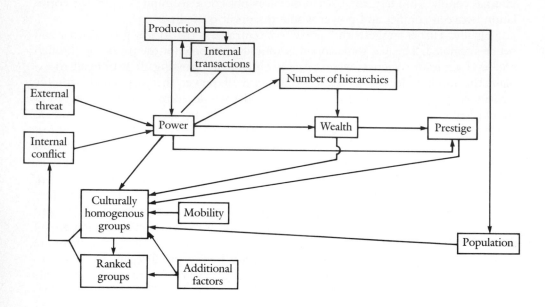

bution of *WEALTH* and *POWER* and *PRESTIGE* in previous equations) multiplied by amount of discrimination against minorities *(DISCRIM)*. The shapes of these relationships are indicated as either logarithmic or exponential, and the weights (W_1 and so on) are in diminishing order of importance. The sheer size of population (W_1) is the most important, reflecting the idea that large populations tend to diversify. Similarly, differentiation of occupational specialities increases cultural diversity, while low rates of mobility (the negative sign on the exponent) promote the consolidation of group boundaries.[13] Another powerful factor (W_2) is the total amount of inequality in the society; Turner proposes that after an initial period of differentiation due merely to group size, the inequality of wealth and power becomes at least as important in differentiating status groups.

This theoretical model is only a sketch, and no doubt needs expansion. One set of factors that should be added to a complete theory would state the conditions that produce distinctive languages, since this is a major source of ethnic group differences. Very long-term processes would seem to be involved here, as indicated by research on the history of languages and their differentiation from one another. Ethnic group diversity is one of the most important kinds of cultural group diversity in modern societies; among the factors that produce it is migration from a foreign territory. Hence, a *MIGRATION* variable should also be added to Turner's model (weighted by the structural differences between the host and origin societies,

---

[13] It is not clear to me why this should be the weakest factor determining group formation.

since these structures determine the degree to which the group's cultures differ).

Proposition 3 only tells us how strong a tendency there is to form culturally distinct groups. An additional Proposition 4 is needed to explain how they come to be ranked among themselves:

$$(4) \qquad RANKGROUPS = W_1 [\log (CONSENS)] \times W_2 (CULTGROUPS^{exp})$$

This says that the degree of ranking among groups is determined most importantly by the amount of consensus in the society about value standards *(CONSENS)*, multiplied by the degree to which culturally distinct groups have already formed *(CULTGROUPS,* as determined by Proposition 3).

This, again, is a useful effort at stating a general causal theory about an aspect of stratification that hitherto has been only described or categorized. It appears too simple to be complete, however. I suspect that inequality—especially the concentration of power—may directly enter into this process to determine group ranking.

Turner (1984: 189) also provides an equation for social mobility. It is quite complex, but may not actually be complex enough for this subject. I omit it here in lieu of further discussion of the topic in Chapter 12.

TURNER'S OVERALL MODEL OF STRATIFICATION

The various factors in Turner's theory reappear in different equations. This means the processes are linked together in a system to some extent. Changes in one part have ramifications spreading throughout. This means the model is to some extent a self-propelling, dynamic theory, implicitly a theory of social change as well as of static comparisons of stratification. (For the implications of this point, see Appendix B on computer simulation.) The theory is very ambitious, and as its author explicitly states, it is only an effort to pull together current theories as a basis for further development. Rather than attempt this here, I present only the general model of relationships among the parts of Turner's theory.

SEX AND GENDER STRATIFICATION

Before about 1970, the existence of male-female stratification was virtually ignored. It was assumed that women had the same status as their husbands or fathers, since their role was a domestic one—as part of the male system of stratification. Studies of social mobility never bothered to include women, and evidence on women appeared only incidentally in studies focused on men. With the rise of the feminist movement, it became apparent that there has existed, for a very long time, a blatant form of inequality along the lines of sex or gender[14]: men and women differ consid-

---

[14] It has become common to distinguish between the older term, *sex* and a term generally preferred by feminists, *gender*. *Sex* tends to imply the biological differences between males and females, while *gender* is used to pick out the cultural, socially created definitions of what males and females are. However, I do not believe the reliance on *gender* analysis is sufficient, because it directs attention away from a crucial feature of the *relationships* between men and women—sexual behavior itself. Although this is reduced to a minor feature in some theories of gender stratification, I believe this is a crucial omission.

erably in their occupations, wealth, and political power, as well as personal defer-ence, status, and freedom of behavior.

Sex and gender inequality has become a major field of research, but its limita-tion is that the research is largely descriptive rather than explanatory. Patterns of occupational and economic discrimination have been documented, and on the micro level there are descriptions of the way males and females interact in conversations and in nonverbal gestures. These patterns are not usually explained, except some-times by social psychological theories operating on the individual level. Some theo-rists (such as Chodorow, 1978, who uses neo-Freudian theory) have proposed that females and males undergo different patterns of early childhood development. Oth-ers speculate that males and females are socialized into different cultural roles (for instance, Gottfredson, 1981), the girls expected to become wives and mothers and fill other nurturant and helping roles, while males are expected to become dominant, aggressive, career-oriented, and so forth. This may be so empirically—at least, some of the time—but it begs the question of what causes these cultural expectations to exist. Socialization theories also have the weakness of being unable to explain vari-ations or social change; if this model were correct, it would have been impossible for the feminist movement to arise and protest sexual discrimination.

What is needed is a comparative and structural theory of different patterns of sexual inequality. Feminist issues are essentially issues within stratification theory, although they add a new dimension or application to that theory. Sexual stratifica-tion is especially complex, because it involves virtually all the dimensions of stratif-iction, plus some of its own. It concerns the unequal distribution between males and females of power, wealth, and prestige. But the status-group dimension is dif-ficult, because males and females generally associate intimately in the same commu-nities, especially the household and family (in addition to sometimes having some group associations of their own). Sexual relationships, as well as ties of descent resulting from these, make male and female status groups merge. The problem of a theory of sexual stratification is to deal both with this merged structure (an extreme from of "fraternization with the enemy") and with the internal structure of male–female status and power regarding sexual and reproductive matters and within the family and sociable sphere.[15]

Without understanding the social organization of sexual behavior, we cannot explain the patterns of male-female stratification. In any case, the term *gender* is not as "sex-neutral" as we might think. Its etymological roots are Latin *genus* and Greek *genos*, meaning race, breed, kin, or kind (ultimately from *gen*, beget); and it includes such cognates as engender, genital, progeny, and genealogy. Thus *gender* is full of biological connotations; in fact, etymologically more so than *sex*, which comes from the Latin *secus*, a division (from *secare*, to cut or divide).

[15] I do not mean to dismiss the individual, social psychological level. Cultural differences among men and women, and cultural styles involved in their interaction, certainly do exist; they are just not an adequate basis for explaining the entire structure of sexual stratification. Part of any theory of stratification is its consequences for the outlooks and behaviors of individuals in different positions, that is, a theory of class cultures. This is treated generally in Chapter 6 as an application of microsociology. I would suggest that these same microprocesses, applied to the particular historical circumstances of males and females, also explain what is distinctive about sexual cultures.

ECONOMIC-MARXIAN THEORIES

The oldest lineage of theories for explaining sexual stratification is Marxian. To be more precise, we should say *Engelsian,* since it was Friedrich Engels (1884/1972) who published, after Marx's death,[16] a theory which relates sexual inequality, as well as erotic behavior itself, to strucutral changes in the economy across world history. There are archaic evolutionary and anthropological assumptions in this theory, which make its details no longer relevant. But the general theme—that economic structure determines sexual stratification—has been developed in several modern versions. One line of argument (Sokoloff, 1980; Hartmann, 1981) points out that housewives— the most common female role—are misleadingly classified as "out of the labor force." Instead, they provide hidden, unpaid, domestic work which serves a crucial function for capitalism in reproducing the labor force by feeding, clothing, and caring for husbands, as well as bringing up the next generation of workers. The inference is drawn that the sex-role segregation of women is a function of the capitalist system, which it serves to uphold. Nevertheless, this is not a sufficient *explanation* of why this arrangement exists. Sexual inequality did not begin in capitalist societies; there are versions of it in many tribal societies (especially those with a "warrior complex"—see footnote 22), and some of the most extreme sexual inequality can be found in medieval agrarian societies (Blumberg, 1978, 1984). And sexual inequality has not disappeared, or even much diminished, in socialist societies. For this reason, capitalism cannot be taken as the cause of sexual inequality. Feminist theorists, recognizing this, have argued that there is a separate cause, the system of "patriarchy" or "patriarchal domination" (Mitchell 1971). This does not provide an explanatory theory either, however, but merely restates the question under a different name. What we wish to know is: what conditions produce greater or lesser amounts of male domination? And do any conditions produce female domination or equality?

A more useful line of analysis investigates the actual variations in the positions of women in different societies. Because of the availability of compilations of anthropological studies, there is a tendency to make comparison only across the tribal level (for example, Sanday, 1981; Sacks, 1979), though some studies have ranged more widely (Chafetz, 1984), and some analyze differences among women within industrial society (Huber and Spitze, 1983). These theories tend to have in common the premise that sexual stratification reflects the relative access of females and males to economic resources. The most sophisticated of these theories is that of Blumberg (1984), illustrated in Figure 5-4.

The crucial feature in this model is women's economic power—essentially, their income and their possession of property. The more economic power women have, the more freedom they have in their personal lives. Where women have relatively high economic power, they have more choice over their own marriage partners; over their freedom of divorce, and of premarital (and even sometimes extramarital) sex; and over their ability to control their own fertility (which usually means limiting the number of children). Economic power also brings women authority within the

---

[16] See Collins, 1985: 56–62, 117–18) for a discussion of who should get the credit for this theory. In general, there is a tendency to overstate the importance of Marx and ignore the contributions of Engels.

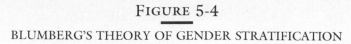

FIGURE 5-4

BLUMBERG'S THEORY OF GENDER STRATIFICATION

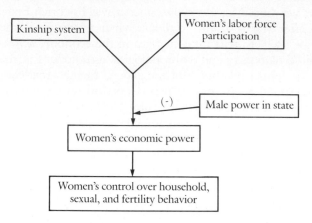

household and sometimes (as in horticultural tribes) local political power. When women have low economic power and depend heavily or exclusively on their husbands or fathers for a living, men control women's sexuality and fertility. Usually women become baby-producing machines, undergoing repeated childbirths; and there are tight male constraints on female sexuality, demanding virginity outside of marriage (for females, but with a double standard allowing permissiveness for males). Under these condition women have low authority in the household; they lack all outside political participation and power; and there is a higher level of physical oppression in the form of wife beating. Blumberg cites empirical evidence to show all these consequences of high or low economic power, from both tribal, agrarian, and industrial societies. Modern evidence (for example, Huber and Spitze, 1983) bears out the importance of these factors, usually in terms of women's income relative to their husbands'.

It is still to be explained why women may have high or low economic power. Blumberg proposes a series of factors. The *kinship system* is one ultimate condition. Where women are able to inherit property, their economic power is higher than in a kinship system in which inheritance is strictly through the male line; thus matrilineal systems favor women's economic power more than patrilineal systems. Another factor of kinship systems is whether women live with their own kin (*matrilocality:* the husband visits or comes to live with his wife's family) or women move to their husband's family household or community *(patrilocality)*. Matrilocal systems enhance a wife's power, since she has her own male relatives around to protect her; patrilocal systems leave a women isolated from allies and reduce her power. This helps account for the extremely subservient position of women in such patrilocal (and patrilineal) societies as medieval China or India.

Labor conditions are a second set of factors. In societies where women's work provides the main part of economic subsistence, women's economic (and hence social) position is higher. Thus in many hunting-and-gathering tribes, where women provide most of the staple food supply through gathering (as compared to the more episodic food supplied from men's hunting), women have relatively favorable positions. Their position is also favorable in primitive horticultural tribes, where women usually plant and harvest the crops. At the opposite extreme, women's position is lowest in agrarian societies, where agriculture has been taken over by men doing the heavy work of plow culture, and in pastoral societies, where herding is men's work. In these societies, women tend to be excluded from the sphere of basic economic production and become low-status and subservient domestic workers.[17] In industrial and agrarian societies, women may sometimes enter the labor force in greater numbers, while at other times they are largely excluded or kept in menial jobs. The difference, Blumberg proposes, is the *surplus of male or female labor*. When there is a shortage of men, women will be recruited to do formerly male work (as in factories during World War I and II). When there is a surplus of male labor, women are forced out of these jobs and into the domestic sphere.

Finally, Blumberg points out that these economic conditions can be overridden by sheer political power. Although women sometimes (as in some tribal societies) are active in local political associations, men usually control the larger, military-based state. Hence, the state can intervene to force women into the domestic sphere by prohibiting their economic participation or their ownership of property (as happened, for example, when European colonial powers gained control of African horticultural societies which had formerly allowed a broad economic and social role for women).

This theory is an attractive one, but it has certain weaknesses. The theory is meant to explain sexual stratification, but it has to assume that sexual stratification already exists at several places in the model in order to explain what happens next. It states that the male-dominated military state can override women's economic power; but why is the state male-dominated? It proposes that a surplus of women's labor allows women to enter male occupations, while a suplus of male labor drives women out. This assumes, again, that males have precedence in the more desirable positions—a factor which needs to be explained. It also shows that when women's work involves the crucial economic activities of the society, women have more economic power; but why does work become stereotyped into "women's work" and "men's work" in the first place?[18]

Finally, there is the factor of matrilineal and patrilineal inheritance, and of matrilocal-patrilocal residence. These kinship variations are undoubtedly important, but

[17] In agrarian societies, women are often engaged in a different form of economic production, especially spinning and weaving cloth, a major household industry. However, women in this kind of household production usually do not retain control of their economic property, but produce for the males who control them. Women household workers were thus probably the first form of exploited labor in a quasi-Marxian sense, although they were not the first in capitalist societies.

[18] Blumberg and others have proposed that a primary determinant of women's work is whether it is compatible with breast-feeding and child-care responsbilities. The argument here is based primarily on tribal and especially hunting-and-gathering societies. This is not a full explanation, since it is possible, hypothetically, that if women were powerful, they would limit their child bearing or assign child rearing to a special class (which could include women wet nurses for young children). The model is especially weak in explaining why there are sexual stereotypes of jobs in industrial societies, where the image of women carrying their babies to work in the fields is no longer applicable. We might well suppose there is a political or other stratification process which determines the sex stereotyping of jobs and that compatibility with childrearing emerges as a subsequent rationalization.

they themselves need to be explained. It is possible that they are themselves the product of the system of sexual stratification. We may also question whether this part of the theory has much relevance to industrial societies, where households are generally bilateral (inheritance on both sides) and neolocal (the couple move away to live on their own). If we followed only this line of argument, we would have to conclude that the industrial family system eliminates the main factors which were ultimately responsible for either male or female power. Hence, we have to invoke other factors to explain the continued existence of sexual stratification.[19]

A THEORY OF SEXUAL POLITICS

If sexual stratification is a version of stratification in general, the more abstract principles of stratification theory should apply to it. We have already seen that this is a complex issue, involving the dimensions of economic wealth, political power, and the organization of status communities. Status communities are internally stratified for both males and females, yet intimately held together by sexuality itself. The general approaches of Lenski, Weber, and Turner nevertheless give us some leads. We may expect that the distribution of power is going to be a major determining factor (see Figure 5-5). Furthermore, since power in many societies is organized at the family and household level, we may expect family politics to affect the positions of men and women. Finally, since a crucial feature of politics is alliances, we may expect that sexual relationships enter into it to the extent that sex is a basis of alliances.

I have proposed (Collins, 1971, 1975: 225–59, 1986: 267–322) a comparative theory of sexual stratification, in which political factors play a crucial role. A basic premise is that male military force has been a crucial resource in sexual stratification. This is based on the generalization that men are on the average (but with individual exceptions) larger and stronger than women and hence have usually been able to monopolize fighting.[20] The effect of this, however, is not a constant but a variable; the theory is *not* proposing that "(belligerent) biology is destiny." Male military monopoly is a variable because the organization of warfare has itself varied among societies. In some societies, warfare has been scattered and inconsequential for strat-

---

[19]There are some similar problems in another comparative theory (Guttentag and Secord, 1983), which focuses on the sex ratio as the main determinant of sexual stratification. Where there are more men than women, it is proposed, women are highly valued, hence men control them tightly as wives and mothers. Virginity is prized and sexual morality is stressed. Women do gain some countervailing power because their favored market position allows them to choose among men for their husbands. Where there are more women then men, on the other hand, sexual controls become lax, divorce is allowed, and women cannot achieve economic mobility through marriage so they go into the labor force (including becoming prostitutes). Although the data demonstrate that the sex ratio does have these effects, it is not a sufficient basis for a general theory of sex stratification. The model assumes that men control the occupational sphere, instead of explaining why this is the case. Also, it is limited to the cases in which women's value (in the eyes of men) is only as wives and mothers. The model explains different versions of women's position in male-dominated societies, rather than when and how male domination exists.

[20]There are some variations here which would repay study. There is evidence, for instance, of women warriors in the period of Viking migrations, especially in Iceland. See Blumberg (1984) for a suggestion regarding myths of "Amazon" societies.

ification; in others, it has turned the household itself into an armed fortress; in still others, it has been monopolized by a professional army and police force, disarming the civilian male population. These produce important variations in sexual relationships. The general model is represented in Figure 5-5.

The type of economic production determines the extent to which a society has property and permanent territories or settlements. Where these exist, along with other geopolitical pressures, warfare becomes important (whether as raiding or conquest of other societies or as defense against them). When warfare is important and when politics is organized around kinship groups, marriage politics is emphasized for making alliances. This, in turn, motivates males to control females as sexual property whom they can use for exchanges with other groups. When women are controlled in this way, males and females have distinctive cultures and are allocated different work roles. High status in such a society goes to families which most strongly control females, especially in their sexual behavior. There is another effect of kinship structure as well: the type of household and kinship system determines the extent to which women are subject to organized male force in their household; and this also affects the sexual property and sexual status situation.

Evidence for this theory is drawn from comparing these factors across the range of human societies, generally following Lenski's categories. Military structure in low-technology tribal societies (especially hunting-and-gathering tribes) is usually unimportant. All males are armed but there is no state and little property, and permanent

FIGURE 5-5

COLLINS' POLITICAL THEORY OF SEXUAL STRATIFICATION

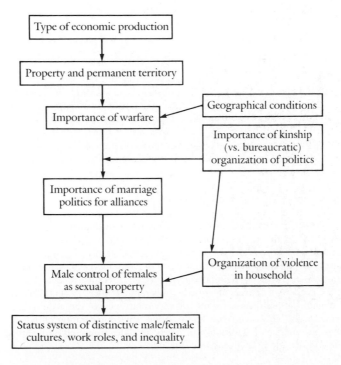

conquests of territory are rare. Economic stratification is low, since these societies exist near the subsistence level. Marriage politics is accordingly of little importance for alliances. There is little reason, then, for anyone to attempt to control sexuality, and sexual relationships tend to be relatively unrestricted.[21]

In typical horticultural societies, there is no permanent state, but males of particular kinship groups tend to be organized as bands of warriors. This makes marriage politics important for alliances; but the situation is mitigated by the fact that economic stratification is modest and all males are armed; hence there is no division between social classes. In these societies, male and female work spheres tend to be sharply divided. The ideology of sexual division may be extended to the whole cosmos, with everything classified as either male or female, supported by barriers in the form of beliefs about magical pollutions caused by entering the sphere of the wrong sex. Sexual behavior itself tends to be fenced around with elaborate taboos regarding menstruation, intercourse, and childbirth. (See Paige and Paige, 1981, for examples, and a theory of these sexual rituals as forms of communication about political alliances.) These are the types of societies in which women produce much of the economic subsistence by their gardening. The men often live in an exploitative relationship with the women; sometimes this is reflected in terroristic religious beliefs and an emotional atmosphere of hostility (which may be manifested in severe physical abuse of women, female infanticide, and wife-raiding).[22] Horticultural societies are not uniformly of this sort, however; in some (as in isolated Pacific island societies), there is little external military threat, and the generally demilitarized situation favors the freedom of women, whose position is enhanced by their economic resources (as in Blumberg's theory).[23]

In agrarian societies, sexual stratification reaches its peak. Class stratification now appears in an extreme form; the economic surplus is fairly large, but it is appropriated by a military aristocracy. The male population now becomes divided into an upper class, which usually monopolizes the bearing of arms, and an oppressed peas-

---

[21] The emphasis of the theory is on the causal variables in Figure 5-5, not on the "stages" or types of societies (hunting-and-gathering, horticultural, and so forth). The latter are important only insofar as they affect these variables. Examined in more detail, we can find variations within any of these types. Hunting-and-gathering tribes of the Australian desert, for example, placed relatively strong emphasis on military feuds and alliances, and hence had a very elaborate system of marriage politics; male-female roles were accordingly rather sharply distinguished, and a complex system of domination by older males existed (Elkin, 1979). Johnson and Hendrix (1982) provide a partial test of the theory, but restricted their study to comparisons among tribal societies. They find patrilineal (versus matrilineal) and patrilocal (versus matrilocal) kinship structures to be the most important determinant of male dominance over sexual behavior; the degree of stratification and political complexity of the society had significant but weaker effects. This analysis did not operationalize the key political variables, the importance of warfare and of marriage politics, nor the effect of these upon kinship structrure.

[22] Murphy (1959) refers to this as "the male supremicist complex." See also Harris (1974: 70–93). It might also be called an almost overt "war between the sexes," thinly disguised by religious ideology.

[23] In some instances, warfare has enhanced the position of (some) women. When men are away much of the time fighting distant wars (rather than fighting locally), women tend to become the home base around which the property system is organized (Ember and Ember, 1971). When there is a stalemate in the power struggle among males, women of important lineages can acquire independent political power as intermediaries. This occurred in the Iroquois war confederation, in which men put women in a position to veto the rise of ambitious war chiefs, in order to preserve equality among the (male) members of the confederation (Collins, 1986: 294–96).

antry or slave population, which does the work. This shifts the nature of marriage politics and the position of women. Since only the upper class now is politically active, marriage politics is important only for upper-class family alliances. For this group, marriage politics is very important indeed, since the state itself consists of nothing more than a network of families and households owing allegiance to superior lords and connected by dynastic marriages. Here women are treated as bargaining tokens to bring advantageous marriages, and their sexual behavior is rigidly controlled to enhance their value as brides. This is where the dual sexual standard prevails, since dominant upper-class men can accumulate many women (in the form of slaves, harems, or concubines), while women are controlled as sexual property to be exchanged by men.

In the lower classes, on the other hand, the men are disarmed and reduced to powerless laborers. Marriage alliances are irrelevant for them; sometimes, in fact, they may be unable to marry at all (or, in the case of slaves, sexual relationships may be enforced breeding, as on the Roman slave plantations; Weber, 1909; Patterson, 1982). While women of the upper classes are pampered but enclosed as sexual objects, women of the lower classes are relatively free because they are used as workers, especially as domestic servants for the higher classes. Lower-class women are considered to have no sexual honor and are subject to sexual exploitation by men of the higher classes.

This is an oversimplified picture of sexual stratification in agrarian societies. A fuller picture would add the members of intermediate levels, such as merchants and wealthier peasants; these groups typically tried to model themselves after the status system of the aristocracy and thus to impose rigid controls over women's sexual behavior, including severe penalities for loss of virginity. Another simplification in the ideal type is that it gives only the static pattern (as found, for example, in medieval India, China, or the Islamic states). But there are elements of change to be found in various periods of agrarian societies. In Republican Rome, in medieval Europe and in medieval Japan (the Heian period; Morris 1964), women of the aristocracy were, during certain periods, able to manipulate marriage politics to gain a considerable increase in their personal status, as well as in their sexual freedom (Collins, 1986: 297–320). Some of these developments were episodic and disappeared as political conditions shifted (as in Rome and Japan), but some (notably the European aristocratic idealization of courtly love and of the "lady") left an effect which served as an opening wedge for subsequent improvements in the status of women generally.

There is a sharp change in the position of women with the coming of "modern" societies: middle class women in general began to be idealized; the belief spread that women were morally superior to men (which was the reverse of the traditional belief, when men virtually monopolized religious life); and polite standards of deference in front of women (being on one's best manners) emerged as the mark of high social status. At the same time, this new "Victorian" role for women left severe liabilities in the economic sphere: women were supposed to be beloved wives and mothers, idealized and nurturant, but protected from the "rougher" aspects of masculine life.

This change can be explained by the political theory (see Figure 5-6). The characteristic structure of the agrarian state was the feudal-patrimonial household, a kind

FIGURE 5-6

SEXUAL STRATIFICATION AND THE PRIVATE MARRIAGE MARKET

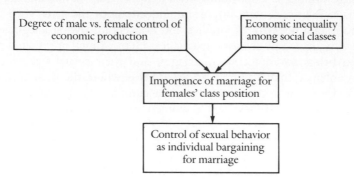

of armed castle or fortress in which the aristocracy dominated by the direct rule of armed guards. This immediate presence of male force is what made male dominance so powerful. The emergence of the bureaucratic state disarmed the household (the kings literally tore down the castles of the nobility and disarmed their followers), substituting a professional army of specialists and placing the enforcement of law and order in the hands of the police. This had two consequences for sexual stratification. One was that women were less subject to immediate male violence; where previously women were more or less casually available to sexual assault unless guarded by their own families, there now was an impersonal police and court system which could protect them (even, hypothetically, against the use of force by their own husbands, although such developments were slow in coming).

The other consequence was that marriage politics ceased to be important. Bureaucratic careers and party politics took the place of dynastic alliances. It was no longer important for families to control the marriages of their children. An individual marriage market appeared instead of the older political negotiations. But, though individual men and women could find their own mates (and an accompanying ideal of marrying for love arose with this situation), they did this with unequal resources: males controlled the economic positions, and hence a woman's position in a class-stratified society depended on the status of the husband she found. The "Victorian" sexual morality was the result of this situation, since it was in women's interest to restrict sex to marriage. A major source of the sharply differentiated sexual cultures of males and females that have prevailed in industrial societies until recently is the way that the two sexes bargain with quite different resources on the individual marriage market.

A final variant (as far as historical experience goes until now) has occurred as some women have been able to acquire economically remunerative careers of their own. This has reduced their dependence on husbands for their economic and status position. A result has been not only increased autonomy in the domestic sphere, but greater sexual freedom and a breaking down of the "Victorian" sexual morality which rigidly controlled sexuality before. (This is in keeping with the latter part of Blumberg's theory, as well.) Change in the economic independence of women is the major factor behind the "sexual revolution" of recent years.

This political theory of sexual stratification is incomplete in some important respects. It is based on historical comparisons across the range of societies. But a crucial issue concerns change within the most recent type of society. Once the bureaucratic state appears, there is a shift to a private marriage market. But what determines whether this will be a "Victorian" marriage market, with women honored but only insofar as they make good marriages into the higher social classes through controlling sexual morality and idealizing their roles as housewives and mothers, or a "liberated" marriage market, in which men and women with their own careers bargain freely for emotional and sexual ties which they can institute or break off at personal preference? Political changes in the past have determined sexual stratification by affecting marriage politics; but, when we are in a society in which marriage no longer has political significance, there still can be major variations in the economic aspect of sexual stratification. The question arises, what determines women's economic resources, which all theories agree is the crucial factor affecting current sexual stratification?

Unfortunately, on this point all theories are too closely oriented to conditions emerging from comparisons among tribal and other historical societies to give us much lead in predicting how much economic discrimination there will be in an industrial society and when breakthroughs occur. A general orientation from a political theory of stratification, nevertheless, suggests some leads. The movement of women into hitherto male-stereotyped jobs has occurred most noticeably at certain times coinciding with upsurges of feminist politics. The initial breakthrough of a few token women into the professions came in the late nineteenth century, a time when women were first admitted to previously all-male universities; this coincided with the movement for women's votes. The second wave of feminism was in the 1970s, as a spin-off of the participation of women in the radical Civil Rights and antiwar movements on college campuses in the 1960s; this resulted in another wave of token integration of women into high-status occupations, and the sexual desegregation of medical, law, and other professional schools. After the initial successes, both waves of feminism tended to settle down, with the overall level of economic inequality between males and females still very great. In theoretical terms, the crucial point may be that political movements are central, both in cracking the sex stereotyping of particular jobs, and in mobilizing women to change career aspirations.

Another theoretical lead is that the structure of occupations themselves is shaped by social factors. What are called the "high status professions," for example, are occupations that have an internal political structure of self-governance through professional associations; these associations act to provide "closure" or "monopolization of opportunities" by setting their own credentials or tests for admittance. They become truly "strong" professions by getting the state to back up their licensing monopoly by legal sanction (as in the law prohibiting the practice of medicine without a license). Politics does not directly monopolize occupations for males, however; but something like this "closed" structure exists in the way the medical profession is internally segregated into licensed segments: nurses (who are largely female) and doctors (who are largely male). Similarly, the biggest sector of female employment is secretarial work, an occupation which became exclusively female around the turn of the twentieth century, with commensurately low pay. Why segregated or "closed" occupational structures of this sort exist remains a challenge for stratification theory and is a crucial piece in the puzzle of modern sexual stratification.

EDUCATIONAL CREDENTIAL STRATIFICATION

The most obvious form of stratification in the industrial societies of the late twentieth century is by education. Public policy for equalizing opportunity has centered on access to education. Much of the quantitative research on stratification has looked at the various factors determining individuals' access to schooling. Studies from the United States and other industrial states show that education is a stronger predictor of occupational attainment than parents' social-class background. These facts have often been interpreted to mean that we have arrived at the age of meritocracy and that, while stratification still exists, it depends on the individuals' skills and achievements rather than on their inherited backgrounds.

But there are a number of reasons to doubt this interpretation. Although education is the strongest known predictor of occupational attainment, it is not an overwhelmingly strong predictor. Education and parents' social class together explain only about 40 percent of the variance in occupational levels (Blau and Duncan, 1967); the majority of occupational ranking is apparently due to something we have not measured. Moreover, although there has been a massive expansion of schooling in virtually every society (and especially in the United States, where 75 percent of the population now graduates from high school and nearly half attends college), the overall amount of social mobility in society has remained constant throughout this century (Blau and Duncan, 1967; Boudon, 1973; Featherman and Hauser, 1978). Expanding the amount of education has not reduced inequality, either of opportunity or of the differences in power, wealth, and prestige among the occupations themselves. The United States is as fully stratified as it was 60 years ago, when a much smaller percentage of the population was being educated.

This persistence of stratification is conventionally explained by two premises: that the skill levels for jobs have risen due to changing technological demands of modernity, and, as a result, individuals have to get more and more education to keep up with skill requirements. This may be called the *technocratic* explanation. The other premise, which is less fashionable but is sometimes advanced in order to explain why the rate of social mobility has not changed despite the expansion of the role of "meritocratic" education, is that individuals differ in their genetically determined intelligence. Hence the lower class cannot do well in school and ends up with the occupational positions (or the unemployment) it deserves. Similarly, poverty in the black lower class, it is alleged, is due to genetic inferiority (Jensen, 1969; Herrnstein, 1973. This may be called the *genetic* explanation.

The genetic explanation is not hard to refute. It does not account for the fact that women have generally lower occupational and income levels than men, as there are no differences in average intelligence. Although blacks in the United States score an average of 15 points lower on IQ tests than whites, there is no evidence that this is a hereditary difference (Taylor, 1980). Cultural learning accounts for much of the individual differences in IQ scores; the best estimates, from studies of identical twins who are reared in genuinely different environments, are that most IQ is environmental, and no more than 17 percent is hereditary (Taylor, 1980: 75–111). Moreover, IQ scores mainly seem to test school skills. They are best at predicting educational achievement, but have little value in predicting the success of individuals after leaving school (Collins, 1979: 28–29). IQ scores, like education itself, seem to be an item of modern culture.

The *technocratic* theory is independent of the genetic theory, and could be true even if the genetic explanation is false. However, the evidence does not favor the technocratic theory either. This theory proposes that (1) the skill requirements of jobs have risen continuously during the twentieth century and the jobs with the highest educational requirements are those with the highest skill requirements; (2) schools provide the needed technical skills, and (3) by implication, societies with the highest levels of education in their population will have the highest economic growth rates. Evidence on all three points is largely negative (Collins, 1979: 1–48).

First, the educational levels that employers ask in order to hire an individual for a job have risen enormously in the twentieth century. Sixty years ago a high school diploma was rare enough to be sufficient qualification for most management jobs. Today, entry jobs at management level demand a Master's degree in business admin- istration. But this does not tell us what the skill requirements actually are. To be clear, let us call these *credential requirements*. Our question is, do credentials reflect skills? Surprisingly enough, it has not been easy to measure just what the skill re- quirements of jobs actually are. Requirements are often vague and estimates are subjective. If we go to organizational studies, which have actually observed the way people act on the job, we see that employees actively attempt to control the way they are evaluated and to protect themselves from pressure to maximize effort and output. The jobs whose outputs are easiest to measure are those with standardized physical products, such as the number of pieces turned out in factory work; but these are the jobs with relatively low skill levels.[24] Complex, innovative work, and management-professional work, typically involve uncertainties or interpersonal ne- gotiations, and the skills involved in this are not easily measured. The higher the level of the job, or the more complex the organization, the more difficult it is to measure output, since the failure or success of the organization is due to the inter- action of many individuals and environmental contingencies and the contribution of a particular person is inextricably mixed with that of the organization as a whole.

For these reasons, there is no clear evidence that skill requirements have changed during the twentieth century. Popular arguments have been made on both sides that unskilled jobs are disappearing, to be replaced by high-skilled jobs. On the other hand, it is alleged that the trend of mechanization and bureaucratization is toward "de-skilling," eliminating the skilled crafts and other jobs with personal initiative and replacing them with mindlessly repetitive work. (Braverman, 1974). Assertions of what the skill requirements of jobs are is largely the result of organizational pol- itics; jobs are manipulated by the people in them in order to either maximize control of subordinates or to evade control from those above. There has been a shift to white-collar jobs and away from a preponderance of manual labor, but it is not clear that this means a shift towards higher skill requirements; it may only mean that more jobs are involved in the "soft" sector of organzational politics and bureaucratic complexities, where actual "skills" and "output" are even more difficult to assess.

---

[24] Sales is another area where output can be precisely measured. Here neither educational level nor skills measures predict the effectiveness of a salesperson working on commission; the major factor is simply the motivation to make money (Collins, 1969).

Since employers themselves cannot know whether the skill levels have actually shifted, their use of rising educational requirements may be based on a social myth.[25]

If this is the situation, how then do individuals make their careers in organizations? They are supposed to be rewarded for their "achievements," but how can this happen if achievements are so difficult to measure accurately? Studies of organizational careers (Collins, 1979: 29–31; Kanter, 1977) show that, among other factors, management careers are largely a matter of organizational politics, of getting into a "fast track" where visibility is high, and of becoming a member of the network or team which gains organizational power and rises together. There is also a matter of luck in the sense that upward movement occurs at times when there are many vacancies, either because new positions are created or because there are relatively few applicants; while movement is blocked when the preceding cohort is large and has filled the vacancies (Grandjean 1981). Business careers are favorable when the economy as a whole is expanding; whereas individual careers suffer when their organizations do poorly in a decline in the business cycle.[26]

Second, evidence also largely contradicts the claim that schools provide needed technical skills. Studies of what is learned in school show that the content of the curriculum is largely nontechnical; that students generally cram for exams and do not remember material long afterwards (Becker, Geer, and Hughes, 1968); and that school experience (at least in American schools) is largely social rather than intellectual. Studies of the classroom show that it is an organizational environment just like any other. As any teacher (or student) knows, the major concern is maintaining (or evading) control. In American schools, cheating on examinations is widespread (Gallup, 1979; California State Department of Education, 1986). In short, students (and teachers) act just like workers and managers in organizations, attempting to control how hard they must perform and manipulating the standards by which they are assessed.

If this is the case, then where do people learn how to perform jobs? The evidence is strong that most job skills are learned on the job itself (Collins, 1979: 16–17). This is true especially of the highly technical jobs involving machinery: people learn to be mechanics by working with machines, not by taking classes (even classes in a trade school).[27] Even in the high-prestige professions, such as medicine and

---

[25] Some studies (Berg, 1970) have nevertheless put a numerical value on the skill levels of various jobs or measured the ratings of performance. These studies have found that individuals with high levels of education usually do not perform better than those with moderate (or sometimes even low) level of education, and that in the U.S. economy as a whole shifts toward "higher skilled" (that is, white-collar) jobs have not happened as fast as the rise in educational levels. If we take these measures of "skills" as accurate, they imply that such changes in "skill requirements" have not been the factor which has driven up the level of educational credentials.

[26] This carries over into the public sector as well. Academic careers, for instance, were favorable in the 1960s, when the economy was booming and universities were expanding; in the 1970s, economic depression and the end of university growth meant fewer positions were available at the same time that an expanded cohort of new Ph.D.'s, produced in the expansion of the previous period, was competing for them.

[27] It would appear that the bureaucratic setting of schools, even trade schools, displaces attention from learning itself into extraneous issues of paperwork and control. On-the-job experience avoids this extra layer of activities while providing contact with those networks that facilitate use of the skills. For this reason, the success rate of on-the-job training is much higher than that of formal school training for

law, the actual performance skills are learned by practice, rather than in professional school. What is learned in the classroom is background material—in fundamental science or in legal theory—while the actual skills of how to diagnose patients or operate in court are learned once the professional begins to practice. Probably for this reason, grades in professional school do not predict professional success. This is characteristic of grades in general: they are highly predictive of how well a student will do at the next level of schooling, but do not distinguish between the success or failure of the individual after finally finishing school. Grades, like IQ tests, appear to be bureaucratic assessment devices, useful within school organizations, but not transferable to other organizational environments (Collins, 1979: 17–21).

Third, if education were providing the necessary technical skills, we would expect that the society with the highest level of education would have the greatest economic growth rate. Comparative evidence shows that this is largely untrue.[28]

This evidence does not fit well with the image that we live in a "high-tech" society characterized by scientific advances and constant introduction of new technology, such as computers. This is because a high level of technological innovation does not necessarily require great technical expertise in the population.[29] Most innovation is carried out by a small number of experts. Furthermore, the very fact that something is technically innovative means that it could not have been taught, since the skill itself had to be invented. This is illustrated by the development of the personal computer in the 1970s by college drop-outs (who nevertheless happened to have good on-the-job training from working in the electronics industry). Although the U.S. educational system is ineffective in teaching widespread technical skills,[30] the economy as a whole is still a world leader in technological innovation. This is because the widespread availability of machinery and other technological equipment (such as electronics) fosters the crucial input—informal and on-the-job training. Additionally, although the average levels of American education are mediocre, the system is so large that at its very highest level universities and technical laboratories contain an adequate minority of the skilled experts needed to keep the society going. The fallacy of the technocratic theory is to assume that educational

---

manual skills. Informal training in which individuals merely pick up the skill by being around others who can do it (the way most Americans learn to repair a car) is actually superior to formally established training programs, even on the work site (Collins, 1979: 16–17).

[28] Collins, 1979: 14–15; though see also Walters and Rubinson, 1983. There is only one level at which educational expansion seems to consistently make a difference for subsequent economic growth: when a society starts from virtually no educational system at all and builds an elementary school system. This is probably because the shift from an illiterate to a literate population does provide skills which allow the creation of modern commercial, industrial, and administrative organizations. The importance of education for economic growth, then, is not at the levels of high schools or universities, which is where most of the growth in education has occurred in the richer societies of the twentieth century. The contribution of education to economic takeoff in the United States is, for the most part, more than a century in the past.

[29] Surveys indicate that scientific and technical knowledge in the U.S. population is relatively low. (Peterson, 1986) This is in keeping with evidence that achievement test scores of American students are also low and actually dropped during the most massive period of educational expansion in the 1960s (Collins, 1979: 198).

[30] American students score near the lowest in the industrial world on mathematics and science (Stevenson, Lee, and Stigler, 1986).

credentials in general represent technical skills or technical demands. The crucial input of advanced technology into our society comes from a small educated group, plus a larger group (yet probably still a minority) of informally trained practitioners.

CREDENTIAL INFLATION AS STATUS COMPETITION

How then can we explain the massive expansion in schooling in the twentieth century and the concomitant rise in educational credential requirements for jobs? I have presented a theory (Collins, 1979) based on education as status competition. Education (for the most part) does not provide technical skills, although it may be mistakenly interpreted as doing so. This appears to be a convenient myth, a legitimating ideology. Education has become the offically accepted criterion for inequality. It is able to fill this role because education has traditionally been a mark of cultural status. The earliest schools in ancient and medieval agrarian states were largely for priests or for the cultivated gentleman (Collins, 1977). (Women were generally excluded from education in these male-dominated societies.) The Hindu or Islamic school taught students to memorize the holy scriptures; the ancient Greeks became cultivated by learning to recite Homer's classic poems; the medieval Chinese, by learning elegant calligraphy. Although the literacy provided by these schools might be of use in administrative jobs, the official purpose of education was generally opposed to merely technical or practical uses; this was incompatible with the status ideal of the educated man, who was supposed to show off his religious qualifications or his artistic cultivation (Weber 1922 / 1968: 1000).

In the twentieth century, two things have changed. Education is no longer officially legitimated as religiousity or personal cultivation; instead, the legitimating ideology has shifted toward the technocratic one in which education is preparation for skilled jobs. However, this is a change only in the content of the legitimating ideology; education remains a mark of high cultural status, even though we now claim that status is supposed to imply occupational skill. The other change is the sheer number of persons who are educated. This has grown from a tiny minority to systems in which (in some places, such as the United States and the USSR) a very high proportion of the population spends many years in schooling.

This expansion in numbers, as we have seen, is not due to the demand for technical skills coming from the economy. It is instead a political process: the expansion of schools has been due to pressures from the population to expand opportunities to acquire status. The United States has gone the farthest in this direction for several reasons: it lacked a centralized state control over education, as well as an officially established church, so that decisions to found new schools and universities could be made locally rather than by a central authority. Competition between different religious sects, ethnic groups, and local governments has resulted in educational expansion; the combination of decentralized democracy and a market for status credentials has made education into a kind of business, selling opportunities for educational degrees. While the possession of education was once confined to relatively upper-status groups (clergy and some of the leisured gentry), the creation of this competitive market made the whole system dynamic. As the older educational credentials became more widespread, they no longer carried the same connotation of elite status. Job requirements began to shift, requiring higher credentials since more educated people were available for jobs. The high school diploma, at the turn of the twentieth century a mark of substantial middle-class status, had become so common by mid-century that it was becoming a minimal requirement for many working-class jobs. College degrees were no longer elite and advanced professional degrees have thus proliferated. This may be described as a process of "credential inflation," analogous to the way a monetary currency loses its value if more of it is printed (Collins, 1979).[31]

In the process, the contents of the culture which is taught in schools has changed. The old religious and humanistic culture of the schools has largely been superseded. Ideologically, the new mass school is interpreted as inculcating technical skills, although as we have seen, this hardly fits the facts. It would be more accurate to say that modern mass education has largely become a system of bureaucratic formalities, filling up courses with almost arbitrary contents so that grades and test scores can be recorded, degrees collected, and students advanced through sufficient levels of credentialling to enter the job market. Modern education is thus a hodgepodge of ingredients: some scientific and technical courses, some remnants of the old status culture in the humanities, and an accretion of new subjects created within the expanded educational bureaucracy itself (one of which is sociology). For some individuals—especially those who are going to become university teachers or researchers in these subjects—very high levels of expertise are achieved, but this is largely internal to the bureaucratic school system itself. The same subjects, for most students, are merely arbitrary materials which they use to accumulate grades for degree credentials. This situation is largely responsible for the peculiar cultural tone of the late twentieth century: there is a proliferation of specialized cultures which are meaningful only to the experts within each area. The overall system is supposed to be technologically efficient and productive, although the realities of progressing through the educational bureaucracy and subsequent jobs make most people realize that as a practical matter it is not so. Periodic proposals for educational reform have a ritualistic quality, since few people are willing to openly face the way in which the system itself is based on a technocratic myth and is producing marks of cultural status whose value is purely relative, fluctuating with the sheer number of people who possess them.

This conflict theory of education is often mistakenly supposed to propose that education merely passes along the parents' social status. This is not so. It proposes

---

[31] Comparative evidence of educational expansion around the world indicates that in the late twentieth century virtually all societies, whatever their economic level, have expanded their school systems. (Ramirez and Boli-Bennett, 1982). Meyer (1977) interprets this as a process of international prestige-seeking. Education is part of the cultural image of "modernity," which all states try to emulate. Historically, much of the original foundation of public school systems was due to power-prestige rivalry of the sort treated in geopolitical theory (Chapter 4). States like France after its defeat by Germany in 1871, or England after losses in the Crimean War, instituted or reformed their public school systems in what they believed was an effort to catch up with militarily more powerful societies. This explanation does not account for the situation in the United States, however, which developed a far more massive school system than any of the European states (and generally earlier than most of them), but was not militarily threatened by a more educated society. Educational expansion in the United States requires something like my explanation in terms of decentralized competition, especially as fueled by the rivalry of multiple ethnic groups. For an analysis of the complexities of the origins of different kinds and levels of school systems (including religious schools, public schools, and universities) see Collins, 1977, 1981d.

that the educational credentialing process has become a prime basis of stratification: an individual's occupational attainment depends to a considerable degree (although not totally, as we have seen) on what degree level is achieved, *and also* on the value that such a degree has in relation to all the other degrees existing in the competitive market for status. This argument is different from that of Bourdieu and Passeron (1970 / 1977) that education reproduces the system of stratification by turning parents' economic capital into children's cultural capital, which in turn determines the next generation's economic position. This model would imply that no social mobility is possible through education, whereas we have seen that this can occur. The credential theory, rather, states that education *creates* stratification. Expansion of the educational system is driven by the competition for status, and educational credential requirements for jobs are driven by the supply of credentials in the population. The shape of the modern stratification system itself is the result of this status competition. There would be just as much inequality among positions, even if there were a maximal amount of intergenerational mobility. In fact, it is likely that the higher the mobility, the more intense the struggle for status credentials, and hence the inflation of jobs requirements would continue at an even higher rate.

THE SINECURE SOCIETY AS THE SOLUTION TO KEYNESIAN UNEMPLOYMENT

How is it possible that a society can afford a system like this? If education is not providing technical skills, then it would appear that employers are wasting their money by hiring educated workers, and that the society as a whole is wasting its money in supporting a massive school system in which the expense grows yearly as credential requirements rise and people spend more and more of their lives in school. Nevertheless, I would argue, the inflation of educational credentials is actually supported by the modern economy and even fills an underlying demand with it. That demand is for jobs and for purchasing power. The underlying problem of the modern capitalist economy is that it tends to replace workers with machines; hence there is a chronic problem of unemployment, as well as the Keynesian problem that the public's purchasing power is kept down. This is one of the sources of periodic economic depressions. Conventional economics argues that this tendency is counteracted by economic growth: as some jobs are eliminated by machine production, new jobs are created as new products and services are invented. This may be so, but nevertheless the growth of new jobs does not usually keep pace in this way with those eliminated, for the new products may be produced with even more technology-intensive equipment and less labor. Most of the creation of new jobs in the twentieth century has not been in the private industrial sector, but in public employment—government agencies and, especially, the school system itself (Collins, 1979: 194–95).

This is actually Keynes' solution to unemployment and underconsumption: the government should use its power of taxation to create new jobs. This proposal has been politically controversial, since it violates the official ideology that work should be productive. Nevertheless, this has taken place covertly. The growth of employment in the bureaucratic sector and in the school system has operated to create jobs and keep consumer demand up. Despite periodic movements of conservative politics, which advocate cutting out bureaucracy and governmental waste, this source of employment and consumer demand is built too centrally into the economy itself to be cut. There are minor shifts back and forth in government and educational budgets, but any severe cuts produce an economic downturn, which brings a swing in the other direction.[32]

The modern economy is based on creating positions so that people can have work. Analytically, we might refer to these as "sinecures," in that the role of most bureaucratic positions is not to produce any physical output, but merely to keep the system going in the Keynesian sense. At times the escalation of educational credentials proceeds so rapidly that it seems absurd, and people become cynical or alienated from the lengthening routines of the bureaucratic school system; nevertheless, the economic system cannot do without these jobs. Moreover, the expansion of educational credentials—and of the bureaucratic job-positions based on them—does not remain constant. Technological innovation and business competition to cut labor costs is continually going on; hence, the "Keynesian" need to counteract this with creation of new jobs is always present. There is probably a cyclical shape to this process over time: during periods when conservative politicians are in power, labor is especially squeezed and government budgets are cut; eventually this brings an economic downturn through lack of consumer demand, which reverses the trend and results in new sinecure creation. This in turn brings prosperity (and probably monetary inflation, too), which eventually brings a political shift to the right, bringing back the conservative politicans, and the process repeats itself.

The possessors of bureaucratic "sinecures" are not exactly doing nothing. Though their work is not productive, it nevertheless is a time-consuming activity, it is taken up with maneuvering over matters of administration, personnel management, the evaluation of credentials, and other bureaucratic career formalities. It might be described as "political labor," as opposed to the "productive labor" of the working class. These are, of course, analytical categories; the same job may involve both "productive labor" and "political labor" in varying proportions. As credential requirements have proceeded, the proportion of what is officially called "work" has shifted increasingly towards the "political labor" end. Because modern technology is extremely productive, it is able to support a large society in comparative luxury (though with some pockets of poverty), while a relatively small proportion of people are actually engaged in physically productive work.

There is every reason to believe this process will go on in the future. The next round of job-displacing machinery is already developing, with robots taking over factory work and other manual labor and computer artificial intelligence (AI) moving toward taking over clerical work. Since the latter is the major province of female employment, we can anticipate a growing crisis in the economic position of women around the end of the twentieth century. The process will not happen all at once, of course. Cost restraints will keep some robots and computers from being intro-

[32]The actual process of economic growth and stagnation is produced by many factors which are not treated here. I am focusing only on the role of educational credentialing and related job-creation, as a central feature in the modern economy. Other factors being equal, growth or contracting of the credentialed, "sinecure sector," will have the effects described here.

duced even where they could best do the job. It may be cheaper to hire unskilled janitors (projected to be a major source of employment in the future) than to buy a robot for the same job. The ownership of robots and of computers, of course, will be concentrated in the hands of those with the most wealth. Thus, we may anticipate that inequality will increase. Countervailing factors to these trends are the continuing need for employment and for consumer demand: too much job-displacement by robots and AI results in pressure for a new round of Keynesian policies. Conceivably, this might take the form of a radical political movement for state ownership and redistribution or for a shorter work week. More likely—in the United States, at least—it will follow our traditional pattern, expanding the educational credential system to take up the slack and create new jobs. This is the form that the economic class struggle takes in a credentialized society.

SUMMARY

1. Weber defined *class* as a set of individuals who share a common situation in a market. The *labor market* separates workers and employers. Some workers' groups acquire special privileges by "closure" or monopolization of opportunities. The *credit market* divides creditor and debtor classes. The *commodity market* separates consumers and sellers of goods. Different degrees of class organization and conflict can take place in these various markets; a full theory should give the conditions for each of these.

2. Weber's category of *status group* is a community who share a common lifestyle and group identity. Status groups can be based upon social classes, but also may cut across or fragment classes if organized along lines of ethnic, religious, or other culture. A *party* or *power group* is a faction specifically organized for political struggle; it may be based upon classes or status groups, or it may be autonomously organized by the structure of interests in power organizations.

3. A full theory of stratification should give the conditions for high or low inequality in six major dimensions. Lenski's theory states that the *distribution of wealth* is likely to be unequal in proportion to the economic surplus it generates beyond what is necessary to keep the population alive, since this surplus is actually distributed according to the concentration of power. Turner's more formal theory is that the concentration of wealth increases with the level of production, but decreases with the number of organizational hierarchies and differentiated subunits in a society (that is, with the organizational dispersion of power).

4. Turner's theory proposes that the *distribution of power* is more unequal when there is external military threat to the society, when production and internal conflict are high, and when there are many internal transactions in the society.

5. Turner's theory breaks status groups into three components. The *distribution of prestige* is determined by the distribution of power and wealth, plus the ideologies according to which people evaluate the importance and skill of positions. The *number of culturally distinct groups* increases with the size of the population and the differentiation of occupations, but it is diminished by the amount of intergroup mobility; it also increases with inequality in wealth and power and with discrimination against

minorities. (A full theory should also include the pattern of migration from other societies.) Finally, the amount of *ranking of cultural groups* is determined by the amount of consensus in the society over value standards, and the number of distinct groups.

6. A theory of inequality should also include an explanation of the amount of *inequality of opportunity* (social mobility) as well as of *inequality of distribution* (the propositions just summarized). Social mobility theory is considered separately in Chapter 12.

7. Economic theory of gender stratification, as proposed by Blumberg, states that women's economic power is the major determinant of their authority within the household and their personal freedom, including sexual and fertility behavior. Women's economic power, in turn, is highest where women contribute the most to economic subsistence, where the kinship system allows women to inherit their own property and when women live with their own kin rather than their husband's kin; but women's economic power is diminished to the extent that there is a nonlocal political sphere or state controlled by men. This type of theory is most applicable to tribal and agrarian societies.

8. Collins' political theory of sexual stratification proposes that warfare has been the main sphere of male advantage and hence that male domination varies with the organization of military force. The more important warfare is for a society and, where politics is organized around kinship groups, more emphasis is placed on making alliances by marriage politics. This in turn brings an emphasis on male appropriation of females as sexual property, the result being distinct male and female cultures and work roles and sexual domination. Sexual stratification in tribal societies is thus influenced by its kinship organization of politics, while in agrarian societies, sexual stratification is centered on the marriage politics of the military aristocracy. With the rise of the bureaucratic state, kinship politics largely disappears.

9. In a society ruled by the bureaucratic state, marriage bargaining is carried out privately by individuals rather than families. To the extent that males control most economic resources, and there is inequality of wealth in the society, marriage is important for a female's class position, and females control sexual behavior as a bargaining device for marriage; this in turn sharply separates male and female cultural spheres and promotes segregated occupations. Explanation is still needed for the degrees of male-female economic inequality found in modern industrial societies. Important determinants may be women's political movements and the political structuring of occupations.

10. Education stratification has been extremely important in the twentieth century. The rising level of education required for jobs, however, is not strongly determined by the technical skill content of education, since that content is typically minor; most technical skills are learned on the job; and the level of credential requirements has risen considerably in excess of changes in job contents. According to Collins' theory, the educational system has expanded because of mass competition for status; and there has been an inflation of educational credential requirements for jobs in response to the mass availability of credentials.

11. Educational credential stratification does not depend on the inheritance of class position by the superior educational opportunities and resources of children of the higher classes. It is a form of inequality of distribution, not inequality of opportunity. High levels of educational opportunity produce high levels of credential inflation and structure the inequality of job positions themselves. Credential inflation is built into the economic structure of advanced capitalist societies as a hidden form of keeping up employment and consumer demand.

PART II

MICRO THEORIES

Chapter 6

INTERACTION RITUAL

DURKHEIMIAN THEORY OF MORAL SOLIDARITY
    Religion as the Archetypal Ritual
    A Formal Model of Ritual
    Intentional and Natural Rituals
    Evidence of Rhythmic Synchronization

GOFFMAN AND INTERACTION RITUAL
    The Frontstage-backstage Model
    Everyday Interaction as Ritual

RITUAL THEORY OF CLASS CULTURES
    Two Dimensions of Stratification
    Other Two-dimensional Theories: Kemper and Douglas
    The Empirical Validity of Two-dimensional Stratification Theory
    The Power Dimension: Frontstage and Backstage Cultures
    The Network Dimension: Social Density and Diversity
    Multiple Causality and Stratification
    Douglas' Grid and Group
    Collins' Historical Typology of Ritual Cultures

CONCLUSION

SUMMARY

I*nteraction ritual theory* is the term I am using for a body of sociological theorizing not always known under that name. It refers, nevertheless, to a well-established sociological tradition, first formulated by Emile Durkheim and developed by Marcel Mauss, Erving Goffman, and others. These writers did not always state their theoretical principles succinctly and formally, and there are various interpretations of what they actually did. In this chapter I will present systematic statements of their central theoretical models.

Durkheim's work was designed to answer the fundamental question of what makes social order possible; it also explains the variations in the kinds of ideas, moral feelings, and social attachments that occur in different kinds of groups. The mechanism that produces solidarity, as well as ideas and feelings, is social ritual. Ritual is best exemplified by religion, but the same model applies to other formal and informal rituals in social life. Goffman took a major step in applying Durkheimian theory to the interaction rituals of everyday life. The next step has been to show how varying conditions in the "ritual density" of life produce cultural differences among social classes. In my own work (Collins, 1975), I have connected ritual theory to the conflict theory of stratification; we shall see that other theorizing and evidence also fits this pattern.

Interaction ritual theory provides a model which is strategically located in sociology, since it both operates on the micro level of personal interaction and connects this level to the macro structure of the larger society and its stratification. Interaction ritual theory (which I will abbreviate as IR theory) presents an alternative to exchange theory, as well as a critique of it. In chapters 10 and 11, we will see the weakness of exchange theory in its "rational choice" formulation derived from conventional economics. IR theory not only recognizes the cognitive and institutional limitations of markets as a basis for interaction, but also shows the mechanisms which produce human cognitions and which make it possible for markets to exist. There is, in short, a ritual exchange theory. This theory can be applied, in my own model of interaction ritual chains, to explain the changing flow of individual motivations and behaviors across the sequence of daily encounters. These encounters make up individual lives, as well as, in the aggregate, the structure of society itself. The IR theory thus contributes to the solution of the micro-macro problem.

DURKHEIMIAN THEORY OF MORAL SOLIDARITY

What holds society together? Durkheim (1893/1964) showed that the fundamental mechanism cannot be merely rewards that people give one another, for this type of exchange relationship presupposes the belief that others will reciprocate rewards. The idea of an initial "social contract" as put forward by Locke or Rousseau is a myth, since some "precontractual solidarity" would be necessary for any binding contract to be possible. Similarly, society cannot be held together merely by coercion (nor can contracts simply be enforced by a coercive state); this begs the question of what has brought about the prior existence of the state and of socially organized coercion. An individual cannot coerce many others alone; coercion is mainly effective when organized in groups. But this brings up again the question of what holds that group together. Again, the answer must be some form of precontractual (or precoercive) solidarity.

Durkheim's analysis is often taken as completed at this point. Parsons (1937) and others have concluded that Durkheim showed the necessary existence of social norms underlying any other form of social action. But "norms" are merely a gloss on whatever solidarity happens to exist and beg the question of what produces this solidarity. Durkheim's works, however, do not merely stop with an assertion of the functional necessity of precalculative solidarity. Durkheim also showed the mechanism by which solidarity is produced and which creates *variations* in the kinds of social feelings and ideas that will exist in different circumstances. I am suggesting that Durkheim does not give a one-sided idealist interpretation of society, in which beliefs determine social structure; he also provides a social materialist interpretation, in which the forms of physical interaction among human bodies determines moral beliefs and symbols. These components then flow in a temporal chain:

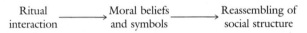

Ritual ⟶ Moral beliefs ⟶ Reassembling of
interaction   and symbols   social structure

The chain can also loop back to form a circle of social reproduction, though other inputs are also possible.

RELIGION AS THE ARCHETYPAL RITUAL

Durkheim's major presentation of the solidarity-creating mechanism is in his last work, *The Elementary Forms of the Religious Life* (1912/1954). Religion gives the clearest example of how social practices create feelings of solidarity. The fact that early societies were permeated by religious ritual and belief is also significant for Durkheim's argument; precontractual solidarity, he argued, is not only logically prior to utilitarian exchanges, but also is historically prior to them.

What is religion, considered empirically? Its fundamental characteristic, Durkheim argued, is not the type of belief it promotes, but the type of action it is. Religions vary widely in how many gods they recognize, in the nature of the gods, even in whether there are gods at all; religions include animistic cults in which spirits permeate categories of nature, as well as philosophical systems in which gods are transcended by Nirvana or an unverbalizable metaphysical Ultimate. What all religions have in common are not any particular beliefs, but the way in which beliefs divide up the world into the realms of the *sacred* and the *secular*. This is not, however, merely a matter of ideas. All religions prescribe certain ways of behaving toward the things that are sacred. These "sacred objects" vary with the particular society. In some tribal societies, certain animals, plants, or places are guarded by taboos and must be avoided or approached only in ritually proper ways and occasions. The sacred objects can also be human artifacts: pictures or emblems of the god, a crucifix, an altar, a church building, a Bible, Koran, or other sacred scripture. Persons can be sacred objects too, at least on certain occasions: the priest in vestments, the tribal initiate who is taboo during a rite of passage, even the consecrated victim of a human sacrifice. And sacred "objects" need not be physical objects at all; they can be actions—such as the act of praying, chanting, or dancing—or ideas, such as theological dogmas, or the idea of God Himself (significantly capitalized to show respect).[1]

What makes this heterogeneous group of things, artifacts, actions, and ideas into "sacred objects" is not any characteristic they objectively have in common, but the way that the group behaves toward them. Behavior toward the sacred is what constitutes ritual; it is action carried out by or enforced by the group, which expresses respect. Durkheim points out that anything at all can become a sacred object; the choice is arbitrary. But having chosen, the group has a device suited to expressing its own identity. Its arbitrary emblems distinguish it from any other group, which has made other objects sacred. The sacred object is a symbol of the society.

Durkheim stated several lines of proof for this assertion. The distinction between the sacred and the secular is not given in nature; it must be created by society. However, there must be something that corresponds to this distinction, that makes it feel realistic to people; so prominent a form of human action cannot be based on a hallucination. Sacred objects are always felt to represent something powerful and worthy of respect, something larger than individuals. But, although humans feel they are dependent on these sacred powers, their gods or totems or spiritual forces, at the same time they feel they participate in them. Tribal cultists feel their totems are their kinfolk; Christians or Buddhists feel there is an element of the sacred inside themselves, whether it is called "soul" or *Sunyata*. But this is exactly the relationship of the individual to society. Society is larger than the individual, but we are also part of it; we depend on it, but it also needs our adherence, just as the gods demand our prayers and our sacrifices, and the totems our ritual respect. The dependence of the individual on society is intimate. Society gives us our language and our ideas; hence it permeates our consciousness. Society distinguishes us from nature. This is the division expressed in the religious distinction between the sacred and the secular.

Another aspect of this dependence of the individual on society is morality. Religions establish moral rules; they define what is right and wrong. Morality is not "natural"—a simple matter of the Golden Rule (Do unto others as you would have them do onto you) or a set of injunctions against killing, lying, stealing, and so

---

[1] It has been argued that Durkheim's procedure is circular (Lukes, 1973: 31; Needham, 1963). Durkheim proposed to find what all religions have in common and discards various elements (belief in a single god, in multiple gods, and so forth) because not all religions have this, until he finally arrived at characteristics which he believed to be universal and fundamental. But in order to do this, Durkheim must already have had in mind some criterion of what constitutes a religion (establishing his universe of "all religions"). Hence, it is claimed, Durkheim only uncovered conclusions which he implicitly held all along. I do not find this criticism convincing. What it shows is that whenever we examine any phenomenon, we engage in a form of *hermeneutics* (see Gadamer, 1975). We can never come to the world without preconceptions, else we cannot pick out anything to pay attention to. This is equally true of the realm of physical science: we could not investigate the nature of fire or heat, for example, without a preconception of what instances of this are. But that does not constrain the physicist to find that "heat" is merely the conception that he or she had in mind to begin with. The concept of "heat" does not include the theory of molecular movement that later developed. Similarly, although Durkheim had to begin with a commonsense notion of what is a "religion," that commonsense notion does not entail the nonobvious points Durkheim derived from his comparisons: religion as ritual action, producing symbols of group membership, and so on. For a further defense of Durkheim and Mauss against their critics, see Bloor (1984).

forth. For religions establish exactly whom is it proper to kill or not to kill: totemic animals (or unborn fetuses) may be prohibited, while enemies, strangers, or victims of head-hunting expeditions can be not only fair game, but group members are positively enjoined to slaughter them. The group establishes when and to whom such rules apply. Furthermore, many of the strongest moral rules have nothing to do with these "realistic" injuries. The Golden Rule is too utilitarian a view of morality. Instead, religions often reserve the strongest injunctions for respecting the sacred objects (including sacred beliefs), and the strongest punishments for their violation. The Judaic-Christian First Commandment is "Thou shalt have no other gods before me," not an injunction against killing or an invocation of moral reciprocity. In a totemic cult, the strongest moral principle is against showing disrespect for the totem, which may even be an act as innocuous as seeing the totem if one is not a proper person to do so. Medieval Christianity was more likely to torture and burn someone at the stake for doctrinal violation ("heresy") than for murder, theft, or rape. In our own society, "crimes without victims"—gambling, drugs, prostitution, prohibited sexual practices—are considered evil not because of practical consequences, but because they are "morals" offences, "vices," evils in themselves. The fact that the content of such offenses is quite variable historically shows that morality is constructed by the social group.

The individual depends on society, then, both for physical sustenance, and for ideas, consciousness, and moral feelings. Religion is moral, because all morality is social. Moreover, society permeates our intimate self, so that it does not feel external, but it also determines what we feel we want to do. Why do we (generally) adhere to principles of morality? Durkheim asked. We might reply that the group demands it and enforces those principles. But this is only part of it. What we consider genuinely moral is not to obey for fear of the consequences if we don't, but obeying because we sincerely feel that is the right thing to do. It is correct to do X (whatever is "right" in a society), even if one incurs a loss for doing it, and it is immoral to violate Y (a moral prohibition) even if one can get away with it. We want to be moral, in short. How can this happen? It is not merely a case of reward and punishment; moral behavior explicitly excludes the realm of utilitarian considerations. We adhere to a standard of morality because we are attached to membership in a group. The strength of moral feelings over practical advantages and disadvantages is the superior strength of this motivation of social belonging over the feeling of not belonging to the community.

Everyone has some feelings of morality, Durkheim is saying, insofar as they are group members. There is of course a further question of what group one happens to belong to, what scope or boundaries it has, and hence what scope of morality it inculcates. Individual self-interest also exists, so that individuals can and do violate group moralities, although in a socially patterned way. We shall deal with these variations later. Here, the issue is the most general conditions which produce standards of morality; and these are found in group membership.

Group membership is not, so to speak, simply imposed on individuals in the process of creating them as human beings furnished with ideas and moral feelings. There are continuing, immediate advantages that individuals derive from participation in the group. The group is most intensely conscious of itself when it assembles to perform a ritual of respect for its sacred objects. Rituals are actually the group worshiping itself. They are special forms of social action which periodically recreate the feelings of membership and which revitalize the sacred objects that symbolize this membership. Participating in a ritual influences the individual in an unconscious, nonutilitarian dimension: it provides a heightened sense of energy and emotional direction. The experience of reaffirming one's membership in the group gives one emotional support; one feels renewed confidence and a greater sense of one's own capabilities.[2] Hence, soldiers entering battle or athletes under the stress of competition often avail themselves of religious rituals to build up their emotions for their task; in the same way, religious participation is often used to generate motivation for the daily tasks of work achievement, especially by individuals trying to move themselves out of a disadvantaged social class by dint of their own effort. Group leaders, in particular, get a special boost of enthusiasm and energy from being the focal center of the rituals they participate in.

A ritual, then, is a kind of energy-producing machine, a sort of social "battery" for charging up individuals. Participating in rituals gives a feeling of strength and support, which individuals can then use in their daily lives. (Hence rituals are particularly likely to be used in emergencies and times of stress; also some individuals make careers out of using rituals to boost their personal success.) Rituals pay off in the form of emotional energy, which also carries with it feelings of morality about what one is doing. Rituals generate feelings of self-righteousness. Thus rituals do, in fact, provide rewards for individuals. This differs from the utilitarian reward-and-punishment model mainly in that it sharply *distinguishes two kinds of rewards:* ritual rewards (and punishments), which come from participation in group rituals and adherence to its sacred objects, versus mundane or secular rewards and punishments (pleasures and pains of ordinary, nonsecular objects and behaviors), which are experienced by the individual alone. In the Durkheimian model, ritual rewards usually override the secular rewards. Ritual rewards are potentially more powerful than any secular rewards and will override them to the extent that ritual solidarity has actually been created. Secular rewards are only operative to the extent that ritual rewards allow them: that is, areas of life may be left in which ritual principles have not been applied, in which the individual is free to follow secular rewards and punishments by utilitarian calculation. It is also possible that ritual group membership may be weak, in which case the realm of secular, self-interested behavior can be more extensive.[3]

A FORMAL MODEL OF RITUAL

Durkheim's discussion is best treated analytically. That is, religion is only a convenient instance in which to understand the general mechanism by which social rituals operate. Furthermore, this mechanism consists of variables, of processes which can take on differing strengths. The amount of social solidarity in any particular

[2] Ritual celebrations such as birthdays or religious festivals even tend to prevent a person from dying on that date. There is a statistical "death dip" for persons affected by such rituals, followed by an upsurge of postponed deaths shortly thereafter (Phillips and Feldman, 1973).

[3] I am going to argue, moreover, that self-interest can often be pursued through the use of ritual motivations and practices. We will see this in the way in which social stratification is organized by social class rituals and the use of rituals as weapons of social dominance.

circumstance is not a constant but a variable outcome of these causal conditions. Hence different social groups can have different kinds and amounts of solidarity, and particular individuals can internalize particular kinds and strengths of group adherence depending upon their personal ritual experience.

In the most general terms, a ritual has the following elements:

1. The physical assembly of a group of people.
2. Their common focus of attention and mutual awareness of it.
3. A common emotional mood.
4. Sacred objects: symbols which represent membership in the group.

These in turn result in:

5. Enhanced emotional energy and confidence for individuals who participate in the ritual and/or who respect its symbols.
6. Righteous anger and punishment against persons who show disrespect for sacred objects.

Let us examine these processes more closely. (1) The physical assembly of the group is the crucial material ingredient of the ritual. Durkheim conceived of this as an actual bodily process. Society becomes emotionally real because these human beings are actually in each other's presence. The larger the group that is assembled, the greater the potential for generating strong ritual effects.

(2) The effects are merely potential, however, unless the second factor is added: a common focus of attention. A large, anonymous crowd of individuals passing one another on city streets does not generate ritual solidarity because it lacks a common focus. However it does do something: it creates a level of excitement for which the "bustle" of large cities is known. This is because the sheer number of bodies creates some degree of awareness of the potential power of the group over the individual. Focusing attention transforms this potentiality into an actuality. This is particularly strong when persons are aware of each other's awareness; they become mutually conscious of each other.

The focus of attention can be created in many ways. What is more conventionally considered to be the essence of a "ritual," namely the "ceremonial" quality of going through certain stereotyped actions, is important only because it focuses each participant's attention on the same thing and makes individuals aware that others are thus focused. A wedding ceremony, an inauguration of an official, a saying of grace at dinner, all are ways in which the group members stop doing what they are doing individually, pay attention to the same thing, and recognize the group in this action. On the most fundamental level, the content of the ceremony is arbitrary; what is crucial is only that it is shared and mutually self-conscious. Thus, any ceremony creates a strong sense of what is the group, and how the individual stands in relation to the group. There is a palpable pressure on individuals in the congregation so that they feel they cannot talk during a church prayer or behave disrespectfully during the playing of the national anthem. Formal ceremonies are important for this reason; but they are not essential. Any procedure that actually focuses attention can serve to generate ritual effects, as we will see in the following discussion of "natural rituals."

FIGURE 6-1

INTERACTION RITUAL

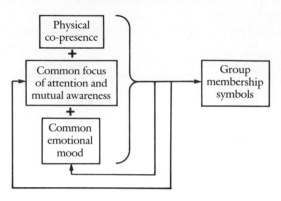

(3) The common mood may also be arbitrary in content. Whatever emotion is shared by the entire group can be an ingredient in building up a strong state of ritual intensity. It may be respect (as in a religious worship), joy (a festive celebration), effort (cheering an athletic team), or humor (telling jokes). It can work equally well with negative emotions; for example, the feeling of sorrow at a funeral is used and intensified, resulting in a renewed solidarity; and anger at the criminal or scapegoat generates solidarity in the crowd at a trial or ritual punishment.[4]

The second process, focus of attention, cumulatively interacts with the third process, the feeling of common emotion. If both of these are initially provoked—by whatever means—a circular relationship is set in motion. (See Figure 6-1.) The spread of a common emotion enhances the pressure for a common focus of attention. (We see this in the feeling of pressure to be respectful during a church prayer or to go along with the mood of the crowd at a public event.) The increase in the focus of attention, in turn, makes each individual feel the emotion more strongly. Successful rituals increase the power of group emotions; they are "batteries" which rev up the social circuits, so to speak, intensifying feelings by contagion throughout the group. Thus, one feels more sorrowful during the course of a funeral than when one first arrived, more enthusiastic about one's football team when caught up in the cheering, more joyous when in the full swing of a party, more pious when maintaining joint silence with a church congregation. Jokes become more humorous when set in a sequence that has the crowd laughing (a process upon which the technique of professional comedians depends).

(4) The membership symbol is whatever the group focuses upon during the ritual. This can be a physical object which is treated with special respect, persons,

---

[4] However, it is worth considering whether specific kinds of emotions give rise to particular subtypes of ritual effects. I suggest that the negative emotions—fear, anger, sorrow—generate stronger and longer-lasting feelings of solidarity than the positive or transient emotions (such as cheering at a football game). The power of religion comes from its concern with negative emotions: situations of death and stress, as well as the implicit or explicit fear involved in respect for sacred objects, whether this is expressed as violent punishment for violation of taboos or the prospect of damnation in Hell.

gestures, words, ideas. Highly intense rituals encompassing large groups or whole communities, which invoke strong emotions, including fear of the implicit threat of death, generate symbols which are held in an especially sacred regard—religious icons, dogmas, and political emblems such as flags. Rituals which bring together smaller and more private or episodic groups may charge with significance the gestures, clothing styles, and forms of talk found in that group. The type of symbol corresponds to the structure or kind of group which produced it. For example, Swanson (1962) found in a cross-cultural analysis that the remoteness and power of the gods symbolized in a society's religion was related to the number of levels of hierarchy in that society. Societies with powerful rulers controlling many layers of government above the masses, tend to mirror this arrangement in the symbolism of an all-powerful chief or creator god; whereas small, egalitarian societies tend to have no hierarchy of gods, but only local spirits with modest powers.

(5) Participation in rituals gives individuals a new fund of emotional energy. This is particularly the case for individuals who are the focus of rituals—the ritual leader, priest, or secular equivalent. Political speeches and meetings focus attention on the politician who is speaking. He or she becomes a symbol of the group, as well as the center of its flow of energy. Charismatic leadership is produced by the ritual process. There is a circular, cumulative relationship here, too: individuals with a reputation for being extraordinary speakers (that is, good focusers of ritual attention) attract many people to their speeches or sermons and create a common mood of expectancy and enthusiasm among them. The greater number and intensified focus increase the emotional energy of the speaker or ritual performer, who in turn is able to be even more "charismatic." What this means is that he or she is able to channel very high levels of emotional energy back to the group—energy intensified by the ubiquity of its shared mood. The charismatic leader has personally become a sacred object. He or she is the pole of the social "battery," through which emotional energy flows from the group and is reflected back to the group.

Symbols are portable in the sense that they can be effective in stirring up feelings of group membership even when the group is not assembled. Believers can carry around the magic emblem, the crucifix, or the sacred scriptures, and recharge their moral battery from them. Similarly, because actions and beliefs can be sacred objects, it is possible to reinvoke the spirit of the ritual in privacy, or even within one's own mind, by focusing one's own attention upon the proper actions and thoughts. Private prayer or silent meditation can have these effects. However, private rituals are secondary to public rituals. The public rituals which assembled the group physically established the sacred objects in the first place and charged them with emotional significance. Once they exist, they can be carried off into privacy by individuals. However, purely private ritual is not as intense as public ritual. Durkheim argued that without periodic participation in the public ritual, the individual loses moral intensity, and the symbols worshipped gradually slip back into being ordinary objects. They must be brought back into the public ritual situation to be recharged.

By the same token, rituals have effects which carry over to the times during which the group is not assembled, and make it possible for members to deliberately reassemble the group. Guided by the emotional energies stored in their bodies and the sacred symbols which remind them of the group, individuals are motivated to come back together and carry out renewed rituals. There is a circular process between assembly and dispersion of the group if sacred objects and emotional energies are generated during the ritual occasions.

(6) Sacred symbols create the basic lines of morality and immorality felt by group members. The most intense commitment is to respecting the symbols of a powerful membership group. Disrespect for these symbols has the effect of defining the violator as a nonmember, as well as evoking righteous anger against him or her. It is important to recognize that this anger is righteous. Members feel that they have a moral right and even duty to punish the violator. This is not a calculated decision based on utilitarian computations of what damages the violator may have done. It is a spontaneous reaction to the way moral sentiments are charged around certain symbols. The ritual "battery" not only gives positive energy to its faithful members, but it also discharges violently against those who have, so to speak, crossed their wires the wrong way. One does not have to act morally and compassionately to ritual violators, since by their ritual transgression they have shown that they are not members of the group. Moral principles of compassion apply only to co-members of the group. Hence, although all groups have an equivalent of "thou shalt not kill" as a rule, this applies only to group members. Nonmembers can be killed with impunity (as killing enemies in war or executing criminals today are not considered murder but highly honorable duties); even more, if they have violated the group's symbols, the moral act is explicitly to hurt them.

Ritually based violence is thus especially severe (Collins, 1981: 133–58). What appears to an outside observer as sadistic torture is believed to be moral behavior by members who have had their ideas inculcated by participation in the group's rituals. Medieval inquisitors burned their victims at the stake in public ceremonies after horrible tortures, which they believed to be for the sake of the heretics' souls: that is, they were offering them a chance to return to ritual good grace by a ceremonial confession and self-sacrifice. Ritual violations are not always treated in such an extreme fashion; as we shall see, there are structural differences among groups which make some much more violent and sadistic in treatment of violators. Furthermore, not all rituals operate with equal intensity. The small-scale rituals of everyday life, involving small and temporary groups, call for much milder punishments of symbolic violations. They are felt to be violations of politeness, respectability, and social competence, rather than drastic moral crimes. But wherever the ritual and its violation may fall along the continuum of intensity, the procedure of punishment is a symbolic one, rather than a utilitarian balancing of pleasures and pains. Such punishment does not fall in the realm of ordinary rational calculation (although sometimes we may pretend that it does, as in modern penal philosophy).

For this reason, ritually based group ties can be both very positive and very dangerous. Individuals who participate in intense rituals feel these to be the most important and meaningful events of their lives. But these same highly intense rituals also create the strongest sense of self-righteousness, and the feeling of a moral duty to punish violators. The intense ritual permeation in traditional societies also resulted in human sacrifices, ritual tortures, and executions. The violators here were guilty of little or no practical transgressions, but their crimes, "victimless" on the utilitarian level, were considered extremely heinous violations on the symbolic level. In our own society, the same general processes operate, although the specific content and intensity of symbolic commitments has changed. In our generally privatized society, one of the few remaining intense rituals centers on sexual property, and sexual jealousy is one of the most common precipitators of private violence. The violence is severe because its perpetrators do not feel they are contravening social restraints on violence; they feel their action in punishing their erring spouse or girlfriend or the intruding lover, is itself a moral action (Dobash and Dobash, 1979).

Durkheim (1895/1982) also pointed out that punishing a ritual violation is itself a ritual. Hence, crimes actually have the effect of holding together society, because they are the occasion for enacting punishment rituals which reassemble the group and reaffirm its solidarity. A legal trial ought to be regarded as a ritual rather than a practical procedure for establishing guilt or innocence. The more heinous the crime, the more effective the ritual, since it creates a widespread moral sentiment in the population and focuses group attention. Severe crimes thus provide very good ingredients for subsequent rituals. Durkheim did not add the point, but we could extend this analysis to say that since punishment rituals are so effective, they may be actively sought out or even arranged. Searching for scapegoats is a tactic that privileged groups can use effectively to restore solidarity with a traditional social order (for instance, in the rhetoric of "crime in the streets" used by conservative politicians today). Political scandals also have this group-mobilizing dynamic—indeed, far more than mundane bread-and-butter issues of politics. Scandals, however, can be turned against either side in a partisan struggle; they can be mobilizing weapons for the oppressed as well as for the dominant classes, depending upon who is the focus of the scandal.

INTENTIONAL AND NATURAL RITUALS

The neo-Durkheimian theory of rituals has a very wide application. We have already discussed a large variety of rituals. One set includes religious ceremonies, political speeches, judicial trials, and criminal punishments. In Bergesen's (1988) terminology, these are "macro-rituals," not because they take place in macro situations (in fact, they occur in a limited space and time, and hence—like all rituals—are relatively "micro"), but because they are oriented toward the larger macro order. They invoke the entire society, the entire state, and possibly the entire cosmos in religious rituals. The group that enacts the ritual is a sample from the society at large. Also, I would add, they focus on emotions which imply the greatest power of the group over the individual, especially the threat of death and violence and organized protection against these. Emotionally and cognitively, they have the largest and most political focus. Their symbols, whether religious or secular, always include the elements of extreme power and extreme dependence.

Another set of rituals refers to smaller but permanent groups: funerals, weddings, and other rites of passage, as well as feasting and gift-giving celebrations such as (in our society) Thanksgiving, Christmas, and birthdays. The majority of social science research has been done on rituals of this sort. Durkheim's theory was initially picked up by the so-called British school of social anthropologists, led by Radcliffe-Brown (1922; 1952: 117–77), which studied such rituals as the focus of tribal societies. These rituals are usually carried out by family groups and other pseudo-kin as neighbors and friends. The intensity of local group rituals is generally lower than in macro rituals (although funerals temporarily can be quite moving), since the groups involved are less powerful and less potentially coercive. These rituals often consist of the ritual exchange of material gifts—that is, rewards raised above the level of utilitarian objects by their symbolic significance.

Even more private and low-key are "interpersonal rituals"—the little ceremonies of everyday interaction, first studied by Erving Goffman (1967). For the most part, these bring together episodic, temporary groups; they constitute ritual communities only for short periods of time, and the symbols they generate are not of very high intensity. Violation of ceremonial propriety here brings scorn and perhaps a breaking off of relationships, but not violent and self-righteous punishment. Such rituals, though, are not without larger social significance. Though they are mild and taken for granted, they are pervasive throughout everyday interaction; and added together in a mass, they shape the pattern of social inclusion and exclusion, which makes up the mundane reality of stratification as it is acted out on the micro level. Some private interpersonal rituals, however, can be quite intense. Falling in love fits the pattern of a high-intensity ritual between the two lovers, making them both into sacred objects for each other. Love is a private cult of mutual worshipers. For this reason, violation of the symbols of this private commitment can bring forth a very strong emotional reaction, including the violent outbursts that are felt to be just punishment for violations of sexual property.

I would like to propose another distinction that can be drawn between any of these types of rituals—"intentional" versus "natural" rituals. Durkheim's model provides a set of conditions—the physical assembly of a group, a common focus of attention, a common emotional mood—which automatically, even "mechanically" produce certain results: intensification of emotion, charging of symbols with membership significance, and so forth. Now, these conditions may occur deliberately, because a ritual was intentionally carried out, or they may occur spontaneously and accidentally. In either case, the results follow from the intensity of the ritual conditions: larger groups, stronger focus of attention, and more powerful emotions result in stronger feelings of group membership and more intense respect for its symbols. Whether rituals are intentional or occur "naturally," makes no difference for their results. The only difference is that with intentional rituals, the members are explicitly aware that they are carrying out a ritual, and they are conscious of their sacred objects as being specially worthy of respect. In the case of natural rituals, the same results happen, but people act upon them unconsciously, without awareness of what they are doing.

Intentional rituals are institutionalized. They are part of the explicit cultural repertoire. Often they are regularly scheduled: church services on holy days, annual patriotic ceremonies, formal ritual when encountering high officials, or periodic family celebrations. Others are explicitly available when certain events come up (wedding rituals, funerals, political speeches). Other occasions have ritual qualities, but are not explicitly recognized as rituals. Goffman's interaction rituals of everyday life are an example; no one had recognized the little stereotyped routines of greetings and departures (saying "How are you?" when the question is not asking for a report on one's health, and so forth) as rituals until Goffman pointed out their structural similarity to better-known formal rituals. Even more significantly, the ritual model can be extended to virtually the whole of sociable conversation. Carrying out casual talk, Goffman (1967: 113) points out, is the creation of a little temporary cult, worshiping the reality of what is being talked about for the moment. It assembles a little group, focuses attention, and builds up a common mood; what is talked about becomes part of a symbolic realm, rather than the practical realm of mundane activities. These fleeting rituals of everyday life, charged with Durkheimian symbolism, produce the lines of social acceptability and unacceptability which determine the solidarity of social classes and the borderlines between them.

Natural rituals are not necessarily confined to casual interactions in everyday life. Large-scale political movements, especially as they happen in crowds, also have the shape of natural rituals. A political speech is not always regarded as a ceremonial occasion but can operate very powerfully as a ritual. In fact, formal, intentional political rituals are usually less emotionally impelling than spontaneous political rituals. That is because a regularly scheduled political ceremony—an inauguration, an opening of parliament, and so forth—is made routine and starts with relatively low levels of emotional excitement, which the ceremony itself then attempts to augment. Spontaneous political gatherings, though, would not happen in the first place unless there were some dramatic or emergency situation that drew people together; hence, they start with higher emotional energy, which can be revved up still further and attached to new symbols: often the person of a charismatic leader, who becomes an incarnate symbol of the group. A social movement might be defined as the spontaneous ritual gatherings that bring its members together. Movements are relatively "uninstitutionalized," as long as they have no permanent organization, property, written records, and the like. What holds them together is mainly their symbolic capital, that is, the shared symbols (sacred objects) and the emotional energy of their members, which is initially generated by spontaneous rituals and which leads to further reassemblings of the group. These, in turn, further intensify energies and the sacredness of its symbols for its members. A natural ritual of this sort, if successful, tends to turn into an intentional ritual. The history of religions (the original followers of Jesus, Mohammed, Gautama Buddha, and so on, and their later transformation into churches) provides many examples of this pattern. It also happens in the realm of politics (and today, in the realm of popular entertainment).

Social movement theory can thus be recast in terms of ritual theory. The question is what enables mass rituals to begin and what determines to what extent they prosper or fade away. Conflicts between movements and established authority is part of what generates emotional excitement and hence group mobilization. Conflict itself has a complex ritual structure, between its two opposing sides as well as within each side. These "material means of emotional production" are the ingredients of a ritual version of conflict theory.

The concept of natural rituals needs to be broadened in one more important way. The model of ritual ingredients (Figure 6-1) contains a set of causal variables: the amount of physical copresence, the amount of focus of attention, and the amount of common emotion. When these are features of a particular situation, locally organized in time and space, it can be readily recognized as a ritual (if perhaps a natural rather than an intentional one). But Durkheim was also fond of using these same variables in a more macho fashion, as they occur over greater periods of time and larger amounts of space. That is, we can characterize an entire society (or any group within it) in terms of how much physical density of interaction there is within it, how much common focus of attention, and how much common emotional sentiment.

In *The Division of Labor in Society,* Durkheim (1893/1964) used these factors to set up an ideal type distinction between two polar forms of society. The "mechanical solidarity" form has high physical density (people are constantly in each other's presence), a common focus of attention (people are all doing much the same thing, and are aware of the same environment), and similar emotions (because their common activities and environment make them feel much the same way most of the time). The "organic solidarity" type is at the other end of the continuum: physical density is low (because people are spread out or have erected barriers of privacy among themselves), they have different foci of attention (because they are doing different tasks in the division of labor), and they share few common moods (because of the foregoing conditions). As a result, Durkheim theorized, the two types of society have quite different kinds of ideas and moral sentiments, what he called their "collective conscience" or "collective consciousness." (See Figure 6-2.)

In the "mechanical solidarity" type of society, people have very concrete, reified ideas; their ideas are strongly felt symbols representing group membership, and deviations from conformity to them are punished by spontaneous emotional reactions. Group pressure for conformity is high. The group has a very strong moral and cognitive presence, reflecting its strong physical presence. Boundaries between insi-

FIGURE 6-2

DURKHEIM'S MECHANICAL AND ORGANIC SOLIDARITY AS DIFFERENT FORMS OF THE RITUAL VARIABLES

	Mechanical Solidarity	Organic Solidarity
Copresence (social density)	high	moderate or low
Focus of attention	low diversity	high diversity
Common emotion	strong ($\longrightarrow$ pressures for conformity)	weak ($\longrightarrow$ individualism)
Membership symbols	concrete, reified	abstract, relativistic
Reaction to symbolic violations	righteous anger; punitive ritual	avoidance or restitution
Attitude to nonmembers	distrusting	routinized trusting

ders and outsiders are very clear and strongly felt; solidarity toward insiders is balanced by distrust of outsiders.

In the "organic solidarity" type of society, people have more abstract ideas, since they cover a wider range of situations. Symbols of group membership are not so strongly felt, and punishment for deviations are less violent and emotionally compelling. Boundaries with outsiders are less clear, and there is less internal solidarity as well as less external distrust. Moral principles, instead of being particularistic and reified, as in the "mechanical solidarity" type, are more universalistic and relativistic.

In this theory, Durkheim is using the same variables as in his later theory of rituals. The only difference is that here he has applied the variables to the macro structure of society as a whole; the resulting states of consciousness are also the same as in the ritual model, except that they are imputed to the consciousness of everyone in the society. Durkheim's use of the term "collective conscience" for this result was unfortunate, and it set off a long debate over whether he was positing a mythical "group mind" over and above particular individuals. His theory does not need to be interpreted in this way. The dependent variables in the theory can be seen as empirical states of the consciousness of individuals: in one set of circumstances, their ideas are concrete, reified, morally absolutist, distrusting of outsiders, and demanding conformity of self and others; in the other set, their ideas are abstract, relativistic, individualistic, trusting, and so on.

The important point is that the ritual model, as a set of causal conditions, works just as well when applied on the macro level. That is, we can characterize not just a particular occasion as having high ritual density, focus, and so on, but also any larger swath of experience in time and space. Some individuals or groups of individuals live in circumstances where they are constantly in the presence of other people, all doing the same thing, maintaining a high focus of attention on each other and sharing common moods. As we shall see (in the discussion of Mary Douglas and of class culture theory), this is common both for particular social classes and for entire societies. We can say that the ongoing experience of these people's lives has "high ritual density." Other people, living in circumstances where they are not constantly in the presence of the same people, where they have little common focus of attention and common moods with the people they encounter, can be said to inhabit lives of "low ritual density." "Ritual density" is being used here as a macro variable. It is obvious that the extension of "ritual" to these cases is a version of "natural rituals," rather than "intentional rituals." Natural rituals of this sort, on the spread-out, macro structure of people's lives, provide an extremely important tool for explaining people's beliefs, feelings, and behavior. This extension of Durkheimian theory provides a basis for a ritual theory of the entire range of sociology, without giving up the micro perspective on the human actor and the interactional situation as the central feature of our explanation.

EVIDENCE OF RHYTHMIC SYNCHRONIZATION

This may be an appropriate place to bring in some empirical research on the microdynamics of interaction. The neo-Durkheimian ritual model (Figure 6-1) posits that shared focus of attention and shared emotional mood are cumulatively reinforcing. Goffman finds tacit rituals in everyday elements of social behavior as brief as conversations. The validity of this theory is supported by some detailed research, although it was carried out without this perspective in mind (for an overview, see McClelland, 1985; Gregory, 1983).

Films of conversations show that speakers and listeners both tend to time their bodily movements to the rhythm of the words being spoken (Condon and Ogston, 1971; Kendon, 1970, 1980; Capella, 1981). The body movements are rapid and subtle: nodding the head, blinking eyes, and other gestures at a rate of about five a second. They are too rapid to be seen by the normal eye and become visible only when a film shot at 24 frames per second is played back frame by frame. Much of this research has centered on interactions between mothers and babies. Neonates as young as a few weeks or months synchronize vocalizations and movements with those of adults (Condon and Sander, 1974a, 1974b; Contole and Over 1981), long before they learn to talk. This suggests that rhythmic synchronization may be the basis of talking—an outgrowth of natural interaction rituals. Electroencephalographic recordings reveal that synchronization can occur between the rhythmic brain waves of adults who are conversing, as well as between infants and adults (Condon and Sander, 1974a, 1974b). Synchronization does not always happen; for instance, it was less likely to happen in conversations between black and white adults than between whites, apparently because different speech rhythms are involved.

The interaction ritual model does not state that synchronization necessarily occurs. What it proposes is that concentration of attention and common mood, once started, becomes more intense, so that people become "locked into" the ritual and engrossed by the reality it creates. Initial orientation and other dispositional factors are crucial for getting the ritual mechanism flowing. This experimental research for the most part did not deal with such factors, but attempted to isolate interactions in which the synchronization reached high levels (mothers and their children being a very common such instance). The research also varies in what aspects of interactional synchronization it studies. So far we have referred to the timing of gestures and brain waves. But there is also evidence of conversationalists synchronizing various features of their voices: the pitch register and range, loudness, tempo, and the duration of syllables (clipped or drawled sounds) (Gregory, 1983).[5] Moreover, there is a tendency for talkers to adapt their speech patterns and rhythms to one another as their conversation goes on (Gregory, 1983; Jaffe and Feldstein, 1970; Warner, 1979; Warner et al., 1983). This process does not continuously build from the beginning to the end of the talk, however; it becomes more intense during particular times. Synchronization may fade, only to build up again, and so on. This pattern makes sense if talk is a negotiation, flowing in and out of closer sympathy among the partners.

The above examples are all what I have called "natural rituals." More explicitly, ritualistic activities show even more obvious efforts at synchronization (such as sing-

---

[5] These are referred to as "nonsegmented" qualities of speech, in contrast to "segmented" qualities which produce the vowels and consonants. The latter convey overt phonetic messages, what we ordinarily consider to be the language. The former are paralinguistic; they are different ways of speaking which can be used at any time regardless of words which are actually formed. Synchronization of "segmented" qualities could happen only if both persons said exactly the same thing; hence it is the paralinguistic, "nonsegmented" features that are crucial for most interactional synchronization.

ing the national anthem together, praying in unison, and so forth). One study of a political "macro ritual," a political demonstration, showed that the microcoordination of movements among the demonstrators was much higher than a comparison group of ordinary pedestrians, and greater even than a marching band (Wohlstein and McPhail, 1979).

An important point is that the synchronization—at least, on the micro level— is largely unconscious. Synchronized gestures occur within time segments of 0.2 seconds, but humans are capable of overtly reacting to a stimulus only in 0.4 or 0.5 seconds at the fastest (Kempton, 1980). Only slow playback of film frames reveals these patterns. Other synchronized behaviors, such as brain waves, or voice pitch range (how narrowly or widely the micro tones vary) are not even noticeable without specialized instruments. How, then, are people able to synchronize? The implication is that they have gotten into the same rhythm, so that they can anticipate where the next "beat" will fall and where their interactional partner will make the next "move" or "stress." This is called *rhythmic entrainment* (Chappla, 1981). It occurs because human actions are themselves rhythmic, with components ranging from the very rapid flux brain waves and muscle vibrations to heartbeats and breathing. The actions involved in social interaction are especially rhythmic (particularly speech, but also the micro gestures indicated in the studies described).

Individuals who get into the flow of an interaction have made a series of minor adjustments which bring their rhythms together; hence they can "keep the beat" with what their partner is doing by anticipation, rather than by reaction. McClelland (1985) proposes that this synchronization is a major source of pleasure in social interaction. If so, this explains why people are attracted to social rituals, and why such rituals generate feelings of solidarity. The symbols which represent these interactions hold deep connotations of pleasure for group members, and this helps make them "sacred objects" to defend, as well as reminders of group interactions that members would like to reestablish in future encounters.

GOFFMAN AND INTERACTION RITUAL

Erving Goffman coined the term *interaction ritual* as the title of a collection of his early papers (1967), and much of his work is an application and extension of the Durkheimian ritual model to new materials. He refers in key passages (1967: 47; 1959: 35–36, 69–70) not only to Durkheim but to Radcliffe-Brown, the leader of the British school of social anthropology. Goffman shifted the focus of Durkheimian theory from the macro to the micro level. I have already shown that Durkheim's works contain a very important micro mechanism, in the theory of rituals. But Durkheim himself tended to work on the level of macrosociology, on the society as a whole, and his analyses have usually been interpreted on that level. Goffman not only showed that the ritual model could be applied to very small-scale, temporary groups and their fleeting acts, but also began to refine the theoretical details of the mechanism by which rituals operate. His frontstage-backstage model points to some of the material conditions, as well as maneuvers and latent conflicts, that go into performing rituals. His later work on *frames* and *framing* adds refinements to the meaning of *focus of attention* within the ritual model. Goffman discovered "natural rituals," although he did not use that term. His work also gives the ingredients for a more subtle theory of how rituals operate.

THE FRONTSTAGE-BACKSTAGE MODEL

Goffman's most famous book, *The Presentation of Self in Everyday Life* (1959) is often referred to as containing the "dramaturgical" model of society. Life is like theater in that it consists of performance, with performers and audience. Whatever is acted on the stage is taken as reality for the moment that the performance is going on. This model seems to be a radical relativism, since it sees reality as fleeting moments of social construction which fade away once the performance is over. However, Goffman intends his model to be taken in a more Durkheimian fashion. The dramaturgy is a ritual. It creates a sense of shared reality, but that reality is not necessarily fleeting. Insofar as the ritual is successful, it creates social symbols which are charged with a moral force. Participants come away from a ritual believing in those symbols, at least for a time. Social reality is not only being constructed but also reproduced and kept in place. Thus, rituals could be said to have a coercive quality.

Furthermore, the stages on which everyday-life's "theater" is performed are real, physical places.[6] Reality is constructed in layers. The material world is the basic level. On it, people come together as real physical bodies and perform rituals which generate a secondary level of reality, social institutions, and socially constructed selves. "Frontstages" and "backstages" are *regions,* areas of physical space. A *frontstage* is the place where a performance goes on; it is physically arranged with various "props" in order to make a certain impression and facilitate a certain kind of performance. A *backstage* is a place that is not visible from the frontstage. It is where the material implements for organizing and preparing the frontstage are kept, for cleaning up afterwards, and for hiding the refuse and the dirty work. (Some of this may literally be the physical garbage, like the kitchen in relation to a dinner party; Goffman also deals with the social "garbage" that is cleaned up backstage.) The backstage is also the place where the performers gather before and after the performance, to rehearse and plan, and later to recapitulate and unwind. Sometimes specific places are set aside for frontstages and backstages: living rooms, board meeting rooms, sales display rooms, office reception desks, as the one type; kitchens, bathrooms, storage areas, as the other. But the same space can also be changed from one function into the other over time: the bathroom is cleaned up for dinner guests, just as the official meeting room is taken over by the sweepers after the convention is gone. (That is to say, physical work is done to make some space temporarily a stage.)

Goffman's *Presentation of Self* is a synthesis of empirical studies, both by other researchers and by Goffman himself. Goffman's analysis implicitly reveals the

---

[6]"All the world is not a stage—certainly the theatre isn't entirely. Whether you organize a theatre or an aircraft factory, you need to find places for cars to park and coats to be checked, and these had better be real places, which, incidentally, had better carry real insurance against theft" (1975: 1). Goffman's model is not idealist, since ideas are constructed upon material arrangements. Goffmanian ritual theory may even be integrated with a Marxian or conflict view. As we shall see, social classes differ in their control of the "material means of emotional production" or "means of reality construction."

implications of frontstages-backstages for a stratified society. His main examples are relations between workers and managers, salespeople and customers, professionals and clients, and hosts and guests. In each case, power or status is the central content of the rituals performed.

The studies of workers, for example, deal with the well-known phenomenon of the informal group which controls its own work pace. The workers organize them selves as a "team," in Goffman's terminology, which makes sure that individuals do not embarrass the rest of its members by acting as "rate-busters"—showing that work can be done much faster than the level the rest of them are maintaining. When the boss is present, the workers put on a show, pretending to be busy and attentive. This is a frontstage situation. When the boss is away, the backstage situation takes over, in which workers may make snide remarks about the official organization and do the staging work which enables them to maintain a united front. Goffman also points out that there is another side to this structure. Managers, too, have their own backstages: their private offices, their executive lunchrooms, and even their own bathrooms with personal keys. In their privacy, managers can be more casual than when they are confronting workers; they too can make jokes and distance themselves from the official reality of the organization. But when they appear frontstage, they are giving orders in the name of the organization and put on a performance to act out their authority.

The situation of giving and taking orders, then, is the ceremonial center of the work organization. Goffman points out that it is a ritual, rather than merely a practical part of getting work done. Managers are often ineffective in controlling the workers; the informal group with its own control of the work pace is evidence of that. Workers are merely giving ritual deference when the bosses are present. The managers often know this, but they go through the ritual nevertheless. Goffman describes the order-giving ritual as a theatrical performance, in which both sides know their parts: the boss acting authoritatively and expecting compliance; the workers acting as a dutiful audience and applauding the performance. Reality-constructing, Goffman says (1959: 9–10), is essentially accommodative—a shared performance.

This is a Durkheimian ritual: assembling the group, going through certain activities to momentarily focus attention and mood, thus creating a shared symbolic reality. The reality in this case is the organization itself. Although bosses are not necessarily very effective at controlling workers, the order-giving ritual nevertheless is crucial for acting out the existence of the organization, and keeping it as a reality in people's minds. Bosses and workers, by the parts they play in this ritual performance, are also reenacting, and hence socially reproducing, their identities in the organization.

Goffman's other empirical illustrations give similar lessons. Salespeople and customers similarly meet on a carefully prepared frontstage and retire to backstages in which they plan their strategies of selling or buying. There is both an accommodative ritual on the frontstage and a divergence of interests which is expressed mainly on the backstage. Relations between professionals and clients also show this division. The high-status professions are those which are particularly good at maintaining the ritual impressiveness of the stage on which they encounter their clients. Doctors meet their patients in carefully prepared consulting rooms, make their entrances through their own private back corridors, and tightly manage the information which gives them control of defining the reality of the situation. Judges have their own backstage areas behind the courtroom, so that they encounter plaintiffs and defendants with the most dramatically imposing stage setting on their side. All these examples show how power and status is enacted in the realm of work. A generalization which emerges is that the occupations with the greatest power and highest ranking are those which have the greatest control over the stage setting in which they meet other people. Their "dirty work" is taken care of by assistants, often invisible, and they are able to take part in rituals on their own terms with the greatest physical resources for appearing impressive.

Goffman also deals with staging in private life. His most vivid examples come from the sociability of the upper classes, since they have the most material resources to put on impressive performances and also the strongest motivation to make themselves appear impressive. Parties, formal receptions, dinners, and the like have their own frontstages and backstages. What is being enacted via the clean table linen, the freshly cut flowers, the elegant cuisine, and so forth is the status of the participants and particularly those who are the center of this sociable activity. Sociable occasions have the structure of natural rituals. The symbolic reality created is the social identity of people who take part—that is to say, their ranking in the order of society as indicated by their elegance and taste. Aesthetics and entertainment thus take on symbolic values, representing the groups which typically socialize in that fashion. The accumulated cultural memories of participants are what enables them to judge further social gatherings for their implicit ranking.

EVERYDAY INTERACTION AS RITUAL

Goffman's work indicates that the entire structure of society, both work and private sociability, is upheld by rituals. Furthermore, it shows that this structure is ritually stratified. The self is socially enacted through rituals on frontstages, separated from backstages. One's home—especially the bedroom and bathroom—serve as backstage areas for hiding the less impressive aspects of one's self, for getting rid of dirt and garbage (literally), and for putting on a frontstage self in the form of clothes, makeup, and hair styling. These same places also are psychological backstages, where one can plan, brood, and complain about frontstage social relationships of past and present, as well as act spontaneously without concern for the proper impression one is making. Conversely, part of the frontstage self is the mood one tries to get into, the facial expressions that ones wears, and the style of one's talk.

This regionalization of the self has implications for social relationships. People's personal ties are more intimate to the extent that they take place on backstages rather than frontstages. Moreover (although Goffman does not go into this), we can readily see that there is a hierarchy of frontstages and backstages: workers out of sight of their boss are on one kind of backstage, while the same individuals at home with their families are on a more intimate backstage, and what transpires between husband and wife in bed is still more intimate. Nevertheless, even the most intimate of situations still has a ritual structure to it, and Goffman comments (1959: 193–94) that even sexual intercourse is in some sense a staged performance.

Goffman analyzes situations as rituals centered on the self. Conversation is itself a ritual. Natural rituals are found even in the most casual and ordinary interactions of everyday life. There is the assembly of the group (most commonly, two people), the shared focus of attention (the actual intention of talking), and a shared mood, which builds up as the participants become drawn into the topic. Initially, the mood may be only a shared desire to be sociable; subsequently, if the conversation is successful, it is enhanced into whatever tone of humor, anger, interest, or anything else which emerges with the flow of talk as people become engrossed in it.

The result of this conversational ritual is that it creates a little temporary cult, a shared reality consisting of whatever is being talked about. This of course is a major respect in which humans differ from other animals: we can take leave of our immediate physical surroundings and invoke a symbolic world of ideas referring to elsewhere or to abstractions or fantasies which have no real physical locus. Goffman points out that once the conversational ritual is in full swing, it builds up its own pressures which control its participants. The topic has to be respected and at least temporarily believed in; it has become, for ever so short a time, a sacred object to be worshiped. Goffman describes this by saying that the conversation is a little social system with its own rules, which acts to protect its own boundaries, keeping the mundane surrounding world outside. Another way to put it would be to say that the circular reaction between attention and common mood is building up, so that the topic becomes more impelling as a focus, and the mood becomes successively stronger. A humorous conversation becomes funnier along the way, so that almost any remark, introduced at the right time, becomes occasion for laughter. Complaining about one's boss, one's job, political enemies, or the like becomes a ritual affirmation of the point of view shared by the talkers, so that sins are magnified and every detail becomes viewed in darkest perspective. The conversation as a ritual reality now demands that the individuals respect the mood that has built up. Its criterion is not whether what one has said is correct; in fact, one violates the ritual if one too bluntly questions a point, takes a joke literally, or fails to go along with the proper mood of sympathy in listening to someone's bragging or complaints. Goffman goes so far as to describe a conversation as a psychosis-like state, temporarily entered into, in which the only reality that counts is that which will keep the relationship going among the talkers.[7]

Not all conversations are equally engrossing, of course. This is the same as saying that the factors that produce natural rituals are variables which can be of lesser or greater strength in any particular interaction. If people cannot get started in a sufficient focus of common attention and common mood, the conversational ritual will not take off. The social tie between those individuals will fail to be built up. Also, conversational rituals which are going well enough up to a point may run

---

[7]"Talk creates for the participant a world and a reality that has other participants in it. Joint spontaneous involvement is a *unio mystico,* a socialized trance. We must also see that a conversation has a life of its own and makes demands on its own behalf. It is a little social system with its own boundary-maintaining tendencies" (Goffman 1967: 113). Habermas' theory (1984) of communicative competence (which I have discussed in Chapter 1) misses the point of Goffmanian ritual, regarding it as a purely Machiavellian effort at deception; for Habermas, it is merely an obstacle to be overcome by rules of truthfulness, honesty, and sincerity of intentions. But in real social relationships, what one converses about does not have to be true, honest, or sincere; in fact, one can ruin a conversation by not entering into the mood of bragging, joking, complaining or whatever is arbitrarily constructed in that little focus of attention. In Habermas' ideal world, according to Goffman, social relationships would not be possible.

down, either because of ritual violations (which Goffman treats under the topic of "alienation from interaction," 1967) or for other reasons. The fact that rituals sometimes work well and at other times badly or not at all, however, does not imply that the model is of only limited use. The very distinction between the occasions when it works and those when it doesn't is what creates dividing lines in the social structure, separating people who have strong social ties from those who do not. The model creates the network structure (which might also be called the Weberian status group organization) of society.

A conversation as a whole is a natural ritual. There are also some more formal elements within it. Goffman points these out in the case of greetings, departures, and other stereotyped procedures that we usually think of as "politeness." Saying "Hello," "How are you?" "Goodbye" and so on does not convey any information; these are not real questions or statements. They are ritual formulas, which focus the common attention of participants on the point that a conversational interaction is about to begin or end. Why should we tack these rituals onto the boundary points of conversations? Actually, we only do it in certain circumstances: where there is a "polite" or sociable relationship among the talkers, and not when it is merely a matter of a practical transaction (with a store clerk, for example). These very quick greeting and departure rituals indicate that we are developing the interaction into one specifically focused on the participants as group members. Ending the conversation with a ritual closure carries the message that we exit on good terms as interactants, available to pick up the relationship again in the future. We might say they are "relationship rituals." Of course, the entire natural ritual of the conversation is really about the relationship between the talkers (although it also implies something of how they are related to other groups in the society which use some of the same symbols). But greetings and departures convey nothing more than a consciousness of how the relationship is being enacted now and one's identity as a capable interactant.

RITUAL THEORY OF CLASS CULTURES

One of the most far-reaching applications of the Durkheimian theoretical tradition is to explain the different cultures of individuals in a stratified society. Durkheim compared whole societies for their collective conscience as a whole, and his model of religious ritual took sacred objects as symbolizing the entire society. However, the main variables in the theory can be treated more analytically. Any particular group, even a social class, can be characterized in terms of its amount of social density, focus of attention, emotional contagion, and the resulting group symbols loaded with moral sentiments. The concept of natural rituals enables us to examine the ritual density of different parts of the same overall society, and hence to produce a neo-Durkheimian theory of class cultures. Goffman, in extending Durkheimian ritual theory to everyday life, enables us to see the detailed mechanisms of interaction that make up the varying experience of members of different social classes. I have set out this theory in *Conflict Sociology* (Collins, 1975: 49–224). The following is an updated version.

TWO DIMENSIONS ON STRATIFICATION

Stratification has two basic dimensions: vertical and horizontal. Accordingly, we need two explanatory mechanisms. The result is a multidimensional theory of stratification, which has many empirical and theoretical advantages over a unidimensional scheme.

(1) Power is organized in the everyday experience of giving and taking orders. Hence, a theory of power stratification derives from the consequences of Goffman's frontstage-backstage model for different participants.

(2) A different type of everyday relationship exists between social equals. This is the realm of friendship and sociability. In empirical everyday life, it consists of Goffman's conversational rituals. But why is this a dimension of stratification rather than an aspect of life that escapes from hierarchy and inequality? Because this "horizontal" interaction nevertheless has stratifying antecedants and consequences.

For people to interact socially, they must be attracted to each other. If there is freedom to choose one's friends, there is an implicit market in which individuals will gravitate toward those whom they most wish to interact with. But because this freedom is shared by everyone else, sociable groups will form among those for whom the attraction is reciprocated. Less attractive persons will be excluded or less warmly received, and hence will gravitate toward forming their own groups. A completely open, "egalitarian" society without constraints on interaction will become stratified to the extent that there is variation in the resources that make individuals attractive. Where do these differing resources come from? One possibility is that they carry over from the *power* hierarchy (including its resulting wealth or cultural differences); in that case, the sociable or "status" dimension is a secondary consequence of the power dimension. (This is one interpretation of Weber's theory of the relationship between economic classes and status group communities.)

Another possibility is that the resources that attract persons to different sociable groups come from an autonomous realm of culture. In this case the horizontal status dimension cuts across the power dimension. Status groups then are not inherently ranked. For example, ethnic groups may split social classes, and each may claim superiority over the other. This is a case of a horizontal conflict, which greatly complicates the analysis of class conflict on the vertical dimension. On the sociable ("horizontal") dimension, there is stratification *inside* or *in relation to* any particular group: some persons are more popular than others (they "have more status"), others are less popular, and some may be outcasts. But the outcasts of one group might be the popular centers of a rival group (and, in fact, are very likely to be so if the groups are in conflict). Here we have local stratification, which cannot be generalized into stratification of the whole society, unless one group is clearly dominant over the other.[8]

In addition to this popularity or "status" process within a sociable group, there is another aspect of the horizontal social structure which has stratifying conse-

---

[8] Sociologists often assume this is so, but I think this is done for analytical convenience rather than empirical accuracy. Jews and Gentiles, Protestants and Catholics, or hoods and grinds in a high school are not necessarily ranked in relation to each other, even though there is a popularity ranking *within* each group.

quences. The different kinds of horizontal organization of people's lives results in different cultures. That is, people inhabit network structures that vary in the amount of social density, focus of attention, and the other variables of Durkheimian theory. Hence the horizontal, sociable dimension of class cultures can have predictable consequences, alongside those of the vertical or power dimension.

The sociological literature on stratification does not always make it clear there are two dimensions. Usually one dimension or the other is taken to be the basis of stratification, and the other dimension is ignored or interpreted within the single model. American researchers have typically ignored the power dimension in favor of the status dimension. For example, Gans (1962) characterizes different social classes as more cosmopolitan or localistic, culturally sophisticated or unsophisticated. These are the Durkheimian consequences of different positions on the network dimension of society. Bernstein (1971–75) also directly applies the Durkheimian model to the speech codes of different social classes. Blau (1964) reduces power to a consequence of popularity in a market relationship among formal equals who differ in expertise or other status attributes. This view eliminates any coercive aspect of power.

The European tradition tends to see stratification only along the vertical dimension of power. This includes the Marxian tradition which ultimately founds power on economic property, as well as the Weberian variant (and its mixtures with recent Marxism) which allow for some independence of coercive political power, as well as the formation of cultural groups based on this hierarchy (for example, Bourdieu, 1984). But empirically, cultural groups (status groups) are not so closely derived from the vertical dimension. Theorists who are exclusively oriented toward the vertical dimension try to sidestep this, often by asserting that the vertical dimension is what counts "in the last instance." Or else the disparities are treated as functional for maintaining the system of vertical domination by obscuring its true nature. But this is functionalist teleology rather than a true explanation; left-wing functionalism is no more acceptable theoretically than is conservative functionalism as far as producing an adequate explanation of what people actually do.

The solution is to recognize that there are two dimensions of stratification. These may *sometimes* interact (for instance, under some conditions the resources derived from vertical hierarchy affect the market relationships of forming horizontal sociable groups; popularity in status groups may also feed back into producing coercive dominance); but now the theory can specify when and how this happens. It also leaves room for independent effects on each dimension.

OTHER TWO-DIMENSIONAL THEORIES:
KEMPER AND DOUGLAS

The two dimensions of stratification are explicitly recognized by some theorists. Kemper's theory of emotions (1978) picks out the same two main dimensions of interaction: the vertical power dimension and the horizontal status dimension. Kemper theorizes that individuals' positions on each of these dimensions determine what kinds of emotions they will experience. Secure self-confidence, fear, or hate result from interactions among powerful and powerless persons; happiness, anger, or depression result from interactions of attractive and unattractive persons in status relationships. Kemper's confirmation of the two-dimensional model is valuable, both because it incorporates a large realm of microconsequences into a stratification theory and because it shows the theory is congruent with much empirical evidence.

The two-dimensional model also emerges in Mary Douglas' (1966, 1973) theory of group cultures. Douglas, a social anthropologist, works explicitly in the Durkheimian tradition. She elaborates the Durkheimian model on the macro level of whole societies by arguing that societies vary not only along the dimension of *mechanical* and *organic* solidarity, but also on the dimension of how tightly stratified they are internally. This, in effect, introduces the vertical dimension into the horizontal comparisons of classical Durkheimian theory. Douglas refers to the two dimensions as *grid* (vertical) and *group* (horizontal). As analytical concepts, they can be applied as well to different sectors within the same society. This has been done by Douglas herself, as well as by Basil Bernstein (1975, in regard to different educational systems) and David Bloor (1983, in the social groups' underlying the production of different forms of science). Douglas's model rejects an evolutionary interpretation of Durkheim; hence, it is particularly useful for explaining historical differences in the stratified culture of various societies. We will treat her model in more detail below.

THE EMPIRICAL VALIDITY OF TWO-DIMENSIONAL STRATIFICATION THEORY

Empirical evidence of class cultures, although plentiful, suffers from the propensity of researchers to conceptualize stratification unidimensionally. Researchers have paid far more attention to dependent variables—the consequences of stratification—than to the actual dimensions of stratifying conditions themselves. Particularly pernicious is the tendency to lump different independent variables in a composite index of social class: as if, say, education, income, occupational prestige, and other factors were all equivalent to each other. In fact, some of these are indicators of the vertical power dimension, others of the horizontal status (or network) dimension. In what follows, I will attempt to indicate how the major empirical findings support the two-dimensional ritual theory of stratification. This depends on interpreting what the causal variables really refer to. My contention is that the evidence is strongly congruent with their theory, although it rarely explicitly tests it.[9]

THE POWER DIMENSION: FRONTSTAGE AND BACKSTAGE CULTURES

1A. PRINCIPLE OF ORDER-GIVING RITUALS   The experience of giving orders makes people self-assured, proud, or even arrogant, and they identify themselves with the official ideals in whose name they give orders. Conversely, the experience of taking orders from other people makes people fatalistic, externally conforming but privately alienated from authority and the official ideals in whose name they are given orders.

---

[9] The struggle over control in organizations is strongly influenced by this set of principles, as we shall see in Chapter 13.

Giving and taking orders is a Goffmanian frontstage situation. Order givers dominate the performance, attempting to make themselves look impressive and in control. Hence, the personality style that emerges from the experience of habitually giving orders: individuals identify the role and the organization with their own ego. This is partly the result of the focus of the order-giving ritual; the order giver, as the focus of attention, hence becomes a sort of organizational "sacred object," a symbol of the organized group.

Order takers also participate in the ritual, but in a more passive or controlled fashion. They must take the role of respectful audience and must make at least a show of the intention of complying, however they actually behave when the order giver is out of sight. Hence order takers become externally conforming, but lack a sense of control over their own fate. This is the reason for the attraction of gambling and superstition often found in order-taking classes. Order-takers' egos are oriented away from the official organization and its rituals because these are the situations in which they suffer most ego loss. Order givers acquire a frontstage personality, the order takers a backstage personality, because those are the spheres in which their ego rewards are the greatest. We might also say that order giving is a ritual in which those in power attempt to impose their view of reality upon others. But because of the alienation from having power imposed upon them, the order takers give only perfunctory deference to those official ideals and ignore or criticize them privately in their backstage group. Order givers, however, must make a stronger commitment to their official ideals if they are to represent them in a ritual; hence order givers end up indoctrinating themselves even more than they indoctrinate others.

This is congruent with evidence from studies of occupational groups (for example, Collins, 1975: 61–87; Gans, 1962, 1967; Kohn, 1977; Kohn and Schooler, 1983; Kanter, 1977). Professionals, who have the greatest power and autonomy in their work and who present themselves in public with the greatest emphasis upon their authoritativeness and impressiveness, are also the most identified with their own work. They idealize their job and consider it a "calling," a contribution to some larger goal rather than a way of making a living. This is particularly noticeable among medical doctors, scientists, and academics. High-ranking officials of organizations also are most likely to identify with the organization and with the ideals that find their way into the ritualistic speeches they make. Identification with the job decreases as one descends the hierarchy of power and is lowest among workers who are purely order takers. The same principle should also apply in other organizations, outside the realm of work (voluntary associations, communities, the family). Those with most power in these spheres have the most frontstage identification with their organization's official ideals, while those with least power are most withdrawn from it psychologically. There is evidence for this regarding voluntary associations, such as trade unions and political parties (Berelson and Steiner, 1964: 378–80); the application to the family or to informal groups is a hypothesis.

Several complexities can be introduced into this basic principle. The experience of giving and taking orders constitutes a continuum. Some persons do nothing but give orders; others do nothing but take orders. Yet others take orders from their superiors and give them to their own subordinates. The sheer number of order-giving and order-taking experiences can vary, both within a single organizational position and between different spheres of an individual's life (for instance, at work and at home). Experiences will also vary over an individual's career (as he or she grows up, leaves one position for another, and experiences mobility). The severity of the authority can vary, from mild and disguised to direct and coercive. Hence, the following additional principles apply:

1B. PRINCIPLE OF RITUAL COERCION   The more coercion and threat there is in order-giving rituals, the more deference is demanded of order takers from order-givers, and the more accentuated are the results of principle 1A.

This implies, among other things, that societies (such as medieval aristocracies or contemporary dictatorships) or organizations (such as the military) which use more overt violence to back up order giving will have more ritual obeisance between the classes. The dominant class or rank will be correspondingly more arrogant and egotistical; the lower class, more externally conforming and personally alienated. The lesser visibility of class divisions in modern "Americanized" societies is due to the "softer" forms in which order-giving rituals are carried out.

1C. PRINCIPLE OF ANTICIPATORY SOCIALIZATION   Expecting to become an order giver in the future makes individuals tend to identify with the class culture of order givers, even if they are currently order takers. Conversely, expecting not to move up in the future makes individuals identify against the order givers' culture.

This is the well-known principle of anticipatory socialization. However, it operates only in an upward direction; persons will acquire some order givers' attitudes, identifying with official values, before they have moved up; but they rarely anticipate moving down (even if there is an objective likelihood of it happening), and they resist preliminary identification with order takers' attitudes (for evidence, see Collins, 1975: 74–75). Kanter (1977) found that lower-ranking managers in a business corporation tended to be enthusiastic about their jobs, and to identify upwards when they were attached to bosses who were regarded as having good promotion chances and as power brokers who could take their group of subordinates upward with them. Conversely, those persons in "dead-end" jobs, who had given up hopes of promotion, were more oriented away from the organization and toward their private lives; they were cynical and critical of the plans and ideas of the "power movers" who were passing them by. This last point suggests that in a mobility-oriented situation, even the failure to move up (rather than the actual experience of being an order taker) can produce the order takers' culture.

1D. PRINCIPLE OF BUREAUCRATIC PERSONALITY   The experience of taking orders from some people and giving orders (or ritually representing the organization) to other people generates a stereotyped, rigid, and external identification with the organization's rules and procedures.

This means that persons who are in the lower-middle of the chain of command will have a distinctive cultural stance. Often this is referred to as the "bureaucratic personality." These are persons who are subject to a mixture of both the order givers' and the order takers' culture. They identify with the organization officially, since it is a ritual performance required by their job. But though they enact their organizational role in a way which conforms externally, they do so without concern for the larger purpose of the organization. They do not identify with the organization as they would an activity which they were personally responsible for and they could create and develop plans for in the way higher professionals and top managers (or upward strivers) do. Thus, low-level supervisors tend to have a perfunctory, role-following style. It is also found among personnel who represent the organization to the public: window clerks in government agencies, bank tellers, service personnel in stores and restaurants. These persons are order takers in relation to their bosses, but in relation to the public they have the initiative in managing the "frontstage" ritual of their occupation. The ritual staging is a necessary part of their jobs, and it is the one area which is under their control. Hence, they tend to enforce their organizations' rules and procedures in a rigid and perfunctory way, to the extent that it gives them power over the persons they interact with.

Kanter (1977) points out that working women are often stereotyped as bureaucratic personalities, concerned with petty enforcement of rules and lacking initiative and vision for the organization's purposes. But this is the result of women being confined largely to lower-level supervisory positions or first-line "frontstage" representatives of the organization—positions of order taker vis-à-vis their organizational superiors, with little chance of promotion, and a sphere of power only in the petty enforcement of rules and routines. Kanter shows by comparison that this stereotype is not based on gender per se, since men in similar positions are similarly "bureaucratic," while women in positions of greater power take on the style of order givers.

THE NETWORK DIMENSION: SOCIAL DENSITY AND DIVERSITY

2A. PRINCIPLE OF SOCIAL DENSITY   The greater the experience of social density, the more individuals will conform to the group's customs and beliefs, and the more they will expect conformity from others.

Social density means the extent to which a person is physically in the presence of others. It is one of the ingredients of the Durkheimian model of rituals; the emphasis on conformity that follows is the result of ritual in which behaviors and ideas become charged with moral significance as symbols of group membership. According to this principle, the range of experience across an individual's years can be regarded as a dimension of natural ritual, the social density of experience in a more macro dimension, rather than as a particular incident.

At least one aspect of this principle has been widely noted in various branches of sociological theory. Homans' social exchange theory (Chapter 10) includes as a basic principle the fact that the more individuals interact, the more they will like each other and expect conformity to group standards. Homans failed to explain why this is so; the Durkheimian ritual model provides the necessary mechanism. Homans added the proviso that the participants must be equal, not ranked, for this result to follow. That is to say, principle 2A *Social Density* is modified by principle 1A *Order-giving Rituals* in the ritual theory, which gives the results of asymmetrical rituals, with one side giving orders and the other taking orders. The order-taking side tends to be alienated from the ritual, and conforms only externally, whereas the order-giving side internalizes the "sacred objects" resulting from the ritual. Homans' theory picks up the last point in the form of its assertion that the group leader is most likely to exemplify the group's values. This is based on empirical evidence, but Homans interpreted the direction of causality incorrectly. For him, leadership is due to

this greater exemplification to the group's values; whereas the conflict theory of rituals points out that the leader's self-indoctrination is due to a greater involvement in order-giving rituals.

There is a considerable range of evidence to support this "horizontal" principle: social density leads to conformity. It has often been noted that small towns, and other isolated communities with a high degree of mutual surveillance, have a strong or even stifling atmosphere of conformity (Gusfield, 1975). Durkheim (1893) took this observation about the taboos of tribal societies as one of the groups for his general principle of social density effects. Urban dwellers have less densely interconnected networks and less traditional attitudes (Fischer, 1982). One of the major determinants of juvenile delinquency is the degree to which teenagers are distant from or close to their parents (Hirschi 1969) (a factor which operates irrespective of social class, the vertical dimension). Similarly, the amount of teenage premarital sex is correlated with distance versus closeness to parents (DeLamater and Mac-Corquodale, 1979). Conversely, creativity among artists and intellectuals typically has, as one of its antecedents (though not the only one), a prolonged period of isolation in youth, and the adult habit of working in privacy (evidence reviewed in Collins, 1975: 273–74). That is to say, creativity is the opposite of conformity to group traditions; hence low social density (at least, from the surrounding society, if not from others in a creative network) is necessary to break the pressures for conformity.

This principle also applies to the typical experiences of different social classes. Though it is hypothetically separate from the hierarchy principle (order giving and order taking), empirically there is a tendency for members of the lower social classes to live in situations of greater social density. In their work, they are more likely to be under close surveillance by peers and superiors; in their home and leisure, they tend to be more often in the presence of family and group. Privacy both at work and outside is more generally associated with the higher social classes. Hence, the greater emphasis on conformity found among the working class. But this conformity is to the local group's standards and does not necessarily mean conformity to the standards of an official organization or to the ideals of a higher social class. These higher-class ideals are often more abstract and relativistic (principle 2B *Social Diversity*) than working-class customs and symbolic values. There is an element of class conflict in the rejection of such "sophisticated" attitudes as tolerance of religious, political, or sexual nonconformists, liberated roles for women, nontraditional psychological methods of education and child rearing, and treatment of penal offenders—issues on which working-class persons are generally found to be more conservative (Curtis and Jackson, 1977: 303–13; Rubin, 1976; Gabennesch, 1972).[10]

---

[10] Kohn *et al.* (1971, 1983) present relevant evidence, although without disentangling the dimensions of principles 1A, 2A, and 2B. Workers who are closely supervised (and who have less complex work) are more likely to bring up their children to follow rules, attempt to get good grades in school, and generally conform externally. Their own values and behavior are similar. Workers who are less closely supervised (1A *Order-giving Ritual* and 2A *Social Density*), or who supervise others (1A), and who have more complex work (2B *Social Diversity*) are more likely to value independence and creativity rather than rote conformity. (In fact, though, working-class children turn out to do less well in school and conform to work standards less. The results are expressing the ideal wishes of parents more than actual behavior. Middle and upper-middle class parents go beyond external, rote conformity, to emphasizing

The vehemence of the reaction to nonconformity is the result of both principles 2A *Social Density* as well as 1B *Ritual Coercion*. That is, the extent to which group members will become righteously angry and inflict violent punishment on violators depends on the actual coercive force of the group. The emotional tone in the ritual interaction (the third ingredient listed earlier in "A Formal Model of Ritual") is what is operative here. If it is based on violent threat, either from inside the group (its own hierarchy) or outside the group (protection against outside dangers), the reaction to deviance will be correspondingly charged with violence. The more egalitarian and voluntary the group, the more its disapproval of symbolic violations will take the form of shunning rather than violent reprisal.

2B. PRINCIPLE OF SOCIAL DIVERSITY   The diversity or uniformity of communications determines whether the group's symbols will be abstract or concrete, reified or relativistic. That is Durkheim's second ritual ingredient, the amount of focus. On the macro level of natural rituals, this is affected by the extent to which an individual participates in a diverse network, as opposed to always being exposed to the same people and the same situations. Durkheim (1893) described this as a high or low division of labor, a description of the entire society; he cited as evidence the fact that religions in small tribal societies are concrete and personify the religious forces, whereas larger differentiated societies have philosophical religions with abstract religious beings, while more complex industrial societies move still further in the direction of abstract moral and scientific principles for their world views.[11]

The most important application of the principle, however, is at the level of the experience of particular individuals and groups. Again, there is a correlation with social class (although this principle can vary independently of 1A). As an empirical generalization, members of the higher social classes have more diverse contacts, both in their occupations and in their social lives. Working-class sociability is more confined to family, neighborhood, and a long-term circle of friends; whereas the more superficial sociability of clubs, formal banquets, parties and the like is more characteristic of the middle and especially upper-middle to upper classes. Both work and sociable spheres are generally more diverse and cosmopolitan for the higher classes. Hence, the empirical correlations found between social class differences in political

internalized values and self-direction. The alienation of order takers expected in 1A shows up in the actual behavior.) This may be confounded by the order takers in the work sphere reporting on their behavior as order givers in the home context. Following principle 1A, they give more emphasis to the home role, whereas order givers identify more with their work. Closeness of supervision also indicates social density; here the greater emphasis on external conformity is what follows from principle 2A.

[11] Durkheim also theorized that the sheer size of society determines its division of labor; hence by a second link in a chain of inference, Durkheim could assert that a larger society produces an abstract rather than a concrete collective conscience. This point has been criticized on the grounds that large societies (like traditional China or India) do not necessarily have an abstract collective conscience; nor do particularistic religion and its secular equivalents, such as nationalism and racism in politics, necessarily fade away in complex modern societies. But the Durkheimian principles we are interested in here are still valid, because: (1) we are concerned with the link which states that diversity of experiences produces more abstract symbols, not with the prior link that sheer size of society produces diversity (which need not always be true). (2) As we have seen, the Durkheimian principle may be applied to particular groups and individuals within a society, so that different cultural symbols can exist at the same time, corresponding to different groups.

attitudes and religious beliefs, and the style of thinking in general (Collins, 1975: 67–77). In the realm of aesthetic tastes, the higher social classes hold reflexive and relativistic ideas as to what constitutes "art," while the lower classes reject intellectualized art in favor of what seems unreflectingly pretty, sentimental, or colorful (Bourdieu, 1984; Gans, 1971).[12]

Bernstein (1971–75), using an explicitly Durkheimian conception, has shown that members of the middle class tend to speak in a more abstract, context-free speech code, while members of the working class speak more typically in a concrete, particularistic style, relying on the assumption that the listeners are part of the same group context. Since speech has a major effect on thought (Chapters 7 and 9) we can infer that these classes have correspondingly different mentalities. Although Bernstein does not independently measure the social density and network diversity of different social classes, it appears that principles 2A and 2B are the operative influences in his results.

Survey research frequently finds education rather than occupational position to be the prime determinant of these attitudinal and behavioral differences (Curtis and Jackson, 1977; Fischer, 1982). Why should this pattern exist? Education itself is a form of diversification of social contacts, a separate sphere of group experience added to home, sociability, and work. Probably more importantly, it affects the ritual focus of life experience by an emphasis on written communications. Reading and writing is a way of focusing attention on distant persons with whom one communicates (who may even be anonymous), as well as on the abstract content of symbols themselves. But abstract content cannot be entirely decisive, since readers of traditionalist books (such as persons who assiduously reread the Bible, the Koran, or right-wing political tracts) will be reinforced in nonrelativistic and nonabstract attitudes. The sheer amount of time doing paper work and communicating in this non–face-to-face fashion increases the level of diversity of communications in a person's everyday experience. The association between education and cosmopolitan attitudes is probably due to the propensity of educated persons to undertake more written communication and more reading.[13]

Again we see differences within the same general class level. The more intellectual professions, although included among the order givers, both spend more time working alone and, because of the paperwork they do, have a greater diversity of communications than do line managers, whose daily work consists mainly of personal meetings (Kanter, 1977). For this reason, there is a split in the higher social classes between those who are more liberal on general cultural issues and those who are more conservative.

---

[12] Bourdieu, however, lumps all his causal variables into a general category of hierarchy, supported by cultural capital, and does not distinguish between the effects of power (1A) and network diversity (2B). According to Durkheimian theory, it is the latter that is the operative factor. Bourdieu's main distinction within "the fractions of the dominant class" is between inherited and acquired cultural capital. Significantly, the latter (the professional-academic elite, who came up via education) are much more likely to have tastes which are intellectualized, reflective, and relativistic, whereas the upper class based on inherited wealth is more likely to ostentaciously simply display their dignity and opulence.

[13] Education can also be nondiversifying and conformity producing, if individuals spend most of their time in a high-density, highly ritualized group such as a fraternity or sorority, and little in abstract communications. A hypothesis worth testing.

In general, we can visualize the class structure not only as a vertical dimension of power but also as a set of communities with different horizontal characteristics of density and network diversity. Using Durkheim's model of religious symbols as a reflection of the self-worship of society, we can say that the Weberian status groups built horizontally within class levels are a set of symbolic cults. Though there sometimes are macrocults more or less shared across the society (which may be forcibly promoted by the upper classes in the interests of ritual domination and legitimacy), localized groups and strata are, in varying degrees, mutually exclusive and even antagonistic cults. They worship their own gods in the forms of different moral, political, and aesthetic beliefs; customs and styles; and even different forms of speech and thought.

Groups in the more localistic, less diverse networks reify their customs and beliefs more strongly, taking them as absolute and actually existing; while persons in more cosmopolitan locations are more likely to see them abstractly and relativistically, as conventions which are adopted under different conditions. The localistic groups also tend to be suspicious, distrustful, and even fearful about the outside world beyond their own circle. This is a consequence of their type of ideas. Their group structure induces them to think concretely, in terms of particular individuals and places, and so the complexities of the outside world are not available to them in terms of abstractions. Thus, the only way they can deal with larger social forces (such as economic and political forces, and natural processes explainable by scientific abstractions) is by projecting personification onto the unknown. In tribal societies, this took the form of occult forces symbolized in taboos; in more complex societies, localized, noncosmopolitan persons tend to personify larger social processes as religious punishment or diabolical intervention, or as the activities of nefarious persons or groups. Since there is a degree of localism in everyone's social networks, almost everyone occasionally invokes individual scapegoats in accounting for uncontrollable processes of the social macrostructure. The tendency to do so, though, varies according to the diversity of network structure which individuals inhabit.

MULTIPLE CAUSALITY AND STRATIFICATION

The evidence just discussed shows a pattern of relative differences. A given cultural trait is found in a greater percentage of one social class than another social class, yet it is not found throughout a particular social class. This is not merely the result of errors of measurement. As is often the case, the technical issue masks a substantive theoretical problem. The fact that predicted differences are merely relative tendencies indicates that the hypothesized principle, although true, is not the only causal process operating. What can the other causes be?

It is likely that much of the additional causality in the situation is actually the same causal principle, but operating in a fashion that we have not specified very precisely. Principle 1A predicts that persons who give orders tend to identify with their official organizational ideals. This will be found to be true a certain percentage of the time. If we knew the pattern involved in how long a person gave orders and what amount of time they gave them, we could state the principle more precisely: that is, how does the principle "giving orders leads to official identification" behave as a dynamic process? How long until it takes effect? Does it reach a plateau? (See Appendix B on dynamic simulation models.) The principle of anticipatory socialization (1C) puts a time element into this model. There is also past experience. Many people will have a history of having taken orders at some time in their lives, later moving on to giving orders (or vice versa). Also, a person can move from situations of high social density to lower social density and so forth. We need "time laws" for how these carry-over effects operate. There is some evidence (cited in Collins, 1975: 75) about some of these carry-over effects for certain cultural outcomes. The amount of unexplained variance could doubtless be reduced if such principles could be more precisely written in terms of time effects, intensity effects, and how long they last into new situations. My guess is that most of these effects are only of moderate length, and that people become largely socialized into a new class situation within a few years. However, they may also be continuously subject to a mixture of circumstances; in which case, their thoughts and behavior will be a mixture of these current forces.

There is a second route by which these same variables may have mixed effects upon individuals. That is, they are influenced not only by the class culture of their own milieu, but by the class culture of the people they associate with. Culture is to some extent transmissible from others: children pick it up from their parents and adults pick it up from their friends. For this reason, a parent's social class will have attitude effects, independent of the individual's own class situation. There is reason to believe that the culture of one's friends has a similar effect (some evidence is in Collins, 1975: 81). It should be emphasized that these are also class effects, though they are transmitted at second remove. They might be called "transmitted class effects," which are passed on through network connections. Prediction will thus be improved by knowing about an individual's network position, not only in terms of its density and diversity but also in terms of the class anchorages of persons near to that person in the network. (Chapter 10 deals with this under the transmission of cultural capital in interaction ritual chains.) An improved theory will have to state the relative weight of each of these lines of influence. I would guess that current conditions and immediate past conditions are most powerful, but we don't know yet how to write the principles of how these different influences combine.

The overall picture of stratification that emerges is a complex one. But the complexity is on the empirical surface; the number of principles that generate it is relatively small. All individuals are subject to a number of different conditions: their current, past, and future expected positions with regard to order giving and order taking (1A), social density (2A), and network diversity (2B); and the indirect transmission of the same three variables as they have affected the individual's acquaintances. Furthermore, order giving, density, and diversity can operate in different degrees at work, at home, in sociability, and so forth. Each individual's overall cultural stance is a mixture, or summation, of all these class influences.[14] This means that it is quite possible for every individual to be unique. No person's position in

---

[14] An additional indirect transmission effect may be via the cultural media: reading, television, or other entertainment. Thus the cultures transmitted would be those of the classes that control these media. But persons of different indigenous cultures select their preferred media, so that these media effects are probably not a major additional influence. Their precise weight has not been determined, though it has been argued that they have brought about a homogenization of class cultures in the later twentieth century. The argument should be taken with some caution, though, because it has been alleged by every generation since about 1500 A.D., possibly with some justification, but class differences still remain.

the grid of influences is likely to be exactly the same as any other person's, although there will be relative similarities. This model of stratification does not force everyone into a mold of a limited class pattern. The class determination of culture and behavior may be quite strict and predictable, but the precise combination of strengths of different direct and indirect factors determines each person to be different in some respects.

How many class cultures are there? The answer must be that it depends on how many distinctions we are willing to make. Potentially, there could be as many class cultures as there are individuals; though of course, they may also coalesce into particular cultural (and associational) lumps. It is the business of a more macro-level theory to show the conditions under which this happens and to what degree.

Roughly speaking, we may sketch the structure of modern class cultures across a grid. (See Figure 6-3.) On the vertical dimension is the amount of order giving versus order taking; on the horizontal dimension (or dimensions) is the Durkheimian pattern of social density and diversity (for convenience, they may be combined into a predominant continuum of high conformity–low cosmopolitanism to low conformity–high cosmopolitanism, although the other combinations also exist. There may not be very sharp borderlines between either the vertical power dimensions or the horizontal Durkheimian dimensions, nor need people be very conscious of the distribution of cultural attributes across the society. (An individual's consciousness is largely micro, while the pattern is macro; individual's awareness of macro is notoriously distorted by class cultures and by ideology.) In fact, there are at least a half dozen or more major cultural clumpings. Most important are distinctions within the same approximate level of order-giving power. For instance, there are at least two different versions of the working class: a highly localistic, conformist and traditionalist group, and a cosmopolitan "action crowd" or underworld.[15] At the other end of the class structure, there is a division between a more cosmopolitan, relativistic and libertarian upper-middle class, and a more traditionalistic and conservative group of order givers. Since it is the higher social classes who are most active politically, this division is probably of the greatest importance for modern politics, since it constitutes the distinction between liberals and conservatives (both of whom attempt to muster support by appealing to the interests or cultural prejudices of the lower-ranking classes).[16]

[15] Certain urban occupations among order takers—street vendors, shoeshiners, doormen, and so forth— have a high degree of cosmopolitanism of social contacts. Hence their greater cynicism and relativism about prevailing ideals and laws. Their cosmopolitanism is not the same as that of respectable upper-middle-class professionals, however. The latter group is more oriented toward abstractions because of their heavy use of print media, which reduces face-to-face contacts and tendency to personification. (This implies that the tendency to abstraction comes from the social density variable, principle 2A, rather than diversity, 2B. Print media also reduce the emotional contagion aspect of natural rituals, further reducing emotional commitment to prevailing group culture.) At the middle level, where interactions involve more horizontal negotiation than order giving or order taking, salespeople and other traveling occupations (for instance professional athletes) have a cosmopolitan diversity of contacts; but it is on a personal level rather than with the lower social focus of attention in written communication. These occupations are highly cosmopolitan but with high social density, hence their own peculiar cultural complex. The different dimensions of this grid deserve to be better explored empirically.

[16] Psychological development models tend to ignore all the dimensions of class cultures. Piaget proposed that cognitive development proceeds from concrete, context-bound operations in small children, up to

FIGURE 6-3

TWO DIMENSIONS OF CLASS CULTURES

Order givers	Authoritarian upper class	Cosmopolitan upper class
Mixed egalitarian	Conformist middle class	Cosmopolitan middle class
Front-line supervisors	Bureaucratic personality	
Order takers	Localistic working class	Underworld or "Action Crowd"
	High ritual density	Low ritual density

DOUGLAS' GRID AND GROUP

A related multidimensional model in the Durkheimian tradition is that presented by Mary Douglas (1966, 1973). Douglas rejects Durkheim's evolutionary stage formulation of "mechanical solidarity" and "organic solidarity," by reinterpreting these as dimensions which may be found not only among tribal societies, but in other types of societies as well. She reformulates the Durkheimian categories as a continuum between high and low *group*—that is, strong or weak emphasis on the boundaries between the society and outsiders. She adds a second, cross-cutting dimension, which she calls high or low *grid*—the extent to which there are hierarchical boundaries inside the group between different ranks. (See Figure 6-4.)

This is largely the same distinction I made between the power dimension (1A series) and the horizontal, network dimension, but incorporating the variations of social density (2A) and diversity (2B). Also, whereas I formulate the model on the micro level in terms of the experience of particular individuals, Douglas formulates it on the macro level, as a characteristic of the entire society.

Combining the two dimensions, we find the following divisions: *High group, low grid* refers to unstratified societies, isolated from the outside world and highly conscious of their external boundaries. They tend to occur in environments with

abstract and relativistic ones in adults; Kohlberg claims a similar developmental sequence for moral judgments. However, Kohlberg's own data (Kohlberg and Gilligan, 1971) indicate that most adults never reach the "highest" stage of abstract operations. This is what one would expect, because of social class differences (especially on the "horizontal" part of the grid). Gilligan (1982) has attacked Kohlberg's model as a male version of morality (and of cognition), citing evidence that women tend to have more person-oriented, contextual morality. Gilligan, too, is unaware that the Durkheimian model predicts greater person-oriented morality for people whose social contacts are mainly in high density, low diversity groups: an apt description of the traditional milieu of the housewife. Alleged male-female differences, from a sociological viewpoint, are actually results of the different patterns of men and women usually allocated to a society in which men dominate the formal organizations. Hence we do not need a biologically reductionist model of gender differences. Insofar as children, too, differ from adults in their cognition and moral judgments, this can be attributed to the fact that they occupy a situation of low diversity and high social density compared to adults.

FIGURE 6-4

DOUGLAS' GRID AND GROUP

	Low group	High group
High grid	Competitive, fluid stratification Emphasis on pragmatism and luck	Rigidly stratified society Rank-conscious, complex world-view
Low grid	Individualistic Privacy-oriented Secular	Sharp external boundaries Ritual concern for enemies and pollution

scarce resources, so that members have to rely on each other for support. Their rituals are concerned with preventing pollution; their symbols emphasize the distinction between what is clean or unclean, often in the form of dietary restrictions and taboos regarding the bodily orifices. This is because the human body is taken as a symbol of the social order and reflects its structure—the basic Durkheimian theory of symbolism. Members are fearful of outsiders, which is symbolized by fear of poisoning. Problems are met by scapegoating and witch-hunting, and conformity is backed up by threat of expulsion from the group.

In the *high group, high grid* society rigid internal stratification is added to strong external boundaries. Because of greater complexity of society, concepts become more complex and abstract; it is less easy to symbolize the entire society in a simple dichotomy of inside-outside (pure-impure). Rituals, instead of centering on pollution, are concerned with promotions and demotions, atonements for offenses, rites of passage between various statuses. Elaborate theologies and scholastic subtleties make up the mental atmosphere.

The *low group, high grid* society has considerable rank stratification, but group boundaries are weak. There is little to keep people together. (In my terminology, social density is low.) The social landscape consists of fragmented, unstably shifting coalitions in conflict with each other. (This is the model Paige and Paige [1981] apply to sexual and reproductive rituals in tribal societies, viewing them as devices used for negotiating alliances and checking political loyalties.) Members are cynical about rituals and use them in Machiavellian fashion for short-term gain. Alienation from the power holders who enforce rituals is high. The world view centers on luck.

The *low group, low grid* society has relatively little stratification, and lacks strong group boundaries. Its culture is individualistic, pluralistic, and secular. There is little alienation because stratification is mild or easy to evade; but there may be considerable anomie, since no binding standards exist. (Alienation is presumably the result of high grid, anomie of low group.)

Douglas developed her model by comparisons among tribal societies, but it is analytically abstract and can be applied to groups within modern societies as well. Douglas suggests that different groups show varying concerns over pollution and its modern equivalents in styles of dress, long versus short hairstyles, and other ways of accepting or controlling nature. Her model has been explicitly adopted by Bernstein (1971–75), who characterizes different kinds of educational systems along the *grid-group* dimension. Similarly, Bloor (1983) suggests that communities of scientists fall into different parts of this two-dimensional scheme. Hence, they have different amounts of commitment to upholding Kuhnian "normal science": a *high group, low grid* community of intellectuals reacts to anomalous research results and ideas as forms of pollution to be guarded against; a *low group, high grid* community uses them competitively for their advantage; and so on.

This work is suggestive but not entirely conclusive. Douglas does not distinguish clearly between causes and consequences, but uses the typology globally to characterize various tribal societies and other groups. That is, she does not separately measure the group boundaries and internal hierarchy, but tends to infer the group structure from the kinds of rituals and beliefs it has. Bloor proceeds similarly in applying the *grid-group* model to scientific communities.

COLLINS' HISTORICAL TYPOLOGY OF RITUAL CULTURES

A somewhat more systematic model is Collins (1975: 161–218), which applies the power and network dimensions to various historical types of societies, and derives their cultures from the kinds of rituals found in each. The historical typology is modified from Lenski and Weber (Chapter 5). The basic principles as to which rituals will exist are a combination of principles 1A *Order-giving rituals*, 2A *Social density*, and 2B *Social diversity*. (See Figure 6-5.)

Where there is *low inequality* and *high social density*, rituals center on group inclusiveness. Typical cases are the participatory religious rituals of unstratified tribal societies: group dances, feasts, and celebrations which symbolize the boundary between the animistic spirits and the outside world. The more isolated and undifferentiated the group (that is, the *lower the diversity of focus*), the more reified these symbols and the stronger and more "superstitious" the belief in them. Where the emotional tone is a *high degree of fear* regarding the environment (as in the case of external military threats from other tribes, or natural disasters or resources crises), the more these rituals are infused with emotion, and the more vehemently there is punishment of symbolic violations. These rituals are most common in tribal societies, but there are modern equivalents in the private, family sphere: usually with low inequality, low fear (because of low environmental stress) and modest social density, for example family dinners (Thanksgiving), gift-giving solidarity rituals like Christmas and birthdays, as well as celebration rituals like political holidays (Fourth of July, Bastille Day, Cinco de Mayo, and so forth), and festive parties and celebrations (New Year's Eve, St. Patrick's day).

Where *high density* societies have *high inequality*, their rituals take the form of *deference rituals*. High-ranking persons (such as tribal chiefs) and their accoutrements (symbols of royalty and power) are subjects of much bowing and scraping. There is an atmosphere of impressiveness, backed up by fear. But in this case it is not fear of outsiders or natural catastrophes, but fear of the punishment that can be wreaked by the powerful elites themselves. Rituals in this case ought to be regarded as part of the resources of class domination. The impressiveness of chiefs, kings, priests, aristocrats and the like is enacted on a Goffmanian frontstage, constructed of mate-

FIGURE 6-5

COLLINS' TYPOLOGY OF DEFERENCE CULTURES

High social inequality

	Low social density	High social density
Low diversity	Ostentatious public display of rank	Coercive, highly visible deference rituals
High diversity	Perfunctory obedience to rituals	Sophisticated manners Subtle rank-consciousness

Low social inequality

	Low social density	High social density
Low diversity	Informality in social groups	Group inclusion rituals Conformity to tradition
High diversity	Private, unritualized interactions	Fads

rial resources: the elaborate costumes, buildings, throne rooms, as well as the art and music of religious ritual designed to awe the audiences and exalt the position of the central performers on these stages. Stratification in such societies is to a large extent due to control of the *material means of impression management,* a concept extending Marx and Engels' (1846/1947: 39) "control of the means of intellectual production" to include the "means of emotional production" and hence of the Durkheimian solidarity symbols which are the result.

The *high inequality, high social density* combination is sometimes elaborated by *high diversity:* this is the case in complex authoritarian kingdoms, such as the courtly society of Louis XIV's Versailles and other Absolutist states. The diversity takes the form of multiple rankings among the courtiers and aristocrats. A certain cosmopolitanism and sophistication accordingly sets in (principle 2B), in which rituals are used as frontstages to be manipulated for private intrigues. Rituals are even more elaborate, however, since they represent numerous rankings in the society. Degrees of deference are finely distinguished, and there is much maneuvering and bickering

over petty precedence (see Morris, 1964, on medieval Japan). Again, modern equivalents can be found (though usually with less intensity, since direct coercion is less
commonly used to uphold stratification): for example in the finely graded status
symbols in the modern corporation, and the organizational politics that goes with
the pursuit of rank (Kanter, 1977).

The complex processes of historical change usually referred to as "modernization" are best seen as shifts in several of these variables. *Inequality* (1A) has generally
lessened since the peak reached in medieval agrarian societies of aristocrats and com-
moners, though seldom dropping to the low degree found in some primitive tribal
societies. Modern stratification is less often backed up by sheer military force of a
dominant aristocracy (though this is found in militaristic regimes, totalitarian party
regimes, or racial supremicist regimes); where this is the case, the inequality component of rituals greatly reduces the intensity of deference expected, and the severity
with which violations are punished. More importantly for the modern trend in public culture or manners, has been a shift away from high *social density* (2A). Both
tribal and agrarian societies tended to pack people together closely; with little privacy in households and low geographical mobility, most people were under high
surveillance from their communities. In the patrimonial household, work was carried
on generally in the living area and sociable activities usually took place there too;
hence there was much less possibility for multiple spheres in which interactional
conditions might vary (along the dimensions of 1A, 2A, 2B). The rise of the private
household, of sociable spheres outside the home, and the separation of the workplace has increased the amount of privacy in modern societies, although this has
affected the middle and especially upper-middle class more than the working class.
The working class, though, has achieved a moderate degree of privacy by being able
to withdraw from their subordinate position in the work place into the privacy of
their local and domestic circle. The anonymity of urban mass society and the privacy of automobiles have also contributed to this greater privatization.

The most important result is that the ritualization of the collectivity has greatly
declined. The inescapable social density experienced by medieval people has given
way to a voluntary social density, chosen by individuals when they wish to attend
religious, political, or entertainment events. There are exceptions, of course: totalitarian regimes and some mass movements attempt to recreate traditional solidarity
by coercively enforcing participation in public rituals. But where this pressure is not
applied, individuals tend to withdraw into privacy. This is because most rituals in
stratified society have an element of coercive imposition to them and demand deference from their audiences. Freed from constraints to be present at rituals, modern
persons tend to choose to withdraw. The result is what I have called "the Goffmanian revolution," a shift in the standards of deference and demeanor from compulsory
deference rituals to a voluntary encounter of individuals. Each person is relatively
(not absolutely) freer to put on a frontstage self under conditions of one's own
choosing. The ironic result is that no one is able to extract very much deference:
though each person can try to manage impressions to his or her own benefit, everyone else is doing the same, and people can withdraw from encounters where they
are overmatched. Hence the trend towards informality in personal relationships,
sometimes referred to as "Americanization," because these structural conditions were
first reached in the mid-twentieth century United States.

CONCLUSION

All the variants of neo-Durkheimian theory may be seen as analytical extensions of the elements of the ritual model. Recall its ingredients: the assembly of the group, the focus of attention, the intensification of a common emotion, and resulting symbols of group solidarity. The concept of natural rituals enables us to use these as variables to characterize the experience of individuals (in principles 1A, 2A, and so on) or of entire groups or societies (in Douglas' grid-group and Collins' historical typology). In the individual case, we get the culture of each individual; in the latter case, we get the kind of rituals and beliefs that dominate in that society.

Goffman's innovations, when we see them in a theoretical light, are important for every aspect of the model. His studies took place in a time when the social factors affecting group assembly were shifting toward a radical voluntarism of social density, as compared to the inescapable social density of the past. In regard to the focus of attention, Goffman's dramaturgical model shows us that material means and deliberate tactics are important determinants of what interactants will focus upon and with what intensity. These conditions determine how much people will accept the realities thus socially constructed and how impressive those realities will be. He also pointed out that chief among these realities is the social impression of the self. The fact that these selves may also be ranked shows us a link between ritual and the stratification of society.

Goffman's staging model also casts light on the everyday basis of group formation and group division. Frontstage presentations are often put on by teams who thereby have a group solidarity from their common activity in the backstage as well as on the frontstage. This is an important variant on the Durkheimian factor of group assembly. Everyone present at a ritual is not affected by it in the same way. Teams of performers are even more tightly linked to each other than audiences are to the sacred objects of the performance; the team loyalty is more specialized, more manipulative and instrumental. It tends to stratify the performance team against the audience and to make the ideals they portray into an ideology of their domination. Goffman's model is especially useful when it is linked to the Dahrendorf-Weber model of stratification by power. The ritual procedures of giving orders make such a sharp distinction between order givers and order takers as to constitute one of the two major dimensions of the culture-producing experience (principle 1A series).

Despite these complexities, the ritual model of society still may seem crude in comparison to the subtle and fluctuating experiences of subjective experience. But Goffman is equal to this challenge and, in his later work (1974, 1981) on emergent levels and frames in the structure of the focus of attention, showed how quite subtle stage identities can emerge within momentary fragments of a conversation. We will meet this in Chapter 8.

I have added a further variant within the Durkheimian model: although any emotion held in common can be an ingredient with ritualistic effects, particular emotions generate their own special types of ritual consequences. Emotions of threat, especially of violence or death, are especially important. They raise the level of fear in the group, and hence the vehemence with which persons indoctrinated with the ritual will cling to its symbols and the ferociousness of their punishment of violators.

Since the implication of violent coercion is always in the background of organized power (the enforcement potential of the state), this is particularly important for rituals which link together the micro to the macro structure of society.

SUMMARY

1. Durkheim's theory of religion may be stated more generally as a theory of ritual production of moral solidarity. The elements of a ritual are (1) physical co-presence of a group; (2) mutual awareness of a common focus of attention; (3) a common emotional mood. Once begun, (2) and (3) recycle and intensify. The results are (4) symbols or "sacred objects" representing membership in the group; (5) emotional energy for participants; (6) righteous anger against violators of the sacred symbols.

2. *Formal rituals* are intentional ceremonies. They may be macro or micro, invoking membership in entire communities or small groups. *Natural rituals* are any form of interaction which can be characterized by some degree of co-presence, common focus, and common mood. Hence any experience of social interaction produces a high to low degree of membership symbols, emotional energies, and pressures to conformity, depending on the amount of copresence, focus, and mood.

3. Durkheim's *mechanical solidarity* type is characterized by high ritual density, which results in a strong and particularized "collective conscience," consisting of concrete and reified symbols, intense punitive ritual against violators, a sharp sense of group boundaries with distrust of outsiders. *Organic solidarity* derives from the more moderate or low ritual density of differentiated interaction and is characterized by individualism, abstract and relativistic ideas, and routinized trust of distant social relationships.

4. The micro basis of rituals appears to be due to rhythmic synchronization between persons in interaction, which can occur at a physiological level that is more finely tuned than persons can be consciously aware of.

5. Goffman studied rituals which hold together small or temporary groups in everyday life. A ritual is performed in a material setting analogous to a theatre, with a *frontstage* region on which the intended performance takes place and a *backstage* where preparation and recuperation occurs and incongruous elements are kept hidden. Ritual performances take place in work situations—especially in acting out the power of order givers and in giving a show of compliance by subordinates—and in sociable situations, especially in the aesthetic self-presentation of the higher social classes. Any successful conversation is a ritual which creates a temporary common reality (usually with an unrealistic content) in which the talkers become engrossed, and which expresses their personal relationship.

6. A two-dimensional theory of class cultures can be built from these micro elements. On the *power dimension,* persons who give orders identify with their frontstage selves and hence with the organizational or institutional symbols which are being enacted. Persons who take orders tend to be alienated from frontstage rituals and identify more with their private, backstage selves. The amount of coercion intensifies these effects. Expectation of moving up into positions of power causes anticipatory identification with order-givers' culture; blocked opportunities foster

attitudes similar to the order-takers' culture. Persons who both give and take orders acquire a mixed culture, often taking the form of a "bureaucratic personality" of stereotyped conformity to organizational rules.

7. On the *network dimension:* The *principle of social density* states that the more that individuals are physically in the presence of the group, the more conformity is given by self and expected of others and the more violent and emotional the reaction to deviants against group tradition. The *principle of social diversity* states that uniformity of communications produces concrete and reified symbols; diversity of communications produces abstract and relativistic symbols. The cultural effect of education and of participation in written media occurs by increasing the level of diversity and abstractness of communications.

8. Social classes must be analyzed by cross-classifying power and network dimensions. Individuals may have unique cultural combinations due to their amount of experience at different levels of power, density, and diversity; as well as by memories of past experiences, anticipation of future experience, and indirect transmission of class cultures from the persons they associate with.

9. Mary Douglas' dimensions of *grid* and *group* cross-classifies these same underlying Durkheimian variables in order to explain the sacred symbols and the concerns over pollution found in various societies. Collins similarly applies the typology of power, density, and diversity to explain the kinds of rituals which have predominated in different historical situations.

Chapter 7

SELF, MIND, AND SOCIAL ROLE

THE SOCIAL SELF
  The Clouded Mirror
  A Basic Debate: "I" vs. "Me"

THE "ME" SIDE: ROLE THEORY
  Social Action as Role Taking
  Role Sets and Role Strains
  Role Identification
  Role Learning vs. Role Making

EXPECTATION STATES THEORY
  Personality as Situational Expectations
  Status and Behavior Cues
  Do Expectation States Explain Stratification?

THE SOCIOLOGY OF THINKING: MEAD AND PEIRCE
  Peirce's Three Components of Signification
  The Generalized Other
  The Generalized Other Is the Source of Universal Signs
  Criticisms of Mead
  Thought as Internalized Conversation
  Further Developments of a Sociology of Thinking

SELF AS A SACRED OBJECT
  Goffman on Face-Work, Deference, and Demeanor
  A Historical Question: What Produces the Modern Cult of the Self?

MULTIPLE OR UNITARY SELF?
  The Self as Modern Myth
  Is There a Core Self?

SUMMARY

Among the first efforts of American sociology to carve out a territory for itself was the theory of the social self. It marks the inroads of sociology into psychology, dealing with a topic that appears at first glance to be preeminently individual. What could be more intimate than one's own self, and hence amenable at best to psychological, rather than sociological, analysis? The classic American theorists, Charles Horton Cooley and George Herbert Mead, writing in the early twentieth century, showed otherwise. In their theories, the self would not exist without society.

This topic opened up many ramifications. Sociologists have studied what aspects of self are influenced by social groups and how much self-protection is left for one's egotism. Social structure can be seen as made up of a variety of selves in the form of roles; these roles involve both coordination with each other, as well as strains and conflicts. How one sees others and also oneself is determined by expectations as to how people will perform in these roles. On another level, we may go inside the self to pick apart its components. George Herbert Mead called these the "I," "me," and "generalized other," actually a whole flock of such items which make up a kind of society inside the self. This leads to the theory that the mind itself is an internalized conversation and that thinking can be explained sociologically. Finally, we consider a different approach to the self: the interaction ritual tradition from Chapter 6, developed especially by Erving Goffman. It proposes a startling conclusion: the self is actually a myth, believed in because *modern* (but not earlier) society worships the individual self as its most important sacred object.

THE SOCIAL SELF

The self is not a private or personal entity, nor even strictly the individual human body. It is, first of all, a viewpoint, one that always involves other people looking upon the self from outside. How can this be proved? Mead offered the argument that when one is engrossed in action, there is no sense of self; one is caught up completely in what one is doing—playing a game, working, talking, making love. (The last is not literally Mead's example, however, since he wrote in the prudishness of the post-Victorian era.) The sense of self is present when one is more reflective; when one is looking at oneself as well as doing. This implies a point of view, a self which is doing the looking as well as a self which is seen. The viewpoint is provided by a sense of society, the viewpoint of others.

There has been by now much empirical research on how people describe or define their selves (Rosenberg, 1979). The results demonstrate that who one considers oneself to be, depends on one's social position. The kinds of categories used and the traits which are relevant vary by how the individual is related to society. For example, adults are likely to identify themselves by their occupations; this is especially true in the higher occupational levels and least likely in the lower levels. Children systematically go through various stages of self-identification (Gottfredson, 1981). One of the earliest traits seized upon, in our culture, is gender: by age two or three, children answer the question "what are you?" by saying (emphatically) that they are a girl or a boy. This is a social pattern, not a biological one. For at such a young age, there are no physical differences between females and males that have any relevance for behavior. (Differences in size and strength do not appear until near puberty, and sexual activity is minimal until later.) Typing one's self as a girl or boy, then, is due primarily to the fact that other people emphasize this distinction, and hence create a social self that is fundamentally gender-based.

One's physical body can of course become a relevant part of one's self. But it has to *become* relevant, because it is socially relevant, not because it is intrinsically so. Among intellectual adults, for instance, or organizational administrators, physique is not likely to be very salient; instead the crucial identifications are what scientific specialty one works in, what books one is the author of, or what administrative position one holds. Physical traits of one sort (being 6 feet 5 inches tall and weighing 220 pounds) are a more crucial item of self-identification if one is an aspiring professional athlete; traits of another sort (being brunette, good-looking, sexy) are important if one is active in pursuing a lot of sexual affairs. There is evidence, too, that in the realm of sexual encounters, women are more likely to identify their selves with their physical appearance, while men identify somewhat more with their achievements (Safilios-Rothschild, 1977: 35–36). This pattern occurs at a particular historical time in a particular society, and it can be explained by the relative resources that males and females typically have in relation to the larger system of stratification.

THE CLOUDED MIRROR

No wonder, then, that Cooley (1902) called his social model "the looking-glass self." The mirror is an eminently social thing. You look in the mirror to see how *others* see you. To be able to see the image in a mirror as oneself is a very human accomplishment. (For this reason the French psychoanalytic theorist Jacque Lacan [1966] places great emphasis on the "mirror stage" in the development of the small child.) Our human self depends upon some internalized capacity very much like that which enables us to interpret a mirror image as if we were in the place of someone else looking at us, a capacity which animals seem to lack (although chimpanzees, which are very near to humans, do respond more to mirrors than other animals). One would not have a self without society; the closer one is to the "animal" level of nonreflective action, the less self one has.

The general premise is that we see ourselves as others see us. But one's self-image is not a literal looking-glass self, because one interprets what one sees in the mirror. There is abundant evidence (Rosenberg, 1981: 597–98) that individuals' judgments of themselves are correlated with a group's judgment of them. For example, students' rating themselves and each other on intelligence, physical attractiveness, self-confidence, and likeableness turn out to have self-judgments similar to the group's judgments. But the similarity is even higher between self-judgments and *what individuals thought the group believed about them* (the "reflected self"). There is strong evidence that people believe others think more highly of them than they actually do, and in general believe that other's judgments about them are congruent with their own (Rosenberg, 1981: 600–601). In short, we are influenced by other people, but we distort what we think other people believe, in an egocentric direction.

That is one way in which individuals are insulated from group pressures on their selves: they misperceive what the group believes about them. This happens only to a degree, however; though some egocentric distortion occurs, the group is often powerful enough to make even negative judgments come through to some extent. Another source of insulation is when there are various groups in a society, and the individual has some choice which ones to orient toward. Many studies have shown (Wylie, 1979) that members of groups subjected to discrimination (blacks, Jews, women) do *not* typically have low self-esteem. How is this possible? Self-esteem depends on the judgments of groups which are most highly valued by the individual and which the individual believes have the most accurate knowledge of him (Rosenberg, 1981: 598). Blacks, Jews, and others escape the negative self-consequences of discrimination by segregation in their own groups. Conversely, when individuals are a minority in the context of some other group, their self-esteem suffers. This seems to be true even if their own group is not a "minority" generally, but only locally: not only Jews in Gentile neighborhoods and schools, but Protestants in non-Protestant neighborhoods, and Catholics in non-Catholic neighborhoods suffer this effect (Rosenberg, 1981: 608–609, 612). The same has been found for various ethnic groups and for children of different social classes: those of higher classes have lower self-esteem in lower-class schools. Deaf children have higher self esteem when their parents are deaf than hearing and when they attend schools for the deaf than when they are in a normal school.

We can see here a structural pressure flowing from these social-psychological processes. Insofar as groups think most highly of individuals like themselves, there is a disadvantage in self-conception for "minorities" who come into those groups. Since individuals tend to act to protect their self-esteem, they are likely to shun these experiences, and to seek out groups like themselves. The end result is to maintain the segregation of society. This is a marco consequence of microsociology.

A BASIC DEBATE: "I" vs. "ME"

Mead's (1934) analysis goes beyond Cooley's by breaking the self into various components. This approach has come to be called *symbolic interactionism*. The looking-glass self is what Mead calls the "me", the self as seen from the point of view of others. The grammatical part of speech "me" implies passivity, being an object. The "I," on the other hand, is always the subject of a sentence; it is the active agent, the doer rather than an object of perception or recipient of some action.

The "I" is not only active but self-reflexive. It stands over against the world and is capable of dealing with it as "things out there." Because it is separate from the world, and not merely another object among the objects of the world, it is capable of reflecting on the world. The "I" is even capable of standing over against the self, of making its own "me" an object of its own consciousness, of reflecting on oneself. This self-reflection would not be possible unless the self were split into at least two components, Mead's "I" and "me." (Mead adds a third, the "Generalized Other," which we will consider later.)

The "I" is the part of the self that provides freedom. It is spontaneousness, the source of creativity and innovation. Mead stresses that the "I" is not to be identified with one's physical body. The true self is a cutting edge in time and viewpoint that is always out in front of where one physically is. You can prove this to yourself by paying attention to what you are doing in physical activity. Running after a ball, or moving an arm from one place to another, you do not concentrate on where your limbs are now, but on the place you are trying to get to.[1] You project yourself out in front of where you are now. If you don't, and try to go through the motions mechanically by concentrating on your current bodily positions, you will be a clumsy runner or ballplayer. This ability to project oneself out in front makes one able to ride a bicycle, and lets one stop floundering in the water and know how to swim. This same sense of the places one is going is what gives us the ability to drive a car; good drivers can squeeze through a narrow opening while looking straight ahead, because they can "feel" where the sides of the car are. This proves that the physical body is merely an extension of the self, as one learns to move towards goals in space; for a good driver, the car becomes merely another extension of oneself, a larger body made out of metal that one temporarily inhabits. For this reason one can imagine that one might lose part after part of one's physical body and still feel one has a self. The self is not the body, but one's "project" into the future. This same projectedness of the self holds in purely intellectual activity as well as physical movements. It is there in social activity too.

Based on the distinction among parts of the self, there are several directions in which sociological analysis can proceed. We can concentrate on the "me," the social self, and examine what is constructed. Or we can concentrate on the "I", the spontaneous side; in this case we get a sociology of process, dynamics, and movement. The "me" sociology is the branch of symbolic interactionism called "role theory." The "I" sociology is the other branch, most strongly represented by Herbert Blumer, which opposes the social determinism of role theory (and every other kind of determinism in sociology), in order to stress the negotiated, emergent, situational quality of human society as a product of human freedom. In the next part of this chapter, we shall deal primarily with the "me" side, since this has been the most prominent approach in the sociology of the self. Blumer's emphasis on the "I" has given rise to a different type of social psychology, focusing on the situation and the reality-construction which takes place within it. In this approach, the self becomes too fluid to be an object of attention. We will consider this approach and its intellectual relatives in Chapter 8.

I should stress that these two approaches in social psychology are matters of relative emphasis, not absolute divisions. Both have the possibility (although they do not always take it up) to bring in elements from the other side. It is a matter of genuine theoretical disagreement, though, how important the various elements are

---

[1] This is borne out by research in physiological psychology (Pribram 1971). The human nervous system is organized, not by monitoring each movement step by step, going from point A to point Z, but rather in reverse: one checks on the goal state Z, and how far away one is from it, and makes moves to bring it closer. In other words, the human nervous system is a cybernetic control system, based on feedback from goal states, not a mechanical feedforward system (as discussed in Chapter 2).

in real life and whether the basic processes are rather fixed and determinative, or highly fluid and interpretable.[2]

Finally, there is yet another theoretical focus: the internal relationships between the parts of the self ("I," "me," "generalized other"), which make up the process of thinking. Instead of being concerned with external society either as roles or as fluid negotiations and interpretations, we focus on what is happening inside the individual. We will take up this topic later in Chapter 7, after discussing the role theory.

THE "ME" SIDE: ROLE THEORY

Role theory deals with the effect of society upon the individual self. But also vice versa: it is concerned with how society is put together out of individual roles. This is one of the two main symbolic interactionist theories about society. Its viewpoint is from the micro angle; it is a view on how society is constructed from the ground up, rather than from the top down. Symbolic interaction is a micro view of macro.

What is a role? The term "role" is a metaphor taken from the theater; it is a part that one plays. An important structural point is that *roles always come in pairs or larger combinations*. There is no such thing as a single role by itself. Mead (1934) liked to use examples from sports. The role of the baseball shortstop is meaningless without the complementary roles of teammates playing first base, pitcher, catcher, and so forth. Not only that, the roles of one team depend on roles of the opposing team: pitcher, shortstop, and so forth have nothing to do without the batters of the opposition. This gives us another proof that the self is social: roles that one identifies with are always part of a network of connected roles and are meaningless in isolation from the others. It is true that one might practice throwing a baseball against a wall, or play golf by oneself, but these are instances of individuals' having internalized a social role so that they can practice it while filling in the social side in imagination.

The complementarity of roles is a valuable point. The realm of sports, to be sure, is an artificial one, because sports have a rule book which clearly spells out how the various roles are to act toward each other. Such rules are not necessarily at all clear or fixed in ordinary life. But the principle of complementarity of roles still holds. In order to learn one role, one must learn the complementary roles, too. This is obvious enough in the case of the shortstop, who must know what the pitcher, batter, and first baseman all do. Less obvious, but equally significant, is the case of gender roles. When a small child identifies herself or himself as a girl or boy, she or he has learned not one role, but the conception of both genders. She or he has learned which one she or he is supposed to play, and which one she or he is *not* to play (Money and Ehrhardt, 1972). Gender roles are not only complementary; one of their distinctive features (found in some kinds of roles generally, but not in all) is that they include a taboo on the complementary role behavior. This separateness

---

[2] These two approaches are sometimes referred to as the "Iowa School" and the "Chicago School" of symbolic interactionists, although actually their proponents are spread over quite a few locations. (See Stryker, 1980; Jonathan Turner, 1986: 333–52.) What I have called the "me" side has also been integrated into functionalism, especially by the influence of Robert Merton, whereas the "I" side is quite hostile to functionalism.

of gender roles is learned first; whereas the complementariness of genders (that is, the way males and females act toward each other—erotic behavior) is not usually learned until much later.

SOCIAL ACTION AS ROLE TAKING

The idea of complementary roles suggests an important point about how social action is carried on. Mead (1934) stresses that individuals in a social interaction align their actions with the actions of their role-partner. An employee knows how to interact with the boss, and vice versa, because each one knows what the other's role is. Learning a new job means learning role interactions, and learning them from both sides. Not absolutely and completely from both sides, however; the employee does not know everything that the boss does, (and vice versa), but only those parts of the boss role that interact with the employee.

Mead called this interactional process "taking the role of the other." It means that mentally the bosses project themselves into the role of the employees, anticipate what the employees should be doing and are going to do in response to the bosses' own action, say, checking up on the day's work. Similarly, the employees project themselves into the boss's position, anticipate what the boss will do, and align their own actions accordingly. Social life works smoothly because people know the complementary sets of roles for themself and those around them and "take the role of the other" inside their own heads every time they come into contact.

There are some debates over this theory. Mead seemed to think that it is a comparatively easy and routine matter to take the role of the other. Because the roles are complementary, we get an image of society as a well-rehearsed play, with everyone playing their parts according to the script. Goffman (1959, 1969), on the other hand, uses the image of the theater but in a very different sense. The different role players are not necessarily so harmonious; each of them has their own private backstage, where they prepare to impress others with their role and to use their roles to try to manipulate others in their own interest. Goffman comes out closer to a conflict view of interaction, while Mead sees the process as basically harmonious. Mead's predecessor, Cooley (1902), voiced an even more benign view: because the self is social, he asserted, there can be no such thing as egoistical self-interest; the individual self is part of society and can do nothing against society. Cooley was an unusually naive person, however; theoretically, his mistake is that he identifies the self entirely with the "me," omitting the "I" that might attempt to manipulate the "me," and the rest of society, in its own interest.

The theory of social interaction as playing roles seems to imply a static society. Though one version of role theory takes this stance, it is also possible to interpret symbolic interactionism in a different vein. That is, once individuals come into a situation, they do not merely take preexisting roles. Mead said that they align their actions by each taking the role of the other. Here "role" might merely mean putting oneself in the other's place. There need not be any preexisting script; or if there is, they could throw the script away. Blumer (1969) stressed that all interactions have this quality, at least potentially. Role taking is a general and all-purpose device by which individuals construct new social actions as well as replay old ones. By alternating mentally back and forth between the stance of oneself and of the other person, one can try out various actions in the mind. Here is a stranger: shall I start up a conversation? Let me project myself momentarily into his viewpoint: does he want to be disturbed? How will he respond if I say "X"? Then back to my own viewpoint: how will I respond if he says "Y"? And so forth. The outcome of this process (occurring on both sides) is that we work out a way of acting that will get us through the situation. At the end of it we may have constructed a new role, such as friends, enemies, persons who shared a brief encounter, and so on.

ROLE SETS AND ROLE STRAIN

A role set refers to the combination of different roles that any particular individual plays. Having a large role set is especially characteristic of persons in complex modern society. Almost everyone has one or more roles to play as a family member (for instance, parent and/or child, spouse, sibling, nephew to a niece), worker (in relation to order givers, order takers, co-workers, clients, customers, salespeople, the public), citizen (voter, taxpayer, subject of police), club or organization members, and so forth.

Most of the theory of role sets has been devoted to role strains that emerge as one tries to coordinate the playing of these different roles. One type of strain that has been studied deals with "man in the middle" roles, such as the foremen in industry. Here there are individuals who both work with lower-level employees and try to be on good terms with them, but also report to high-ranking supervisors, for whom they are responsible for getting certain tasks carried out. The foremen are pulled both ways, by the workers to take it easy and interpret rules loosely and by the managers to press hard and be strict. This is one kind of role conflict found in hierarchical organization. Essentially it is a role-theory version of one of the strains of class conflict.[3]

Another type of role strain which received a good deal of attention (Merton, 1968: 422–38; Goode, 1960) is concerned with the meshing of "horizontally" related roles. That is, individuals participate in different spheres: home, work, the public community, various clubs, and so forth. Suppose one is a mother, wife, and school teacher, each with its own complementary roles played by other people. Everything is fine as long as these complementary role-persons keep distinct. But what happens if this school teacher has her own son assigned as a pupil in her class? That creates a role strain, because the personal relationship of mother-son gets in the way of the impersonal relationship of teacher-pupil. (This is an example of conflict between Parsons' pattern variables of specificity and diffuseness, Chapter 2.) Both mother and son feel pulled both ways, with resulting embarassment or other pressures.

What are the consequences of role strain? At the level of the society, we might conjecture that social arrangements are usually worked out so that these strains can be avoided. I say this is a conjecture, because there is no systematic evidence that

---

[3] Role theory, generally speaking, sees a fairly harmonious world and does not deal with the major form of class conflict between managers and workers. Characteristically, it is concerned with psychological pressures on the middle group, not with conflicts of real interests between order givers and order takers. Here again Goffman is closer to conflict theory.

this is so. Historically, family and nonfamily roles were often combined, with little sense of strain: "nepotism" was not considered a threat, but rather the normal course of affairs. If we were to argue as a functionalist (as did Merton), we might claim that social structures would change in the direction of reducing role strain. But it is not clear that this actually happens to any great extent.

The utility of the role-strain model may be more on the individual level. It shows mainly the effects of society upon the individual, not of the individual upon society. It indicates how personal discomforts can be the result of structural positions. In this light, the concept of "role strain" might be a diagnostic tool in a kind of applied sociology or "socioanalysis," parallel to psychoanalysis.

ROLE IDENTIFICATION

All the different social roles that one plays each creates a self as subjective counterpart. Which self does one most identify with? This is the question of role identification or role merger. The most elaborate theory along this line has been developed by Ralph Turner (1976, 1978, 1979–80; see Jonathan Turner, 1985b: 369–88 for the most accessible exposition).

Some roles are felt to be purely external, mere social games that one has to play for some time period. Other roles become part of the self, an inescapable part of one's self-definition. The degree of embedding one's personal self in a social role is highest, according to Turner's theory, according to two sets of conditions.

First, one identifies most strongly with roles which have the most power or other rewards, roles which one is most capable at playing, and roles which are most intrinsically enjoyable. Role identification is also increased by making sacrifices to learn or enter a role. Turner also believes that unresolved role strain increases one's tendency to identify with that role, as if the problems of the role get inside one's mind, and won't go away. This last point suggests that although people prefer to identify with pleasurable roles, nevertheless the process is not completely under individual control.

A second set of factors are social conditions which coerce an individual into identifying with a given role. Thus, the more extreme the ranking of a role, either very high or very low, the more likely other people are to identify oneself with it, and hence not to allow one to escape the social identification. Not only are high-ranking persons trapped in their jobs (like celebrities or politicians), but also very low-ranking persons. Someone who is stigmatized by a handicap, a criminal record, or minority status, for example, finds it hard for other people to treat him or her any other way except in that role, and hence that person will end up identifying himself or herself with that role. This part of the theory follows the Cooley-Mead "looking-glass self": you see yourself as others see you.[4]

The structure of the group will have an effect on this pressure to identify oneself with a given role. The more tightly circumscribed the group and the more clear-cut

---

[4]This may follow from the more general principle that a self trait becomes salient to the extent that it stands out from the social context. Boys in a schoolroom containing a majority of girls are most likely to identify themselves by sex, and vice versa. Similarly, children who are younger or older than the majority of classmates, or who have unusual size or hair coloring, also pick out those traits to describe themselves (Rosenberg, 1981: 611–12).

the roles are within it, the more pressure there will be for individuals to play their roles and identify with them. Conversely, the openness of multiple groups in modern society allows individuals to pick and choose which roles they want to play and to exercise more psychological distance in identifying their personal selves with them. Another factor is how public the role is and how visible its activities are. Public and highly visible roles, according to Turner's hypothesis, are roles that people end up identifying with more strongly. This may be true, although Goffman would add that public roles usually have backstages attached to them; hence people who play very visible public roles may develop multiple personalities, capable of throwing themselves into one identification when "on stage," but preserving another part of the self for privacy. Of course, if the group is all-encompassing with no privacy, there is no way to avoid identifying totally with the public role.[5]

ROLE LEARNING vs. ROLE MAKING

Another controversy deals with the question of how solid or changeable roles are. Obviously roles had to be created at some time, but role theory tends to deal only with roles that are already firmly existant, and the question is only how individuals come to fit into them. Role theory thus gives considerable weight to learning roles, and especially the role learning that goes on in childhood, called socialization. According to this view, by the time a child has matured, he or she has learned a repertoire of the basic social roles, and need only play them out in appropriate situations.

The opposite viewpoint is that roles are not simply learned but also made. In Blumer's vision, even old roles have to be enacted, and re-made, every time they are played. Ralph Turner (1968) called this creative aspect *role making*. Thus there is role making within short-run situations. Role making can also be a historical event. An example is the gender roles that children learn. According to research carried out in the 1950s and 1960s (Gottfredson, 1981), children learn that females can take the adult roles of secretary, nurse, entertainer, housewife, or a few others. If role-socialization were all there is to it, these roles would simply be passed on continuously to the present. Instead, in the 1970s role-conceptions (at least in some parts of American society) changed, and the restricted set of "female occupational roles" was broken down so that girls can now conceive of themselves as business executives, lawyers, and other traditionally "male" roles. There is no doubt, then, that roles are not static and that they can be changed. Sociological theory has not progressed very far, however, on the question of how and by what process role change comes about.

It is possible to combine the two viewpoints. Some of the time roles are stable and are learned by socialization; at other times, roles become negotiated and changed, either within a given situation or by a historical shift in the definition of a role. The

---

[5] This last condition is what in terms of Durkheimian ritual theory (Chapter 6) constitutes a situation of high ritual density. It therefore produces very strong conformity to the symbols of group membership. Insofar as the self is a symbol also produced by the group ritual experience, this structure would lead to a strong sense of the propriety of being that person, and none other: the equivalent of strong role-embeddedness in Turner's theory.

question is: under what conditions and to what extent does each occur? The two existing sides of the debate have not provided many leads on this. One side does not consider change at all. The side which emphasizes social fluidity does not explain why, in fact, much of the time things do not work out as fluid and why there is so much routine and repetition. In general, it does not seem reasonable to suppose that all aspects of roles are equally amenable to renegotiation and redefinition. Some roles are more trivial or superficial than others; it is easier to redefine the manners used between employees and their bosses, for example, than to change the amount of money each one is paid or who gets to give orders and who has to take them. The theory of roles by itself does not shed much light on this issue, especially because it generally ignores power and the resources that uphold it. Carrying out roles is not purely a mental process; it involves material conditions as well. In other words, playing roles is not just a matter of interpersonal agreement at the micro level, though that is one element that enters into it.

EXPECTATION STATES THEORY

A related issue is how people perform in their roles. Their behavior is affected by group pressures but mediated by internal processes, which are the subject of *expectation states theory*. Led by Joseph Berger, Morris Zelditch, and others, a large body of experimental studies have been carried out in small groups to test and elaborate the theory. The original theory dealt with how power and prestige emerge in small task groups—that is, laboratory groups which have been given some collective problem to solve. The research of Bales and others (Bales and Slater, 1955) had already shown that initially unranked groups typically develop a task leader, who participates more than others and has more influence, and that once developed this group stratification remains stable. Berger and his associates (Berger, Conner, and Fisek, 1974) went on to explain this result by the theory that the participants develop *performance expectations* about how others as well as themselves will behave. These expectations are based on how well they have done on tasks in the past.

Persons whom the group expects to perform well, then, will take the lead in subsequent activities, and their leadership (the plans they put forward, the directions they give) are accepted by others. Persons who have performed poorly in the past, on the other hand, are not expected to take the lead, and their suggestions are generally not accepted when they do make them. It was discovered, however, that even in ostensibly equal groups, some people took more initiative right from the outset, even though they had not yet established a "track record" on the task. This led to an elaboration of the theory: it was recognized that status characteristics affect expectation states, even though they have nothing directly to do with the task. High-ranking military personnel, for example, were given leadership roles even in experimental groups that had nothing to do with their official duties; males were repeatedly observed to get leadership roles over females, whites over blacks, and higher-ranking occupations over lower; age and education also had similar effects (Berger, Wagner, and Zelditch, 1983). Even being perceived as good-looking operates as a status characteristic, so that good-looking people are given more opportunities to take the lead in a group and are evaluated as performing better even if their actual level of performance is the same (Berger, Rosenholtz, and Zelditch, 1980; Webster and Driskell, 1983).

These *diffuse status characteristics,* it is theorized, affect expectation states about how these individuals will perform on tasks. High status cues lead to power and prestige in the problem-solving group, even if the diffuse characteristic is irrelevant to the task; moreover if there is some relevancy, the connection becomes even stronger. Berger et al. formulated this as the principle of *burden of proof:* people assume that diffuse status is relevant to any task, unless some special circumstance is introduced to show that it is *irrelevant.* If the actors have multiple status characteristics (for instance, they are high on some traits and low on others), the group's expectations about them combine this into an overall rating.

Persons have expectations about themselves as well as about others. These self-expectations or subjective power-prestige ratings are determined, not just by how well one has done on past tasks, but by the communications one receives from others in the group. One feels highest subjective self-expectation when one has been praised by someone who ranks high in the group, and lowest self-expectation when one is criticized by that high-ranking person. This process is independent of what one actually thinks of the evaluator; one may rank the evaluator low, but if one perceives that his or her structural position in the group is high, his or her opinions count strongly in one's self-image nevertheless (Webster and Sobieszek, 1974).

PERSONALITY AS SITUATIONAL EXPECTATIONS

An extension of the theory (Johnston, 1984) argues that personal attributes—such as shyness, hostility, warmth, aggressiveness, and so forth—are actually socially constructed expectations about how particular people are going to behave. They are stable and appear to be attributes of the individual, mainly because people develop these expectations about themselves, just as others develop the expectations about them. Like performance expectations in a task group, these personality expectations affect the way individuals are treated, as well as the way they themselves act. To say that some people are "timid," for example, is merely to summarize the expectation (held by themselves and others) that they will not take initiative and not perform well. Berger, Wagner, and Zelditch (1983) point to evidence that individuals behave inconsistently if they are put in grossly different situations; the reason they tend to act consistently and show the same "personality" is because they in fact usually interact with the same people or in the same kinds of situations. "Behavioral 'traits,'" Berger et al. (1983: 61) argue, "are not part of the individual in any 'deep' sense, rather they are reactivated by interacting with the same individuals under the same recurring conditions." Personality might also be regarded as a situational expectation which generalizes, just as is shown by the evidence that expectation of performance in one task group tends to generalize to performances on quite different kinds of tasks (Webster and Driskell, 1978).

STATUS AND BEHAVIOR CUES

Expectations can be formed on the basis of actual performances (as in the experimental task group); but we have seen that they can also be created by the sheer status attributes that individuals bring to the group. Berger et al. attempt to generalize this to all kinds of situations of face-to-face interaction. How do people know what is the status of the person they are interacting with? Sometimes they are explicity told: in the experimental group the experimenter may actually tell them the rank, education, or other traits of the person in the next cubicle; or in real life, people introduce themselves or have information told about them. These are *indicative* cues. There are also *expressive* cues, signs given out which indicate something about one's social rank, sex, education, and so forth (from styles of dress, speech pattern, bodily appearance).

Among these expressive cues, Ridgeway, Berger, and Smith (1985) pick out what they call "task cues": nonverbal behaviors such as how fluently one talks, whether one takes the initiative in speaking, the tone of voice one uses, and whether one makes eye contact and who breaks off eye contact first. They call these "task cues" because these presumably provide information that is relevant to the task. I would suggest, however, that this is misleading terminology. Eye contact, speech, and so forth are expressions of personal self-confidence; these might be relevant to performing a task, if that is what the group is about, but they are more likely styles of interaction relevant to all social situations, including purely sociable ones, and probably reflect one's degree of acceptance by the group or one's previous ability to dominate.[6] The theoretical conception of Berger et al., however, seems to remain wedded to their original experimental design in which laboratory groups carry out some collective task; hence everything is interpreted as if it were an indicator, near or remote, of practical performance abilities. It would bias the issue less, however, to simply call these nonverbal expressions "behavior cues."

The generalization that emerges is that "the level of task cues that one actor displays in relation to another is a direct function of his or her expectation advantage (or disadvantage) relative to the other" (Ridgeway, Berger, and Smith, 1985: 965). This means that low-status people speak more hesitantly, maintain less eye contact, and so forth when they are interacting with high-status persons, whereas high-status persons manifest the dominant nonverbal cues; and the reason for this difference is that their status gives them expectations about themselves and each other which in turn causes the nonverbal, expressive behavior, as well as any other kind of behavior (such as task behavior). Furthermore, if people enter the situation equally ranked in regard to race, sex, occupation, education and so forth, the nonverbal cues they give off (speakingly hesitantly or fluidly) will have an *effect* on their power and prestige behavior and on the assessment of their task capacities. In other words: status leads to inner expectations which lead to dominant or subordinate nonverbal cues; and nonverbal cues lead to expectations which (among other things) determine task performance and how it is assessed.

DO EXPECTATIONS STATES EXPLAIN STRATIFICATION?

The expectations states program began with a model of performances in work groups and traced inequalities to the different contributions of individuals to the group's work.[7] There is something artificial about this starting point; the laboratory

---

[6] In the interaction ritual chain theory given in Chapter 10, I suggest that these same nonverbal behaviors are indicators of "emotional energy," derived from previously successful interaction encounters.

[7] In this respect, expectation states theory is similar to the starting place of Homans' and Blau's exchange theory, discussed in Chapter 10.

studies were set up so that the group as a whole had a task to perform, and individuals' contributions were clearly measurable and apparent to everyone. But this is not the normal situation in real life, even in the realm of work. (Nor is it what leisure-time sociability is like.) Workers and bosses typically have different priorities about what they are trying to achieve; for many, the object is merely to receive their pay, minimize their discomfort, or expand their realm of power and control. Hence contributions to the group are not usually very relevant; the collection of individuals are more likely to bargain or manuever against each other, than trying to achieve something collectively. Like Homans' and Blau's exchange theory, Berger and his followers seem to imply that stratification is justified because persons are given power and prestige for what they contribute to the common good. But this is not what the social world is actually like. In the real world of factories, offices, stores, army troops, and the like, power is not a reward for collective contributions but a resource—based on politics or property—that already exists to begin with and that, in fact, brings people together into an organization in the first place.

The expectation states theory, though, is superior to exchange theory in a number of ways. It moves away from merely asserting that power and prestige are returns for contributions, by noting that diffuse status characteristics brought in from outside the group already affect the way people are evaluated in the group and the opportunities they are given to make suggestions and influence others. There is, I would suggest, a certain ambiguity in the way this evidence is analyzed. The theory might be interpreted as implying (though it does not come out and say it directly) that blacks, women, and other low-status individuals are not given any leadership chances because their status traits carry over from previous performances: status is merely a mnemonic device, indicating success or failure on past tasks. This would be in keeping with the basic equitable-reward-for-performance theme that underlies this whole research tradition and which is also a fundamental assumption of exchange theory.

When the issue is couched in terms of women or blacks, this interpretation seems absurd. It implies that individuals who are discriminated against deserve the discrimination because they performed badly in the past. It would be more reasonable to make an alternative interpretation and say that expectations are autonomous (or can become autonomous) from past performances. Expectation, in fact, can be a kind of bias, a reality-construction of self-perpetuating privilege. This seems borne out by the evidence that persons about whom expectations are high are evaluated high, *for exactly the same performances on which low-status persons are evaluated low*. The original theory of expectation states, as based on evaluation of performance, is undermined; in its place, the more recent version of the theory focuses on the autonomous power of the cognitive expectations themselves. This implies that there are other inputs into expectations besides past performances; if these inputs are a tradition of prejudice against certain categories of persons, the theory must go further in order to explain how such prejudices arise, and what changes them. And the internal structure of mind, which looms so large in the theory, needs to be further explored in its own right.

THE SOCIOLOGY OF THINKING:
MEAD AND PEIRCE

Most thinking takes place in language. But language is a social act; in fact the most typical and ordinary social action is having a conversation with someone. In George Herbert Mead's (1934) theory, thinking is an internalized conversation, taking place with imaginary others.

We have already met some of the elements of Mead's theory of the self. At least in the adult person, there is an "I," the active agent; the "me," the self as object with various characteristics, as seen from the point of view of other people; and the "generalized other," which is the internal facility to take the standpoint of other people. We have already seen how, in role taking or role negotiation, the "I" mentally tries out different versions of the "me" to see how they coordinate with what is being attempted by the person with whom one is interacting. This trying out of possible roles is done mentally, under the eyes of the "generalized other," which acts in the crucial position of observer and judge of what is a successfully enacted "me." Thinking is an interplay between these various parts of the self.

PEIRCE'S THREE COMPONENTS OF SIGNIFICATION

Mead's theory of thinking derives from the work of the pragmatist philosopher Charles Sanders Peirce. According to Peirce (1897/1955), language, or any kind of conscious meaning, involves 3 elements:

1. A *sign,* which may be a gesture or a vocal sound (or for that matter a visual emblem such as in writing or in art).

2. The *object* to which the sign refers.[8] For the simplest case, we may consider this to be a physical object (as the word "chair" refers to the thing chair), although we will see that an object may be a good deal more complex, dynamic, or abstract. Anything we can refer to, that is, all words except pure connectives (like "to" or "a"), can become an object because it can be treated gramatically as an object.

3. The *idea* which the sign invokes. This is an internal meaning in the mind. For a successful communication, the same idea is invoked by the sign in the minds of both the speaker and listener, the sender and the receiver of the communication. The meaning, in short, must be socially shared if it is truly to be a meaning.

Peirce stressed that signs themselves are never isolated, but always invoke each other. That is, there is a system of signs which is implied whenever any particular isolated sign is used in communication. (See Figure 7-1.) Signs are linked to each other in several dimensions:

1. *Semantically:* any particular word is reminiscent of other words in the language: "chair" can remind one of "sofa," "armchair," "chaise lounge," and so forth, as

---

[8] In the French structuralist version of linguistics, deriving from Saussure, *sign* is called the *signifier,* and the *object* is called the *signified.* See the discussion in Chapter 9.

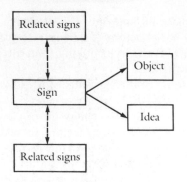

FIGURE 7-1

PEIRCE'S THREE COMPONENTS OF SIGNIFICATION

well as other words with similar sounds and spellings ("Charlie," "chariot," or "rare," "care").

2. *Syntactically:* the grammatical relationships among words makes one expect a certain kind of word after another kind of word: a verb to be followed by an object noun, and so forth.

3. *Pragmatically:* isolated words are always part of a surrounding flow of thought or action. One would not say "chair" out of the blue; it is always part of a discussion, a request, perhaps a language lesson, a joke, or a number of other possibilities. It is this larger context or flow which picks out the word to use at that particular time. The train of thought is more important than the individual word and its meaning: in fact, its meaning is the way it fits into the larger context. Peirce stresses that this flow of thought or action, this dynamic context, may be largely unconscious. As long as the inferences from one statement to another, from one part of the action to another, go along smoothly, the persons involved may scarcely pay any attention to them. Only when there is a difficulty, when something is blocking the smooth flow of action and inference, must one concentrate on exactly what words to use, which signs to choose, or how to interpret the signs that other people are using. Whenever signs are used, then, they always imply both interconnections among themselves, and a dynamic situation in which there is a flow from one sign (and action, and emotion) to another.

THE GENERALIZED OTHER

Mead added the point that communication itself is possible only because of the social organization of the self. Signs (such as spoken words) can mean the same thing to both speaker and hearer only because each is able to take the role of the other. This is done because all people have a "generalized other," by which they are able to empathize with the other, to put themselves in the other's place and thus to see (or "feel") what the sign refers to.[9] Without the "Generalized Other," signs would not communicate anything.

The "Generalized Other" is not a part of the self in the same way as "I" and "me." It is not a kind of self, like the latter; nor is it an object. It is never used as an object, mentally or grammatically. It is invisible and characterless, except in the sense of what "it" can do. ("It" is a metaphor here.) Mead sometimes refers to this "Generalized Other," especially in his philosophical writings on metaphysics and epistemology (Mead, 1938) by such phrases as "acting with reference to him[one]self" (1938: 367), "exciting the attitude of the other" (1938: 376), "an indefinite group . . . where that group includes the individual himself as an other" (1938: 389), "the organized group reaction of the individual over against himself" (1938: 432). This variation implies that the term "generalized" had no special technical significance in his usage. The "Generalized Other" is a capacity to take a viewpoint, to be an audience, to read meanings from signs from that other person's point of view, especially when the particular person is rather vague.[10]

THE GENERALIZED OTHER IS THE SOURCE OF UNIVERSAL SIGNS

Signs depend on the social nature of the mind in another respect as well. Signs are usually universals, but the world as we experience it, moment by moment, meets us only as particulars. It is not "chair" in general that we sit down upon, but only a particular chair at a particular time and place. The sign universalizes by making all different chairs equivalent; it does this by using the same vocal gesture, or written word, in a great many different situations. It is our use of the sign that generalizes, not the existence of such categories "in nature" waiting to be recognized as the same, for there are many possible ways that we might divide up the universe. Some viewpoints might not recognize chairs at all (for some people they might be just furniture or, for a primitive tribesman, strange objects), while others might distinguish various kinds of objects one can sit on without lumping them all together.

---

[9] This is not done merely by pointing to the object. You can illustrate this quite readily with your pet cat: if you point at an object and say its name at the same time, the cat usually won't associate the object with the name; more likely the cat will look at your finger instead of at the object. Pointing itself is a sign gesture, whose meaning (to look in the direction the finger is pointing) is something that must be acquired by some prior act of communication. Moreover, Peirce's point must be considered, that the meaning of a sign is not usually just in its relationship to an isolated object, but in its "horizontal" meanings to other signs (words, parts of sentences) and to trains of thought and action.

[10] Mead (1938: 376) also occasionally introduces the notion of a "generalized actor," who is overviewing alternative actions to a goal and various "specialized actors" who are assigned different responses, actual or mental. The "generalized actor" is not a "me," but it has more of the qualities of the "Generalized Other" than of the "I." Is the "Generalized Other" always a person? Mead claims that when one is absorbed in action there is no self, no person. The same may be true in a nonactive mode. Buddhists claim as their central truth, based on the experience of meditation, that there is no self; Hindu orthodoxy celebrates the same experience as the annihilation of individuality and the absorption of the self in a larger Self. Meditative experience might be interpreted in Meadian terms as making dominant the mental audience, the reflective, nonmoving aspect of self, while feelings of personhood as well as focus on any concrete objects are transcended. Hence a "Generalized Other" or reflection-capacity can exist without being a person; it may be an emergent mental level beyond ordinary self-reflection.

This is a very important feature of signs, and one that we so much take for granted that we usually fail to see that it is an important human accomplishment that needs to be explained. The natural world consists only of particulars; the mind-world in which we think consists largely of universals. And since we tend to see the physical world through the veil of our mental categories, we transform that world, too, into instances of universals. We see the world as full of meanings, because our normal use of signs to refer to things and to think about them to ourselves makes us impose those meanings over everything we notice.

Mead's solution to this issue is that the universal nature of signs comes from the "Generalized Other." We take the attitude of the "Generalized Other" toward the signs (words) that we hear others using, and for that matter toward the words that we use ourselves. We treat those signs as if they call forth the same response in everyone—every possible person who could experience them. This universalizing attitude of the "Generalized Other" makes signs universals. We mentally take the attitude of all persons toward these signs, and that makes their objects into universals, or, to be more precise, into particulars which are instances of universals.

Conversations, of course, are not only about physical objects. It is only the more banal parts of our lives in which we spend much time talking about such things as chairs. The "object" in the above tripartite scheme of object-sign-meaning can be anything at all which a sign may be used to refer to: from actions, intentions, and emotions as well as abstractions, other words themselves, or the self. By referring to other words and meanings, signs can be reflexive and can build up many levels of reference-upon-reference. In the sentence: "What do you think you're doing?" most of the words (especially "what" and "doing") have "objects" that can be indicated only by a fairly complex set of sentences referring to other sentences. Similarly, most of the sentences in this paragraph (or this book) are full of signs whose "objects" would have to be unpacked at many levels of reference. (I encourage you to take any sample of sentences, such as those heard in ordinary conversation, and see what kinds of "objects" their signs are referring to.) The mental world built up by language is a multilevelled, emergent world of reflexive meanings. This quality is what makes an experience uniquely human. By contrast, the world of most (or all?) animals is relatively flat and "one dimensional," confined to the physical plane and its particulars, with only very limited reference from one part of it to another. The human world has veritable thickets of meaning-reference, going off in several dimensions, away from the sheer physical surface of reality. If Mead is right, this is all fundamentally due to our capacity to take the stance of a "Generalized Other."

The generalized other underlies every aspect of communication and thought. It constitutes signs as universals, and it enables us to project ourselves empathically into the position of another speaker in order to discover that particular meanings and objects are being referred to in that instance. The "Generalized Other" is also important for the speaker in working out the flow of what to say. This may happen rapidly as one goes along and need not involve conscious premeditation. One thinks of what to say next by taking the role of the other and assessing the reaction to what one has said so far. Mead leaves room here for interpreting nonverbal signs or other responses from one's listener, as guides by which the speaker decides whether the words are having their intended effect; but mainly this is an internal process, imagining what effects those words would have on the speaker, if someone else had said them. In any case, the responses that one reads on the listener's face have to be interpreted, and this again involves an imaginative leap into the other's place.

CRITICISMS OF MEAD

Mead's theory is not immune to criticism. As we shall see, the ethnomethodologists implicitly suggest there is a limit on how much of this agile jumping back and forth between roles of listener and speaker really can take place. For it could easily enter an infinite regress, if someone wanted to come to a definite conclusion as to what certain signs mean. Supposing a speaker is picking out her words in order to get a meaning across: she takes the role of the other, to see how they look from the other side. But that other, if the model is correct, is taking the role of the speaker in order to ascertain the meaning of the words, so the speaker has to take the role of someone else taking the role of herself. And that isn't all: this last "herself" is taking the role of the other, and so on continuously. There is no fixed point at which the meaning is ultimately given, but an infinite regress of role takings. The ethnomethodologists point out that human cognitive capacity is limited, that people cannot handle even a relatively small number of reflexive loops. And in fact, according to ethnomethodological investigations, people do not usually even try to be very reflexive. If a listener does not understand the meaning of what is being said, the usual procedure is to let it pass and assume that the meaning will emerge later. It is only when there is a fairly severe disruption of meaning that people will interrupt the flow and reflexively comment on it by asking for clarification. As shown in a famous ethnomethodological experiment (Chapter 8), a person can deliberately disrupt someone's communication by doggedly asking for clarification at all possible points, setting off the reflexive spiral toward infinity.

The same would presumably apply to a speaker, who is checking on whether he is getting his meaning across: Garfinkel's results (on listeners, not speakers) imply that the speaker *assumes* there is a normal flow of meaning, without getting into any of the reflexive loops that would ensue if he sought to get inside the other person's head in any realistic way. Goffman, too, with his theme that interaction is largely frontstage ritual—a pretense of keeping up appearances—would agree that neither speaker nor listener normally has to do very much real empathizing with the actual stance of the other, as long as both maintain a polite veneer of doing so. This is not to say that breakdowns do not occur in the communication of meaning: overt instances in which speaker and/or listener has to actively check whether the meaning is getting across. But ethnomethodological studies of what happens in cases of such breaches and repairs (Scott and Lyman, 1968) show that people do not go through extensive efforts to fully take the role of the other, but instead use ritualized, quick formulas for apologies and other retreats which skip over the breach and go ahead again, safely on the conventionalized surface.

Nevertheless Mead may be on the right track regarding the nature of meanings. Words are not just sounds in your ears or in your heard when you are thinking "in words." Your own grunts and noises to yourself don't carry the freight of words which mean something, that is, call forth a referent. This may be an image of something visible and contactable, but it could also just be that a word calls forth other words (or at least echoes with them) and certain kinds of sentence flows. Words have this extra quality because they are embedded in a larger system and also because they imply the point of view of everyone. This might be called a further consequence of the "generalized other." And we see that the "generalized other" is not an object, but a capacity for experiencing a certain kind of event.[11]

Words are thus loaded with what we might think of as a penumbra of neighboring mental actions (which might well be brain actions). (Here I am filling out Mead with Peirce, as well as with Saussure, whose structuralist theory of linguistics is sketched in Chapter 9.) They reverberate "horizontally" in semantic echo chambers, and forward in time into grammatical and pragmatic flows of speech actions (and possibly other bodily actions as well). They also reverberate with a special aspect of reflexiveness, the feeling that each word means the same universally from the point of view of the "Generalized Other."

Whence comes this capacity to take the stance of the other? Mead relies on it heavily to explain mind and language, but that does not explain itself. Mead has a mystery in the very center of his system. Language cannot be responsible for the ability to take the stance of the other, because language itself requires the ability to do that. Perhaps the way out of this conundrum is to recognize that there is another process which already links human organisms to each other. It is presymbolic and emotional. Furthermore, it involves communication: emotional signs and vocal expressions, such as those which pass between infant and parents: crying, cooing, soothing, laughing, phatic interest, and the more basic growls, purrs, and other tones humans use (as well as other animal species in their own ways). These all call out the same response in listener as in sender. It is out of this connectedness, presumably, that language arises, as the most primitive kind of "natural ritual" (discussed in Chapter 6). But the problem remains: why is it that when humans engage in this presymbolic communication, it passes on into symbolism, whereas this is not the case with animals? The problem still remains to be solved.[12]

THOUGHT AS INTERNALIZED CONVERSATION

Conversation with other people is a form of thought, in fact the prototype of internalized thinking. To think silently, "in one's head," is something that children learn to do *after* they learn to talk. External talk already contains all the crucial elements of thought: significant symbols and the capacity to take the stance of one's interlocutor or listener, as well as (in more mature persons) the stance of a generalized audience.

---

[11] Of course I have made "Generalized Other" an object in the preceding paragraphs; but this is a higher order of reflexivity, in which any word can be analyzed in the abstract sense and may stand as the object or predicate of a sentence. My point is the "Generalized Other" is not an object on the same prereflexive level as are chairs or even selves ("me's"). Mead's argument casts light on existentialist philosophies like those of Heidegger (1927/1960) which stress that this aspect of the human self *(Dasein)* is not the same kind of entity as any other object in the world.

[12] Wiley (1986) refers to this as "the symbolic capacity miracle" and proposes that its marvelous nature is what gave human beings the idea that there is something sacred in their mundane world.

What happens in internal thought? Mead presents the model of a subvocal speaker with an imaginery audience. Mead's favorite examples all deal with physical action: a thinker takes images of oneself as object ("me"), and tries them out in various situations—going through the door, driving a car, and so forth. The "generalized other" operates as audience to these alternative "me's", which presumably judges the outcomes of these trains of imaginery action and thus chooses a course of action from among them.[13] The same process would hold in social action (mentally trying out different things to say, overtures to make) or intellectual action (different lines of thinking to try out).

There can be very rapid changes of stance within one's mind, as one's thoughts switch from one train of connections to another. Mead stresses that thinking involves the rapid interchange of points of view. Not only are there multiple object-selves ("me's", each corresponding to a particular proposed train of action), but also multiple stances of observer upon these. One can identify first with one possible "me" in action, then with another on the stage-play of one's mind. And implicitly the universal meaning of the words referring to the environment—even physical objects such as doors and cars—also contain a viewpoint from the generalized other: in fact, this seems to be a *more generalized* "other" than is involved in the merely "local" self-observing that goes on in mentally watching one's particular proposals for action. Mead seems to have been insufficiently systematic in laying out the different kinds of reflective stances one may take, instead lumping them under a single "generalized other."

Internal conversations do not have to be laborious. When adults think smoothly and without difficulty, much of the process of internal conversation is short-circuited. One understands almost immediately how the end of a train of thought will come out (that is, how the sentence will flow off) and hence can judge whether that is the train to follow or to switch to something else. One can rapidly shift between objections, alternative ideas, or skip ahead to conclusions. Moreover, trains of thought can associate "horizontally" because, as we've seen, words invoke other words of similar meanings or sounds, as well as connecting syntactically and pragmatically. Much of these associations can occur unconsciously or nearly so, because they happen smoothly and rapidly, with nothing to disrupt the process and make us pay attention to it. This implies, incidentally, that "unconscious" does not have to mean ideas which are repressed or forbidden to enter conscious in the Freudian sense; much of our mental action is unconscious, because it is a penumbra of language-connections that surrounds whatever we are concentrating upon. The mind should not be viewed as a lighted chamber above ground and a dark chamber below, but as a searchlight amidst a cobweb, focusing on different places in the net of connections.

FURTHER DEVELOPMENTS OF A SOCIOLOGY
OF THINKING

A sociological theory might go further to try to explain why someone thinks the thoughts that come to mind at any particular time. If thinking is internalized

---

[13] I say presumably because the "generalized other" seems to be featureless, without criteria by which to make a selection or to facilitate the aims of the "I." These are obscure points in Meadian theory.

conversation, it must be made up of elements from past conversations and future or hypothetical conversations that one expects or wishes to have. Thus the "inner conversations" one has with oneself must be connected to the networks of social interaction in which one takes part. Presumably the more attracted one is to certain parts of these networks, and the ideas that are exchanged there, the more one is motivated to think those ideas to oneself.[14] Some of these implications are discussed in the theory of interaction ritual chains at the end of Chapter 10.

SELF AS A SACRED OBJECT

A different approach to the nature of self and social roles is taken by Goffman. We have already seen (Chapter 6) that Goffman follows the Durkheimian theoretical tradition, applying Durkheim's analysis of religious rituals to the interaction rituals of everyday life. The self, then, is another aspect of these rituals. For Goffman, the self is not so much a private, individual attribute, as a public reality, created by and having its primary existence in public interaction.

Goffman (1967: 47) leads off this analysis by referring to Durkheim's theory of the soul. In Durkheim's sociology of religion, we may recall, God represents society. Most religions have a conception of the soul, a sacred part of the individual, which is related to the God or gods, the totemic animals or spirits, however the religious sphere is conceived in that society. The individual soul is regarded as kin to the gods or totems, or is created by them, and is spiritual or immortal and goes to join them after death. According to Durkheim, this represents the fact that the individual's consciousness (and especially his or her moral sentiments) are created by society, and that society is constantly within him or her. Goffman (1967: 47) summarizes: "the individual's personality can be seen as one apportionment of the collective *mana*, and . . . the rites performed to representations of the social collectivity will sometimes be performed to the individual himself."

From this, Goffman derived his notion that the interactions of everyday life are rituals, which create a collective reality. Furthermore, in modern society, these rituals center especially around the "worship" of the self. What does this mean? Goffman spelled it out in two early papers.

---

[14] Peirce (1868/1955: 238–49) stressed (although Mead seems to have given little significance to the point) that the connections among ideas are emotional as well as purely associative and grammatical. Peirce did not sharply distinguish emotions from other kinds of thought, because emotions themselves have a "logic": they are an "inference" from one idea to another (for instance, going from something dangerous to being afraid of it, or from somebody saying something disagreeable to an angry rejoinder). Emotions are part of the flow of mind from one related meaning to another. Consciousness itself, Peirce suggested, can be regarded as a particular kind of emotion, namely attentiveness. Normally it is very mild and attached to certain sign-relations. The amount of attentiveness presumably changes in various social situations (including imagined ones). Only when the smooth and easy inference is blocked, when the automatically expectable way of feeling at the next moment is contradicted by something in the situation, does the emotion burgeon up into consciousness. Thus emotional weightings may be the medium by which social situations affect what one thinks about at a particular time.

GOFFMAN ON FACE WORK, DEFERENCE, AND DEMEANOR

One is called "On Face Work," (originally 1955, reprinted in Goffman, 1967) with the revealing subtitle: "An Analysis of Ritual Elements in Social Interaction." There Goffman says everyone is constantly engaged in presenting a "line", acting out a certain view of what situation one is in and what kind of person one is. Other people react to each other's "lines," and depend on one another to keep up social reality by keeping up a consistent "line." Notice, the "line" one takes, the "face" one presents, does not have to be realistic, but it has to be consistently maintained so that other people will be able to know what to expect and how to react to it. Hence a ritual code exists, requiring individuals to maintain a consistent face, and also to help others in maintaining their own faces. Thus, although there certainly can be competitive and deceptive elements in interaction, Goffman's main point is that all these depend on a more basic *ritual cooperation* in upholding the enactment of a shared reality.

In other words, people accommodate to each other's constructions of their social selves. They tend to accept the way they define what they are. The politeness of everyday interaction is largely oriented toward protecting these self-definitions. The ritual code calls for people to avoid threatening topics in conversation, to avoid questioning claims that people have made about themselves, and to show tact in overlooking errors in what one's conversational partner has said. What Goffman calls "face work" in conversation includes not insulting others, not getting into disagreements but rather covering up differences of opinion by polite assent or ambiguous expressions, and avoiding lulls or "embarrassing pauses" which would reveal a lack of interest in the other person's line.[15]

In "The Nature of Deference and Demeanor," (originally 1956, reprinted in Goffman, 1967), Goffman uses evidence from a mental hospital to prove his point by comparison. What we consider to be mental illness, Goffman argued, is the violation of the ceremonial rules of everyday life. Extreme and consistent violation of these rules is what gets one put in the mental hospital in the first place. The worst violators are put in the "back wards," while those who are considered less "ill," or on the road to recovery, are placed in a "good ward," where the ceremonial rules of ordinary interaction are better observed. Moreover, the staff of the mental hospital defines the mental health or illness of its inmates as what kind of *self* they have, although the actual behavior they use to rate mental health is their adherence to ceremonial rules. This indicates that interaction is seen as an expression of one's self. Persons on the back wards, who tear off their clothes, defecate on the floor, drool, growl, curse, or otherwise violate the ceremonial standards of polite society, are also showing no regard for the self-image they are expected to display. By this compari-

---

[15] Goffman points out that people can and do engage in conversational games in which they deliberately try to embarass one another, "one-upping" them with insults or catching them in pretensions and inconsistencies. But this is only possible if a cooperative game is being played at a more fundamental level. A really "cutting" remark is one that "hits home" because it cleverly twists the rules of the conversational game. It is not a blatant and hostile statement like "You are an idiot!", but typically a play on the other person's words which turns them in a self-deflating direction. Only by playing the game of mutual, accommodative reality constructing can these subtle twists be added in a competitive direction.

son, Goffman shows that the self depends on—one might also say, is created by—the acceptable use of the ritual of ordinary social etiquette.

There are two sides to this etiquette of the self. *Deference* is the ritual behavior which one expresses toward others; *demeanor* is the self which one gives off. Thus one's own self is linked to other people's selves through interaction rituals.

Deference consists of acts of respect for other people's selves. Goffman subdivides this into various kinds of rituals. "Presentational rituals" are ways that one expresses regard for others; they include salutations, invitations, compliments, minor services (holding a door, passing the salt, giving the time of day). All these are ways of showing that one has regard for other persons, as individuals worthy of some respect. Goffman implies that these actions do not have to be sincere. When one greets another by saying "How are you?", it does not have to be motivated by a genuine concern for the other's health; all that is necessary is polite adherence to the formula, indicating that one recognizes the other as an individual self. "Avoidance rituals" are forms of polite distance, allowing others the privacy of their backstages, not intruding on the intimacy of things they wish to keep private (including the way they have fixed up their physical appearance), allowing them to get away with conversational exaggerations and "white lies."

Demeanor is the expressive aspect of the self, oneself as seen by others. It consists of the clothes one wears; the care one takes to control the way one looks and smells by bathing, perfuming, and combing one's hair; one's posture and facial expressions, as well as the kinds of things one says. This is a presentation of one's self for others to see. But it also has an indirect message, indicating how much respect one is giving the other person. To dress up for an encounter and to be on one's best behavior show not only that one is trying to put forward an impressive self, but that one has enough respect for the other to offer one's best self to them.

Interaction, then, is a process of exchange between ritually enacted selves. Each person makes deference to the other's demeanor self, and receives back in return deference which helps one to uphold one's own demeanor. One's personal self is partly based on other's reactions via deference to one's demeanor. Each individual relies on others to complete one's picture of one's self.

All this consistutes a ritual, nonutilitarian dimension of social behavior. Goffman (1967: 73) quotes Durkheim: "The human personality is a sacred thing; one dare not violate it nor infringe its bounds, while at the same time the greatest good is in communion with others." The polite aspects of everyday interaction are rituals in the same sense as the religious ceremonies of the community, only on a smaller scale. Instead of worshiping the whole society or group, as symbolized by its gods and other public sacred objects, however, these everyday rituals express regard for each person's self as a sacred object (Goffman 1967: 95; echoing Durkheim, 1906/1974: 58–59).

A HISTORICAL QUESTION: WHAT PRODUCES THE MODERN CULT OF THE SELF?

Goffman's analysis leaves the historical question unanswered: why and under what conditions does the cult of the self emerge? Goffman is describing manners of polite interaction which are located especially in the higher social classes in some recent civilizations. But the individual self was not always regarded in this way.

Durkheim's nephew and collaborater, Marcel Mauss (1938/1985) sketched a history of the self. In tribal societies, individuals are sacred only as they are absorbed into religious rituals; the self consists of playing a part in a kinship-based symbol system, often taking on an identity passed along from ancestors. Here the old sense of the word "person" was dominant: it meant a *persona* or mask. In later civilizations the self began to be regarded as something interior and individual; Mauss attributed the first influences in this direction to Roman law and to Christianity with its inner conception of the soul. But only in modern Western society, with its liberal political ideas, does the private self with its inalienable rights become the basic category of selfhood.

Subsequent scholarship (the essays in Carrithers et al., 1985) has modified Mauss's picture somewhat. Some tribal societies have more of a fusion of self with role, while others have more scope for individuality; complex civilizations like China had a variety of perceptions of the self, some of which are like the Western conceptions. But Hindu and Buddhist religions went in the opposite direction, absorbing the self into a transpersonal religious experience. There does not seem to be any straight-line evolution from tribal to modern societies. All that we can say is that modern Western societies place an unusual emphasis on respect for the rights of a private individual, at the same time making inner intentions the criterion for legal obligations. Together with the rituals which Goffman noted, and the modern tendency to psychologize the individual, this adds up to what might be called a modern Western "cult of the self."

How can we explain these various conceptions of the self? Durkheim (1893/1964: 402–404) provided one theory. The collective conscience reflects the structure of society. In a world of small, isolated tribal groups, social structure was symbolized by concrete and particularistic representations: local gods and spirits. As societies became larger and the division of labor more complex, symbols of society became more abstract. The spiritual realm receded further from the concrete, material world. The many gods were absorbed into one supreme God or still further into a universalized, featureless spiritual principle. In modern industrial societies with a complex division of labor, the only thing that everyone has in common is their role-playing capacity, their self. Hence the worship of society becomes the worship of the self (Durkheim, 1978/1966: 366).

A second hypothesis is that the worship of the self is due to the increased ability of persons for Goffmanian staging. A wealthy capitalist society provides more material assets, including more of a repertoire of clothes, better housing, more private rooms, autos and other transport. All these can be used as staging devices, so that individuals can show themselves to audiences when and how they choose. There is more material control of frontstages on which to present the individual self and more privacy into which the performers can retire when they do not wish to be viewed. This is a major change from the conditions of most tribal and also medieval agrarian societies, where housing was meagre, privacy nonexistent, and most people were constantly in the presence of others (Collins, 1975: 161–87; Ariès, 1962). Hence it is the material conditions of modern society that promote the cult of the self.

There is also a more conflict-oriented, political explanation. Wiley (1985) has argued, in criticism of the Durkheimian line of theory, that respect for the individual does not automatically follow from a complex division of labor. Granted that individual role playing may be the only remaining attribute which everyone has in common, why should the individual be respected rather than taken as a cog in the machine? The nature of capitalist labor markets would lead to treating the individual as a commodity, while bureaucracy similarly reduces the individual to a site for the imposition of rules. If there is a respect for the individual, it has come from political processes: specific laws giving individual rights, civil liberties, citizenship and the welfare state. It has been the success of the democratic revolutions which has won these liberties. The medieval agrarian societies showed scant respect for individuals, subjecting them to judicial torture, public mutilations, and executions (Collins, 1984). If these offend our modern moral sensibilities, it is because democratic politics overthrew the autocracies and established legal guarantees of the rights of the individual.

The several hypotheses need not be incompatible. The conflict explanation indicates why the individual would become immune from traditional authoritarian violations of the self, but it does not explain why there should be a positive cult worshiping the self. The materialist staging argument shows some conditions which allow the presentation of more favorable self-images, but does not tell us why other people accept these presentations. The Durkheimian theory of the universalization of the moral conscience provides the missing moral element, although it does not specify all the conditions for realizing it in the realm of the modern self.

The several lines of hypothesis appear to be implied in multidimensional models of culture which we have already met in Chapter 6. Mary Douglas' typology of grid and group, and Collins' historical dimensions of status cultures, indicate there is both a vertical (political power) factor, and a horizontal (group structure) factor. Douglas (1973) generalized that where there is *high group* (strong local group boundaries), the society is highly conscious of pollution and takes strong ritual precautions against individuals endangering the group by their symbolic actions. This implies, I think, that the group intrudes on the self, allowing little conception of individual autonomy. Symbolically, the individual is merely the locus of magical currents from outside. Where there is *high grid,* the society is very rank conscious. It can be inferred that higher-ranking individuals are allowed to have selves, which must be worshiped by the others in elaborate deference rituals (Collins, 1975: 161–87); whereas lower-ranking persons have severely degraded selves and may be subject to ritual mutilation and torture.

In this perspective, the modern society in which Goffman situated his analyses has relatively low group structure, with moderately high grid. That is to say, our societies have numerous, weakly bounded groups with plural and overlapping memberships; while stratification is moderately high, mitigated by the political rights won in the struggle for democracy. The result is the Goffmanian cult of the self. We should modify this conception by recognizing that the intensity of this cult varies with stratification. Individuals in the higher social classes, especially public figures built up by the concentration of material means of impression management in the mass media, are given an exaggerated veneration for their individuality; while lower class persons, and those subjected to the people-processing effects of bureacratic organization and the pressures of capitalist labor markets, are allowed very little individual self. The sacredness of the self is a focus for struggles between opposing forces.

MULTIPLE OR UNITARY SELF?

The major contemporary version of symbolic interactionism (Rosenberg, 1979; Stryker, 1980; Ralph Turner, 1979–80) takes it for granted that there is such a thing as the self. The normal condition of the healthy individual is a central, stable self-conception. As Rosenberg (1981) argued, this is shown by virtually all studies of mental illness. A fragmented self is abnormal; low self-esteem or a weak self-conception are implicated in virtually all psychological problems. Neurotic behavior usually can be interpreted as a defense against threats on the self, a form of protection from having to be conscious of some area of felt inferiority or danger.

The reality and importance of the self may seem obvious. Nevertheless, it has been challenged by a number of important theories. The most extreme challenge comes form Goffman. For him the problem is not that there is no self, but that there are too many. Multiple, fluctuating, situational selves are the rule, not the exception. There are occupational selves and other roles that one plays in various contexts (family, politics, and so forth), usually with no sense of difficulty or strain from this multiplicity. Furthermore, there are numerous fleeting contextual selves: the self one makes up temporarily as a traffic unit, when walking on a street or occupying a bus seat as part of a group in a public place (Goffman, 1971). There are numerous selves that one briefly animates during the course of a conversation: different voices that one speaks in while joking or narrating what someone else (or even oneself) has said on another occasion (Goffman, 1974, 1981; also see Chapters 8 and 9). There are game-selves, identities that one takes up in order to take part in a contest or entertainment. Goffman (1961) pointed out, moreover, that having "fun in games" happens when one becomes engrossed in the role, so that one is no longer conscious of role playing but is spontaneously absorbed in whatever the game-world takes as immediate reality. Here, it is "losing oneself," rather than maintaining a stable self-conception, that constitutes normal, adaptive behavior.

In a companion article, Goffman (1961) introduced the concept of "role-distance." Here we have a further complexity in modern social life: not only do people play multiple and fleeting social roles, but they often play these roles in a double fashion, simultaneously enacting the role and distancing themselves from it. Goffman cites such observations as children who adopt an attitude of disinterest while riding on a merry-go-round, as if to display that they are too old to be engrossed in this "little kid's" amusement. The phenomenon is extremely widespread. A major part of the contemporary culture of personal styles, extending at least as far back as the first half of the twentieth century, is the "cool," ironic, mocking attitude toward social roles. The "punk" styles of the 1980s are only a particular version of the common practice of communicating one's alienation, or at least distance, from ordinary role-engrossment. Our modern heroes, both in the entertainment media and in everyday life, are those persons who communicate by little gestures and styles that they can stay cool under pressure, aware of the demands of the role but able to stand back from it and keep it subordinate. Our public heroes have had their jaunty cigarette holders or their baseball caps turned at a rakish angle, their mocking smiles or half-contemptuous pouts, which set them off and show them as superior to the demands of interaction, able to play the game and stand above it at the same time.

We might argue, however, that all this role-distance shows that there is a true self, and that is what these heroes of the gesture are displaying by refusing to be caught up completely in their roles. But Goffman (1961: 152) denied this interpretation. To display distance from one role is only possible because we inhabit a social structure with multiple roles; we use roles elsewhere as a background that frees us from being completely caught up in the obligations of the role right in front of us. It is only the structure of *modern* society, Goffman is implying, that makes possible role-distance, and hence this appearance of a self which stands above roles.[16]

THE SELF AS MODERN MYTH

Insofar as Goffman is applying Durkheimian theory of rituals to modern life, we may push the implication one step further. Durkheim's sacred objects, the gods of a society, do not really exist in themselves; they are merely symbols reflecting the structure of society. If the self is the central sacred object of modern society, it is correspondingly unreal. The self in Goffman is not something that individuals negotiate out of social interactions; it is, rather, the archetypal modern myth. We are *compelled* to have an individual self, not because we actually have one but because social interaction requires us to act as if we do. It is society that forces people to present a certain image of themselves, to appear to be truthful, self-consistent, and honorable, when in fact the same social system, because it forces us to switch back and forth between many complicated roles, is also making us always somewhat untruthful, inconsistent, and dishonorable—in short to be actors rather than spontaneously the roles that we appear to be at any single moment. The self is real only as a symbol, a linguistic concept that we use to account for what we and other people do. It is an ideology of everyday life, used to attribute causality and moral responsibility in our society, just as in societies with a denser (for instance, tribal) structure, moral responsibility is not placed within the individual but attributed to various spirits or gods.

Goffman's denial of the ultimate reality of an inner self is an extreme position, but there are others which support it. Role theory itself implies that the subjective self is multiple rather than constant. Insofar as people have multiple roles, they must have multiple selves. Ralph Turner argues that the self is lodged more in some roles than in others, but this does not rule out the possibility that it may be partially and

---

[16] Goffman (1961: 152) explicitly draws on Durkheim in his put-down of the "common-sense" position on the self. "There is a vulgar tendency in social thought to divide the conduct of the individual into a profane and sacred part, this version of the distinction strangely running directly contrary to the one Durkheim gave us. The profane part is attributed to the obligatory world of social roles; it is formal, stiff, and dead; it is exacted by society. The sacred part has to do with 'personal' matters and 'personal' relationships—with what an individual is 'really' like underneath it all when he relaxes and breaks through to those in his presence. . . . The concept of role distance helps combat this touching tendency to keep a part of the world safe from sociology."

in different degrees lodged in many places at once. George Herbert Mead's account of the self is explicitly pluralistic; there are numerous "me's," including not only more enduring social roles, but fleeting imaginery "me's" which are used mentally to try out various courses of action. In addition to these "me's," there is the "I," which is fluid and uncrystalized, lacking any content at all. Even the "generalized other" may be plural, since as Goffman points out (especially in his "Frame Analysis," described in Chapter 8), there are many different group structures; some of these exist only in fleeting situation to which one momentarily orients one's mental standpoint.

Among classic theories, Freud proposed a divided self: ego, id, and superego. Even though he suggested that the healthful goal of psychotherapy was to develop the conscious ego and give it control over the primal drives of the id as well as over the moralistic superego, this appeared to be a distant and utopian end, which Freud himself despaired of reaching. Most extreme of all is the premise of Buddhist philosophy (Conze, 1967: 122–43) that there is no self. What people take to be their self is merely the realm of illusion, the attachment of human cravings to mere "name and form" of the world of the senses. The Buddhist conception is a sophisticated one. It holds that we build up our conception of the world by taking fleeing sensory impressions as if they were permanent objects, whereas it is our subjective mind which is carving up the flow by imposing verbal names and sensory forms upon it. Our own "self" is just another such illustory conception: illusory insofar as the true reality is a primal flux, which one would directly experience if one stopped imposing names and forms upon it. The experience of wordless meditation, directing consciousness to itself without these subjective impositions, escapes from the illusory sense of self. We might give a sociological interpretation of this form of meditation: insofar as words and concepts come from society, the process of separating oneself from all social influences and turning consciousness inwards reveals the world as it exists without socially structured cognition. Significantly, this primal reality does not include a self.

The issue can be approached from many angles. Philosophers have argued on various sides: Hume declared that we never encounter the self in experience; Kant, that it is a "transcendental illusion"; Sartre, that a major component of the self is "nothingness." Sociological positions that we will meet in upcoming chapters are relevant. Ethnomethodology (Chapter 8) and a micro-macro analysis (Chapter 11) imply that the self is a reified concept which is merely constructed outside of the fundamental reality of situational experience. Goffman's frame analysis (Chapter 8) further dissolves the self into layers of situational orientations. The self seems to have an objective and enduring reality, because in our society we constantly refer to other people's intentions and because we often may reflect about our own selves. But these may be merely words.[17]

---

[17] Goffman's (1971: 366) most explicit definition of the self is as follows: "The self is the code that makes sense out of almost all the individual's activities and provides a basis for organizing them. The self is what can be read about the individual by interpreting the place he takes in an organzation of social activity, as confirmed by his expressive behavior." Significantly, this definition comes in the midst of Goffman's most important discussion of mental illness. The healthy "self" is not depicted as some inner state of integration, but rather a social interpretation of how one is living up to ritual obligations. People only begin to define someone as "mentally ill" when that person does not mesh with other

The theory of interaction ritual chains (Chapter 10) proposes that our acting as well as thinking may be explained by situational flows of emotional energies and culture capital. Hence self-reflection may not be generally necessary for action. Conscious reflection on action would only come up when there are conflicts or unusual difficulties. Reflection on the nature of one's "self" in these situations would be yet a further degree of difficulty. Persons who habitually reflect on their selves are likely to be quasi-paralyzed from action. Self-reflection is certainly possible, but it may be a neurotic loop. Perhaps this is the reason why mental health difficulties, as Rosenberg argued (1981), tend to involve problems of self-conception. It is not that a healthy self-conception is normal; but rather that normal social action involves little or no reflection on the self at all. Having to reflect heavily on the self is already a sign of difficulties. Furthermore, it may be chasing a chimera. If there is no single, enduring entity which answers to the name of "oneself," then searching for the self is an endless enterprise. Numerous, maybe infinite, situational selves can be found. Moreover, since "self" is generally a reflexive grammatical construction, concern with oneself can lead to loops upon loops, reflections on reflections, chasing an end-point which recedes forever in the distance. Perhaps for this reason the resolution of psychotherapy often involves breaking away from the involutions of the therapeutic process itself (what the Freudians call "resolving the transference").

IS THERE A CORE SELF?

These arguments for the situational nature of self (more accurately, selves) seem to me significant. However, it may still be possible that there is a "meta-self" or core self as well as these various situational selves. A reason to believe this is that virtually all theories, including those which propose plural, situational selves, seem to imply such a core self.

Goffman, the most extreme expositor of multiple selves, nevertheless seems to admit a kind of director behind the scenes, choosing which self to enact at each moment. In his early work on the labelling theory of mental illness, Goffman (1961a) argued that the bizarre behavior of patients in total institutions (organizations which enclose all aspects of their lives) can be interpreted as a defense of the self. Where the social situation is all-encompassing and is attempting to impose a new conception of the self—first, to force one to admit that one is "mentally ill" and then to build a new "healthy" self—individuals are still striving to maintain some vestige of control, even if it means violating the demands of the institution in the most outrageous ways. This implies some inner self to be defended, behind the selves which society constructs and deconstructs. And in Goffman's last work (1981), he argued that the individual makes a choice among various "footings" that can be taken in the flux of situations and verbal stances:

> What the speaker is engaged in doing, then, moment to moment through the course of the discourse in which he finds himself, is to meet whatever occurs by sustaining or changing footing. And by and large, it seems he selects that footing

people's framework of meanings: ". . . the individual's failure to encode through deeds and expressive cues, a *workable* definition of himself, one which closely enmeshed others can accord him through the regard they show his person, is to block and trip up and threaten them in almost every movement that they make. The selves that had been the reciprocals of his are undermined."

which provides him the least self-threatening position in the circumstances, or, differently phrased, the most defensible alignment he can muster . . ." (Goffman, 1981: 325).

"The least self-threatening position in the circumstances" even makes a reference to "self." But what kind of self is this, over and above any situational self?

Conflict theory, as well, seems to need a conception of self as motivator. It proposes that behavior is driven, to a considerable degree, by self-interest. For example, Principle 1A in Chapter 6 says that persons avoid or act to protect themselves against having to take orders from others. The class struggle of everyday life takes place on frontstages which individuals project in order to present their best self-image. This indicates multiple selves, in the eyes of others, but it also implies that there is a "stage-director" self, which selects what staging to do and what self to present.

It does not follow, however, that the core "self" is of the same kind as the selves which can be "self-images" or have "self-esteem." The core self which chooses footings and stages, which learns Buddhist meditation, or which follows its "self-interest" is not an image. It is explicitly contentless. Moreover, it does not (apparently, or at least usually) involve self-consciousness. If self-consciousness occurred at this level, it would probably be a loop which is totally incapacitating for action. (Though perhaps this is what is involved in the more intense levels of meditation.) The core "self" can be conscious but usually only of the outer environment or of verbal thoughts; sometimes it is conscious of some image-self, arising from situational action or from our uses of language terms referring to "self." But these are selves on different layers. It is an error to confuse them and to attribute the contents of situational selves to the core motivational center. Only by its contentlessness and its lack self-consciousness is it able to act as stage-director and motivator among all these situational selves.

It may be that we can arrive at a more penetrating conception of this inner layer of "self." The outer layers, I have suggested, are fluctuating, multiple, and situational. They are given a "mythical" unity because of our uses of language, and are elevated to enormous respect, especially in the psychiatric concerns of today, because of the Goffmanian rituals focused on them. But the surface self, or rather the responsibility for formulating innumerable surface selves, is the "sacred object" of modern society. The "core," or directing "self," however, may be a misnomer. It is an analyst's premise that we use to make theoretical sense out of our explanations of what people actually do and say. It may be that the unity of situational selves is due merely to one's physical body, and that the directing principle is merely a version of the animal tendency to take the most favorable route within situations as they come along. The only difference is that for the human animal the landscape is no longer merely physical, but is overlaid by symbols and verbal constructions. This adds a fluctuating haze, which we take for more solid objects than are really there.

SUMMARY

1. The self is a combination of at least two viewpoints: a self which is doing the perceiving as well as a self which is perceived. Individuals tend to define their self by a social position or category that is most relevant to them. A person's self-

image is influenced by other people's opinions about him or her, but in a somewhat distorted fashion: individuals are most influenced by what they believe others think about them, rather than by what others actually think. One's self-esteem is most influenced by groups which are most highly valued by the individual; individuals also protect their self-esteem by avoiding groups in which they rank low.

2. In George Herbert Mead's theory, the "I" is the part of the self which is active and self-reflexive, capable of making itself (or anything else) an object of its consciousness. The "me" is the passive part of the self, the self as seen as an object. The "generalized other" is the viewpoint of society within the individual.

3. Roles always come in pairs or larger combinations; learning one role always involves implicitly learning what the complimentary roles do and how one is to act in relation to them. Action is carried out by taking the role of the other, or *role taking,* putting oneself mentally into the role of the persons one is interacting with in order to anticipate what they will do.

4. A role set is the combination of different roles which one individual plays at different times. Where one must deal with a situation which invokes several of one's roles simultaneously (such as a mother who is also a teacher who has her son in her class), the result is role strain.

5. Individuals identify their self with the role which gives them the most power and other rewards and which they are most capable of playing; but also, individuals are coerced into identifying with a role to the extent that it is very visible, ranked very high or low, or is part of a tightly organized and omnipresent group.

6. A theoretical issue concerns the extent to which roles are learned through socialization and then merely carried out, or are created in new forms (role making). Though the latter does occur, the theory is not well developed as to how and when.

7. Expectation states theory shows that individuals develop performance expectations about how well they themselves, as well as others, will do on tasks. These expectations affect both future performance and evaluations. Persons who are expected to perform well take the initiative and are given leadership roles by the group. Diffuse status characteristics such as official rank, gender, race, or physical attractveness also influence people's expectations about how individuals will perform, even when these characteristics have nothing to do with actual capacity. Persons who have high status are evaluated more highly than low-status persons even if they perform the same on a task.

8. An individual's "personality" is not an enduring set of attributes, but expectations about how one is to perform in a given situation. Status is communicated by overt information and by nonverbal expressive cues, which are given off according to their expectation advantage or disadvantage relative to the other.

9. Thinking takes place by means of signs (such as words). In Mead's theory, it is an internalized conversation between the parts of the self. Signs have a universalized meaning, picking out not just some particular object or event, but referring to it as a more general kind of item. Signs thus enable the thinker to transcend the immediate here-and-now and to see the world as enduring objects and processes; signs fill the world with meanings. Universal signs would not be possible without the "generalized other." This is the part of the self which takes the point of view of any possible other person. Acquiring a generalized other is a crucial part of the development of a child into a human being, capable of using language, thinking, and interacting by taking the role of the other.

10. Mead's theory has been criticized for emphasizing the cognitive and reflexive nature of the self too heavily, although human cognitive capacities appear to be more limited. Another unsolved problem is to explain how humans acquire the capacity for consciously taking the role of the other in the first place. The "generalized other" may actually involve a number of different kinds of reflective stances.

11. Goffman proposes that the self is the object of everyday rituals such as *deference,* which gives respect to other people's selves, and *demeanor,* in which one expresses an idealized self to others. This constitutes a Durkheimian cult of the self, which becomes the main sacred object in modern society. However, this respect given the individual self appears to be most characteristic of the higher social classes and public figures who control the means of impression management.

12. Many theories propose that a stable, unified self-conception is crucial for normal psychological health. Goffman, however, emphasizes that there are numerous fleeting contextual selves, that the most enjoyable activities are ones in which the conscious sense of self is lost in the role or activity, and that distancing oneself from roles is typical of modern culture. The idea of a "true" or inner self apart from society is a myth, which we believe in because it is the focus of the modern cult of the individual. Mental health problems arise from over-reflexive loops concerning self-conception, which are themselves rooted in social interactions. The question remains whether there is a central "self" which guides the individual through the various surface, situational selves.

Chapter **8**

DEFINITION OF THE SITUATION AND THE SOCIAL CONSTRUCTION OF REALITY

DEFINITION OF THE SITUATION
   The Sources of Situationalist Theory
   Blumer and Symbolic Interactionism
   Applications of Social Constructionism
   Criticisms and Further Directions

ETHNOMETHODOLOGY
   The Background in Social Phenomenology
   Garfinkel's Cognitive Radicalism
   The Procedures of Commonsense Reasoning
   Cognition vs. Emotion

IMPLICATIONS OF ETHNOMETHODOLOGY
   1. Human Cognitive Limitations
   2. Weakness of Overcognitive Theories
   3. Application to Artificial Intelligence
   4. Social Order and Change

GOFFMAN'S FRAME ANALYSIS AS A RECONCILIATION OF
   RELATIVISM AND OBJECTIVITY
   Frame Analysis
   Out-of-frame Activity and Frame Breaks
   Human Society Is Built Up by Transforming Frames
   Goffman's Answers to Symbolic Interactionism and Ethnomethodology

CONCLUSION: IDEALISM AND RELATIVISM IN THE CURRENT
   INTELLECTUAL WORLD

SUMMARY

The theories examined in the last chapter tend to assume a relatively fixed social world. This world is made up of roles and selves; even if the self is interpreted as changing and situational, the world is objective and more or less stable. The more radical positions treated here tend to dissolve reality itself into something fluctuating, unknowable, or constructed by humans. The older version of this constructional radicalism is a variant of symbolic interactionism; its emphasis is upon the *definition of the situation*. More recently, there is an even more thoroughly constructionist position, developed by ethnomethodology and some other versions of social phenomenology. These positions burst on the scene in the mid-1960s, with the appearance of Peter Berger and Thomas Luckman's *The Social Construction of Reality* in 1966, and Harold Garfinkel's *Studies in Ethnomethodology* in 1967. Erving Goffman also concerned himself with this radical constructionism, though approaching the issues from a more conservative position. Goffman's later work constitutes a compromise position, which recognizes multiple levels of reality without getting caught up in infinitely relativistic ones.

At its extreme, situationalism and the social construction of reality virtually eliminate the objectivity of the world and negate the possibility of any definitive knowledge in sociology (or in any other branch of science or scholarship). The popularity of these positions has gone along with a widespread movement among modern intellectuals to disavow the traditional philosophy of scientific positivism. Whether this complete disavowal of any objective knowledge is reasonable, however, remains to be shown. The radical constructionist position verges on the slogan "it's all in your mind"—at least, whatever is not in one's mind is unknowable. This may be a self-defeating or self-undermining position. But the apparent subjectivism of these positions is limited by several features. These are not solipsistic positions, since they assert that knowledge is socially, rather than individually, constructed. Society, interactions, and situations are central in the creation of reality, fluctuating or impossible to pin down as it may be.

Furthermore, the most prominent of these movements in sociology are by no means strictly philosophical. Both symbolic interactionism and ethnomethodology have placed a very strong emphasis on empirical research of the most naturalistic kind. They have been critical of more posivitistic research methods for jumping too easily to the realm of questionnaires, attitude measurements, and statistics, rather than examining the flow of natural life, of social experience as it actually happens. And in taking the situation and the social construction of reality as their themes, these positions have attempted to get to the essence of these phenomena, to show the principles on which they operate. The ethnomethodologists in particular have tried to state the principles by which humans carry out reasoning in everyday life and have discovered some important generalizations. As we proceed, I will attempt to show how these contribute to a larger corpus of sociological knowledge.

DEFINITION OF THE SITUATION

"If men define situations as real, they are real in their consequences." This is the so-called Thomas Theorem, enunciated by W. I. Thomas in 1928 (Thomas and Thomas, 1928: 572).

The Theorem has far-reaching implications. Thomas stated it in the context of a concern for social problems. If immigrants are regarded as unintelligent, shiftless, and incapable of achievement, the consequence is that they are not given decent educational and occupational opportunities. They end up being relegated to a lower-class lifestyle, thereby making the definition initially asserted actually come true. As Merton (1949) later renamed it, the process is a "self-fulfilling prophecy." Here Thomas's Theorem is applied to explain the effects of racial and ethnic discrimination, juvenile delinquency, and failures of social mobility in the class structure. Presumably it could be applied (although the issue was not part of much social consciousness until the 1970s) to the definition of females as emotional, concerned only with clothing styles and domestic affairs, and incapable of achievement in the "masculine" realms of business, politics, or the professions.

The definition of the situation, however, does not merely apply to these instances of discrimination and failure of achievement. It indicates a principle of how the entire social structure is put together, both in its positive and dominant aspects as well as in its negative and subordinate ones. All social reality is defined; power comes from the ability to control the definition of situations. A man pretending to have a gun can order his victims around just as effectively as if he really had one, provided that they believe he does. Robbers have effectively held up banks and stores by brandishing a paper bag, or with a hand in a pocket, by convincing others that it is a weapon or a bomb. Conversely, even a real weapon may be ineffective if the victims do not recognize it or refuse to believe the threat is serious. The robber attempts to get compliance by the threat of using violence, which is far more effective than actually having to use violence itself. But if the victims are deaf and blind, or otherwise fail to recognize the threat, they can't be coerced into cooperating with the robber.

The example may seem extreme, but it holds the key to an analysis of authority relations generally. Governmental power depends upon certain persons being defined as powerful. As long as politicians can get others to believe in the effectiveness of their "clout," they can get compliance, which in turn can be used to pay off or punish those who cooperate or fail to cooperate. As soon as the reputation for power slips, the followers and the coerced alike desert the leaders, thereby hastening their fall from power. Definitions of the situation are thus particularly crucial in political situations. This holds especially true for the power of dictators who rule by violent threat. It is crucial to be on the right side of such dangerous persons as long as they are in power; but when their power slips away, it rapidly becomes crucial not to remain onboard a sinking ship, hence there is a rush to join an opposing coalition when it looks like it will take over. Similar phenomena seem to apply in military conflicts; battles are won and lost at the moment that the soldiers of one side go into a panic, which in turn ensures their defeat (Collins, 1988).

Because of the importance of these dynamics of defining the situation, politics and war have a very volatile quality. As long as definitions of power situations remain stable, the authority of a state or the invincibility of armed force may seem immutable. When changes occur, however, they tend to happen rapidly, in dramatic incidents. The central role of definitions of situations is responsible for the sudden rhythm of revolutions.

THE SOURCES OF SITUATIONALIST THEORY

W. I. Thomas worked out his basic position while collaborating with the Polish sociologist Florian Znaniecki on *The Polish Peasant in Europe and America* (1918–20). This was the first major empirical work in American sociology, a study of the lives of Polish immigrants. (The most important interpretation of this intellectual history is that of Wiley [1986] which I will draw on here.) Znaniecki, trained as a philosopher in the neo-Kantian tradition, brought to this research a theoretical interpretation deriving from idealism. American social science prior to this time was heavily influenced by Darwinian biology, which explained behavior as the result of evolutionary adaptation and biologically based instincts within the individual. Thomas and Znaniecki replaced this biologism with the concept of the "attitude," the human capacity for symbolic interpretation, and hence for creating new situations. In addition to the "attitude," which is intrasubjective, there are also "values," which are intersubjective, the culture shared by the group. Ideally, attitudes and values would match, the social being reflected inside the individual. However, it is more usual for there to be a discrepancy between the two levels. The culture imposed by society may differ from the interpretations of a given individual. This is especially likely to happen when there is international migration, such as that experienced by Polish-Americans in the early twentieth century, when individuals from one culture move to another. Social harmony can be restored either by socialization—changing attitudes to conform to the prevailing social values—or by loosening up the existing values to allow for the new interpretation by individuals.

The "definition of the situation" is implicit in *The Polish Peasant*. Wiley (1986) sums up the underlying message: "If the Poles define themselves as American, then they will become American. . . . On this premise, the American Poles, and all the other new ethnics, had the psychological capacity to assimilate, over time, American life. . . . There would be no need to regiment them or deny their rights." Thomas and Znaniecki thus turned sociology in a more liberal direction. Instead of condemning the immigrants for their inferior biological inheritance, sociology shifted to an emphasis on situational factors and on the dynamic possibilities of change. George Herbert Mead, who was also active on the liberal, reform-oriented side of politics in that era, similarly developed a concept of the self as active, reflexive, and capable of creatively constituting society; this self emerges out of the biological level, but then transcends it. Herbert Blumer's synthesis of these positions in the 1930s created symbolic interactionism.

BLUMER AND SYMBOLIC INTERACTIONISM

The philosophical input to Thomas and Znaniecki's work was German idealism. On the American side, there was also a native philosophical tradition. This was pragmatism, developed by Charles Sanders Peirce, William James, and John Dewey, and brought into sociology through the influence of George Herbert Mead. For pragmatism, truth is not a correspondence between subjective ideas and externally existing objects. Truth is not a relationship at all but a practical criterion of action. Ideas are true if their consequences are such that they enable someone to carry out some action successfully. Your idea that there is a chair at the other side of the room is true if you are able to sit down in it. This treatment of ideas in terms of their consequences has an echo in Thomas's Theorem (". . . they are real in their consequences"). However the pragmatists, and especially William James (their most famous spokesman), had an individualistic emphasis. Thomas went on to stress that situations are socially defined. This concern for social definitions of reality was built into a full-scale theory of human thought and interaction by Mead and Blumer.

Mead was not a sociologist but a philosopher. He developed a social theory of the mind, but he wished to use this to cast a new light on traditional philosophical problems in epistemology. Mead's central interests are revealed in his *Philosophy of the Act* (1938). Here, Mead defended a physical science view of the material world and showed how the mind emerges naturalistically from the physical level. For Mead, this was a philosophical battle, using pragmatism to undercut the idealists who dominated American philosophy at the turn of the century (Schneider, 1963; Kuklick, 1977). All his arguments are directed at showing that one can't even perceive or conceive of objects in the physical world, without the ability to use universalizing symbols produced from social communication and the stance of the Generalized Other. Mead's works are somewhat disappointing if we are looking for much analysis of how complex social action takes place. Mead is always showing the mind as figuring out how to take a walk, jump a ditch, or some other bodily action, rather than how the social world is negotiated. Mead also did not seem to show much interest in how abstract thinking takes place, but only thinking at the level of crude physical action. In this respect, Mead represents the style that made pragmatists generally seem crude to their philosophical opponents. But in the context of traditional philosophical discussion (as practiced by Berkeley, Hume, and Kant) the crucial issue was the reality of the physical world. Mead set out to prove the reality of this world against the idealist emphasis on the mind by showing that the mind itself can only exist as it derives from action upon the physical world.

For this reason, Herbert Blumer is the central figure in creating a symbolic interactionist position within sociology. What makes this complicated is that fact that Blumer always asserted that he was merely expounding Mead's ideas, that he was merely a disciple of Mead. But Blumer took the crucial step of taking Mead out of the philosophical context and using him for issues within sociology's intellectual field.[1] In recent years a debate has been emerging on how different Blumerian sym-

---

[1] Mead was never president of the American Sociological Society (later renamed the American Sociological Association, to improve the acronym). It would seem paradoxical if America's most distinguished

bolic interaction is from Mead's own position. Where Blumer maintained that he was merely following Mead's own theories, McPhail and Rexroat (1979) and Lewis and Smith (1980) have charged that he distorted Mead's message (for replies, see Blumer, 1980; Johnson, 1983). The critics depict Mead as much more of a behaviorist, while Blumer's symbolic interactionism stresses the role of the mind in redefining social situations. Another way to put it would be to say that Blumer principally stresses the "I," the creative, emergent aspect of the self, whereas the rival interpretation of Mead stresses the "me," the relatively fixed parts of the self that are internalized from social roles. In actuality, there are two different schools of thought inside sociology, both calling themselves "symbolic interactionism" and both claiming to represent Mead's true position. The debate has gone on between Blumer's version on one side and those who have developed the type of role theory found in Chapter 7.

It is clear that Blumer's position is different from Mead's; but role theory is different too. The difference, above all, is that Mead's concerns were philosophical and only used a social conception of the mind in order to answer philosophical questions.[2] Blumer necessarily had to orient toward different disciplinary issues when he took Mead's content out of philosophy. As Wiley (1986) put it, sociology was detaching itself from biology, hence pushing "upwards" to the autonomous symbolic level. In philosophy Mead was combatting religious idealism in the name of scientific naturalism, showing how the mind and its emergent and reflexive properties comes from the physical world. Blumer did not need to stress this physical grounding of the mind, and so he slanted it the other way, to continue Thomas's definitional sociology with its stress on the autonomous and creative capacities of the mind. In the process Blumer so much identified Mead with sociology (and since Mead was never popular among philosophers), that almost everyone has forgotten that Mead was operating in a different intellectual arena.

Let us examine Blumer's position, then, as a creative development of Mead in its own right. He proposes three fundamental premises.

(1) "Human beings act toward things on the basis of the meanings which these things have for them" (Blumer, 1969:2). Meanings are not intrinsically in things in the world; they have to be defined before they have any human reality. This applies to other human beings (a mother or a store clerk), social organizations (a school or a government), to ideals (democracy, honesty), as well as physical objects themselves (a chair to sit in, a piece of furniture to admire). Everything that people act upon or that has an impact upon them must go through the process of subjective meaning.

---

sociological theorist never won this honor. But in fact, as a philosopher, Mead was not perceived during his lifetime as part of the sociological discipline, and he probably was not a member of the A.S.S. Blumer, on the other hand, was elected president and was a dominant figure in sociology's intellectual life for over 40 years.

[2] Lewis and Smith (1980) are correct in perceiving a difference between Mead and Blumer, but they muddy the issue by claiming that Blumer was actually influenced by other philosophers, especially Dewey and James. However, the crucial influence is sociological: Blumer wished to use Mead's ideas to deal with the issues raised by Thomas and Znaniecki. Blumer's first notable publication (1939) was an extensive analysis of *The Polish Peasant*, pointing up its flaws and the need to go beyond it.

(2) "The meaning of a thing for a person grows out of the ways in which other persons act toward the person with regard to the thing" (Blumer, 1969: 4). Meaning is not merely individual and subjective, but social.

(3) "The use of meanings by the actor occurs through *a process of interpretation*" (Blumer, 1969: 5). Meanings are handled flexibly as actions are worked out. The social communication which constitutes meaning (premise 2) is itself an interpretive process, as individuals imaginatively take the role of the other to work out a way of dealing with each other (explained in Chapter 7). People are not merely pushed around by psychological or social conditions. Each individual has to interpret whatever factors there are in the situation, to give them a meaning, and thus to work out a course of action in regard to them. Society, roles, social institutions, or values should not be reified, as if they were objective things or autonomous forces impinging on the individual. Society exists only in action; it is whatever people work it out to be, at a particular moment in time.

Human action is created in the process of interpreting meanings. Blumer uses Mead's analysis of the self as consisting of the "I," "me," and "Generalized Other." In Blumer's version, the "I," the active self, imaginatively tries out various "me's," images of the self, as engaged in different possible actions, while the "Generalized Other," as internalized witness, acts as the audience conscious of these imaginary play-actings within the mind. But Blumer stresses that interpretations are always going on in this process. Everything must be defined, including the self. The human being is able to be an object for one's own action, one's own reflection. Because the "I" can try out different "me's" in imagination, one can step back from the self, have distance from the self. One is not trapped in a social role, since one can detach oneself through the process of interpretation. Different "me's" can be imagined and tried out. Similarly, one can put oneself in the place of the other and imagine various selves that are being launched on the other side of the interaction. One can interpret other people, just as one interprets oneself. Every person, and hence every situation, can be interpreted and reinterpreted.

In effect, Blumer has developed a more radical and far-reaching version of Thomas's Theorem. Not only are situations determined by how they are defined, but every element within the self has a similarly fluid quality. Everything, internal and external, must be interpreted if action is to take place; everything is subject to the ruling process of definition. Blumer is strongly critical of any theories in sociology or any other social science, which fail to take account of this crucial process of self-interaction. No matter what is being done, it always depends on the individuals involved making indications to themselves as to what they will act toward, interpreting the world and covertly mapping out lines of action.[3]

---

[3] "Self-indication is a moving communicative process in which the individual notes things, assesses them, gives them a meaning and decides to act on the basis of the meaning. The human being stands over against the world, or against 'alters' . . . the individual points out to himself and interprets the appearance or expression of such things, noting a given social demand that is made on him, recognizing a command, observing that he is hungry, realizing that he wishes to buy something, aware that he has a given feeling, conscious that he dislikes eating with someone he despises, or aware that he is thinking of doing something. By virtue of indicating such things to himself, he places himself over against them and is able to act back against them, accepting them, rejecting them, or transforming them in accordance with how he defines or interprets them" (Blumer, 1969: 81–82).

One objection that may be offered is that the social world is not always so novel. People repeat the same actions over and over again many times, like a grocery clerk ringing up prices. This repeated behavior is, in fact, what constitutes social roles. Blumer replies that even where there is this repetition, the symbolic interactionist process of interpretation is still going on. It only happens that people make the same interpretations over and over again; when this happens routinely, they may barely pay attention to the process of interpreting and fail to notice it is occurring. But without these interpretations, the action would halt. Meanings may be carried over from previous situations; the grocery store is defined as a place for buying groceries because individuals carry over and renew the interpretations they have made from the last time they were there. But reinterpretation is always possible; the grocery store may rapidly turn into a situation where there is taking place a flirtation, or a holdup, or a fire, or many other emergent meanings. Reality is volatile. We can construct it in a repetitive, stable manner, but we can also change its nature in an instant.

APPLICATIONS OF SOCIAL CONSTRUCTIONISM

The situationalist theory stemming from Thomas and Blumer has been influential particularly in the area of social problems. A major position in the study of deviance stresses that deviant identities are socially constructed and that categories of what is considered deviant are socially defined. The *labelling theory* of deviance (Lemert, 1951; Goffman, 1961a; Becker, 1963; Scheff, 1966) proposes that it is the process of being caught or threatened that turns an individual into a deviant in his own eyes. Bizarre actions or violations of normal interaction, if they lead to psychiatric treatment or incarceration, make an individual acquire an identity as "mentally ill"; illicit actions by teenagers, if followed by arrest and jail, make them "delinquents"; the experience of being in jail, and of being checked up on by police and parole officers, cuts one's ties with "straight" society and launches one on a career as a criminal.

Labelling theory has given rise to considerable research, and has been both widely supported and criticized. It is true that the procedures designed to apprehend, help, or cure "deviants" often do not work; courts, jails, and psychiatric facilities have relatively low rates of success, and in many ways make problems worse. On the other hand, labelling does not always operate in this way; not all jail inmates are recidivists, nor do all juvenile delinquents go on to become adult criminals. In certain areas, such as homosexuality, it has been proposed that labelling by the authorities is not a crucial process at all (Warren and Johnson, 1972). Further, the authorities do not necessarily aggressively apply labels to all cases that come before them; many juvenile offenders are let off informally, without labelling, and people tend to resist labelling someone as mentally ill, despite bizarre behavior, until it becomes too disruptive to put up with.

These objections do not disprove the labelling theory of deviance, but they put it in a more limited perspective. They indicate that (1) labelling sometimes occurs, but not always; and (2) when labelling does happen, it sometimes creates long-lasting deviant identities, but with considerable variation in their strength. The implication is that there are several processes going on, of which labelling is only one.

Other considerations determine whether and how forcefully labelling occurs in a particular case; and once there is labelling, other factors can enter in which may shape one's identity in other directions, including back toward nondeviant status. As usual, we have a multi-factor world. Blumer's definitional perspective would agree with this; if certain situations can define one's identity as deviant, nevertheless one has the capacity to reinterpret the situation subsequently, and further interactions can emerge and change.

Another version of the social construction of deviance does not focus on how individuals get labelled, but points out that the categories of what is considered deviant in the first place are constructed by society. Becker (1963) describes the history of drug laws, which outlawed opiates, marijuana, and other substances and thus defined their users as criminals. Gusfield (1963) similarly shows the interests of particular status groups in the campaign to outlaw alcohol, thus creating a category of criminal deviance which prevailed officially in the United States during the Prohibitionist period of 1920–33. Homosexuality is socially constructed as deviant in this respect by particular societies at particular times in history. What Schur (1965) calls "crimes without victims" (gambling, prostitution, abortion, ingestion of forbidden substances) are especially amenable to this analysis; special agents or interests, which Becker (1963) calls "moral entrepreneurs," rather than agrieved members of society, act politically to get these categories of deviance officially established. This aspect of the theory of social construction of deviance appears to be generally valid. It has a different, more macro, focus than labelling theory, which concentrates on the careers of individual "deviants."

CRITICISMS AND FURTHER DIRECTIONS

There is no doubt that the definitional perspective refers to an important phenomenon. But the theoretical formulation leaves several problems still to be resolved.

(1) What is a situation and its definition? The notion of "situation" is usually expressed in common-sense terms. We presumably know what the situation is of being in a grocery store, being in a holdup, and so forth. But there is a theoretical problem here. Do people actually define situations simply by using ordinary, commonsense language? One alternative, expressed by the ethnomethodologists, is that people in fact may not usually pay much attention to the precise definition of what is going on, as long as it goes on smoothly. The elements of a "situation," then, may be more simple and basic than all the verbal terminology that the symbolic interactionists seem to imply. Part of the problem is that the symbolic interactionists have not looked closely at exactly what situation defining really is, but have been content with giving a common-sense label to what they assume is going on. This is one of the points of contention between the ethnomethodologist and the symbolic interactionists.

(2) A related issue is that symbolic interactionists appear to rely exclusively on cognitive processes as defining situations. Situations are what people *think* that they are. An alternative is that situations, to a considerable extent, may be more *felt* than thought. Emotion more than cognition may be the crucial aspect of the way people act in situations. As proposed by interaction ritual theory, people may delineate

situations primarily in terms of deference to themselves or others (the power dimension) and of closeness or distance between the persons involved (the ritual density dimension). These emotions may be conveyed by the sheer physical aspects of the situation which generate ritual density and by the way that physical surroundings, words, and gestures give off symbolic resonances of the power and membership ties of the people present. Hence the processes that define a situation may be largely these emotional resonances, which may be registered without much conscious attention, rather than verbal definitions of what is going on.[4]

(3) Who defines a situation? Blumer assumes that individuals define their own situations. In whatever way other people may define it, individuals can redefine it in their own way. There is, of course, a process of symbolic interaction, taking the role of the other in order to anticipate what they are going to do and hence to take into account other people's definition of the situation. But other people's definitions of the situation can be redefined by each individual. How then is any definition of the situation agreed upon by all participants, since they all have the capacity to veto it and impose their own? Blumer proposes that there is a good deal of covert negotiation and that people are able to work it out. But if this process really goes on, it may be doubted that people actually arrive at the same definition of the situation. In that case, we would have to ask, whose definition really counts?

Other versions of this theoretical tradition assume that other people can define a situation for the individual. Thomas's Theorem is vague as to who defines the situation, but the applications by Merton and by labelling theory are that minorities, deviants, and so forth are stuck in disadvantaged careers because others are able to impose definitions upon them, even defining their selves from outside.

I have suggested above that the evidence indicates the labelling theory is partially true, but that there are other processes involved. Blumer opts for the stance of sheer creativeness, in which the individual can overturn any existing definition of the situation (or of one's self) and create a new one. The labelling theory goes in the opposite direction, assuming there are some especially dramatic, fateful situations in which a label is imposed from outside: the definition made at one point in time sticks for a long time thereafter. Blumer's version of creative re-definition could then come in to overcome this externally imposed kind of definition.

(4) The question thus arises: when and under what circumstances do which persons have the capacity to define a situation? Blumer's creativity is a phenomenon that sometimes happens, but he himself admits that it does not happen always. Routine is also possible, if people redefine situations the same way over and over again. The trouble is that Blumer's theory is not only indeterminate but that it is indeterminate in an indeterminate way. Sometimes people are innovative and sometimes routine: but when are they which?

Blumer's theory of creative redefinition of situations depends on a particular model of the development of self. The individual is assumed to have arrived at a stage at which there is a flexible "I," capable of standing over against any existing

---

[4]This position can be made congruent with the ethnomethodological one, if we assume that a situation will be taken as normal as long as these emotional resonances are automatic and undisturbed. If a verbal definition is introduced that does not fit these underlying emotions, or if the interaction is otherwise disturbed, then the definition of the situation becomes problematic, and some remedial action will be taken. As we shall see, the ethnomethodologists do not agree with the symbolic interactionists about the nature of such remedial action.

"me," and viewing imaginary alternatives through the vantage point of an abstract "Generalized Other." Presumably small children, who have not yet arrived at much reflexive consciousness, would not be able to redefine situations so easily. But as we can see from the theory of ritual density and its application to various communities and class cultures (Chapter 6), it is not only children whose circumstances limit their reflexivity; any persons who live in conditions of high ritual density tend to reify their group's customs and symbols and have strong emotional reactions against non-conformity. The type of reflexive self which Blumer assumes as normal, in fact, only exists widely in the higher social classes in complex societies. The theory of ritual density thus gives us one answer to the question, when is routine and when is reflexive redefinition of situations likely to occur?

The theory of interaction ritual chains (in Chapter 10) also indicates how situations can be an emergent property, while at the same time being theoretically determinate. Every situation is the coming together of two or more persons, each bringing their baggage of emotional energies and cultural capital. If we examine the situation from the viewpoint of only one individual, there is no way of predicting what will happen. The outcomes actually depend on how their emotional energies and cultural capitals match in relation to each other. But if we view the situation as the mixture of these resources brought by all participants, then there are some determinitive principles (indicated in Chapter 10), which state what can be expected to happen. Challenges to routine will happen only when an individual's resources, and especially one's emotional energies, have built up from previous chains of recent interactions, so that one feels capable of rejecting definitions imposed by someone else. Conversely, low levels of emotional energy from one's recent interactional experiences should result in passively accepting others' definitions of the situation.

ETHNOMETHODOLOGY

There are various versions of social phenomenology, but I will concentrate on ethnomethodology as the most important. Ethnomethodology, and especially its founder, Harold Garfinkel, have an extremely controversial reputation in sociology. Ethnomethodology is widely regarded as a cult, centering on outrageous theoretical claims and bizarre, nonscientific "experiments." It is also often claimed to be boring and commonsensical, poring over the details of everyday life in their endless banality. How can these two opposing charges be reconciled? A further feature is that the writings of ethnomethodologists are difficult, philosophical, and abstruce. An important passage from Garfinkel can illustrate the problem:

> The Analyzability of Actions-in-context as a Practical Accomplishment. . . . For members doing sociology, to make that accomplishment a topic of practical sociological inquiry seems unavoidably to require that they treat the rational properties of practical activities as "anthropologically strange." By this I mean to call attention to "reflexive" practices such as the following: that by his accounting practices the member makes familiar, commonplace activities of everyday life recognizable as familiar, commonplace activities; that on each occasion that an account of common activities is used, that they be recognized for "another first time"; that the member treat the processes and attainments of "imagination" as continuous with the other observable features of the settings in which they occur;

and of proceeding in such a way that at the same time that the member "in the midst" of witnessed actual settings recognizes that witnessed settings have an *accomplished* sense, an accomplished facticity, and accomplished objectivity, an accomplished familiarity, an accomplished accountability, for the member the organizational hows of these accomplishments are unproblematic, are known vaguely, and are known only in the doing which is done skillfully, reliably, uniformly, with enormous standardization and as an unaccountable matter. (Garfinkel, 1967: 9–10)

A little later Garfinkel (1967: 10) adds that "the unknown ways that the accomplishment is commonplace . . . is . . . an awesome phenomenon." He is placing tremendous emphasis on the importance of seeing something about ordinary life, something that we usually cannot see and that sociologists miss as well. His mission is to wake us up to this phenomenon. Garfinkel is trying to create a new topic for sociologists and a new way to study it. He throws down the gauntlet to conventional sociology, undermines its research methods, and substitutes new ones. But Garfinkel is not merely a methodologist. He and his followers have made important substantive discoveries, which have major ramifications in sociological theory. His theories and his methodology alike present the most radical challenge to existing sociology. We shall see, though, to what extent ethnomethodology in its most radical form can stand on its own, or what can be gained by bringing its discoveries back into the reconstruction of current sociology.

What is this new topic that Garfinkel would have us study? A clue is provided by the word "ethnomethodology" itself. "Ethno" indicates the "ethnography" of something, the study of some phenomenon in its natural setting. Anthropologists study "ethnobotany," which is the way that people in various cultures (especially tribal societies) classify the plants in the world around them, or "ethnomedicine," which is their folk beliefs and practices regarding medicine. "Ethnomethods," then, are the way that people use "methods" in everyday life; and "ethnomethodology" is the discipline that studies these practices. There is a subtle twist here, directed at social scientists, since they are the people who are most concerned with studying "methodology": in this case, the surveys, experiments, statistics and so forth by which they carry out their research. Garfinkel is saying that ordinary people are practitioners of methodology too, without being self-conscious about it. Ordinary people observe the world around them and make inferences about it. *Everyone* is a lay social scientist (and conversely, Garfinkel charges that social scientists are not so special). "Ethnomethodology" is thus sometimes referred to as *the study of commonsense practical reasoning.*

Why is it important to study how people in ordinary life reason about their world? Garfinkel offers two main reasons. One is that the social world does not really exist, objectively, except as people construct it. Here he is following the tradition of social phenomenology. The second reason to study practical reasoning is that the way in which people account for their world is the same thing as the way in which they act it out. Practical reasoning or "ethno-methods" are, according to Garfinkel's hypothesis, the key determinants not only of what people think but also of what they do.[5]

---

[5] We might add a third reason for Garfinkel's concern with practical reasoning. He wishes to show that social scientists, for all their claim to "scientific" method, are fundamentally relying on the same "folk

THE BACKGROUND IN SOCIAL PHENOMENOLOGY

Phenomenology as a philosophical movement began in the early twentieth century with the German philosopher Edmund Husserl. Husserl's concern was to arrive at the "essences," or general forms, of all consciousness. In order to do this, it is necessary to strip away all specific contents of consciousness, to "bracket" them, to not entertain the question of whether they are real. Husserl was after, not *this* chair or *this* cat, but the general features that would comprise the consciousness of any object at all. Husserl hoped thus to found a universal science of consciousness, since it would deal with forms which are absolutely necessary in any experience whatsoever. He never arrived, to his own satisfaction, at the fundamental laws of all consciousness. But he did influence other thinkers who applied the phenomenological method to investigating the forms of particular areas of experience. Among the philosophers who took up Husserl's program were the existentialists, Martin Heidegger, Jean-Paul Sartre, and Maurice Merleau-Ponty. The most immediate route into sociology, however, came via the work of Alfred Schutz, who attempted to apply the phenomenological method to the social world.

Schutz (1962: 3–9; 207–59) proposed a number of features which he claimed are the fundamental aspects of the consciousness of everyday life. Some of the more important ones are:

(1) *Reciprocity of perspectives*. Each person makes certain assumptions about the world, assumes that anyone else who is there is making the same assumptions and that each one is assuming the other is assuming the same thing. If they were to switch positions, presumably each one would see the world as the other did.

(2) *Objectivity and undeceptiveness of appearances*. A person assumes that the world is what it appears to be, and that it is factual and objective, not something that has been subjectively manufactured. Doubt is suspended.

(3) *Typifications*. The kinds of things that happen in one situation are taken as instances of the kinds of things that have happened before and that will happen again in the future.

(4) *Practicality and goal-directedness*. People experience a situation as something they are doing, a project they are working toward in the world; their sense of their self as working toward a goal is experienced as their total self.

(5) *Stock of commonsense knowledge*. Persons interpret their situation by using a stock of symbols, such as the words in their language, and other cultural knowledge. This knowledge is socially based and is assumed to be obvious to everyone. Garfinkel later referred to it as "What Anyone Knows."

Schutz does not mean that this is the only way that people can experience reality, but this is the most prevalent form, wide-awake "ordinary reality."[6] There are multiple realities, but these are when individuals withdraw from ordinary social life, for example in sleeping, dreaming, delirium, drug intoxication, religious experience. Each of these presumably can be mapped out phenomenologically, too.

methods" to constitute the reality of the things they are studying. Sociologists have no privileged viewpoint; hence the aspect of ethnomethodology which attacks conventional sociology, and which is a major reason for the outrage Garfinkel provokes.

[6] Schutz's description of the attitude of everyday life has not been accepted by everyone. Goffman (1974: 6) comments sceptically that Schutz's pronouncements were only suggestions that still remain to be demonstrated.

As we shall see, Garfinkel adopted Schutz's analysis of everyday life, but took it in a far more radical direction. For Schutz's world has the quality of being banal; he only calls our attention to its banal features. It is a world that is not problematic. It is intersubjectively based on a common culture, through which individuals interpret their experiences the same way, at least almost all the time (Schutz, 1940/1978: 134–135; 1932/1967). The most interesting feature of Schutz's analysis is that it points to the prevalence of *glosses,* ways in which one partial feature of reality is taken as indicating the fuller reality which is not seen. We live in the present and experience only little fragments of the social world. Most of what we assume is there is inferred from the little that we actually see. We assume that someone we are talking to is a bank president; we assume that there is a corporation called "General Motors" though all we ever see is a car salesman. But although there is a vast unseen world which people take for granted on the basis of glossing fragments that we do see, the existence of this larger world is not really called into question by Schutz's analysis. Though we don't see it, there are no problems with its reality, and society moves along in stable patterns.

This is the version of social phenomenology presented by Berger and Luckman in *The Social Construction of Reality* (1966). Combining Schutz with a rather static version of Durkheim and Weber, they argue that the social world is socially constructed by the processes of thinking in everyday life. But the world that arises from this looks like the conventional categories in a sociological textbook. There are institutions made up of roles and legitimated by a set of religious or quasi-religious beliefs regarding fundamental reality. Individuals carry around this set of cultural interpretations because they have been socialized into that culture by growing up in it as children. Although the world is socially constructed, this construction works smoothly and uniformly, guaranteed by the prevalence of a common culture. The vision is not far from Parsons's social system with the accepted culture minimizing conflict, disagreement, multiple realities, or individual initiatives.

GARFINKEL'S COGNITIVE RADICALISM

Garfinkel shares Schutz's views of the commonsense knowledge that goes into the everyday interpretation of social reality. But he goes beyond this to add two important discoveries of his own.

INDEXICALITY   Everything has a context, which must be taken into account in order to make sense of any particular thing. That context is crucial, but it has to be taken for granted that people know what it is. This is the phenomenon of *indexicality.* Any particular item of significance is an "index" for what lies beyond it. If we shift our attention to what lies beyond, then the same problem repeats itself: there is a further context, which is again taken for granted, and so on.

The strongest examples of this contextual embeddedness are certain verbal terms that linguists call "indexical expressions": words like "I," "you," "here," "there," "now," and so forth. It is impossible to define the meaning of these terms without falling into circularity. The word "you" means something different, depending on whether *you* are saying it to *me,* or vice versa, or to someone else. But here is Garfinkel's point: despite our inability to define such terms with scientific "objectivity," we are perfectly capable of using them in everyday life. And in fact, we are so used to this, that we become upset if anyone calls attention to their indexical quality.

Garfinkel illustrates this by a series of "experimental" studies with real-life situations. He stresses, however, that these are not "experiments" in the conventional scientific sense (which is something he is calling into question) but "aids to a sluggish imagination" (Garfinkel, 1967: 38). For example, he has his students engage someone in conversation, but to call for clarification for everything that was not completely clear. The results ran like this:

> On Friday night my husband and I were watching television. My husband remarked that he was tired. I asked, "How are you tired? Physically, mentally, or just bored?"
> (S) I don't know, I guess physically, mainly.
> (E) You mean that your muscles ache or your bones?
> (S) I guess so. Don't be so technical.
> *(After more watching)*
> (S) All these old movies have the same kind of iron bedstead in them.
> (E) What do you mean? Do you mean all old movies, or some of them, or just the ones you've seen?
> (S) What's the matter with you? You know what I mean.
> (E) I wish you would be more specific.
> (S) You know what I mean! Drop dead!

(Garfinkel, 1967: 43)

In every case, the subjects soon became exasperated, as if tacitly recognizing that such questioning could, in principle, go on *ad infinitum*. Garfinkel demonstrated the same point by having students report a conversation they had had, and then write down explanations of what was really meant by what was said. When Garfinkel asked them to go back and add more detail, explaining what they meant by their explanations, they could do this, and do it again and again as he asked for further clarification. But they became increasingly unwilling to do so, because they recognized that the task was endless (Garfinkel, 1967: 26). They recognized that to literally state in words all that was implied was impossible.

The entire social world, Garfinkel goes on it claim, is like this. It is a set of indexicalities, which are taken for granted. They are rarely called into question, and when they are, the questioning usually stays on a superficial level, accepting fairly quick and easy clarifications instead of pursuing the search for objectivity to its end. For there is no end: the search for objectively definable reality is a bottomless pit. This lends an extremely radical quality to Garfinkel's depiction of socially constructed reality. But Garfinkel is not asserting some form of Oriental mysticism; he is pointing up a major feature of social life: that people *avoid* having to recognize indexicalities, though they must deal with them all the time. This is above all what ethnomethodologists study. "The earmark of practical sociological reasoning, wherever it occurs, is that it seeks to remedy the indexical properties of members' talk and conduct. . . . I use the term 'ethnomethodology' to refer to the investigation of the rational properties of indexical expressions and other practical actions . . ." (Garfinkel, 1967: 10–11). We shall see next the way people "remedy" this indexicality by the use of interpretive procedures, although in principle there is no real remedy.

REFLEXIVITY   The other central point of Garfinkel's theory is the phenomenon he calls *reflexivity*. People interpret what is given in each situation as instances of something more general, but what this "something" is never appears, except in particular situations. The general and the particular are reflexively or circularly tied to each other. An illustration of what Garfinkel means by this is given in the quotation at the beginning of this section, the long and very tightly packed sentences beginning with *The Analyzability of Actions-in-Context*. Let us unpack this with the aid of another of Garfinkel's "experiments."

In this case he examined a group of researchers, who were working on files from a psychiatric clinic. Their job was to code the materials in the patient's files, as to what features of their biographies (reported in the files) were associated with how much and what kind of treatment they got in the clinic. Garfinkel points out, though, that in order for the researchers to sort out the "data" into different categories, they had to assume they already knew how the clinic was operating. In order to describe how the clinic was operating, they were supposed to be carrying out this research; but in order to carry out the research, they had to assume they knew how it was operating. Without this, they could not know that, for example, the pieces of paper in the file had been placed there by an intake clerk, a psychological tester, a psychiatrist, and so forth. In order to interpret the data as an instance of something, they had to already know what the more general thing was that it was an instance of. (If this sentence sounds circular, that is a reason why Garfinkel refers to this phenomenon as "reflexivity.")

Similar examples can be cited. Garfinkel studied the way jurors in a court case come to a decision and concluded that they used the same "reflexive" modes of reasoning. They assumed that someone was innocent, or guilty, because they acted in certain ways that were taken as instances of the way an innocent or a guilty person would act. One does not merely see the action, but one sees it as an instance of some more general kind of thing. This presumes we are already acquainted with what this general "thing" is. But we never encounter general "things" in real life; all we ever get are some particulars, which we always interpret as if they were instances of this general thing. We never see the "medical clinic," but only particular people doing particular things, which we make sense of by assuming that they are part of the "medical clinic." Similarly, in a study of a coroner's office (Douglas, 1967), the medical examiners decide whether a death is a suicide or not, by whether the deceased had done certain things that are typical of suicides (being despondent, leaving a note). But this is based on the inference that all the other "suicides" which had these qualities were in fact really suicides; but those prior "suicides" had been judged as such by the same process of reasoning.

We could always go into further detail, and look at the evidence more skeptically and closely. But this never leads us to generalities, but only to further instances, which are still reflexively constituted: we understand what these are instances of by already assuming we know what their general category is. Moreover, a tacit rule of daily life is that we do our best to figure out what things are in a practical and reasonable way. We do not waste infinite amounts of time in trying to decide whether our characterizations of things are beyond any possible doubt; juries have to come to a conclusion, coroners have to move the bodies through, people have to get their work done, as best they can.

The phenomenon of reflexivity is entwined with that of indexicality, but adds several twists to it. One is Garfinkel's claim that the procedures by which people account for what is going on are also the way social reality is created in the first place.[7] This implies a very cognitive view of reality. It is alleged that the way people think about social reality, after the fact, is the same way it was constructed in the first place. We shall return to this point, for it is one of ethnomethodology's assumptions that is never demonstrated and may well not be true (or only partially true).

Another facet of reflexivity is that the ordinariness of the world is socially produced at the same time that our awareness of this process is censored. Ordinariness is not something that is objectively there. People are constantly engaging in cognitive practices to make the world ordinary, to treat whatever happens as if it were just another instance of something familiar and commonsensical. The fact that we have successfully made our experience ordinary keeps us from seeing how we did it, or even *that* we did it. We might say that we have objectified or reified the ordinariness of life. This makes Garfinkel's theory parallel to Hegel's and Marx's accounts of alienation: our experience is created by a human subject who then is oppressed by his or her own creation as if it were an alien thing. The major difference is that Garfinkel does not ascribe this alienation to capitalism or a particular stage of human history, but to a universal set of human practices of practical reasoning. Reflexivity is buried in the "natural attitude."

Nevertheless, we cannot claim that this embeddedness is absolutely universal. For one thing, Garfinkel himself and his followers detach themselves from the natural attitude, at least during the times when they are analyzing it. Schutz, too, although he did not penetrate as far into the phenomenon as Garfinkel did, also achieved a break with merely naturalistic thinking. The world is not always taken as ordinary by all people and all occasions. Buddhist meditators and other mystics have devised deliberate methods for withdrawing the mind's assent to ordinary assumptions about reality and have claimed to experience an illumination by looking at whatever transpires without putting any interpretations upon it. Garfinkel seems to admit this possibility but only grudgingly so. His own enterprise indicates the possibility of breaking the natural embeddedness in the ordinariness of things. But at a meta-level the same problem reinstates itself. Though one can detach oneself from other people's assumptions of the ordinariness of the world, nevertheless when we study them as ethnomethodologists we are engaging in our own normalizing procedures, interpreting what we see as an instance of some more general procedure of interpretation, which we already have a conception of. We could have, then, the hyper-ethnomethodologist studying the ethnomethodologist, and the hyper-hyper-ethnomethodologist studying the hyper-ethnomethodologist, and so on: except that the problems of infinite regress indicated by the discussion of indexicality would, as a practical matter, soon bring this to a halt.[8]

---

[7] Ethnomethodologists' "central recommendation is that the activities whereby members produce and manage settings of organized everyday affairs are identical with members' procedures for making those settings 'account-able.' The 'reflexive,' or 'incarnate' character of accounting practices and accounts makes up the crux of that recommendation" (Garfinkel, 1967: 1).

[8] It should be apparent by now that Garfinkel's use of "reflexivity" is not the same thing as Blumer and Mead's phenomenon of self-reflection. For the symbolic interactionists, the capacity of the "I" to stand

I am not certain that Garfinkel and the other ethnomethodologists have fully addressed this problem. They declare that social science is impossible because of the reflexivity issue; but they seem to feel secure on the next level of studying presumably universal processes of everyday reasoning. Moreover, this may be a valid stance to take, as a practical matter; the ethnomethodologists certainly have advanced our understanding of this part of the social world by their researches. But it seems to me that if they have the right to assert their findings about practical reasoning, then other sociologists have the right to assert their findings about other aspects of social behavior, with no less justification. For all of us, there is mainly a pragmatic justification.[9]

The same sort of argument is raised now with regard to all the sciences. Garfinkel and his students (Garfinkel, Lynch, and Livingston, 1981; Lynch, Livingston, and Garfinkel, 1983) in recent years have given much of their attention to the practices of scientists as they actually go about their work. Scientific "discoveries," even in the physical sciences, are inferences, usually drawn from some intermediary body of laboratory equipment, about some "reality" which is actually priorly conceptualized by the social discourse of the scientists (Knorr-Cetina, 1981; Latour and Woolgar, 1979; Knorr-Cetina and Mulkay, 1983.) Scientific reality is thus reflexively constituted, too. This line of argument has become influential in the philosophy as well as the sociology of science, as it fits well with the lines of thinking developed by Kuhn (1970) and Feyerabend (1975), as well as certain aspects of Goodman (1978) and other "post-positivists."[10]

---

back from its various "me's," from the world, or from anything else is the source of creativity and freedom. Garfinkel's reflexivity, on the other hand, refers to a source of the paradoxical, taken-for-granted, constraining quality of life. It refers to a box we can't get out of, because we see everything through our preconceptions. Blumer and Mead's reflexivity is optimistic; Garfinkel's is pessimistic. Nevertheless, we might say that Garfinkel's reflexivity would not be possible without Blumer and Mead's; it is the capacity of an ethnomethodologist, as an "I," to distance himself or herself from ordinary practical reasoning, to make others an object, that allows their analysis. Symbolic interactionists' reflexivity is at the core of any cognitive operations, at least at the higher levels of conscious attention. Symbolic interactionists and ethnomethodologists, generally speaking, are rival positions in current microsociology. Each is able to focus on something that the other one misses. A truly comprehensive theory of human cognition will have to assemble pieces from both of them, as well as from ritual theory.

[9] Richard Hilbert (personal communication) points out ethnomethodologists draw on the same folk methods as the traditional sociologists. The main difference is that the ethnomethodologists become conscious of these methods and make them the topic of study. Ethnomethodologists do not deny the validity of these methods, but merely suspend belief in them.

[10] Mehan and Wood (1975) provide the following argument, drawing on Garfinkel, on Pollner (1974), as well as on anthropological materials. Among the Azande tribe in central Africa, people frequently make decisions on the basis of a magic oracle. A chicken is ritually killed, and the corpse inspected for signs of what action to take. But how do the Azande deal with cases where the chicken oracle is falsified by future events, when it claims that it will rain, for example, and the weather turns out clear? Instead of impugning the validity of this way of forecasting the future, the Azande simply reframe the issue: if the prediction came out wrong, it was because the chicken was not killed correctly in the first place. The procedure remains correct; it is just that this was not a correct instance of its use. Mehan and Wood argue that this procedure of reasoning is used by people in modern "rational" civilizations, too. It is directly paralleled in Kuhn's (1961; 1962) depiction of the way scientists behave when their experiments do not come up with the expected result. They do not immediately decide the theory was wrong; they assume instead that the experiment was not carried out correctly, that the test tubes were insufficiently clean, that the electrical wiring was malfunctioning, or many other practical difficulties.

Two points can be made in commentary on this. First, Garfinkel is defending a position that has existed in philosophy since the time of Kant, that we never see the world directly, but only through the screen of our presuppositions, our prior concepts. This is true, and Garfinkel documents in new ways what some of these presuppositions are and how they operate. But the existence of this cognitive screen between ourselves and the world does not imply that there is no world "out there," nor that in some ways the world itself cannot affect, select, and even change over time what those presuppositions are. A totally relativitistic or subjective conclusion is not warranted.

Second, there is a major empirical and theoretical problem raised by Garfinkel's own characterization of everyday practical reasoning. Where do these prior categories, typifications, glosses come from? Garfinkel shows that people already have them in mind so that they can interpret their experience through these lenses. Are people's minds, then, just filled with culture? Where does the culture come from and what modifies it?

I believe there is an inconsistency here between two sides of ethnomethodological theory. One side implicitly stresses a common culture and gives it great weight in determining our perceptions of the social world and hence (if accounts determine practical action itself) our actions as well. This position does not seem to me far from that expressed by role theorists like Ralph Turner, that individuals carry around a mind full of pieces of roles, out of which they put together their daily interactions. But Garfinkel (1967: 66–70) also attacks such theories for making out the human actor as a "cultural dope" who merely complies with the preestablished common culture. He argues instead that people only assume there is a cultural rule for behavior and avoid testing the consequences of not abiding by this assumed rule.[11]

Elsewhere, Garfinkel and others (Cicourel, 1973) point out that although people believe there are rules operative in society, in any real situation the individual must interpret whether and what rule to apply. Invoking rules is itself the result of an interpretive procedure. If we were to theorize that there are rules which tell us which rules to apply in what cases, we would still have to say when and how people know they should bring their meta-rules into action. This leads to an infinite regress of rules, which people are cognitively incapable of handling.

Ultimately, then, there is a contradiction between the line of inference from reflexivity which concludes that people interpret everything that happens via their stock of common culture and the phenomenon of indexicality, which defines that

These conditions are then manipulated and the experiment is repeated until it finally comes out "right." Anyone who has worked in a laboratory can testify to the accuracy of this description.

[11] Garfinkel illustrates this with another of his "experiments": students were sent to a store with instructions to bargain for items, even though the presumed "norm" in American culture is that the prices marked are fixed. Students found, in fact, that they could get away with offering 25 cents for a $1.00 item; that they rarely encountered negative sanctions for breaking this "norm"; that in fact they often were successful at getting the price reduction. They also reported the most anxiety before the first time they attempted to bargain; subsequent attempts were often described as enjoyable (Garfinkel, 1967: 69). Garfinkel (1967: 69–70) concludes: "one can make a member of the society out to be a cultural dope . . . by portraying the member of the society as one who operates by the rules when one is actually talking about the anticipatory anxiety that prevents him from permitting a situation to develop . . . in which he has the alternative of acting or not with respect to the rule. . . . Indeed, the more important the rule, the greater is the likelihood that knowledge is based on avoided tests."

any knowledge can be completely objective and formal. The "common stock of knowledge" is tacit, not explicit, and contextual rather than universal. I think that the real force of Garfinkel's position comes down on the indexical side, since he himself never describes the stock of common culture as having any specific content; nor does he say how people acquire this culture. It makes more sense to assume Garfinkel is talking about people's assumption there is a common culture, rather than its actual existence.

THE PROCEDURES OF COMMONSENSE REASONING

Garfinkel describes ethnomethodology as the study of the procedures people use to remedy the indexical nature of social life. People do not confront the indexicality; they avoid it, and thereby sustain the sense that all is as it should be. Some of these procedures are the following:

(1) *The et cetera assumption.* People commonly refer to things in their world, or actions they or someone else take, by a short-hand mode of expression. To this is implicitly or explicitly added the proviso that "I could go on in greater detail along this line." People take this ability to provide the "et cetera" for granted, although in fact no one ever does. The fact of indexicality shows why they never do. Garfinkel's breaching experiments in which people took things literally in a conversation shows how upset people become if the et cetera assumption is not allowed to operate.

(2) *Waiting for clarification.* People do not insist that everything should be clearly understood at the moment they hear or see it. Generally they will wait to see whether what is said later casts light on what went before to make it meaningful. Garfinkel (1967: 79–94) dramatizes this by an experiment in which students were told they were testing a new method of psychological counseling. They were to ask a series of questions about some personal problem, which could be answered "yes" or "no," by a counselor in the next room. Actually, the "counselor" was an experimenter who was merely giving random "yes" and "no" answers without regard to their questions. In effect, the students were given meaningless answers to such issues as whether they should drop out of school, what career to pursue, whether to get married, and so forth. Garfinkel found that even when answers seemed bizarre, the subjects tended to accept them as meaningful, waiting for further clarification in later answers and reinterpreting what was presumably meant by earlier answers in the light of the way they interpreted the later answers. Garfinkel also reports that the subjects, when informed at the end of the experiment that the answers they received were meaningless, were profoundly shocked. They had constructed a coherent view of the world from this information, and it was very unsettling for them to give up the basic assumption that a meaningful reality could be constructed by the methods of commonsense reasoning they were using.

(3) *Offering accounts.* When something happens that people genuinely do not expect or cannot make sense of, they quickly move to rectify their sense of disturbed reality. They offer "accounts," excuses that others accept as putting their sense of reality back into order (Scott and Lyman, 1968). They offer an apology or an explanation: they were not paying attention, didn't know what they were saying, didn't mean to do it, or even were deliberately lying or playing a trick. People find making cognitive amends of this sort very important; it turns a meaningless world back into

a meaningful one and restores the sense of normalcy. We might also say that it shields people from realizing the indexicality that underlies everything they do. Even if, in fact, there was no good reason for the other person to do or say what they did, it makes things right that they now have come back to normalcy and are claiming to offer an excuse. People want each other to give obeisance to their belief in a common reality. For criminals to admit that they were "temporarily insane" or that they had "made a mistake," "done the wrong thing," is important for all of us because it restores a sense that everyone now is acknowledging what is normal; and this becomes more important than what was actually done. (For example, it greatly mitigates a criminal sentence.) The same applies for the little lapses and misunderstandings of everyday life.

Ethnomethodologists also generally accept Schutz's list of attributes of the "natural attitude," but as procedures that people follow. Garfinkel's breaching experiments are designed generally to reveal people's use of these procedures by observing how they act when they are not allowed to use them. Reciprocity of perspectives was violated by having an experimenter go into a restaurant and treat a customer as if he were the head waiter, insisting that he show the experimenter to a table, bring a menu, hurry up the service, and so forth. The customer's protests that he was not the head waiter were treated merely as if he were trying to avoid serving the experimenter. The customer reacted with a sense of deep anxiety to this breaking down of shared reality. The customer, a physics professor, later said that he hadn't been so shaken since a rival had denounced one of his theories years earlier (Garfinkel, 1963: 226). A similar result was found in fake medical school interviews in which students were shown films of a boorish and ignorant applicant who was then described as highly rated by medical school admission boards (Garfinkel, 1967: 58–65). Here, too, the subjects of the experiment used various species of commonsense reasoning to try to reconstruct their view of the boorish applicant to bring it into congruence with the apparent reality that he was "a successful applicant." All these subjects showed considerable anxiety during the time when their faith in their commonsense understandings was shaken; when they were finally told of the hoax, their relief from tension was dramatic and emotional.

COGNITION VS. EMOTION

This brings up a final point in regard to what ethnomethodology is revealing. In almost every case, Garfinkel shows that there are fairly strong emotions that will be released if normal interpretive procedures are breached. Conversations in which indexical expressions are not allowed to pass end up with angry denunciations.[12] The physicist taken for a head waiter was extremely shaken; students who couldn't judge a medical school interview according to their common sense became anxious; students who had been hoaxed into constructing a coherent reality out of a random series of "yes" and "no" answers were upset when told their constructions had no

---

[12] (S) How are you?
   (E) How am I in regard to what? My health, my finances, my school work, my peace of mind, my . . . ?
   (S) (Red in the face and suddenly out of control.) Look! I was just trying to be polite. Frankly, I don't give a damn how you are. (Garfinkel, 1967: 45)

foundation. Even when students were experimenting on themselves, they became anxious or hostile when they suspended ordinary procedures for constructing the meaning of events around them. For example, students were told to merely observe what goes on in their homes, without taking them as instances of some larger meaning that lay behind them. Instead of seeing the people there as "father," "mother," and so forth, they saw such things as "a short stout man entered the house and kissed me on the cheek . . . the older woman shuffled around the kitchen, muttering" (Garfinkel, 1967: 45). Students reported that it was hard to sustain this detachment and that it would "explode"; and then they found themselves being drawn back into ordinary attributions of a larger reality.

When the students, in a further experiment, went on to act as a polite guest in their own homes, their families tended to react with incredulity and hostility. They were accused of being mean, inconsiderate, selfish, nasty, and impolite. Yet what they were doing was being unusually polite, asking for things, not helping themselves without permission. One woman went into a tirade when her daughter asked politely if she could take some food from the refrigerator. It is clear that the experimenters were not being offensive by their impoliteness or inconsiderateness, but by the opposite. They were not breaking cultural "norms," but adhering to them too carefully. This suggests that people's sense of normalcy (in this case, that of the students' families) is based on a familiar routine which no one disturbs. Any extensive disturbance creates anxiety, and if someone's actions seem to be responsible for it, that person becomes the target of righteous anger. There is a moral obligation to follow ordinary procedures of reality constructing and not to interfere with people's sense of commonplace reality.

This raises a question: how do people know what is normal and habitual? How is this encoded in their minds, so that they can recognize what is normal and what is a violation of it? The problem is that Garfinkel has shown this cannot be encoded simply as a set of cognitive constructs, a set of rules or images of what things ordinarily should be like. All this knowledge is tacit, contextual, indexical, not an objective, generalized part of the "culture." But what does it consist of?

My suggestion is that Garfinkel is actually close to the Durkheim-Goffman model of interaction rituals at this point. Recall in that model cognition is on the surface and the emotional contagion of interaction is in the underlying depths. Garfinkel's experiments show us a series of social interactions in which people take things for granted and do not press for any clear evidence of shared meaning, but they react vehemently when their feelings of normalcy are disrupted. This looks like a version of "natural rituals" (Chapter 6). The "how are you" conversation cited in footnote 12 is a violation of a common Goffmanian ritual. "How are you?" is not meant to communicate any information, but is merely a symbol of common membership in the loose fraternity of acquaintances. The angry reaction to the disruption of the ritual is just what we would expect when the symbols of social membership are rejected. This is even more apparent in the experiment where students breached household normalcy by being too polite. Implicitly, they were rejecting the tacit symbols of familiar membership; hence the families reacted with righteous accusations that the students were being hostile. The surface of actions and words in everyday life are not primarily tools for rationally understanding reality, but symbols which assure a comforting sense of group membership.

What, then, holds society together? Garfinkel's work implies two answers. One is that reality is held together because no one questions it. It is not so much a common commitment to certain values and beliefs, as a set of procedures by which people avoid calling reality into question. Indexicalities and reflexivities are potentially always present, but we avoid seeing them, and we act quickly to repair any breaches in the dike that let the anxiety-provoking unfoundedness of our world leak through.

It is true, of course, that sometimes people deliberately do try to break down common routines. A great deal of modern art and literature is designed to be provocative in just this sense; the "guerrilla theater" of the 1960s was explicitly based on confronting people in real-life situations, such as having actors come off the stage and dragging the audience into participating in the play. In everyday life, people amuse themselves by playing jokes and tricks. On a more serious level, political rebellions are successful when they can shake up the sense of inalterability of the enforcement chain that upholds a government or a political coalition; that is, political movements try to overcome the sense of anxiety Garfinkel points to as keeping people from testing what can actually be done. Garfinkel is overstating people's embeddedness in the existing routines of the "natural attitude." I think it is more accurate to describe this embeddedness and its supporting defense against anxiety, as one factor in a multi-factor situation. Sometimes and in some respects people do break down routines and even deliberately play on the indexicality of things. This can be done in many different contexts: private joking, public art and entertainment, intellectual analysis (such as Garfinkel's own), and political activism. More attention needs to be paid to the conditions under which people do break down routine in these various ways and when they will reinforce routine and punish breaches of it.

I think it can probably be said that it is impossible to break down all aspects of routine at the same time; certain kinds of things have to be taken for granted, so that other aspects can be called into question. A political movement to overthrow the state questions the reality of the enforcement coalition, but at the same time it must uphold the more mundane routine of local communication which makes it possible for the oppositional group to carry out its own practical activities. Modern art and guerrilla theater still trade on the background existence of a world in which bills get paid and contributions are made to support artists; ethnomethodologists can focus on indexicality as an intellectual matter, but they can't avoid taking the natural attitude when they leave their office and go home. This suggests a possible hierarchy of embeddedness, of routine and routine-breaking activities within one another. This is the subject of Goffman's frame analysis.

The other answer to the question of what holds society together is emotion. It is not so much that people reason their way consciously to conclusions about the ordinary world and how they should interpret it and behave in it. They follow routines whose existence cannot be cognitively formulated with any definiteness. I am suggesting that this "X-factor" which underlies social life is largely emotional. People react to the physical actions of others around them and to the sense of emotional mood which accompanies any situation. These flows of emotions uphold routines and break out in the vehement reactions people feel to the violation of routine procedures. When, however, emotional energies of particular people build up in ways that make them especially forceful, they can lead to breaches of ordinary routines and efforts to impose another reality. The mechanisms by which this happens are explained in the theory of interaction ritual chains (Chapter 10).

Implications of Ethnomethodology

Despite appearances to the contrary, ethnomethodology is not merely an esoteric specialty, migrating away from the concerns of mainstream sociology. There are several ways in which it adds to some major theoretical concerns.

1. HUMAN COGNITIVE LIMITATIONS

The findings of ethnomethodology depict the human being as engaged in a particular style of practical reasoning. The human mind's capacity is very limited, compared to the infinite problems associated with indexicality and reflexivity of everyday experience. People follow strategies designed to reduce these difficulties: they ignore difficulties as much as possible; they interpret whatever they encounter as if it were instances of the normal and do not pursue the question of whether this is really true; they let puzzling or meaningless things pass, relying on the strategy of expecting that they will clarify themselves eventually, if necessary. In short, they process information so as to keep routine social actions going without questioning them and to construct a comfortable sense that there is a common reality.

This emphasis on cognitive limitations undergirds a perspective that has been proposed in several other areas of social science. The organization theorists March and Simon (1958; Simon, 1957) point out that managers cannot keep tabs on everything at once; they cannot simultaneously be certain that every employee is doing a job properly, according to the rules, with the maximal amount of speed, cost-savings, safety, innovativeness, and courtesy. Instead, they concentrate on trouble-shooting any area which comes up with a special problem. All other areas, as long as they maintain a routine level of normalcy, are left as a taken-for-granted background. This strategy March and Simon refer to as "satisficing" rather than "optimizing"; hence their position in general is called "neo-rationalist." The neo-rationalist strategy is a special case of the interpretive procedures which Garfinkel documents everywhere.

The experimental psychologists Tversky and Kahneman (1974; Kahneman et al., 1982) show a parallel result. People make decisions in ordinary situations, not like idealized scientists testing alternative theories, but by following a strategy like those found in ethnomethodology's interpretive procedures. Given the fundamental nature of Garfinkel's position, it has good claim to be considered a general picture of the nature of human cognition.

2. WEAKNESS OF OVERCOGNITIVE THEORIES

It follows that theories which see the human being as storing and processing large amounts of cognitive information cannot be accurate. Symbolic interactionist role theory is weak insofar as it assumes that people carry around in their heads a prescription for every role they might play or encounter. Ralph Turner (1968), for example, theorizes that people have learned a large repertoire of role conceptions (although these cannot cover every detail). They use these to recognize what roles other people are playing, and they can make up their own roles by drawing upon various elements of these stocks of role-culture, so that they can communicate to their audiences exactly what roles they are playing. They know the role of the professor, the role of being aloof, of being friendly, and so forth; so then they can put together a specialized role of being, say, an aloof professor; and they can recognize when someone else is playing this role (see Jonathan Turner, 1986).

The ethnomethodological conception of cognition implies several criticisms of this theory. People's cognitions are limited; situations are indexical and not generalized; people assume normalcy rather than working it out precisely. Hence people do not make much effort to figure out what role is being played, but instead assume that whatever it is, is normal, unless something goes wrong. When that happens, the role is not specified according to preexisting culture, but only a few repair sequences are drawn upon to go back to the oblivious sense of normalcy. It should be added that Ralph Turner's theory is not based on evidence that people really do share a large repertoire of role elements. Some research which has been done in this area, asking people to specify what they think a role consists of, finds that different people have quite variable conceptions of roles (Morgan and Spanish, 1985; Leiter, 1980: 78).

An alternative is that people have only a few fundamental items in their repertoires of interactions: for example, the ability to recognize someone as friendly-unfriendly, high status–equal status–low status,[13] perhaps also work-nonwork situations, and a few others. These elements, moreover, may be encoded from physical postures, emotional flows, and unconscious labelling of cultural items as familiar-unfamiliar, rather than from more conscious, higher-order cognitive processing. I suggest in Chapters 9 and 10 that the underlying, pared-down repertoire of interactional routines can be laid out according to the interaction ritual model. Recent work by ethnomethodologists (Schegloff, 1986) casts this in different terms, but also stresses that the "surface" of ordinary role conceptions is generated by more basic elements. Since almost everything social is enacted through conversations, these basic elements of social competence would include such procedures as: (1) knowing who gets to talk and who listens, (2) who gets to give orders, and (3) who gets to ask questions and make requests.

With a set of basic elements of this sort, it would not be necessary for everyone to carry around in their heads detailed conceptions for what a "professor" does, a "student," a "waiter," a "customer," and so forth. They need only pick out the normalcy of the situation as one, for instance, in which someone else gets to talk while the others make a polite show of listening (a classroom situation) or in which someone gets to make requests which another carries out (a restaurant). The advantage of this model is that it does not require an unrealistic overloading of the actor's cognitions, and it is compatible with the limited-cognition strategy documented by ethnomethodology and its parallels noted above. It also avoids the overly static im-

---

[13] That is, order givers, order takers, or neither. The friendly-unfriendly dimension is the Durkheimian ritual result of recognizing the border between members and nonmembers.

plication of conventional role theory, which assumes that an actor already knows what the role conceptions are in that culture. The basic-elements model, on the other hand, implies that people can quickly learn to adapt to any new situation, and create new "role variants," by using a few basic skills. They recognize deference, equality, conversational turn-taking, and keep up a sense of normalcy while they focus on any special procedures that are needed to avoid disruptions.[14]

There are many other current theories whose inadequacies are shown up in light of the ethnomethodological model of cognition. One of these is Habermas' (1984) proposal for an ideal speech community in which all hidden assumptions of speech actions are brought out into the open and criticized until full agreement is reached. The weakness is that Habermas is proposing the infinite regress into indexicalities that Garfinkel shows is impossible and that people as commonsense reasoners strenuously attempt to avoid. Giddens' (1984) structuration theory attempts to ground macro structures in the interpretive practices of everyday life. But Giddens conceives of these practices as invoking rules and cultural conceptions which are not located in time and space. That is, he underestimates the crucial feature of indexicality and gives a model of the actor as mentally loaded with all the culturally defined features of society.

Finally, it should be noted that French structuralism (to be treated more fully in Chapter 9) may be criticized for its reliance on naive ethnomethods in its own "research." The structuralist method for discovering the fundamental structures of a society's code consists of examining various patterns in the culture (for instance, its myths or its advertisements) and discerning a pattern in them. But this is a particularly strong example of Garfinkel's "documentary method of interpretation": a human subject imposing a pattern on materials which may in fact be quite random and heterogeneous. The work of Lévi-Strauss, Barthes, and their followers may be more of an unwitting Garfinkelian experiment (like the subjects of the fake counseling experiment described previously) than a valid way to reveal mental structures which "objectively" exist.

3. APPLICATION TO ARTIFICIAL INTELLIGENCE

The effort is now under way to program a computer which can simulate human intelligence. It has turned out to be an extremely difficult task to match the actual methods by which humans think (Dreyfus and Dreyfus, 1986). Instead, the most success has been had by building so-called "expert systems," which store information and a set of search procedures in specialized domains. For example, a computer program may be capable of diagnosing particular forms of illness from inputs of medical test data. But this is a limited situation, in which the problem is already prestructured. The general human capacity to define its own situations and to interact with people still remains to be solved.

---

[14] It implies, also, that one does not need to learn a special role of "arrogance," so that one can combine it into being an "arrogant professor." One almost certainly does not refer to the social definition of "arrogance," mentally rehearse it for its effects upon others, and then act it out, nor is "arrogance" a reciprocal role in the sense that the recipient has a prescribed way he should behave. Behavior of this type, rather, is something that observers may pick up when they reflectively characterize what they have seen, but not a deliberate role of the actor.

I would strongly suggest that the problem of artificial intelligence will only be solved by taking into account the best sociological models of how human cognition operates. It must build upon the model of *limited cognition* and the strategies that humans use for constructing and normalizing social reality.[15] The ethnomethods revealed by Garfinkel and others will have to be formally stated and put into an operative program. Some steps in this direction are indicated at the end of Chapter 9.

4. SOCIAL ORDER AND CHANGE.

The microsociological processes uncovered by ethnomethodology also have macrosociological consequences in three areas: bureaucratization, political tactics, and disorderly and episodic social change.

BUREAUCRATIZATION   On the level of organizations, ethnomethodology corroborates the research finding that formal rules and regulations operate only statically and clumsily. Bureaucratic formalities are circumvented by an informal structure whenever its tasks demand speed or adaptiveness to circumstances. Rules are relied upon mainly when the achievement of goals has low priority, compared to the mere ritual enactment and stability of the organization. Bureaucratic rules are not so much guides for effective behavior as items of communication by which organization members justify what they have done in case it is questioned. In ethnomethodological terminology, rules are used to build accounts in case of troubles. Bureaucratic elaboration of rules is a false effort at precision and control; it merely results, as has been empirically found in organization studies, in yet further elaboration of rules to cover the contingencies which it inevitably misses. Ethnomethodology thus helps explain the process of bureaucratization (see Chapter 13; also Hilbert, 1987).

POLITICAL TACTICS   Politicians and other power-wielders make their careers by taking advantage of people's limited cognition and their practical ethnomethods. Those in power rely on people's unwillingness to call the accepted order into question. This is often mistakenly interpreted as the legitimacy of a given order. Ethnomethodology suggests, however, that it is merely the "natural attitude" in the face of the general constructedness of things social. *Any* social order becomes accepted as long as it has been in existence long enough to seem routine or normal. Moral legitimation, appealing explicitly to emotions and ideals, is only added onto this cognitive acceptance of an assumed status quo. In many cases, this idealized legitimation may be largely or entirely lacking. Ethnomethodology implies that any society will become accepted, no matter how coercive, cruel, or stratified it is, provided

[15] One strategy in artificial intelligence is to build models of "scripts" which humans presumably follow in given situations. A well-known theory (Shank and Abelson, 1977) formulates a "restaurant script," giving the moves an actor follows to order a meal. Such scripts resemble the role models which I have criticized above as overly cognitivized. The behavior of a person in a restaurant might well be simulated on a more basic set of elements involving deference relations, conversational turns, and rights to make requests. Such a computer program would avoid the problem of having to incorporate innumerable routines for every kind of social situation, as well as the likelihood that in real situations special features would be found that the program could not handle. The ethnomethodological model suggests a more parsimonious and powerful algorithm.

that it appears stable.[16] The strategy of a conservative politician, then, is to rely on people's cognitive aversion to becoming aware of the arbitrary nature of social order and to saddle critics with the onus of appearing to be absurd, in precisely the way that individuals who perform Garfinkelian breaching exercises appear to be outrageous.

Ethnomethods are also prominently used by politicians in conflicts with each other. In debates, skilled politicians control the verbal construction of reality by manipulating the underlying organization of topics and the taking of conversational turns. A skilled debater can deflect opponents' statements and charges in a public meeting or a negotiation by playing on indexicalities: asking opponents to define terms and invoking other gambits which descend into the infinite regresses Garfinkel points out. Shifting frames (in Goffman's sense, see following section) can also be used to deflect attention from embarrassing topics. Michels' Iron Law of Oligarchy (Michels, 1911/1949), which shows how organizational leaders maintain themselves in office even against the interests of their followers, is connected to this use of the ethnomethods for reality constructing.

SOCIAL CHANGE IS DISORDERLY AND EPISODIC   There is also an implication on the most macro level. If social order is based on an arbitrary routinization of whatever arrangements happen to exist at a given time, then we should not expect a society to have a great deal of structural coherence. Any society, or any historical time in the world system, is a concatenation of the changes which have built up by accretion. Wallerstein makes this conception central to his view of the world system, which always contains different "eras" existing simultaneously: as if the abstract "stages" of industrial capitalism, feudalism, tribalism, and so forth all existed at the same time and interacted with each other, producing still messier combinations. Similarly, within a given society, the coexistence of ethnic groups is like a set of time capsules which carry over routinized cultures from previous historical epochs. Higher social classes become status groups by cloaking themselves in traditions of the past, thereby relying on remembered routinization as a basis of their presumed legitimacy. These traditions are spread to lower ranks of the stratification system by the process of cultural emulation and individual mobility.

Social change, when it occurs, tends to be dramatic and episodic. Instead of gradual movements of "progress," routines are clung to as long as possible. Changes

---

[16]Thus even individuals who are members of oppressed groups will tend to accept their niches in that order. An example is the ritual tortures applied to pubescent women in some tribal societies (Paige and Paige, 1981), such as cutting off the clitoris while chanting to cover up the girl's shrieks. The actual ritual is carried out by the older women of the kinship group. Similarly, older women acted as executioners of female slaves in the fertility rites of the ancient Germans (Davidson, 1981: 61–62). The fact that such individuals act as agents to oppress members of their own groups is sometimes cited as evidence that there is no sexual oppression in such societies. This version of anthropological relativism, in the guise of cultural determinism, is actually just an atheoretical description masquerading an an explanation. To say that people behave in this way because the culture prescribes it is merely to assert the description again as if it were an explanation of itself. I am suggesting that there is real physical and psychological oppression and that it is "normalized" by the prevalence of the natural attitude. Some individuals, like the older women who have risen to a secondary rank of power by lording it over young girls, find a secondary gain for themselves within this taken-for-granted system. A similar process explains the "loyal retainer" type found within slave and servant populations in extremely stratified societies.

occur in rapid periods of revolution, war, or political overthrow of a dominant group. Social movements, like the labor movement in the early twentieth century, the civil-rights movement in America of the 1960s, and the feminist movement of the 1970s, tend to win what changes they make in a rapid period of enthusiasm. Historical change is parallel to Garfinkel's picture of micro interaction alternating between long periods of routine and the building up of troubles which result in a rapid restoring of order by offering accounts. If the micro-macro connection of these events were to be worked out in more detail, it would likely be the case that the ethnomethods on the micro level are the foundations of both the long periods of structural stability and the rapid periods of change.

GOFFMAN'S FRAME ANALYSIS AS A RECONCILIATION OF RELATIVISM AND OBJECTIVITY

FRAME ANALYSIS

Erving Goffman's *Frame Analysis* (1974) establishes a way to mediate between the hyperrelativism of the positions we have just considered and the objective determinism of conventional sociology. Goffman operates on the same turf as the symbolic interactionists and ethnomethodologists, and in some ways he is extending their analyses. But he is also explicitly critical of them. On the one hand, he argues that exclusive emphasis on definition of the situation, and on Schutzian reality construction, are too radical. They reduce the world into whatever the human mind happens to construct at a particular time. On the contrary, Goffman defends the "realistic" view that the physical world exists and has a primary reality. Society, too, is external and prior to the individual. Even situations have a structure to them, a set of contingencies and constraints that may enter into the definition of the situation, but which are not merely created by the defining process. They are something that participants arrive at, rather than merely construct.

Goffman also criticizes the reality construction–definitional view for not going far enough. To speak of "the" definition of the situation, in the manner of the symbolic interactionists, misses the multidimensional and layered nature of situations. It is not just that different people might have different definitions of the same situation, but that each participant can be in several complex layers of situational definition at the same time. (The fact that these layers have a structure in relation to one another is one of Goffman's reasons for arguing that they are not simply created by the observer.) Similarly, Goffman (1974: 26) attacks Schutz and his ethnomethodological followers for giving primacy to the "natural attitude" of "everyday life," as if this were a single reality that people construct. For Garfinkel, the everyday commonsense world may sit over an abyss that people try to avoid seeing, but as long as people keep things intact it has a banal unity to it. Goffman wishes to show that everyday life is not that simple, yet people are quite capable of dealing with complexities as a matter of ordinary common sense.

Goffman's *frames* are designed to support both these points: avoiding complete relativism but showing multiple realities. This is done by a set of levels, each of which is built upon another. The multiple nature of realities comes from the way frames can be built upon frames, while the whole is anchored because some frames are more fundamental than others. Goffman uses several metaphors here: framing in the sense of putting a frame around a picture, and a larger frame around that (or a smaller one within it), and so on. Another metaphor is "keys" and "keyings," as if a musical tune were transposed from one key to another. Both of these can be called transformations of one reality in another. The major levels are primary frameworks and transformations.

PRIMARY FRAMEWORKS   Goffman's *primary frameworks* consist of

- The natural world of physical objects in which people live, including their own bodies.
- The social world of other people and their networks of relationships.

TRANSFORMATIONS   A strip of activity in these primary frameworks can be transformed in numerous ways. "Keys and Keyings" are ways that people perform a strip of activity, but in such a way that it is taken at more than face value. These include:

- Make-believe: a theatrical performance, children imagining, and so on.
- Contests: special activities that one performs for the sake of an athletic event, a board game, a bet, and so forth.
- Ceremonials: weddings, birthday celebrations, church services, and all the other special bits of behavior which are enacted for their symbolic significance rather than as ordinary-life actions.
- Technical redoings: Here Goffman refers to actions people perform so that the activity itself can be tried out, practiced, or observed, without being seriously committed to it. Examples are practices (for a play, for a game, for a ceremony, even for a real social event such as a job interview); exhibitions; psychotherapy in which past events are recapitulated; and experiments.
- Other, more complicated and arcane "keyings" of ordinary activities that can occur.

Quite possibly there are no limits on how far such transformations might go. Transformations can be made of transformations: for example, someone might be practicing for a make-believe play, which is about a wedding ceremony, which the participants are really only going through as an experiment. This gives us five levels of transformation embedded in each other (including the physical activities of the people involved as another frame). Reality, in short, can become very complicated. Yet, Goffman points out, people rarely have trouble with this kind of multiple realities. They know what frame is related to what, and they can easily fall back into a more primary reality if any trouble arises. They know how long they have to practice, and how to stop the play if a fire breaks out in the theater.[17]

---

[17] Jonathan Turner (personal communication) points out a possible contradiction between these multiple frames and the ethnomethodological theory of limited cognitive capacities. Why isn't holding complexly embedded frames in mind an instance of cognitive overload? Turner argues that the fact people can do this indicates that they could also hold very complex role prescriptions in memory too—which is the conception of role theory presented in Ralph Turner's theory in Chapter 7, but which I have

A second kind of transformation Goffman calls "fabrications." These are cases where people try to induce false beliefs about what is actually going on. Examples range from spying and military espionage through the more mundane frontstage-setting of jobs and of status impressiveness in sociable life. These add layers of reality onto ordinary activities, both because ordinary appearances are made to represent something that they are not and also because the participants can now have several layers of reality to pay attention to. At a minimum, people who give a deceiving appearance must be aware of (1) what their appearance is supposed to look like; and (2) what they are actually hiding and how they have transformed it. Matters become further complicated when the observer on the other side becomes an active part of the game and tries to penetrate the "cover" to discover what is actually going on. Now the reality multiplies to include (3) what the observer actually knows about (1 and 2), and perhaps (4) what the perpetrator believes the observer knows. Higher level complexities here can sometimes be added on (Goffman, 1969; 1974: 156–200).

OUT-OF-FRAME ACTIVITY AND FRAME BREAKS   The foregoing are ordinary multiple realities encountered in social life. The everyday human being is thus something like an actor, concerned about staging a performance. But things do not always, or even usually, go flawlessly. This does not bother us much; we are used to this staged nature of much of social life, and we make allowances for people's difficulties as actors. When something happens that disrupts a performance, or just does not fit within the frame we are trying to be in at the time, we usually ignore or speedily repair it. When a dog wanders into a wedding ceremony, someone quietly tries to shoo it out while others ignore the frame break. When children interrupt adults' conversation, the latter may attend briefly to the kids and then pick up where they left off. Sometimes, however, extreme troubles break down a frame entirely; the performers become flustered, or the setting breaks down so badly that the performance cannot go on. This is considered very disturbing, often scandalous, but it testifies to the power of more primary realities over the contrived ones.

HUMAN SOCIETY IS BUILT UP BY TRANSFORMING FRAMES

Why is this analysis of frames important? Goffman's examples often deal with the lighter, more frivolous parts of life: entertainment, playing, ceremonies, sociability, the arts. But this cultural realm is distinctively human, a level of consciousness in which animals do not participate. A key characteristic of the realm of culture is precisely this feature of transforming ordinary actions into something seen in a different light. Goffman does not emphasize the theoretical importance of framing for creating the various aspects of human society. But let us consider some possible applications.

THE NATURE OF LANGUAGE AND SYMBOLISM   Talking or writing, seen from the level of primary frames, is merely making certain physical gestures with the

---

criticized from the point of view of cognitive limitations. It may be, though, that multiple framing is a step-by-step process in which one remembers only the most recent steps. In an emergency, people tend to drop all the frames and go back to a very simple program for dealing with physical safety. Thus multiple framing perhaps does not violate the principle of cognitive overload.

mouth and tongue or certain marks on material objects. Culture transforms these actions, sounds, and sights into meanings, an emergent level which wholly supercedes the primary, physical level. Language is thus a reframing of sounds and visual sights into words and meanings.

SOCIAL ORGANIZATION   Organizations and institutions are patterns which link individuals together as occupants of positions, owners of property, possessors or subjects of authority and other rights. In everyday life, though, any organization or institution appears merely as people carrying out some activity in some place. It is a social reframing which turns a man or woman in a room into an organizational member working in an office: it is the same strip of activity, but transformed into a certain social frame (one which Goffman does not discuss). Thus we may say that "organizational framing" is crucial for our ability to enact the larger structures of society.[18]

RITUAL   We have seen the importance of ritual (the Durkheimian theory in Chapter 6) for creating feelings of group membership and moral obligations. But any ritual involves some type of physical activities, which are given a new meaning as ceremonial actions. Ritual is thus a special type of framing. A more adequate theory of rituals could be developed by taking into account the different kinds of framings and reframings which occur, thus making some rituals religious, others secular; some explicitly ceremonial, others "natural rituals" which are not recognized as such. Some rituals are more powerful than others, which may be due to the amount of transformation they undergo. A hypothesis is that the relatively less transformed rituals have more powerful emotional and symbolic effects.[19]

PLAY AND ENTERTAINMENT   Leisure activities are important as personal pleasures and because they further divide people into culturally distinct groups via the stratification of culture. Playing, watching dramas and games, and most other cultural activities are reframings of ordinary actions to see them in a new light: they are "play" and "not serious," with clear boundaries marking them off from ordinary behavior.[20] But also they can be regarded as "peak experiences," culturally "higher"

---

[18] Conversely, people who are in an organizational setting may momentarily drop their working attitudes and lapse into informal, personal relationships. One may say "I can't say anything official, but just between you and me . . .", thus reframing the situation which an instant before was an official one. This may be seen as a transformation on a transformation, creating an informal level of organization upon a previously existing formal level.

[19] Chapter 6 proposed that class cultures are partly determined by the different kinds of participation of classes in rituals: it was suggested that the order-giving classes develop "frontstage" personalities because they exercise power through rituals, whereas order-taking classes have "backstage" personalities because they withdraw from the official world of rituals which is used to dominate them. From the point of view of frame analysis, this appears too simple. In general, the higher social classes are involved in complex reframings of rituals and develop sophistication about the performance problems of highly transformed situations; the lower social classes are involved in ritual on a lower level of transformation and are both more naive about rituals as well as more distrustful of them. There are of course many possible types of individual experience in frames and reframings, which create a variety of individual outlooks spread across the dimensions of class cultures.

[20] It is noteworthy that the first things small children learn are to talk and to make-believe or play. Both of these are distinctively human techniques of reframing. George Herbert Mead's social theory of the self (Chapter 7) regards them as stages in the movement from egocentricity toward full social role

than mundane reality; this seems to happen especially when something is transformed by looking at it through an aesthetic frame, as an instance of art. Bourdieu's research (1984) shows that people are stratified especially by the amount of aesthetic reframing they do: the higher social classes value "sophisticated" art which reframes ordinary objects into "art," while the lower classes need a much more blatant frame of "prettiness" in order to regard something as art. Here again frames are crucial not only in creating different realms of human experience, but in stratifying social groups.

INTELLECTUAL COMMUNICATION   The intellectual realm, including science, is a special attitude toward the other realm of experience. Anything ranging from parts of the physical world on through the social world, including the complex reframings of aesthetics, can be subject to additional reframing as a topic for intellectual analysis. Very high order levels of reflection upon multiple transformed experiences can be achieved, as in philosophy or in ethnomethodology. Intellectual life exists as a very complex reframing activity. Not surprisingly, it gives rise to social communities of intellectuals, whose ultrareframed outlooks of life tend to mark them off from other persons.

CONVERSATION   People's most common activity is talking, especially as a sociable activity. The nature of talk involves a complex shifting of frames, as people set up topics of conversation, maneuver over the implied relationships among the conversationalists, make jokes and insults, bargain, engage and distance themselves toward their words and each other (Goffman, 1974: 496–559; 1981). Sociable conversations take the rest of the world of social frames and transformations and replays them as the contents of talk. This "relaxed frame space," in Goffman's words, is the basis of informal, personal relationships. "Personality" in the private sense thus is the end result of the proliferation of frames upon frames that make up a complex modern society.

GOFFMAN'S ANSWERS TO SYMBOLIC INTERACTION AND ETHNOMETHODOLOGY

Despite his criticism, Goffman adapts many of the points of the reality constructionists, while extending them in a new direction. He even defines "frame" as an element out of which definitions of situations are built up (Goffman, 1974: 10–11). At the same time, "frame" is made equivalent to the phenomenologists' bracketing of the contents of experience to look at the devices by which we give it a certain reality status (Goffman, 1974: 3). We might say, too, that the frame (or nested set of frames) puts greater detail into the "contextuality" within which Garfinkel stressed human perceptions always occur.

Goffman, however, wishes to make all this more structured. Definitions of situations, precisely because they are built up by transformations, have to respect the other frames out of which they are built. They have to move to "adjacent" frames, so to speak, rather than arbitrarily defining any situation any way at all. Vis-à-vis

taking; but it may be that the capacity to do reframing of ordinary activity is more fundamental and, in fact, the key to becoming human.

the ethnomethodologists, Goffman rejects the more extreme implications of indexicality and reflexivity. Contexts can be spelled out by specifying the surrounding frames. The reflexive nature of our reflections on social reality is merely another frame to pay attention to, not a place to become transfixed so as to keep us from seeing anything else about these various levels (Goffman, 1974: 11–12).

Goffman's solution to the problem of reality is this ordered connection among the frames. One layer rests on another. Despite the ambiguities which can arise, and the ways in which people can switch frames and inadvertently or deliberately confuse one another, people can almost always break out of the more complex levels of framing and return to a lower level. The primary framework of the physical world is always there; so is a primary level of the social world. Goffman's view is thus compatible with a materialist view of the world and even with political economy or conflict theory, with its stress on property, physical resources of organization, and coercion. Goffman never mentions this theoretical connection; his own intellectual resonances are more on the Durkheimian side, as we have seen. But here, too, the bottom line is human bodies moving in the physical world, coming into different degrees of proximity and thereby creating the effects of social density and emotional contagion, as spelled out in interaction ritual theory.

I have stressed that Goffman connects the levels of higher mental life, of conscious transformations into constructed realities, "downwards" to the physical frame in which they occur. His model goes in the other direction as well. Any physical or social activity can be transformed "upwards," by reframing it. There is no intrinsic upper limit to the amount of self-conscious reframing that can be done. It is for this reason that extremely high-level transformations can be reached (like Garfinkel's commenting on his "breaching experiments," as well as other intellectuals commenting in turn upon Garfinkel's comments, and so on). Human life has a creative, open-ended quality—but only at the "upper end."

I would suggest that many problems are cleared up if we see that analysts are referring to different parts of the framing continuum (see Figure 8-1).

The ethnomethodologists examine the world of social routine at its most commonsensical. This is where the "natural attitude" prevails. Garfinkel argues that most people try to avoid becoming conscious of the cognitive practices which make this ordinary, for to be conscious of this would throw one up to the highest level, where everything becomes arbitrary. Garfinkel ignores the fact that each level is grounded in another one. But whereas people are reluctant to make a huge leap across several levels of framing, a gradual ascent is possible (such as for intellectuals who entertain their analysis at the highest level of reflexive consciousness, having worked their way up through progressive levels of sophisticated awareness).

Symbolic interactionists are little concerned with the mundane world, but concentrate on the dramatic shifts which can occur in definitions. But this power of actively intervening in defining situations only occurs against a background of a certain routine, at the medium-high levels where situations have already been dramatized as especially exemplary of some larger reality. Goffman stresses, to the contrary, that if one drops back to much lower levels of framing, situations become much less amenable to anyone's definitional activity.

Goffman's own ambiguities about the nature of the self (Chapter 7; see also Goffman, 1974: 573) can be seen in this light. Goffman typically stresses that the

FIGURE 8-1

THE FRAMING CONTINUUM

HYPERRELATIVISTIC CONSCIOUSNESS
Ethnomethodology's reflexive analysis

COMPLEX FRAMING GAMES AND DEFINITIONS OF SITUATIONS
Symbolic interactionist definitional dynamics

SOCIAL ROUTINES
Ethnomethodology's "natural attitude"
Practical activities

PHYSICAL WORLD AND SOCIAL ECOLOGY
Durkheimian grounding of interaction rituals

human self is multiple and dependent upon the kinds and levels of situational activity that is happening at the time. Here, I think, Goffman is mostly pointing to what happens in highly transformed bits of activity: complex stances that can be taken in talk, in performances, in self-reflection or psychiatric contexts. Moreover, given the fact that the sequence of transformations is opened-ended "at the top," the search for the "ultimate self" will never come to an end in that direction. However, if we go in the opposite direction, back toward the human actor as a physical being in a social world of other human bodies, we can come to a core self in the living organism that is trying to orient itself through these successive laminations.

CONCLUSION: IDEALISM AND RELATIVISM IN THE CURRENT INTELLECTUAL WORLD

In my opinion, Goffman's levels of realities offer a breath of fresh air on the current intellectual scene. There have been strong tendencies in recent years toward idealism and relativism, of denying there is any objective reality, of asserting that realities are merely subjective or cultural constructs which exist in endless profusion and among which no intellectually valid choice can be made. This is concentrating on the highest, most reflexively transformed end of Goffman's continuum, and ignoring how these levels themselves emerged out of the physical and social world. At the same time, it would be undesirable to return to naive positivism, which sees only a single-levelled objective world "out there" and ignores any problems of human subjectivity and especially the way subjective reflections can affect what is seen of the world.

The philosophy of science has been paralleling (and following) the tracks of the sociology of science, showing the ways in which the world is always interpreted through a presupposed intellectual context. To stop here, though, and conclude that there is no objective world because we always see it through a context, is unwarranted. We have still to ask: where did this intellectual context emerge from? It is generally believed to be social; this in turn raises the question: what is the nature of this society and how does it affect ideas? Here we need to push beyond the higher, reflexive levels of Goffman's continuum to see how those reflexive levels themselves have emerged as transformations of more naturalistic activity.

To follow this up would require an excursion into the sociology of science. I would like to mention only that the sociology of science can and should be multi-levelled (Collins, 1975: 470–523; Knorr-Cetina and Mulkay, 1983; Whitley, 1984). It does not reduce scientific (or other) intellectual ideas directly to the physical world, but introduces social organization as a shaper of intellectual communities. Here again there is a further set of layers: intellectuals' ideas do not merely reflect those of groups in the larger society (such as social classes) because what makes them intellectuals is participation in a specialized network of other intellectuals. Ideas are, rather, weapons of domination and marks of membership for factions within the intellectual community; at the same time, these ideas can be turned upon both the physical world, the social world, and even upon themselves, thereby giving rise to varying degrees of reframing. Issues of relativism and validity can be understood in this fashion, while still recognizing the objective existence of physical world, and various organizations of the social world within which the intellectual frames arise.

The sociology of science thus can incorporate the increasing sophistication that comes from neo-idealist and constructionist viewpoints, while still retaining an objective world in which this all occurs. Though our knowledge is open-ended, it also can have an objective character, by understanding the hierarchy of transformations itself. The same lesson applies more broadly to all issues of the social construction of reality. The most important aspect of multiple realities are not those that exist among competing intellectuals, but those that exist in people's minds because they are of different social classes, occupy organizational positions, and move through different conversational gambits in their daily lives. But there exists a larger frame around them: the physical world in which they are organized in time and space. Their relation to this material world, especially through property, and to each other through emotional memberships and enforcement coalitions, grounds all the reality constructing which goes on. The various macro and micro theories expounded in other chapters of this book, where valid, are compatible insofar as they mesh into particular levels of this continuum.

Summary

1. The Thomas Theorem states that the way people define a social situation determines how they will behave in it.

2. Herbert Blumer developed the basic principles of symbolic interactionism: people act toward things according to their meanings; the meanings are not intrinsic, but are socially constructed; human beings create their actions by interpreting meanings through a process of making symbolic indications to oneself.

3. Developing upon George Herbert Mead's position, Blumer proposes that the "I" imaginatively rehearses courses of action by trying out different "me's" in various situations. Any situation is potentially novel because the actor can reinterpret any of its aspects.

4. Situational theory is criticized for assuming that people always pay attention to verbal definitions of situations; for overemphasizing cognitive rather than

emotional or unconscious factors in action; and for overemphasizing individual freedom, although some individuals and groups have more power than others to define situations. Individual creativity and freedom may occur only under particular conditions, especially high degrees of reflexive consciousness, and emotional energy or initiative.

5. Ethnomethodology studies the practices of reasoning in everyday life, the methods by which people make inferences about the world and themselves in it.

6. Alfred Schutz's social phenomenology proposes a number of basic principles of consciousness in everyday life, including the *reciprocity of perspectives,* the *undeceptiveness of appearances, typification,* and *goal-directedness.* Individuals make interpretations by drawing upon a *stock of commonsense knowledge* in their culture; and rely heavily on *glosses,* by which partial features of reality are taken as indicating the full reality which is not seen.

7. Harold Garfinkel produced a more radical version of social phenomenology by stressing *indexicality:* everything is embedded in a surrounding context that must be taken for granted in order to know what it is. If one tries to state explicitly the assumed background, this leads to a still further context which is taken for granted, and so on. To avoid this infinite regress people use the procedures of commonsense reasoning.

8. Garfinkel also stresses *reflexivity:* we live in a world of particular situations, though we use general concepts to interpret them; but these general concepts are never directly seen, but only illustrated by alleged examples of them. There is no escape from this circular relationship.

9. Garfinkel claims that the procedures by which people account for what is going on, are the way social reality was constructed in the first place. The ordinariness of the world is not given, but is socially produced, although people censor their awareness that they have actually done this cognitive work. Reflexivity is hidden by "the natural attitude."

10. In commonsense reasoning, persons add an implicit "et cetera clause" to everything, although (because of indexicality) this could never be filled in. In Garfinkel's "breaching experiments," persons become upset when asked to actually fill in these endless details.

11. People assume that meanings will eventually emerge and do not insist that everything be meaningful the moment they experience it. Only when something happens to disturb their sense of the normal flow of action do they examine social reality; usually they offer "accounts" which quickly restore the sense of normalcy. The world is held together, not by common agreement on a single reality, but because people refrain from questioning it.

12. Some implications of ethnomethodology for sociology may include: (1) the importance of emotions in determining taken-for-granted aspects of social life; (2) a demonstration of human cognitive limitations, paralleling the conception of "bounded rationality" in Herbert Simon's organizational theory; (3) a criticism of theories which rely heavily on cognitive definitions of reality; (4) a set of features that a successful computer artificial intelligence program would have to incorporate; (5) congruence with a macrosociology emphasizing coercive power and bureaucratic routinization in upholding a stratified social order, together with sudden, revolutionary changes.

13. Erving Goffman's *frame analysis* avoids the extremes of sheer physical objectivity and subjective relativism, by a set of levels building upon one another. Human beings orient first to the *primary frameworks* of the physical world and human bodies within it; they then can construct *transformations* which change the meaning of activity into make-believe, contests, ceremonials, deceptions, and other reformulations. Transformations can be built on transformations, resulting in very high levels of complexity. The framing continuum is in principle open-ended at the "upper" end, but grounded in an objective physical world at the "bottom."

14. Transformations give rise to performance problems in staging these levels of reality. This analysis adds onto Goffman's earlier model of frontstages and backstages in the presentation of self.

15. Framing is important because it transforms bare sounds and gestures into meaningful language; it constitutes social organizations by reframing situational activities at work, authority, or membership in a larger structure; it is the basis of social rituals as well as human social symbolic culture. Complex levels of framing are involved in intellectual life. The kinds of social relationships enacted by ordinary conversation are conveyed by the level of framing shared by the participants.

Chapter **9**

STRUCTURALISM AND SOCIOLINGUISTICS

FRENCH STRUCTURALISM: THE LANGUAGE-MODEL OF REALITY
  Saussure
  Lévi-Strauss
  Semiotics
  Deconstructionism
  Evaluation of Structuralist and Post-structuralist Theory

CHOMSKY'S GENERATIVE GRAMMAR
  Transformational Grammar
  Sociological Theory of Language
  Speech Act Theory
  The Turn-taking Model

GOFFMAN'S SOCIAL ECOLOGY OF LANGUAGE
  Footings
  Sudnow's Embodied Talk
  Childhood Learning of Speech

TOWARD A GENERAL THEORY OF LANGUAGE

SUMMARY

FRENCH STRUCTURALISM: THE LANGUAGE-MODEL OF REALITY

The strongest claims for the importance of language have come from the movement of French intellectuals generally referred to as *structuralism*. This movement is actually broader than being limited to those who accept that label for their work. Most make obeisance to the early twentieth-century linguist Ferdinand de Saussure, but do not necessarily accept the lead of the anthropologist Claude Lévi-Strauss and the psychoanalyst Jacque Lacan. At varying distances are the structuralist Marxists Louis Althusser and Nicos Poulantzas, the historian Michel Foucault, the literary critic Roland Barthes, as well as "deconstructionists" such as Jacques Derrida. But even deconstructionism and other forms of "semiotics" remain part of the same intellectual universe, constituting a sort of "second generation" of structuralism extending earlier lines of analysis. This later work actually converges with hermeneutics, an interpretive analysis which has sometimes been regarded as an opponent of structuralism. (In structuralist terminology, we may say they are all working out of the same "problematique": see the Box titled "Structuralist Terminology.")

The basic structuralist strategy is to regard language as the model for all of reality. It is not just that we see reality through the lens provided by our words. This would be a kind of subjective idealism. Instead, the structuralists propose that reality is itself a language, whose underlying structure it is our task to decode. Reality is objective, not subjective; and some structuralists go so far as to declare they are "anti-humanists" and practitioners of a "philosophy without a subject." That is to say, reality is a "text" (see box) which we may read. Linguistics is the fundamental science, giving the method for reading any of these texts. Various practitioners apply the method to different areas: Lévi-Strauss to myths and other items of culture in primitive societies; Barthes to literature, and then to advertisements, automobiles, and other artifacts of modern life; Lacan to dreams and products of the human unconscious; Foucault to history; Derrida to philosophies; Althusser and Poulantzas to capitalism.

SAUSSURE

The basic ideas of structuralism are taken from Saussure (1915/1966). He was concerned with shifting the focus of linguistics from purely historical concerns with the way languages have developed, the search for the common ancestor of modern languages, and the etymology of words. These "diachronic" studies (see box), he argued, piled up particular facts but gave rise to no general theory, no science of language. Such a theory would have to be "synchronic," to show language as a *formal system,* a set of relationships among different words and parts of speech. Saussure, influenced by the sociological theory of Emile Durkheim, pointed out that language is not individual, but a collective representation. It has a force imposed by

STRUCTURALIST TERMINOLOGY

French structuralism has developed a distinctive vocabulary, which has now spread rather widely in the intellectual world, including to the post-structuralist and Marxist sectors. Some of the key terms are the following:

sign: an element in a linguistic system, uniting an acoustic image or "signifier" with the concept that it stands for.

text: any unified ensemble of signs which may be interpreted by structural analysis. A "text" may be not only a written document but any spoken, visual, or other collection which can be subjected to the same treatment.

discourse: the activity of producing and interpreting signs.

projection or *project:* human action taking its direction from a given starting point (though not necessarily aiming at a given end).

parole and *langue:* literally "word" and "tongue," but meaning language as it is spoken in the contingencies of ordinary life *(parole)* and language as an underlying, systematic structure *(langue)*.

binary opposition: a contrast between two parts in a system, especially between the presence and absence of a given element. Saussure proposed that language is built up out of binary oppositions between phonemes; Lévi-Strauss attempted to generalize this to all aspects of culture.

diachronic and *synchronic:* a system of changes in time, as compared to a system of simultaneous relations. "Diachronic" is sometimes further distinguished from "historical," in that the former shows the systematic model of changes, whereas history is the full panoply of concrete details resulting from this abstract structure.

problematique or *problematic:* (used as a noun) the basic model or set of ideas behind the actual thoughts of any particular intellectual generation. According to Althusser, a problematic changes only occasionally, in a moment of "epistemological rupture" *(coupure èpistémologique)*.

moment: a particular phase of argument within a larger theoretical complex. The term is used to imply that all aspects of the theory are connected together and that selecting one part for attention is an abitrary interruption of the overall flow.

social formation: term coined by Poulantzas to replace "society." "Social formation" is meant to convey that any given historical society combines economic, political, and ideological structures of several different types (corresponding to different historical stages in the basic structural-Marxist model). The dominant mode of production is what gives its name to the particular social formation (for example, "capitalist," "feudal," and so forth).

society: there are correct and incorrect ways of speaking, which are not determined by the individual. Hence Saussure distinguished between *parole* (words, the way language may actually be spoken on various occasions) and *langue* (the basic structural rules of language itself). Ordinary speech may not quite live up to basic language rules, but it is derivative of them. This underlying structure, imposed by society, should be the topic of linguistic analysis.

Saussure goes so far as to call language "the collective mind of the community of speakers" (1915/1966: 96). Like Durkheim in his work *Suicide,* Saussure criticized theories which reduced language to the influence of climate, race, or Tarde's theory of imitation (1915/1966: 150–51). Language is a phenomenon *sui generis* and a social institution like other rites and customs which represent the identity of a group. Unfortunately, Saussure did not go further and actually apply Durkheim's theory in any detail to see that speaking itself can be analyzed as an interaction ritual and that words constitute "sacred objects" conveying a sense of group membership. The fact that words operate on this level beyond practical reasoning, and serve as a foundation for it, shows why every language is essentially arbitrary, and yet is strongly felt to be a proper, even morally sanctioned form of behavior. Saussure stressed the point, without explaining it; as we shall see later in this chapter, Goffman's theory of interaction ritual and of talk eventually laid out this connection.

Language is arbitrary in the following way. Out of the large number of sounds that the human vocal apparatus can make, each language selects a few and makes them into units of meaning. The phoneme "fa-" in the English word "father" is a different choice than the French phoneme "pe-" in "pere." The choice is arbitrary. But once it is made, it operates as part of a system: "fa-" stands in opposition to all other phonemes and cannot be confused with them. It is the set of distinctions or oppositions that is crucial, rather than anything intrinsic about the elements themselves. "Fa-ther" does not in any way resemble the human persons that it represents, any more than does "pere." But once that set of sounds is used in a certain way, it acquires a structural position in the language, by opposition to all the other phonemes that it is not. The originally arbitrary sound elements take on a meaning because of their relationships inside the language system.

Language, then, is a system of signs. A sign unites an image (which may be acoustical, the sound of a spoken word, or visual, the way it is written), with a concept that it represents. "Father" and "pere" are signs in different systems, each corresponding to a different spoken-written image but referring to the same concept. Notice that Saussure does not build his system merely out of relationships between "names" and "things." It is concepts, mental entities, to which words correspond, rather than necessarily to physical objects in the world. (Thus in more elaborate versions of structuralism, signs themselves can become the objects of other signs.) Also, the sign intervenes between the concept and the word image. Signs are not isolated, but are strung together in a system. They relate logically both to that which they are not (that is, other signs in a system of oppositions), and to other signs which are connected with them through various associations and common usages (as the word "father" is connected to "fatherly," "fatherland," and so on).

More complex systems of formal linguistics have arisen since Saussure's day, and now the older historical linguistics has been largely neglected. The important elements which have been developed into structuralism are not in the technical side of linguistics, however, but in the basic concepts: the notion of a system of arbitrary elements which take their meaning from their relationship to other parts of the system, the distinction between history and underlying structure, and the corresponding method of going beneath the surface to the "model" beneath.

LÉVI-STRAUSS

Saussure's most immediate followers were a group of Russian "Formalist" literary critics, together with the Prague School of linguistics, whose most influential representative was the emigré Roman Jakobson (see Jameson, 1972). The method became famous in social science largely through the work of Claude Lévi-Strauss, who incorporated some of the ideas of Jakobson and Saussure but applied them beyond language itself. An anthropologist, Lévi-Strauss was in the French tradition which regarded sociology as the theoretical and generalizing side of ethnographic field work. He thus followed directly in the lineage of Durkheim and Mauss in comparing and synthesizing studies of tribal societies. His first major work *The Elementary Structures of Kinship* (1949/1969) was in one sense a continuation of the theory Mauss had set forth in *The Gift* (1925), a Durkheimian version of exchange theory.

Lévi-Strauss went on to make a similar analysis of kinship systems. Kinship is based on a system of exchange among families; giving a woman in marriage creates an obligation to return another woman in marriage at a later time, and thus creates a long-term bond between the families involved. Just as Mauss showed that ceremonial gifts created social ties which then made it possible for more mundane economic exchanges to take place, Lévi-Strauss argued that the exchange of women created the structure of tribal societies within which other economic and political transactions could take place. Lévi-Strauss follows Durkheim's theme of the precontractual basis of solidarity: beneath the level at which rational, self-interested bargaining takes place, there has to be another level which established the framework of interaction in the first place. This is a level of ceremonial exchange relations; in the case of a tribal society, it is made up of marriages.

Lévi-Strauss' early work was more clearly related to Mauss and Durkheim than to Saussure, but some Saussurian themes were already present. Lévi-Strauss described the kinship system as a structure of signs, a form of communication. That is, the exchange of women among families is a communicative act. It is intrinsically social and human rather than biological. All mammal species find mates, but only humans build up a network of kinship relationships out of the mating process. Moreover, the exchange is symbolic; it expresses social relationships and contains a reference to the future, when the exchange is to be repaid by a marriage in the other direction. Lévi-Strauss speaks of the incest taboo as the beginning of human society, the dividing line between humans and animals. He means this in the following sense: the incest taboo forces humans to go outside their own family of procreation in order to find mates and thus to overcome the tendency for society to remain a series of isolated, self-reproducing groups. (Some species of animals may have some version of incest avoidance too, but without establishing network ties.) The incest taboo is the break between "nature" and "culture" because it creates a system of communication among families. The first signs in that system of communication, Lévi-Strauss argued, were perhaps not words but the women who moved between the groups. They were living reminders of the groups they had come from and to whom the family owes a mate in return at some time in the future.

Kinship, then, is in some sense a language system. Lévi-Strauss then went on to distinguish different languages. The formal rules of kinship in different societies—

which for example require a man to marry his father's sister's daughter, or his mother's brother's daughter, or follow yet some other marriage rule—make up different grammars, as it were. Each is implicated in a different system of communication. Lévi-Strauss distinguishes short cycles and long cycles, ones in which two families are braided together in back-and-forth exchanges, and ones in which many families exchange indirectly through a chain which eventually circles back to its starting point. Lévi-Strauss' structuralism emerges in the emphasis he places on the underlying logic of the system, as opposed to what actually happens in the details of everyday life. Not all families will happen to have a father's sister's daughter for every son to marry; some will have too many daughters or too many sons; others will have blank spaces due to deaths or infertility. Also the rules of exchange can shift, and fights and ruptures can occur between families. Nevertheless, Lévi-Strauss argued, the underlying structure of the system tends in a certain direction, and families which follow that structure will end up, over a period of generations, becoming more strongly linked to others than families which fail to follow the structure. The payoff is that they will become "rich" in marriage alliances with the power, wealth, and prestige that follows from this. This is parallel to Saussure's distinction of "parole" and "langue": the everyday details and accidents of marriages are an accidental surface, comparable to the way people actually speak; the underlying structure of the kinship system is comparable to the formal structure of the language itself.

Lévi-Strauss subsequently went on to develop his structuralist theory explicitly. He proposed that any item of culture in a society—its kinship, the way its campsites were arranged in space, its songs and form of art, its religion—might be "decoded" to find its underlying structure. At one time (1958/1963) he hypothesized that each society would turn out to have the same particular structure underlying *all* the different items of its culture. But he then abandoned this ambitious project to concentrate on tribal mythologies. In *The Savage Mind* (1962/1966), Lévi-Strauss set out to show that so-called "primitive" societies think in just as logical a fashion as modern Western ones; it is only that they use a different form of language. Tribal myths are actually coding schemes, laying out the basic categories of the universe and grouping different objects together under these categories. This is what modern science does, too, but under the guise of causal relations. "Primitive" thought, on the other hand, is concerned especially with the different categories of animals and objects in the world of nature and with the connections and the disjunctions between them and the human world. Hence the numerous myths of animals and birds which talk, propagate the first people, engender different items of culture, and so forth. Lévi-Strauss worked out a series of analyses under the general title "Mythologiques": *The Raw and the Cooked, The Origin of Table Manners, From Honey to Ashes, The Naked Man*. These drew largely on comparisons among the myths of various native American tribes, using one myth to elucidate another (for example, a jaguar might be related to eating raw meat in one myth, while another spoke of humans killing a jaguar with a bow and arrow). By this means, Lévi-Strauss attempted to show the underlying structure of categories related to one another and thus make sense out of the universe.

Lévi-Strauss' structuralism came to emphasize the full range of parallels with Saussure's linguistics. The analyst looks for the underlying language code beneath the surface combinations of elements in which history and ordinary narrative are expressed. There is a historyless, synchronic structure from which the myriad combinations of the empirical world are generated. Lévi-Strauss appeals both to the aim of creating a generalizing science, as well as to antipositivist critiques of science. The empirical surface of society cannot be explained in a determinative way any more than can the innumerable sentences that are actually spoken. (Here Lévi-Strauss parallels Chomsky's linguistics.) But we can arrive at a scientific system at the level of the underlying model. At one point, Lévi-Strauss (1964/1969) claimed that such a structure might actually be produced by a computer. He also draws the parallel with the fundamental on-off choices of computer circuits by stressing that the underlying codes are in the form of *binary oppositions*. Out of a series of such binary oppositions the more complex cultural forms are built up.

SEMIOTICS

Related to Lévi-Strauss' structuralism is the field called semiotics. *Semiotics* is the science of signs, that is to say, any system of signification. Semiotics derives both from the linguistic theory of Saussure, which stresses that signs are arbitrary and derive their meanings only from oppositions to other arbitrary signs used in a system; and from the pragmatism of Peirce, which viewed signs as part of an ongoing process of human action. The latter approach was extended by the French literary theorist Roland Barthes (1964). Barthes argued that objects of everyday life, such as an automobile, could become signs and communicate meanings. Thus an automobile can convey a message about the social status of its owner, about worldviews, and so forth. So can any item of culture, ranging from styles of dress or food to popular entertainment, like professional wrestling.

In his later works, Barthes (1974) refined his position to avoid the implication that material objects in the world are nothing more than parts of a cultural "language." It is not the objects (the automobile and so forth) that are the subject of analysis, but rather the *discourse* or *text* which are about the objects. Barthes came to conclude that clothes are not themselves immediately signs but rather that they become subject to the signs of the world of fashion; that is to say, the cultural world of talking and writing about clothes gives the clothes themselves a social meaning. Following a Marxian tradition of criticizing mass culture, Barthes referred to the culturally represented object (as opposed to the material object itself) as a "simulacrum": the object as permeated with the ideological meanings of the system of consumerism. Baudrillard (1981) has applied this critique to the advertising world, which, he argues, has reduced all material objects to their "sign value" so that their use as real objects is forgotten.

Other semioticians have gone further in laying out a multilevelled theory of signs (see Gottdiener, 1985). Umberto Eco (1976) pointed out that objects can be used by individuals not only as signs but also as indexes (a term Peirce used to refer to features which convey some implication without being symbols of it: for instance seeing a short bowlegged man is an index that he is probably a jockey). Hence objects can be signs without taking part in a system of communicative signalling. An object has a primary function and a second-order social meaning, which may be called *signification*. Going further, an object may be explicitly produced to intentionally signal a message; in this case, there is not only signification but *communication*.

Moreover, communication brings in a larger cultural system or code, which exists already independent of particular material objects that can be made sense of within it.

Eco (1976: 27) pointed out that an automobile, for example, can be analyzed on five different levels. It can be described (1) as a material object of certain materials and shape, (2) as a tool whose function or use value is transportation, (3) as possessing a certain economic exchange value, (4) as a sign of social status, and (5) as a cultural object (word, idea) in a system of verbal discourse. Level 5 is the usual realm of semiotic analysis, where cultural codes exist; and level 4 is also a kind of semantic code, in which automobiles of different sort mean social rank. But levels 2 and 3 can also be made into signs, and hence incorporated into the meaning system on level 5: in this "transfunctionalization" the automobile as transportation (level 2) can now signify speed or movement; and the auto as economic value (level 3) can signify an aspect of the capitalist system (a commodity, a product of surplus value, and so on). Thus any one material object can become involved in a multiplicity of systems of signs and meanings, as well as possess a noncultural reality. There are a multitude of codes coexisting in social life, and cultural perception is *polysemic* (characterized by multiple meanings).

DECONSTRUCTIONISM

The structuralist movement eventually generated its own criticisms as well as opposing movements fighting over the same territory. Language is still generally taken as the basic model of reality, and all other areas of (social) science assimilated to it. Thus the psychoanalyst Jacque Lacan (1966/1977; see Kurzweil, 1980) proposed that the child is born into a symbolic order, and the Freudian categories of libidinal stages and conflicts must be recast in terms of linguistic problems in the child's mind. This parallels a tendency within the work of Lévi-Strauss and other structuralists to see psychoanalysis as the model for a science which decodes underlying structures. Lévi-Strauss himself proposed that the psychoanalyist is the modern equivalent of the tribal shaman: the shaman did not so much cure people of real ills, as make their troubles *thinkable* within a framework of mythical categories. Louis Althusser (1965/1972; 1971), too, incorporated Freudian categories in the Marxian framework in arguing that history can be "overdetermined" by several different underlying causal forces and that a particular historical event can be a "symptom" or "condensation" of numerous conflicts, as in the moment of revolution.

But many of these same theorists have disputed whether they should be called "structuralists." Some of the points at issue have been these three. First, whether the strict application of Saussure's and Lévi-Strauss' models are appropriate. In particular, Lévi-Strauss had laid emphasis on *binary oppositions*. But is the world really always made of dichotomies? Can there not be other categories mediating between extremes? In any case, the strict set of oppositions seems too rigid, too much of an imposition of Lévi-Strauss' personal predelictions on the world.

Second, Lévi-Strauss had declared himself a seeker of the fundamental science, of the universal categories of the human mind, or of a general science of models. "Deconstructionist" thinkers like the philosopher Jacques Derrida (1967/1976) have declared that this goal maintains a traditional illusion. For Derrida (joined by the literary theorist Julia Kristeva and by Barthes in his later work), the world consists of nothing but "discourse" or "text." Signs do not point beyond themselves to a world out there, because the world always comes to us pre-interpreted by signs. One set of signs merely signifies another set of signs. Derrida makes all thought radically historical: it is an interpretation at one point in time of the texts laid down at a previous point. The world itself is a "text." We can never arrive at a definitive interpretation of it, because we are always in the process of producing a new text, which will be subject to yet later analysis.

Third, "deconstructionism" thus pushes toward an endless historical relativism in which we can never get outside of a system of signs. It is a kind of structuralist critique of structuralism itself. In the other direction, structuralism is criticized because it is too confined to the world of signs. Althusser denied he was a structuralist because he insisted on the material nature of the structures which Marxist analysis uncovers in capitalism. Michel Foucault (1961/1965; 1963/1973; 1975/1977; 1976/1978) analyzed the history of madness, of insane asylums, of sexuality, and of other aspects of early modern culture with an emphasis on the underlying social mentalities which were expressed in each of these phenomena. But Foucault parted company with the structuralists, despite similarities in their analyses, both because he disavowed rigid formulae for the underlying structure and especially because he came to feel that structuralism neglected power. Items of culture are products of stratified societies, structured by power and the domination of groups and individuals over others. The somewhat ethereal quality of structuralist systems neglects this and hence should be repudiated.

EVALUATION OF STRUCTURALIST AND POST-STRUCTURALIST THEORY

The biggest weakness of structuralism is that it promised more than it could deliver. Lévi-Strauss claimed that he would produce a science, that he would, so to speak, "crack the genetic code" that underlies human societies. He did not succeed. His lengthy analyses of myths contained interesting and plausible interpretations of thought within tribal societies. But the analyses went on endlessly, without any particular order, and did not arrive at any model except for Lévi-Strauss's very abstract and disputable claims that culture is built up by series of binary oppositions. His followers eventually decided that he did not have to answer and moved on to deconstructionism, semiotics, and other positions, which have not arrived at a definitive code either. We can see several more specific indications of Lévi-Strauss' failure.

For one thing, he changed his mind as to the generality of the code. In the 1950s (1958/1963), Lévi-Strauss was proposing that each society had its own *particular* code, underlying all items of its culture. This appears to be an extension of his theory of kinship, which was based on separating out *different* forms of kinship systems. But apparently Lévi-Strauss was never able to demonstrate that such a code existed for each society. In the 1960s, we find him taking a different tack: that there is a *universal* code of the human mind, which may be found by analyzing tribal myths. But this too was a failure. At least, Lévi-Strauss never demonstrated what such a code would be; and his claims for universality were undermined by the fact that he was really showing that the mode of thought in tribal societies, though "logical" in its own way, is quite different from the scientific mode of thought in modern Western societies.

It is also striking that Lévi-Strauss and the other structuralists, although drawing upon Saussure for a general model, never ventured to incorporate language itself into their analyses. They analyzed myths, kinship systems, psychoanalytical symptoms, and so forth but did not look directly at the structure of languages. The reason, I think, is because language would not have demonstrated what they were looking for. In fact, there are well-described structural differences among various types of language around the world: inflecting, isolating, agglutinative, polysynthetic, as well as other dimensions of language structure (Sapir, 1921). But these structures are not neatly correlated with other aspects of the society (not even something as basic as the complexity of the society itself). This fact would have violated Lévi-Strauss' early search for a particular cultural code in each society; while the deep differences among types of language creates a series challenge for any claim that there is a universal structural code.

In general, it is peculiar that the structuralist thinkers have borrowed linguistic theory as an analogy, or rather as an inspiration, but they have neither kept up with the technical advances in linguistics itself, nor have they contributed in any important way toward unifying sociological principles with those of linguistics. To find genuine advances in sociolinguistics, we need to move away from the structuralists themselves toward those sociologists examined in the latter part of this chapter. Interestingly, the connection which was initiated between Durkheim and Saussure has been developed, but more through the Durkheimian side of social rituals than through the Saussurian side of formal structures.

The major weakness of the structuralism and its post-structuralist continuations, in my opinion, is that its real model is not so much linguistics as literary criticism. Beneath the new terminology, the work of almost everyone reviewed so far in this chapter—from Lévi-Strauss and Lacan to Derrida and Foucault—consists of reading some aspect of society as if it were a novel. What does it express? What was the author thinking? In these cases, of course, there is nothing like a single "author," so a fictitious mind is invented, which is then projected into a realm of underlying "structure." But there are innumerable ways that different viewers might interpret any historical or cultural complex; hence it is no wonder that the search for "the" code turns out to be inconclusive. Derrida and the deconstructionists implicitly admit this by making it all completely relativistic, thus giving up hope that "the" code might ever be found.

The positive contributions of structuralism are less in any particular structures they have uncovered than in some features of their basic approach. They provide a valuable distinction between the empirical surface, whether it be called "parole," "myth," or "history," and the underlying "model" or "structure" which produces it. This helps us to solve some of the social science problem of explanation in a world which is changing, complex, and particular. In a time when prevailing intellectual fashion tends to go in the direction of relativism and idealism, structuralism provides a midway point. Science is possible, but on the level of models; reality as derived from these, on the other hand, will always have a quality of particularity and indeterminateness that we cannot overcome. I am also sympathetic to the structuralist point that these structures are beyond the level of the individual, that our individual human consciousness is not the ultimate level of analysis, but is on the level of the empirical "parole" that is a product of deeper structures. Our individual minds are on the surface, not the depth. Structuralism warns us not to stop our analysis on this superficial level but to push to a more fundamental level of structures from which it derives.

Structuralism's program is still valid, although its substantive results (except perhaps for aspects of Lévi-Strauss' theory of kinship) are not. Fortunately there is a sociology which can fill in the spirit of this program.

Chomsky's Generative Grammar

One of the most famous developments in the social sciences in recent years has been Noam Chomsky's "generative grammar." In two important books (1957, 1965) Chomsky carried out a revolution in linguistics which has had repercussions in philosophy and psychology, as well as in sociology. Chomsky's work was revolutionary because it broke with the behaviorism that had previously dominated linguistics. The task of linguistics had been seen merely as describing the ways the people behaved when they spoke different languages. Chomsky, however, argued that the task is to go deeper, to show how to formally represent languages which are already very familiar to their speakers—languages like English, French, or German—rather than describing exotic tribal languages. His point is that linguistic science should not merely pile up endless detail about various languages, but should penetrate more profoundly into the nature of language in general. He believed that this could be done by examining a language that we already know quite well on the surface level, such as our own intuitive understanding of English.

Part of Chomsky's revolution, then, was a break from the narrow positivism which identified science merely with empirical description. Chomsky was felt to be a liberating influence by social scientists who wished to dig into the nature of the subjective world; Chomsky helped produce the turn toward cognition in psychology, as well as inspiring the outburst of phenomenological and interpretive theory in sociology. Chomsky can also be regarded as something of a triumph for structuralism. Although he himself is not a French structuralist (his work was independent of and parallel to that movement), Chomsky provides one of the strongest examples of how a "deep structure" can generate many different surface structures. We have already seen that French structuralism took language as its model for all of reality, but without making much contribution to linguistics itself. Chomsky provides exactly that contribution, which has provided some of the best evidence that a structuralist position actually has some validity.

Chomsky's task may be thought of as the problem of writing out the rules for a computer to produce sentences of a *natural language* (that is, a language which some group of people spontaneously uses; often abbreviated NL). That is not to say that Chomsky was interested in programming computers to speak; his own work goes back before the recent upsurge of interest in computer artificial intelligence (AI), and he was highly critical of early work in this area. But the computer analogy makes it easier to see what he was doing. He wanted to find the answer to the question: what rules is the human brain following in order to construct proper sentences?

Chomsky has formally stated, using mathematical concepts, a number of different systems for constructing sentences. His aim was to show that certain kinds of systems, although initially appealing, do not work very well to produce all the sentences that we count as good English, and that to adequately account for all sentences we need a system which he calls "transformational grammar." This is not the same term as generative grammar, which refers more inclusively to all such systems which Chomsky tried out. In other words, Chomsky's task was to create different systems of rules which would generate all possible sentences in a NL (hence generative grammar).

One of the generative grammars which Chomsky tried out and rejected is what he called "finite state grammars" (which we might think of as "left-to-right" systems). In this system, the speaker chooses a word to begin with (say the word "The"). Every word that comes after this (to the right of it) is constrained by what came before it (to the left of it). So after "The" one has a choice of words from a list that can come after "The"; man, dog, hamburger, shovel, and so on. Suppose you choose "dog"; now the choice is what kind of words can come after "The dog." Again, there is a list: has, woke, took, said, snarled, had, gives, gave, and so on. When you choose a word from that list, there is still a further possibility for the next place in the sentence, until finally the sentence is finished (for instance, "The dog has a collar.") This sound fairly straightforward, but it is easy to show that many sentences in English can be produced only clumsily in this way and some cannot be produced at all. "Anyone who says that is lying" is a sentence in which the left-to-right construction "Anyone . . . is lying" is broken up by an embedded clause "who says that." We can make this even more complicated by embedding yet another phrase (or even more), such as "Anyone who says that those people are here is lying." In these examples, words are separated from those on which their choice depends. It is not a matter of what is just to the left of them in the sentence, but some kind of connection "in another dimension." To put it another way: our brain is not a computer with a set of lists of words that can be used in particular positions in sentences; and if we try to program a computer to search through in a "left-to-right" fashion, it will be very slow and clumsy in producing sentences and will be unable to produce many sentences that human beings can with ease.

Chomsky is well known as a critic of traditional behaviorist models in psychology. Language is not built up merely by associating one word with the words that can come next. In the same way, it is not correct, he argued, to assert that languages are simply learned by associating words with particular objects. The problem is not merely that there are many words which do not correspond to any object at all ("the," "and," "is," "of," are obvious examples) but so are many verbs and abstract nouns: for instance, "correspond" or "problem"). The behaviorists held a simplistic view of language in assuming that its primary constituent consists of nouns and adjectives (and concrete ones at that). Chomsky believes instead that grammar (also called syntax) is more fundamental than individual words themselves and certainly more important than nouns. Concentrating on nouns gives the world a misleadingly static and concrete appearance, when in fact our own world is extremely dynamic and mental.

Small children learn language very quickly, relative to the complexity and extent of the system they are mastering. This is a marvelous achievement, Chomsky points out, which we take for granted simply because almost everyone manages to do it. But it is the most complex piece of learning that anyone accomplishes in one's life. This cannot be done by painstakingly learning the meaning of every distinctive sentence and associating it with things in the world. Children by the age of four or five have heard only a small proportion of all the possible sentences in (let us say) the English language. But these children can recognize and understand many sentences that they have never heard before, can tell the difference between sentences which are grammatical and those which are not, and can form and speak innumerable sentences which they have neither spoken nor heard.

Language use is creative, Chomsky stresses. It is not merely a business of memorizing thousands of associations between words and objects and millions of different ways words can be put together in sentences. Rather, there is a deep structure which produces all the different combinations. This consists of a finite set of rules, which operate on a finite (but possibly quite large) set of words, to produce an infinite variety of sentences, most of which one has never heard before. This means that some of the rules must be capable of being applied over and over again, including in the same sentence. This is the meaning of saying that language structure is *recursive*. (The way that phrases can be embedded in other phrases, as shown previously, is an example of this very important property of language.)

TRANSFORMATIONAL GRAMMAR

After trying out various formal systems, Chomsky concluded that the most adequate one for generating all possible sentences is what he calls *transformational grammar*. The details of this can be quite complex, and the following will give only a few of the rules to give some of the flavor of this analysis:

1. Sentence $\longrightarrow$ NP (noun phrase) + VP (verb phrase)
2. VP $\longrightarrow$ Verb + NP
3. Verb $\longrightarrow$ Aux (auxiliary) + V
4. V $\longrightarrow$ (talk, walk, give, sing, . . . etc.)
5. Aux $\longrightarrow$ Tense (+ modal) (+ have + en) (+ be + ing)

The arrow ($\longrightarrow$) means that what is to the left consists of what is to the right of the arrow, and the parentheses enclose lists from which one item is to be chosen.

Following these kinds of rules, one comes up with a set of items that Chomsky calls "underlying strings." It should be noted that these are not yet sentences, though they are the materials out of which sentences are constructed. One of these strings might be: the + man + Present Tense + may + have + en + open + the + door. By application of a *transformational rule,* this string can be used to generate both the active sentence "The man may have opened the door," and the passive sentence "The door may have been opened by the man." (Notice that for the left-to-right method given above, these two sentences are produced in quite different ways and have nothing to do with each other.) But the transformational rule still isn't enough to produce real-life sentences. Words consist of particular grammatical

FIGURE 9-1

CHOMSKY'S MODEL OF TRANSFORMATIONAL GRAMMAR

Initial element ⟶ Phrase structure rules ⟶ Transformational rules ⟶
⟶ Morphophonemic rules ⟶ Recognizable sentences

elements, but they may not be spelled or pronounced literally the way the rules generate them. What in Chomsky's rule system for verbs is represented "open + en" is actually spelled "opened", just as "be + s" is spelled "is." So Chomsky adds another set of rules which he calls "morphophonemic rules" which convert the underlying string into pronounceable sounds (phonemes) or into letters (when the sentence is written).

We can see now why Chomsky emphasizes the difference between the deep structure and the surface structure of language. In Figure 9-1, there are several different levels that have to be gone through before the underlying structure is turned into a recognizable sentence in the English language (or presumably any language). There are family relationships between different sentences: actives and passives, assertions and questions ("Did the man open the door?"), positives and negatives ("The man did not open the door"); and various combinations of these are all produced by different transformations of the same underlying string. The surface structure often may hide the deep structure.

There are some important limitations on Chomsky's theory. It is concerned with *syntax,* the structural relationships among parts of speech, and tells us virtually nothing about *semantics,* the meaning of communications. This would limit its application by interpretive sociologists, who place great emphasis on subjective meanings in the construction of social realities.

Chomsky's appeal is in a different direction. His theory is a very strong example of the structuralist view of reality. The empirical world as we experience it is infinitely varied. What laws can be stated are not about this surface level, but about the underlying structure which generates all its possibilities. Chomsky's structuralist model is both determinative, in the sense that people must necessarily follow these structural rules, but also free, in that it leaves room for human choice and creativity. We are free to choose many different elements and transformations, and thus we can create an infinity of different sentences, many of which have never been heard before. But we do this within a framework of determinative rules. According to Chomsky, it is because we are bound to use this small number of rules that we can readily understand all the new sentences that people can produce.

One reason that Chomsky has been received so favorably in the social sciences is because this may be a good model for the way in which society works in general. There are an infinite variety of different social institutions and different actions that individuals may take vis-à-vis their fellows. It may be impossible to explain just why this particular combination of institutions or behaviors happens to have occurred at each time. But according to an analogy with Chomsky's generative grammar, all this variety of the social surface is nevertheless produced from a much smaller set of basic procedures or rules. Just how this analogy works out in practice, though, remains to be seen. Some theorists, such as Habermas (1984) and Giddens (1976) have proposed that society is in fact constituted by language (people communicating with each other), so that the rules by which societies are constructed may simply be applications of the properties of language itself.[1] And some of the ethnomethodologists, such as Sacks (1972), have claimed that knowing how to behave socially is really a matter of knowing the meaning of words, for instance the meaning of being a "mother" in relation to a "baby" and so forth. But no one has yet proposed a theoretical system for society which actually specifies a general set of rules like those which Chomsky has given for the English language.

We might say there are two versions of the Chomskyan analogy for society. The "weak form" of analogy says that society has a surface structure and a deep structure which generates it. The surface structure is the empirical details of each society's history; the deep structure would be given by any successful general theory which shows the processes which produce each of those specific forms. In this sense, any general sociological theory is attempting to spell out the deep structure of society.

The "strong form" of the Chomskyan analogy goes much further and claims that Chomsky's theory is not just a general inspiration for what a successful theory might look like, but actually gives us specific guidance in building that theory. In particular, it proposes that language itself is the key to social structure and that some version of transformational grammar itself should give the rules for constructing societies. There are two problems with this strong form of the analogy. One is that Chomsky's own linguistics has run into controversy over the question of how far it may be generalized. Chomsky himself claims that the deep structure of language is universal, in the sense that all languages are built upon certain innate capacities of the human brain. He argues this because of the fact that children learn languages so readily, despite the very great complexity of the system they are acquiring and the limited amount of learning time they have available. Chomsky is aware that languages around the globe differ in many ways from English, but he believes that they all must have the same underlying deep structure, which is merely specified or transformed in particular ways to make up the particular languages (Chinese, Hottentot, Arabic, English, and so on). But this was largely a matter of faith on Chomsky's part (since he did his own work on English); and more recent investigators, notably Comrie (1981) have argued that the deep structures of various languages do in fact have important differences.

Now, if language is supposed to constitute society, the strong analogy to Chomskyan linguistics has a problem. If the deep structure of language really is universal, then there is a problem of explaining why societies are different from each other. Presumably different transformations are applied; but why should these transformations be done in different ways? At a minimum, the theory is drastically incomplete on this point. On the other hand, if Comrie and other critics are right, then different language structures underlie different societies. This is close to a position which Lévi-Strauss (1958/1963) once held, when he claimed a common structural "code" underlies all the different elements of a society—its art, kinship system,

---

[1] These theorists recognize, however, that there are nonlinguistic aspects of society. Habermas wishes to give primacy to "communicative action," but he sees it as undermined in modern societies by "nonlinguistic steering mechanisms," under which he categorizes money and power. I think Habermas has chosen the wrong examples; money and power are both grounded in forms of communication (though they are ones he does not approve of), whereas he neglects the physical substratum of social interaction itself.

mythology, and so on. But Lévi-Strauss never succeeded in showing that such a code existed for each society; and it is notable that he never tried to show that the language was itself an instance of this societywide code. Also there is evidence (Sapir, 1921; Kroeber, 1963) that the type of language does not correspond to the type of society (for example, that complex language structures are often found in simple, tribal structures and simplified languages in complex industrial societies). This may not be conclusive in that these comparisons are made in terms of the surface structure of the grammar rather than by analysis of Chomskyan deep structures, but it suggests that the model of language providing the code for the social structure is probably not true.

There is also another objection to the strong form of the Chomskyan analogy. It is questionable whether language really is the key to social structure. This is a rather idealist position, claiming that mental, communicative actions determine everything else. It is undoubtedly true that human minds and communications are an essential part of society, and that they enable us to build forms of interaction far beyond what any other animals have done. But this is not the same thing as saying that knowledge of language or of mind is enough to explain the forms that societies take. Our view of macrosociologies (see Chapters 4 and 5) has already shown that the sheer physical arrangements of material goods are crucial in determining power, political mobilization, and organizational forms (see Chapters 12 and 13). Material conditions affect the construction of reality, through the use of goods for putting up frontstages and backstages, as well as in the material production and propagation of ideas and symbols themselves. Durkheimian theory proposes that the sheer physical arrangement of human bodies in various degrees of spatial density, along with the propagation of emotions among people focusing their attentions, is crucial for producing not only social solidarity and boundaries versus outsiders, but also shapes the symbols with which people think. We might go so far as to say that language is itself shaped by social interaction. The Chomskyan model may not go deep enough; even its deep structures may turn out to be derivative of still "deeper" sociological situations.

Cicourel (1973) proposed that Chomsky's distinction among levels can be used as an analogy, although Chomsky's own model cannot be taken literally. From the point of view of ethnomethodological research (see Chapter 8), the deep structure is something that the linguist infers from the fact that the surface structure is indexical: what people actually say implies that they have more information than is immediately displayed. Chomsky's transformational rules are only logical devices is the eyes of the observer and do not explain how performance it itself produced. Moreover, the surface level involves meanings, which cannot be ignored as in Chomsky's syntactical model. Cicourel proposed instead that language, or any other situational behavior, has two levels analogous to Chomsky's: (1) *interpretive procedures* are analogous to deep structures, since they constitute the person's sense of what social organization there is. For Cicourel, these deep structures appear to be nonverbal. (2) *surface rules* are analogous to Chomsky's surface structure of language; these are the "normal" forms of behavior and talk that people arrive at in situations. Cicourel stresses that explaining ordinary behavior by "norms" is like taking the surface structure of language utterances as if it somehow produced itself. Instead, ordinary life gives the impression of being consensual or "normative" but only because people have used a deeper structure of procedures to interpret what the situations are and what sorts of behavior will get by as normal in them. The meaning (and not just the "grammar") of specific situations and actions is thus produced by application of "deeper" procedures.

This is a promising perspective, although it remains on the level of very abstract theoretical relationships. Let us see what else in sociological theory can help fill it in.

TOWARD A SOCIOLOGICAL THEORY
OF LANGUAGE

Let us begin by examining Chomsky's model again. Chomsky argues that a sentence is formed by the speaker first choosing the topic, forming the phrases, applying a transformative rule (which turns it into an assertion, question, active or passive, positive or negative, and so on) and finally adding the phonological trimmings so the words are pronounced in acceptable form. (see Figure 9-1). But is this in fact the way talking really happens? For one thing, it is hard to imagine what an initial topic of a sentence might be, apart from the nouns and verbs that express it. (Or apart from some previous flow of conversation, as verbally expressed by a conversational partner or oneself.) Even more importantly, it is hard to believe that the "transformational component" comes near the end. Can we really make up a "neutral" statement, and then later decide whether to affirm it or deny it, assert it or ask it as a question? I would be inclined to say that the transformational component actually happens first: the speaker decides first what kind of utterance to make and then goes to the topic, which is virtually indistinguishable from the phrases in which it is couched. This is all the more likely when we understand that Chomsky's transformations are part of a very important aspect of language called *speech acts*.

Chomsky's generative model seems to be a logical reconstruction, rather than the time-order in which a sentence is really produced. His only proof that speakers start with a topic and end with an utterance is that sentences can formally be taken apart in this way. But most topics make no sense without being "transformed" in Chomsky's sense. Chomsky seems to believe in the existence of thoughts prior to words, but this is a view of the human mind which several modern thinkers, including Wittgenstein, Goffman (and implicitly George Herbert Mead), deny as an unsociological view of mind.

Another way to say this is that the deepest structure of the mind is not the topic or even the phrase structure rules, but what Chomsky called the transformational component. Consider the sentence: "What?" You might utter this in the course of a converstion, when you haven't heard what the other person said. This may be taken as an abbreviation for "What did you say?" or "Say it again, more loudly." Or it could even mean: "That's unbelievable. You don't really mean that?" The central point in these nuances of meaning, though, is that you are questioning the whole previous utterance. The main force of your "What?" is that it is a *question*, rather than a topic which you have incidentally transformed into a question. If it weren't a question, it would be no topic at all.

SPEECH ACT THEORY

This kind of questioning is a good example of a speech act. The theory of speech acts derives from work in the philosophy of language by Ludwig Wittgenstein and John Austin, and it is part of what is more generally known as the "pragmatics" of language. Wittgenstein (1953) was attempting to break down the view of language, held by the logical positivists (a group to which he had previously belonged), that a sentence is either true or false depending on whether it corresponds to a state of facts in the world. Austin (1962) formulated a set of categories for speech acts which are not simply declarative sentences or questions and cannot be evaluated as true or false. He called these "performatives," sentences which do not state something (or ask for information) about the world, but which actually *do* something in their own right. "With this ring I thee wed" or "I hereby name this ship the Queen Mary" or "I bequeath all my worldly goods to my daughter" are not statements which are true or false, but are social actions. They bring about a social state of affairs which did not exist before the words were said. Austin laid down a number of categories of such speech acts, including verdicts, (of judges, umpires, teachers assigning grades, and so forth) exercises of powers to appoint, name, vote, or orders, promises, bets, and other ways of committing oneself.[2]

Austin added two other categories which are of special interest to us. One includes various ceremonal social actions such as greetings, farewells, thanks, applause, curses, toasts. Austin rather infelicitously called this category "behabitives," presumably meaning "relative to social behavior"; Searle (1970) renamed them "expressives." In any case, this is exactly the territory where Erving Goffman has made many of his classic analyses. These speech acts are actually little rituals of everyday life which establish or perpetuate personal relationships through the cult of the self and its ties to other selves. Saying "Hello" is not a sentence that can be produced by Chomsky's generative grammar at all, since Chomsky's system (despite his antagonism to raw empiricism) is in the spirit of traditional positivist philosophy. But saying "Hello" is socially an extremely meaningful statement, as you can tell by failing to say it when it is expected. As Goffman points out, it ratifies a state of friendly relationship between persons and opens the way for friendly or at least polite talk. Again, we see the speech act as primary, setting the stage within which the more expository kind of language may take place.

Austin's final category is "expositives," which bring speech acts onto the home ground of traditional declarative talk. Expositives are statements in which speakers explicitly comment on how they are declaring something. "I repeat that. . . .", "I would argue that. . . .", "I insist. . . .", and "I would conclude that. . . ." are all ways of referring to one's own exposition of something about the world. They make conscious what the speaker is doing in the declarative speech. This is useful sometimes as a "roadmap" to a complex argument one is making made by summarizing

---

[2] Later speech act theorists, such as Searle (1970), divided performatives into "commissives," in which one commits oneself to an action; "directives," trying to get the hearer to carry out an action; and "declaratives," which define institutional reality. Nonperformative statements, such as old-fashioned assertions of a state of affairs, Searle calls "assertives" or "constatatives." Habermas (1984) reorganizes these into still a different classification.

and emphasizing what has gone before or foreshadowing the main points of the argument to come. What is interesting is that expositives are saying explicitly what Chomsky's transformational component builds into the grammar of speech. "I question whether. . . ." and "I deny that. . . ." are the same kind of thing as making a question or a negative sentence. My point is that Chomsky's "transformations" are actually speech acts.

Let us add two emphases. (You might want to be conscious here of how these very sentences are doing various kinds of speech acts.) One is that expositives can be implied rather than explicitly stated, as in Austin's examples just given. Even a simple declarative sentence "The man saw the cat." actually has two messages. There is the message about some state of affairs in the world, involving a man and a cat. But there is also the implicit message: "Listen! I am saying something to you." The latter is the underlying speech act in virtually every kind of speech. It is a social act, which sets up and makes possible the more "surface" level of meaning (about the man seeing the cat).

My second emphasis is that speech acts are more fundamental than topics, phrases, or any other portion of language. The speech act is the deepest structure, and it sets in motion everything else. A truly successful generative grammar in Chomsky's sense would have to start here and derive the rest from it. This is what Goffman's later work was driving toward. Before coming to this, we must examine a related development in sociolinguistics, the conversational analysis carried out by ethnomethodologists.

THE TURN-TAKING MODEL

Some ethnomethodologists have taken Garfinkel's injunction to study the local production on social phenomena as the grounds for a research program on conversation. Using cassette tape recorders, these researchers have made recordings of the way people actually talk in real-life situations. Transcripts of this material shows that talk as it really happens is much messier than in the idealized, hypothetical statements which Chomsky and other formal linguists use for their analyses. People frequently start sentences over in the middle or run sentences together, fail to speak grammatically, slur their words and in other ways fall short of the ideal. Nevertheless, people are generally able to understand one another well enough to keep conversations going and to negotiate some kind of social order. How is this done? One focus has been on the way that people are able to arrange it so that talk takes place in turns, so that one person speaks while the other listens. This implies some mechanism which is more fundamental than what is being said itself; without this mechanism for alloting turns, talking could not take place.

Sacks, Schegloff, and Jefferson (1974) developed a set of rules which talk seems to follow. The main rules are that one person talks at a time; at the end of a turn, the speaker selects the next person to talk, which could be oneself again (self-selecting) or someone else in the group. If it is a two-person conversation, then the choices are narrowed down. What might sound on the surface like a long monologue is actually a series of turns, in which the same speaker keeps selecting himself or herself to have the next turn. One of the less obvious implications of this model is that people must not merely listen to what the other person is saying, but also (or possibly even instead) monitor when a turn is about to come to an end, so that they can get the next turn. In other words, conversationalists are attending to something "beneath the surface," rather than merely trying to catch the meaning of what is being said. In fact, it is less important to do the latter than the former; a conversation can go on smoothly if all participants notice where the turn breaks are and act accordingly even if they don't pay attention to the meaning, whereas conversation will break down if they notice meaning without noticing turns. Because people do this, Sacks et al. are able to show empirically that turns generally go off quite smoothly, usually with less than a second of time in between the moment one person stops talking and another begins. (In fact, the next speaker often starts up an utterance even before the last speaker has come to an end, so there is a very slight moment of overlap.) People do not always catch the meaning in what is being said, but they are very good at picking up their turn to speak: this illustrates that the mechanism of social interaction is deeper than the meanings of utterances.

This is a formal, somewhat idealized model, and variations do occur. Sometimes people get into a struggle over who is going to get the next turn; they interrupt one another or both start talking at the same time. Or a turn may end without anyone taking the next turn; hence an embarrassed pause, a "dead space" in the conversation of 10 seconds or so may result. But these can be seen as derivative phenomena, built around a normal turn-taking mechanism. We can see this because struggles over the turn do not happen just anywhere during a conversation, but at the point at which a turn break is happening, at which several different persons each selects himself to speak next (which may include the last speaker trying to be next speaker, to get two turns in a row) and because long pauses are felt to be embarrassing, not the way talk is implicitly supposed to go. In both cases, the mechanism is there, but something extra happens to keep its results from working out smoothly.[3]

GOFFMAN'S SOCIAL ECOLOGY OF LANGUAGE

In his later writings, Erving Goffman, who pioneered the study of everyday life interaction, turned to criticizing and reformulating the research which had grown up about conversation. He did this particularly in his last book, *Forms of Talk* (1981), as well as in his earlier *Frame Analysis* (1974). Conversational analysis is built around the concepts of *speaker* and *hearer*. These are formal designations for the persons who take turns, as well as make utterances and responses. One such analysis concentrates on *adjacency pairs*. These are statements which break Chomsky's mold, in that they don't make sense when taken as an isolated utterance, but do make sense when both sides of the conversation are put together. A typical adjacency pair would be:

A: "Can I borrow your hose?"
B: "Do you need it this moment?"
A: "No."
B: "Yes."
(Goffman, 1981: 7)

---

[3] There is by now a wide range of studies in what is called "conversation analysis" or "discourse analysis." See Atkinson and Heritage (1984) and van Dijk (1985).

Goffman broadens the social basis of this analysis. Speaking and hearing are not the fundamental units of a conversation, but are products of the more fundamental structure of the situation. For instance, bystanders who are in sight and earshot of a conversation, even though they are not "officially" part of it, nevertheless have an effect on what happens. If there is a bystander, then the person who is speaking will have to take account of whether this is the kind of thing the bystander should be hearing. There are really three parts here: speaker, the addressed recipient, and the unaddressed recipient. Any of these subcombinations of persons can engage in interaction that goes on at another level than what is actually said. There can be "collusion," "byplay," and "crossplay" such as the listeners' raising their eyebrows subtly to indicate they are distancing themself from what the speaker is saying or the way it is being said.

Goffman's point is not just to add some subtleties of nonverbal communication onto the conversational content. His vision is that *conversation always is part of a larger frame of interaction*. Only if the larger frame is properly handled can the conversation take place; and just how that large frame is set will determine what kind of conversation can proceed within it. Most of the time we don't notice this larger frame, because it is routine and can be taken for granted; that is why Goffman is at pains to pick out instances when it is not quite routine, and hence intrudes in the form of "byplay" and the like. But even when there is nothing disruptive about the larger frame, it has to be there to make the conversation possible. (An example would be having the privacy and other situational appropriateness for having a casual chat). Goffman is saying that talk needs to be analyzed "from the outside in," with the larger frame setting the conditions for what can emerge within it.

Now what determines the larger frame, with which the analysis should begin? There are several layers here, which (making more explicit that Goffman refers to only in passing) we can call (1) the physical world, (2) the social ecology and (3) the institutional setting.

(1) Often talk arises or takes on meaning from the relationship of participants to some event or task in the physical world around them. The talk which occurs when individuals are repairing a car ("There." (pointing to the problem); "Hand me that.") or playing cards ("Three spades.") is not understandable at all unless one knows what is being done physically, and often this requires being right there on the spot and looking under the hood of the car from the same angle as the speaker, or looking at one's own cards and listening to what other people have implied about their cards from the way they have bid. This embedding in a *particularized* physical world is an instance of what the ethnomethodologists called "indexicality:" these statements have a meaning only in that context, which is not transferrable or generalizable. Goffman concludes that the basis of language is not a primal intersubjectivity, a meeting of minds, but rather a common focus on a physical scene of action. The anchoring of the mind is outside ourselves, and communication at its most primitive derives from the way several people anchor themselves to the same physical world they are acting in.

As we shall see, this does not mean that Goffman is a "physical reductionist," with a purely external, behaviorist view of talk. Rather, he is saying that mental levels are emergent from this most fundamental, physical frame and they are always anchored to it through one or more transformations. There is a mental level, but it is not a free-floating realm, and it is not the primary reality but a derived one.

(2) We have already seen that Goffman takes as the social basis of any conversational situation the physical bodies of the people who happen to be present, whether they are actually all talking to one another or not (that is, bystanders must be included). This might be called an "ecological" perspective, since Goffman is looking at human beings in the aspect in which they are animals, just as a biologist would look at birds or mammals who are in range of each other. Goffman asserts that people must always pay attention to other human beings in their presence; each one needs to check out the others, if only to see if it is safe to ignore them.

One piece of evidence Goffman brings to make this point is the kind of utterance that he calls "self-talk." These are the outcries, mutterings, and so forth that people utter in the presence of others but without being in conversation with them. For example, it is embarrassing to behave incompetently when there is someone else around. Hence one makes a "ritual repair," implicitly directing it toward the other people around. Suppose you are walking down the sidewalk and suddenly realize you have to go back to get your car keys. The reason you say "Oh, damn!" and shake your head, as you spin on your heel to go back the way you came, is because you are embarrassed in the eyes of other people for your abrupt change of direction. Implicitly, you and everyone else recognize that people take notice of the way others walk; when someone does something that looks "crazy" (like abruptly turning around), it is necessary to give a reason for it. That is what is conveyed by swearing or by the facial expression which says, "What a stupid mistake I've made!" As with apologies in general, this kind of putting blame on oneself actually serves to *raise* one's status as a social interactant, after a temporary fall, because it shows that one recognizes one has made a mistake, and hence distances oneself from the previous self which made the mistake.

The same applies to any other violation of what is the expected, normal flow of public order. Talking to oneself (thinking out loud) and then suddenly discovering there are other people present, calls for just such a ritual repair. It violates the social demand that we should show ourselves as competent and self-controlled persons; hence we need to do something to reestablish ourselves by communicating to the bystanders. This might be referred to as a kind of "ecological order." As Goffman puts it, even "when nothing eventful is occuring, persons in one another's presence are still nonetheless tracking one another and acting so as to make themselves trackable" (1981: 103). We human beings, just as sheer physical bodies, share a certain animal level of interawareness: each is potentially dangerous to another, as well as potentially someone who might be of aid (by calling out a common danger, for instance), and hence we are "primed," perhaps even biologically, to pay attention to how other persons are behaving. Whenever people do something that is abnormal, they set up a flicker of attention among the others around them, because they are giving off a sign that they are not quite under control and may in fact be dangerous. Hence, to reassure others and ward off their possible fear of our "craziness," we communicate little ritual repairs disavowing our mistakes, and thereby making ourselves normal bodies walking down the street, whose behavior can be taken for granted.[4]

---

[4]This process is particularly noticeable in male-female interactions. Here, the primal physical possibility in any situation is sexual attraction or even sexual assault. Hence this potential is always implicitly checked, even if only to establish the "normalcy" of a non-sexual relationship.

Goffman believes that this analysis explains most of the cries and sounds that we make whenever we mess up, ranging from spill cries to threat startles and revulsion sounds. There is a similar social significance in the grunts we make when we are straining muscularly, the cry of pain when something hurts, even moans of sexual pleasure or the audible glee when we are happy. He argues that we make such sounds mainly in the presence of other people and that these sounds are meant to communicate something. Though it might seem that we merely blurt out one of these sounds because we cannot help it—because we are just spontaneously trying too hard, feeling hurt, ecstatic, or the like—Goffman argues that the same analysis applies as in the case of embarrassing situations. We have shown ourselves to be less than completely competent or completely in control; hence we feel the need to utter an expression to other people, to *detach oneself from the responsibility* of being the sort of person who is weak, hurt, or even off in one's own world of pleasure. These sounds are not sheer asocial expressions, but arise following some action which other people will notice. They rectify this privitization by constituting an "invitation into our interiors," not "a flooding of emotion outward, but a flooding of relevance in" (1981: 121).

This is strange conception, since we usually believe that we occupy the primal vantage point of our own private experience, which we then can choose to express outwards to other people. Goffman, however, denies that private experience is primary; the social situation is always the center of the action and of attention.[5] Whenever we have something happen which takes us temporarily out of the social realm (for instance, when we are turned on sexually so that we pay no attention to anyone else) or when we fall short of expected competence (by feeling pain or muscular strain), the return to social awareness always triggers a need to reestablish contact. These expressive cries, grunts, and groans explain to other people why we had taken leave of them. Goffman's theory depends on the empirical pattern that we make such noises mainly in the presence of other people, not when we are alone. But sometimes we also make these noises in solitude. Goffman's argument implies that these solitary instances are derivatives of the social ones, that we can cry by ourselves, or grunt in muscular effort, because we are performing before an imaginary social audience. Presumably, if a person had never been socialized, they would not only be unable to talk: they would also be unable to make these kinds of nonlinguistic expressions.

(3) The institutional setting is a frame which arises inside these two outermost frames: the physical world and the ecological copresence of physical human bodies. We can see the significance of the institutional setting by looking at the limitations of the kinds of conversational analysis which ignores it. The turn-taking model, for instance, only applies to informal conversations, in which the participants themselves must arrange, or negotiate, who gets the sequence of turns. But there are other kinds of interactions, organized by different turn-taking rules. There is the formal lecture, for instance, which not only gives one speaker a certain amount of time to

---

[5] This argument is also shared by Wittgenstein (1953) in his attack on the notion of purely private experiences. See Bloor (1983) who interprets Wittgenstein in a thoroughly sociological way, as congruent with Durkheim. Goffman, too, is following basically a Durkheimian analysis here, especially as Durkheim's theory of rituals deals with the emergent consequences of certain high density, highly focussed microecological patterns.

talk, but also may have a chairperson who calls upon the persons who are allowed to ask questions. There is the theatre or the musical recital, which have their own ways of alloting turns. There are formal rituals, such as a church service or wedding, in which the turns (and frequently what is said in them) are rigidly programmed in advance. There are also situations of hierarchical authority (an army drill, a corporate board meeting, and so forth), in which there is a ranking according to who is allowed to initiate conversation by giving orders, asking for reports, and so on. These institutional frames determine the kind of talk that can take place within them.

A sociological theory should be able to explain why one institutional frame rather than another may be in existence at a given time, and why it has the allocation of turns and other restraints on talk that it does. Cicourel (1986) shows that in a medical organization, for example, every situation includes a bureaucratic frame, which implicitly involves the kinds of activities elsewhere in the organization that are being anticipated and coordinated, as well as whatever is immediately going on. Notice that a free, casual conversation does not escape the institutional model but is itself constituted by certain institutional conditions: namely there must be a situation which is *away from* the more formal types; there are certain arrangements that call for informal talk—such as being invited to a party; there may also be prior sociable relationships among the persons involved, as when talk is called for when running into an acquaintance on the street. These institutional frames have further levels of complexity within them, which Goffman explicates via his discussion of "frame space" or "footing."

FOOTINGS

Goffman proposes to replace both the turn-taking model and the speech act theory by a more deeply sociological approach. The constraints on how one speaks and replies are not in the formalities of language, but in the realm of social relationships, in how one must display one's self with respect to others. Instead of turns, talk is organized into "moves," which may take a good deal more, or less, than a full turn as speaker. Austin and Searle's speech acts are in the right direction, but their essence is not captured by analyzing single utterances for their illocutionary force. These are only particular kinds of moves in a social situation. To make a command, a performative (like christening a baby) may take much more than one utterance or turn at speaking, and the speech act is not really finished until the move is over. Alternatively, one might take several speech acts within the same utterance, packing one's "turn" with several different moves.

This helps explain, incidentally, a point which is mysterious in turn-taking theory. Exactly how long is a turn? The turn-taking model dealt with this after the fact, by assuming it was however long it turned out to be in that instance, when someone gave up the floor or grabbed it again. Goffman's model goes deeper, because it tells us that a turn comes "up" for reassignment at the point at which one of these moves is completed. This seems to contradict Goffman's point that moves can take several turns to accomplish. The implication is that there are different levels of moves, so that there can be moves within moves. Some particular range of moves is what constitutes the length of turns.

Goffman in effect makes turns derivative of speech acts, and both are derivative of social moves. Social action, in short, is more basic than talk. Speech is embedded in ritual, and one moves through talk by displaying a self to others. Goffman's late works are continuous with his early model in *The Presentation of Self in Everyday Life* (1959). Though his terminology has changed (frames, frame space, instead of frontstages and backstages; footings instead of presentation of self), his later arguments are more sophisticated elaborations of his earlier ones. There are two main components: self and stage. We will take stage first, since self depends on it.

STAGES AND FRAME SPACE   Any situation, as it has become organized through social moves up to that point in time, constitutes a frame, a socially defined reality (which itself is a transformation of some prior or more basic reality). Take, for instance, a public lecture, which Goffman once analyzed before a packed auditorium while giving a lecture. In the lecture, there are "multiple selves in which the self of the speaker can appear" (1981: 173). There is the self as enunciating its own current beliefs or desires; but also there is the self as a figure within the talk; and the self as animator—the self who delivers a performance in the situation (the lecturer as lecturer). It is clear that the animator is not the same person as the self as enunciator, when someone reads someone else's lecture; but that is only a reminder, because even when you are reading your own lecture, it is one self that is the reader, and another self whose voice is making a statement. The lecturer as lecturer has certain staging requirements to worry about: speaking loudly enough, making sure the microphone doesn't tip over, and so forth, while the enunciator is simply involved in making certain points. These roles are embedded in each other, and one can distance oneself from various of them, as well as inadvertently break frame (for instance, when one stops lecturing to say "I'm running out of time so I'll skip the next page"). Skillful lecturers keep up interest and make their talk charming by playing on the ironies of using one role against another; clumsy lecturers botch the transitions and the whole performance fails to grip the audience's attention to the reality that is being constructed.

Audiences, however, do not need total deception. They are usually aware of mundane physical contingencies, in case there is a fire in the theater, for instance. And primal social monitoring always goes on concerning the solidarity or hostility of the human animals around them. Humans have the capacity (which is perhaps their distinctive humanness) to be aware of transformations and emergent levels of reality, and even to enjoy multi-level alternations. An important theoretical point emerges by examining the conditions when these alternations feel clumsy and distracting: perhaps it is losing rhythm between audience and speaker, the crucial ingredient in maintaining any social ritual. Goffman thus seems to be showing what is meant by the key feature of "focus" in interaction ritual theory.

Goffman (1981) elaborates this analysis by examing the errors made by radio announcers who often become inadvertently hilarious by the way they break frame to apologize for a mispronunciation or *double entendre,* and then make the situation worse by still further frame breaks they get into by trying to correct their previous breaks. Goffman is not merely describing radio shows or analyzing the source of humor. His theoretical point is that frames build on previous frames, so that even errors do not so much destroy the social situation as give rise to a new situation, a transformation of the old one. The complexity of reality (and of talk) comes from this "emergent" quality. Further, the radio announcer illustrates a "frame space" which is tightly prescribed, so that errors in it are both highly visible and create a lot of anxiety when they occur. The comparison between this extremely "staged" situation and the informality of everyday conversation, highlights just in what that "informality" consists: the freedom of frame space in which we ordinarily move. Friendly talk allows for a maximal amount of reflexive frame breaking.

Goffman is telling us more precisely what the difference is between frontstages and backstages in his earlier model. That is, formal situations (or frames) are ones in which the structure is very consciously and deliberately manipulated to have a certain effect by performers on an audience. All the words to be said may be tightly scripted (as in a radio show or a wedding ceremony), but that is not crucial (since ad libbing may also be scripted in). More fundamentally, there is a preplanned set of slots in which certain speech acts are supposed to take place: an announcement, an introduction, a sermon, a joke, or so forth. The more formal the situation, the more the performer tries to hide any notion of the performance process itself, so that attention will be concentrated only on what is on the stage. This is, so to speak, the most intense state of a Durkheimian ritual, in which only the sacred object produced by the ritual commands the audience's attention, and the fact that it is a ritual is forgotten. Such "extreme frontstages" are hence most vulnerable to embarrassment by frame breaking.

From here, we can go down through a continuum of increasing informality, allowing for more collusion between performer and audience in putting over the performance, and hence more tolerance for frame breaks. At the other end are personal conversations, in which both participants more or less interchangably take the stage, as well as sympathetically participate in what the other person is trying to put on. For this reason, informal talk does not have to maintain much "successful" structure, and its talk can be full of interruptions, mis-speakings, or speech acts which change course in mid-stream or don't come off. Such is the "backstage," which we can now see does not only consist of performers' shop talk about the more formal performances they have put over on other people or that they have witnessed (and perhaps wanted to puncture) as audiences. This does not mean that friendly talkers are exempt from problems of framing/staging. It still remains necessary to dramatize one's point of view in order to get it across and to perform ritual repairings when things go wrong. It is just that informality consists of mixing together the performer and audience so thoroughly that neither has many secrets from the other—that is, secrets in the problems of performing (whatever information about other things they may be hiding from the other). There can be plenty of performance failures here: in fact, the sharing of such failures as they actually transpire is what makes up the "informality" of the talk, and the sense of ease and intimacy of selves that goes with it.

Goffman argues (1981: 240) that "frame space" is a more precise referent for what older sociological theory called "norms." Social constraints are not encoded in the form of verbal prescriptions, but of something deeper. These are not rules that people have learned to carry around in their heads, but are ways in which situations unfold, so that participants feel they have to behave a certain way or make amends for not doing so. The frames are the constraints, and even when they are broken, the situation that then emerges remains constraining in a predictably transformed way. Similarly, Goffman (1981: 321) sees "role" as an imprecise concept; on finer examination, it (for instance, the role of the lecturer or of the radio announcer) really consists of multiple voices and a way in which changes in footing are managed.

SELF AS CONVERSATIONAL MOTIVATOR   We have already seen (Chapter 7) that Goffman regards the idea of a unitary self as a myth. Nevertheless, something analogous to this is involved as a motivational principle to account for the way people move through frame spaces. Goffman states this as it applies to talk, beginning with a criticism of Chomsky for assuming there is only a single, verbal deep structure:

> The underlying framework of talk production is less a matter of phrase repertoire [that is, Chomsky's categories] than frame space. A speaker's budget of standard utterances can be divided into function classes, each class providing expressions through which he can exhibit an alignment he takes to the events at hand, a footing, a combination of production format and participation status. What the speaker is engaged in doing, then, moment to moment through the course of the discourse in which he finds himself, is to meet whatever occurs by sustaining or changing footing. And by and large, it seems he selects that footing which provides him the least self-threatening position in the circumstances, or, differently phrased, the most defensible alignment he can muster. (Goffman, 1981: 325–26)

The "self" that selects the "least self-threatening position" or "footing" in the interaction as it unfolds is the core motivational unit. It is a thread through all the various selves that are enacted, which can be exalted or threatened by the way the performances are carried off. But the content of this self probably cannot be discovered. Since all these interactional frames are a series of embeddings upon the primal reality of living creatures in the physical world, we could argue that the underlying "self" is simply the awareness residing in one's physical body, as one tries to deal with the other physical bodies around one. But this, in turn, spins off many levels of self-presentation, performative exigencies, frame breaks, transformations, and so forth, which split off the stances of many "selves," most of them quite temporary. The underlying, motivating "self" has no enduring description, but is simply the human capacity for negotiating all these performances and transformations.

SUDNOW'S EMBODIED TALK

Goffman's implicit idea that the body is the center of the organization of talk is supported by an unusual analysis by David Sudnow called *Talk's Body* (1979). Sudnow, a former student of Goffman as well as an ethnomethodological follower of Harold Garfinkel, had provided a subjective phenomenology of the experience of learning to play the jazz piano (Sudnow, 1978). Music is a form of communication, and it even has written "instructions" (notes) and verbal explanations (from a piano teacher). Nevertheless, the musician only uses these as an introduction into the world of music; to actually become a performer, and especially in the free-form of jazz improvisation, these crutches have to be thrown behind, and the musician has to plunge into the playing in a way that has no verbal referent. Sudnow called his book on jazz playing *Ways of the Hand,* because he felt, when he became proficient, that his hands knew what sounds they were producing, and that his mind simply had to watch them. In fact, it was only when his hands could play jazz "on their own," without having to be mentally coached, that the music came out well at all.

In *Talk's Body,* Sudnow showed there is a close analogy between talking and playing improvised music. He began by reflecting on the similarities between playing on a piano keyboard and typing on a typewriter keyboard as he was writing his book about jazz piano. In typing, too, the hands "know where to go" without the mediation of a set of verbal instructions on where to put the fingers. The same holds, Sudnow argues, for speaking. Speaking is embodied, rather than primarily mental. He describes the thoughts that sometimes may precede verbal communication as "like rubbing the hands and stretching the fingers as you approach the bandstand and ready yourself to play . . . it literally *feels* as though there is much to say. . . . As I come to the typewriter this morning, my interior monologue buzzes with the sounds of my topic, like an orchestra tuning up, even chaotic in the multitude of noise. I must choose a mode of expression, a style of making movements, so that my arrangement of places might become part of yours as we come to think 'thoughts' together" (Sudnow, 1979: 58).

Language is not basically a set of nouns, adverbs, prepositions, and other formal parts of speech. These are merely the ways that we intellectually analyze speech. We use them to learn a foreign language; but that is why it is so hard to actually speak a language when we are suddenly abroad after spending months in the artificial atmosphere of a classroom. To speak, we need to throw our self into the talking, this Meadian language of gestures, in just the same way that the jazz pianist throws himself into the music to be produced. Meaning, in both cases, emerges as we go along. Sudnow describes both cases as a matter of getting into the flow of a rhythm.[6] Because this rhythm can be shared, other people can listen and understand. Listeners succeed when they are able to get into the same pacing as the speaker, anticipate where the talk is going. "A way of listening is a way of using the body to take hold of a course of movements . . . what we need for an approach to intersubjectivity is an embodied description of the course of gestures instead of a cognitive attack on the program of minds" (1979: 83). Sudnow is elaborating a version of Mead but without Mead's emphasis on nouns as the principle form of shared symbol. Instead, Sudnow points to the *process* of coordinating these physical gestures we make with our mouths and the rest of our bodies. "Describing my experiences at typewriter and piano, I find no good use for an analytical conception of 'the thought,' for from the standpoint of *doing* sounding movements or those versions of sounding movements we call 'thinking' or 'singing to oneself,' there is only process—thinking, not thoughts; melodying, not melodies" (1979: 57).

Like Goffman, Sudnow shows us a bodily self, fluidly moving through social situations, including above all the situations of speaking. The two analyses are com-

---

[6] It is because of these shared rhythms that turn-taking is well-coordinated: "I say: 'I'll talk to you *la*-ter,' and as I especially delineate the pacing of '*la*-ter' with a precisely accented undulation, you tightly latch on to the pulsing of my moves and place your 'Goodbye' on the next downbeat to end the phone call" (Sudnow, 1979: 114).

plimentary. Goffman stresses the multiple levels of transformations that can be built, but always upon a core of the physical co-presence of human animals in a place; Sudnow stresses that these human animals are engaged in action and in fitting rhythms together. This reinforces the interaction ritual model; in Chapter 6, we saw that there is evidence for the coordination of emotional rhythms among interactants. Durkheim's emotional contagion, a crucial ingredient in producing ritual states of solidarity, is further specified as a rhythmic phenomenon; the collective symbols which result are Sudnow's shared meanings. Sudnow adds the emphasis that these "meanings" do not have to refer to objects, nor to preexisting thoughts, but instead emerge in the interaction itself. For that reason, they are well suited to "symbolize," in the Durkheimian sense, membership in the group of interactants more than anything else. Sudnow, like Goffman, has given more evidence for the primacy of the social.

CHILDHOOD LEARNING OF SPEECH

Sudnow and Goffman converge also on the issue of how language is initially learned. Goffman (1981: 151) notes that sociological theory has not yet explained how a child is "socialized" into acquiring a self. Presumably it is done through language (see Wanner and Gleitman, 1982; Corsaro, 1985). But adults talk to small babies in a complex, not a simple way: they imitate a babyish tone of voice and speak *for* the child, not to it ("Does baby want a nice teddy bear?"). This is a fairly elaborate embedding of social roles. Hence it is clear that the child is not simply following Mead's process of acquiring a "me" and a "Generalized Other," but a process of learning how to decode and perform embeddings. Baby talk may involve a simplified grammar and vocabulary, but "its laminative features," Goffman asserts, "are anything but childlike" (1981: 151).

Sudnow (1979: 81) similarly emphasizes the way that adults bring the child into their own ritual *activity:*

> The parent listens to his child's attempt to assemble a correct greeting to the aunt who has just arrived for a visit. But adults attend not so much what the child says as the fact that the child is coming to speak competently now, and we have a meeting pleasantly opened with a coached ritual performance. Both parent and aunt watch the child now stammeringly and now smoothly putting together a more or less passable greeting. They watch the child form up the mouth, forming up theirs in sympathetic appreciation, following the course of the child's pacing-and-placing gestures, leaning forward into the gestures, taking the movements by the hand and stumbling rather than dancing with them as they come out. This is 'listening so as almost to aid the production.' It is one form of intersubjectivity, one way to fit yourself into another's actions. (1979: 81–82)

Language learning is like music learning: getting into the right rhythm so that social interaction can be carried off together.

Goffman argues that the child psychologists Piaget and Vygotsky have an unsophisticated notion of what is involved in *egocentricity* (1981: 95): the alleged stage in which the child can see the world only from his or her own perspective, without taking account of the viewpoint of others. This would have to be reformulated in terms of the interactive self-audience relations which Goffman shows are fundamental in all social relationships. Becoming socialized as a human being, including learning to speak, may be largely a process of learning how to do framing and of fitting one's framed activities together with others.

TOWARD A GENERAL THEORY OF LANGUAGE

We have reviewed various elements of a theory of language. Chomsky alone provides a systematic model, although we have seen its shortcomings from the point of view of speech act theory, ethnomethodology, Goffman's social ecology, and Sudnow's embodied speech. Can a formal theory of language, comparable to Chomsky's, be built up from sociological elements?

There is reason to think that it can. Goffman in particular converges with parts of Chomsky, corrects him in others. Social action is creative and emergent, just as language is for Chomsky. It can produce infinite varieties, many of which are totally new but which people can deal with almost routinely nevertheless. However, Chomsky regards this as mysterious, this creativeness and ability to recognize and produce language forms that the individual has never heard before; hence he falls back on the "Platonic" postulate of innate language structures in the brain. For Goffman, Sudnow, and other sociologists, language is not innate in the brain, because it is not fundamentally the expression of individual experiences outwards, but an originally social, external form of action, which can sometimes be turned inwards. It is a series of emergent structures, each building upon and making reference to those "beneath" and temporally prior to them. Because human beings are capable of this kind of reflexive building upon prior interactions, they can generate new levels of social reality, one form of which is speech.[7]

Chomsky's model of the sequencing involved in putting together a sentence might be reformulated something like this (compare Figure 9-1). First comes monitoring of the social situation; it may be spoken or unspoken, but always involves some physical relationship among the persons who might communicate (even if they are at a distance). The social situation, in turn, may make other aspects of the physical setting especially salient: as objects or grounds for tasks, action, or observation. Thus at any point in verbal interaction, the appropriate move or speech action may be simply to point, touch, or otherwise refer to some part of the physical environment. (In a more reflexive mode, these gestures oriented toward the physical world are transformed into nouns and units in constative speech acts; but the more primitive move does not require the formalization of a noun or a grammatical assertion. Chomsky's noun phrase, then, is itself a speech act, simultaneously calling attention to an object pointed at, and to the person assertively doing the pointing.)

---

[7] Ontogenetically, the individual learns language by being born into a flow of social actions, from which the "meaning" of verbal gestures emerges. This in turn provides a base from which further meanings may be learned or created. Historically, too, we might propose that languages gradually built up by accretion from prior, more primitive speech actions, the later words taking their meaning by their reflexive reference back to ones already socially established. See Gillian Sankoff (1980) for a model of language as emergent in this sense.

Social actions always take place in time; they are a chain of events.[8] The social relationship at any particular instant determines what speech acts are appropriate at that time. This local time context also provides topics, insofar as something may be in the course of being talked about (or it may have been talked about in the past between these persons): both of these are instances of the flow of *cultural capital,* which happens not only over longer periods of time but within the second-by-second movement of speaking and listening. Another source of topic can come from outside the words of the conversation, in that one can talk about the immediate situation, or even comment on the talk itself or on the social relationship. (The speech acts which are felt to be appropriate are made so by what I have glossed in Chapter 10 as "emotional energy.") The speech act force is controlling, in the sense that it selects what topics to follow up or when to begin a new topic.

Chomsky's model then reduces to a special case, where a verbal topic is already in flow. The previous speaker has said something, for instance: "I saw Tom yesterday." Tom becomes a topic that they will converse about, if there is a particular kind of social relationship here: if the two speakers are part of a group of mutual friends, if it is not embarrassing to their relationship to talk about him (for instance, if one of them has not just broken up with Tom), if speaker and hearer are motivated to keep up a certain level of intimacy between themselves, and so on. Depending on these social conditions, a speech act will be engendered, which might come out in the form of a question: "Oh, how is Tom?" or "What did he say?" The speech act both selects the topic and puts it in a particular form (in this case, a *leading question* inviting the first speaker to go ahead and talk some more about it). A different social relationship would produce a different speech act, such as "I don't want to hear about it," or "Oh, I've got to go to the grocery store before it closes."

In comparison to Chomsky's disembodied model of talk, one should note that the topic is not inside the speaker's head and then pops out in words; rather, certain words in the social interaction (that is, *outside*) lead to a continuation or disruption of the topic. The "transformative component" is also social, and it determines whether this external, on-going topic is to be made a further topic or not. Presumably this then sets in motion something like the process Chomsky describes of casting it into appropriate phrases. But contrary to Chomsky's logical dissection of the sentence, the "transformations" of making it an assertion, denial, question, and so forth are actually chosen before the phrasing. (Though the phrasing may be lying ready at hand in what the previous person had said, as in the case of adjacency pairs.) To ask a question, for instance, depends on the mutual orientation of persons to a topic or task; the social right and motivation of one person to interrogate the other; a boss asking for a report; a subordinate asking for advice; in informal discussion; a social relationship of sufficient intimacy allowing rights of curiousity or of sufficient respect to have rights to ask for repairs; the power and motive to interrupt the other; the motivation to act the part of a good audience by expressing interest; and so forth.

---

[8] The interaction ritual chain model given in Chapter 10 puts this process in a larger social context. Goffman's microanalysis of moves made by transient selves through emergent frame spaces fills in the fine-grained detail of what takes place in any particular interaction.

The social structure of situations is crucial for determining the speech acts within them, and hence for triggering the rest of the speech production. Three major types of talk situation are important:

1. *Work or practical situations.* Here reference to the physical world is often central, sometimes in cursory and abrupt form (Wittgenstein's [1953: 8–9] construction workers calling "Slab!"). The structure of task action, and social relationships of authority and cooperation among participants dominate the selection of topic and speech act.

2. *Formal ceremonies.* Here there is an explicitly enforced focus on the speech acts themselves, as indications (or creators) of particular social relationships. Examples of ceremonies and corresponding relationships range from weddings, christenings, church services, and inaugurations, to minor greeting and departure rituals. Performative speech acts are constituted by such ritual situations: we might say that performatives are especially Durkheimian forms of speech. Ceremonial talk is Goffmanian territory as well; it involves extra transformative rules, including both explicit announcements of how the ceremony is to be carried off, as well as metacommunications about the staging as it is in process.[9]

3. *Conversation.* This is talk for its own sake, which is to say, talk as expression and medium of personal relationships. This is the most free-form type of talk, with the greatest flexibility of frame space. Here talk is most fully guided by the components of the interaction ritual chain: the flows of emotional energy coming from the market attractions among talkers to sustain a particular level of social intimacy, and the cultural capitals of the speakers.

We might envision a formal model of speech, analogous to Chomsky's transformational model, as a set of rules programmed into a computer. This is the aim of artificial intelligence, except that in this case, the program is not an unrealistic "expert system," but an actual model of the human being. It would take the form of something like Figure 9-2 (compare this to Figure 9-1). The model is schematic, and would have to filled in with many subroutines for the details of each portion of action.

In words, the model may be summarized as follows:

1. Monitor persons present as human animals: are they threatening or friendly? If normal, proceed to (2); if threatening, proceed to monitor for ritual repairs; if repairs are not forthcoming, take defensive action or withdraw. If undecidable, continue monitoring. There is also a self-observation loop, not included in the diagram, by which the actor examines his or her own behavior from the point of view of others present and initiates Goffmanian ritual repairs when any actions are judged abnormal in others' eyes. (1) is always in operation, and overrides all other actions if the situation becomes nonnormal.

---

[9]This part of the typology bears an analogy to Habermas' (1984) category of speech actions as "regulatives." However, Habermas goes no further than to interpret these as speech controlled by social norms. Habermas makes culture the ultimate determinate of social action, whereas the model proposed here shows how culture and feelings of propriety are themselves generated by the interaction ritual chain. Habermas, in other words, does not penetrate beneath the level of ideology to what produces it.

FIGURE 9-2

SCHEMATIC COMPUTER SIMULATION OF CONVERSATION

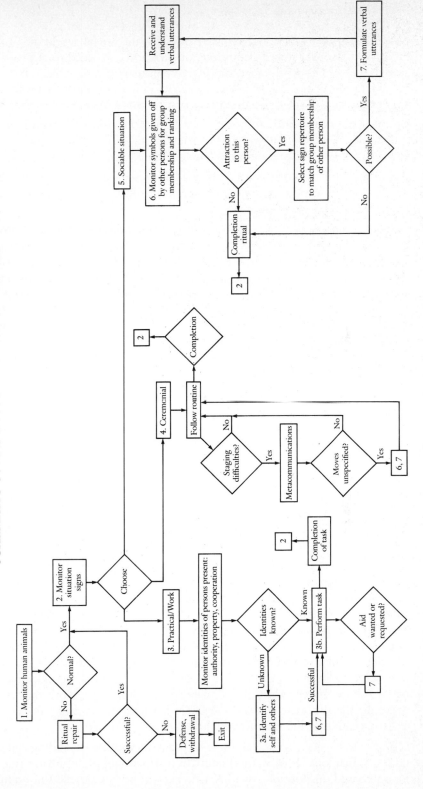

2. Monitor current situational signs in physical and social world and match with store of previously stored definitions of situations. Proceed to appropriate situational action: (3) work/practical; (4) ceremonial; (5) sociable. Like (1), (2) is always tacitly in operation and can override any on-going situation, that is, if a higher priority problem occurs in (1) or (2), the actor reverts to that level.

3. Monitor physical world, authority, and task cooperation relationships, matching with generalized definitions and particular identities of persons. If particular identities of persons present are lacking, initiate (3a). Otherwise proceed to (3b).

   3a. Search for authority/cooperation identities of persons present. Proceed to self-identification and membership-establishing loops as necessary (6) and (7). On completion proceed to (3b).

   3b. Perform practical task action. Initiate/respond to work talk in flow of task. Draw upon subroutines for referring to physical objects/actions, and for formulating socially meaningful utterances (7). On completion of task, return to (2). [Note that all situational types (3–5) draw upon the generalized interactional and talking routines (6–7), except that task-oriented talk can skip the social monitoring level (6) and proceed directly to speech acts (7). That is because practical action per se can draw directly on the immediate physical environment and physical action toward it; this also results in Wittgensteinian short-circuiting of the "Chomskyian" level of speech production itself.]

4. Follow prelearned ceremonial routine. Where ad libbing is called for within the ceremony (that is, specific moves are left unspecified), go to (6) and (7). If staging difficulties emerge, repair with metacommunications about on-going moves, using (7). [This calls for monitoring emergent levels of Goffmanian frame space.] On completion return to (2).

5. Engage in conversation on topics set by one's own attraction toward social membership in status level indicated by other persons present (using 6), and drawing upon (7) to formulate utterances. Conversation is completed when cultural capital and motivational energy for that situation is exhausted; return to (2). [See model of interactional markets in Chapter 10 for further detail.]

6. Monitor the symbols (verbal and nonverbal) presented by other persons for what group memberships they connote, the ranking of those groups, and the power of the interactant implied in their connections to enforcement coalitions. Select verbal symbols from one's own repertoire of cultural capital which represent membership in the highest ranking group one can make claim to, according to one's current level of emotional energy (stored from previous rounds of membership and dominance/subordination encounters). If the repertoire of signs in one's cultural capital is inadequate to carry out verbal interaction, give deference or withdraw. If repertoire is adequate, proceed to (7). [Note that (6) and (7) make up the slot in which the Durkheimian interaction ritual model (Figure 6-1) is operating in the interaction.]

7. Monitor last speech act/social move of previous speaker (including self) for turn-taking transitions. Follow modified Chomskyian rules for putting together sentences, based on flow of previous sentences of self or others. On completion of

speech act (which may be a sentence), recycle (6) as necessary and (7). Completion occurs as specified in (3), (4), or (5), or when overridden by new problems in (1) or (2).

SUMMARY

1. French structuralism analyzes society as a language or system of signs, which take their meaning from their relations with each other, especially as a set of distinctions or oppositions.

2. Lévi-Strauss searched for ahistorical synchronic structures out of which the varying historical surface of societies are generated. He proposed that the underlying code consisted of binary oppositions. Later practitioners of *semiotics* and *deconstructionism* argued for a multi-level theory of signs, and have regarded the world itself as an endlessly analyzable text.

3. Chomsky's generative grammar proposes a *deep structure* of underlying strings and transformation rules, by which the innumerable set of sentences in the *surface structure* of a language are produced. This model has inspired theories, such as those of Giddens and Habermas, in which society is generated by linguistic rules. Other theorists, such as Cicourel, take deep structure and surface structure as an analogy for constructing a theory of situational interpretations and behaviors.

4. *Speech act theory* points out that utterances do more than convey information; they also perform actions and express social relationships. Speech acts are at a deeper level than Chomsky's deep structures of language.

5. Ethnomethodological researchers developed the detailed examination of conversation in everyday life, and formulated underlying principles such as the turn-taking model by which conversationalists tacitly control the order in which they speak. People are usually better at attending to the turn-taking mechanism than to the actual contents of what they are saying to each other.

6. Goffman proposes that conversation is possible only because it arises within a surrounding frame of interaction. (1) The most basic frame is the particular physical world that is the site of practical activity. (2) Within this, human bodies tacitly monitor each other's animal presence to maintain a sense of safe normalcy. Most of human expressive activity is oriented toward presenting oneself as a normal social interactant on this level. (3) More elaborate social institutional frames are built up reflexively when the more fundamental levels can be taken for granted.

7. For Goffman, speech is embedded in ritualized moves by which an individual displays a defensible self to others. Complex frames, built up from previous settings, can generate a multitude of situational selves; some are more formal, others allow informal or intimate interplay in which performance problems are shared with the audience.

8. Sudnow argues that talking is fundamentally a bodily activity, in which humans attempt to fit together a common rhythm.

9. A general theory of verbal interaction proposes that each person goes through a sequence of monitoring successive levels of physical and social reality (as in Goffman's frames), which provide the context for what is said. This may be represented schematically in a computer simulation.

Chapter 10

SOCIAL EXCHANGE AND RELATED THEORIES

HOMANS: BASIC PRINCIPLES OF EXCHANGE THEORY

EXCHANGE THEORY AND POWER: BLAU AND EMERSON
    Exchange Theory of Power
    Criticisms

FROM SOCIAL BEHAVIORISM TO RATIONAL CHOICE
    Homans' Behaviorist Propositions
    Rational Choice
    Assessments

INTERACTION RITUAL CHAINS
    Interactions Are Durkheimian Rituals
    Market Opportunity, Cultural Capital, and Emotional Energy
    Encounters Change or Reinforce Individual Resources
    Interaction Ritual Chains and Exchange Theory

HEISE'S AFFECT CONTROL CHAINS
    Criticisms and Extensions

SUMMARY

Exchange theory has one of the clearest lineages of cumulative development of any line of theory in sociology. It is generally acknowledged to have been formulated by George Homans and developed by Peter Blau, with subsequent refinements by Richard Emerson and others. An elaborate program of empirical researches has been carried out developing such aspects of the theory as "distributive justice" and "power-dependency." This theory and research has sometimes been criticized for the narrowness of its assumptions and its area of application. But it has been and remains a theory with grand ambitions to apply to all aspects of sociology. We will assess these claims and accomplishments in this chapter.

However, there are several complications concerning terminology. "Exchange theory" was in fact practiced before the name existed. Its main area of application had been in studies of courtship and marriage, notably by Willard Waller (1937), who formulated the concept of a "marriage market" and some principles of relative attraction in love relationships. Later research linked the power of husbands and wives to their relative economic and other resources. This research on love and marriage has been explicitly incorporated by the exchange theorists. Parallel to marriage markets, personal relationships have been both analyzed as bargaining on "friendship markets," by exchange theorists such as Blau (1964), and incorporated into conflict theory as well (Collins, 1975; 1981a). Thus it is possible for exchange theory to overlap with conflict theory; however, other aspects of exchange theory, especially in Blau's discussion of norms and power, converges with functionalism.

Another complication is that there are two very different traditions of exchange theory (see Ekeh, 1975). The term is conventionally used for the Homans-Blau-et al. lineage, which consists almost entirely of American social scientists. There is also another lineage, developed largely in France and by anthropologists, which produces a theory of social structure as exchange. This lineage is older than the American lineage, going back to Marcel Mauss' study of *The Gift* (1925), and used in Claude Lévi-Strauss' (1949) theory of tribal kinship structures as different arrangements of the exchange of women (also sometimes called "alliance theory," since it stresses the political nature of such alliances). The two versions of exchange theory are conceptually quite different: Mauss and Lévi-Strauss come from the Durkheimian tradition (Chapter 6) and argue for the symbolic nature of exchange, while Homans and Blau connect themselves with the positivist traditions of behaviorist psychology and economics and make exchange eminently rational. We have here a clash between two opposing traditions: the Durkheimians, as we have seen, maintain that utilitarian exchange is a surface phenomenon which cannot take place with ritual-symbolic solidarity; Homans and Blau operate on precisely the level of utilitarian calculation which the Durkheimians criticize. I will refer to the French tradition as "structuralist exchange theory," and reserve consideration of it until Chapter 12.

This family of theories also differs over the issue of what kind of psychological mechanism exists at the basis of exchange, and how much emphasis should be placed on the individual level. Homans and some of his followers are strict behaviorists, attempting to reduce everything to individual behavior without referring to subjective, mental states. Blau has been less concerned with psychological mechanisms and placed his attention on the macro process of exchange itself. More recently, the term "rational choice theory" has begun to creep in as an alternative to exchange theory. Instead of Homans' behaviorism, proponents of this position regard exchange as a process of rational assessment of rewards and costs by human beings who make conscious calculations. Still other relatives of exchange theory are models which reject both behaviorism and conscious calculation as the basic motivating process of human beings. Instead, exchanges are guided by emotional processes and symbols which individuals pass around in conversations (which we might call "conversational markets"). This leads us to the theory of interaction ritual chains formulated by Collins and to Heise's affect control theory.

HOMANS: BASIC PRINCIPLES OF EXCHANGE THEORY

Unlike most other areas of sociological theory, exchange theory developed initially from the empirical side more than from the theoretical side. Blau is a well-known researcher in the area of organizations and related fields. Homans worked in organizational research too, though his best-known study is in the distant field of medieval English history (Homans, 1941). Homans developed his theory, not so much from his own research, as from an effort to synthesize and draw out the underlying principles from the variety of sociological and anthropological studies done early in the twentieth century. This might be called the "first wave" of empirical social science: starting after World War I, anthropologists like Bronislaw Malinowski, Arthur Radcliffe-Brown, and Raymond Firth were bringing back detailed field reports on behavior in tribal societies. Industrial sociologists had invaded the factories to observe the behavior of workers, while other sociologists (including an ex-anthropologist, W. Lloyd Warner) were studying the status system of American communities.

Homans inducted his theory from these materials. That is not to say he simply "let the facts speak for themselves," for facts never say anything until approached with a question in mind. Homans himself, in writing about his methods (1967), is quite clear on the point that theory is only somewhat loosely coupled with empirical evidence. He approached the anthropological and sociological researches available to him in the 1930s and 1940s with an interest in theory derived from reading Pareto; and later he was goaded into making his own theory more comprehensive after being challenged by Parsons' conceptual scheme, which Homans felt was definitely the *wrong* way to go about building a theory (see Homans' very revealing autobiography, 1984: 91–166, 321–31). But being interested in building a theory is not the same thing as being constrained to see in the data only what one already has in mind. It is equally clear that Homans (and as we shall see, Blau) was very impressed with certain patterns in the data he first looked at and that he made these the basis of his subsequent theoretical generalizations. Induction in this sense certainly has a value: it enables one to find theoretical principles that one didn't already know. On the other hand, being overly impressed with a particular type of research finding may limit one's later vision; this also turns out to be a problem with both Homans and Blau.

In Homans' case, the research which seems to have provided his starting place was the famous "Mayo studies," carried out under the direction of the industrial psychologist Elton Mayo at the Hawthorne electric equipment plant in the 1920s and 1930s. The Mayo studies were a breakthrough in several respects. They discovered the "informal group," the personal connections among workers which underlies the formal structure of the organization. The informal group has its own leaders and its own standards of behavior, which often go counter to those of the formal organization. In particular, workers set their own informal rate of work, independently of how hard the managers wish them to produce, and control one another to conform to the informal rate. This discovery gave rise to the so-called "human relations school" of management, which placed emphasis on gaining the workers' confidence informally in order to improve production. For a while it was believed there is a "Hawthorne effect," that is, workers improved their production just because the staff (or Mayo's research group itself) was paying attention to them as persons. It turns out that the "Hawthorne effect" is inaccurate, or at least does not happen very often (Carey, 1967). Informal groups turn out to be hard for outsiders to manipulate, especially against their own economic interests. But the inner structure of informal groups does certainly exist, as the Mayo researchers found them, and on this aspect Homans built his theory.

To explain such patterns, Homans (1950) offered a series of propositions. First: *the more that people interact, the more that they will like each other*. And vice versa: *the more that people like each other, the more they will interact*. Second: *the more that people interact, the more their sentiments and actions become alike*. In other words, they build up "norms," common beliefs and ways of acting. The group acquires a common culture.

What we have here is a set of causal loops. These may be diagrammed as a system model following the method of Chapter 2 (although Homans himself did not do so):

Interaction and liking flow in a circle. The more that people interact, the more they will like each other, which causes them to interact even more. There is a second, reinforcing loop, since interaction causes people to create a common culture, which in turn is yet another incentive for them to interact. Homans intends this model to explain how any group at all gets started and builds up its culture and structure. Presumably the workers at the Hawthorne plant, thrown into the same work place, began interacting, and hence ended up forming a group in this way with its own norms (such as controlling how hard its members work).

Is this model realistic? There are two immediate problems. One is apparent from the flow chart. If liking increases interaction and vice versa, then both the amount of interaction and liking should increase to infinity. The loops are positive feedback, and hence their outcome in a computer simulation would be explosive growth, reaching infinite amounts of interaction and liking. That is unrealistic; though we can believe that a group might get started in this way, there is some upper limit to how much individuals will want to interact, and how much they will like one another. After all, the Hawthorne workers formed a group mainly on the job, and they were not necessarily very close friends. Homans implicitly recognized this problem, and in his later system (1961) formulated a principle to deal with it. This is the principle of *marginal utility,* borrowed from economics. It states that the more persons possess of some particular reward, the less rewarding are further increments of that reward. In other words, interacting with certain people is rewarding; but after having built up a level of interaction so that individuals see a lot of each other, further increases in interacting among them become less desirable. The amount of interaction in the group reaches its limit, and no further growth in intensity occurs. The same holds for the other processes linked to the interaction loop: common sentiments and behaviors build up as liking reinforces interaction, but these level out at some point, so that the group has a common culture which remains fairly stable.

The other caveat, also discovered by Homans himself, deals with the conditions under which the first proposition is true. Is it always the case that people who interact will like one another? Not necessarily, if the interaction is not rewarding to one or both of them. Homans proposes that *the interaction will be mutually rewarding only when the persons are equal; if they are unequal, the one with lower rank or power will find the exchange unpleasant and will avoid further interaction.* Homans derived the point empirically from the role of the maternal uncle (mother's brother) in tribal societies with patrilineal kinship (Homans 1984: 158–60). In these family systems, a boy's father had authority over him, and hence their relationships tended to be rather formal and distant. But these same societies tended to encourage a warm bond between a boy and his mother's brothers, who would protect and support him in various tribal rituals. Homans formulates the point: unequal relationships are unrewarding to at least one partner, hence the result is avoidance, while equal relationships allow the principle to play itself out, that interaction leads to liking.

Homans seems more successful in explaining the negative than the positive part of the boy's relations with his adult kin. The unrewarding effects of being subjected to power explain why the boy is distant with his father. But the lack of authority relationship over him by his maternal uncles does not explain why they should build up a bond, especially as ritualized as it is in these tribal societies, where the mother's brother helps him through his initiation ceremonies and so forth. Homans says (1984: 158–59) that a child is brought up to believe he should act warmly toward his mother's brother and vice versa; but Homans is not satisfied with an explanation based merely on socialization and wants to show why that pattern should be taught in the first place. He states that many boys (and uncles) may not actually feel the warm sentiments called for, but act the appropriate way anyhow because of fear of punishment for violating a tribal norm. That is to say, the pattern of boys avoiding their fathers and relying on their maternal uncles builds up in enough cases so that it becomes recognized as a tribal custom; then "what many families do in fact becomes in time what every family ought to do" (1984: 159). In short, *what is conventional becomes normative.*

But this does not solve the problem. In fact, it multiplies the issue into two problems. First, it still doesn't tell us why boys in patrilineal tribes should especially like their maternal uncles and vice versa. We can understand why they fail to get along closely with their fathers; but why should their mothers' brothers be picked out, of all the other people in the tribe, to become especially close to? It is even more mysterious why the mother's brother should feel he should interact a great deal with a small boy. Nor is this really an equal relationship: the adult man is protecting the boy, who cannot repay the favor, except with affection. Homans himself admits that many boys and uncles don't feel this way, but are coerced by the norms of the tribe. Second, Homans thinks he has solved this problem sufficiently so that the behavior takes place habitually; hence it then becomes obligatory. As we shall see, this is a weak explanation of moral beliefs and obligations; it does not capture the points that Durkheim made in showing the level of ritual interactions operating beneath the level of rational calculation of rewards and punishments. Homans fails to see that interaction can operate on two different levels and that rewards can be of two qualitatively different sorts.

With these caveats accepted, Homans' other principles do seem realistic. They even have a practical application: if one wants individuals to become friends, one should arrange for them to interact with each other a good deal but also make sure that no one has power over anyone else, so that they interact as equals. A bunch of new kids in a school classroom will eventually build up liking for each other and formulate a group culture, provided these conditions are met. This means that they have to spend time together: the process will work more powerfully, the more they are kept in each other's company, away from the distractions of other groups (and previously formed relationships). And they have to actually interact, that is, carry out some activities together, rather than merely sitting in the same room. This occurs especially strongly if they are subject to a common stress, such as undergoing an arduous task together or being exposed to a common emergency. Principles of group dynamics of this sort are now routinely applied in group psychotherapy and other situations.

Another feature of the group explained by Homans' theory is the position of the group leader. The leader is the person who conforms most to the group norms, in other words, the individual who represents the ideal attitudes and behavior in the group culture. Homans' leader is not an innovator or an individualist. He substantiates this with various kinds of evidence. For example, in William F. Whyte's famous study *Street-Corner Society*, the leader of a tough Italian-American slum gang was the person who was toughest of all, who did everything best that the group believed in. This was confirmed by other studies of small groups in laboratory settings, where the kinds and amount of interaction were carefully recorded by observers sitting behind one-way windows (Bales, 1959). These studies found not only that the leader conforms to the group norms but also has more social contacts within the group, both initiating and receiving communications. The leader, in short, is the individual who interacts the most with the members of the group. It follows from Homans' second principle that the leader would also be the person whose sentiments and activities are most similar to the group's own.

Homans developed a number of conclusions from these analyses. All these examples convinced him that the operative principles in social relationships are psychological laws. In his book *Social Behavior: Its Elementary Forms* (1961), he laid out these principles as versions of the behaviorist psychology developed by B. F. Skinner. At the same time, he interpreted these principles as versions of those in economics. Homans thus reunited two branches of the utilitarian tradition (which derived originally from Adam Smith and Jeremy Bentham), which emphasized that society is built out of the commonsense, rational behavior of individuals, especially as they exchange rewards. How does the exchange model emerge from Homans' basic principle that interaction leads to liking, and vice versa? Homans interprets this to mean that as individuals interact (in egalitarian relationships), they reward one another, which causes them to repeat the interaction (a behaviorist principle). Also, being rewarded by the other, causes the actor to give rewards in exchange (the exchange principle).

Homans argued that the basic laws of sociology are psychological laws and attacked Parsonian functionalism in particular for obfuscating the search for true explanatory principles. This was a major point in the outbreak of the micro-macro issue in sociology, an issue which has ramified into sufficient complexities that it deserves a separate treatment (Chapter 11). Homans' work has been the starting point for a number of theories and research programs, including the refinements of Homans, Emerson, and others in exchange theory; for the connections to network analysis made by Karen Cook and others; and for the general program of rational choice theory. These developments make Homans perhaps the most successful of modern sociologists in his actual influence upon practicing researchers.

EXCHANGE THEORY AND POWER: BLAU AND EMERSON

Like Homans, Blau began with empirical work, especially in organizational research. Blau's first book, *The Dynamics of Bureaucracy* (1955), is a study of a government welfare agency. Previous organizational studies of blue-collar workers had found an informal work group which controls the place of work; Blau found a similar informal group controlling the pace of work among white-collar workers. He focused particularly upon the relationships involving "old-timers," veteran workers who gave advice to new-comers and received deference in return. This was one prime example of exchange relationship. Blau also noticed that conversational relationships had a distinctive pattern over time. When individuals first meet, they try to make themselves as impressive as possible; Blau interpreted this to mean they try to make their exchange value as high as possible so that others will want to interact with them. After they establish their attractiveness, they then become self-deprecating, informal, or modest such as by making jokes at their own expense. Blau interpreted this to mean that one does not want to "price oneself out of the market"; having established one's exchange value, one then makes oneself approachable so that someone else can afford to be intimate with them.

Blau (1964) went on to generalize a set of principles, a number of which are taken from Homans (1961):

1. BEHAVIOR IS DETERMINED BY EXPECTED PROFIT.   That is, an action is performed if it is expected to be rewarding; it is discouraged to the extent that it is expected to incur costs. Profit is the expected reward minus cost. An application is that people will interact with those individuals from whom they expect to get the

most rewards (for instance, the pleasure or usefulness of interacting with them), relative to the amount of costs they must put out (the amount of deference they must give). A man may find it very pleasurable to interact with a beautiful woman, but she may exact a lot of deference (especially if she has many men chasing her). An implication is that individuals will tend to become friends with people of approximately equal status. If the rewards are very unequal toward one side, the other person will have to give a great deal of deference, which is not conducive to friendship; people do not voluntarily enter into such exchanges, if they have alternatives; hence they will gravitate toward exchanges with equals. Also involved here is (1a) *the principle of marginal utility* (already invoked by Homans): the beautiful woman who has lots of admirers is already satiated and does not need one more, hence she is unlikely to strike up a friendship with just another ordinary man. This process, however, applies mainly to informal friendship relationships. In work settings, people may not have a choice, and they cannot avoid unequal interactions. It is out of this that Blau develops his theory of power.

2. THE NORM OF RECIPROCITY.   Blau finds it necessary to explain why people reciprocate a reward, that is, why when someone gives a reward the other person feels obligated to give a commensurate reward in return. Why not simply take the reward and give nothing back? People in fact do not usually do this (although sometimes they do cheat or steal). Blau proposes that this is because there is a social norm of reciprocity: a feeling that it is *right* to reciprocate a reward. A corollary is (2a) *people become angry when the norm of reciprocity is violated.*

We should note that the norm of reciprocity is not itself a principle determined by exchange of rewards. It is on a more fundamental level, a process which makes possible exchanges in the first place. (It is equivalent to Durkheim's precontractual solidarity, discussed in Chapter 2.) Blau wishes to derive the norm itself from behaviorist principles; he does this by arguing that people begin to reciprocate rewards because it is rewarding to do so. The additional force of the norm, its obligatory nature, and the anger which results from violations of it, can be explained by an additional postulate: *what is habitual becomes obligatory.* Moral norms are thus supposed to develop because of the sheer repetitive pattern of behavior. Here, too, Blau gives a more elaborate statement of Homans' arguments.

3. THE NORM OF FAIR EXCHANGE.   People expect that the ratio of rewards and costs should be the same for both sides. That is, they do not expect that everyone should get equal rewards; Blau's image of the human being is not a socialist or egalitarian one. Rather, it is that people expect everyone to get the rewards they deserve. Those who put in more effort or make greater contributions should receive more rewards, whether in the form of wealth, esteem, or power. Again, there is a corollary (3a) for violations of the norm: *people become angry when they perceive someone has gotten more rewards than are deserved; and they feel guilty when they themselves get a reward that they did not earn.*

Presumably the same issues could be raised about this "norm of distributive justice" as about the norm of reciprocity: namely, how is this norm itself to be derived by behaviorist principles of reward and punishment? This question is seldom asked, however, and the principle tends to be taken as an empirical given. Research has been carried out to show to what extent people actually hold this belief and how they judge the justice or injustice of the actual inequalities found in modern society (Alves and Rossi, 1978; Form, 1985). This research, however, merely establishes an empirical point rather than an explanation of what causes this norm to exist. It may also be noted that the research concentrates on the modern United States, a capitalist society in which this principle is a widely stated public standard (some might call it an ideology) justifying inequality as long as it is "earned." We might question whether the same principle would operate in a socialist society committed to egalitarianism or in a traditionalist society in which inequality is conceived of as supernaturally given or a privilege of the strong over the weak. And even in our own society, there is some evidence (Deutsch, 1985; Form, 1985) that not everyone agrees on a strict standard of inequality as proportionate to one's achievements. Why this is so remains to be explained.

The Homans-Blau formula has also been criticized by expectation states theory (Chapter 7). The general principle is that an actor is regarded as justly rewarded by an exchange partner if they have the same ratio of rewards to costs (for instance, their pay in relation to how hard they work or how much skill they contribute). But expectation states theory notes that person A cannot tell whether B is overrewarded or not, if—as is often the case—A only knows how hard A works, but doesn't know about B (who may be A's boss). Furthermore, even if A knows that the ratios are equal, it still may be true that both of them are overrewarded (neither is really working very hard for the pay), or both are underrewarded, or both are getting their just deserts. These questions cannot be answered without some *local frame of reference:* a standard of the local group which sets a level of reward in relation to inputs. Furthermore, there is a reverse process: the fact that rewards are distributed in a certain way sets up expectations that highly rewarded people have the status traits that justify getting those rewards. This has been shown experimentally (Cook, 1975; Harrod, 1980): expectations normalize to fit whatever rewards are given, and people's performances change accordingly. Jasso (1980) proposes a logarithmic "justice evaluation function," which indicates that people react more strongly to being underrewarded than overrewarded. This implies that self-interest is working more strongly than a disinterested attachment to the ideal of justice, since the guilt which Homans proposed for being overrewarded in relation to one's efforts does not manifest itself very much.

4. BALANCED EXCHANGES IN SOME SOCIAL RELATIONSHIPS TEND TO PRODUCE UNBALANCED EXCHANGES IN OTHER RELATIONSHIPS.   Actors strive to achieve balanced exchanges, to obtain an appropriate return of rewards for their costs and efforts in each interaction. But the costs of any particular exchange usually include rewards foregone by not exchanging with someone else. To marry Bill is to forego marrying Tom, and to be close friends with Sally means less time for socializing with Wilma. Balancing one exchange relationship tends to make other exchange relationships unbalanced. Blau proposes that the dynamics of social life follow from this process, as individuals strive to balance their exchanges, but in doing so unbalance other relationships, which can be repaired only at a cost to yet other relationships, and so forth. It is not entirely clear logically, however, why this necessarily is the case. I think Blau is responding to an empirical observation, that in fact relationships are often unequal (which is to say the world is stratified), and that people are

disgruntled as a result (which follows from principle [3] on fair exchange). Since Blau does not want to admit any sources of inequality except those in exchange itself, he adds this postulate, with its argument about foregone opportunities.

Blau's undertone does recognize the social world as conflictual. He sees social life as a competition to impress others, so that they will exchange with us. He also stresses the corollaries to principles (2) and (3), that nonreciprocity or unfairness lead to anger and retaliation. These result in a vicious cycle of conflict, since the other side is now motivated to retaliate as well.[1] Blau adds a series of principles on conditions that mobilize conflict, which are very similar to Dahrendorf's model (Chapter 4). Conflict increases when the aggrieved persons are concentrated rather than dispersed, when they are in communication with one another, and when they share collective experiences which result in an ideology or "counter-norms." Once conflict begins, the experience of solidarity can make opposition into an end in itself.

TYPES OF REWARDS   People are ranked by the kinds of rewards they can give to others. There are four main types: (1) money; (2) approval—that is, friendship, group belonging; (3) esteem—giving deference to others; and (4) compliance—taking orders from someone else. Blau comments that money is least usable in social exchange, hence exchange is determined largely by the other three. This seems an overly narrow judgment; what Blau seems to have in mind is that people do not control others by giving them money in *sociable* relationships, although they obviously control them in this way in the realm of work. In general, Blau avoids anything to do with material conditions or class relationships in the Marxian sense.

The general model is that persons who have none of the other rewards to give must give compliance or deference to other people in return for their more highly valued rewards. Put the other way, compliance can be extracted by those who have highly desired rewards that they can withhold. This is the source of power. For instance, the old-timer in the bureaucracy gives advice (a desired reward) to newcomers, who in turn must repay with deference or compliance (since that is all they have to give in return). This model can be stated in more detail, as has been done by Emerson (1972).[2]

1. The fewer the sources of rewards for actor A, the more dependent A is upon a given source of rewards. (Emerson calls the extreme version of this a *unilateral monopoly*, in which A has only one place to go for a particular type of reward.)

---

[1] It is not clear, in terms of the theory, whether the retaliation is motivated by a kind of reciprocity—in which exchanges can be balanced, but in a negative direction—or by a generalization of nonreciprocity to both sides. In other words, is fighting just a negative exchange, following the principles of reciprocity, or is it a breakdown of reciprocity? If the former, we are in the peculiar position that reciprocity does not break off, except at one arbitrary point, but only changes direction. This implies that the enemies now will become satisfied because their relationship is balanced by the evils they do to each other. According to the theory, this would reduce anger and make them like this exchange. This does not seem to be an accurate description of what actually happens in conflicts. The other alternative, that there is no longer any reciprocity, also has difficulties, since it makes it difficult to explain why there should be a cycle of conflict.

[2] Emerson draws on both Blau and Homans to state a series of formal propositions in quasi-mathematical symbolism. Actor, reinforcement, value, alternatives, costs, dependence, balance, and other terms are defined carefully as forms of numerically measured behavior. See J. Turner, 1985b: 287–305 for the most succinct overview of the work of Emerson and his collaborators.

2. The more different kinds of rewards actor A gets from a particular source, the more A is *dependent* on that source.

3. The more *uncertain* A is that a reward will be forthcoming from a particular situation, and the fewer the alternatives for getting this reward, the more A is dependent. This is a version of B. F. Skinner's (1969) experiments with animals, which shows that pigeons who get their food by pecking a bar, will peck especially hard if they only get rewarded occasionally, and there is no other way to get food. In the human situation, presumably Mr. or Ms. A has to give especially great deference if they are dependent on someone but are unsure how much that person will reward them.

EXCHANGE THEORY OF POWER

Power emerges from exchanges, then, in which one individual (or side) has services that the other side wants, while the latter has nothing to give in return but compliance. Further, the dominant side must have a relative monopoly on those rewards: there are no alternative ways to get them. And the rewards must be highly desired—subordinates cannot do without them. Blau's paradigm case is always the expertise of the leaders; this is highly desired and needed by the subordinates, who cannot do their work without it, and there is no alternative place to get it. Curiously, Blau's model would work better if he took money as the central reward in work organizations: then compliance would follow (that is, the sale of labor-power) in return for money, which propertyless workers lack and need in order to live. This brings Blau's model uncomfortably close to Marx's, however, which is probably why he avoids this obvious truth about the exchange relationship in most jobs. Blau does not say anything about how the leaders got their monopoly on rewards, but the image of the world he wishes to present is a basically equitable system. He wants to claim that the leaders earn their esteem and power by the expert advice they give and the expert services they provide to the group, which the rest are too inexperienced or incompetent to provide for themselves. If he were to focus on money, its possession by capitalist employers, and its nonpossession by propertyless workers, he would have to explain how the former acquired their money in the first place. He could, of course, fall back on the claim that they gained their money by the services they provided; but this is an implausible characterization of property relationships in a capitalist society.

INSTITUTIONALIZED ROLES   In Blau's model of organization, leaders provide services of expertise to followers in return for compliance. As long as the leaders' costs are proportional to their rewards, the inequality is accepted as fair. Blau means by this that the bosses are perceived as deserving higher pay, either because they are better trained (Blau accepts educational credentials at full ideological value), more expert, or more essential to the organization. It is possible, of course, for these exchanges to grow unbalanced (see Blau's rather tortuous argument, discussed previously, as to why this should occur). As a result, conflict may occur between subordinates and their bosses, and something like class conflict will break out if the conditions for group mobilization are also present.

More normally, though, workers accept bosses' authority as legitimate and see compliance as a fair exchange. Moreover, through the process by which what is habitual becomes normative, compliance to authority becomes a norm enforced by workers upon each other. Again, this seems an inapt derivation, insofar as most research on workers' cultures show that what they enforce upon each other is not the *bosses'* authority and values, but the workers' *own* standards of controlling and slowing down the work pace (Etzioni, 1961/1975).

Behavior patterns, according to the theory, are institutionalized as roles. General norms emerge, which make it possible to create new organizations without an initial period of competition. Once people become familiar with work roles, they no longer have to go through the process of competing with one another to display their reward-giving value, and negotiating over relationships of how much compliance is to be given for how much expertise. That process is the elementary basis of social organization, according to Blau; it is presumably what happened in the "cave-man stage" when a society was first formed. But now relationships of leaders and followers are institutionalized in general norms, so workers enter a new job and know what compliance they are expected to give, without actually negotiating with their boss or having to be shown just what superior expertise the bosses are supplying to the organization.

At this stage, direct interaction between leaders and followers declines. The norms rather than direct experience tell the classes what they get from each other. The members of the lower class get fewer personal rewards (for instance, sharing status by associating with the higher ranks), but they incur fewer costs since they have to give less deference by associating with their peers. In this way society differentiates into strata.

COMPLEX EXCHANGE SYSTEMS   The same relationships emerge at a higher level among organizations rather than among individuals. Organizations engage in exchanges, governed by their relative resources and by norms of reciprocity and fairness. The society as a whole becomes stratified by the same kind of differentiation that characterizes its individuals. Overall solidarity is generated by "generalized media" of exchange: norms or laws which codify the principles of exchange into abstract principles. Individuals learn these norms by being socialized into society's system of common values. Possession of these norms then makes it possible for exchanges to take place at a distance, instead of through direct interaction. In this way, the entire society is held together by exchanges. For Blau, the macrostructure is the multiplication of the microstructure through the building up of interpersonal exchanges into roles, of roles into organizations, and of exchanges among organizations at the most macro level. Holding it all together are not only the actual rewards which are exchanged, but the abstract norms which tell individuals (or organizations) what rewards they are presumably getting from others' contributions, even if there is no concrete evidence of it.

CRITICISMS

It must be admitted, I think, that Blau jumps all too readily to an idealized vision of macro exchange in which not only every individual but every organization gets its fair return for its contributions. Blau repeats the functionalist theory of stratification. Blau seems to have generalized too far from his study of the *informal* relationships among workers in a bureaucracy—none of whom actually had any *formal* control over each other. He mistakes this informal exchange system of advice and deference from the more formal structure of control enforced by the possession of property. For Blau, the formal structure merely crystalizes the informal structure; whereas in reality, these tend to be quite different forms of organization. For all the importance of informal relationships at work, these relationships would not exist at all unless there were a preexisting organization, which is usually based on property ownership backed up by the coercive power of the state.

It is true that Blau adds a conflict dimension in which normative violations can give rise to protest movements, and eventually to revolutions (which supposedly restore equitable exchange). But this seems even too idealized a view of conflict: as if no one ever fought for their self-interest but merely for equity. The image of giant capitalist organizations all trading fairly among themselves, with no one ever making a profit or getting ahead of the others, also seems very naive.

Blau does raise the possibility that rewards may be extracted by coercion rather than by being exchanged for other rewards. He comments, however, that this is a minor factor and ignores it in his systematic theorizing. The omission is general among supporters of exchange theory: an unwillingness to look at the coercive, and ultimately military, aspect of political power, and hence an obliviousness to how coercion and threat are actually organized. Blau and Emerson analyze power as the result of dependency of some persons on others who have a monopoly of rewards; but this is still a positive and peaceful exchange, not a coercive one. Moreover, Emerson (1972; see J. Turner, 1985b: 296–99) proposed that unbalanced exchanges, in which one partner is more dependent on an exchange than the other partner, will move in the direction of greater balance. Since dependency produces power, this is tantamount to saying that power relationships over time lead to the reduction of power, which is empirically rather dubious. Similarly, Emerson believed that a one-sided monopoly over resources gives way over time to a division of labor, in order to reduce the power of the monopolist. This might be a more equitable outcome, but Emerson seems overoptimistic in believing that it actually happens. In fact, coercive relationships as well as positive exchanges link individual actors together, especially in the realm of the state, and coercive power structures tend to have rather strong staying power. To comprehend how coercive networks operate it is necessary to broaden exchange theory to include the factors considered in Chapters 3 through 5, as well as 12 and 13.

A major weakness of Blau's theory, I would suggest, is not so much the basic principles of exchange, as the way that Blau short-circuits them and substitutes sets of norms which are supposed to summarize their results. He departs too readily from Homans' strategy of "bringing men back in," of grounding human arrangements in the actual rewards and costs of human beings negotiating in concrete situations. Instead, Blau interprets behavior as following from quasi-mythological exchange relationships that were made in the past, or that everyone knows about anyway; so it no longer has to be tested whether bosses actually owe their power to the contributions they make to the organization. In short, Blau drops exchange too much from his theory, at exactly the points where he ought to use it to be skeptical of the ideological definitions of what work is actually like or what relationships between organizations actually are.

FROM SOCIAL BEHAVIORISM TO
RATIONAL CHOICE

Many of the principles stated by Homans, Blau, and Emerson are not necessarily concerned with exchange at all, but with individual motivation. Homans modelled his principles on behaviorist psychology. Although he coined the term "social exchange" (Homans, 1958), he later regretted his identification with that term and referred to his position by what he regarded as its more fundamental characteristic, "social behaviorism." Behaviorism was an attempt to be extremely objective about human action, to describe its laws without having to refer to the subjective state of the individual. The human mind is taken to be a "black box"; since we cannot look inside other people's minds, we must build up our theory by what we can observe of their behavior. Homans followed this route. Blau later took over most of Homans' principles, but eased the assumption that we can't look inside the black box of subjective states. Emerson, finally, returned to something closer to the original behaviorist position.

Homans' basic propositions, which are the basis for the other systems, are as follows:[3]

1. *The Success Proposition: The more often a particular action of a person is rewarded, the more likely the person is to perform that action.* In other words, behavior is determined by one's history of rewards.

2. *The Stimulus Proposition: If in the past the occurrence of a particular stimulus has been the occasion on which a person's action has been rewarded, then the more similar the present stimuli are to the past ones, the more likely the person is to perform the action or some similar action now.* Hence, when someone is in a situation similar to a previous situation, that person will do what was rewarded earlier.

3. *The Value Proposition: The more valuable to a person is the result of an action, the more likely he is to perform the action.* Stronger rewards control behavior more than weaker rewards. But the value of a reward is also determined by past experience, as in the next proposition.

4. *The Deprivation-Satiation Proposition: The more often in the recent past a person has received a particular reward, the less valuable any further unit of that reward becomes for him.* Eating too much candy will make a person sick of it for a while. Similarly, someone who receives plenty of social esteem is less moved by it than someone who normally gets little attention from other people.

5. *The Aggression-Approval Proposition: (a) When a person's action does not receive the reward he expected or receives punishment he did not expect, he will be angry and become more likely to perform aggressive behavior, and the results of such behavior become more valuable to him. (b) When a person's action receives the reward expected, or especially greater reward than expected, or does not receive punishment he expected, he will be pleased and become more likely to perform approving behavior, and the results of such behavior become more valuable to him.*

---

[3] I take these from Homans (1974: 11–68), which is the second edition of his 1961 book.

What Homans has in mind here is action toward other people, rather than toward the physical world. It is true that if you are used to your car starting when you turn on the ignition, you may become angry if it doesn't start; and you may slam your hand down on the dashboard, since, as Homans says, the results of aggressive behavior are particularly valuable to you at that time. But I suspect that most people don't behave this way with inanimate objects. People do seem to be special, even though Homans' behaviorism would not allow him to recognize this. It is primarily when a *human* fails to reward our behavior as we have come to expect in the past that we become angry. Similarly, when someone does meet our expectations we find it particularly rewarding to deal with them; and when someone gives us *more* than we expect, we are grateful. I doubt that this applies much to our dealing with physical objects.[4]

The Aggression-Approval Propositions are designed to lead into the exchange part of the theory. This is particularly so of part (b), since this implies that when people build up a pattern of exchanging rewards with each other, they come to like each other more, and each successive reward becomes more valuable to them. This should be especially so if people get more than they expect (which is Homans' quasi-behaviorist way of saying that they get more than they feel they deserve). Part (a) of the proposition gives the negative side: if people get less than they expect, they become angry; and *then* they go on to build up a fight, because it is especially rewarding to them to perform aggressive actions. Actually, we might question whether the last part of this strictly follows. It may feel good to strike out at somebody who has frustrated us, but if they punish us even more severely, our action did not turn out to be rewarding after all. Clearly some additional contingencies have to be added. Also, the Aggression-Approval Proposition is modified by the Deprivation-Satiation Proposition. Even positive exchanges do not go on building up closer and closer ties forever; eventually we become satiated by the rewards, and they become less valuable.

6. *The Rationality Proposition: In choosing between alternative actions, a person will choose that one for which, as perceived at the time, the value of the result, multiplied by the probability of getting that result, is greater.* We choose our actions, according to this model, by a combination of the most likely reward and the most valuable reward. As we shall see, there are technical difficulties in exactly how people know this. Things are clear enough when choosing between something highly desirable and highly probable versus something we dislike and don't much expect to happen. But what about mixed cases, where one action will almost certainly lead to a small reward, whereas another action has a bigger payoff but is more of a long shot? Homans' Rationality Proposition declares that we somehow are able to calculate these two probability-payoff mixes and choose the higher one. This is one place at which the behaviorist model appears to need to be supplemented by a better theory of the human mind.

---

[4] Why humans should have this particularly emotion-arousing quality is not explained in Homans' theory, or any of the exchange theories. It is explained better in the Durkheimian theory of interaction rituals, which explicitly deals with human feelings of group membership and moral obligation.

As we have seen, Blau is not so concerned with these issues on the level of individual motivation. Where Homans was explicitly trying to reduce the macro aspect of sociology down to the micro principles of psychology, Blau accepts Homans' principles in a looser form and devotes most of his attention to the level of social exchange. Blau is thus more macro than Homans (an issue we will discuss more generally in Chapter 11). Emerson, finally, is something of a synthesis of Homans' micro behaviorism and Blau's macro exchange, which is stated in more technical detail than either of them. For example: "The greater the uncertainty of A ever receiving a given reward in a given situation and the fewer alternative situations for receiving this reward, the greater is the dependency of A on that situation" (Emerson, 1972). Here we can see that Emerson has taken the *probability of getting rewards* from Homans' and Blau's rationality propositions and defined it as "uncertainty"; and, together with Blau's formulation of market alternatives, put this together into a general model of dependency. Further propositions and theorems connect this to a model of power in various kinds of exchange networks.

RATIONAL CHOICE

Yet another variant of the exchange theory tradition emphasizes rational choice. This is a broader slogan than "exchange theory," although it does have an affinity with the model of the human being used in economics; indeed, sometimes it is referred to as "the economic program" in sociology. But here the crucial aspect is not the macro structure of the large-scale market, but the micro level: the model of individual action. Although the advocates of rational choice theory see Homans as one of their predecessors, they are critical of Homans in certain respects, too. Rational choice focuses on the individual actor as being able to consciously choose among alternatives in a fashion consistent with his or her best interest. This is a major break from Homans's social behaviorism, which attempted to eliminate consciousness from its model and refer only to overt behaviors. Rational choice theory, though, is explicitly a model of human cognition in social situations.

Lindenberg (1985) provides a succinct overview of this approach, and its contrast with rival models. The individual human being is like *homo economicus,* economic man, buying and selling goods and services according to the laws of supply and demand. This individual acts rationally, keeping down costs and maximizing profits. These are social costs and profits, however, not merely economic ones. Moreover, Lindenberg points out, the sociological theory of rational choice does not have to follow economic theory at all points and is not necessarily saddled with all the assumptions made by traditional economic theories. The human individual does not have to be omniscient, able to judge all possible alternatives in order to choose the best one; he or she is not obsessed with money and material consumption, but pursues a wide range of rewards, including social ones. What is central about this rational individual can be summed up by the acronym RREEMM (Lindenberg, 1985: 100):

Resourceful: man can search for and find possibilities; he can learn and be inventive.

Restricted: man is confronted with scarcity and must substitute (choose among alternatives).

*E*xpecting: man attaches subjective probabilities to future events.

*E*valuating: man has ordered preferences and evaluates future events.

*M*aximizing: man maximizes expected utility when choosing a course of action.

*M*an.

In contrast, Lindenberg (1985: 101–102) proposes that the *homo sociologicus* of traditional sociology is SRSM:

*S*ocialized: man internalizes role expectations (norms and values).

*R*ole-playing: man acts according to situational role-expectations.

*S*anctioned: man is guarded against deviancy by the sanctions of others in case socialization is not perfect.

*M*an.

Finally, there is a kind of *homo empiricus* of ordinary survey research, OSAM (Lindenberg, 1985:102):

*O*pinionated: man forms an opinion about everything.

*S*ensitive: man's opinion is easily influenced by others.

*A*cting: man acts directly on the basis of his opinions.

*M*an.

Lindenberg goes on to argue that RREEMM is much preferable to the other images, SRSM and OSAM. Only the rational choice individual (as I will refer to RREEMM) has any freedom or dignity. These individuals are inventive and for-ward-looking, have a mind which can evaluate what goes on and are endowed with willpower and the ability to make choices. Furthermore, they make intelligent choices, maximizing gains and cutting losses, and are not merely pushed around by culture or other people. There is an element of caricature in Lindenberg's opponents, of course; the rather superficial survey-researchers' model is depicted as if human beings were nothing but a bundle of opinions, without any substance of their own. But Lindenberg does put his finger on the relative advantages and disadvantages of the different positions. The rational choice model is more firmly founded in the real world: human beings do have real interests and hence a real basis of action. The social structure is not reified as some superimposed culture floating down from the clouds, but is nothing more or less than the sum total of all individuals interacting, exchanging, or otherwise maneuvering in pursuit of their real interests by following their own evaluations and perceptions.

There is a further element of realism in that individuals are restricted. There are real conditions of scarcity: there is a material world, as well as such goods as power or prestige, which cannot be shared equally by everyone; and there are choices which individuals must make among alternatives. Individuals are free and capable of think-ing for themselves, but they exist in a world in which things are not attained merely by wishing. Individuals are fully cognitive, but cognition does not rule the world. This means that a rational choice model can be elaborated in the direction of the hard material and structural constraints impinging upon individuals. It can develop a theory taking full account of the individual and individual subjectivity, but is not trapped into overestimating the power of the individual.

ASSESSMENTS

I would agree with Lindenberg on the strong points of the rational choice model, which is to say more broadly the strength of the entire exchange theory tradition. But various warnings must be registered.

In addition to the general strategy of rational choice, this approach usually brings in a good deal of baggage from conventional economics. These include joint utility functions, which sneak back into the collective-functionalist viewpoint and eliminate the advantage of analyzing individual interests, as well as the tendency to bring in assumptions about the openness of the market, equilibrium pieces, and other concepts which are of dubious application. Economists have sometimes directly applied their models to social phenomena. Gary Becker (1971, 1981), for example, has developed economic theories of discrimination against minorities, of crime, educational attainment, and the family. These theories have not been very realistic, however. *The Economics of Discrimination* (Becker, 1971) shows that it is inefficient for employers to discriminate (since they get the best pool of workers by being meritocratic) while it is majority-race workers who benefit by excluding minorities. The implication is that employers do not discriminate against blacks, and what discrimination does occur must be the white workers' fault.

Becker's (1981) analysis of the family has a similar tendency to let theory override empirical reality. The basic model proposes that people maximize a mathematical quantity, made up of all the "commodities" (that is, goods, pleasures, values) that they can gain from the use of their time: children, prestige, health, altruism, envy, sensual pleasure, and so on. They will invest their time, inside and outside the home, in order to maximize the productivity of their time over the sum of their activities. Furthermore, Becker assumes that this sum for the family is a "joint utility function"—it is the total of what both husband and wife (and children) produce with their time that is maximized. Individuals are not out for themselves, and no account is taken of their self-interests. (Hence any sexual stratification or conflict within the family is assumed away by definition.) Becker derives various implications from this. Using a well-known argument in the economics of specialization, he "proves" that the joint utility for the family is maximized if only one spouse works outside the home, while the other specializes in housework. Becker claims that he is not being a traditionalist, since it makes no difference to his theory whether it is the man or the woman who is the "housewife" as long as somebody is. (Why women get stuck with this role is not accounted for; since the market can do no wrong, it cannot have anything to do with discrimination against women for jobs.) The theory clashes again with empirical reality, unable to explain why the historical trend has been toward a *majority* of women working outside the home.[5]

---

[5] See Stinchcombe (1983) for a critique of this book. Stinchcombe summarizes the basic problem: "Becker likes to reason from outrageous assumptions" (1983: 468). For example, Becker argues that parents want their children to make the maximal amount of money when they grow up, in relation to parental investments in them; hence parents will invest *less* in their education and health, if the child is bright, white, or otherwise advantaged, because the latter factors substitute for education and health. He claims that public expenditures on compensatory education for the poor are misguided, since he assumes that parents will *reduce* their other assistance to their children to make up for what they are getting in schools. (This is a nice example of blaming the victim.) He attempts to derive a theory of when societies

All this is not to say that market-exchange theory might not validly be applied to the family, but it cannot be an unmodified version of neo-classical economics. The relationship between sociology and conventional economics is analyzed further in Chapter 12. In general, we should note here that the rational choice model of the individual does not necessarily imply that we must also adopt the conventional economic approach to the market.

The entire exchange–rational choice school of thought tends to have too narrow a conception of what human action is about. What is being exchanged, or what is the source of status or the center of motivation or evaluation, is too often construed in narrow utilitarian terms. Blau's or Emerson's exchanges focus on practical advice or contribution to a work project as the higher-valued reward for which deference or compliance is given.[6] This is far too limited. A realistic exchange theory must include the more prominent human goods, especially emotional payoffs of solidarity and belonging, as well as dominance as a pleasurable emotion in itself, and the symbolic versions of these things. An extension of this kind is incorporated in the market aspect of interaction ritual chains.

The exchange school has a poor track record in dealing with stratification, and especially with coercive power. Its theories of stratification look like a functionalist justification for inequality as a reward for the superior contributions of those in power. Its lack of concepts for dealing realistically with power resources (including the emotional aspects of group mobilization), make it look naive by comparison with the macro theories of stratification, political and economic conflict treated in Chapters 3 through 5. These weaknesses are perhaps not intrinsic to the most fundamental model of the rational actor motivated by seeking favorable exchanges. The self-interested component of this, in fact, could be a grounding for a conflict theory. But the additional assumptions typically brought in when these theories dealt with power or with the macro structure have thus far sidetracked that potential.

The rational choice–exchange tradition has also tended to be rather narrow on the micro side. There is little in the way of treatment of the self, mind, consciousness, language, situation, or the social construction of reality—in short, the subjects treated in the rest of Part Two of this book. There is nothing intrinsic in the basic conception of exchange that would prevent the development of the subjective side. But the prevailing tone has been narrow and cramped, even if it has repudiated some of the dogmatic extremes of behaviorism. For that reason, the exchange theory tradition has a reputation among other theoretical camps for lack of subtlety and vision regarding the truly human aspects of life. I do not think that this is a necessary

---

will have polygynous families (one husband, many wives), predicting that polygyny declines over historical time because it is correlated with the amount of childcare provided by the family versus by the larger community. In fact, polygyny rises and falls in a bell-shaped curve from hunting-and-gathering economies up to agrarian ones (in their upper classes) and then declines (Blumberg and Winch, 1972). Polygamy is actually connected with social stratification, a phenomenon which pure market theories have difficulty in dealing with realistically.

[6] Similarly, expectation states theory (Chapter 7) focuses rather narrowly on the expectations that arise from individual's contributions to performing a task (and contributions only to collective group enterprises, at that). In this sense, ES theory has some of the same weaknesses as rational choice–exchange theory.

consequence of the fundamental theory, but it does represent a weakness in the way it has been applied.

My comments so far have been directed toward the more superficial weaknesses of exchange theory, regarding ways in which it has been applied in an overly narrow fashion. However, there are some deeper problems in the central model itself, which must be faced if the theory is to be seriously used as an explanatory theory.

The basic model describes individuals as calculating rewards and costs, along with their expected probabilities of occurring, and thereby choosing the best course of action. But there are technical difficulties in actually carrying this out. As Heath (1976) pointed out, there is a problem of the incommensurability of different rewards (and of costs). How do we decide how much deference is equivalent to how much effort, or love, or advice, or any other reward? The problem is finding a *common metric* by which to measure these various things. The formula adopted by Homans and Blau, that the likelihood of a behavior is determined by its profitability (rewards minus cost), multiplied by the probability of each, exascerbates the problem. For a reward—say deference—is on one kind of scale of "more or less," and a probability of occurrence is on another kind of scale. The two scales have no common units, nor conversion factors. Multiplying the two together results in hybrid units which have no meaning; we cannot say, strictly speaking, that a moderate probability of achieving a low amount of love is a total worth more, or less, or even equal to, a low probability of achieving a moderate amount of advice. Without a common metric, the basic images of the rational, exchange-calculating actor turns out to be metaphorical, without any precise meaning.

There is also the problem of the limits of human cognition. It has been pointed out by organizational theorists (March and Simon, 1958: 136–42) that it is not possible to be completely rational, in the sense of calculating every alternative and choosing the best one. Even a computer cannot do this for a complex situation, like a game of chess; the number of chains of possible events is too large to handle. Lindenberg spoke of the rational actor (RREEMM) as "maximizing," but this is inaccurate. March and Simon proposed that the term "maximizing" or "optimizing" should be replaced by "satisficing": that is, real-world actors cannot maximize every possible good. When they are faced with a complex situation, like managing an organization, they cannot simultaneously maximize everything at once. Instead, real people follow a strategy of allowing actions to remain routine, as long as things meet a "satisfactory" level; this frees attention to concentrate on just one area, or to troubleshoot when things turn up that drop beneath the satisfactory baseline. The lack of a common metric, mentioned in the previous point, is one of the contributers to the limited cognitive capabilities of real-life human beings; so is the prevalence of processes with uncertain outcomes. That does not mean that individuals give up on trying to gain rewards and avoid costs; but they move in those directions only in a mushy and imprecise fashion, rather than with the kind of mechanical exactitude which the Homans-Blau model seemed initially to promise.

In view of these limitations, it might seem that rational-exchange models ought to be abandoned altogether, in favor of a purely interpretive-subjective approach, or a purely cultural analysis, or avoiding the individual-micro dimension entirely. This seems to me too drastic a solution. Individuals do have motivations in social situations, and they do seem to choose favorable alternatives and avoid unfavorable ones. The strengths of the exchange theory approach make it worth salvaging to the extent that we can. It may be possible, in fact, to connect it, even to approaches which have traditionally been regarded as its enemies. The analysis of limited cognitive capacities, for example, was stated within the utilitarian-rationalist camp itself; it meshes, interestingly enough, with a totally different approach, ethnomethodology (in Chapter 8), which also places great emphasis on the consequences of human cognitive limitations, and goes on to formulate principles of how human beings operate in the face of these limits. We may even argue that the solution of the problem of a common metric for different choices and probability expectations lies on a level deeper than cognition, namely emotion.

The weakness of exchange theory is that it has cut itself off from the rest of sociological theory and espoused a narrow utilitarian vision, combined sometimes with a functionalist ideology. But these are not necessary features of an exchange theory. For example, as we will now see, elements of symbolic interactionist emphasis on situations, and the Durkheimian-Goffman ritual theory, can be set in the context of exchange principles.

INTERACTION RITUAL CHAINS

The interaction ritual (IR) chain model (Collins, 1981a; 1975: 133–60) retains the focus on individuals who are seeking their most favorable exchanges in a social market. It differs from conventional exchange theories in several respects. Its *social psychological basis* is neither behaviorism nor rational choice, but interaction rituals; hence the focus is on situations and the symbols and emotions which are generated in them. *What is exchanged* is broadened from advice, compliance, and other utilitarian goods; in the IR chain model, individuals are seen primarily as seeking symbolic and emotional payoffs, conveyed in conversations, often unconsciously. And the *tie-in to the macro level* is different; *power* is not described as resource dependency, but as membership in a coercive enforcement coalition. This last point will be discussed in Chapter 11 on the micro-macro connection; we turn now to others.

INTERACTIONS ARE DURKHEIMIAN RITUALS

The basic unit of interaction is the natural ritual, in the sense explained in Chapter 6. Every interaction has some degree of ritual quality, insofar as it has the ingredients: the copresence of two or more persons; their common focus of attention and the sharing of a common emotional tone or mood, both of which intensify over time (recall Figure 6-1). The result is that whatever content they have focussed upon becomes a symbol representing membership in that group.

RITUALS SYMBOLIZE GROUP MEMBERSHIP   Any object at all can become a group membership symbol. The high intensity rituals of large groups, as enacted in religious and political rites, produce sacred objects and beliefs loaded with devotion and loyalty. Moderate intensity rituals of everyday conversation also load membership significance into words, gestures, clothes, and aesthetic styles; the culture of everyday life comes to connote membership in informal groups. Such group memberships may be visualized in concentric circles around each individual: nearest are idiosyncratic interpersonal cultures linking together special friends or family members, surrounded by more general cultural styles of everyday life which tie together social classes or their fragments as status groups.

Let us set the model in motion over time. Where do the ingredients come from that make this IR model possible? One source is the previous rituals those persons have taken part in. In a conversation, the most frequent form of natural ritual, the common focus of attention, is largely due to these persons having been in previous conversations (with each other or with someone else) that have given them certain verbal symbols that represent a certain kind of group membership. If those symbols match, these persons will now be able to focus on them and use them as the basis for a further ritual: in other words, they will be able to have a conversation. The same kind of cyclical relationship happens with emotions, carried over from one conversational ritual to facilitating the next.

Notice that conversations are not primarily cognitive, in the sense that their ostensible purpose is to convey information, express social rules, or allow people to calculate an exchange. The cognitive content of talk is the surface, merely the fuel that is burned up to make the ritual go. To put it another way: it does not make any difference to a successful conversation whether what the talkers are saying is true, sincere, or well expressed. It does not have to be believed or even understood! All it takes is that an energetic flow of talk is set off, one speaker spurring the other on. At the end, they may have talked total nonsense, or at least gross exaggeration, or sheer fantasy (which is what the most enthralling conversations usually are), and neither person may have caught much of what the other one meant; but if they were able to become engrossed (that is, there was a strong build-up of focus and emotional tone) they will come away from their encounter with a warm feeling of satisfaction and an intensified social tie. The nonsense they talked about will carry a symbolic weight and may act as material for getting a future conversation going. This is part of what it means to say conversation is a ritual.

IR CHAINS IMPLY SOCIAL RANKING   We now have a set of persons walking around at any given point in time, each carrying a set of symbols from their previous encounters. A symbolic item, such as a way of talking, a topic, an idea, can have been passed along from one encounter to another through quite a large network of people; at any given point in this chain, each person will have some sense of what that membership is, based largely on the emotions it is capable of setting off. These groups represented by symbols are usually ranked or stratified. Some of these groups have more power or property than others; that is to say, conversations or other ritual encounters take place among persons who belong to various social classes, who hold various positions as order givers or order takers in formal organizations. Hence the cultural symbols people acquire from their encounters are coded with significance, not merely as membership in a "neutral" set of groups, but as groups which have different degrees of power and economic resources.

MARKET OPPORTUNITIES, CULTURAL CAPITAL, AND EMOTIONAL ENERGY

Stated more formally, every individual who enters a social encounter is loaded with three items. What happens in the encounter depends on the match of these resources among all the persons who are there. For clarity, we will take it first from the point of view of person A (see Figure 10-1 page 363).

1. SENSE OF MARKET OPPORTUNITIES   Each individual has an awareness of how many persons they know with whom they could be interacting. In some situations, such as a cocktail party or other social gathering, some persons will know many people, others few; hence there is a difference in their market opportunities in that situation. Another obvious market situation is the process of seeking out sexual partners, whether it is called "finding some action," "dating," or "the marriage market." This part of the theory is similar to Blau's exchange theory, which points out that persons with low market opportunities are dependent upon the few contacts which they do have. We may add, conversely, that persons with high market opportunities are more likely to shop around for their "best deal."

Blau (1964) stated that persons who have more resources in the market have power over those with less resources; this is a generalization of the point made by Stendahl and other writers on love, that the person who is least attracted to a relationship has power over the person who is more in love. This is true, but there is an alternative: the person with better market position simply pays little attention to others with low resources. Dependency doesn't develop because the "stars," whether in the sexual realm or in cocktail party conversations, aren't interested in spending time with people at lower levels of attractiveness. Because of this tendency, people tend to separate into informal status groups made up of persons of approximately equal rank, instead of forming vertical cliques that cut across social ranks (Collins, 1975: 135–39).

For this equal-status-group structure to happen, though, depends on *how open the interpersonal market is* in that society. Where there is a great deal of freedom for people to choose who will associate with whom, the result of people seeking their best deal will be that approximate equals will end up associating with each other. That is because individuals with lower resources may try to associate with persons who are highly attractive; but the latter, as long as there are plenty of market opportunities for them, will not be very attracted to a relationship until they hit on one that pays them back equally to their own resources. That leaves persons with moderate or low resources to make their best deal with whomever will have them, which should eventually turn out to be at their own level.[7]

It is important to see that there is structural variation in how open the market is. Modern urban, wealthy societies tend to allow quite wide market opportunities for friendships and sexual partners. Historically, in agrarian or tribal societies, the number of persons who are nearby may be very circumscribed; hence individuals' market opportunities may be quite limited. Since they cannot shop around very extensively, they may be forced to make their sociable and sexual exchanges among unequals, resulting in more pervasive dependency and deference relationships in everyday life. The general decline of deference in modern life may be due to a large extent to the greater openness of the interpersonal market.

However, there are some spheres of modern life in which individuals' market opportunities for interactions are quite limited. One is for small children: in the

---

[7]The working out of these market tendencies takes time, of course, and at any given moment people may still be discovering what their resources are (or are mistaken about their opportunities and attractiveness). Hence there can be plenty of interaction among unequals, and here is where the Blau-Stendahl principle of love-dependency applies. To the extent that there are many market opportunities, though, these kinds of dependency relationships are temporary. Where the unequal relationship continues, it is presumably because the market is not open.

family, or perhaps in their neighborhood, there can be only a few choices of play-mates; hence unequal-dependency relationships are more common at this age of life than later. Another limited-market context is in formal organizations: the organization itself (and the places in it where people work) determines how many people of what sorts of ranks will be in contact with one another. The organization, so to speak, skews the interpersonal market within it. This does not mean that an individual's sense of market opportunities becomes irrelevant in that context. On the contrary, even having only *one* choice of whom to interact with is a significant factor in how someone will behave. To repeat: the sense of market opportunities is a *variable;* where it is high, one will shop around for the best deal; where it is low, one has to settle more immediately for the line-up of resources that presents itself.[8]

2. CULTURAL CAPITAL   We now must consider the resources that people have in the market. Whatever those resources are, they must somehow be conveyed in the immediate situation if they are to have an effect.

2a. *Generalized Cultural Capital*   This is person A's repertoire of symbols charged with group identification. In plain language, it is the range of things A can talk about, the kinds of ideas A has, and A's ways of expression. It is also A's ability to recognize these symbols are used by other persons talking to A, or as given off by their physical appearance and the style of their surroundings. These symbols are weighted by the ranking in terms of power and property of the social groups they connate.

I refer to these as "generalized" cultural capital because they are symbols which have come loose, so to speak, from any particular person and which simply convey a general sense of group membership.

2b. *Particularized Cultural Capital*   In contrast, particularized cultural capital are the symbols which have a special memory component, connected with particular people. It is part of generalized cultural capital to be able to talk in an upper-middle-class style; it is part of particularized cultural capital to be able to remember people's names and what they said last time one talked with them. Generalized cultural capital is like a kind of monetary currency, which can be widely used, even with strangers; particularized cultural capital is quite useful in keeping up a conversational ritual, but only with certain people. Hence it is more like an exchange by barter. As people get to know one another better, they can convert generalized into particularized cultural capital. Also, particularized connections allow them to acquire new generalized cultural capital.

---

[8] What we call someone's "personality" includes as an important component what kind of market opportunities for sociable relationships one is used to. I am suggesting that "personality" is situational, and may shift fairly rapidly when one's market situation shifts: that means both one's own market opportunities, and the opportunities of the persons whom one typically encounters. This is practically obvious in regard to the sexual component of personality, but it applies also to persons' general gregariousness in sociable relationships, "the friendship market." To the extent that someone's personality seems constant, it is because that person is in a constant milieu, in which their's and others' market positions do not shift.

2c. *Reputation*   A crucial aspect of individual A's particularized cultural capital is not only what A knows of the identities of other people, but what other people know of A's particular identity. In ordinary language, this is one's reputation. But it has a dimension which is far more important than the personality traits which usually go under the label of "reputation." One is known as being a worker in such-and-such a department of a particular organization; another is known to be the boss. This particularized information, passed around in everyday conversations, constitutes a crucial resource (or lack of resources) governing what will happen in the next encounter. That is because knowing people by their organizational location places them at a certain point in the power-enforcement coalition. One's reputation is a part of the self that one has no personal control over. It is one's location in the social structure, which circulates in the conversations of everyday life, but among other people's conversations rather than one's own. For other people, someone's reputation is merely another item of particularized cultural capital to fuel their conversations. But when one of those persons comes to encounter someone previously talked about, it operates as a pre-shaped resource, positive or negative, for the match-up in that situation. Thus one's self depends upon market interactions which one has not even taken part in.[9]

3. EMOTIONAL ENERGY   A third factor, which exchange theories have usually neglected, is emotion. It is important not merely because the IR chain model requires some emotion in order to start rituals operating. Emotional energy is also the individuals' motivating force. The feelings they have make them want to talk with certain people, or to avoid them; it determines how long an encounter will go on, and how much they have to say to each other. It also determines much of who will have the initiative in the encounter, who will be able to pick the topics, and who will win the arguments, dominate the discussion, make the jokes, as well as give or take the orders.

Why can't all this be governed simply by the cultural resources individuals bring to the encounter? There are several reasons. Culture is not a set of rules which tells individuals how to behave; it is simply a set of symbols which have to be activated in each situation. Emotions call up the symbols and charge them with energy.

There is a deeper reason why culture or cognition cannot operate in the absence of some motivational force. Human beings have limited cognitive capacities. We are able to keep only a limited amount of information in mind at one time. Also, as we have seen in discussing rational choice theory, it is impossible to calculate complex

---

[9]These various kinds of "capital" should not be confused with the term "human capital" used by economists (Schultz, 1961). "Human capital" means the skills which human beings have for carrying out economically productive activity; it is instrumental, whereas "cultural capital" is the resources persons have for making social ties and conveying group memberships. The debate over the roles of education and "technocracy" hinges on the distinction between the two kinds of "capital"; "human capital" theorists believe that schools provide mainly technical skills, whereas "cultural capital" theorists attempt to disprove this and show that schools pass on the culture of dominant classes (Bourdieu and Passeron, 1970; Collins, 1971, 1979). The term "cultural capital" was originated by Bourdieu. I have broadened it to include the particularized, as well as the generalized, form and the ritual mechanisms that produce these cultural identifications in everyday life. In my original publication (Collins, 1971), I used the term "status group culture" rather than "cultural capital."

contingencies in any precise way. There is no common metric for multiplying probabilities times the values of incommensurate outcomes. In other words, how do we decide whether to go for the status payoff of impressing an important person, at the cost of some personal obeisance, or to have a more egalitarian conversation with someone of lesser importance, especially in a situation in which neither outcome is completely certain? We humans do in fact make such decisions all the time, mostly without consciously thinking about them; when we have to consciously bring them to mind, often we are incapacitated and cannot make up our minds. I suggest that emotion is the unconscious common denominator: one line of action feels more right than the other. There is more emotional energy in one direction than in the other.

Emotional energy means a very general quality of emotion underlying the specific emotions. It is not a specific quality of love, hate, joy, and so forth, but the amount of emotional power that flows through one's actions. The relationship between emotional energy in general and the specific emotions is a theoretical and empirical problem which remains to be worked out. Emotional energy in its general form is the quality of confidence, enthusiasm, warmth and assertiveness with which one carries out one's actions. It is not a constant, but changes from one situation to another. We might say, from the point of view of a broadened exchange theory, that emotional energy is the motivating force that moves one through a series of interactions on the social market. This brings us to the dynamic part of interactions.

ENCOUNTERS CHANGE OR REINFORCE
INDIVIDUAL RESOURCES

Person A and person B come into an encounter, carrying their senses of market positions, their general and particularized cultural capitals, and their emotional energies. Various things can happen. If their cultural capitals permit, they can focus their attention on a common subject and begin to parade cultural symbols past one another: in short, they can mount an interaction ritual of several subvariants. If their particularized cultural capital identifies them as co-members of a formal organization, and the situation involves business to be done, they will enact their appropriate order giving, order taking, or negotiation. If, on the other hand, their particularized identities do not match in this way, they are more in a market rather than an organizationally structured situation. Matching of cultural capitals now counts for whether they will be able to have something to say to one another at all, while their relative market positions influence to what extent they will want to.

Each item of cultural capital that person A brings into the interaction is monitored by person B for the group membership that it implies. Most importantly, B judges the relative social rank of these groups, connoting the social ranking of person A. There is a special recognition of symbols which imply personal membership in an enforcement coalition. Person A similarly sizes up person B. None of this, I stress, has to be done consciously; the symbols are operating as ingredients of the ritual, giving each person a certain degree of impressiveness and attractiveness.[10] On

---

[10] As indicated in Chapter 6, there are two main dimensions of interaction: power (vertical) and status (horizontal attraction). For simplicity, here I am giving only a very general model of dynamics, which could apply to the relative position of either dimension.

FIGURE 10-1

THE INTERACTION RITUAL CHAIN

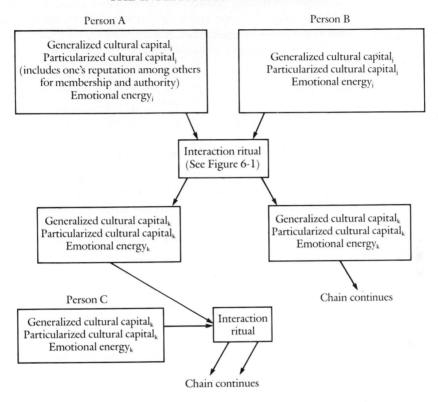

the basis of this mutual tacit monitoring, the interaction proceeds. The outcomes are an altered lineup of generalized and particularized cultural capital, and of emotional energy, for both A and B:

1. *Whatever generalized cultural capital A communicates to B is now part of B's repertoire.* Cultural capital thus increases over time, provided that B is associating with persons who have different cultural capitals and are not merely repeating the same over again. Particularized cultural capital also increases or is reinforced.

   Emotional energy is changed via the following processes:

2. *If A dominates the ritual, A's emotional energy increases and B's emotional energy decreases, proportionate to the degree of domination.* A comes away from the situation feeling more confident, more energetic; B comes away feeling less confident, more depressed. How strong these effects are, and what complexities may cut across them, has not yet been well studied. The main effect is that A will now have at least slightly more emotional energy, which A will be able to use to dominate the next interaction; while B will have at least a slight decrement, reducing the chances that B will be successful in B's next interaction.

This situation described in (2) applies only to deference rituals, in which one individual is able to dominate the other, either by superior organizational position (particularized cultural capital indicating connection to an enforcement coalition) or sheer surplus of generalized cultural capital (impressive things to talk about) and of emotional energy. Rituals may also be egalitarian, with no one having the power to control the other. But even in egalitarian exchanges there still can be a gain or loss of emotional energy:

2a. *If A has much more cultural capital than B, and also A has alternative people that A could interact with* (that is, A's position in the conversational market is better than B's), *then A will spend little or no time interacting with B.* What interaction does take place is on a superficial level of conversation and is relatively unsatisfying.[11] Hence B loses emotional energy. Note, though, that A does not (usually) gain emotional energy by rejecting B.

2b. *If A and B have similar market positions,* so that both want to interact with one another in egalitarian ritual, they will be able to carry out a successful interaction ritual. The ritual process itself intensifies emotional energy. *Hence both A and B emerge with greater confidence.* How long these energy flows last in daily life has not been measured. Probably it can be contravened by the next encounter; but over a period of many encounters, if the emotional outcomes are similar in each, there is perhaps a cumulative effect, leading to some individuals becoming quite dynamic, others depressed and withdrawn, and still others in between.

2c. *The successful ritual in (2b) is still further modified by the ranking of the groups implied in the symbols used.* If A and B carry out an interaction ritual in which the symbolic content implies their mutual membership in high-ranking groups (that is, they are successfully showing off), both will come out with an especially high level of emotional energy. On the other hand, A and B may have a successful ritual but incorporating cultural capital which implies merely local or unpowerful group membership. There is still an emotional increment, but not a large one.

---

[11] What people will say in a conversation is predictable from their relative market positions and resources, together with the kinds of relationships implied by the type of talk itself. Various kinds of talk are differently value-weighted by the kinds of social relationships they imply. The following categories are arranged roughly from situations of impersonality, to those of greater intimacy and trust (Collins, 1975:114–31): (1) practical talk as part of the work situation; (2) commenting on some facet of the external world; (3) discussing political, religious, or other areas of value commitments; (4) talking about entertainment, or doing entertaining talk (such as joking); (5) gossiping about events of personal acquaintances; (6) narrating one's own experiences and feelings.

Talk which is relatively more frontstage or backstage in the Goffmanian sense correspondingly implies lesser or greater commitment to one's conversational partner. Hence some kinds of talk "costs" and is "worth" more than others. How far up or down this continuum of impersonality versus intimacy one situates one's conversation depends on the market situations of the participants. A weak level of mutual attractiveness keeps the talk at relatively "superficial" or impersonal levels; a high level of mutual market attraction moves the talk to the more personally binding side. In some situations, individuals who have temporary surges of emotional energy may attempt to negotiate a closer relationship by moving the conversational topic to a different level. Whether this succeeds or not, however, depends on the resources and motivations of both sides.

In addition, the *market opportunities* of A and B may also change as the result of their interaction. If they have not interacted before, their successful meeting adds to each one's sense of market opportunities. They may also indirectly acquire new market opportunities by references to third persons or introductions. Some existing market opportunities could also be lost, if the outcome of the interaction is that one of them decides not to interact with the other person again.

INTERACTION RITUAL CHAINS AND EXCHANGE THEORY

The IR chain model broadens the application of exchange theory and also helps solve some of its weaknesses. The difficulty of finding a common metric for different rewards and probabilities is solved by postulating emotional energy as a common denominator. Similarly, limited human cognition in decision-making situations can be incorporated by focusing on the ritual nature of interaction.

The IR chain theory also helps explain one of Homans' earliest principles: the more people interact, the more they will like each other, provided that there is no power difference between them. Homans later interpreted this as due to the mutual exchange of rewards. The Durkheimian ritual model is at least partly equivalent to Homans' formulation. The ingredients of interaction are broken up into physical copresence, plus a common focus of attention and a common mood, which result in turn in collective symbols and feelings of group solidarity (what Homans calls liking). The reason this process becomes stronger and stronger over time is that the symbols which result from one interaction (that is, ideas held in common) make it all the easier to focus mutual attention the next time and, thus, to carry out an even more successful interaction ritual. Homans' model is then a kind of skeletal outline of the Durkheimian process. What the ritual theory adds, besides detail on how the interaction has its effects, is the point that a successful ritual results in feelings not just of liking but of moral obligation.

This helps explain a puzzle that both Homans and Blau wrestled with: the issue of reciprocity. In their model, persons A and B like each other the more they interact, because each wishes to reward the other for the rewards they have just received. But why should they feel a need to reciprocate in the first place, instead of just taking their payoff without having to pay for it? Blau had to fall back on the argument that what is habitual becomes obligatory, though this does not seem to be always true, and does not follow from his utilitarian principles in any case. More generally, Blau just assumes there is a norm of reciprocity, a feeling that one ought to return a favor, and that this gets exchanges going in the first place. The Durkheimian ritual theory, on the other hand, gives a causal mechanism for exactly when people will feel this obligation and when they will not. In the IR chain model, an interaction does not have to be a deliberate exchange of rewards; its crucial element is rather the focus of common attention and the emotional contagion that goes with it. The interaction itself may be rewarding, primarily because of the joint experience of a successful ritual and the heightened emotions that it produces for all participants, rather than because the participants are taking turns rewarding each other.

When someone feels the obligation to return a favor, then, or when someone becomes angry because someone else failed in this obligation, it is because a prior ritual solidarity had already been established. Not all situations fit this condition: if persons have not gone through much high-density, ritually focused experience, they are not likely to feel much obligation toward each other, and instead they will approach their interaction in a spirit of competitive self-interest. To put it in other terms: when people share the same symbolic status system, they are motivated to make fair exchanges with each other; if they do not have the same "cultural capital," they do not feel this obligation and may try to turn a profit at the other's expense, possibly even by fraud or coercion.

Blau's version of exchange theory, as we have seen, was too ready to fall back on assumed social norms and short-circuit the actual process of bargaining that takes place among individuals. IR chain theory does not rely on general social norms, but focuses only on what emotional solidarity is actually created by particular groups of people. Cultural capital is not something that is spread uniformly over the whole society, but is produced and used by individuals in particular encounters; it ties together only particular networks, rather than everybody. Instead of assuming solidarity and reciprocity everywhere, we are able to see just where it will be found and where it will not.

The IR chain model also links exchange theory with the more subjective and interpretive models in microsociology. For example, it offers an explanation of the symbolic interactionist principle that behavior is determined by the definition of the situation. In the IR chain models, individuals go through their daily lives from situation to situation. They enter each one with a stock of cultural capital and emotional energy, which is then reproduced or changed, leading them into the next situation. In principle, what each individual will do in their next encounter is determined by their cognitive (cultural) repertoire and the emotional energy to activate it. But one cannot predict what will happen in any situation from knowing about one individual alone. It is the *combination* of persons who come together which determines what ritual will ensue (if any ritual at all), how long it will last, and who will dominate it. In this sense situations are emergent. But it is an illusion to regard them undetermined, an illusion which arises when a social psychological theory focuses on the viewpoint of only one individual.

HEISE'S AFFECT CONTROL CHAINS

A theory which parallels at least some of the interaction ritual chain model is Heise's (1979, 1987) affect control theory. Heise blends several ingredients. From psychological experiments with balance theory, he takes the principle that an individual's attitudes change in order to remain in maximal cognitive balance. (That is, if one is told that a good person did a bad thing, either one's attitudes toward the bad thing change in a positive direction, or one's evaluation of the person changes in negative direction.) From symbolic interactionism he takes the principle that action is determined by the definition of the situation, and the general viewpoint that action is constructed in an ongoing process rather than given in a static structure. In Heise's model, individuals carry a set of cognitive categories in their minds, which are loaded with evaluations. That is, individuals know their social world consists of mothers, children, soldiers, fire fighters, bankers, and so on and of various levels of prestige, power, and excitement associated with each of these.

Initially each social category has an evaluation on three dimensions: good to bad (which the theory calls "Evaluation"), strong to weak ("Potency") and active to passive ("Activity"). As action takes place, these evaluations shift. If someone learns, for example, that "the mother hit the baby," their evaluation of the mother shifts from good toward bad, while the other dimensions (strong, active) also shift. Through an extensive program of research, Heise and his colleagues have assembled "dictionaries" of hundreds of words, which people used to categorize people, actions, emotions, and other parts of social descriptions. There is an Evaluation, Potency, and Activity (or EPA) score for each category, ranging from +4.5 (the most highly valued, powerful, or active) to −4.5 (the most disvalued, weakest, most passive), with zero as the neutral point. A mother has a profile, in the American subculture that Heise tested, which is quite good, quite powerful, and neither active nor passive: 2.3 1.9 0.0; while a child is good, somewhat powerless, and very active: 1.9 −1.1 2.5.

With this data, it is possible to write equations which predict the outcomes of different combinations of actors, objects, and actions. Supposing "a mother whips a child." Whipping has an EPA profile of −2.2 0.4 0.9 (that is, it is quite bad, slightly powerful, somewhat active). Combining this with the profiles for mother and child, we predict that the mother will be viewed as somewhat bad (−1.3), powerful (1.5), and active (1.2). The image of the child changes too: it becomes regarded as less good than before (slipping from 1.9 to 0.9), even weaker (−1.1 to −1.9), and less lively (2.5 to 1.7). Part of this result is unexpected, since not only the mother but the child loses goodness as the result of participating in a negative action. But Heise suggests that this is empirically accurate, even if we might think it unjust: it is part of the phenomenon of "blaming the victim."

The preceding is a simple version of impression-formation processes, which are at the center of the affect control model. In a more complex version, more information is provided about the people and their actions: status characteristics such as old, rich, Catholic; personality traits such as shy, proud, friendly; and moods such as angry, elated, sad. These modifiers have their own loadings in terms of evaluation, potency, and activity, and make up more of the "dictionaries" of concepts that people carry around in their heads. When added into the equations of who does what to whom, they add more detail but act in the same way as the basic model (Averett and Heise, 1987).

These processes may be applied to predict various aspects of how people think, feel, and behave. In the preceding example, we have been concerned with the way an observer will react to seeing other people in action (for instance, what one would think about the mother whipping the child). In addition to such "impression formation," these processes also may be used to predict how one would expect other people to behave. We would generally regard "the mother whips the child" as an unlikely event, because it results in changing the baseline identity of the mother too far from normal.

Perhaps the most important application is for determining what people actually do, rather than their observations or expectations regarding other people. In each situation, actors monitor their own stocks of social categories and match them with the persons they are encountering. For instance, a mother encountering a baby consults her set of possible actions, each of which is loaded with a set of affective ratings. The same applies to a patient encountering a doctor (or vice versa) and to any other combination of social categories. Choosing from this list, one picks the action that will most closely confirm one's existing sentiments about oneself and one's set of categories of other people. That is, the EPA profile of the action chosen is the one which will leave the EPA profile of oneself (say the mother) and the object (the child) as close to their starting points as possible. "Whipping" is not very likely to be chosen, because it results in such a sharp deflection in identities; whereas some action like "soothing", "feeding," "carrying" would more nearly maintain existing identities.

Heise's model constitutes a chain of events. One person acts, and then another acts; after each action, their feelings about themselves and each other are either confirmed or shifted. Hence these feelings are *transient* and link together situations as a chain. The social definition of each situation shifts as the result of the last situation and of the mixture of persons who are put together. Heise's affect control theory differs from the more traditional cultural model in which unchanging rules and norms determine people's behavior. Instead, each situation can be different from the last one because it emerges out of a chain of past events. People behave in terms of their situated identities and the identities which they have learned from recent experience of the other persons around them. Moreover, although the basic categories are cognitive, the affects activate them in any particular situation. As Heise (1987) sums up: "the affective system provides a way for storing much of the cultural heritage of reasoned action. People do not have to solve each problem anew, they do not even have to understand the logic of old solutions; they have only to acquire sentiments, and then they produce reasonable action as if by instinct."[12]

CRITICISMS AND EXTENSIONS

One apparent problem with Heise's affect control theory is that it is difficult to see how individuals could come to bring themselves to perform acts that are uncharacteristic of standard roles. If mothers are always good, how could they possibly ever act out of role? Presumably the whole social structure would remain static.

---

[12] The emotions that people experience is derived in Heise's model in an interesting way. There are two levels of affect which a person feels in any situation: the *fundamental sentiments* (the EPA profile) associated with the identity of oneself and the person one is encountering; and a *transient feeling* which is connected to the action that takes place. Interestingly enough, when the action is normally congruent with the basic sentiments (the mother feeds instead of whips the baby), the emotion that is actually felt is minimal. It is only when something happens which violates one's identity, or else confirms it extremely strongly, that emotion is felt. The emotion is then selected in the same way as an action. The action of a child being whipped by the mother needs an emotion which corresponds to a movement from child-before-whipping into child-after-whipping; comparing these two profiles, we find a difference of $-1.0 -1.5 -0.5$, and the modifiers that will generate this difference corresponds most closely to the EPA profiles of afraid, flustered, or horrified. These are the emotions, then, that the child will feel. Another possibility that causes emotion is when someone has experiences that very strongly reinforce his or her fundamental identity; for example, when a child feels especially loved, cared for, and entertained. Insofar as individuals carry around certain kinds of emotions from one situation to another, this is because they have a modified sense of their own identities and consider themselves "outraged," or "calm," or the like. Heise (1987) interprets Collins' (1981a) "emotional energies" as such long-term modifications of one's self-conception.

Heise (1987) modifies the earlier theory to answer this point. There can be different subcultures, which gives different EPA profiles to various roles; hence persons from different families, occupations, genders, social classes may apply different sentiments to the situations they see before them. Various combinations of persons encountering one another may define the identities differently; and even if they pick the same categories, they may have different EPA profiles attached to them. This, of course, would set in motion further developments in the affect control chain, as people change their EPA profiles according to what happened in the last event. Conflicts can emerge, with the consequences of redefining people's identities through labelling, blaming the victim, and perhaps provoke withdrawal into one's own subculture, or retailiation.

Heise's theory would need to be expanded, then, to include an explanation of how different subcultures emerge in the first place. It also needs to be amalgamated more fully with a market model of interaction, which would show which persons attempt to interact with whom, and whom they have less attraction toward. Heise's affect control theory, as it stands, explains what happens once people get in a situation where they are motivated to act toward certain people in terms of certain identities, but tells us little about why one person gravitates toward them. Heise's only motivational mechanism is homeostatic, in the sense that it proposes how people try to maintain stable identities for self and others. This would have to be expanded to add the kinds of motivations that move people in social markets: seeking the best payoff in social membership and power that is available to them out of alternative possibilities.[13]

Another difficulty is how people happen to define the situation in the first place, so that they know which identities of themselves or others are salient. Situations in formal organizations (for instance, the sick person in the doctor's office) may often solve this problem if some practical activity is sufficiently urgent; but in sociable or casual situations different identities may equally apply. And even at work, what happens if the person one encounters can be treated equally well as "secretary," "co-worker," "acquaintance," "woman" (in relation to a man; or in relation to another woman), "newcomer," and so on?[14] In Heise's research, these possibilities are preempted, since he presents his respondents with a list of situations which are already verbally defined. (Most of the evidence for Heise's model has been confined to pencil-and-paper responses to hypothetical persons and situations, rather than actual observations of what people actually do, think, and feel in real situations, although some studies have successfully predicted behavior in laboratory experiments.) This is another "external" context which needs to be completed in order for the affect control theory to be set in motion. Heise (1987) thus attempts to borrow from some other models of how situations become defined.

---

[13] Heise, however, questions (in a personal communication to the author) whether people always seek the "best payoff." He conjectures they do so when they are maintaining good, powerful identities, but may avoid the "best" and even seek the "worst" when they have negative identities, such as neurotic, crazy, or depressed.

[14] In terms of a market theory, which identity became salient would depend on one's emotional energies and market position, which would determine whether one felt the best deal would come from interacting with someone sociably, sexually, in strictly business-like practicality, in a power confrontation, and so forth.

Heise's model, although driven by affect, loads up the individual with long "dictionaries" which they carry in their heads, listing hundreds of social roles, actions, descriptions, traits, and moods, each with its own EPA profile. Of course it is not literally true that everyone has memorized a long list of these words with numbers attached; Heise is implying that these affective loadings are unconscious and that they are built in not as numbers in our memories but as emotional propensities attached to certain ideas. We might question, though, whether the human mind really does shuffle through several thousand words in order to come up with the right match for the situation, and then produces the action or emotion that corresponds to the appropriate vector. This is a great deal of cognitive processing, and it might strain human capacities to have to do this—at least quickly enough to react normally in a situation as it presents itself. Perhaps these lists of words are labels that we apply after the fact, while the behavior is generated by some more compact set of ways for reacting to people in situations. (This might be something like the model of generative element in interactions given at the end of Chapter 9, in the proposed computer simulation of Goffman's model of interaction in Figure 9-2).

Heise's theory seems to imply that people cannot act until they have learned the culture, which gives them the appropriate categories for defining identities. We might question, then, how it is that children learn to behave in the first place, before they learned the culture? Furthermore, since affect control theory proposes that emotions come from a process of comparing outcomes with identities, and choosing emotions which correspond to the shift, how can children have emotions before they learn the words for them? If the affect control model is correct, "emotions" do not really exist in the same sense before and after children learn the cultural labels. This is a fairly radical suggestion. Alternatively, we can suppose that children have a different, pre-cultural way of acting and feeling, and that this mechanism makes it possible for them to learn.[15] But if so, then it is conceivable that this "primitive" mechanism still remains present later and is only overlaid by the mature cognitive processes which Heise describes. Here again we see the possibility that Heise's model (or at least his long "dictionaries" of cognitive terms), may be a "surface" level which is produced by a smaller number of generative elements "beneath" it.

SUMMARY

1. Homans proposed: the more that people interact, the more they like one another, and vice versa, provided there is no inequality in power. The more that people interact, the more similar their sentiments and activities become. These processes occur because individuals exchange rewards.

2. Blau theorized: behavior is determined by expected profit (rewards minus costs). Rewards are returned because there is a *norm of reciprocity;* people become angry when reciprocity is violated. Blau attempts to explain this norm behavioristically by the principle that what is habitual becomes obligatory. Balanced exchanges

---

[15] In contrast, the interaction ritual chain model is precultural, in the sense that ritual interactions generate symbols, as well as recycle symbols which may already exist.

in some social relationships tend to produce unbalanced exchanges in other relationships, resulting in conflicts and change.

3. Power derives from the dependence of some persons on others for scarce rewards. Power is highest when one actor has a unilateral monopoly and when rewards are uncertain.

4. Homans stated his principles in terms of behaviorist psychology, later elaborated by Emerson. A key is the *rationality proposition:* the actor chooses the behavior which has the greatest payoff in value multiplied by probability of attaining it. This has led to a theory of rational choice, which applies principles of economic theory to social behavior.

5. The exchange-rational choice line of theory has been criticized because it has focused too narrowly on practical activity or advice as a source of power; it is weak in dealing with coercive power resources; it fails to provide a common metric by which individuals may compare different rewards and costs; its model of the individual calculating maximal expected payoffs violates the limits of human cognitive capacities.

6. Exchange theory can be broadened to meet these problems. In the theory of interaction ritual chains, interactions are natural rituals which generate symbols of group membership. Symbols from previous interactions imply relative group rankings. Individuals bargain implicity over the exchange of ranked membership symbols.

7. Individuals enter an interaction carrying (a) a sense of their market opportunities, the number of other possible interactions; (b) generalized and particularized cultural capital; (c) emotional energy, a level of confidence and initiative ranging from low to high. Individuals move toward those interactions which have the highest attraction in emotional energy. The extent to which any combination of persons will interact is determined by the match of their market opportunities, cultural capitals, and emotional energies.

8. Cultural capital is circulated through a network of interactions. An individual's emotional energy increases or decreases depending on whether she or he is accepted or rejected in ritual participation and is dominant or subordinate in the ritual. These processes are enhanced by the ranking of the group membership symbols in the larger chains of society. The result of any interaction is to change or reinforce the lineup of individual resources.

9. Heise's affect control theory proposes that individuals carry mental categories of persons and actions, which are emotionally loaded on three dimensions: good to bad, strong to weak, and active to passive. Individuals perceive the social world as a series of events, which change their transient impressions of persons to reflect the actions taken. Actors construct their own action by categorizing social objects in their environment and choosing the action toward them which is most consistent with their current emotional loadings for self and others.

PART III

MESO THEORIES

Chapter 11

THE MICRO-MACRO CONNECTION

HISTORY OF THE MICRO-MACRO QUESTION
    The Micro Attack on Macrosociology: Homans and Psychological Reduction
    The Micro Attack: Symbolic Interactionism and Social Phenomenology
    Recent Developments on the Micro-Macro Issue

THE NATURE OF MICRO AND MACRO

REDUCTIONISM
    Is Microsociology More Empirical?
    Micro Reduction or Micro Translation?

THEORIES OF MICRO-MACRO LINKAGES
    Giddens' Structurationism
    Habermas' Colonization of the Lifeworld
    Rational Choice and Exchange Models
    Interaction Ritual Chains

CONCLUSION

SUMMARY

The micro-macro issue has become an important topic in recent years. Historically, Emile Durkheim launched the modern discipline of sociology with a sharp claim for the autonomy of sociology from psychology. Not everyone agreed, but there was relatively little controversy over micro and macro issues until the 1960s, when Homans launched an explicit drive to reduce sociology to social behaviorism. The attack on macrosociology was joined by several versions of interpretive microsociologies, including symbolic interactionism and ethnomethodology. The issue has never been settled. Several militant microsociologies continue their war against macrosociology, although they disagree sharply among themselves over the nature of the microsociology to be put in its place. And macrosociology has gone ahead, largely oblivious to the onslaught. But the controversy has been theoretically fruitful. Most important theorists since the 1970s have turned their attention to the issue. In general, their stance has been that sociology must be able to construct macrosociology on a micro basis. There are varying approaches how this is to be done. There are already payoffs in understanding the processes of social action, and in arriving at a more realistic and more penetrating view of the macro structure.

HISTORY OF THE MICRO-MACRO QUESTION

Durkheim was concerned with establishing sociology as a discipline with its own focus and subject matter. Above all, he did not wish it to be taken as a branch of psychology, which was also emerging as an empirical discipline in the 1880s and 1890s. In *The Rules of the Sociological Method* (1895), Durkheim laid down the principle that sociology deals with a reality *sui generis,* of its own kind. "Social facts" are not merely the experiences of individuals, but are characterized by exteriority and constraint. We know we are in the presence of the social because it imposes limits on what we can do. From this follows a methodological principle: we can best observe these social constraints by watching what happens when they are violated. Society is aroused; it becomes righteous and punishing. From this follows Durkheim's theory of deviance and social control. Most of Durkheim's works can be recognized as arguments in favor of the social over the psychological. His famous *Suicide* (1897) is designed to show that even this intimate act is determined by social currents which make it more or less common and, conversely, that society is what gives meaning to living. *The Elementary Forms of the Religious Life* (1912) attacks psychological theories of religion, such as those which derive the belief in spirits from the experience of dreams. Religion is founded instead on the social structure, and God symbolizes this exteriority of society, just as the soul represents its penetration into the individual.

Most of the classical sociologists took a similar position. Comte, Marx and Engels, Toennies, Pareto, Spencer and the social organicists—all of these had concentrated on the macro structure of society and attempted to state its determining laws on that level. Durkheim stood out only by the explicitness of his attack on psychological reductionism, and by the cleverness of his attempts at proving the autonomy and priority of social structures. Simmel, too, although he is regarded as a forerunner of the modern microsociology of everyday life, held that sociology studies the forms of sociation, a formal realm analyzable in its own right. The only major European sociologist who departed from this consensus was Weber. In his major systematic work (1922/1968: 3–31), Weber begins with the categories of social action and declares that society is built up out of the interpretations of individuals. But this did not pose a challenge to the macro tendencies of sociology, since Weber himself laid out his action theory only in his methodological writings. In his substantive work, he operated as a historical comparativist, concerned entirely with large-scale structures of religion, state, and economy. Weber's writings on action theory were picked up by the Austrian Alfred Schutz (1932/1967), who connected Weber's ideal types to Husserl's phenomenological philosophy (see Prendergast, 1986). Schutz attempted thereby to show how the entire social world is built up subjectively. But Schutz's work only became influential decades later, after he had migrated to the United States, through his students Peter Berger and Harold Garfinkel.

Only on the American side of the Atlantic was this dominance by macrosociology seriously challenged. Cooley, Mead, and their followers actually concentrated on the microsociological realm and built up theories of the social self and mind. Nevertheless, the micro-macro dispute remained latent. Cooley (1902: 88–97) had taken a potentially very radical stance by claiming that society is in the mind. But he himself went on to treat society as a natural and harmonious meeting of minds, a great democracy in which everyone gets together to construct all social institutions for mutual benefit. Similarly, Mead seemed to see no theoretical problems in the emergence of macrosocial institutions from his microsociology of the self. Mead was a philosopher, not a sociologist, although active in liberal social reform movements which appealed to the education of the individual as the solution to social problems. This political stance is perhaps responsible for Mead's apparent belief that there is no problem in going from the smaller to the larger arena. It was only later, in the 1950s, that Mead's views were taken to more radical conclusions by his former student Herbert Blumer.

A kind of orthodoxy was established for a while by Talcott Parsons (1937, 1951). Parsons ignored the American symbolic interactionists, but he was conscious of a need to develop a comprehensive sociology which would include both the micro level of individual action and the macro level of large-scale structure. Parsons took the categories of action theory from Weber, Pareto, and from economics. Parsons' (1937) basic action scheme has four elements: the actor chooses (1) *means* to arrive at (2) desired *ends,* while constrained by (3) the *environment* and following (4) *social norms.* The mean-ends scheme is the core of economic rationality. The environment is left over from the heritage of biological schemes, and Parsons largely ignored it. Social norms are what Parsons interpreted as Durkheim's exteriorly constraining social facts, a category to which he assimilated the religious and status factors in conduct stressed by Weber.

In his later work, Parsons (1951) steadily expanded the importance of the social shaping of action. The ends of action are not random, but are set by society's values (for instance, economic success in a modern capitalist society). Choice of means is dictated, too, by social roles. Gradually the action elements were swallowed up.

Parsons' emphasis was heavily on the macro side, since it is the overall structure of society which determines roles and norms, and the cultural system which determines the ultimate values of ends. Nevertheless, all this was to be attached to the individual as well. Parsons did this by adapting a neo-Freudian theory of personality. The superego, a combination of moral conscience and personal ideal, is developed inside each child's psyche through the process of socialization. Parsons conceived this in conventional Freudian fashion, as the resolution of the Oedipus complex and the identification of the child with the parent (to be precise, with the parent's superego). Thus society's norms and values are passed down from generation to generation. Individuals enter into this theory of the social system, but largely as passive material on which the social content is stamped.

THE MICRO ATTACK ON MACROSOCIOLOGY: HOMANS AND PSYCHOLOGICAL REDUCTION

In the 1950s, a rebellion against macrosociology was building up. One of Parsons' younger colleagues in the Harvard Department of Social Relations, George Homans, sharply rejected Parsons' attempted grand synthesis in *Towards a General Theory of Action* (1951; see Homans' autobiography, 1984: 300–303). Homans had been studying interactions in small groups. In 1961, he radicalized his position. Homans' *Social Behavior: Its Elementary Forms* (1961, 1974) declared not merely that the laws of small groups are the fundamental principles of sociology, but that the general principles of all the social sciences are the laws of behavioral psychology. All human groups and institutions consist of the actions of individuals in relation to each other. Analyzing a series of empirical studies, Homans showed that in each case the behavior could be explained in terms of the frequency with which people's actions were rewarded and punished, together with intensity or value of those rewards and punishments, and the expectations of receiving them in various situations. For example (Homans, 1961: 164–80), sociometric choices in a group are determined by the rewards that alter gives to ego; the similarity of alter to ego; and the value of alter's contributions to the group, which in turn is rewarding to ego insofar as ego is a group member.

In his presidential address to the American Sociological Association in 1964, "Bringing Men Back In," Homans declared himself a psychological reductionist. The prevailing positions within sociology had lost the human element in a series of remote abstractions. The social system does not do anything; only real people do things, and in fact it is their repeated behaviors that constitute social structure. Homans attacked functionalism, insofar as functionalism declared that social institutions exist because of the functions they serve for maintaining society. Where this is not a tautology, it merely means that certain arrangements serve functions for certain real people: in other words, that it is rewarding for those persons. Homans (1984: 344–45) thus reinterpreted Merton's (1949/1968) famous functional analysis of why the corrupt political "machine" persists by pointing out that it is rewarding for business executives who get favors from the politicians, and for the politicians who are paid off by the business executives. In general, Homans felt that functionalism was empty, lacking in real causality because it ignored the processes impinging on real people's behavior.

Homans' attack on macrosociology thus arose in the context of an attack on functionalism as the macrosociological paradigm.[1] His advocacy of B. F. Skinner's behaviorist psychology also followed from Homans' acceptance of the methodological strategy widely touted at the time (Braithwaite, 1953; Nagel, 1961). Science produces "covering laws" which subsume particular patterns of events under general propositions. Sociology "reduces" to psychology, in the sense that its explanatory propositions turn out to be those of psychology. Homans himself showed, in numerous instances, that sociological patterns could be explained in this way. Reduction does not deny the reality of the social patterns. It merely insists that they are on a different level than the laws that explain them: they are the material to be explained, the empirical surface as opposed to the theoretical depth.

A considerable debate followed Homans' pronouncements. Homans' evidence, it was pointed out, came from small groups existing within larger structures—businesses, schools, communities—which set the context for the group behavior. Hence Homans was taking the macro structure for granted, which made possible the micro behaviors he observed. Homans replied (1984: 341) that these larger structures themselves exist only as repeated patterns of social behavior. Even if the individual members come and go while formal organizational patterns persist, nevertheless at no point in time does the organization or community ever exist without people enacting it. Homans distinguishes between *individualistic sociology,* which explains how individuals create structures by their interactions, and *structural sociology,* which shows the effects of these structures on the behavior of individuals. But the propositions involved are the same ones: in the former case, individual behavior is the independent variable and structures are the dependent variables; in the latter, the order of causality is the reverse. This is not a vicious circle, but just a different part of the sequence in time.

Other critics (Blain, 1971; J. Turner, 1974: 242–57) argued that Homans' psychological principles do not cover everything a sociologist wishes to know. It may be true that people are motivated by expectations of reward and cost as they interact with one another; but what determines whether they will reward and punish one another in a particular way? Homans himself gives an example (1984: 340): states with freely elected legislatures tend to have independent judiciaries. This relates two structures to each other. But both the elected legislature and the independent judiciary are patterns of individual behavior. Once instituted, these patterns are maintained because new individuals are rewarded for following the pattern and punished or otherwise incur costs for not following it. But how did the institutions get established in the first place? Again, this was done through the behavior of individuals,

---

[1] At about the same time, Homans had attacked Lévi-Strauss' structuralism. Lévi-Strauss (1949/1969) had interpreted cross-cousin marriage systems in tribal kinship for their structural consequences in integrating families through long chains of exchanges. Homans and Schneider (1955) argued instead that these marriage practices existed because they maximized rewards for the immediate group members, and attempted to prove this by analysis of the comparative evidence. Although Homans does not say so, I would suggest that this dispute with Lévi-Strauss is one of the sources of Homans' own exchange theory. Lévi-Strauss' theory of kinship (which in turn came from Mauss' 1922 theory of gift exchange) concerns indirect exchange, a structured pattern above the level of individuals. Instead, Homans proposed that society can be reduced theoretically to direct exchange links, driven by individuals' calculations of expected rewards and costs. See Ekeh (1975).

acting in circumstances in which they expected rewards for setting up certain institutions and costs for not setting them up. The structural connection between legislatures and judiciaries means only that the existence of one determined the rewards
and costs of the other in such a way as to favor behavior in creating and sustaining
the other.

To explain situations, in other words, is only to explain the histories of rewards
and punishments experienced by individuals. These histories can take many shapes.
Hence they are on a level of greater empirical detail than the covering laws of psychology, which apply over and over again to these different configurations. Structural sociology, for Homans, is merely a psychologically informed history. It is only
out of laziness, or lack of information, that we do not perform this reduction of
institutions to the histories of individual reinforcements which made up their basic
reality. The institutions—legislatures, judiciaries, businesses, schools, and so on—are
only a convenient shorthand for these processes.[2]

THE MICRO ATTACK: SYMBOLIC INTERACTIONISM AND SOCIAL PHENOMENOLOGY

Homans' work came from the positivistic side of social science. The psychology
which he adopted as sociology's "covering laws" was that of B. F. Skinner, the most
extreme of the behaviorists, who denied anything could be said about what goes on
inside the "black box" of the mind. Homans' theories have been most popular with
the researchers who carry on laboratory experiments with small groups. For the
most part, Homans' followers have been content to develop his micro propositions,
and have stayed clear of the debate over the reduction of macro structures to psychology. The most extensive attack on macrosociology, however, has come from a
very different version of microsociology. Homans, and above all Skinner, are on the
"hard" side, emulating the mathematical principles of physical science and concentrating on behavior and its determinative laws. At the same time that Homans was
launching his attack, the advocates of the "soft" approaches were mounting theirs.
In a series of papers going back to the 1950s and before, Herbert Blumer advocated
a symbolic interactionist theory based on the teachings of George Herbert Mead,
and incorporating many of the emphases of William I. Thomas, Florian Znaniecki,
and other members of the Chicago school of the previous generation. (The most
important of these papers are collected in Blumer, 1969). But whereas his predecessors were content to leave sociological concepts of the macro structure unquestioned, Blumer formulated a sharp attack on virtually all branches of existing sociology.
Like Homans, Blumer was hostile to functionalism and to Parsons' abstract categories. He also attacked statistical sociology, as carried out by questionnaire research.

In both cases, Blumer made the argument for greater empirical realism. Functionalism deals with structures, values, norms: but where are these? In what ways

[2] Homans himself began his scholarly career as an historian, with an account of the system of rural land
holdings in thirteenth-century England (Homans, 1941). His work was almost entirely descriptive and
attributed the two different field systems found in England to those brought from the continent by two
different groups of invaders. Homans later (1984: 187–88) commented that history has no general
laws, except that people act according to general psychological laws in specific historical circumstances.

are they empirical, Blumer asked? In fact, when sociologists carry out field-work, they observe real people in some situation, making interpretations of what is going on. People put themselves mentally in the place of the other and attempt to work out a course of action which will take account of what the other is expected to do. Social behavior is negotiated, situation by situation, not imposed by some hidden structure. The abstractions of functionalism are merely ways of categorizing what has happened after it is over, and do not capture the real processes by which this behavior has come about. Macro structure, in other words, is unreal. The empirical basis of any true sociological theory must be the interpretive behavior of people in real situations. This interpretation and communication is done by means of symbols, which are themselves the products of interaction; hence Blumer's label, "symbolic interactionism."

The same criticism applies not only to functionalist theory but much of the work in sociology which claims to be empirical. Survey researchers claim to be discovering "attitudes" by asking respondents questions. The questions usually refer to hypothetical or abstract statements, such as whether one believes racial segregation is desirable. Blumer comments that such questions have little bearing on the central matters of social life because people act only in concrete situations. Whatever they may say in the abstract about their views of race relations, politics, or any other issue, social life actually flows through a series of real-life encounters. In each instance participants have to work out their own interpretations of what is happening and how they will behave in relation to the others. Blumer denies that static "attitudes" exist over and above these situations and govern what people do in them. The researcher administering a questionnaire is merely interacting with people in another, somewhat artificial, situation, eliciting responses which are determined by the interpretations made by participants of how one should deal with a researcher.

SITUATIONAL REDUCTIONISM VS. PSYCHOLOGICAL REDUCTIONISM   Blumer's attack on macrosociology is in some ways more radical than Homans'. Homans left the macro world intact, but as a history of individual reinforcements. Blumer denied that most of what we claim to know about the macro world is empirically true; it is merely a set of interpretations that people make in situations. Blumer also denied the stability that Homans claimed to find on the level of psychological principles. The situation, not the individual, is fundamentally determining. The interaction of individuals makes up situations, and this interaction has a negotiated, and hence emergent, quality. Though one can specify the nature of the individual, using Mead's theory of the self and mind, this turns out to be radically social (see Chapter 7). The individual is fundamentally constituted by interaction. Blumer practices *situational reductionism,* as opposed to the *individual* or *psychological reductionism* of Homans. The individual or psychological level is not ultimate, since it too takes on significance only as it enters into situations. Individuals must be further analyzed into the stances that they work out across the flow of situations; psychological principles (such as reward and punishment) are themselves subject to situational interpretation.

Blumer's attack on macrosociology was pitched at the level of the social, not the psychological. It advocated, in effect, that microsociology (rather than psychology) should take the place of the unrealistic abstractions of macrosociology. Perhaps for this reason, Blumer's general approach has had a larger theoretical following in sociology, at least as far as the micro-macro issue is concerned. The 1960s and 1970s saw an upsurge of microsociology. This included the experimental social psychology following Homans' exchange theory, but this was quite positivistic in spirit and continued a research tradition that went back several decades before. The hallmark of the more radical microsociology was its emphasis on everyday life. An attack on positivism built up, drawing on many sources. Blumer's criticism, that quantitative survey research dealt with artificial entities and missed the prime social reality of situational negotiations, was part of it. Laboratory studies were also criticized as unrealistic. Some other contributing themes came from the student political revolts of the period, which brought a shift toward left-wing theorizing, and regarded both positivist research and functionalist theory as defenses of the status quo. There was also a general movement in philosophy toward dissatisfaction with positivistic accounts of science. These last two influences did not necessarily favor microsociology, since they could just as well advocate a more left-wing (or more historical and interpretive) version of macrosociology; and in fact these did appear. But for sociologists already interested in microsociology, these influences provided an additional rationale for rejecting both traditional macro theories and quantitative research methods.

GOFFMAN'S INFLUENCE   The leading practitioner of the sociology of everyday life was Erving Goffman (1959, 1961, 1967, and many other works). Goffman showed what could be accomplished by a field researcher, operating with no other instruments than sensitive eyes and ears, who avoided construing the situation by asking artificial questions and merely observed what people did. Goffman was particularly good at ferreting out the backstage of interactions, aspects that would never come to light in the artificially observed groups of the laboratory. Goffman was not hesitant to use literary sources, popular entertainment, etiquette books, advertisements, and a host of other unorthodox sources of data on people's ideas and behaviors. Although some of these are themselves quite artificial, Goffman made the distinction between artificial and natural "realities" itself a focus for his research. Thus he ended up (Goffman, 1974, 1979) with an understanding of a central dimension of social life that could never have been achieved by sticking with traditional positivist conventions of what was acceptable scientific data.

Goffman's influence was felt to be tremendously liberating by sociological intellectuals chafing under the narrow restrictions of positivist methodology. The door was opened for qualitative field research on the full range of real life whose study had hitherto been ignored or regarded as unscientific. With the breakdown of positivist dogma, wide-ranging philosophical interpretations could be made of this material, rather than the strict search for empirical generalizations in statistical form or physics-like "covering laws." It should be noted, though, that Goffman himself retained a rather conservative theoretical stance on what he was doing. He never construed his work as an attack on macrosociology. In fact, as we have seen (Chapter 7), he was actually applying Durkheimian theory to the level of situational interactions. It is possible to turn Durkheim's theory into a microsociology, but Goffman did not take this slant either. He presented his own sociological self as the practitioner of a modest specialty, merely picking over the details of some unimportant parts of social life, while the main work went on elsewhere.[3]

SOCIAL PHENOMENOLOGY AND ETHNOMETHODOLOGY   For all that, the study of everyday life did become popular. This could not have happened if it were a minor sideshow, but sociologists now invested it with a larger significance. It was felt to be mounting a major challenge to the dominance of macrosociology as well as of functionalism and positivism. Blumer's critiques of mainstream sociology and Goffman's empirical studies were the major forces popularizing microsociology. But the theoretical leadership was soon seized by an even more radical stance. The manifesto was written by Peter Berger and Thomas Luckmann, whose *The Social Construction of Reality* (1966) summed up in its title the new attitude. Based on the social phenomenology of the philosopher Alfred Schutz (1932/1967) Berger and Luckmann argued that reality itself is not something that is there for researchers to investigate, but something that is produced by people in everyday life. Hence the major subject for sociologists to study is not social institutions and macrostructures, since these do not exist independently of human reality-constructors. It is, rather, the principles of social phenomenology. Sociologists should examine the structure of social experience itself.

The most elaborate examination of this structure has been carried out by the movement of ethnomethodologists. Its founder, Harold Garfinkel, like Berger and Luckmann, had studied with Schutz in New York City at the New School for Social Research in the 1950s. These sociologists constituted a wave of Schutzian social phenomenologists. We have examined the major theoretical findings of this work in Chapters 8 and 9; here I wish only to note the impetus that ethnomethodology gave to the micro-macro dispute. Ethnomethodology is radically situational. Its entire focus of attention is on the methods that people use in commonsense, everyday reasoning. One of these folk methods is to "gloss" most of the implications and assumptions in the background of what they are doing at the moment. People do not generally call into question the larger social context, or the meaning of the things that other people refer to in conversation with them. This happens not because those contexts and meanings are secure and well known, but precisely for the opposite reason: because they are not well understood and, indeed, in principle may be undiscoverable. People take the larger society for granted because this is a convenient way to proceed, not because it has any firm reality.

Garfinkel (1967) and his followers apply the same point to sociologists. Like other intellectuals and scientists, sociologists use the same procedures of common-

---

[3] "I make no claim whatsoever to be talking about the core matters of sociology—social organization and social structure. Those matters have been and can continue to be quite nicely studied without reference to frame at all. . . . I personally hold society to be first in every way and any individual's current involvements second; this report deals only with matters that are second" (Goffman, 1974: 13). Characteristically, though, Goffman defended himself against the charge that his stance is politically conservative because it diverts attention from the conflict of social classes: "I can only suggest that he who would combat false consciousness and awaken people to their true interests has much to do, because the sleep is very deep. And I do not intend here to provide a lullaby but merely to sneak in and watch the way people snore" (14).

sense reasoning, the same ethnomethods, as the people they study. There is no privileged position for sociological analysis. The "society," "organizations," "institutions," "groups," "norms," and so forth that we talk about are merely so many glosses. The ethnomethodologist thus might study (as Garfinkel himself did: 1967: 18–24, 186–261) sociological researchers as they administered questionnaires, coded the answers, and came up with a research report. At every step of the way, the researchers were engaged in commonsense assumptions, and their final depiction of reality was in fact a series of glosses, a gloss-upon-a-gloss-upon-a-gloss. Cicourel (1974) also carried out such studies of demographic research on fertility, as well as a thorough critique of the distortions introduced by quantitative methodology (1964). At one point, ethnomethodologists (Leiter, 1980) spoke of themselves as a meta-discipline beyond sociology, whose aim was to destroy the illusions created by sociology. Others, taking a politically radical stance (Mehan and Wood, 1975) argued that by using the language of social class, sociologists were helping construct the inequality of society; and that they could engage in abolishing inequality by ceasing to contribute to this kind of reification.

Arguments at that extreme are no longer much heard. But ethnomethodologists continue to emphasize that everything sociologists are interested in is "locally produced." Micro reality is the only true empirical reality. No one ever escapes from micro reality, because this is where we live, every minute of the day. Even sociologists and other intellectuals are merely making constructions of macro reality from the micro reality they inhabit. Ethnomethodology is sometimes regarded as a philosophical position, but this is a mistake. Although one of its roots is in phenomenology stemming from Husserl and Schutz, it also can claim to be the most empirical side of sociology. Its tape-recordings of everyday life interaction, and the principles which are inducted from them (for example, Schegloff, 1968; Atkinson and Heritage, 1984) are doubtless the most carefully observed and most primary, first-hand data which sociologists have concerning their subject matter.

RECENT DEVELOPMENTS ON THE MICRO-MACRO ISSUE

A large portion of sociology simply went ahead with its traditional line of work, whether in macro theory or in quantitative research, untouched by these claims. Some macrosociologists even struck back. Coser (1975) charged that ethnomethodology and popular forms of quantitative survey research, although ostensibly enemies, were actually both examples of the same fallacy: both were specialized methods of research, but lacking in substantive theory which can explain the range of relevant social events. Gouldner (1970: 390–95) and others declared that modern microsociology is an evasion of the political dimension of the social world, which can only be understood on the macro level. He depicted the popularity of both Goffman and the ethnomethodologists as a phenomenon of modern culture, dropping out from social concerns and turning attention inward to the private realm or even the subjective fantasies characteristic of the psychedelic counterculture.

In retrospect, these reactions appear polemical, missing the intellectual substance of what the movements in microsociology were attempting to do. Virtually all the recent efforts to produce a comprehensive sociological theory have tried to incorporate the lessons of the newer micro positions. The debate over reductionism, at least in its extreme form, has died down; but the issue remains strong as to how micro analysis is to be coordinated with macro analysis, and how much of each side must give ground to the other. Many theorists still take a strong stance that macro-sociology must give up much of its traditional formulations in the light of micro-sociological critique.

There are a number of different issues which have gotten mixed together over the years of debate. (1) What *are* micro and macro phenomena? Different theories set the dividing lines in different places and against different conceptual backdrops. (2) Is reductionism possible? If so, to what? And if not, can some milder form of micro translation be carried out? (3) What is the connecting link between micro and macro? That is to say, what theory should we use at the micro level and what does it imply about connections (if any) to the macro level?

THE NATURE OF MICRO AND MACRO

Various theorists have construed the micro and macro levels in different ways. Homans regards the micro as individuals engaging in activities according to the laws of psychology. For Blumer, the micro level is the situation: a social interaction, characterized above all by the interpretative—that is, cognitive—activities of inter-actants. For Goffman, too, the micro is situational, together with the structure of the experiences of individuals in it (although Goffman is more hesitant to character-ize that experience as merely cognitive). For Garfinkel, the micro is the local situa-tion in which commonsense reasoning takes place: unlike in symbolic interactionism, it is not necessarily interactional, even having a solipsistic quality to it, and it is certainly episodic. For some ethnomethodologists, the micro is the conversation, or even some portion of it (such as the pair of utterances). Some other theorists (for instance, Coleman, 1986), approaching the issue from a more macro stance, have argued that the micro is the individual person, while the macro is the quantitative pattern found among individuals.

At first glance, the macro level appears simpler to define. Most of the microso-ciologists take a commonsense definition of macrostructure: it is "society," or "insti-tutions," or whatever macro theorists want to characterize it as (for example, Parsons' social system). But most micro theorists are highly critical of the reality of this macro level. For Homans, macro structures are merely repeated patterns of individ-ual activities, explainable by psychological principles; at best, Homans implicitly ad-mits that what is macro is the unique historical patterning of these reinforcements experienced by individuals. For Blumer, the macro is really a situational flux; for Garfinkel, it is a gloss, implying its dubious (or at least unreachable) reality. Goff-man is willing to declare his belief in "society" as a macro reality, but he never says what it is. Coleman's definition of the macro as the quantitative pattern would pre-sumably be rejected by all of these theorists (except perhaps for the taciturn Goff-man); for Homans, numbers merely hide the real individual agents and their psychology; for Blumer, numbers hide the situational interpretations that are really happening; for Garfinkel, they are yet another gloss.

There is even another variant, approximated by Berger and Luckmann, in which the emphasis on the cognitive construction of reality is so strong that it presses right through the micro level and comes out the other side. If reality is socially constructed, even the individual and the situation are constructed, too. There is nothing but the process of construction, which is larger than, or logically prior to, the individual experience. Hence this construction is in some sense objective, itself a macro object. This version of extreme microsociology thus turns into a kind of trans-individual Idealist philosophy, coming close to the versions known as transcendental idealism (Fichte, Schelling, Hegel).

How one characterizes micro and macro, then, seems to depend on what one's substantive theory is. I would propose a more general solution. Micro and macro should not be taken as absolute categories, but as the poles of a continuum. Various levels of analysis can be more micro or more macro, depending on whether we look "up" or "down" from them. What is the dimension here? Let us take some examples. No one would doubt that a nation-state is macro. The world system is even more macro. From that point of view, a state could be viewed as relatively micro, as one of its components. Organizations, such as business firms, are still more micro, though of course they are quite macro from the point of view of small groups and situational interactions.[4]

The underlying dimensions are apparently time and space. The most macro entities are those which cover the most territory and last the longest. That is why Wallerstein's (1974, 1980) study of the capitalist world-system, covering (as projected) the years from 1400 to 1980 is more macro than Barrington Moore's (1966) comparative study of half a dozen major revolutions, although that too is a very macro analysis; and Michael Mann's (1986) study of power from tribal societies through the present is even more macro still. Although the two dimensions are not usually explicitly distinguished like this, we can see that a study might be very wide in one dimension (either time or space) but considerably narrower on the other dimension. A chart for locating possible objects of sociological analysis is given in Figure 11-1.

The horizontal dimension is the amount of time focused upon, ranging from a few seconds, through minutes and hours, days, weeks and months, years and centuries. The vertical dimension charts the amount of space, from a few square feet (enough room for a single person), through local regions (the size for a small group), larger compact regions (inhabitable by a crowd or organization), up through a few miles (the site for a community), hundreds of thousands of square miles (the base for modern territorial states), and even the surface of the globe. Anything sociologists have studied can be located on this chart. Generally, most topics fall along the diagonal axis, since we tend to study things which are approximately the same size in both dimensions. Thus at the most macro end are studies of long-term social change in the entire world system; near this are some histories which focus on very long changes in more compact structures (such as particular states or institutions). At the level of the smallest spatial unit, that occupied by the individual human body,

---

[4]We can see now what is unsatisfactory about Goffman's glib assertion that "society" is primary, since "society" can be taken to mean anything above the level of the isolated individual experience. The externally structured nature of an interaction, however fleeting, would constitute "society" in a generic sense. We can then accept Goffman's position, with its Durkheimian overtones, without going all the way to believing in the primacy of the social system on a larger level.

FIGURE 11-1

TIME AND SPACE AS LEVELS OF SOCIOLOGICAL ANALYSIS

SPACE SCALE (SQ. FT.)	TIME SCALE					
	SECONDS (10^0–10^1 SEC)	MINUTES–HOURS (10^2–10^4 SEC)	DAYS (10^5 SEC)	WEEKS–MONTHS (10^6 SEC)	YEARS (10^7–10^8 SEC)	CENTURIES (10^9 SEC)
One Person (1–3)	Cognitive–emotional processes	Meaningful events; work; repetitive and intermittent behaviors			Careers; life histories	Genealogies
Small Group (3–10^2)	Eye-contact studies; microconversational analyses	Rituals; group dynamics; exchanges; bargaining				
Crowd–Organization (10^3–10^6)		Crowd behavior		Organizations: informal; formal	Organizational structures and histories	
Community (10^7–10^{10})				Social movements	Communities	
Territorial Society (10^{11}–10^{14})					Political, economic, demographic, and stratification patterns (mobility rates etc.) "cultures"	Long-term social changes

Source: Collins, 1981b.

there is a form of analysis which follows this through a long sequence of time: this is the study of careers or life histories. It is macro in time, although micro in space.

There is another clustering at the micro end of both dimensions. We might notice that the realm of "social psychology" has somewhat ambiguous boundaries. Most small group experiments take a few hours, although some reassemble the group over a period of days. The length of naturalistic, everyday life studies appears to vary with the theoretical tradition in which they are carried out. In principle, Mead and Blumer were dealing with situations of relatively short duration (minutes or hours), although much of the field work done by symbolic interactionists has concerned work roles or deviant identities, which are believed to be formed through intermittant interactions spreading over periods which may be as long as months. Not much attention has been paid to time spans in sociological theory, but the presumption seems to be in symbolic interactionist theory that (1) sometimes very brief but dramatic episodes can have major effects, and (2) the negotiation of roles in small groups is usually worked out within a few weeks.

The more radical microsociologies and their accompanying research methods have shifted the focus of attention to the shorter time periods. Goffman studied situations lasting for minutes or less. Conversational analysis has focused on recordings of talk which may take as little as a few seconds. Recently, there has come a development of ultra-micro studies, such as Thomas Scheff's analysis of video tapes of emotions, in which processes happen so rapidly (in tenths of seconds) that they cannot even be seen with the naked eye unless the tape is played back frame by frame (unpublished studies at UC Santa Barbara); or Mazur et al.'s (1980) measurements by instrument of emotions and eye contact in interactions.

Let us now attempt to answer the question, what is micro and macro? Clearly, what is macro is that which is more spread out in time and space. It is a pair of directions in a two-dimensional continuum. Some versions of the micro-macro relation rely more heavily on one dimension than the other. Coleman's (1986) suggestion, for example, that the micro is the individual, and the macro the quantitative sum of individuals, ignores the time dimension. Individuals are taken as if they were timeless, enduring units, as are the structures which they add up to. I think this is a bias introduced by the way survey data is typically analyzed: as if individuals have certain traits (for example, social status, education, race) or attitudes, which combine into overall patterns in the population. The butt of Blumer's critique of quantitative research was precisely this atemporal bias.

The more radical microsociologies claim that fundamental reality lies in the short time periods. There is also a tendency to claim it must be very highly focused in a small space, whether it is the individual's body (or mind) or a slightly larger territory of face-to-face interactants.[5] Can we settle this claim? The time-space chart shows us

---

[5] We might notice, in the middle of the diagonal, that crowd behavior is the largest space of the micro sociological topics, and social movements is one of the smallest of the macro topics. Both have a relatively fluid quality, compared to other areas of sociology. But crowd behavior is usually on a scale of minutes to hours, while social movements are spread out across many people in different places and may last for months or longer. Characteristically, crowd behavior has been one of the specialties of symbolic interactionists, while social movements have attracted more structurally oriented macrosociologists, including conflict theorists who often use quantitative research techniques.

the two continua could both be extended to the infinitesimally small, although practically speaking there is little sociological (or even psychological) subject matter very much smaller than the size of a human body and probably shorter than fractions of a second. The issue, ultimately, is not whether what is smaller is more fundamental, but what level of time and space contains the substantive mechanisms which drive the others. If we are to push for micro reduction or micro translation, to what level should the reduction (or translation) take place? Since we have a continuum, it could move from any larger level to any smaller one, on either or both dimensions. We might want to argue that the world system can be reduced to the behavior of particular states or economies; or more plausibly, that political structures ought to be reduced to a series of organizations, or even to informal networks within organizations. Coleman's (1986) argument that the macro structure (by which he seems to mean population distributions at approximately the upper-middle levels of size and time span) is composed of individuals (or rather their attributes persisting across medium periods of time) turns the micro-macro question into a vertical link across the right-hand side of the time-space chart.

The real energy of the micro-macro dispute has come from the more radical micro positions. Homans sounds more micro than Blumer and Garfinkel, in one respect, since he aims to reduce sociology to the principles of psychology, while symbolic interactionists and ethnomethodologists wish to stop at the level of the situation. Homans, in other words, is more micro on the space dimension. But his psychological principles, dealing with a series of reinforcements and expectations about rewards and costs, relate to a period over time, on the order of days and perhaps longer for most human activities. What gives the symbolic interactionist position its volatile quality is its focus on a much more micro time unit, while moving up slightly on the space dimension to insist on the group situation as fundamental. Within the situation, the determining factors, according to symbolic interactionists and ethnomethodologists, may well operate within seconds (or even fractions of seconds).

The issue, though, is not to be "more micro than thou." It is to decide which level has the most powerful theory in its consequences for other levels. To decide this we must move on to other considerations.

REDUCTIONISM

Why should anyone want to reduce one level of analysis to another? Homans argued that this is scientific procedure, to subsume the more complex but messy and idiosyncratic "surface" pattern of empirical realities to fundamental processes which generate them. We might well agree with this as a goal of theory building. But it remains to be shown that these general principles are micro (or especially, micro psychological). The thrust of virtually all the reductionist programs has been that there are no such principles on the macro level, and macro theorists have created artificial entities. For Homans, Blumer, Garfinkel and others, the "society," the "state," the "social class" and so forth are merely words used by an analyst, constructions or glosses upon the reality which is actually micro.

Macrosociologists, on the other hand, mount two main defenses. Some argue that microsociology in fact does not contain all the causal laws in sociology; that the macro level has laws of its own which cannot be reduced to micro principles. Some even go so far as to deny that microsociology has any valid, or at least important, laws on its own turf; in other words, microsociology is trivial. This is a dispute over which is the ultimately more powerful level of theory.

There is also a pragmatic defense. Durkheim had argued that sociology does not reduce to psychology, just as in the physical sciences, physiology (the principles of the functioning of living bodies) does not reduce to chemistry (the principles of combination of matter). That is to say, physiologists can go ahead and formulate principles about the structure of the circulatory system, the operation of the heart, and so on, which are valid scientific generalizations; they do not need to refer these to the chemical constituents, nor to wait for chemical research to show how bodily functions operate. The pragmatic part of this argument is that students of the macro level can go ahead and do their research and formulate their generalizations without depending on micro researchers. This is true in the physical sciences, and we can argue that it is true in sociology as well.

But the years since Durkheim wrote have given a twist to the argument. For the fields of biochemistry and molecular biology have emerged, engaged in precisely the derivation of macro physiological processes from micro chemical ones that Durkheim said was unnecessary for the advance of science. Does this invalidate Durkheim's argument? Yes and no. It suggests that the posited autonomy of macro levels from micro ones does not necessarily hold, even if there are general principles formulated on the macro level; these might well be reduced or at least linked up with principles on the micro level which define the detailed causal mechanisms. On the other hand, Durkheim's argument still holds, but in a weakened form. It becomes a pragmatic strategy of scientific division of labor. Workers in the macro fields can go ahead on their own, formulating their own generalizations. The one field does not have to wait for the other. Only at some future time, possibly, will the micro-macro connection be made, once theory is well advanced on both levels.

There is a good deal of strength to this pragmatic interpretation of the autonomy of macrosociology. Macrosociologists have not generally found that they needed micro principles in order to proceed with their work; theories of the state, of the world system, of the structure of stratification have been formulated quite well based on macro-level research. This will probably be true for some time to come. But it should be recognized that the pragmatic arrangement does not tell us ultimately where the truth lies. Micro reduction might still be accomplished at some time in the future, like the emergence of biochemistry within physiology. And indeed we might argue that some of this is already starting, such as in the micro-based theory of class cultures given in Chapter 6.

The pragmatic argument rests on the answer to the question: what difference does it make whether we can cast macrosociology in micro terms? A pragmatic answer says knowledge can proceed just as well—or even better—if we let each level pursue its own goals for a while. The argument for reduction says that the micro level does indeed make a difference because it is more empirical and less distorted by ideologies or false abstractions.

IS MICROSOCIOLOGY MORE EMPIRICAL?

The term "empirical" means that which is experienced. Firsthand observation is the primary criterion of empirical reality. But experience always is the experience of some particular human being at some particular time and space. Thus micro-situational reality is the ultimate empirical reality.[6]

However, this is not the way "empirical" is normally used in social science. There is a tendency to claim that only "hard data," that is, quantitative counts or measurements are empirical. Frequently both micro-descriptive accounts and macro-historical studies are dismissed as "nonempirical" because they are not quantitative. This however is a rather inept use of words. Historical events are no less real than questionnaires; neither one can claim to be more empirical than the other. But micro observations of natural experience are in a privileged position, because this is exactly what "empirical" means: firsthand experience. Everything else is constructed from this. So-called "hard data" are not primary data at all, but represent observations which have been transformed many times.

Take for example a study of social mobility. Typically this is done by interviewers persuading a number of persons to spend a few minutes (or hours) answering questions. They are asked to name their father's occupation, their own occupation, their level of education, and so forth. After that the answers are coded (in another situation), put into computer storage, subjected to various statistical manipulations, and finally written up in an article with tables which claim to represent "the empirical reality." What we actually have are the products of one micro situation (the interview) being transformed through a series of other micro situations, and resulting in a series of markings on paper which are read by readers in yet another micro situation. There is no way to escape this: you, the reader of this book, are always living in a micro situation, and you are reading this within one of those micro situations. No one ever steps out of a micro situation to directly observe the macro level.

What difference does this make? At a minimum, it means that "hard data" cannot claim to be the primarily empirical reality. It is something which is constructed from the true empirical reality, micro experience. But having disposed of the unfortunate arrogance of quantitative researchers, might we not have to concede that they can maintain the substance of their position with a pragmatic defense? Their data is not primary; it merely summarizes the primary data. But if this summarizing is done fairly and accurately, where is the harm? Moreover, we can turn the pragmatic argument against the microsociologists. Some claim (for example, Cicourel) that a truly empirical account of social mobility would have to take apart the glosses, so that we can see all the micro details of how careers are actually made. "Father's

---

[6] Paradoxes emerge, though, regarding very small slices of space and time. Not only are paradoxes associated with the reality of the infinitesimal, but since human beings cannot observe anything at all below a few tenths of seconds and spaces on the order of a millimeter (at least without instruments, which introduce their own distortions), there is a lower limit to how micro we can go. And in fact even these very small units of time and space are somewhat artificial constructions, since they are always embedded in a large visual and experiential context. It would be safer to say that the micro situation has to have contours of at least normal human bodily size and attention span.

occupation" only takes a second to say, but in reality it means thousands or millions of interactions which took place over a period of years. The same is true of one's "own occupation," one's "education" and so forth.

To describe all these interactions in the kind of detail that the ethnomethodologists provide for a bit of conversation would take an impracticably long time. It would take at least as long to describe, for each respondent, as it actually took to happen. Actually the whole survey would take very much longer, since it would have to devote research hours to every individual lifetime in the survey; and furthermore, a detailed micro analysis of each fragment usually takes much longer to perform than the event itself. Thus, if we had a video tape recording of every moment of all these people's lives (and their parents' lives), we would have the true primary data for a social mobility study; but the entire world population for several generations would have to turn into sociologists if a study were to be carried out in full ethnomethodological detail.

Although microsociologists sometimes argue as if attaining a full empirical description were the point of research, it is not necessary to be stuck with either this extreme or staying with the conventional glosses of quantitative research. A complete micro description of any large-scale process would not only be impractical, but it also becomes tedious. Much of the elan has gone out of radical microsociology in recent years, because its detailed descriptions of social processes do not seem to add much to more conventional summaries of what goes on. Micro detail may be empirically more real, but it is only preferable to summaries if it captures crucial processes which are missed at the more summary level. This means that (1) microsociology has to formulate its points as theoretical generalizations, rather than merely rest its claim to superiority on its greater empirical directness, and (2) empirically microsociology, too, must sample and summarize micro situations rather than try to describe all of them.

What does microsociology add, then, that looser macro summaries miss? There are two major claims: freedom from ideology and reification and bringing the human agent back in.

IDEOLOGY AND REIFICATION   The more cognitively radical microsociologies argue that traditional macrosociology deals with words which are taken to be things. It turns processes—interactions of many human beings—into fictitious entities, the people who enact politics into "the state," the sum of all the interactions on a territory into "the social system." It is often claimed that there is a conservative bias to this. Proponents of existing privileges exalt the "society" over the individual and claim that the latter has an immutable reality. To see that these "entities" are not static at all, nor even real in their own right, is an act of liberation. I think there is some validity to this exposé. Sociology too often unthinkingly reflects the words of everyday life for talking about the macro structure, and these words are loaded with ideologies. The meaning of "state" carries such connotations as "maintaining law and order" or "serving the will of the people;" if we translate these into the microprocesses that actually go on, we can see the particular and antagonistic interests of police, politicians, bureaucrats, social classes, minority groups, and so on. The shift toward a more micro level of analysis, whenever we are dealing with ideologized and reified public "realities," is always a move toward greater sociological realism.

But there is an obverse side to this argument. The microsociologies are generally weak in their own fashion on ideologically loaded issues. None of them has an adequate theory of power, of coercive force, or of property. The Homans tradition attempts to deal with this, but feebly, reducing power to an exchange of resources in which one party has more to offer than the other. This is little more than the same optimistic interpretations put forward on the macro levels by functionalist theories of stratification. But if the Homans behaviorist model is couched too narrowly to deal with the nasty and negative sides of society, the cognitive approaches are almost entirely unable to conceptualize these phenomena at all. The symbolic interactionists place such a stress on voluntarism and situational interpretation that it might seem a miracle that anyone could be able to coerce anyone else. Ethnomethodologists dismiss power as just another gloss, or at best a form of talk that goes on in situations (Clegg 1975). None of these positions is able to deal with the issue of why some people have power rather than others, why some situations are more unequal than others, or how to explain occasions when, in Mao Zedong's words, "power comes out of the barrel of a gun."

I am sympathetic to the effort to improve the realism of macro concepts by eliminating their ideological distortions, and believe that a move toward the micro side aids this. But this ideological omission of micro theories must be remedied. If microsociology is to succeed, it must have its own theory of power and property. Otherwise microsociology can be charged with being another kind of ideology, naive individualism.

HUMAN AGENCY   Homans' major point was "bringing men back in." Similarly, Blumer argued against macro theories because they lacked the dynamism of people negotiating and making interpretations in situations. This is a crucial point. Whatever is the nature of what people do, it is only on the micro level that they do it. Macro structures never do anything. Whatever reality they may have, it is a reality of relationships among people. Yet it may be possible to state generalizations about macro structures: that a given structure is correlated with another structure (for example, Lenski's 1966 generalization that agrarian systems of production have more inequality than either industrial or horticultural systems of production, and that the concentration of political power determines the degree of inequality in the disposal of the economic surplus). But there is no causality in these principles. Only people can act, and they only act in concrete situations. Since macro structures are abstractions from the empirical realities of people across many situations, whatever causality there is in structural relationships must come from the actions of people in them.

I am suggesting, then, that any theory of social change, on however macro a level, must involve a crucial component: the motivating forces of individual people. But more than this. We should not take it for granted that if structures do not change, the people who make them up do not do anything. Instead, those people are repeating the same behaviors, generating the patterns that we call "structure." This, too, must be explained. There must be a micro component which tells why (that is, under what conditions) people maintain the same patterns of behavior. A micro theory of motivations must enter into any comprehensive macro theory, both to provide the energies for change, as well as the glue that holds things together when they do not change.

MICRO REDUCTION OR MICRO TRANSLATION?

The strongest claim of the reductionist position is that the theoretical principles or generalizations of sociology turn out to be nothing more than the principles of micro theory. When macrosociology is analyzed through the lens of micro theory, there is nothing left over.

Is this true? Let us leave aside the questions of *which* micro theory is the one to do the job. I would also like to avoid limiting macro theories to a specific instance. Homans and Blumer both had in mind functionalism, which is a fairly weak version of macro theory since it has virtually no causal principles in it. Homans (1961) did go through a series of empirical studies, but they are studies of small groups and do not touch the larger macro structures of society. Homans (1984: 341), moreover, admits that there is macro structure, when he says that institutions are the histories of reinforcement of large numbers of persons. He merely asserts that history has no general principles, hence what is left are psychological ones. But this is disputable. If we go to more serious macro-historical sociology (as in Chapters 3 through 5), we can find a number of generalizations relating one structure to another.

A real test of reductionism would be to try it. Instead of making a purely conceptual argument that the micro is more fundamental than the macro, or about the distortions introduced at either level, we can take a range of macro theories and see whether they can in fact be reduced to micro processes with nothing left over. I have carried out this experiment (Collins, 1981b), using as materials the collection of several hundred propositions in *Conflict Sociology* (Collins, 1975). These propositions attempt to summarize the major causal and structural principles of various theorists (including my own, but also formulating generalizations from Lenski, Barrington Moore, Weber, organizational theory, and so forth).

The result turns out to be that micro translation is to a certain extent possible, but there are three irreducible macro factors left over. These are (1) the extent of *space* involved in a process; (2) the extent of *time* the process takes; (3) the *number* of people or situations involved.

To analyze a state into micro processes, for example, is to refer to the way in which some people (officials, rulers) exercise the threat of physical violence over a territory. Though we nowhere reify the "state" in this analysis, nevertheless the sheer expanse of physical space is a crucial variable, affecting how difficult it is for rulers to maintain control, what control arrangements they use, and also the degree of vulnerability of one state to conquest by another.

Second, processes spread out in time, and the amount of time for something to transpire is itself a crucial variable. For example, there is the following proposition (Collins, 1975: 218):

> 6.81 The more efficient the technology of transportation and communication, the greater the potential diversity of communications, and the lower the potential level of surveillance.

This is part of a series of propositions, based on historical comparisons, concluding that the status system of communities—the patterns of deference and demeanour rituals prevailing there—is determined by the amount of cosmopolitanism experienced by individuals and by the amount of group density or individual privacy. (The underlying generalizations are those given previously in Chapter 6 as the "Principles of Social Density and Social Diversity"). But although the aim here was to take a theory of what is usually glossed as "the status system" and turn it into a series of micro processes experienced by individuals, nevertheless some irreducible macro factors entered in. The "efficiency" of the technology referred to in 6.81 can be unpacked into the amount of time that it takes for people to communicate across a given amount of space. But the technology can always be observed at some particular point in time and space: we see a telephone, writing implements, automobiles, horses, and the like, always within some micro situation. Technology itself is micro, since it is empirically observable.[7] But the use of technology gives certain patterns of speed at which certain human interactions take place. Among other things, technology can actually link various micro situations (for instance, at opposite ends of a telephone wire) together, or make it possible for people to move from one situation to another. The degree to which a variable in a causal statement is micro or macro is thus itself a variable. This is the same as saying that time is an irreducible factor in our causal statements, even if we try to translate everything as much as possible into micro-situational processes.

Third, there is the number of people or situations involved in a process. The number of people is not just the same thing as the amount of space, since a space could be closely packed or largely empty. Thus we have the following principle:

> 2.2 *Cosmopolitanism.* The greater the diversity of communications one is involved in, the more one develops abstract relativistic ideas and the habit of thinking in terms of long-range consequences. (Collins, 1975: 75)

"Diversity of communications" means whether one experiences a number of diverse situations over time, as compared to experiencing the same kind of situation over again. The sheer repetitive experience of the same situation can also have major consequences:

> 1.1 The more one gives orders, the more one is proud, self-assured, formal, and identifies with the organizational ideals in whose name one justifies the orders. (Collins, 1975: 73)

Not only the number of situations, or of times a situation recurs, is fateful, but so is the numbers of people who are in these situations, (as indicated in the "Principle of Social Density," Chapter 6).

What is striking here is that I was making the effort to formulate a theory which would be maximally based on micro-situational behavior. But even on the micro level, it is impossible to avoid some reference to factors which transcend the situation: the numbers of situations of a certain type that individuals experience, the spread of these situations across time, and the number of people involved. At the more macro levels, the numbers of people (and of course of situations) becomes quite large. It is precisely this variation in number that makes up some of the crucial factors on the level of organizations, networks, markets, and states.

---

[7] But some kinds of technology spread out in space: the observable roadway which stretches off to the horizon, and—we know from experience—beyond; the telephone wires which do the same. Human modifications of the physical world, themselves activities occurring in micro situations, nevertheless leave real marks on the macro world, precisely insofar as that world is physical space.

CONCLUSIONS ON REDUCTIONISM   I conclude that *complete micro reduction* is impossible. On pragmatic grounds, it is not necessary, insofar as macrosociologists can go ahead with their theories of the state, social change, organizations, and so on, without reference to micro theories. But that is merely provisional. These theories offer only crude approximations, since they are dealing with "things" that are not really entities at all, but are summaries, and sometimes ideologically distorted glosses, on the behavior of real people in micro situations. The people in situations give the causal force to all explanatory principles, including at the most macro level. A truly comprehensive and grounded theory will ultimately have to translate macro principles into combinations of micro principles. But the effort to carry out translation with what principles we have so far reveals that irreducible macro variables pop up: space, time, and number.

The macro structure exists only as the aggregation of micro situations in space, across time, and in the number of situations of various kinds and of people who take part in them. We can see this from the time-space table. Everything horizontally to the left and vertically to the top is contained within everything to the right and bottom of it. Larger expanses of time and space are made up of smaller bits of time and space. Thus all macro topics of sociology contain within them all the micro topics of smaller segments of the time-space scale. The micro are the empirical building blocks of the latter. But there is a sheer structural property to the time-space framework itself (along with a third factor, not included in Figure 11-1): number of situations and persons. Ultimately, a truly precise sociological theory may be built by translating our commonsensical, reifying, and ideologically loaded summary terms for what happens at the macro level into statements of how individual, situational events are aggregated along these three dimensions.[8]

It has been questioned whether we have yet precisely formulated the factors at the most immediate micro level. The micro processes which I have used to reduce macro theories are themselves on the level of situations, or rather aggregates of situations, spread out across a certain amount of time. There is a still more micro level, such as that focused upon in conversational analysis, which turns up its own units and propositions. Schegloff (1987) has suggested that even on this level, we may not have arrived at the ultimate units out of which others are to be aggregated. This may well be so. It is also worth contemplating, though, that the principle "more micro than thou" is not the criterion for theoretical centrality. If we want the dynamism of human action at the center of our sociological theories, then we must find the appropriate point on the micro-macro continuum at which this can be formulated; and its principles may be at the situational level, but not much below

---

[8]"If the sum of all possible empirical evidence in sociology consists ultimately in a set of 'filmstrips' giving the sensory and subjective experience, moment by moment, of every person who has ever lived, then macro-references can arise only in these ways: (1) each strip consists of micro-situations, but it runs on in time (for a lifetime), and hence gives the aggregates of situational experiences that make up micro-histories; (2) often people at particular points in time refer to the future or past of their own 'filmstrip,' or to some aggregate of other people's filmstrips, whether individually or in the form of a reification; and (3) there is the sheer number of micro-strips of various sorts, their configurations in space, and their lengths in time" (Collins, 1981b: 99).

it. Thus the principles of conversational analysis, although applying to very short units in time (for example, Schegloff's response pairs) may turn out to depend on some surrounding cultural context which is slightly more macro (though still situational). (See in this light Chapter 9 on language.)

A final comment. You will notice that this book itself is organized beginning with macro sociology and then proceeding to micro sociological theories. There is a practical reason for this sequence. The macro theories can generally be explained without raising any micro considerations. But the reverse is not true. Macro theoretical issues are constantly creeping into the discussion of micro theories. Homans' exchange theory, as we have seen, was initially formulated from research on small groups, often within the settings of communities or businesses; it branched off from organizational and community sociology. Homans added the push toward psychological laws as a theoretical program, but the tendency of most subsequent exchange theorists (like Blau) has been to go the other direction, toward larger networks of exchange. Homans himself borrowed certain traditional formulations from functionalist macro theory, including the "norm of equal exchange" and his functionalist explanation of inequality. Thus although Homans made the most explicit claim for micro reduction, the macro themes and contexts of his own work tend implicitly to undermine it.

Similarly, the ritual theory has had to make analytical shifts from macro, historical-comparative evidence to micro-situational models. It is an argument for shifting Durkheim in a more micro direction, following Goffman (Chapter 6); at the same time, we have seen how it links back to the macro, producing a theory of class and community cultures. We have continued to see these macro intrusions: social role theory (Chapter 7) links with larger, nonindividual structures, and the theory of self as sacred object has a historical and even political dimension; reality-construction models (Chapter 8) tend toward a macro-cultural or macro-subjective vision as well as toward a situational and individualist view; the sociology of mind and language (Chapter 9) has as one of its branches French structuralism, which sharply denies that it is micro, although it claims not to be located in macro time and space either.

What this implies, I think, is that macro has a certain precedence over micro. This may seem contradictory, in that I have just argued that at least a partial micro reduction, or micro translation, should be carried out of macro theories. But the attempt to do so comes up against the irreducible macro factors of time, space, and number. We may turn the micro-translation formula around to stress its other side: every micro situation is embedded in a larger context. But let us not call this larger context "the macro structure" and let it go at that. Instead, we should dwell on the point that every micro situation is surrounded by other micro situations, stretching off to the horizons of past and future, and in physical space. Micro situations are analytically central, but the actual contents of any micro situation is affected by its *macro location, among other micro situations*. In this sense, micro depends on macro, perhaps even more than the other way around. A better way to put it is to say that the micro-macro link, when analyzed, is really a micro-micro link: *macro is the medium through which micro situations are connected to each other*. This gives us a clue for what we may expect from substantive theories of the micro-macro connection.

THEORIES OF MICRO-MACRO LINKAGES

GIDDENS' STRUCTURATIONISM

Giddens (1976, 1981, 1984) offers a multidimensional model which is explicitly dynamic. Macrosociology is the institutional level; its theoretical weakness is to assume that human agents can be safely ignored, as if they were programmed to automatically follow the necessary routines. Microsociology is the level of human actors; but action theory has no way of accounting for the fact that structured social action is relatively stable and it has an extension in time and space. Giddens proposed that the gap may be overcome by the notion of the *double hermeneutic* or *duality of structure*. Micro and macro, agent and structure mutually constitute each other in an ongoing, temporal fashion. He proposed there are actually two aspects of the macro dimension, *structure* and *system*. These can be identified as follows (Giddens, 1981: 172):

> Structure: recursively organized rules and resources, having a virtual existence outside of time-space.
>
> System: reproduced relations between actors or collectives, situated in time-space.
>
> Structuration: conditions governing system reproduction.

There is a domain of rules and resources which is shared by the actors in a given society. Rules are social conventions of how to behave; resources are "capabilities of making things happen" (Giddens, 1981: 170), which include the various aspects of power. Rules and resources have a "virtual existence," somewhere outside of space and time. The "system" is a concrete instance of these rules and resources, as actually put into practice by a given, historical group of people.

The micro level consists of human action, in which actors draw upon rules and resources. These give a structuring quality to their actions. At the same time, the system is being structured, as it has no concrete existence prior to action. Action of human agents gives a dynamic quality to social history, since they can change the system as well as the underlying rules and resources. Actors can change these dual aspects of the macro structure, however, only within limits, constrained by the existing rules and resources. In particular, even though actors are knowledgeable and capable, they do not know the unintended consequences of their actions; and they operate in a context of unintended consequences of the actions of other people. This is part of the double hermeneutic. The macro structure depends on the actions of human agents, which in turn acts back upon both the agents themselves and future states of the macro structure. Micro and macro levels mutually constitute each other in a process over time.

There are several weaknesses in Giddens' model. Although it is multidimensional in much the same way as Alexander's and Parsons' schemes, like them it places the analytical emphasis on the side of ideal factors. It sees human action as structured by rules of how to behave, even though such "rules" have been criticized (by the ethnomethodologists and by ritual theory) as analyst's constructs and as ideologies of everyday life (see Chapters 6 and 8). Giddens, along with Alexander and

Parsons, puts these cultural rules into an autonomously existing sphere, a kind of ethereal stock-pile somewhere outside of time and space. Concretely, what Giddens has in mind is the cultural tradition of a society. For example, a tradition of political democracy is one of the crucial cultural resources which determines whether a particular state will undergo a revolution (Giddens, 1984). However, I would suggest that although this may be adequate as a macro level description of what has happened in certain historical sequences, it is not a very penetrating analysis, particularly from the point of view of a theory which tries to lay bare the micro-macro connection. Giddens does not make the extra effort to see whether the realm of rules and cultural traditions can be micro-translated into more fundamental processes.

A similar point could be made about his rather general category of resources. These include such things as having power, property, organizational position, and social status. But these categories remain too much on the surface of sociological analysis. It is hard to conceive of them existing outside of time and space, unless we adopt an idealist position which sees power, position, and so on as merely the human actors' relation to certain commonly shared ideas. My conclusion is that Giddens has not attempted micro-translation seriously enough. His autonomous macro level includes not only time and space, but also a realm which transcends both of these. I doubt the reality of this transcendental realm of rules and resources, and suggest that what Giddens is referring to here empirically can be reduced to aspects of the behaviors of people in situations within time and space.

HABERMAS' COLONIZATION OF THE LIFEWORLD

Habermas (1981/1984) too has adopted much of the Parsonian imagery of the social system, while giving it a critical twist. He conceives of the macro structures of society as integrating mechanisms for individual action. But as these macro structures change with different stages of evolution, so does the relation between micro and macro. In primitive tribal societies, micro and macro are closely related, with most action taking place through the kinship system. As economic and political institutions differentiate out, the macro structure takes on more autonomy. Eventually, in capitalist society, macro autonomy turns back against the micro to "colonize the lifeworld."

The lifeworld of everyday experience can be described as forms of communicative action. Speech acts of various sorts (constantive, regulative, expressive, and strategic; see Chapter 9) are the modalities in which people enact social relationships. However, in addition to this level of action in the lifeworld is a realm of impersonal communicative media, money and power. Habermas uses the phrase "the colonization of the lifeworld" as an analogy to the colonies established by an imperialist power over primitive tribal societies. Modern capitalism, with its own logic of economic competition and its bureaucratic power structures, is an alien force intruding upon individuals' communicative actions. The micro-macro relation, for Habermas, is less a theoretical problem than a substantive issue of political strategy; it needs to be solved in order to liberate people and to continue the evolutionary trend toward rationality.

The weakness of Habermas' evolutionary conception has already been noted in Chapter 1. As a contribution to the micro-macro issue, I would suggest again that it is insufficiently penetrating. The so-called impersonal media of money and power are taken for granted as macro entities, without attempting to analyze them further into their actual constituents in human encounters within time and space. The problem that Habermas points to under the term "colonization of the lifeworld" may be real, but he does not adequately characterize what it really consists of, and his theory offers no solution of the practical issue either.

RATIONAL CHOICE AND EXCHANGE MODELS

The preceding models have their intellectual lineage in the idealist and functionalist camps, with a dash of recent Marxism thrown in. There have also been efforts to make the micro-macro connection from the positivist side, by extending exchange theory.

Blalock and Wilken (1979) follow Homans, Blau, and Emerson in conceiving of society as built up by exchanges among rational individuals. But instead of Homans' appeal to the psychological behaviorism of Skinnerian operant conditioning, the model of the actor adopted here is that of economic theory. Actors have an array of subjective utilities and expected probabilities: they have a set of preferences for various outcomes and beliefs as to how easy it is to attain them. Individuals exchange with one another in order to maximize their gains while minimizing their costs, according to the probabilities that they see for getting what they want.

A quite complex model, formally diagrammed, emerges from this. The micro-macro linkage is built up by conceiving of groups as collections of individuals who engage in aggregate decision making. In other words, a group of people can be treated as an individual at yet another level. Through a mechanism of rationally guided exchanges, they arrive at a collective decision. The group as a whole, then, has a higher-level set of subjective utilities and expected probabilities and engages in exchanges with other groups, based on the same principles that govern exchanges among individuals. Power is analyzed in terms of goals, beliefs, resources, and mobilization of various groups. The long-term historical reproduction of society is then modelled, following Stinchcombe's functionalist feedback loops (see Chapter 2).

Blalock and Wilken's main example of macrosociological phenomena is American race relations, blacks and whites as groups acting in relation to each other. This limits the applicability of the model, since formal organizations (and especially coercively powerful ones, like the state, or economically dominant ones like large businesses) are rather different than unorganized racial communities. In short the macro structure does not emerge here as very structured. As in exchange theory in general, there is no very realistic way of dealing with power in its coercive mode. There are also shortcomings on the micro level. The actor is treated as completely rationalistic.[9]

---

[9] Blalock and Wilken refer briefly to the concept of "satisficing," the strategy of organizational actors pointed out by March and Simon (1958). But Blalock and Wilken downgrade this to a minor variant within the more general model of maximizing and describe satisficing as occurring only when information is lacking. They give little attention to the central point that human information-processing capacity is limited, and hence that a purely maximizing strategy is the exception, rather than the rule.

Although the general intent is to follow Homans and ground all macro in micro, Blalock and Wilken are not able to carry this out consistently. They use the argument, taken from Homans, that there is a universal "norm of distributive justice," a belief that people ought to receive as much in an exchange as they give. This norm, as well as other norms for specific situations, are taken as given, contextual factors affecting exchange and behavior. In their model, Blalock and Wilken make no effort to explain why norms exist, nor do they take account of variations in such patterns and show the conditions which produce them.

Another effort to use rational choice theory as the link between micro and macro levels is Hechter (1983). Most other approaches begin from the micro level and regard the macro as problematic. In contrast, this book is the product of macrosociologists who are concerned with building down from historical structures to the micro ground. Hechter argues that the holistic, structural concepts which are sociology's home base, nevertheless are undertheorized. Macrosociology, he points out, frames its problems more often in terms of the social problems and political issues of the day than in terms of intellectual concerns with valid explanatory theory. To do so, it must admit human agency, and thus overcome its bias against individualistic explanations. Normative explanations and structural constraints are not enough; we must find room for self-interested individual actors. The problem is to connect the two levels: to show how group solidarity and other "normative" phenomena are actually the product of individuals making rational choices in their own interest.

The various chapters of this book apply this interpretation to particular areas. Hechter contributes a theory of group solidarity. He argues that solidarity is not automatically or mysteriously given, as it seems to be in the normative model, but is instead a variable, which has specific causes and which can be empirically investigated. He chooses data on the party-voting loyalty of members of legislatures as a comparative base on which to develop his theory. Solidarity is due to the group's capacity to mediate individual goals, together with the group's resources for monitoring compliance and for providing selective incentives. These conditions seem to fit the empirical data on voting loyalty. But the data are not highly micro, in that they select out from the flow of face-to-face encounters that make up the micro world only a few instants in time: the votes themselves. Given this, how do we know that the micro reality would actually sustain the processes implied in the rational choice model? Would we actually see individual legislators calculating incentives and responding to conditions of surveillance, or would we find instead the processes of meaning construction or emotional attachment postulated in other micro theories?

Hechter and his colleagues assume too readily that the rational choice model is coextensive with a micro level of explanation. For example, Freidman's chapter on why workers strike provides a complex, formal model of the contingencies that presumably enter into an individual's decision. But this ignores the problems of information overload and of the limits on human ability to make complex calculations, which are precisely the issues which have emerged recently among economic theorists themselves. Hechter, however, (1983: 187) is aware that rational choice theory is only a halfway point toward the ultimate solution of the micro-macro issue.

INTERACTION RITUAL CHAINS

The interaction ritual (IR) chain model of the micro-macro connection (Collins, 1981a; 1975: 133–60) differs from the preceding cognitive models, since it does not make social structure into a set of rules or mental objects that actors carry around in their heads. Cognitions are explained as arising situationally, as the result of processes of interaction themselves, mediated by emotions. We have seen the dynamics of IR chains in Chapter 10. Each social encounter is a natural ritual of varying strength. A successful ritual (such as a conversation) creates or recreates a temporarily shared reality, ideas which act as symbols of group membership within that little group. Individuals move through their daily lives in a chain of interaction rituals, coming away from their last encounters with their particular blend of *cultural capital* and *emotional energies;* these in turn become the resources which each person uses to negotiate their next ritual encounter. Interaction rituals are the micro experience out of which macro social structure is formed.

INTERACTION RITUAL CHAINS AND LOCAL MACRO STRUCTURE   Macro structure enters IR chain theory in two ways. First, each social situation is part of two (or more) chains of IRs, the past experience of the several participants. The encounter is, so to speak, the intersection of the personal "filmstrips" of these individuals' life experiences. The filmstrips are spread out in macro dimensions, since each one carries across time; the different filmstrips are spread out in space; and there are a number of such existing strips, which together make up the society. Moreover, the sheer number of such strips or IR chains of various kinds is a crucial feature of the macro structure, which influences what happens in individual situations. This is because it is the number of such strips that surrounds any one person that makes up her or his *market opportunities* and hence determines who will be able to encounter whom and what kind of interaction she or he will be motivated to have.

All social institutions are made up of chains of micro interactions, spread out in time, space, and number. But any particular interaction ritual is dependent upon other interaction rituals, and hence the local micro situation is influenced by the macro structure, the layout of other micro situations around it. Cultural capital and emotional energy carry over from previous situations; and their usefulness for negotiating a relationship in *this* here-and-now situation depends on the match-up with the cultural capital and emotional energy that other participants bring to the situation. People's market opportunities are also a characteristic of how they fit into the larger macro pattern around them. This does not mean that everything in the entire "society" or the entire "culture" influences every interaction. It is rather the *local macro structure,* the network of experiences and relationships right around any individual, that is the crucial nexus of the macro-micro connection. When we say that there are macro effects upon micro, this means only that micro interactions *elsewhere* have an effect on the micro interaction *here*.

MICRO-TRANSLATING POWER AND PROPERTY   A second way in which interaction rituals connect micro and macro is through the principle that individuals can sense each other's place in the social class and organizational power structure of society. We might object: how can we introduce "power," "social classes," and "formal organizations" into the analysis, if we are approaching everything from a strictly micro viewpoint? All these categories need a micro-translation, which we must now provide.

Power Is Membership in an Enforcement Coalition.   Individuals do not wield power (at least not very much) alone; no matter how strong one is, an isolated individual can always be overpowered by an organized group. The decisive factor is to be able to command an organized group. That power of command, though it ultimately contains a crucial element of coercion, is not enacted by coercion itself. Even a military dictator does not have to go armed to the teeth; he (virtually all military dictators have been men) orders his followers to kill or imprison anyone who disobeys him. Even highly coercive power is a form of social communication; the dictator, like the army or police commander, uses his armed subordinates to enforce discipline on each other. That is why discipline is regarded as so crucial in a coercive organization. The commander cannot allow his ability to get his way to slip away from him. He must be sure that enough armed supporters will obey his orders so that the others will not dare to disobey.

In terms of game theory, the problem of power is what Schelling (1963) called "tacit coordination." The group is more powerful than any individual in it. But an individual can command a group by coercive threat, as long as a sufficient number cannot unite to oppose him. How is this done? Schelling suggests it happens because the commander controls the channels of communication; he makes sure that commands to use coercive force go through him alone, and he prevents any group from autonomously forming their own circle which might agree to use their force together against him. Power is surrounded by ritual in a special sense: the person who gives orders must appear to be in command, capable of calling on enforcers to punish anyone who disobeys. He (or she) must give off the tone of self-assurance, even ruthlessness. Hence encounters between subordinates and a commander are rituals which express, above all, that membership here is ranked between order givers and order takers.

Power is never absolute. Precisely because it depends on controlling the tacit coordination of the group, power is vulnerable to symbolic disruptions, which may escalate into loss of the ability to keep an enforcement coalition together. Dictatorships usually fall suddenly, in a panic, due to a wave of belief that the dictator no longer has the support of his troops. When that happens, individuals no longer feel they are in danger from his enforcement coalition and no longer have to obey; not only that, they may actually feel it is dangerous to keep on his side, once a new or revolutionary coalition emerges, which will coerce anyone who does not join it. Schelling (1963) calls this the "tipping phenomenon." Here we have an instance in which micro theory explains a macro phenomenon. Because coercive structures are based on this mode of interaction, fundamental political change is episodic and "revolutionary," occurring in sudden leaps and not in smooth transitions.

What does this discussion of dictatorships and revolutions have to do with power in ordinary social life? It gives an extreme example, a pure case, of the phenomenon of the enforcement coalition, which underlies all governmental power. A democracy, too, is upheld ultimately because no one is able to overthrow it; anyone who tries will be put down by the army, and any army faction which rebels will be overthrown by the loyal soldiers. I am stressing that this is the core phenomenon; sentiments of legitimacy come after the enforcement coalition is established and do not determine it. An army does not have to share the political sentiments of the government that they uphold; often, in fact, the military or police are quite out of sympathy and may talk of intervening against the civilians. As long as the armed soldiers are organized in such a way that they cannot form their own coalition, but instead always get orders through an external, civilian source, they are structurally unable to avoid using their weapons to enforce existing authority over any rebels, even within their own ranks. The sentiment of legitimacy, I am suggesting, has at its core the feeling that the only safe side to be on is the existing center of authority. Through Durkheimian rituals, this sentiment in time is embellished with moral beliefs that this authority is right and proper. But this is only the outer dressing. A government with a strong enforcement coalition can create legitimacy for itself; a government with moral legitimacy, which cannot maintain its enforcement coalition and falls into internal military dissention, loses its power to command and eventually its sentimental legitimacy, too. The point is important because the center of any society is its state (or whatever organization of armed force there may be, in the case of stateless tribes). Every individual, for safety's sake, must somehow be oriented toward the dominant enforcement coalition. Those persons who are at the top of the enforcement coalition are persons to be feared or respected, whom one must convince of one's own loyalty.

Micro-translation of Property.   Given the existence of this state enforcement coalition, other organizations and social arrangements can be established which use it to back up their local authority. *Property* is the major way in which this is done. From a micro viewpoint, property is not merely an object. It is, rather, a *social relationship* between three parties: the owner, nonowners, and the enforcement coalition or state. As a fourth element, there is the object which is property. In plain language these are: the person who owns something (for instance, a factory building); the people who do not own it, and who do not have the right to enter the building or use it except with the permission of the owner; and the police who will arrest anyone who violates the property. The police here are just one end of an enforcement coalition. If the nonowners fight back against the police, the latter will call for reinforcements and eventually (if resistance is large enough, as in an insurrection, say, or a very militant union strike) on the army to back them up. Other parts of the network who make up the enforcement coalition are the courts, jailers, and government officials, who back up each other's orders.[10]

Most of the time this power is not actually called upon. Usually it suffices for the person with property to give orders, which will be obeyed, lest the next link in

---

[10] Stinchcombe (1968: 158–63) defines legitimacy in this way, the ability to call on a network of enforcers to back up one's power. Weber (1922/1968: 901–40) connects the legitimacy of the state with its power prestige in relation to other states. The implication is that the officials at the head of a state are felt to be legitimate by their subordinates inside the state only to the extent that the state itself is militarily powerful enough to maintain itself in the world arena. For this reason states tend to break down internally after suffering defeats or strains externally. Victories or defeats in foreign policy raise or lower the legitimacy of whatever political faction happens to be in power at the time. Hence internal politics can be explained, at least partially, by the dynamics of international geopolitics. See Collins (1986: 145–66).

FIGURE 11-2

PROPERTY IS UPHELD BY AN ENFORCEMENT COALITION

Excluded non-owners/non-employees

the enforcement coalition (the police) be called. This means that individuals tacitly monitor the enforcement coalition and do not usually take any rash actions against overwhelming force which can be marshalled against them. The power tied up in property (more precisely, this kind of relationship to the enforcement coalition) can be further delegated downward. The factory owner can use the power of his or her money to hire managers, who in turn hire submanagers, who in turn give orders to assistants and workers. There are various complexities in the operation of power within organizations which will be treated in Chapter 13. Here, the only important point is that there is a long chain of enforcers behind anyone with power. The manager who gives instructions can threaten various sanctions if they are not carried out; ultimately, he or she can get the disobedient subordinate's pay docked (a form of control through deprivation of property rewards) or transfer him or her to a less desirable job. If the rebellious subordinate resists, ultimately the high-level enforcers can be called upon.

All Interaction Rituals Contain Tacit Rankings in Enforcement Coalitions. The symbols which are passed around in everyday rituals connote membership at some level in one of these enforcement coalitions. Because some symbols have been charged up through rituals involving managers, they may connote membership in a middle, or an upper range of power, or may connote negatively one's lack of such membership in the higher classes. They may also carry the culture of rebellion or of withdrawal into privacy characteristic of order-taking classes (see Chapter 6 on the ritual basis of class cultures). Every conversational ritual gives its participants a tacit sense of where they stand in the power and property rankings of society.

This, however, does not usually take place consciously. People must always monitor the dominant enforcement coalitions, at least when they are around situations involving power or the overt threat of force; for example, when they come into contact with a police officer or a court official, or when they are involved in exchanges over property (such as working for someone else in return for pay). Ordinary people do not want to take on the organized and armed power of society, unless they have a feeling they can get away with it. If much of the time, in our own American society, we have little consciousness of the threat behind enforcement coalitions, it is because we go along with a routine in which almost everyone obeys most of the time, or at least avoids provoking its overt action. (But in other societies, such as coercive military regimes, people are more conscious of what is the safe thing to do in their everyday lives.) Through routinization, enforcement coalitions fade into the background. They are taken for granted, but not ignored; whenever trouble arises—a threat to property, an instance of insubordination to power—people very quickly are aware of what is the safe side to be on. This process is similar to the ethnomethodological principle that people usually take social arrangements for granted, until trouble arises.

Particularized Cultural Capital Is More Important for Power and Property than Generalized Cultural Capital.   The existence of two different forms of cultural capital (as discussed in Chapter 10) implies that there are two dimensions to networks of personal contacts. It might seem that the generalized form of cultural capital is the more important. But from the point of view of micro-translation of macro structures, particularized cultural capital is more important. For organizations are always concrete: it is a particular business or a particular government agency that exists. In micro-empirical reality, it exists only as a repetitive set of encounters among certain people, perhaps with particular buildings or vehicles which are the property of the organization. But the property is appropriated by its tie to an enforcement coalition, and authority within an organization is a set of relationships among a chain of *particular persons.* Though the generalized cultural capital may contain such symbols as "the manager," in fact the only way that people know that *this particular person* is the manager of *this* organization is because they have been introduced by someone else in the chain of command, ultimately leading up to the property holder or the governmental enforcement coalition. It is people's particular memories, then, that constitute each other's social identities in formal organizations.

This gives a micro-based criterion for distinguishing between formal organizations and the informal and less structured relations that occur among acquaintances or strangers. Formal organizations are based on chains of particular memories, embodied in individuals' particularized cultural capital, which give specific relationship identities. Mere friends, acquaintances, or strangers on the street do not have this particularized connection to an enforcement coalition (though they may have particularized memories of each other, and hence can deal with particularized as well as generalized cultural capital).

Individual reputations or identities are passed around in conversations not involving the individual who is talked about. The social structure is thus reproduced in at least two ways: directly, by being enacted in the network of conversations itself; and at a distance, in the reputations which are circulated elsewhere. The extent of such reputations is an important part of maintaining power in an enforcement coalition. Since power is a tacit coordination game based on appearing to be in a position which no one dares to challenge, a widespread reputation in these distant interactions makes an individual's power appear to be all the more unshakeable, thereby making it unshakeable in fact. Conversely, when one's reputation becomes negative—one is talked about in distant circles as being no longer able to hold the enforcement coalition together—one's power tends to be undermined, even if the rumor initially is not true. Distant reputation and direct ceremonial domination are two aspects of power.[11]

INTERACTION RITUAL AND SOCIAL CHANGE   Social structure is enacted situation by situation. It is stable to the extent that people interact with the same persons, or at least the same kinds of persons. That is to say, the distribution of individuals' cultural capitals and relative emotional energies remains approximately the same. Different mixtures of persons produce new ritual outcomes and are one of the causes of structural change.

CONCLUSION

There are other micro-macro models. Burt (1983) combines a symbolic interactionist model of role-taking at the micro level with a network view of macro structure. Burt's "structural theory of action" will be treated in Chapter 12. Another important area is organizations, which occupy an intermediate, meso level between micro and macro. The substantive connection between the levels—as well as the importance of space, time, and number as the basic macro variables linking micro interactions—will be seen again in the explanatory propositions in Chapter 13.

Some headway has been made in translating macro theories into micro components. The better macro theories, I would suggest, eliminate or greatly reduce reifications and display their true causal mechanisms as people acting in micro situations linked in the irreducible macro dimensions. The major payoff of work upon the micro-macro connection, however, has been in an unexpected direction: it has given us a better understanding of the micro side. Micro situations are embedded in chains of other micro interactions, and it is this chain-linking that is crucial for determining what individuals will do in each situation. This dependence of micro on macro (at least "locally") penetrates to rather intimate levels, including a person's thoughts and emotions. It is worthwhile to think through again the topics of the "micro" chapters of Part II from this point of view.

I would also suggest that micro-macro analysis has a payoff for applied or "clinical" sociology. Unlikely as this might have seemed while we were wandering in the conceptual thickets of the micro-reduction argument, when we emerged at a chained

---

[11] The relative weight of each has not yet been measured. Possibly in property-based organizations, the direct enactment of power outweighs the effects of distant reputations for power; in military-based states, the power of distant reputation may be more salient.

model of interactions we acquired a means of diagnosing many of people's personal problems. Psychological theories and psychotherapy, I am suggesting, are weak because they look for sources inside an individual. But if what people feel, how much emotional energy they have, and what they think and talk about in interactions are determined by the intersection of interactional chains, then an adequate diagnosis and treatment depends on a sociological perspective. Instead of psychoanalysis, what is needed is "socioanalysis." Depression, mania, and other personal difficulties result from situational patterns as particular individuals get caught in their unique interactional markets and hence generate and regenerate a particular pattern of emotional energies and cultural capital. Granted, it may be easier to diagnose such problems microsociologically than to cure them, since the latter involves treating not only an individual but somehow changing his or her relationship to an entire network. But any solid practical payoff must begin with a solid understanding of the source of the problem. Here, too, sociological theory has fruitful work to do.

SUMMARY

1. Durkheim argued that society is a reality *sui generis* (of its own kind), which cannot be reduced to individuals, because it consists of "social facts" which are exterior and constraining.

2. Homans argued that all human groups and institutions consist of individual human actors, and that the general principles underlying any social phenomenon are the laws of behavioral psychology. Explaining institutions is to explain the histories of rewards and punishments of real human beings.

3. Blumer's symbolic interactionism also attacked macro theories, especially functionalism, by arguing that structures, values, norms and other macro entities are not empirically real. The empirical basis of any sociological theory is the interpretive behavior of persons in situations. Blumer advocated *situational reductionism* rather than *individual reductionism;* the individual is only an abstraction as well, and psychological principles are themselves subject to situational interpretation. Empirical research on everyday life inspired by Goffman, and ethnomethodological studies of the construction of social reality, gave support to the micro-reductionist position.

4. The micro-macro distinction is a continuum, ranging from very small to very large segments of time and space. Recent sociology has expanded both ends of the continuum, pushing macro up from national societies to the entire world system and many centuries of historical change and studying micro phenomena that occur within individuals at less than tenths of seconds. Which level of this continuum is most appropriate for sociologists to focus upon is not a matter of which is more real, but which has the most explanatory power for other levels.

5. A pragmatic argument for the independence of macro levels is that research can discover macro principles, without having to wait for research on more micro levels. A stronger claim is that macro levels have irreducible causal principles of their own, or even that microsociological levels are trivial, or are themselves determined by the macrosociological situation. For example, patterns of micro behavior are said to be determined by the stratification system.

6. Microsociology is the fundamental empirical material since everyone, including sociological researchers, lives in the world of micro experience, and macro realities are constructed or inferred from this micro data. Sociological concepts (such as "father's occupation" in a survey question) are glosses or summaries of thousands or millions of micro interactions taking place over many years. However, the extreme micro reductionist program of describing everything in full micro detail is impossible, since it would require very long periods of time. Microsociology, too, must sample and summarize micro situations and show the value of its analysis through theoretical generalizations. Its major strengths are avoiding conservative ideological reifications of macro entities and incorporating human agency.

7. An exercise in translating sociological principles into micro processes shows that micro-interactional principles are always involved, but that there are three irreducible macro factors: (1) the extent of space, (2) the amount of time, and (3) the number of persons, situations, and processes involved. The ultimate causal laws of sociology, including both processes which reproduce patterns, as well as those which change them, would take the form of the combination of micro processes across space, time, and number.

8. The contents of any micro situation is affected by other micro situations in past or anticipated future time and by reference to or carry-overs from other persons elsewhere in space. Thus every situation is affected by its macro location among other micro situations; the structural relationships among micro situations is a macro effect upon micro.

9. Several theories attempt to specify the substantive content of the micro-macro connection. Giddens' structuration theory proposes that agent and structure mutually constitute each other. Individuals construct micro action by drawing upon rules and resources which exist outside of time and space; their actions in turn can change the macro system, but only within limits. Habermas proposed that the lifeworld of individuals has lost its autonomy due to "colonizing" encroachments by modern capitalism and bureaucratic power structures. Rational choice theories analyze levels of collective decisions emerging out of individual choices. Hechter's model proposes that social solidarity is due to the group's capacity for mediating individual goals and monitoring compliance.

10. Interaction ritual chains theory incorporates the local effects of macro structure upon micro situations via individuals' market positions, the cultural capital circulated between persons, and the emotional energies which build up or die down across situations. Power is based on membership in an enforcement coalition; property is a social relationship of owners to such enforcement coalitions. The sense of group rankings tacitly transmitted in interaction rituals is based on symbols of membership in such coalitions. *Particularized cultural capital* (the reputation of particular persons for being connected in particular organizational networks) is more important for power and property than *generalized cultural capital* (the stock of general topics and cultural knowledge which individuals use for conversation). The latter is more important for informal, status-group connections.

Chapter **12**

NETWORK
THEORIES

NETWORK ANALYSIS
    Varieties of Network Structures
    What Can Network Theory Explain?

NETWORK EFFECTS ON INDIVIDUAL ACTION AND BELIEF
    Cohesion
    Structural Equivalence

NETWORK THEORIES OF SOCIAL TIES
    Structural Exchange Theories
    Mauss and Gift Exchange Systems
    Lévi-Strauss and Tribal Kinship as Exchange
    Marriage and Friendship Markets and the Modern Status System
    Blau's Theory of Intergroup Integration
    Theories of Social Mobility

NETWORK THEORIES AND ECONOMICS
    The Crisis in Economic Theory
    Markets and Hierarchies
    Sociological Reformulation of Economics
    Markets as Mutually Monitoring Producers' Cliques

NETWORK THEORIES OF POWER
    Structural Dependence and Power Brokers
    Enforcement Coalitions
    Combinations of Enforcement Coalitions and Exchange Theories of
      Power
    Community and National Power Structures

SUMMARY

NETWORK ANALYSIS

Network analysis is a relative newcomer on the theory scene. The study of networks has been around for some time, but it was used largely as a descriptive technique. Though its methods have grown increasingly sophisticated, some scholars have called it "a technique in search of a theory." The interest of network analysis has seemed to be where it provides empirical information which bears on some substantive controversy in another area. For example, a traditional theory of urbanization (Nisbet, 1953) proposed that the tightly woven communities of rural and small-town life disappear in urban society, leaving the city-dweller as a mass of anomic individuals. It turns out that this is not true, neither in African cities, where individuals maintain connections to their tribal homes (Mitchell, 1969); nor in North American cities, where individuals have their own circles of friends, often of greater breadth and density (especially in the higher social classes) than in rural communities (Wellman, 1982; Fischer, 1982.) Other studies have used network analysis to describe the concentration of political power in communities, and to mediate between pluralist and elitist theories of power (Laumann and Pappi, 1976).

Recently network analysis has emerged as a style of theory in its own right, and one with large ambitions. Part of its ambitiousness comes from a growing awareness of the connection between networks and market or exchange theories. Markets and networks are two conceptions of how individuals link together into a larger social structure. For this reason, they are on the cutting edge of theory in attempting to unite micro and macro into a single model. Both provide a way to deal with real people coming together in situations. Since these interactions exist in a context of other interactions, what happens locally depends, at any rate to a degree, on what happens elsewhere; thus macro affects micro. And conversely, the overall structure is nothing more than the way the total number of interactions are patterned in time and space: macro is constituted from micro. Markets and networks make it possible to conceptualize the larger structure in a nonreified way and to built it up from the behavior of real persons.

These models picture individual actors as both free and constrained. Human beings have the capacity to create or negotiate whatever they can at any moment in time. But they always act in a structured situation, so that the consequences and conditions of their creativity and negotiation are nevertheless patterned by larger relationships beyond their control. The network perspective avoids not only reification of the macro structure but a disembodied view of micro interactions by showing structures as patterns among individuals. Moreover, network theorists have suggested that their principles cut across the micro-macro dimension, applying equally well to relationships among persons, organizations, or still larger units such as states (in other words, to networks of networks).

Theories of networks and of markets occupy a strategic position in building general sociological theory. For this reason, I think, sociological theories of this sort have had great ambitions. Exchange theory, a version of market models, was the first to militantly push the micro-macro issue, and its proponents have attempted to construct macro theory from a micro basis. Network analysis has been touted as the solution to the problems that have limited exchange as well as virtually every other approach.

The network approach proposes a major revision in our way of looking at society (Burt, 1982; Wellman, 1983). Much of sociology, especially on the empirical research side, has tended to deal with attributes of individuals—race, sex, age, social class, education—as if these were the fundamental building blocks of society. In survey research, we examine how some of these traits affect others (for example, the effects of race or sex upon social mobility, the effects of education on prejudice, and so on). The trouble is, these are abstractions from what is really going on in social life. Social life is relational; it is only because, say, blacks and whites occupy particular kinds of patterns in networks in relation to each other that "race" becomes an important variable. To regard race as a cause of social mobility is misleading, since it is really the pattern of network connections around persons of different races that makes this trait significant. The same is true for an individual's sex, social class, or education. None of these is an intrinsic or perpetual determinant of anything else; each is only a convenient shorthand we use to refer to a pattern of network relationships which exists at some time in history. When the network structure changes, then some other traits become salient, rather than race, sex, education, and so forth. If we merely study the correlations among traits, as in conventional multivariate data analysis, it is like putting living matter through a centrifuge: we come out with isolated chemical molecules, but all the structure is gone. The truly fundamental sociological theory, then, must focus on network patterns, rather than on the traits that are picked up by them at various points in time.

I believe the theoretical potential of network analysis is real, but several issues must be overcome first. Principles of exchange theory have sometimes been incorporated within network models, although in some respects the theories are also rivals. There are serious difficulties with market theory, and with the conventional economics to which it is related. Network theory is promising because it explicitly recognizes and avoids these weaknesses of market theory. Networks offer a superior way to analyze the phenomena that we usually think of as exchanges or markets: repeated exchanges among the same people constitute a network. The main task is to make network analysis more theoretical—to formulate it in terms of conditions which bring about varying results and to reformulate market theory so that it can operate within a network context.

The network conception of the social world has considerable advantages (see Wellman, 1983). It does not assume an idealized market, but shows precisely who exchanges with whom, and with what regularity. The network description is actually a more precise version of the market relationships around any given individual. Ego's network comprises all the exchanges that are possible *for that person*. Usually, Ego's market is not wide open; frequently Ego has only a limited set of possible exchange partners. Does this invalidate the market model? No, but it gives the market model a more specific application. Ego still bargains for the best exchange, and the principles of the various exchange theories tell us which one that will be. All that is ruled out is the assumption made by economic theory (but not usually by sociological exchange theorists) that the full set of exchanges on the open market create a general price at which everyone converges. More precisely, we can say that how much of an open market exists around Ego is a variable. Network analysis tells us to what extent Ego's market choices are open or limited,[1] and hence where separate, local "prices" will occur. Network analysis tells us about structures in which individuals go "off the market" in permanently repeated relationships, and hence about power hierarchies and interpersonal property relationships.

VARIETIES OF NETWORK STRUCTURE

Network analysis began as a descriptive technique. Researchers collect information about ties among individuals (or any other social units, such as organizations). They can then describe the network of relationships, in either of several ways. We may take the point of view of the individual, the "Ego network." In this case we ask: How many direct or indirect ties does Ego have to other people in the network? Is Ego isolated or central? What kind of ties does Ego have? Alternatively, we may try to characterize the overall shape of the network. In this case we must describe: How densely or loosely connected is it? How centralized or decentralized? How many gaps or holes are in it (individuals who are not connected?) And are the relationships transitive or intransitive (that is, are ties reciprocated in both directions, or do they go one way only)? (See Figure 12-1.)

A number of different techniques have been used to describe networks, to analyze data, and to make theoretical inferences from them. (A good summary is Marsden and Laumann, 1984). *Topological* models use the mathematical idea of structural equivalence: two actors are equivalent to the extent their relationships with other actors are identical. The mathematical model maps various actors onto social positions, in what is called "homomorphic reduction" or "many-to-one mapping." One such approach (White, Boorman, and Breiger, 1976) produces "blockmodels," diagrams of rows and columns in which the positions are the cells, and which show how closely or distantly incumbents of those positions are related to actors who are in other positions in the blockmodel.

Another type of network model uses *graph theory*, which represents individuals and their connections as a set of nodes with paths among them. Such models can search for cliques or "maximal connected subgraphs," individuals who are all directly and reciprocally connected to each other (that is, each pair chooses one another mutually). Such completely tight-knit cliques are rare, though, and the method has expanded to deal with cliques of varying degrees of completeness and cohesion. It is also possible to describe a path through a graph from any individual to another; the shortest such path is called a "geodesic," using a metaphor from geography. One can then analyze the presence of strong or weak ties among individuals, including the amount of indirect ties needed to connect any two individuals together.

A third method for analyzing networks uses measures of *social distance*. This approach has the theoretical advantage that it can deal with the degrees of social

---

[1] Strictly speaking, network analysis would give us this information if it provided a full description of everyone that Ego encounters. In practice, network research usually asks for the persons that Ego deals with most frequently. Even this gives us a certain amount of market information, since these persons are the part of the network about whom Ego has most often to make market choices.

FIGURE 12-1

VARIETIES OF NETWORK STRUCTURE

A is directly connected to B and C.
B and C are indirectly connected to each other.

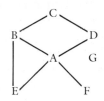

A is central.
F is relatively isolated.
G is completely isolated.
B and C are structurally equivalent.

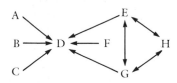

E and G, E and H, and G and H
are transitively connected; all
other connections are intransitive

relationship between individuals: instead of counting a tie as simply present or absent, it can examine finer gradations, such as how often one person sees another, how intimate they are, and so forth. There are numerous technical problems here, though, since one must be concerned with whether there is a standard metric for measuring such degrees of relationship, as well as scales which divide the "social distance space" into multiple dimensions. This kind of network analysis, although it seems intuitively more subtle and realistic, has had more complex methodological problems than the other approaches. Hence the simpler kinds of approximations have been more often used.

WHAT CAN NETWORK THEORY EXPLAIN?

Network theories can be applied to a variety of topics and on different levels of analysis. Starting from the most micro level, we can examine how individuals' locations inside networks affects the way they behave, think, and feel. At a larger level of analysis, we are concerned with the patterns of networks that make up a society (or some part of it). This is a very extensive application of network theory, since entire social structures can be seen as networks of people who repeatedly interact. The question is, how can we move beyond descriptions of such networks, to theoretical explanations of why networks (that is, social structures) take particular forms?

One type of theory here actually derives from a version of exchange theory. This is not the American branch of theory, deriving from Homans and Blau, but a French version which goes back to Marcel Mauss and was developed by Claude Lévi-Strauss (see Ekeh, 1974). This is sometimes referred to as "structural exchange theory"; its focus is not on the individual motivations produced by a person's position in a market, but on the repetitive pattern of *who* exchanges with *whom,* and thus on the shape of social connections. Mauss and Lévi-Strauss applied the model to gift exchanges and marriages in tribal societies. I suggest that similar (though of course modified) processes apply to the ceremonial-cultural exchanges that make up the status stratification of modern social life, which may also be conceived as "friendship" markets and marriage markets. Peter Blau's more recent structural theory of intergroup integration is related to this type of theory, since it too is concerned with the structural conditions which affect how often friendship ties or intermarriages of a certain sort can occur.

Much of the theoretical work on these kinds of models of social ties has concerned their *structurally static* aspects. Mauss and Lévi-Strauss have focused on the large-scale structures that result from particular kinds of gift exchanges; Blau tells us, conversely, how the overall pattern of group sizes affects who can exchange with whom. There are also some *dynamic* implications of such theories, as when Lévi-Strauss proposes that certain kinds of kinship exchanges result in a "kinship revolution," breaking down the exchange pattern and giving rise to a stratified society and the rise of the state. For modern society, the area of social mobility theory can be best seen as a complex set of theories which include both static and dynamic aspects and which operate on both micro and macro levels. We will see how the network perspective helps to build general theory across several of these levels of analysis.

There are two further areas of sociology in which network models are now making an impact. One is in the borderline between sociology and economics. In recent years, there have been frequent efforts to import economic theory into sociology, although at the same time some fundamental problems in economic theory itself have received a lot of attention. If economics has been invading sociology, sociology has also been invading economics. Network theories, such as those of Harrison White and Ronald Burt, have been especially prominent in the new "sociology of business" that is now reformulating economic phenomena on its own grounds. Finally, we will look at network theories of power, another frontier area which has been making a good deal of recent progress.

NETWORK EFFECTS ON INDIVIDUAL ACTION AND BELIEF

What kind of networks individuals are in, and where they are situated in them, has an effect on the way they behave and what they think.

COHESION

The more tightly that individuals are tied into a network, the more they are affected by group standards (Whyte, 1943; Festinger, Schachter and Back, 1950; Bott, 1971). Actually, there are two factors operating here, which we can see from network analysis: how many ties an individual has to the group and how closed the entire group is to outsiders. Isolated and tightly connected groups make up a clique; within such highly cohesive groups, individuals tend to have very homogeneous beliefs.

A more recent area of research has been to show the effects of social density on well-being. For instance, individuals who have a dense "support network" tend to have better mental health in reacting to stressful events (Kadushin, 1982), although this also depends on the quality of these personal relationships. This topic has been somewhat isolated from sociological theory, because its primary focus is on social problems; but it does have a theoretical connection. Here the dependent variable is not the homogeneity of belief but an individual's emotional state. The empirical pattern fits the Durkheimian theory that social density promotes group solidarity and moral sentiments. Indirectly, this research supports the IR chain model in which emotional energies are generated by being accepted in the membership rituals of group interaction.

STRUCTURAL EQUIVALENCE

The most explicitly theoretical model of network as source of individual motivation is Burt's (1982) "structural theory of action." Burt's theory proposes that individuals are not simply acting out a generalized culture shared by everyone. Rather, they occupy particular kinds of positions in a social network. The actors' interests are shaped by their network position. Burt refers here, *not* to the immediate effects of the clique that Ego interacts with, but rather to the pattern of individuals who are in similar structural positions elsewhere in the network. Individuals who are central in their own cliques, or who have extensive ranges of contacts, are similar to each other and are different from persons who are peripheral in their cliques or have limited ranges of contacts. Burt ascribes this similarity of persons who occupy similar positions, but are not necessarily personally connected, to a perceptual process. Drawing upon Meadian symbolic interaction, Burt proposes that individuals acquire a "Generalized Other" based on the incumbents of similar positions. This in turn shapes their beliefs and motivations in their own realms.

Burt's model is an impressive one, combining both micro and macro levels of analysis. Although he offers some data congruent with his model of individual behavior, it cannot be regarded as entirely confirmed. It is not clear that individuals actually know about people who are in analogous positions, but with whom they do not actually interact. Burt is breaking away from the classical model which derives the "Generalized Other" from one's own interactions with a multiplicity of others. An alternative explanation may be that the attitudes and behaviors found across similar structural positions are due, not to imitation of a common reference group, but because of the structural properties of interaction itself. People who are central or peripheral in networks probably differ in the sheer "ritual density" of interaction, as well as perhaps in their daily experience as order givers or order takers; and being in networks that differ in their range and density also affects the Durkheimian variables producing the "horizontal" aspects of class cultures (Chapter

6). Burt's model may actually be showing how different kinds of networks affect the micro-interactional conditions which IR chain theory specifies as determining beliefs and behavior.[2]

NETWORK THEORIES OF SOCIAL TIES

STRUCTURAL EXCHANGE THEORIES

So far we have been concerned with the effects of network positions on the individuals within it. We turn now to a more macro-level question: what are the properties of the overall network itself, and its causes and effects? Here we encounter another connection between network and exchange theories. Homans and Blau had argued that social structure consists of the linkages which emerge when people exchange repeatedly with each other. But their focus was largely on the "prices" at which individuals made exchanges. An alternative tradition in exchange theory has focused, rather, on *who* exchanges with *whom,* and thus on the shape of the social connections. This is the French version of exchange theory of Marcel Mauss and Claude Lévi-Strauss. This theory was formulated for exchanges in tribal societies, in which social custom tended to rigidly prescribe the exchange of gifts and of inter-marriages; hence it does not describe an open market but structured and apparently noncompetitive exchanges. The Mauss and Lévi-Strauss models look more like closed networks than markets in the capitalist sense.

From this line of theory we can learn several things. Exchanges in which the "price" has already been set do not tell us much about the motivating pressures on individuals, but they do make up a network structure whose properties can be explained by the kinds of repeated exchanges that make it up. They also show us the relationship between symbolic-emotional exchanges, and more utilitarian or "economic" exchanges. Although the former kind of exchanges are most apparent in tribal societies, they also exist in more complex societies as well. The more important instance of such social ties are the linkages of friendship and marriage which make up the informal and interpersonal side of stratification, the structure of status groups. And the link between such personal groups and occupational positions brings us to a network theory of social mobility.

MAUSS AND GIFT EXCHANGE SYSTEMS

Mauss (1925/1967) concentrated on gift exchanges in horticultural tribes, but his analytical model has wider application. In these societies, he argued, gifts are the basic form of economy, the principal way in which goods and services are traded. His emphasis, however, is on the Durkheimian, ritual aspect of exchanges. Mauss

---

[2]The actors in a network need not be persons, so structural equivalence may also be found on a more macro level. For example, Snyder and Kick (1979) have shown that countries which are mapped into different positions in a blockmodel of transactions in the world capitalist system have different rates of economic growth; and Burt (1983) shows that a corporation's network position affects its profits. These economic applications of networks will be discussed later in this chapter.

points out there is a morality attached to the process of gift giving. Although the gift is, on the surface, freely given, nevertheless there is an underlying obligation. Certain kinds of gifts are owed to certain people on certain occasions; just as in our society Christmas and birthday presents are expected for close relatives, in tribal societies certain festivals, ceremonies, and times of the year require gifts of food, labor services, or luxury objects. In addition to the obligation to give, there is an obligation to receive; it would be an insult to turn down a gift. And there is the obligation to reciprocate on a later occasion, thus setting (or keeping) in motion a cycle of reciprocal links between givers and receivers.

In this way, gifts constitute the social structure, linking people together repeatedly. It is not necessary that the "economy" of gift exchange actually result in any material advantage to anyone; exactly the same kinds of gifts might be exchanged back and forth, so that there is no division of labor involved in it; and equal values (or merely token objects) might be exchanged, so that no one really gains anything. The purpose of the gifts is not the economic advantages of participation in a market, but the social advantages. Gifts link people together both as individuals and as one family or tribe to another. The alliances, the solidarity, is the payoff. Once this solidarity exists, as we shall see, it can be turned to further uses.

Why do people feel this moral obligation to give, receive, and reciprocate gifts? Here we touch a point also raised by Homans and Blau in their utilitarian version of exchange theory. Their model deliberately stays on the surface: people consciously calculate what advantages they get from exchanges, whereas Mauss points out that such calculation is explicitly excluded from giving and receiving gifts. But Homans and Blau run up against the problem that rational calculation does not show that the other person will in fact reciprocate a favor; this has to be taken on faith. (This is related to Durkheim's more rigorous argument, summarized in Chapter 2, that rational exchange cannot take place without precontractual solidarity.) Hence Homans and Blau posit a social "norm of reciprocity" or "fair exchange" which everyone adheres to, thereby violating their own program to derive everything social from individual motivations.

How does Mauss handle this problem? Although his treatment is not carried through analytically, he provides some basic elements. There is a violent sanction for failure of gift obligations: it is an insult and can result in tribal war. But this cannot be the whole answer, since wars and vendettas in tribal societies also have a ritualistic character, seeking a victim from a particular group to pay off an insult or obligation. Moreover, these acts of violence tend to be chains of reciprocity on the negative side: one ritual killing is avenged by another, linking groups together in a long-term social relationship that happens to be founded on enmity. Bourdieu (1972/1977: 177–92), following this line of analysis of vendettas among the tribes of rural Algeria, has even characterized this as an exchange of gifts, of throats to be cut which are "lent" and "repaid." The reason they are gifts is that the family actually benefits socially from having a vendetta: it acquires a certain public reputation, a status honor which cannot be demonstrated unless it has enemies, and especially enemies of sufficiently high rank to make fighting with them worthwhile.

This reveals a deeper process in Mauss' gift exchanges. Gift exchanges properly carried through bring honor; violations of them bring a loss of status. The ideology of these societies usually puts this in magical or religious terms. Things which are given may be conceived as magical, filled with dangerous power over the receiver, until they are appropriately repaid. Or the gift-giving ceremony is regarded as essential for good luck or fertility, for warding off evil, or as an invocation to the gods. The magic power or religious significance of gifts tends to coincide with social identity and status. In the famous Melanesian kula ring (Malinowski, 1922; Mauss 1925/1967), the ceremonial shells bring honor to whoever possesses them, giving them a temporary social reputation, as well as focusing public attention on who will be given them next. The gifts, and above all the persons who give and receive them, are filled with *mana,* an emotional energy that is regarded as magical but socially represents their central position in the transactions of the group.

We may push Mauss' analysis further, and recognize that gift exchanges are rituals in the neo-Durkheimian sense. They assemble the group, focus public attention, and build up emotions. The gifts become sacred objects, symbolizing a crucial social process: the making of social alliances. In this way, we no longer need to invoke a mysterious "norm of reciprocity" floating about in the culture. The sense of obligation is generated by interactions, the ritual aspect of encounters in which gifts are given. This analysis has the advantage that it can recognize variations; instead of assuming that everyone everywhere has an equal sense of this obligation to reciprocate gifts, we can recognize that it varies in its intensity. Some societies (and some individuals within them) place much more emphasis on the status received by gift exchanges, while others are nearer the utilitarian pole of economic calculation, trying to cut the best deal and make a profit.[3]

Mauss distinguishes several versions of gift-exchange systems (see Sahlins, 1972, for another such typology): (1) Permanent linkages between tribal clans in which virtually all goods are circulated by ritual gift exchanges. Mauss (1925/1967: 6) calls this *"total prestation."* (2) *Two-level exchanges,* in which trust is established by ritual gifts, followed by utilitarian bargaining over mundane goods. This is exemplified by the Melanesian kula ring (Malinowski, 1922). Voyagers from neighboring islands first negotiate guest-host relationships with ceremonial gifts; then these relationships are used as trading partners for hard-nosed buying and selling of fish, coconuts, and other commodities. The two levels illustrate Durkheim's notion of a precontractual solidarity underlying and prior to the utilitarian division of labor. (3) *Potlatches,* competitive gift exchanges in which rivals try to shame one another by giving gifts, including lavish and even boastfully destructive celebrations. (No Homansian "fair exchange" here!) This results in an escalating series of exchanges, each trying to outdo the other, until one side goes bankrupt. Mauss describes the potlatch as a kind of credit investment, which must be repaid with interest. It is a tribal version of dynamic, competitive capitalism, since the escalating consumption of gifts requires a continual pressure for economic productivity. (4) Full-fledged *utilitarian markets,* characterized by hard economic bargaining, where the gift-exchange system has been reduced to vestiges in the private sphere in the form of personal gifts, dinner parties, family ceremonies, favors among friends, and the like. (The latter

---

[3] Although this has never been explicitly tested, I would suggest that high ritual density of face-to-face interaction, especially closed local communities, generate much more gift-exchange obligations than situations of low ritual density.

was where Blau documented his exchange model, in the *informal* side of a modern bureaucracy.)

Mauss himself supposed there was an evolutionary sequence among these types, but we need not accept that interpretation. The potlatch, for example, is not a stage which is gone through everywhere, but was found primarily among the coastal tribes of the Pacific Northwest. I would suggest a more analytical explanation: this kind of highly status-competitive gift exchange (that is, ceremonial showing-off for one's guests) exists where there are unusually rich resources in the environment, while no single stratification hierarchy is enforced by a strong state or other form of centralized control. This would explain the most common modern analogy, the potlatch-like parties which wealthy youths like to throw—a status competition in the form of "wild parties" involving ritual destruction of property. A systematic comparison of the general conditions for the range of gift-exchange (and nongift) systems remains to be done.

LÉVI-STRAUSS AND TRIBAL KINSHIP AS EXCHANGE

I have already noted in Chapter 9 that Lévi-Strauss applied Mauss' exchange theory to kinship systems of tribal societies. Families link themselves together by a regular exchange of women by marriage, resulting in a pattern of reciprocal obligations. This is a Durkheimian two-level system, since marital exchanges create the social alliances which in turn structure the distribution of economic goods and services. Lévi-Strauss extended Mauss' model into the fundamental basis of all early societies. For their social structure consists of nothing but kinship; hence these exchanges literally constitute all the social structure there is. Lévi-Strauss also gave attention to varieties of such structures and to their dynamics over time. Societies follow varied rules of kinship exchanges: some prefer matrilateral cross-cousin marriage; others, patrilateral cross-cousin marriage; still others, systems of intermarrying tribal sections; while yet others follow negative rules which specify only which groups cannot intermarry.

Each of these has a structural logic, which Lévi-Strauss attempted to state formally. Some result in "short cycles," which tie together the same pair of families repeatedly over the generations, but leave them isolated from other groups. Other exchange rules bring about "long cycles," which indirectly link together many distant families, thus producing a more elaborately connected social structure. Lévi-Strauss theorized, too, that short cycles were more stable, reproducing the same kind of social structure over the centuries; whereas long cycles had more of a dynamic to them, which eventually transformed the kinship system. This is because long cycles are a kind of "investment" in alliances. Some families eventually acquire many obligations of repayment and become rich in alliances. These families are able to set themselves up as an aristocracy and eventually create the military state which transcends the kinship-based tribal system entirely. Lévi-Strauss' theory of structural dynamics remains relatively undeveloped by subsequent research, as he himself turned in another direction, into systems of symbolism in myths. (But see Lévi-Strauss, 1984; White, 1963; Collins, 1986: 267–321, for further theories along this line regarding marriage politics.)

MARRIAGE AND FRIENDSHIP MARKETS AND THE
MODERN STATUS SYSTEM

All of the models we have considered so far—Mauss' total prestation, two-level systems, potlatches, and Lévi-Straussian kinship systems—are structured by exchanges which link particular individuals or groups together by repeated exchanges. Some of these, such as potlatches and some of the long-cycle kinship systems, are dynamic: the structure transforms itself over time. Others are apparently stable. These models do not focus on the individuals and their motivations for making exchanges, but show the structural consequence of one form of exchange (for instance, the ceremonial part of the kula ring) for some later or parallel form of exchange. The question arises as to the general theoretical use of such models. Do they apply mainly to tribal societies and have no more universal application? I would suggest that they do apply more widely, although with certain variations. Mauss' theory considers small, bounded communities with high ritual density and no state; hence the ritual basis of the status order is strong, while exchanges are used especially for political alliances. Lévi-Strauss' kinship exchanges are found in a similar context and decline with the rise of the autonomous military state. Similar conditions occur only within the private sphere in a modern, state-structured society; hence the scope of our ritual exchange is much more modest.

It is precisely in the private sphere that modern sociologists have found similar linkages based on exchanges. Willard Waller (1937) analyzed the American courtship system as a market, in which young men and women rated each other's desirability relative to their other choices, and eventually settled on marrying the person whose degree of attraction most matched their own. Waller marks the beginning of modern social exchange theory. The structure of the market is quite different than Lévi-Strauss'; the individuals rather than families are doing the exchanging and linking themselves together. Furthermore, Lévi-Strauss focused on the marriage rules, the public conception of who ought to marry whom (cross-cousins and so forth); whereas the modern, individualistic marriage market has no prescriptive rules: the absence of such rules is in fact one of the things that makes it individualistic. Since only individuals are exchanging personal resources, there are no long-term cycles of any sort; nothing carries over to other persons or later generations. Nevertheless, it does constitute a social structure, the structure of the modern family. The couple, having agreed to exchange exclusive sexual attention and emotional tokens ("love"), and to pool their incomes and economic possessions, go on making this exchange day after day, as long as they stay married. This continued exchange, seen in micro-empirical detail, actually constitutes the "marriage" as a structure.

This may seem a fragmented system, isolated exchanges which have no relationship to any other structures elsewhere: each couple goes on exchanging among themselves, parallel but unconnected to other family units. That is true, but there are two areas where connections do occur. The marriage consists in the pair of individuals taking themselves off the marriage market. But the market remains there in the background. The overall structure of opportunities and resources in that market—the various other men and women who were available as partners—motivated this pair to choose each other in the first place; and since some lineup of resources and opportunities is still actually available, its temptations and pressures can sometimes break the marriage exchange through adultery, divorce, and/or remarriage. That is one way the overall structure, even in an individual-choice marriage market, can still affect the structure of its component parts. Even if the individuals go off the "open market" by contracting permanent and exclusive exchanges within a pair (that is, by marrying), the market is still there, exerting pressures to attract them back onto the market (or contrarily, keeping couples married by their lack of resources to go back on the marriage market).

The other large structural connection is via status. The husband and wife constitute a unit of joint social status in the larger society. Their combination of resources, weighted by the general pattern of male-female stratification in the society, determines their status honor as a couple. This is not merely an abstract process of judging prestige. As Weber pointed out, the realm of status is the realm of community memberships and exclusions. (The same thing is implied in the Durkheimian theory of rituals, since it both creates bonds among members and excludes outsiders.) The modern family's social standing is enacted by sociable contacts in everyday life: who gets invited to whose parties, who attends what formal occasions together (dances, banquets, entertainments, weddings). We might notice that these are ceremonial gift exchanges in the Maussian sense: they are not utilitarian, they involve obligations of reciprocity, and their violation results in loss of status and social exclusion. Participation in charities and other public events, incurring personal expense for the "benefit of others," is an explicit version of the implicit trade-off of ceremonial goods for social honor, which tribal societies carried out in a religious guise in the form of sacrifices and other ceremonial donations. Moreover, charitable giving is parallel to Lévi-Strauss' "long cycles." Whereas social invitations and presents produce "short cycles," which merely link persons together repeatedly as local groups, charity is a transaction on trust, which is repaid indirectly through the status one receives from larger and unspecified social circles. As in the case of Lévi-Straussian kinship alliances, the "long cycle" investment in charity is riskier but brings a larger payoff.

A family's social life, even when it is entirely "private," always has this honorific quality. It is part of a market of social connections. The same analysis may be extended to individuals' "friendship markets." Whom one is friends with is socially patterned; there is a tendency for homogeneity of friendships by social class (and by certain occupational enclaves within classes), as well as by ethnicity, age, and sex (Laumann, 1966, 1973; Fischer, 1982). From the macro viewpoint, this is what status groups are: collections of persons who associate together and tend to exclude others. The boundaries do not have to be rigid for this process to apply; status groups in a modern industrial society cluster around certain commonalities, even though their borders are often vague.[4]

We may also do a micro analysis of these friendship linkages. From the point of view of the individual, or of any particular encounter, this market structure shapes

[4]They are less vague at the level of the upper class, however, also in certain sectors such as highly educated professionals and especially intellectuals (Laumann, 1966). This gives a distinctive shape to the status-group structure of modern society: more sharply bounded at the top (though with several competing status realms, especially business wealth versus education), more permeable at the middle class, more localized into purely family and intimate groups in the working class.

the relative attractiveness of particular people one might associate with, as well as provides the lineup of cultural capital and emotional energies which determine what happens in these encounters. In other words, the analysis of *markets as interlinkages* (a macro level 2) gives specific content to the analysis of *individual motivations for making* exchanges (a micro level 1). The cultural capital which makes up the content of conversations is largely a repository of what was said in past exchanges (or retellings about those exchanges); it is a set of words, ideas, and symbols actually circulating through a structural network, which operates to reproduce (and to systematically change) that network. Conversational rituals are the nodes of this ongoing structure of exchanges.

Theories on the macro level concentrate on showing how particular sorts of linkages operate. This includes structure-to-structure patterns, principles of how one kind of structural linkage engenders another. This type of theory is not well developed, although what I have said about Mauss' and Lévi-Strauss' models indicates that systematic comparisons can be expected to turn up more general principles. In modern societies, the exchange-based structures that we know the best are in the sphere of private status groups: the pattern of marriages, the lineup of status groups throughout the class structure, the degrees of cultural homogeneity involved in these. A notable feature that any general theory will have to address, is that, although these structures are generated by exchanges on an open market, the creation of structures themselves takes the form of individual-to-individual linkages which take those persons off the open market. We thus have a paradoxical picture of market and non-market structures coexisting and even determining each other.

BLAU'S THEORY OF INTERGROUP INTEGRATION

A related model of how networks affect the contacts of people within them is Blau's (1977) macro theory of social integration. Blau explicitly abandons exchange theory, because he feels it is necessary to go to a purely structural level, beyond micro exchanges, in order to account for macro structures. His most important principle is that the sheer size of different sorts of groups determines the amount of linkages that can exist among individuals who belong to those groups. If the white population, for instance, is ten times larger than the black population, it follows that white people have a much greater chance of associating with other whites (10 to 11) than with blacks (1 to 11). Conversely, blacks will have a much greater chance of associating with whites (10 to 11) than with other blacks (1 to 11). Accordingly, ingroup associations should be much greater among whites than among blacks.

Another proposition is that intergroup association is promoted to the extent that various individual attributes are cross-cutting rather than consolidated. Assume that persons tend to associate with others who are like themselves. But if there are various dimensions of resemblance, people can associate with others who are similar in race, class, education, religion, cultural interests, and so forth. If these are not tightly correlated, then associating with someone who is similar on one dimension will tend to bring people into contact with persons who are dissimilar on other dimensions. If race and education are not closely correlated, for instance, then associating with persons of similar education will cause people to cross racial lines, and vice versa.

Blau does not actually measure networks in the conventional sense (that is, draw a diagram of who associates with whom across an entire population); instead, he and his followers (Blau and Schwartz, 1984) survey rates of intermarriage or other indicators of contact and correlate them with the relative sizes of these groups in the population. Blau is thus closer to traditional surveys of aggregated individuals; his groups (blacks, whites, and so on) are not actually groups that are known to associate together as a community, but are statistical constructs, individuals lumped together because they share common traits.

Blau's model is nevertheless suggestive, since it is dealing with one set of factors that produce network structure. It is not likely that these are the only factors, however. For example, the above example of interaction between black and white populations in the United States implies far more contact than actually takes place. (Of black married women, 99.0 percent are married to black men [U.S. Bureau of the Census, 1985, Table 11] and patterns of friendship also are largely within racial lines.) This indicates that there are further pressures for segregation, or for maintaining ingroup solidarity against outsiders, which Blau's theory does not take into account.

THEORIES OF SOCIAL MOBILITY

Social mobility is movement within a stratification system. It can be analyzed from various angles. The failure to distinguish among them is one reason why its patterns are still not well understood theoretically, even though social mobility has been heavily studied for many decades.

First, there is *description versus explanation*. Are we merely describing how much mobility there is in a particular society and a particular historical time, or are we developing an explanation of what causes the amount of mobility that takes place?

Second, what aspect of mobility is our theory focusing upon? There are at least three important levels (see Collins, 1975: 430–36, 445–56):

1. INDIVIDUAL MOBILITY   What determines the movement of an individual through the system? Notice that the amount of movement can be divided up into various segments: theories traditionally were concerned with *intergenerational mobility,* tracing social positions (usually occupational class) across from parents to children; but more recently there is much focus on *lifetime* mobility, from one's childhood (or perhaps one's first job) through the subsequent career. Even smaller segments can be picked out, such as research which concerns determinants of one's first job or movement from one job to another. These individual-level models are often referred to as "status attainment."

2. THE STRUCTURE OF POSITIONS   The answer to the first question (what causes an individual's career movement, upwards, downwards, or staying the same) depends in part upon what kind of structure there is to move through. Hence a second level of explanation arises: What determines the sheer numbers of positions at different levels? What determines how many levels there are (whether the structure is tall, with many levels to climb, or flat)? What determines the shape (pyramid-shaped and narrowing at the top, equally broad at all levels, unified or branching off into separate hierarchies, as well as other possible shapes)?

3. MOBILITY RATES   What determines how many, and what proportion, of persons move from their original positions? Here again there are various sub-foci of attention. We might want to explain what the rate of mobility is across generations, or within a lifetime, or even in some smaller segment of it.

Notice that these three problems are on different levels of micro-macro analysis. (1) *Individual mobility* is the most micro in its focus, but it has a macro component insofar as structural factors affect the ways people can move. A popular way to study individual mobility ("status attainment" models) is to treat a mobility study as if it were a survey of the correlation among individual attributes; thus we would study the effects of one's father's occupation, one's own education, IQ, and so forth, upon one's first job, second job, income, and so forth. This has been most conveniently modeled by a path diagram, which connects variables by arrows that indicate the strength of causality from one to another. However, this approach has been criticized from the point of view of network analysis because it is overly individualistic.

That is, social mobility is really movement through a set of networks: some networks make up the organizations in which one works; the labor markets and contacts connect jobs together; other networks constitute schools and the people in them (vertical networks to teachers, horizontal networks to other students, and so on); and still other networks are one's family and friends. The connection between "father's occupation" and "son's occupational attainment" is not really the correlation between two attributes of a person, but the link between father's and son's occupational networks, with the family as yet another network connection between these individuals. Network analysis in general wants to dissolve alleged individual attributes into results of one's relationship to others in a network; it tries to turn cultural and psychological factors, as we have seen, into the effects of cohesion or structural equivalence. (As I have suggested, the IR chain model is one way in which cultures and psychological states are produced by network positions.)

The network approach to individual mobility also stresses the effects of positions upon mobility, without going through the mediation of cultural-psychological effects. That is, the sheer shape and size of the network determines individual movement, irrespective of individual attributes. One such theory is Harrison White's (1970) "vacancy chains." The basic principle is that people usually can get a new position only when a job opens up; but once one vacancy is filled, it opens up a second vacancy from the person who left to fill the first position. In this way, vacancies rather than persons can be conceived as migrating around the system, and individual moves are due to the structure rather than to their personal characteristics.

Notice that explaining individual mobility is no longer merely a matter of a micro-to-micro explanation, as it appeared to be in the "status attainment" model of a correlation among individual attributes. Introducing the structural constraints of networks makes this an analysis of how macro structures affect the movement of individuals within them. Another network model is Granovetter's (1973, 1982) theory of the "strength of weak ties." This is a model of individual mobility, but introducing the individual's network ties (Ego networks) as a key explanatory variable. Granovetter shows that individuals who have many "weak ties" are most likely to find favorable opportunities for career advancement. Here, "weak ties" means ties to people who are not part of one's local clique, as compared to "strong ties" to persons with whom one shares many reciprocated connections and a less tightly interconnected network. This occurs because weak ties connect one indirectly into more remote parts of the social structure than do strong ties which tend to be a closed local group. (Once again, this is parallel to Lévi-Strauss' distinction between "long cycles" and "short cycles.") For purposes of job contacts, casual acquaintances are more valuable than intimate friends, because of their structural connections.

Since we know from studies of social classes that middle- and especially upper-middle- and upper-class persons have more acquaintances and formal organizational memberships, while working-class persons have fewer acquaintances but are most closely attached to their families and friends (Gans, 1962; Laumann, 1966; Curtis and Jackson, 1977), it follows that this is one of the sources of career advantage for the higher classes. Similar patterns affect the career chances of men and women, since males have wider and more diverse contacts through belonging to voluntary associations than women do (McPherson and Smith-Lovin, 1986); women's organizational memberships tend to have a high density of association within the local group and are connections mainly to other women. Lin (1982) modifies the general theory to take account of this sort of pattern by proposing that weak ties are important when they are to individuals who have more resources (that is they connect one to persons with more organizational power who can help or give information about jobs). Having weak ties to persons who themselves lack power is of little use; it is the upward weak ties that count.

Lin (1987) has unified several structural factors into one model. The structure of society can vary in a number of ways. (1) The number of levels of stratification can range from only two up to as many levels as there are persons. Using Blau's theory of intergroup contacts, Lin points out that when there are few strata, most people will have contacts only within their stratum, and weak ties will not be very useful in mobility (which will depend instead on the resources individuals possess). Conversely, where there are many strata, there are many opportunities for weak ties to persons of differing resources, hence the Granovetter effect should be strong. (2) The relative size of the strata can vary from equal (the hierarchy looks like a rectangle the same shape all the way up) to unequal (such as a pyramid broad at the base and narrow at the peak, or a diamond, or other unequal shapes). Generally speaking, equal sizes among strata make possible the maximal number of weak ties across strata for all persons. But the more the shape looks like a pyramid, the fewer chances of mobility-useful weak ties the lower-ranking persons will have, just because there are relatively few persons they can associate with upward as compared to sideways or downward. Thus the network effect of weak ties on individuals is itself constrained by the structural shape of the network.[5]

A theory of *individual mobility* (level 1) thus implicitly leads us to the second level, explaining why the *structure of positions* takes a particular shape. Relatively little research has been done on this level; even the network models have been more

---

[5] One limitation of these models is that they are concerned primarily with upward mobility and ignore downward mobility. But if a high-ranking person interacts with a low-ranking person, it is only the latter who gains some benefit from it in terms of job possibilities. Persons in upper strata, especially strata which are small relative to those below them, will tend to have many structural opportunities to interact with persons who actually do them no good for maintaining or improving their own positions. Possibly this may be one structural source of downward mobility.

concerned with the consequences of structural differences than in their causes. This is true in the vacancy chain model as well; it describes individual mobility as the result of the movement of a vacancy around the system, but it needs a higher-level theory to explain why vacancies occur in the first place and when the rate of vacancies will be high or low. It would appear that a theory of the determinants of structure would have to be a very broad one, since it would require us to make comparisons of whole societies at different historical times. Here social mobility theory becomes one of the consequences of a general theory of stratification and social change, and hence a result of the kinds of theories proposed in Chapters 4 and 5.

Most mobility theory has been very weak on this level of analysis. Models which have been proposed as "general theories" have had a tendency to be parochial to a particular time and place: for instance, models (Featherman and Hauser, 1978; Sewell and Hauser, 1980) which take the pattern of variables leading to progress through the U.S. school system in the 1950s through the 1970s are obviously not very general; they have little application, for instance, to agrarian societies, or tribal societies, in which there is no school system or one which affects only a tiny proportion of the population. A truly general model would have to conceptualize processes which occur in all societies. It would focus, not on education, but on cultural transmission and the different ways it can be structured; on various patterns of network connections and their causes; on the structural pattern of positions into which mobility might take place; and the relationships between all of this and the historical shaping of stratification and social organization in general. The nearest to such a theory perhaps remains that of Bendix and Lipset (1959), which proposes that the sheer amount of structural change in a society, especially creating new positions at the higher level, is the major determinant of mobility, rather than any ideological "openness" of the stratification system. That is to say, the movement from a rural society in which most persons were peasants to an urban industrial society with numerous middle-class positions itself produces mobility structurally, even if the society operated under a hereditary ideology. Conversely, a society in which there is little organizational change is missing the main engine of social mobility, even if its ideology is egalitarian.

Explaining *mobility rates,* the third level of problem for mobility theory, is especially difficult because the meaning of any particular "rate" depends on the answer to the second issue, the kind of structure within which mobility is measured. Here we are focusing on the most macro level of the entire structure, the total number of moves of persons found within that society over some period of time and measured across some range of distance from one position to another. Obviously, a society in which there was a narrow range of positions would have a mobility rate that was not comparable to the rate in a society which had an extremely stratified structure. When social mobility was first studied, in the 1940s and 1950s, most attention was upon these overall rates (summarized in Collins, 1975: 430–35). The research raised more questions than it solved, because it was soon recognized that differences in the structure were itself a prime determinant of the rate. Much discussion focused on "forced" mobility which was due to changes in the occupational structure and attempts to statistically separate out "pure" or "circulation" mobility, which was what was left over when structural effects were removed. This pure mobility was taken to be some indication of the "openness" or "fairness" of the stratification system; mobility which occurred merely because there were new white-collar positions was ruled out as not really relevant.

The search for ideologically pure mobility, though, is probably seeking a myth. The better that we can focus upon the network positions and distribution of resources in a society, the more we can explain the actual mobility of individuals; and by calculating the overall shape of these networks, we may be able to arrive at an explanation of when mobility rates are higher or lower in the whole society. For example, a model like that of Stewman and Konda (1983) combines structural features which produce vacancies together with individual resources. A complete theory of mobility rates will no doubt be very complex, since it must incorporate all three levels of analysis. But the further such a theory advances, the less it leaves for a pure mobility, irrespective of social factors. Ideology about the openness of the society is less important than the actual structural factors which produce the movement of people through networks which make up their careers.

NETWORK THEORIES AND ECONOMICS

Economics and sociology share a wide border. Economic theory uses the utilitarian model of individuals pursuing gains and avoiding losses in the context of a market place in which other individuals are doing the same. In a very general sense, this is the same approach as exchange theory in sociology, although there has been a difference in the kinds of phenomena that economists and sociologists have focused upon. Economic theory attempts to explain prices, amounts of production, and financial phenomena such as the value of money (inflation and deflation). What is called "microeconomics" (not to be confused with microsociology) builds models of the behavior of the individual firm or consumer in the context of these processes; "macroeconomics" deals with the activities of the entire market system over time, including the business cycle, economic growth and depression, as well as the "welfare" and policy implications of various business, financial, and governmental actions.

We have already seen in Chapter 10 how some of the more technical models of economics have been introduced into sociology, although these models have often been unrealistic, especially in dealing with matters of stratification. The sociological version of exchange theory is generally more realistic than economic theory; and this is especially so when we move to structural models—exchange networks—rather than assuming open markets. In fact, at the same time that some economists have been extending their formal theories into sociology, sociologists have launched a counterattack across the frontier and have proposed that the whole issue of markets, including the traditional topics of economics itself, might be better understood by sociological theories coming from network analysis. This has been happening, not only because of the promising position of network theories, but also because conventional economics has a number of weaknesses of its own. This has given rise to a good deal of self-criticism in recent years, and some economists have imported quasi-sociological concepts, such as a theory of markets and hierarchies.

THE CRISIS IN ECONOMIC THEORY

The utilitarian market model has come under attack on its own grounds, within economics itself. As a number of economists have pointed out (Leontieff, 1982; Thurow, 1983; Shubik, 1984), economics is especially weak in dealing with large-scale dynamics of markets: being able to explain and predict the rises and falls of the business cycle; dealing with the unexpected combination of inflation and unemployment, which has been apparent in recent decades; and explaining long-term economic growth itself. A fundamental problem is that growth in the capitalist market system remains mysterious, more a matter of faith than of demonstrable patterns. Which society will be the world leader and which fall behind at any historical point has been a shifting, and inexplicable, pattern for economic theory, since the basic market model only gives an idealized picture of efficiency everywhere.

Other empirical problems are in the area of distribution. Classical and neoclassical economics proposes that the market results in the most efficient and equitable distribution of resources and rewards for both labor and capital. In fact, there is considerable inequality in the distribution of both income and wealth (see Chapter 5), but economic theory is unable to account either for the existence of these distributions or for their changes over time. The forgoing issues are all within macroeconomics, but as Thurow (1983), Leontiev (1982), and others have argued, the theoretical problem is with the underlying structure of microeconomics, the basic model of prices set by the action of the market.

MARKETS AND HIERARCHIES

Some economists have offered revisions in the fundamental theory. Oliver Williamson (1975) proposed a "transaction costs" approach to explain why businesses depart from market principles. Economic actors incur the cost of time and effort in bargaining on the marketplace in order to find the best deal. Furthermore, they are hindered by "bounded rationality" (March and Simon, 1958), the inability to process all information and attend to all criteria simultaneously. On top of this, self-interested agents in the market engage in deception, giving rise to complex information-gathering and trust-assessment games (Goffman, 1969). For these reasons, it is more economical for actors sometimes to go off the market. They do this by forming organizations, which Williamson calls "hierarchies." Instead of bargaining daily for the best price of labor, or negotiating over each task, workers are hired for long times at terms fixed in advance by contract. Instead of shopping around for components at each step of a manufacturing process, the various components are brought into the organization. Williamson offers hypotheses about when economic actors will tend toward the market, and when toward the hierarchy. Uncertain environments result in hierarchy, while routine transactions are left on the market. Single-shot, unique transactions are left on the market because there is no point in internalizing them; repeated transactions are taken into the organization.

Williamson's model is a step in the right direction. We may note that the shift from market to hierarchy is a shift toward repeated transactions, in other words, what sociologists call a network. Williamson thus proposes to make the market/network pattern itself a variable. But Williamson's model has a number of weaknesses. Its vision of hierarchies is idealized, assuming that inside organizations there are no problems of control, no transaction costs, no conflicts, just the sheer efficiency of repeated transactions under agreed-upon conditions. The fact that organizations themselves are often conflictual and inefficient is not analyzed here, although it would undermine the rationale of going off the market in order to be more efficient. (In general, the degree of efficiency of market and organizational arrangements has not been measured, but only inferred.) Williamson's model pays no attention to power, except to assume that power (hierarchy) comes into existence because it is more efficient than market bargaining. It gives the most benevolent and idealized interpretation of the growth of organizations and of monopolies: these are allegedly always due to their greater efficiency, and the possibility that mergers and conglomerations may be forced by sheer financial power of capital is not considered. There are many instances in which transactions do not take place on an open market, but nevertheless are not hierarchies. Customers frequently buy at a particular store, or are loyal to a particular brand, rather than shopping around. Another such network of repeated transactions is found in the links that exist among corporate buyers and sellers in the business economy (Burt, 1983). The revisions of economic theory, in short, do not get far enough away from the underlying assumptions of some mechanism tending toward optimal efficiency, as the sole cause of economic arrangements (Granovetter 1985).

SOCIOLOGICAL REFORMULATIONS OF ECONOMICS

While some economists have been pushing their unreconstructed market models into sociology, sociologists have been proposing theories of the structure underlying and controlling markets. A long-standing effort in this direction, (which we have seen in Chapter 3) is the Marxian model. This uses a market model, but links it to the fundamental institutions of property, class inequality (which forces some persons to sell their labor on the market), and political power upholding the property system (as well as manipulating the market in the direction of favored classes). The dynamics of the market remains a central driving force in the Marxian version of capitalism. The Marxian model, however, has empirical problems of its own. More complex and sophisticated versions, such as those of Weber and Schumpeter,[6] make closure of opportunities, and hence monopolies, a basic process in capitalism from the very beginning. Marx and Engels start out with an almost pure market model (except that there are property-owning and nonowning classes in it) and gradually derive monopoly (in the realm of capital) from the fall of profit in the market. Weber and Schumpeter propose that the market is almost never completely open. For Schumpeter (1911/1961), innovative firms reap profit from their natural monopolies that exist before other competitors catch up. For Weber (1922/1968), not only capitalists but sellers of labor organize into status groups to restrict their numbers, control competition, and set "status-appropriate" working conditions and pay (see Parkin,

---

[6] Though Schumpeter was an economist rather than a sociologist, his model was developed in the same intellectual milieu as Weber's, and it fits well with the Weberian sociological model. See Collins, 1986: 117–42.

1979; Murphy, 1984). It is for this reason that the work force is not the homogenous and expanding proletariat envisioned by Marx and Engels, but becomes divided into self-protecting professions, crafts and technical workers, as well as unions and unorganized workers.

These sociological models seem conceptually more realistic than a pure market model. However, they are suggestive rather than definitive, since these theories do not spell out the answer to the various dynamic problems of economic change, distributional inequalities, the setting of prices, and the behavior of firms and economic actors. Though the potentiality is there, no economics has been worked out yet on the basis of these sociological ideas. It is clear that such a model will have to incorporate *both* market processes and those that restrict the market. Weber's model of closure indicates that some individuals are able to become an organized group *which monopolizes opportunities on the market*. Schumpeter connects monopolization and demonopolization to the sequence of events on the market over time. (He does not pay adequate attention to processes that build up monopoly over time, though his theory of financial power suggests how they occur.) The full theory, then must show how exclusionary tendencies balance against (or blend with) market tendencies.

BUSINESS NETWORKS AND PROFITS   Network analysis has been applied to these kinds of issues by Burt (1982, 1983). His work describes the network structure of American manufacturing businesses in terms of the links among their boards of directors. The result is that firms which are able to coopt their favorite trade partners (suppliers or business customers) thereby generate higher profits. Thus the characteristics of interlinkages affect the distribution of profit in the system. This analysis is a direct challenge to economic market theory. It shows the ways in which firms go off the market, and how this affects a key economic phenomenon, profits. Other analysis (Baker, 1984) shows that in financial markets (the commodity exchange) networks among brokers can sustain separate prices, depending on the size and density of exchanges in the local group—again, a phenomenon which conventional economic theory does not grasp. Models of this sort indicate there is great promise for sociology in operating on the home turf of economics itself.

MARKETS AS MUTUALLY MONITORING
PRODUCERS' CLIQUES

The most sophisticated modern effort by sociologists to build a model of the market economy is that of Harrison White (1981). White is a leading practitioner of network analysis, and his model of the market is an innovative version of networks. He points out that in most areas of production, the producers do not so much try to take over the market from each other, as to make their product unique and hence occupy a distinctive niche. In order to do this, they monitor each other: the Chinese restaurant owner is aware of the other ethnic cuisines in town; car manufacturers try to hit on a unique style and a quality and price level. Whereas conventional market theory says that sellers will compete with each other and drive prices (and profits) down to the lowest level commensurate with costs, White proposes that sellers differentiate rather than homogenize their products. Instead of converging on a single price, they try to find a unique combination of price, quality, and sales volume at which they can operate; hence prices will range across the spectrum, from Rolls-Royces to cheap subcompacts.

The producers in every area constitute a network, because they have to monitor each other in order to see which niches are available. It is not surprising, says White, that organizations which are competitors nevertheless typically form trade associations or even social clubs, ranging from big corporate groups down to local merchants' associations (the Rotary Club luncheons, the Chamber of Commerce, and so on). Competitors must see each other in order to structure their stance on the market. Information gathering is thus an important part of the market, but it is structured quite differently than in classic economics. In the latter, sellers try to find consumers, and vice versa. In White's model, like Schumpeter's, producers do not directly monitor demand (at least not very well); especially when they put out an innovative product (which is the essence of growth in the capitalist economy), they cannot monitor demand because there is no demand yet for the product which doesn't exist. Personal computers, like a long list of innovations before them, had to come into existence first, before a consumer demand could be drummed up. "Demand" is thus a mysterious part of the market, which can be established only by processes of consumer emulation, as long as business itself is booming, freeing up credit and resources so that people can afford to buy "luxuries" which they never had before, and even turn them into "necessities" after they become sufficiently widespread.[7]

White's markets thus are organized from the producers' side. Producers mainly monitor each other. Even their own sales are taken as indicators of how well they are doing in dividing up the market. In White's (1981: 543) words: "Markets are tangible cliques of producers observing each other. Pressure from the buyer side creates a mirror in which producers see themselves, not consumers." White does not draw out the dynamic implications of his model, but they seem to be as follows (Collins, 1986: 117–42). By their mutual emulation (and careful differentiation), producers' cliques can generate business booms through waves of confidence spreading throughout the system. Conversely, the mutually monitoring network of producers can generate a spreading mood of caution or even panic, which brings about recession or depression. The actual situation is complicated by other factors. Financial markets (which are structured by another level of "producers," banks and other generators of credit) operate as another monitoring network, which attempts to direct investments throughout the economy for maximal return; presumably, they too attempt to steer producers into noncompetitive niches, instead of driving down profits for everyone by head-to-head competition in the same arena.

Yet another factor that must be added is the market itself. Even though White's firms tend toward noncompetitive niches, this is not always achieved. Sometimes they end up battling over the same markets (each of the big auto manufacturers has a line of low-priced cars, for example), with the result that sometimes competition

---

[7]Television sets in the United States went from being luxuries in the early 1950s to necessities in the 1970s, just as automobiles shifted from being toys of the rich in the early 1900s to mass products by the 1940s and 1950s. Video cassette recorders (VCRs) are a current product now making the move from luxury to necessity.

does drive down prices and also sometimes businesses are forced into bankruptcy or bought out. White's model, like the other sociological models, must also make room for market processes and show under what conditions they will have varying strengths vis-à-vis nonmarket processes. In other words, White's model is not a complete economic theory, but an ideal type. It shows one set of forces that operate, mutually monitoring producers on the supply side. But there is also a market or demand side, which also varies in strength.

We might ask, then, under what conditions is the market most controlled by producers' cliques, and when is it least controlled or most open?[8] Several possible hypotheses here are: (1) the greater the number of producers, the less ability they have to monitor each other successfully, and the more likely they are unable to find noncompetitive niches. Here market competition will be dominant. Conversely, small numbers of producers can more easily form cliques. (2) Monitoring is easier when some producers are highly visible (for example, an industry leader attracts most of the attention, like IBM in the computer market for many years). (3) Business crises may be due to the failure of producers to correctly monitor the market. This is most likely to happen when a type of product is very new, and the existence of demand can only be judged by the rate of growth of the new organizations that have already entered the field. Here, monitoring can lead to overoptimistic results, because the limits of demand are not visible just from the upswing portion of the sales curve. It is possible, also, that White's theory is most applicable to late capitalism, when there are high levels of intercommunication, which make it easiest for monitoring to take place.

One other notable point, though, is that White's theory seems to be implicitly connected with distinctively sociological factors even on the market demand side. Producers try to find a distinctive market niche by turning out a product that is different from others in quality and price. Although White does not say so, this implies that status stratification is crucial in differentiating economic markets. There are markets not only for high-price–high-quality goods and for low-price–low-quality goods, but also for goods which are cheap imitations of higher quality goods (for instance, there are luxury cars, economy cars, but also cheap imitations of luxury cars). The latter may not seem like a very good deal in price-to-quality ratio, but they make a viable market niche if there is much status emulation, so that the culture of the higher classes is accessible to mass demand in a less costly version. The latter process looks very much like the process of "inflation" in a "cultural market" which we have already seen one example of in the theory of educational credential inflation (Chapter 5). Implicitly in White's theory, as in Schumpeter's, the economy is led by its luxury sector, which generates demand by the very existence of new products. Capitalism thus seems to depend on status competition carried out in the realm of commodity symbolism.

These theoretical developments are relatively new. The sociological theory of business is rapidly making progress and has great potential for explaining economic phenomena. A sociologically adequate theory of the economy will have to include several levels: the network organization of producers (White's mutually monitoring

---

[8] I am indebted for discussions of these points to George Eicholtzli and other members of the Institute for Advanced Study, Vienna, Austria.

niche-seekers); the network of financial organizations, which accumulates money from economic transactions and turns it into a kind of "political" power within the economy by its control of investment and credit; the status structure of the community (especially the distribution of cultural capital), which affects how consumers will respond to price-and-quality differentiation of products; and finally the degree of head-to-head market competition in all this. The overall model will be quite complicated if it is to match the dynamics of the real world.[9]

NETWORK THEORIES OF POWER

We have dealt with power in many parts of this book. Macro theories (especially in Chapters 3 through 5) include the Marxian theory of the state and struggles over its control, as well as Turner's general theory of the conditions for macro distributions of power and geopolitical theory. The order-giving and order-taking model in Chapter 6 shows the consequences of power for class cultures. Blau and his followers (Chapter 10) proposed an exchange theory of power; the interaction ritual chain theory (Chapter 11) treats power as membership in enforcement coalitions.

Network analysis also deals with power. This is not surprising, since power is not exercised by isolated individuals, but only through their relationships with a plurality of others. Hence network theory should be able to lay bare the structural skeleton underlying the exercise of power. It is important to recognize here that there are two different aspects of power. Some theories analyze power as *exchange or resource dependency*. Other theories focus on *coercion* through *enforcement coalitions*. The latter approach has been less developed into explicit models than the former. The difference between the two kinds of power theories is roughly similar to the old debate between functional and conflict theories of stratification. The following sections will sketch out both types of theories. We will also see that in many concrete situations one kind of power can flow into the other.

STRUCTURAL DEPENDENCE AND POWER BROKERS

Cook (1982; Cook et al., 1983) has tried to extend exchange theory to account for the kinds of power linkages that occur in different types of networks. The independent variable-causal factor here is the way resources can be traded in the network. There are two polar types. In a "negatively connected" network, relationships are mutually exclusive. Person A will exchange either with person B or person C, but not both. This is the case, for example, in sexual marketplaces like dating or marriage (and perhaps also in friendships): one pairing excludes making alternative pairings. This kind of "negatively connected network" may also emerge where people are making economic bargains and choosing which of alternative deals they will make (whom they will buy a house from or where they will go to work). The other

---

[9] White's model has proven difficult to work with. Not only is it conceptually a large breakthrough from current modes of thinking; but it is also formulated in a mathematics which is more esoteric than sociologists and economists are used to dealing with. Further breakthroughs toward a more tractable mathematics are called for if the White model is to become widespread.

FIGURE 12-2

THE POWER BROKER

type of network, "positively connected," is where person A deals with both person B and person C: for example, A gets some kind of resource (information or goods) from B, which A can then use to trade with C. In these positively connected networks, some positions might emerge as "broker roles," transmitting resources between more distant locations.

It is generally assumed that the more centralized position will be the most powerful one. The broker can withhold or manipulate information that the more peripheral persons cannot get for themselves; the broker is also less dependent on other positions (Freeman, 1979). The person with the key resource of being the only one able to link together subsystems becomes the focus of a centralized power system. However, Cook et al. (1983) show that this occurs only in positively connected networks. In negatively connected networks, the crucial resource is whether one's alternatives are relatively better than those of the persons one deals with. In Figure 12-2, person A is centrally located; but persons B_1 and B_2 are more powerful. Why is this? It is because A bargains on an equal basis with either of the B's; but B_1 can choose between bargaining equally with A or getting an unequal bargain over C_1, who has nowhere else to go. (The same applies to B_2 and C_2.) Remember, this network is negatively connected, so that every actor must choose *one* partner to interact with. Thus A gets excluded despite being in a central position. The network tends to break up into "decentralized" subsystems, autonomously interacting subgroups.

We have here something more like a "feudal" system than a bureaucratic one. The precise application of this model to real-life structures, though, depends on whether resources in that real-world situation happen to be structured in negatively connected or positively connected networks. Also, in many or most real-life situations, people may exchange both kinds of resources.

ENFORCEMENT COALITIONS

In exchange models, actors are motivated to maximize their profits, and power goes to the individual who has the most to offer relative to everyone else. In a coercive model, however, the primary motivation is not profits but safety. We have seen the rudiments of this model in Chapter 11. A coercively organized group uses the threat of punishment against any dissident member; in a military dictatorship, this means that the loyal members of the army will use violence against anyone who disobeys. The soldiers enforce discipline on each other. The commanders do not command because they personally have superior force, but because they are strategically situated in the network to get others to carry out their orders. As the game theorist Schelling (1963) puts it, the members are involved in a "tacit coordination game." If they all rebelled together, they would be safe; but anyone who is the first to rebel individually puts himself in jeopardy of having the rest remain loyal and hence of being coerced by the others.

Coercion is thus primarily a matter of communications. All individuals tacitly monitor where the dominant enforcement coalition is; their primary motivation is to play it safe, to be a member of that coalition. If a dominant coalition begins to shift, then at some point the safe thing is to abandon it and get into the new winning coalition. For this reason coercive structures tend to be stable and then to change very suddenly in what Schelling calls a "tipping phenomenon," like a board suddenly tipping across a fulcrum. This is evident, not only in revolutions which occur in authoritarian states, but also on battlefields. Combat may be analyzed as a kind of communications game, in which most of the violence is merely psychological, until one side breaks up into a disorganized retreat (Keegan, 1976; Collins, 1988). After the organizational structure of an army breaks down—when it no longer can act as an enforcement coalition to discipline its own men—the army becomes vulnerable to the enemy, and hence it then receives most of its casualties.

Formal models of coercive structures have not been as yet much developed. Theorists like Schelling (1963) and Collins (1975) concentrate on the instance where the enforcement coalition is already in place in a highly centralized form. This is something like Figure 12-3, in which there is a single high commander (A), who issues orders through a chain of command (C), down to the level of armed enforcers (E). There may also be a subordinate population (P), who are unarmed and hence are not part of the enforcement coalition at all. The organization or lack of organization among the unarmed populace (P) is relatively unimportant for the power structure, for even if they are organized to rebel, they would be defeated by the enforcers (E). Hence only when the army itself becomes split or breaks down do civilian rebels make a difference (as is clear in virtually all revolutions: Russell, 1974; Skocpol 1979).

The power of the high commander (A) depends on keeping the loyalty of the enforcers. There are a number of ways in which this can be done: giving out rewards (the spoils of conquest or exploitation, for example), as well as emotional attachment (legitimacy) to the chief. But these are secondary as long as the enforcement coalition itself is capable of coercing any individual member. The "pure form" of coercive power has a "structural skeleton" in which the commander keeps everyone believing that he or she will be obeyed by the great majority of enforcers, hence making it too dangerous for anyone to risk being a dissident. There appear to be several possible mechanisms involved in this:

1. DIVIDE AND RULE   The strategy of keeping any rival commanders from becoming too powerful is divide and rule. There can be separate chains of command down to the enforcers (that is, multiple C's); extra chains (such as secret police: Spy in Figure 12-3) can actually be added to spy on the intermediate commanders; politically, the chief can actually stir up rivalries among commanders, or recruit from mutually hostile ethnic groups, and so on.

2. DIRECT SURVEILLANCE OR VERTICAL CONTROLS   The divide-and-rule tactics are not always found in coercive organizations (although they seem characteristic of the most violent or "terroristic" dictatorships). Many armies do not use them;

and they are absent in many governments, even though every state has a coercive coalition at its core. An alternative mechanism by which discipline is maintained in an enforcement coalition is by vertical controls (dotted lines in Figure 12-3). The chief may be able to maintain direct surveillance over the first-line enforcers, if the group is small enough, or by periodic visits (which is what traditional kings and military commanders did). In very large coercive organizations, much direct surveillance from the top may be impossible, but a psychological version of it can be maintained by keeping the first-line enforcers aware that their fate is in the hands of the central chief rather than their immediate commanders, so that they will not follow their local captain into disobedience. This can be done by frequent rules and directives issued from the center, as well as promotions, demotions, and other rewards and punishments.

3. RITUAL FOCUS OF ATTENTION   Since the maintenance of power in a coercive network is primarily a communications game, a crucial device is to focus the enforcers' attention on the person who is in command. Massive ceremonies, special uniforms, and the impressive pomp which surround traditional rulers and modern dictators are a use of this method. We could analyze this by using the Durkheimian theory of rituals (Chapter 6): the common focus of attention and the building up of common emotions make the leader a "sacred object" who is defended as representing membership in the group. But when the leader is highly coercive, ruling through fear, we must add a special twist on the theory. The dictator is not necessarily popular, and may actually be widely hated. But the very fact that his symbols are the omnipresent focus of attention means that everyone is constantly aware of

FIGURE 12-3

POWER IN COERCIVE COALITIONS

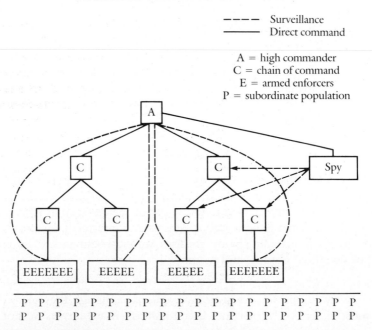

- - - -   Surveillance
————   Direct command

A = high commander
C = chain of command
E = armed enforcers
P = subordinate population

the center of the enforcement coalition. (The cult of the leader evidenced in omnipresent pictures of Stalin, Mao Zedong, Hitler, Duvalier, or other leaders with dictatorial powers becomes understandable from this theory.) In order for rebellion to take place, someone else would have to rival this kind of ritual focus; as long as the dictator maintains a monopoly over ritual attention, the organization of counter-coalitions is severely hampered.

4. COMMUNICATION AND TRANSPORTATION TECHNOLOGY AND ECOLOGY
Finally, the physical layout of material resources for communication and transportation affects the structure of enforcement coalitions. If all the physical channels go vertically from the bottom-level enforcers to the center and back, central power is supported. Horizontal connections make it possible to monitor whether rival coalitions can be created. For this reason, as both Marx and Engels (1848/1985) and Schelling (1963) point out, the political power of the masses is greatly increased when they are brought together in large factories or urban areas. By the same token, authoritarian rulers in rural societies could rely on the difficulties on horizontal connections to maintain their power against rivals; in societies with modern technologies, dictatorial power depends more heavily on using the other mechanisms listed above. The amount of horizontal versus vertical organization can also be due to the actual lay of the land. The ecology of ancient Egypt, for instance, made it easy for a central government to control all local areas via the river, while local commanders could never acquire enough allies to become serious rivals (Mann, 1986: 110). Some areas are thus ecologically "naturally centralized," whereas other territories ecologically favor horizontal splits.

A full theory of coercive coalitions should tell us the conditions under which different degrees of coercive structures will exist and which individuals will have what degrees of power within them. Theory on this degree of explanatory detail is still very rudimentary. I would suggest, though, that there are at least four main kinds of structures to be explained:

1. *Strong centralized power* takes the form in which the center of the enforcement coalition is able to mobilize a large majority of enforcers to put down any dissident.

2. *Nominal power* exists when the ruler actually lacks the channels to discipline rebelling members; but because there are no horizontal channels by which strong rival coalitions can form, the ruler stays in place "by default." Here the communications game might be called "pluralistic ignorance": if the members knew that the ruler lacked support they would be able to rebel, but in the absence of this information they maintain the existing structure.

3. *Fragmented power* exists where no one has been able to create a centralized enforcement coalition, or where some previous coalition has fallen apart among rival centers.

4. *Revolutionary challenge* exists where a strong rival coalition forms against a weakening central authority, threatening a showdown which would "tip" the power structure to the other side.

Our theory should be able to tell us the conditions under which each of these structures exists and when one type transforms into another. (There are of course intermediate types in between these four which would be dealt with in a fuller theory.) I suggest that the ingredients of such a theory exist, but the actual models have not been worked out. Notice, though, that the theory cannot merely explain a movement from (1) *strong centralized power* to (4) *revolutionary challenge* and then back to (1). Revolutionary challenges do not always win, and that too needs to be explained. Moreover, another important path may go from (1) to (3) *fragmented power:* a strong state may fall apart into many local states, or into an ongoing power rivalry in which no side gets very centralized control.

DEMOCRACY AS A DECENTRALIZED POWER NETWORK   This latter alternative is important, because it does not merely describe feudalism or tribalism: a version of it is what constitutes democracy. For a democracy is the structure in which there are permanent rival groups, none of which is strong enough to coerce the others. Under these circumstances, conflict may be routinized into a peaceful competition for command of the state; precisely because no one believes that a single dominant coalition is possible, the various local coalitions try to form short-term alliances in pursuit of limited goals. It is also possible, however, for these horizontal coalitions to escalate into hostile conflict or even civil war. This is a danger of democracy, since it is structurally a kind of contained or limited conflict situation among rivals of approximately equal strength. Here I would suggest that the theory of enforcement coalitions has an important application if we are interested in promoting the democratic form of government. It is a difficult form to maintain, because it depends on a balanced and mutual limitation of conflicting coalitions; a successful theory should help us understand the conditions that allow this structure to exist. I would add incidentally, that here is a potential payoff for the conflict or enforcement coalition approach to power, which is not shared by the exchange-resource dependence theory, since the latter does not give us a theory of democracy.

Finally, we should consider the path which goes from (3) *fragmented power* to (1) *strong centralized power*. In some historical circumstances, this was the rise of the centralized state out of feudalism. But is also represents the disappearance of democracy and its replacement by a centralized dictatorship. Most of the rudimentary theorizing which has been done about enforcement coalitions has concentrated on what goes on inside (1) as it maintains itself over time, and tangentially on the transition from (4) to (1). We need a fuller consideration of the other possible paths.[10]

A final word on the usefulness of enforcement coalition models. The most obvious examples of these come from the realm of violent threats: the military-based state and its revolutions. But there are important applications to civilian structures as well. For example, ordinary politics has an aspect of such coalitions. A political

---

[10] Most research on coalitions has taken the situation to be something like (3) *fragmented power* and has concentrated on the ways in which actors try to keep a single dominant coalition, that is, (1) *strong centralized power,* from emerging. Caplow (1968), summarizing research on triads and larger structures which can be composed out of interlinked triads, shows that individual actors choose to ally with coalitions in the triad, depending on their own political resources versus those of their potential coalition partners and enemies. For example, they will usually play a "balance of power" strategy, in which the weaker two keep the strongest player from becoming so strong that they are swallowed up one at a time. (This would happen, say, if player 1, the strongest, allied with player 3, the weakest, to conquer player 2, the next strongest; the end result would be that player 3 would be alone and defenseless against player 1.)

"boss" within a formally democratic community is someone who has the reputation for being able to give or withhold favors; hence subordinate politicians are "coerced" into giving her or him their legislative votes or endorsements (that is, they say they "have their arms twisted") for fear of being excluded from the winning coalition (Banfield, 1961). The boss may be unpopular, but rival coalitions to unseat her or him may have been difficult to form because of the same structural reasons that apply to violent dictatorships.

Similar phenomena, I would suggest, take place in the realm of business organizations. A version of such coercive threat coalitions are those which carry out corporate takeover bids, or which struggle for control within boards of directors. But also on a less dramatic and more routine level, leading banks and financiers constitute coalitions which dominate business activity through controlling credit. I suggest that this has the "coercive" structure of enforcement coalition theory, rather than the purely "profit maximizing" structure of exchange theory, because open competition is circumvented once strong coalitions are formed. As in enforcement coalitions generally, "the strong get stronger" and the weak are excluded, because no one wants to risk being left out of the winning financial coalition.[11] Business and financial networks thus are centered on communications games which are structurally similar to those involved in the maneuvering over violent enforcement coalitions, even though these are carried out with different resources.

As a third application, I would suggest that internal politics within organizations often has an aspect of enforcement coalitions. The formal structure of "line authority" may be based on direct exchange of rewards, skills, and productive effort; but the informal networks operating behind the scenes, which have much influence over the allocation of personal praise and blame and hence over promotions and careers, can likely be analyzed by using enforcement coalition theory, the same as in politics generally.

In all these applications, it should be stressed that enforcement coalition theory does not merely expect a dictatorial or boss structure. That occurs under certain conditions; but it is also possible for democratic, fragmented, or other decentralized coalition structures to exist. And there can be movement from one structure to another: revolutionary challenges can occur in the realm of financial networks, internal organizational politics, or legislatures, and shifts can occur from centralized to decentralized forms, nominal power, and so forth, or in the opposite direction. To spell out the conditions for these various structural outcomes and dynamics would give us a strong theory of many phenomena not only in government but in business and organizational life generally.

COMBINATIONS OF ENFORCEMENT COALITIONS AND EXCHANGE THEORIES OF POWER

There is nothing in the real world which prevents coercive and exchange processes from both operating. They may even intermesh in the same concrete exercise of power. For example, coercion may be analyzed as a form of exchange: instead of

---

[11] A related example: IBM has been able to set industry standards in the personal computer industry, although it is not the most innovative or best system, because its sheer size makes it the focus of attention for competitors worried about surviving in the dominant technological coalition.

each side offering a positive good to the other, one side threatens to make the other take a loss, if a good is not given up (Willer, 1984; Willer and Anderson, 1981). Coercion is thus the exchange of a (threatened) negative for a positive. Willer (1984) shows how to calculate the rate of confiscation or exploitation that will occur, depending on the balance of positive and negative exchange resources and the network structure of trading partners. In Willer's model, the phase of bargaining—that is, the communication of threats and offers—is more crucial than the exchange itself, since coercion works best when it remains a threat. "Your money or your life" will only generate income for the coercer if the threat successfully extracts money; the same thing holds for slave labor, since a dead slave is of no value.

This type of integration of coercive and exchange theories, though, remains largely on the exchange side. That is, it takes as already given that one party has a certain amount of coercive power and calculates the consequences of this for the exchanges that will follow. It still remains to be shown how that coercive power was generated in the first place, and here enforcement coalition theory is necessary.[12]

Enforcement coalition and exchange power mesh more directly in instances where coercion is used to extract goods, which in turn are used as rewards to bind members into the enforcement coalition. For example, in the ancient Middle East before the rise of the state, temporary war-bands were organized relatively democratically; but when these bands began to take wealth by conquest, the most successful military leader could use these spoils as rewards to attract more followers and bind them into his coalition (Mann, 1986: 99–100). After this point, the coercive aspect of the coalition became inescapable. Conversely, the military commanders in the Roman Empire became able to challenge central authority when they acquired the local resources to pay their own men; while army rebellions broke out at the points when the commander was unable to pay his men (Mann, 1986: 288).[13] Any strong enforcement coalition depends on its "structural skeleton" consisting of the threat of group discipline to coerce dissidents; but this discipline is reinforced to the extent that the common hierarchy is able to add material-resource dependency, an exchange structure reinforcing the coercive structure.

A full theory of power, in all its applications (whether to military states, civilian politics, financial coalitions, or informal organizational politics) should thus combine exchange and coercive coalitions in the appropriate ways.

---

[12] Similarly, Willer (1985) demonstrates that the kinds of exchanges which take place depend on the kind of property relationships which exist. The classical Homans-Blau exchange theory works only if there is private property, consisting of enforceable rights of exclusion, alienation, appropriation, and reciprocity. All of these are rights enforced by a state or other coercive community. Communal property systems, on the other hand, cannot have exchanges because these enforceable rights are lacking.

[13] There is also an interplay between ecological resources and enforcement coalitions. The early state or tribe which conquered (or just happened to be located in) a territory of fertile agriculture, iron or other mineral deposits, or major trade routes, thereby had a resource which they could use as exchange with other areas (Mann, 1986: 116, 124–25). Coercive power conquered or defended the territorial resources in the first place, but once it was appropriated, it could be used to make other groups dependent upon the possessing group. In addition to such "unequal exchange," these states could use their resources to build military alliances, which in turn increased their power to coercively control yet more territories.

COMMUNITY AND NATIONAL POWER STRUCTURES

For the most part, the network approach to power has not yet been developed on this level of theoretical abstraction. It has been applied more concretely, however; I will conclude by giving one of its successful applications. The network approach provides us with the most realistic and sophisticated view yet available of modern mass politics. Laumann and his colleagues have shown that the old debate between reputational and decision-making methods of studying community power was one-sided. Reputational methods found that certain people had reputations for generalized power, whereas decision-making models found that different groups of individuals were involved in different types of political decisions. However, Laumann and Pappi (1976) have shown that in local communities, the people who have the reputation for power are, in fact, powerful when they are linked together into an informal network. The question then becomes a structural one: when do communities have this kind of network structure? Studying the national level of politics (the U.S. government), Laumann and Knoke (1987; also Knoke and Laumann 1982; Laumann, Knoke, and Kim, 1985) find that there are numerous actors (most are organizations) and different structural networks among them in different policy domains. For instance, federal politics about energy issues has a "ring-structure" in which organizations have contacts with those "adjacent" to them on issues of interest, but no organization is concerned with all issues or marshalls coalitions all across the board. (In other words, the center of the "ring" is empty.) In other policy domains, such as medical and health issues, there are different forms of networks.

So far this analysis is descriptive rather than explanatory. But it shows us the materials that a sophisticated theory of politics must explain: organizations are the principal political actors, with complex network relationships among them, which result in various kinds of political events. Knoke and Laumann (1982) propose a set of theoretical hypotheses about some of the structural determinants:

1. The more *centralized* the communication structure in a policy domain, the fewer the number of issues that are generated in a given time, the smaller the number of policy options, the shorter the time for the issue to reach the governmental agenda, and the more likely the authorities to accept the central group's position. Conversely, *fragmented* or merely *locally connected* domain networks generate more issues with more options, take much longer in getting to the decision point, and force no clear outcome.

2. *Polarized* (highly confidential) structures emerge around specific issues when the domain is uncentralized and issues are consummatory (that is emotional and symbolic) rather than instrumental (that is, technical).[14] Such events take a long time to reach any governmental action, and the option finally chosen is likely to be that of the most powerful collective actor (rather than the consensus generated by a network center).

---

[14] How emotional the issues are, however, is not a structural feature of the network itself, but something added onto it. It can perhaps be analyzed in terms of a micro-macro model of emotional flows and cultural capital in interaction ritual chains.

3. *Monocephalic organizations* (those with a powerful decision-making head) are quickest to recognize problems and formulate policies, while *confederated organizations* (coalitions whose constituents maintain autonomy) are slowest to act. Domains with a *centralized communication structure* are likely to have the center filled by either a monocephalic organization or by a governmental agency, while confederated actors are on the periphery; and such monocephalic organizations are especially likely to get their policy accepted by the government. *Polarized issues* tend to make the participating organizations move their internal structures toward being monocephalic.

4. The more *equal the distribution of resources* among actors in a domain, the larger the number of actors involved in any issue, the more likely there are to be opposing positions, the less rapidly the issue will reach the government agenda, and the longer it takes for a definitive decision to be made. In other words, equal resources generate more conflict, and a messier and longer governmental decision process.

Since networks are found among units of any size, these hypotheses apply both to the networks which make up individual organizations, as well as to networks among organizations. If desirable, we could go on to analyze still larger units—networks of networks of networks. The Knoke and Laumann model includes both the level of organizations (which can be monocephalic or confederated—the latter itself containing yet further levels of organizations within it), and the level of issue domains (which can be centralized or decentralized, conflictual or nonconflictual, involving instrumental and technical or consummatory and emotional issues).

At the level of individual organizations, we may assume that whether organizations will be monocephalic or confederated depends on several factors. (1) Control resources, especially material property, are the basis of any permanent organizational structure (Chapter 13). Here we see that highly concentrated resources result in monocephalic organizations, while more equally dispersed resources result in confederated structures. In addition, (2) a high degree of conflict in the issue domain moves organizations away from the confederated and toward the monocephalic end. This is a version on the organizational level of Jonathan Turner's (1984) theory of power distribution (Chapter 5), if we equate conflict with external threat.

Moving up to the interorganizational level of the domain itself, we see that a similar set of factors shapes this larger network. A high concentration of resources favors the centralization of the domain around a dominant organization, while more equal resources decentralizes the domain. Knoke and Laumann draw out some consequences for subsequent political events: there will be less conflict where the domain is centralized, there will be focus on fewer issues, issues will be taken up faster, and favorable governmental action is more likely to follow. Conversely, more equal resources results in higher conflict, a messier and more inchoate process, with more issues raised but more slowly and less likelihood of action being taken on them.[15]

[15] In one respect the "superorganization" level of issue domains is different from the propositions regarding centralization ("monocephalic" organizations) at the next level down. For individual organizations, external conflict produces a trend toward centralization. But at the domain-superorganization level, conflict is no longer an "external threat," but is internal conflict within the superorganization itself. Turner (Chapter 5) proposes that internal conflict also increases central power, though I believe the process is more complex than that, and depends on who wins these conflicts—the centralizers or the decentralizers.

This network theory of power can also be made dynamic. Since the Laumann and Knoke theory combines events and structures in the same model, it promises a truly comprehensive theory in which we may be able to predict both sides of a "power structure"—the events in which power is exercised (or more often, merely fought over) and the shape of the structure itself. I would point out that, if we model the theory as in Figure 12-4, there are some interesting feedback loops. Highly emotional issues, and a decentralized domain structure, result in more conflict; but conflict tends to make organizations monocephalic. In other words, over time the processes that build up conflict tend to undermine themselves.

A similar loop occurs on the other side of the model: a centralized domain, one dealing with purely technical (rather than emotional) issues, will have less conflict. A result is that there is less pressure to maintain monocephalic organizations. Furthermore, highly technical issues probably result in the proliferation of technical specialists (as we shall see in organizational theory, Chapter 13), which will also tend to decentralize the domain. We have two loops, then: one in which conditions for conflict undermine themselves and move toward more centralized and less conflictual situations; and another in which the low-key issues of a centralized power structure also undermines itself in the direction of more decentralized structures.

FIGURE 12-4

DYNAMICS OF POWER IN A DEMOCRACY

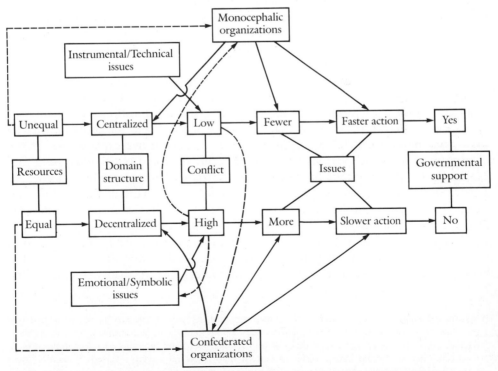

Based on David Knoke and Edward O. Laumann, "The Social Organization of National Policy Domains: An exploration of Some Structural Hypotheses," in *Social Structure and Network Analysis*, eds. Peter V. Marsden and Nan Lin (Beverly Hills: Sage, 1982).

The overall result would be an oscillation between turbulent and somnolent periods in politics.[16]

Further steps in theorizing along this line can benefit from the fact that network and organization theory generally refer to aspects of the same phenomena. In the following chapter, we encounter Perrow's (1984) formula for a "system accident," the combination of a complex interdependence between parts, and a tightly coupled system. In politics, a tightly coupled system would be one in which there is an extremely centralized, hierarchic power structure. A complex system would be one in which issues are not isolated from each other, but overflow in complicated and unexpected ways.

Now, it happens that Laumann and Knoke, describing the structure of some of the issues of U.S. national politics in the 1970s, found that these interorganization systems were by and large "loosely coupled." Although some domains were more centralized than others, there was nothing approaching the extreme of "tight coupling" in Perrow's model. But this is an empirical input: we can easily imagine cases of a centralized or dictatorial power structure that does fit this profile. On the other dimension, Knoke and Laumann tended to find issues that were relatively isolated from each other, although again there were variations here. The United States in the late 1970s (at least for energy and health), then, fit the pattern where no major blowup was being induced. We can imagine a case, though, in which there is a dictatorial (tightly coupled) structure, dealing with complex issues that are interlinked (for example, economic strains, military defeats, and governmental inefficiency). Perrow's model predicts that random interactions within this system, once started in a negative direction, could quickly escalate into a system accident. For some historical cases, this would spell revolution. I would suggest that even short of such dramatic outcomes, periods of political crisis and upheaval can be explained in this way.

I hope that by this point a larger picture is starting to emerge. Sociological theory has started out from a diverse number of viewpoints, but the results of these often converge. Theories of exchange, networks, and organizations are all ways of mediating between the micro and macro levels of analysis; and furthermore, they all have gone beyond general conceptual schemes to substantive explanations of the conditions under which various phenomena occur. It should not be surprising that as they have progressed they have begun to overlap and merge with one another. In a more general way, I suggest that this will hold true of many of the theories and substantive areas we have treated throughout this book. In the chapters of Part III of this book, there are many potential contributions toward theories of long-term social change, social systems in general, stratification, power, and conflict (treated in Chapters 1 through 5 from Part I of this book). At the same time, I hope it has been demonstrated that there are links to the topics of micro theory treated in Part

---

[16] Strictly speaking, just what would result from this model depends on the *rate* at which the different processes take place. If the shift from confederated to monocephalic organizations under conditions of conflict takes place much faster than the shift on the other side from centralized to decentralized organizations, then we would have a different pattern than if the rates were reversed. "Quantity" does transform into "quality"; there are many different outcomes possible, depending on how fast various processes happen. See Appendix B on computer simulation for further details.

II (Chapters 6 through 10). The final chapter, on organizations, illustrates a combination of many of our themes.

SUMMARY

1. Network analysis focuses on social relationships, which are more fundamental than individual attributes. *Cohesive* networks produce homogenous attitudes. Individuals in *structurally equivalent* positions have similar attitudes and motivations.

2. Structural exchange theories focus on who exchanges with whom in repeated patterns. Mauss analyzed ceremonial gift exchanges in tribal societies as systems of personal honor and emotional energy, regarded as magical force or "mana." Gift exchanges are rituals which generate moral solidarity, and produce alliance networks within which utilitarian exchanges can take place. Lévi-Strauss analyzed tribal kinship systems as alliances held together by marriage exchanges of women. In modern societies, gift exchanges and domestic entertainment constitute friendship networks and status stratification.

3. Blau's theory of intergroup integration states that members of relatively smaller social categories have a greater chance of associating with members of larger social categories than vice versa. Intergroup association is promoted to the extent that individual attributes are cross-cutting.

4. Social mobility can be described, and explained theoretically, on three different levels. (1) *Individual mobility* or "status attainment" is movement through a network of positions. It is determined by the extent of vacancies and by "weak ties" which give individuals connections to persons with higher resources. The number of such upward ties is greater when the structure of positions is not pyramid-shaped but has equal numbers at adjacent strata and when there are many strata rather than few.

5. (2) Determinants of the *structure of positions* include the amount of structural change in the society; explanatory theory is not well developed on this level. (3) *Mobility rates* are the result of complex determinants, including all of the factors in (1) and (2).

6. Economic theory based on markets has been weak in explaining large-scale dynamics as well as inequalities of distribution. The "transaction costs" approach offers a revision: uncertainty in repeated bargaining leads to replacement of markets by permanent organizational hierarchies. Network analysis, though, shows there are kinds of repeated transactions which are neither markets nor hierarchies.

7. Sociological theory deriving from Weber proposes that the dynamic of capitalism is a struggle over closure or monopolization of market opportunities. Network analysis shows that profits are highest for firms which coopt trade partners into permanent networks. Harrison White theorizes that markets are made up of mutually monitoring cliques of producers, in which each attempts to find a noncompetitive market niche by creating a unique mix of product quality and product price. Market dynamics are driven by production rather than demand. An implication is that status stratification is important in generating demand for new products.

8. Network exchange theory analyzes power as *structural dependence* on a central network position which acts as broker for scarce resources. This occurs only in "positively connected" networks (those in which individuals can trade with several partners). In "negatively connected networks" (where relationships are mutually exclusive), the system may break apart into decentralized subsystems.

9. Enforcement coalition theory concerns power based on coercion. Coercive threat depends on members of a group enforcing discipline on each other; individuals are motivated to avoid being isolated from the majority coalition. The power of a coercive commander depends on a self-fulfilling reputation. Structurally, this can be done by (1) dividing possible rivals from forming coalitions; (2) direct surveillance; (3) monopolizing a ritual force of attention; (4) control of communications and transportation.

10. Coercive structures include *centralized power* (enforced as described above); *nominal power* in which the ruler lacks resources to discipline subordinates, but they lack communication channels to form rival coalitions; and *fragmented power* in which control resources are decentralized among separate coalitions. The theory of change among these types is not well developed. *Revolutionary challenge* occurs when there is a choice between rival centers of a single centralized power coalition. *Democracy* is a permanent structure of decentralized power resources.

11. Both coercive enforcement coalitions and structural dependency may be involved in the same empirical power structure. Material resources reinforce a coercive hierarchy, and coercion can be used to extract material resources.

12. Power within a democratic government is structured by networks among organizations. Centralized communication structures generate fewer issues and policy options, but are more likely to reach authoritative decisions. High conflict occurs when emotional and symbolic issues arise in decentralized domains; the result is slow government action, influenced by the most powerful organizations more than by the central network consensus. A cyclical process may take place between centralized and nonconflictual, to decentralized and conflictual periods, and the reverse.

Chapter 13

ORGANIZATIONS

ORGANIZATIONS IN SOCIOLOGICAL THEORY
    Approaches in Organization Theory

CONTROL THEORY
    Coercion, Rewards, Internalized Control
    Historical Trends in Control
    Administrative Devices
    Who Uses Which Controls When?
    Control Resources as Core of an Organization's Existence
    The Importance of Property
    Tasks and Control Forms

MOTIVATION, CLASS CONFLICT, ORGANIZATIONAL CULTURE,
    AND DECISION MAKING

ORGANIZATIONAL STRUCTURE
    Is There a Trend toward "Modern" Organizational Structure?
    Woodward and Thompson's Structural Types
    Size and Organizational Structure
    Organizational Hierarchy as Macro Coordination of Micro Activities
    Structure and Control
    Derivation of Woodward's Organizational Types from Control Theory
    Organizational Structures as Ideal Types

ORGANIZATIONS AND ENVIRONMENTS
    Resource Dependency
    The Population Ecology of Organizations
    Organizational Boundaries
    Interorganizational Relations as a Superorganization
    Capitalism and Socialism as Superorganizations

SUMMARY

ORGANIZATIONS IN SOCIOLOGICAL THEORY

The topic of organizations is seldom treated as a part of sociological theory. I believe this is a serious omission, for several reasons.

(1) Many of the major theorists have worked on this terrain. Weber, Michels, and Mannheim among the classics, and in our own times, Blau, Gouldner, Etzioni, Goffman, Herbert Simon, and others have made important contributions to organizational studies. Though in the last decade or two organizational studies have come to be regarded as just another research specialty, we can argue that it is not by happenstance that so many theorists have been interested in them. Organizational analysis has made more progress in cumulating explanatory knowledge than perhaps any other part of sociology; and organizational theory is both continuous with the rest of sociological theory, and a solution to many of sociology's substantive problems.

(2) Organizations are a crucial part of the micro-macro connection. Not only are they in the middle of the range in size and longevity, but as we shall see, organizational "structure" means some people deliberately specialize in the macro ordering of micro processes. Theorists who lack a theory of organizations have a serious problem in this regard. Durkheim and Marx, in their day, had both micro and macro theories (for Durkheim, the ritual density model on the micro level, the division of labor model at the macro; for Marx, alienation of species being as micro, political economy as macro); but both theorists suffered from the inability to connect the two levels realistically. Hence arose the problems of reification of the social structure, or of romanticization of personal relationships, that Durkheim and Marx have been respectively charged with. Currently, the same problems arise with theorists such as Habermas and Giddens, who explicitly attempt to ground macro in micro, but who have no way of formulating the specific contexts in which this actually happens. Organizational theory, on the contrary, gives us a tool to build up specific but limitedly macro organizations from micro interactions. The next larger level, interorganizational relations, can then be added, which itself is a mega-organization, subject to the same kinds of principles found within organizations. This gives theoretical leverage in approaching the large-scale structures of societies or even the world system, rather than merely seeing these as an ideal-typical economic market or capitalist system.

(3) Organizations are the original site of stratification. Social classes are based on different control positions within organizations (including ownership of organizations). The state, as a center for political control, a prop for the property system, and locus of struggle, is a particular kind of organization. The capitalist system itself is a kind of interorganizational network. For this reason, organizational analysis meshes especially well with conflict theory. (Notice, for example, that Dahrendorf developed his theory by drawing upon organizational evidence; Chapter 4).

(4) Most social issues in sociology are organizational problems. Deviance, police, corrections, medical sociology, educational problems, ethnic and gender discrimination, as well as the largest-scale issues of citizen control of the military,

environmental degradation, industrial accidents, nuclear war, and the operation of democracy, are all largely organizational issues. One reason that their discussion is often unrealistic or inconclusive is because they are not recognized as such: organizational constraints are not seen, and realistic organizational options are not recognized. (See Perrow, 1984, for an example of the superiority of organizational analysis for public issues.) Insofar as systematic sociological knowledge has a practical or political payoff, it usually happens through organizational theory.

APPROACHES IN ORGANIZATIONAL THEORY

There are numerous topics in the general area of organizations. In recent years, work within the field has gotten rather specialized. Hence various partial or specialized theories have arisen, reflecting the interests of particular researchers. The classic sociological concerns were with internal processes of power and control; other researchers focused on organizational structures, goals, and technologies. In fact, so much was already known about these topics several decades ago that researchers tended to shift their interest to less explored areas, such as organizational environments, interorganizational relations, and various resource-dependency and ecological models couched on that level. Practically oriented researchers in business and management fields have focused on leadership, managerial decision making, and (especially when concerned with the performance of Japanese versus American organizations) organizational culture. I will attempt to show, though, that organizational theory possesses an underlying unity and that many of the findings in the newer areas of research can be derived from an extension of the principles already established in the older literature. Hence I will begin with organizational control theory and then will point out how more recent discussions of decision making, culture, and class conflict fit into this classic model. Next I will discuss organizational structure and show how it can be derived from micro principles of control as tasks are organized in various kinds of macro environments. Finally, I will deal with various approaches to organizations and their environments, concluding that the most powerful approach here is to treat the organizational environment as if it were a "superorganization," to which we may apply the same principles of control struggles and determinants of structure as we have found operating inside organizations. As a payoff of this approach, I present a theory of how the overall systems of capitalism and socialism may be explained by organizational theory.

CONTROL THEORY

The first major discovery in organizational research, beginning in the 1920s, was the informal group. (A history of this research is sketched in Collins, 1975: 39–41, 286–98.) Workers have their own informal organization, which contravenes formal management and sets its own standards of effort and production. Then Chester Barnard, Melville Dalton, and others discovered that managers, too, have an informal structure and that the exercise of power and the making of careers, as well as the evasion of formal power from below, is an interpersonal and political process.

Herbert Simon pointed to the covert powers of "horizontal" relationships with staff experts, and Crozier, Wilensky, and others indicated the power involved in access to areas of uncertainty. By 1960, a number of theorists (March and Simon, Blau and Scott, Caplow, Etzioni) had produced syntheses of these studies: essentially theories of organizational group-formation and control. This provides a solid core to organizational theory; since that time, research focus has shifted to organizational structure and external environments. Much of these areas too, we shall see, can be derived theoretically from the core of control theory.

Etzioni's (1961/1975) "compliance theory" is a useful place to start. Etzioni proposed that organizations can control their participants in three ways, corresponding to Weber's dimensions of power, class, and status. Etzioni develops his evidence by concentrating only on the orientations of lower participants (workers, clients, inmates). But the theory works more broadly for all organization members, including higher administrative and order-giving staff, and I will state it more inclusively:

1. *Principle of Coercion:* coercive control results in an alienative orientation. Organizational members so controlled will react by resistance, if possible; next, by avoiding the coercing situation; and finally, lacking other alternatives, by dull, minimal compliance. Evidence from prisons, slave plantations, forced labor, and the military buttress Etzioni's generalization.

2. *Principle of Material Rewards:* control of utilitarian rewards leads to an acquisitive orientation. Members comply to the extent that rewards are linked to their behavior, and only to those demands which are rewarded. Workers paid by quantity of production pay attention only to quantity, ignoring quality, material savings, or other goals. Material controls lead to focusing only on the rewards. In the Marxian theory of alienation, this is formulated as a nonintrinsic relationship with the products of labor.[1] Informal membership groups or formal countergroups (for instance, unions) usually emerge to struggle over the rewards.

---

[1] Marxian theory uses the term "alienation" in a different fashion than Etzioni's "alienative orientation." The difference stems from the Hegelian philosophical tradition in which Marx worked, and in the larger economic theory of capitalist dynamics attached to it. Marxian alienation is a consequence of capitalist labor relations. Workers sell their own labor power on a market, and labor is embodied in products over which the workers have no control. Marx's model is not intended to be a theory of workers' behavior; it characterizes, rather, the nature of capitalism and its consequences for the workers, especially their deprivation of "species being," a relationship to the world in meaningful, self-guided work. Etzioni's theory is more limited, although empirically better grounded. It describes a particular kind of organizational members' attitude and behavior as the result of being coerced, especially through the threat of violence, although this would also include threatening and invasive means of supervision, and the threat of economic deprivation. Etzioni's theory is broader and more useful than the Marxian theory, however, in the following respect: it does not automatically assume that capitalism is the only source of alienation; it does not expect alienation to disappear in socialist societies, unless coercive controls are eliminated there; nor does it make the romanticizing mistake of assuming that premodern, agrarian societies were nonalienated. In fact, the worst coercion and alienation is found there. See the following section "Historical Trends in Controls." However, if Marxian theory of alienation is reformulated to stress workers' lack of control over the products of their own work, its insights can be made congruent with organizational control theory. The crucial reformation is that the source of this loss of control does not have to be capitalism, but can also occur from political coercion. Hence state socialist regimes, governmental agencies, and so forth can also engender alienation, and control of power rather than control of capitalism per se is the crucial remedy.

3. *Principle of Internalized Control:* internalization of the goals of the organization by members results in voluntary, self-motivated compliance. Etzioni, who calls this "normative control," gives evidence from medical, scientific, religious, educational, and other organizations which get some degree of internalized control over their participants.

How is internalized control achieved? Etzioni gives several methods, to which I will add some points of my own (Collins, 1975: 298–307):

(1) *Pre-selection and socialization* are means by which organizations acquire members who have already committed themselves to their goals, or by which they acquire that commitment before they become full-fledged members. The church, voluntary associations, political parties and movements, and the high-status professions have an image which enables them to attract precommitted participants. Etzioni does not explain why some organizations are able to draw on this resource; in my view, it derives from the ritual, reality-defining activities of the organization itself, which spill over to the outside world. Such organizations also use socialization in the form of a special status as novices or students, often segregated from the outside world and undergoing ritualized ordeals and initiations. But socialization does not come cheaply; Etzioni himself shows (1975) that it does not work well in the absence of willing recruits, and organizations which are not intrinsically attractive cannot generally use it to overcome the alienative or utilitarian-acquisitive orientations produced if they also use coercive or remunerative controls.

(2)*Order-giving and promotion possibilities* are probably the strongest means of inculcating the organization's ideals. Etzioni does not mention these methods, due to his concentration of lower participants, but there is considerable evidence for their efficacy. Order giving, as we have seen (Chapter 6), is an interaction ritual which commits the order giver to the Goffmanian "frontstage" reality they are presenting. Hence the higher the rank of organization members, the more they are characterized by this form of internalized control. The basic organizational control principles are thus another version of the fundamental principles of class cultures: the Principle of Material Rewards characterizes the basic stance of working-class order takers (1A, *Principle of Order-Giving Rituals,* Chapter 6); the *Principle of Coercion* gives the more extreme reaction of order givers when orders are coercively enfolded (1B, *Principle of Ritual Coercion,* Chapter 6); the order-giving variant of the *Principle of Internalized Control* is the same as *Principle* 1A at the high end of the continuum. The subvariant of internalized control through opportunities for promotion is the same as 1C, *Principle of Anticipatory Socialization,* Chapter 6. The fact that the organizational and class-culture evidence meshes so well is a strong argument for the validity of both parts of the theory.

It is well to stress, at this point, that all the control forms are ideal types, which may be combined in different degrees. Etzioni points out that organizations may be generally characterized by a preponderance of one type of control, but that various kinds of dual-control organizations exist. At the level of individuals, we may similarly see a mixture of controls used. Even normatively controlled professionals and order givers are also paid for their work (and in fact, tend to be paid quite well, precisely because the power given to them enables them to extract higher incomes). Mixtures of control types give rise to mixtures of compliance outcomes (as in the front-line supervisors' style, noted in 1D, *Principle of Bureaucratic Personality*). Since order-giving and promotion chances (anticipation of becoming an order giver) are apparently the strongest source of internalized control, no organization can be expected to have much of it without using these methods.

(3) *Ritual participation* in the group can also generate normative commitment. Conditions include: time spent together, focused on common activities and characterized by a common mood (the same principles as in the "horizontal" aspect of stratification theory, 2A, *Principle of Social Density,* and 2B, *Principle of Social Diversity,* Chapter 6). But group ritual is a two-edged sword. Group solidarity, as Etzioni and others point out, can be antithetical to the organization's official goals, if it is built around the informal, alienated or acquisitive group of lower members. In terms of ritual theory, the common sentiment may be opposition to the order-giving hierarchy. In this case, internalized control extends only through the local group but not to the organization as a whole. In order for the latter to occur, the sentiments must be more uniform and eliminate internal conflict. Only organizations that are fairly egalitarian and lack or minimize a control hierarchy are able to do this.[2] The other possible source of common sentiments arises when the organization as a whole is confronted by an external enemy threatening all members. Thus armies in time of war are able to shift from predominantly coercive control to internalized control, sustained mainly by the enemy (but also supplemented by a reserve of coercion, in case discipline breaks down under stress and chaotic battlefield conditions).

When dealing with internalized control it is essential to bear in mind the question: *whose* ideals are being inculcated? Power-wielders in an organization become personally attached to ideals that uphold their power. But these are not necessarily the ideals of those who set up the organization. Their ideals tend to be extensions of their own egos, so to speak. In coercive organizations, lower-level controllers (for example, guards) tend to identify with control as an end in itself: hence their petty authoritarianism. Group participation and rituals create a different form of ideals. But although this can occur within the organization, it does not necessarily identify with official purposes, but with the group itself. Internalized control within a group of workers may even be turned against organizational officialdom.

HISTORICAL TRENDS IN CONTROL

There is an important historical application of Etzioni's typology. Coercive controls were most widely used in agrarian modes of production (serfdom, slavery), resulting in a preponderance of alienative compliance in such societies. Capitalism, shifting control predominantly to the market, resulted in an acquisitive, utilitarian orientation of limited organizational involvement on the part of the working class. Internalized control, however, cannot be dispensed with in either type of system, since the order-giving hierarchy itself must involve a strong measure of internalized

---

[2] Churches may seem to be an exception to this. But commitment to organizational ideals is strongest among the professional priests, who are ritual leaders and order givers. Among common worshipers, the order-taking aspect is mitigated by the fact that the organization is generally not engaged in any utilitarian task, but mainly in the activity of ritual itself. Hence there are few practical demands on common members, mitigating tendencies to alienation from authority.

control in its own ranks. Is there any historical trend to either increase or decrease the amount of normative, ritualized participation? Arguments have been made in both directions. The Marxian tradition argues that, in effect, normative membership is driven out by capitalism. On the other side, it is claimed that advanced technology has promoted informality and equality among organizational members, and hence brought a shift toward internalized control. Both trend arguments are oversimplified. Though some kinds of technology give rise to this informal structure (see following), these are not the only types of technology characteristic of modern organizations. Hence a variety of control types coexist which can be expected to survive far into the future.

More fundamentally, there is an antithesis between the two major ways of promoting internalized control: via opportunities for order giving or via ritual participation. The former requires inequality within the organization, the latter minimizes inequality. Order giving is a more reliable form of internalized control, though it applies to only a few organization members (plus those who believe in their chances for promotion), and it produces alienation among order takers and those whose promotional chances are blocked (see Kanter, 1977, discussed in Chapter 6). External enemies are rarely available to provide ritual focus in most peacetime organizations, and in any case ritual cannot be used to override the effects of coercive and remunerative controls, some of which are almost always present as well. Ritually based cohesiveness is hard to achieve at the organization-wide level and is easily turned against the organizational hierarchy. For this reason, we can expect that although elements of ritual control through informality will exist in many modern organizations, the power hierarchy itself is the main source of internalized control, and it is in conflict with the other forms of control. Neither a historical utopia nor a dystopia is in sight.

ADMINISTRATIVE DEVICES

Other organizational theorists, notably Simon (1947) March (March and Simon, 1958), Blau and Scott (1962), have focused on the way in which control is organized: that is, rather than on the effects of specific sanctions (as in the Etzioni model), on the methods used by controllers to tell what to do and observe compliance. The two models are complementary and may be combined. Following is my own ordering of administrative devices laid out in this literature:

(1) *Principle of Surveillance:* controlling workers' behavior by watching over them results in compliance to those tasks which are directly observable. It also produces limited involvement and (when combined with coercive or remunerative sanctions) alienation from the organization's ideals. These outcomes can be explained by ritual theory. There is high interactional density, but combined with inequality. As we have seen in Chapter 6, this combination results in an atmosphere of petty deference rituals. The act of being observed is itself the focus of ritual attention and an enactment of authority and subordination. Hence attention is deflected from the task itself to the issue of compliance. The implicit alienation of the powerless results in minimal compliance, merely performing the physical motions demanded. There is also a structural consequence: organizations using surveillance as a form of control must have additional personnel in the control hierarchy, guards or supervisors whose

job is merely to oversee. The ideals with which this control staff identifies (given their position as noncosmopolites, at the bottom of the superior hierarchy) are unlikely to be those of the higher chiefs, but merely control as an end in itself. Hence surveillance is associated with a ritually enhanced authoritarianism.

(2) *Inspecting outcomes:* controlling workers' behavior by periodically inspecting their products (sometimes called "efficiency criterion") results in a concern for the most easily measurable aspects of outcomes. Here workers are given more freedom to do their tasks, but are checked by what they produce. Piecework incentive systems are of this sort, as are examinations and other school assignments. The focus is now on products rather than actions. It is less alienating than surveillance, but it results in a displacement from commitment to larger organizational goals, to complying narrowly with whatever aspect of output is measured (for example, getting grades rather than learning the material). Structurally, organizations using this form of administration must develop a staff for record keeping, producing a depersonalized, paper-work and number-counting orientation. This in itself is often regarded as bureaucratically alienating; but it should be borne in mind that it is a trade-off from the petty authoritarianism of direct surveillance. This method and the next are the essence of bureaucracy.

(3) *Rules and written orders:* controlling workers by general rules of procedure results in impersonality, lowered individual authority, slowness, and low adaptivity. Rules are formulated to cover the most standard procedures, with additional principles to be invoked in case of more exceptional circumstances. Rule-following organizations have the reputation for being slow and unable to deal with unique or new situations. Even if rules exist for exceptional cases, time is spent looking up what these rules are. Thus administration by rules generates a displacement from goals to procedures, and increases the proportion of staff and of time spent promulgating, updating, and searching for applicable rules.

These bureaucratic pathologies are well known. Why, then, are rules used? One reason is that standardized behavior is desired by the organization managers, especially in certain technological tasks. More importantly, rules are a focus for the struggle over control. Higher managers promulgate rules to attempt to control the behavior of lower-down (middle) staff, whom they cannot personally supervise. Rules are part of the answer to the problem "who shall control the controllers?" On the other side, rules often result from conflicts. Formal rules, to some extent, protect workers and clients from the arbitrariness of their bosses and service-providers. Often rules are crystallizations of negotiated agreements ending conflicts: union-management contracts regulating work conditions, safety regulations resulting from law suits, faculty tenure procedures embodying past struggles over academic freedom. The fact that such rules then become part of the bureaucracy, making experience in these organizations cumbersome, does not mean they are easily replaced; conflict groups have fought to get them established in the first place, and usually oppose their elimination. Here we have an unexpected principle: *democratization increases bureaucracy.* An ironic consequence is that movements for limiting arbitrary power also bring subsequent areas of alienation.

It should be added that rules do not enforce themselves. Often rules are evaded or ignored by the informal groups that make up the organization; there may be collusion between higher and lower ranks in the interest of getting the work done or avoiding meaningless activities. Rules thus become part of the ritual sector of the organization, rituals precipitated by former situations of real intensity but now lying latent until new conflicts arise. But evading rules is not the whole reality; many aspects of organizations (for instance, taking courses and getting grades in a school, getting a license at a government agency) are effectively controlled by rules. But there must be activities of real people involved: some other forms of administration have to be combined with rules, so that there is surveillance as to whether rules are being applied or efficiency outcomes are periodically checked by the rules. Probably most common is the mechanism of judgments and appeals by which rules or rule violations are specifically invoked when a conflict arises. Rules thus imply that there will be a structure of the organization specifically concerned with these adjudication activities. (This, of course, is another way that organizations can get sidetracked from their main activities, an aspect of bureaucracies that is both "democratic" in some degree and at the same time alienating.)

Finally, there are two indirect or "soft" means of administering control:

(4) *Information control:* whoever is able to provide exclusive information defining the reality in which the organization is operating will have covert power over what the organization will do; this power increases with the extent of uncertainty in that environment. Simon (1947) discovered this factor in the influence of staff experts and assistants who officially lacked "line authority." Workers, especially maintenance personnel who deal with machine breakdowns, have a similar power at lower levels (Crozier, 1964). Negotiators and go-betweens at the top levels of organizations, especially dealing with complex legal questions or volatile political or financial alliances, have similar covert power (Wilensky, 1956). The important principle is that the more uncertain that reality is, the more the official line authorities must defer to the judgment of the persons who have exclusive access to defining the problem. Managers can attempt to circumvent this problem by developing alternative sources of information and advice; in counterattack, "experts" often organize professionally or informally to present a united front. The distribution of uncertainty in various parts of organizational environments is a major determinant of how much covert power will be spread around. We shall see that this affects the organizational structure of different types of organizations.

(5) *Environmental control:* the more confined the physical setting, the more that members comply with at least minimal organization demands. This type of control cuts across all the administrative devices and sanctions. It is not a primary form of control and needs to be combined with at least some of the others. The most extreme form is a prison or labor camp, where the walls are used to keep the organization together. But rooms in factories and offices or schools also focus attention, make surveillance possible, or reduce monitoring to simply checking who is or is not present. Highly alienating organizations need to use a high degree of environmental control. At the other extreme, occupations which are spread out (traveling salespeople, truckers, police on patrol) are much more difficult for the central administration to control; often such work is spun off into franchise or contract activities. Even if central authority tries to keep control, the organization has a propensity to disintegrate, as in the case of the decentralized feudal lords of the agrarian state. Structurally, we might say that organizations with high environmental control can correspondingly cut back on their personnel in the control hierarchy (see theory of

organization structure following); organizations with low environmental control must invest much more in other control forms or else relinquish control entirely.[3]

WHO USES WHICH CONTROLS WHEN?

Organizations can be characterized by the mixture of control sanctions and administrative devices they use. What determines this? There are two main approaches. One is functional. This is the approach taken by Etzioni, who argues that certain kinds of controls are generally used with certain tasks, because the organization will be most successful. Organizations which do not use the appropriate controls experience strains. Similarly, Thompson (1967) states his propositions with the preface "under norms of rationality," meaning that if one is committed to achieving certain goals, these are the control methods that must be followed. The other approach, in keeping with conflict theory, argues that the controls which are used depends on what control resources are available. It states that the core of the organization is not its tasks but its control structure, and that this is what established the organization in the first place and keeps it in existence.

The functional-teleological approach and the conflict-domination (control resource) approach are not necessarily incompatible, although they have quite different emphases. I will begin with the control resources, and attempt to demonstrate that they are central for the existence of the organization; then I will add what is valid from the task-teleology approach.[4]

CONTROL RESOURCES AS CORE OF ANY ORGANIZATION'S EXISTENCE

What conditions establish an organization in the first place? An organization is an enduring arrangement coordinating people's activities, and we have seen that coordination is determined by various forms of control. To establish an organization, someone must have enough control resources. Coercive power (ultimately, the power of armed force) is the *sine qua non* for establishing governmental and military organizations, as well as their offshoots: prisons, concentration camps, slave plantations, serfdom, and so forth. Possession of property is what makes it possible to establish an organization controlling its members by material reward: that is, by hiring and paying its members. This is the source of business organizations, as well as any other organization (such as a family hiring a housekeeper) using remunerative control. Internalized control, finally, as a source of organization, is found in orga-

---

[3] It may be noticed that police on patrol are subject to little environmental control, but the structural alternatives (just mentioned) applied in other decentralized situations are not used. Hence it is not surprising that an official hierarchy, such as that which stretches from the voters through elected officials to police chiefs down to police officers, has little power to control police behavior in many dramatic instances, such as the use of force on what are regarded as suspects. Many other aspects of organizational analysis are applicable in understanding the police and other social issues.

[4] My own treatment of organizational theory (Collins, 1975: 286–347) is deficient because I followed Etzioni's exposition too closely and accepted a purely functional account of why certain tasks tend to be carried out by particular control forms. The following treatment puts the control theory back in proper perspective.

nizations voluntarily recruiting their membership. People join because they want to, being attracted to the ideal of the group or the activity itself. Examples include clubs and associations, as well as organizations specializing in emotion and culture, such as religions and schools. Conflict organizations, such as political parties, trade unions, or, historically, tribal coalitions or prophetic religious movements, derive their normative power especially from their ritual solidarity against their external enemies. In each case, organizations get established because some people have control resources they can use to build the organization.

Organizations are usually mixtures of control types, though one form may be predominant. The mixture arises because one control resource can generate others. Purely coercive organizations, such as crude military governments, tend to supplement the threat of force with other controls. Weber (1922/1968: 212–15) made a point of stressing the greater durability of coercive organizations which establish legitimacy: that is, acquire some internalized control. As we have seen, though, internalized control is not easy to acquire without giving away power; highly coercive organizations usually make this concession only within their higher ranks, generating some normative solidarity among the coercers, while relying more heavily on sheer threat to keep the lower ranks in line. For this reason, these organizations usually split into castelike levels, subject to different control techniques, as in the aristocracy versus peasantry of feudal-agrarian states. Analytically, the most important point here is that coercive power usually generates the ability to create internalized control, at least to the extent of being able to use the sharing of power (or chances at promotion) as form of control. Coercive power can also be used to organize rituals and set up impressive stage-settings (such as religious buildings, costumes, music and so forth) to appeal to emotions and determine beliefs. This is a weaker form of control if it is combined with continued coercion (since that produces continued alienation), but it probably has some independent effect in the total mix of compliance.

Even more importantly, coercive organizations are usually able to generate remunerative control. Governments acquire revenue that they can use to pay at least the active, controlling tier of their members. In modern government agencies, control by the pay check is so central that there is little difference between them and private business organizations in this respect. How much a coercive organization shifts in this direction is of course a variable. It would seem to depend on (1) the degree to which sheer coercion is checked by other political forces (for example, by democratization) and (2) the size of the material resource base available to the government. Where coercion is limited and the material resources are constricted, there arises a "fiscal crisis of the state" as expressed in modern Marxist theory (O'Connor in Chapter 3).

Conversely, organizations based on property and recruiting by material reward usually can produce derivative forms of control. Any property system is ultimately backed up by the state, and hence rests at least ultimately upon some coercive control. If one set of persons has most or all of the property and another set has little or none, the need for livelihood can turn remunerative control into a form of coercion, as stressed by Marxian theory of capitalism. This coercive aspect is especially likely to come to the fore when working-class rebellion arises, resulting in the property owners calling on the military power of the state to directly protect their property. Within an organization, too, remunerative control can be administered in a more coercive or less coercive manner: by threatening firing or fines (withdrawal or reward) as a negative control, or even by making hired workers submit to physical punishment as a condition of their job discipline.

Remunerative organizations may also attempt to generate internalized control. The considerations here are essentially the same as those applying to coercive organizations.

Finally, organizations based initially or centrally on internalized control (churches, schools, voluntary associations) nevertheless gravitate toward the other forms of control. For any organization to last, it usually must acquire property: a permanent home in buildings, a material base for symbolizing its continued existence, material resources to support a full-time staff. Weber's (1922/1968: 1111–157) analysis of the routinization of charisma essentially makes this point. Charisma refers to leadership in a social movement, a set of voluntary followers of some ideal and its spokesperson. But social movements are notoriously unstable, coming and going on waves of popular emotion, unless they are transformed into a more permanent structure. Weber's prime examples of routinization are the histories of religious movements such as Christianity, Buddhism, and Islam, though the argument applies generally. The permanent structure arises most easily because the movement acquires property by the donations of its members. (Modern voluntary associations, significantly, spend a disproportionate amount of their time in raising money.) From this follows the existence of a permanent staff to look after the property and carry out the organization's activities. There is now a split in the organization, between mere voluntary members and its professional employees. New resources mean new control techniques (part of what Michels was referring to in his "Iron Law of Oligarchy" in political parties; see following). In Weber's terms, raw charisma is "routinized": it becomes a tradition deliberately kept alive by organizational functionaries whose major resource is now their control of material rewards and material conditions of impression management.[5]

THE IMPORTANCE OF PROPERTY

I am suggesting, then, that over time most organizations tend toward a remunerative form of control based on property. Some other directions are also possible. Social movements, based on normative ideals, may try to turn themselves into coercive organizations; this happens for instance when a religious movement becomes powerful enough to capture control of the state (or make itself a new state, as in the case of the Islamic conquest). And we have seen that coercive and remunerative organizations usually try to acquire at least some components of internalized control over some of their participants. But property seems to be central because what makes

[5] Weber distinguishes two directions in which charisma can be routinized: into traditional or rational-legal authority. These indicate the control ideologies associated with two forms of organization: a patrimonial form, in which the organization becomes hereditary property of a family or coalition of households, as in typical agrarian societies; and a bureaucratic form, in which individuals and families cannot appropriate the organizational position itself, but are subject to formal rules and regulations as the administrative control device.

an organization permanent is the property that its controllers hold. Organizations that fail to acquire property usually fall apart fairly quickly. They represent the difference between a coercive gang and a state, between a group of friends or political-religious sympathizers or a cultural fad, on one hand, and a formal association or school or church on the other.

We may arrive at the same conclusion from another point of view. An organization disappears when its property goes away. It is the property that gives its a formal, open, public identity as a "thing" which exists. The officials of an organization are those who have control of its property, who can disperse it as remunerative control to hire staff, to buy supplies and services, and to issue communications bringing the organizational members together. Even voluntary associations, unless they exist in a small face-to-face setting where communication is automatic, depend on this material structure for the enactment of its social reality.

This enables us to answer a point often raised: that the control-resources viewpoint is too "management-oriented," and reflects only the point of view of the bosses in how to control their organizations. The control viewpoint is management-centered, but not because it is pro-management. It can just as easily be used as a critique of management domination of workers. We could also turn it around and ask what resources and administrative devices are available to workers (or other lower participants) to control their superiors. But the answer is, generally speaking, that lower participants do not have as much control resources as their superiors, and that is precisely what gives the organization its structure. (This can of course be variable, and we can find more centralized and decentralized, more undemocratic or democratic, organizations.) But even the conditions which allow workers to evade many forms of control, amply documented in the literature on informal groups, does not eliminate the central form of control: the property structure of the organization itself. Workers often evade rules and regulations, usually do not work as hard as bosses wish them to, and may have quite different committments than those of the official organizational ideals. But the organization can continue to survive with all this, as long as one condition remains: the formal hierarchy remains intact and still hands out its paychecks for minimal compliance.[6]

This view shows us several of the limitations of a functionalist perspective on organizations. The organization may exist, whether or not it is effective at carrying out various tasks. The key is not its functional task effectiveness, but whether control resources still exist. A business organization, using material rewards to keep a labor force on its rosters, will continue to exist as long as its top officials—which is to say its owners—are solvent. Of course, we could introduce the premise of conventional market economics, that an organization will not make profits and stay in business unless it is efficient; but this is not decisive. Just how efficient it has to be depends on how competitive its environment is and on how efficient its competitors are. The

[6] I have overstated the argument in terms of purely property-based organizations, where the power of hiring, firing, and promotion is the most immediate form of control, even if the organization is part of the coercive state. Analytically, we could make a parallel argument in favor of the permanent apparatus of coercion as central to some organizations. For instance, in a prison or concentration camp or a terrorist dictatorship, there may be an informal structure and much normative alienation. But the organization will survive as long as there is a command hierarchy capable of passing along orders to coerce people in particular instances.

analogous point in coercive organizations is even stronger: a government does not have to be effective at anything, as long as it is not challenged by some other coercive power which is stronger than it is. As Meyer and Zucker (1987) point out, there exist many "permanently failing organizations," which persist despite a low level of performance; often the interests of workers or the surrounding community keep an organization going after its owners have given up on its profitability.

We lose sight of the central activity of organizational officials if we regard them merely as "experts" who contribute to the organization by their ability to plan and coordinate.[7] But officials are far more important to the organization in a different way: they administer the control resources that bring members into the organization and keep them at least minimally complying. That is, they hire, conscript, capture, or proselytize new members; promote, demote, or otherwise reward or punish them for their participation; and can terminate their membership in the organization. As long as a chain of controllers has the control resources to hire or otherwise bring in members, the organization will exist; and it will exist even if these managers are totally inept at planning or coordinating anything. Highly technical expertise, although it may be well rewarded in some contexts, nevertheless does not result in people being able to set up organizations or becoming the heads of them; unless the technical experts shift over to direct "line" authority, and especially the financial realms of power in property-based organizations, they remain auxiliary staff whose power is mainly covert.

Analytically, of course, skills at planning and coordinating are also usually operative in organizations. But the central feature of the organization is its control hierarchy; the task aspect of the organization, and whatever functional pressures it generates, is added onto this. Ultimately, it is the control structure that determines whether and in what form the organization will exist. Functional task pressures may feed into this, but as a secondary influence.

TASKS AND CONTROL FORMS

Organization theory is the one area in sociology where a functional approach may have some validity, but precisely because formal organizations are explicitly teleological: and it is because of the control structure that they have this kind of formality and explicitness lacking in other kinds of social organization. We can predict what control forms will be used in an organization by asking two questions: (1) What are the resources (coercive, material rewards, appeals of emotions and ideals) of the persons who established the organization in the first place?[8] (2) What tasks are those persons trying to carry out? The goal-directedness here is open and conscious: what are the organization controllers trying to do?

Eztioni's model (1961/1975), as extended by Collins (1975) takes the tasks specified in the second question and shows what sanctions and administrative devices best fit them.

---

[7]This is the way they are viewed in Blau's (1964) version of exchange theory, accounting for their greater power and higher salaries as the result of their greater contributions. We may recognize here the old functionalist theory of stratification. See the discussion of exchange versus enforcement coalition theories of power in Chapter 12.

[8]The same applies to persons who come later who have acquired control of those central control resources.

Tasks with a high degree of initiative and uncertainty are carried out most effectively by internalized control and information control. Alienating coercive controls or remunerative controls resulting in merely perfunctory involvement cannot motivate personnel to do tasks requiring a high degree of initiative and judgment. Since the outcomes are uncertain, administrative devices must be on the "soft" side; rules and rigid counting of results will not work with innovative activities, and surveillance and environmental control limits the initiative that the job requires. Creative and mental work falls into this category of tasks, as does dealing with emergencies and other unpredictable situations. The task of maintaining control over others is often of this unpredictable sort, and must itself be controlled in this fashion.

Tasks with predictable and standardized products can be carried out effectively by control with material rewards, administered by an efficiency criterion of counting outcomes. As long as there are visible products whose characteristics are known in advance, rewards can be attached to them and output easily measured. In some cases, the actions of producing those outcomes can be effectively spelled out in rules. Much of routine physical work falls into this category: operating factory machines, delivering goods on schedule, as well as much predictable paperwork in white-collar jobs.

Low initiative tasks with highly visible outcomes can be carried out effectively by coercion. But since coercion is alienating, it requires surveillance and environmental control to keep participants from fighting back or escaping. The functionally most appropriate use of coercion is where the persons on whom it is applied are already alienated: prisoners, forced laborers, serfs. In some organizations, such as prisons, the main task of the organization is a minimal one: simply to prevent escape and rebellion. If coerced people are to be used to carry out tasks, those tasks will have to be fairly crude physical activities: the farm work carried out by serfs and slaves, the rock crushing and road maintainance of prison work gangs, the picking up trash used as a punishment for trivial offenses. Creative tasks or those with uncertain outcomes cannot be well motivated with coercion, because more autonomy must be given to the worker than this alienating control will allow. Even machine work of any degree of complexity, even if it has standardized products, is not easily motivated in this fashion, as indicated by evidence that slaves and prisoners have never been very efficient as factory workers, compared to free laborers working for wages.[9]

The model does not say that it is necessary to use coercion to get workers to carry out low initiative tasks. Ditches can also get dug or rocks crushed by paying laborers, or conceivably even by relying on internalized control. The efficiency model here is asymmetrical, in that the more internalized forms of control can substitute for the more externalized forms, but not vice versa. But the organizational controllers may not have the resources to do this. Normative control is nice if you can get it, but it is not widely available, and few organizations can afford to squander it on getting highly routine tasks done. Similarly, remunerative control will motivate the same tasks as coercive control, but persons who possess coercive resources (military dictators, slave-owners, feudal aristocrats, prison guards) will find it cheaper to rely

---

[9] Patterson (1982) shows that historically slaves were often used for crafts work, as in ancient Greece and Rome. But when this was the case, the control system shifted from sheer coercion, characteristic of mines and agricultural plantations, to a version of material rewards: slaves were held out the prospect of manumission, of buying their own freedom with their earnings from their work.

on coercion as long as the tasks are very simple (and as long as some political force does not take their coercive power away from them). Coercive control is not considered morally proper in a democratic society, but it will be used nevertheless where coercers have the power to get away with it.[10]

There are two aspects of functional interconnectedness here. Etzioni (1961/1975) expresses his functional argument about the *congruence of tasks and control forms* as follows: organizations which choose the proper control form for its tasks will survive and prosper; those which choose an inappropriate control form will have a lower level of performance and will either change toward an appropriate control form or else fail and disappear. This is not entirely conclusive, since organizations may continue to survive at a low level of efficiency, as long as their control resources remain intact and if the competitive pressure of their environment is not high. Traditional coercive controls in farming may not be as efficient as remunerative controls, but coerced feudal labor lasted for centuries as long as the aristocracy was not challenged politically or economically; the relatively coerced atmosphere of communist collective farms results in lower output than private farms within the same Soviet societies, but state policy has kept the former in existence and barely tolerated the latter. Hence the extent to which an organization has to move toward the functionally optimal relationship between tasks and controls depends on the structure of power, the distribution of control resources itself.

The other aspect of functional relationship is *between control sanctions and administrative devices.* Here the functional pressures are tighter. Coercive sanctions cannot be used for long if they are not combined with surveillance, and they work best if environmental control is also available. Since coercive organizations are usually willing to put up with a low level of effectiveness, rules can be applied in a rigid way, since speed and adaptiveness are not criteria of success. Material rewards imply some method of recording outcomes. Normative control and information control have their structural requirements, without which they cannot be generated. Within the dynamics of control itself, there are teleological relationships that can be validly said to exist.

MOTIVATION, CLASS CONFLICT, ORGANIZATIONAL CULTURE, AND DECISION MAKING

A number of other topics concerning behavior in organizations have been extensively discussed in the organizational literature (see Hall, 1982; Perrow, 1985; Pfeffer, 1982). Without devoting a great deal of space, I would like to indicate how these may fit into the fundamental theory about organizational control.

---

[10]Milder versions of coercive control are common. Rewards can be used coercively when authorities threaten to take them away; verbal abuse also has coercive effects. These controls are most often used by the lowest-level, "frontline" controllers on potentially rebellious subordinates: prison guards, high school teachers, and other petty despots. Athletic coaches often have this style as well, most likely where the sport itself involves the use of brute force, as in football.

MOTIVATION   The *motivation* of organizational members cannot be approached purely psychologically, since this takes the actors out of their real-life context, which consists precisely in their positions inside the organization. Motivation is what organizational control looks like from the point of view of the individual. We should bear in mind that control theory is a flexible instrument; although it is most typically couched in terms of how managers try to control their subordinates, it also explains the extent to which the latter will comply or evade controls; and it also shows the resources and conditions by which subordinates counterattack and control at least some aspects of their superiors' behavior. There are also horizontal controls (especially through control of information channels), as well as the ritual participation that occurs among members of a group and the exchanges, dependencies, and threats which constitute power within organizations' informal networks. Moreover, control theory is related to the theory of class cultures given in Chapter 6, and to exchange theory and interaction ritual chains (Chapter 10); hence these other aspects of sociological theory can be brought in to spell out individuals' motivations within organizations in more detail.

INTERESTS AND CLASS CONFLICTS   One of the few approaches in recent years that has paid attention to the workers' levels inside organizations has been Marxian theory. Burawoy (1979) has analyzed why factory workers comply with the capitalist system, which comes down concretely to why they put up with managers' controls. He concludes that workers are involved in a "game" in which they juggle the payoffs of their incomes, job security, and informal group membership against the amount and quality of work they are willing to do. Apart from the Marxian frame of reference, however, the patterns are familiar ones, which readily fit the principles given previously concerning control by rewards, promotion possibilities, ritual participation, and various administrative devices. Interestingly enough, in another work, Burawoy (1985) shows that similar controls exist in factories in socialist countries, which suggests that it is the local organization more than the overall economic system that is determining workers' and managers' behavior.

This leads to the more general issue of the interests of persons within organizations. The question comes up in the Marxian context as the issue of "which side are you on?" in what is assumed to be a two-sided conflict between workers and capitalists. But organizations have a number of different levels (upper and middle management, clerical, skilled and unskilled manual workers, as well as further splits among various professions, unions and non-unionized workers, and so on). Empirical researchers following the Marxist approach (Wright, 1978, 1980; Wright and Singleman, 1982) have had to add intermediate classes or "contradictory class locations" based on multiple criteria. Managers who do not own their company (or stock in capitalist enterprises generally) are nevertheless members of the employer class, in some degree, when they exercise power in the pursuit of capitalist profits. But about half of all supervisors today lack significant power, since they do not control the pay or promotion of their subordinates; hence they may be regarded as actually being members of the working class. On the other hand, some workers are not very "proletarianized," since they have considerable autonomy over the performance of their own work. From the point of view of organizational control theory, we should note that Wright is actually placing considerable emphasis on order giving and order taking as an indicator of class position; in fact, he is forced to place many people in "contradictory class locations" because this organizational power distribution is not at all identical with property ownership and nonownership, nor with the classical Marxian category of the production of surplus value.

I would suggest that organizational control theory analyzes the situation more straightforwardly. Persons have interests because of where they stand in the control structure of the organization: order givers versus order takers, with the conflict among their interests becoming maximal the more coercion is used; defense of one's own source of material rewards (which may be specific to only a particular occupation, or even an individual, within the organization); plus the emotional effects of group solidarity and symbolic ideals, as produced by the various mechanisms of normative control. There are multiple interests and hence multiple lines of potential conflict inside organizations, whenever coercive and material controls are differentiated, and when the structure of normative control reinforces local and fragmentary groups. Interests are the result of the distribution of controls, and that in turn is determined by organizational structure (which we will consider next). This is not to say that a Marxian-style confrontation of two major classes is impossible, but only that it occurs only under special organizational conditions.

ORGANIZATIONAL CULTURE   A rather different concern with organizational members comes from business school researchers, who look for an organizational culture which is optimal for efficiency and success. It has been argued that the superior performance of Japanese companies in recent years is due to their distinctive organizational culture (Ouichi, 1980, 1981) that emphasizes group participation and harmonious relationships, as compared to the confrontations between management, workers, and government which are characteristic of American business. Other studies (for instance, Peters and Waterman, 1982) have stressed the person-oriented and forward-looking management styles prevailing in the most successful American organizations. The danger of this approach is in romanticizing the hard realities of organizational life. The actual message is quite similar to the "human relations" approach which appeared following the discovery of the informal group half a century ago; but this was eventually superseded when researchers recognized that informal groups cannot simply be manipulated from the top by bosses' pep talks and that organizational power struggles over controls are still concerned with the actual distribution of power and rewards. Even the success of the Japanese corporations appears to have less to do with their distinctive culture than with differences in the way these organizations are structured, especially in relation to banks and to government agencies, and with favorable conditions in the international economy (Cole, 1979, 1981).

DECISION MAKING: THE GARBAGE-CAN MODEL   Following a period in which economic models of rational actors were applied to organizational decision makers, the theory of decision making shifted toward the opposite extreme. March and Olsen (1976) proposed the "garbage-can model," which stresses that choices are fundamentally ambiguous at every stage of the decision-making process. What gets considered as a problem in the first place is affected by channels of communication and the various actors that control them. What objectives are aimed at is not constant but evolves over time as various possibilities come into view. And the procedures for solving problems are typically not clear. All these factors interact: they are, as it were, thrown together into a "garbage can," which is particularly messy since different problems and goals get mixed together with whatever happens to be there at the time. The policies that come out are merely those which have managed to compete with other pieces of information for the scarce attention of the decision makers.

This model is empirically realistic, but I think that it throws away some of the existing power of organizational theory. Focusing on the minds of decision makers makes us look at things at a micro angle of vision in which situational contingencies loom largest. If we approach the behavior of organizations in a more long-term fashion, the overall pattern in which organizations (and the people within them) operate is predictable from the factors given elsewhere in the theories of organizational control and structure.

Organizational Structure

IS THERE A TREND TOWARD "MODERN" ORGANIZATIONAL STRUCTURE?

It has often been assumed that organizations are tending to assume a particular "modern" form. One candidate is the supposedly universal trend toward bureaucratization. The dominance of paperwork and of formal rules and regulations has been regarded as mercilessly advancing. Weber (1922/1968: 956–1005) regarded this as the most efficient form of control, and hence expected that twentieth-century (and subsequent) societies would be caught in the "iron cage" of bureaucracy. Socialism would constitute no exception; in fact, it would intensify bureaucratization, a prediction borne out by the organizational forms dominant in Soviet societies. Only charismatic movements in political parties, Weber felt, provided any counterbalance against the bureaucratic trend. Schumpeter (1942) extended Weber's pessimism to capitalism itself; the advance of the corporation would drive out the entrepreneur and result in the deading structure of bureaucracy. Neo-Marxian theorists, too, have proposed a predominant trend in this direction. Habermas (1984) has theorized that the personal lifeworld of interaction has become "colonized" by impersonal media of communication, in the form of money and power, leaving individuals pushed about by impersonal bureaucratic forces.

A counterargument, however, has been made that bureaucracy is characteristic only of early capitalism and is being replaced by a more advanced form, sometimes called "post-industrialism" (for example, Hage, 1980, or numerous popular expositions). Modern "high-tech" organizations, based on scientific expertise, become informal and person-oriented rather than thing-oriented, decentralized and democratic rather than centralized and authoritarian. Instead of an iron cage, we are moving toward an organizational utopia.

Neither predicted trend is conclusive. Neither structure has yet displaced the other. The two structural types posited, bureaucratic and expert-participatory, do not even capture the variety of structural types now in existence. Neither theory takes sufficient account of research accumulated in the last 25 years, which shows how and why organizations differ from one another. The factors determining organizational structure—especially goals, technologies, and controls—vary within the same society, and do not fall into a simple historical sequence. Instead of a single-factor evolutionary trend, sophisticated organization theory shows us a multi-factor situation.

WOODWARD AND THOMPSON'S STRUCTURAL TYPES

Comparative research and theoretical synthesis by Joan Woodward (1965) and James D. Thompson (1967), sometimes called contingency theory, indicates there are four major types of organizational structure. Woodward initially demonstrated their existence for industrial organizations, related to their technologies of production. As Thompson, Perrow (1967), and others indicate, the structural types are found across all types of organizations, including those producing only paperwork, as well as military and political control, religious or other cultural outputs, or cultural involvement in voluntary associations. (See Figure 13-1.)

UNIT PRODUCTION   *Unit production* is a form of organization which makes just one or a small number of relatively unique products at a time. Innovative engineering projects are of this type, as are many scientific laboratories; so are movie and theatrical companies. But traditional crafts, too, may take this organizational form, such as companies which manufacture individually tailored suits. These organizations tend to have a low hierarchy of command with few rank levels. Relationships are personal and relatively informal. There is little distinction between line authority and auxiliary staff advisers. Communication is done more by mutual consultation than by formulating rigid rules or elaborate record keeping.

This type of structure comes closest to the type adulated as the "modern" democratic organization. But several caveats must be added. This is not necessarily a "high-tech" organization; it exists in some traditional activities (for instance, crafts, theater), and, as we shall see, very advanced technologies do not necessarily take this form. Moreover, although this organizational type is relatively personal and unbureaucratic, it does not follow that it is democratic. A control structure still exists, based on the power of hiring, firing, and promotion; in some instances, where the number of good jobs is scarce, the bosses of unit production organizations can be dictatorial. The entertainment business is notorious for the petty deference given to directors and producers and for the importance of personal connections in careers. Informality here amounts to personalilty cults around those individuals with power, since there are few impersonal, bureaucratic procedures to restrain them. Scientific laboratories, too, which approximate this model (Latour and Woolgar, 1979) may have an atmosphere of casual informality, but key scientists with personal reputations have a crucial importance for the ability to recommend their subordinates for positions, as well as to legitimate grants of research funds. In traditional crafts organizations, such as the medieval guild, the master-owner of the shop had arbitrary personal authority over his journeymen and apprentices. The informality of personal relationships can be personal authoritarianism as well as personal democracy. The latter depends on a greater equality of control resources among organization members; for reasons that we shall see, democracy often introduces an element of bureaucracy.

FIGURE 13-1

TASK TECHNOLOGY AND TYPES OF ORGANIZATIONAL STRUCTURE

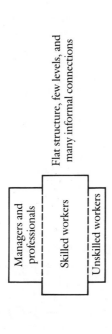

Managers and professionals

Skilled workers

Unskilled workers

Flat structure, few levels, and many informal connections

UNIT PRODUCTION

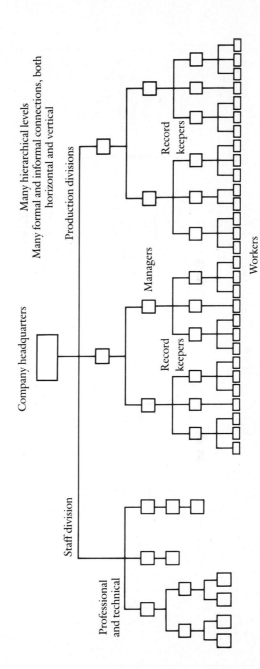

Company headquarters

Staff division

Professional and technical

Production divisions

Record keepers

Managers

Record keepers

Workers

Many hierarchical levels

Many formal and informal connections, both horizontal and vertical

MASS PRODUCTION AND ASSEMBLY

FIGURE 13-1 *(Continued)*

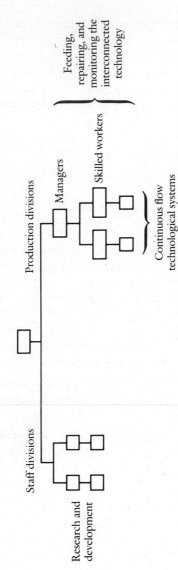

PROCESS OR CONTINUOUS-FLOW PRODUCTION

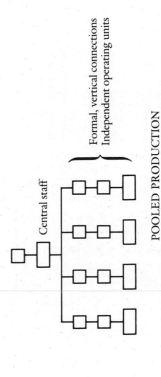

POOLED PRODUCTION

MASS PRODUCTION AND ASSEMBLY   *Mass production and assembly* exists where a considerable number of different items are manufactured or procured and then brought together to be assembled, possibly with the pattern repeating many times as subassembled components are brought together into still larger components. The archetype is a factory manufacturing machinery, especially a complex machine like an automobile. Analogous organizational forms can be found outside of manufacturing; for instance, a modern army in war in a mass production-assembly structure, with soldiers themselves as well as their equipment and supplies constituting the parts to be assembled in various places.

Woodward found that mass production organizations tend to be highly bureaucratic. The structure resembles a pyramid: a central command, with branching suboffices for various geographical or product divisions and functional services. There is a good deal of formal paperwork, much record keeping, formal rules, and written orders. There is a sharp division between line authority and auxiliary staff whose duties are to deal with the record keeping and informational flow. This is the type of organization in which there is most likely to be an informal structure alongside of, and in conflict with, the formal structure. This dual structure makes for great complexity. There are numerous breakdowns in coordination, and typically an elaborate organizational politics exists behind the scenes. Many of the famous organizational studies (Gouldner, Dalton, Barnard, Mayo,) were done in this type of organization; hence we tend to have an image of it as the archetypal bureaucracy.

PROCESS OR CONTINUOUS-FLOW PRODUCTION   This kind of production typically consists in manufacturing a product which undergoes many transformations. Often there is a liquid, such as petroleum, which is refined through a serious of operations. High-tech versions are found in chemicals and drugs, but low-tech versions are also found, as in bakeries, dairy products, soft drinks, distilleries, and other food products. What is organizationally distinctive is that the sequencing is built into the machinery itself. There are few coordination problems, since the machinery itself guides the different components together. Work is highly predictable and is regulated by formal rules. Structurally, these organizations often look top-heavy, with a relatively high proportion of administrative staff. This is because most of the manual work is done by machines; what manual work force remains is primarily involved in monitoring and repairing machines.

Process-production and mass-production organizations are structurally both bureaucratic, but are very different types. Mass production usually has a messy and conflictual bureaucracy, with an informal structure shadowing the formal structure; process production usually has a smooth and nonconflictual bureaucracy, and formal and informal authority tend to coincide.

POOLED PRODUCTION   Where a number of different operating units carry out more or less the same activities in parallel, *pooled production* can exist. The central organization provides a pool of resources for local units and receives other resources or products back from them. Coordination is largely vertical rather than horizontal. Many white-collar organizations are of this type: government agencies that issue licenses, welfare and employment agencies, banks, insurance companies, schools; so are certain material-processing operations, such as retail stores. Since there is little coordination between local activities, the structure can be highly bureaucratic, dominated by formal rules and regulations and devoting most of its attention to record keeping. Here we have yet another type of bureaucracy: an extremely impersonal one, with little pressure to move quickly. Here is found the greatest "goal-displacement" from ends to means, where the paperwork routine becomes an end in itself, taking precedence over service to persons using the organization. In effect, clients become mere material for the organizational record-keeping process.

SIZE AND ORGANIZATIONAL STRUCTURE

Before the discovery of Woodward and Thompson's organizational types, it was commonly believed that the main variable associated with differences in organizational structure is size. Larger organizatitons, it was held, become more bureaucratic. The image of bureaucracy, however, was crude, mixing several dimensions. (1) Larger organizations are more impersonal, with greater use of paperwork, record keeping, and formal rules. This appears to be partly true. *Within* any one of the Woodward-Thompson types, it is probably the case that the bigger organization will have more paperwork and more formal written communications and general rules. Even unit production, when it gets to be large, must have some of this bureaucracy; clearly there will be more formal structure in a giant engineering project of thousands of persons making a rocket ship than in an engineering group of half a dozen. It would not follow, however, that *any* large organization will have more paperwork than *any* small one. A small pooled-production organization may well be much more bureaucratic in this respect than a rather larger unit-production organization. Another caveat is that some types of big organizations respond to size and complexity by elaborating their informal structure. A big mass-production, mass-assembly structure (such as the army or a big manufacturing corporation) is likely to be both highly impersonal on the frontstage, and highly personal on the back stage. As we have seen, whether size will generate this dual formal-informal structure depends on the task type.

(2) Larger organizations have a relatively greater proportion of clerical staff than of frontline production workers. This is another image of bureaucracy as a structure which is inefficient, displacing its activities from output to administration. Considerable research has been done on this question, though much of it is limited by failing to take organizational type into account. Blau and Schoenherr (1971) formulated a mathematical law stating that organizations do increase their administrative component relative to their size, but at a decelerating rate (as they get very big, the rate of growth of extra top-heaviness slows down). But Blau has done all his work in a particular type of organization, governmental agencies which fit the pooled-production type. This principle may not fit organizations in which complexity of interdependence among units increases with size (Anderson and Warkov, 1961).

(3) Larger organizations are sometimes believed to be more bureaucratic in the sense of more centralized. This however does not appear to be so. Chandler (1962) has shown in a historical account of large American corporations that difficulties of coordination increase beyond a certain size, resulting in a tendency to decentralize. This decentralization is not absolute, as giant organizations do not fragment into small ones. Instead, semi-autonomous divisional centers are established, controlling a full range of functional activities. Often these are geographically based, or grouped

around particular product lines. Sometimes both forms of divisionalization are used in a cross-cutting fashion, as in the U.S. Department of State, which has both area divisions (Europe, Africa, and so on) and functional divisions (political affairs, economic affairs, and so on). Divisionalization does not mean the end of bureaucratization, but only focuses certain aspects of record keeping and communications at divisional levels, while retaining other aspects at the overall headquarters. Recent development of superorganizations in the form of business conglomerates (or "multi-profit centers") indicate there is no trend to eliminate or split up extremely large organizations, but only to moderately decentralize some aspects of their functioning. The major control resources, especially finances, however, are kept at the center (and in fact constitute the center).

ORGANIZATIONAL HIERARCHY AS MACRO COORDINATION OF MICRO ACTIVITIES

The preceding propositions about organizational structure are empirical generalizations. These observed patterns can be explained as applications of control theory in different situations laid out by tasks, technologies, and ecological spaces.

A useful perspective is to regard the administrative hierarchy of an organization as a set of positions which specialize in the macro coordination of micro activities which take place at the levels below them. On the micro level, organization members are carrying out various activities: making and assembling different pieces of machinery, for example, or receiving applications for services. The administrators' activities are to coordinate these micro activities across time and space: they take account of what several different people are doing in different places and times, and try to bring those activities and their products into a sequence so that there will be certain results. The administrators' activities themselves, of course, also happen in a particular micro situation, but they are explicitly oriented toward a larger macro slice of activities. Higher level administrators in turn have larger macro slices to coordinate, typically consisting of the blocks of activities coordinated by subordinate administrators.

Perrow (1984) gives a theory of organization structure based on the kinds of anticipated and unanticipated coordination problems that arise with different tasks and technologies. (See Figure 13-2.) He distinguished two dimensions, complex versus linear and tight versus loose coupling. However, his dimension of complex versus linear itself seems to have important subdimensions; based on his earlier statement (Perrow, 1967) and my own analysis (Collins, 1975: 315–29), we may break this down, resulting in three dimensions:

(1) *The degree of uncertainty in each micro activity.* Where this is high, it is harder for an administrator to predict what each participant will be producing. One consequence (according to the *principle of task uncertainty,* page 463) is that bureaucratic controls of activities will be hard to apply, and frontline workers will have a high degree of autonomy.

(2) *The degree of uncertainty in the structural connections between micro-activities.* This depends on how complicated the process is by which different activities depend on each other. Where many parts are needed to be assembled into a product, some administrative activity is called for to schedule their separate production and deliv-

FIGURE 13-2

ORGANIZATIONAL COUPLING, COMPLEXITY, AND SYSTEM ACCIDENTS

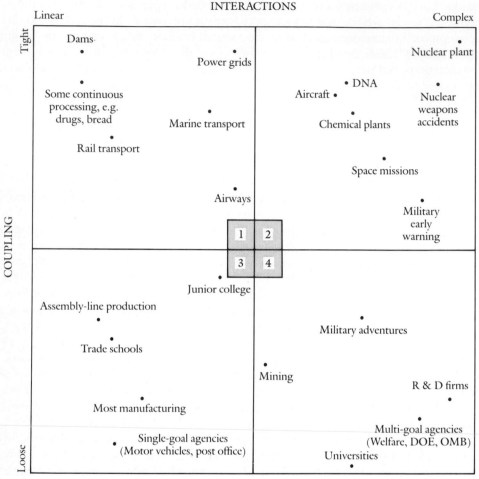

From Charles Perrow, "A Framework for the Comparative Analysis of Organizations," *American Sociological Review,* vol. 32, 1967. Reprinted by permission.

ery. Much of what administrators do is troubleshooting when some needed component is missing. Such breakdowns can occur whenever machines break, human workers are absent or slow or careless, or prior planning was not accurate. Moreover, the effects of breakdowns can multiply if there are complex connections: a needed part itself may come from some other organization or division, which has its own coordination problems. The more such complexity, the more administrators' time is needed to coordinate activities. Administrators deal not only with normal coordination, but with the consequences of accidents; but accidents are more or less expectable according to the degree of uncertainty of coordination.

Perrow (1984) points out, moreover, that some systems are complex, not only because of the planned connections among activities, but because problems can overflow into activities which just happen to be physically nearby. The same equipment may be used for several purposes (for example, maintenance tools in a factory can be used in different production sequences), hence a breakdown in one sequence can cause an unforeseen cramp in a quite different sequence. Or a small fire in one machine system may damage electrical connections which happen to pass nearby but affect quite different operating systems. This kind of "spillover" effect can also apply to humans: an informal network in one part of the organization can make personal connections with that in another part, thus resulting in unexpected channels of communication. Perrow also notes that these kinds of complexities may provide at least short-term solutions for problems. An entirely different sector of the organization can be cannabalized for needed equipment or personnel to fill needs elsewhere, making up for failures or shortages in their own stockpiles. In the longer run, though, these makeshift adjustments tend to cause an unplanned difficulty in the activities elsewhere in the organization, resulting in still further adjustments, and so on. For all these reasons, production sequences can operate differently than planned. The greater the degree of such uncertainty of coordination, the more administrators are needed to devote their energies to dealing with keeping the coordination of activities going.

Perrow (1967) earlier formulated the difference between these two types of uncertainty as whether there are many exceptions to routine in carrying out tasks and whether a regular search procedure is available when exceptions occur. The latter refers us to the realm of macro coordination, searching for solutions elsewhere to problems that crop up in a particular place. Note that the two forms of uncertainty are empirically distinct. A scientific research laboratory may have a high degree of uncertainty in its individual tasks; yet the experiments each member is carrying out depend very little on experiments elsewhere in the organization, as there is no need for materials or information to flow from one to another. Hence higher-level administration may be merely a routine, pooled-production bureaucracy, softening out to an informal structure at the operating level. Where intercoordination uncertainties and micro-activity uncertainties are both high, however (for instance, putting together many innovative parts into an aerospace vehicle, see Perrow, 1984: 258–81) the tasks of administrators multiply (and may be relatively insoluable).

(3) *Tight versus loose coupling* refers to the extent to which activities follow invariably in an inalterable sequence, usually under strict time pressures. Tightly coupled systems, such as many chemical refining processes, as well as hydoelectric dams, usually have only one route for achieving a goal, and each activity must fit into the sequence at the right time. Loosely coupled systems, on the other hand, allow delays and can change the order of sequences without harm, as in the pooled activities of many government agencies.

It is the combination of these three dimensions of activities that determines the shape of the organization structure. Organizations with tight coupling and low coordination uncertainties can afford to have a highly centralized structure, with a few administrators controlling all activities under rigid routines (Perrow 1984: 331– 32). Continuous-flow process production fits this type when the machinery itself guarantees a smooth coordination of activities; so do railroads, where the main problem of keeping up the tight coupling (one train has to get off the track to make way for the next one) is to keep on schedule. At the other extreme, organizations with complex and unexpected interactions, together with loose coupling, must be decentralized: local administrators have the authority to negotiate unexpected relationships; while the loose coupling relieves them of pressure to fit the whole structure together rigidly.

The other two combinations are more problematic. Loosely coupled organizations with routine, uncomplex activities can be either centralized or not, Perrow says, depending on the tastes of organizational elites. A rigid centralization will work, since everything is routine anyway; and indeed this is the structure typically found in single-purpose (pooled production) governmental agencies (licensing bureaus, and so on). Some such organizations, though, are decentralized, as in school systems that give much autonomy to local officials. The difference seems to be in the control resources, rather than in functional needs of carrying out the tasks.

The combination of complex coordination uncertainties and tight coupling, however, is potentially a disaster. Centralization is desirable as a way of keeping up the coordination necessary for the tight coupling; but the complex nature of interactions among organizational components means that when something goes wrong, it is very difficult for a remote hierarchy to respond to it. These contradictory pressures result in elements in both centralization and decentralization: such organizations may vacillate between these poles in successive "reforms"; an informal structure tends to emerge which acts as decentralized power because of the inability of the formal structure to handle emergencies.

STRUCTURE AND CONTROL

The structural theories laid out by Woodward, Thompson, Chandler, and Perrow are all couched in functional terms: the coordination needs and difficulties arise directly out of the tasks being carried out. What is left out is the control structure. But the administrative hierarchy is not merely coordinating tasks; it is also controlling people. At the lowest level, supervisors are engaged less in task coordination (aggregating micro tasks into macro sequences) than in making sure people do their work. The amount of macro coordinating increases as one ascends the hierarchy; but from the point of view of their own superiors, the coordinators themselves need to be controlled. At the same time, subordinates at every level have some control resources to use against their own superiors. Organizational politics involves a mixture of task activities and the struggle over control.

As we have seen, what types of controls are used depends on both the tasks that are being attempted and the control resources that are available. Certain kinds of tasks can be carried out most effectively with certain kind of controls; if cruder or more alienating controls are used, the organization will pay the price (which, however, its controllers may be willing to pay). Having chosen certain control techniques, certain structural contingencies follow. If coercion is used, the organization will have to have large numbers of supervisory personnel—guards wielding the threat of force—whose activites themselves have to be overseen. And since guards are not directly involved in the coordination activities of the organization, and typically have little chance of promotion, the higher authority has to deal with a relatively unmotivated and easily corruptable group of lower controllers. In short, the control structure at the lowest level calls for a secondary control structure at the next level, with similar issues at each level. An organization using coercive threat throughout the control hierarchy (as in a military dictatorship) lives in constant danger of alienating the armed controllers themselves, and hence tends to focus heavily on simply maintaining power.

Control by rewards, the most common form in modern organizations, requires an additional administrative structure in the form of record keepers and payroll administrators. Incentives and concessions made in the form of additional benefits (medical, vacation, retirement) bring with them the expansion of personnel departments and a flow of paperwork to line administrators. Material rewards thus inevitably expand the routinized bureaucracy of an organization.

Normative control takes many forms, not all of them very effective. But organizations may create extensive departments specializing in employee relations, socialization, educational indoctrination, and reviewing qualitifications. Universities, which rely heavily on normative control (along with a bureaucratic reward structure) are permeated with committees to examine personnel qualifications for an elaborate hierarchy of promotions. Administration in some normative organizations thus may be given over almost entirely to control activities, since most of the "productive" activities are left to the control of the participants themselves, and little coordination among micro activities is needed.

The growth of the higher levels of organization structure, then, is not merely a matter of what micro tasks need to be coordinated into sequences. The nature of the controls being used at the lowest levels ramify into yet another component to the administrative hierarchy, whether it specializes in control activities, or whether it is combined with the activity of coordinating administrators. (The latter is more usually the case; though some hypersensitive control systems, such as within the Soviet Union, use a dual hierarchy: Communist Party members are used strictly for control purposes, paralleling the formal line authorities whose duties are mainly the purely functional coordination.) Furthermore, the functional activities of coordination are themselves positions of power, and lower individuals are rewarded or punished in the process of having their activities regulated. Issues of what are appropriate policies for the goals of the organization become entwined with issues of the career advancement of individuals; the administrative coordination structure becomes permeated by the motivations of personnel seeking advancement for themselves, promoting their allies, and deliberately or undeliberately acting against the power interests and career prospects of other factions.

For this reason, the efficiency of administrators is hard to judge. The output of their section of the organization is the result of the work of many persons, and the precise contributions of individuals is often hard to measure, especially as one moves away from the immediate micro focus of productive activities. Numerous contingenices of coordination, including much chance, determines whether an organization or department will prosper or languish. Moreover, in many organizational types it is difficult even hypothetically to set forth in advance a blueprint for what the organization and its managers ought to be achieving. In organizations where activities are loosely coupled and/or highly routine, measurements of expected performances are not difficult; but as organizations move toward the other ends of those continua, the uncertainties mount. But at least here we are in the functional realm, where there are clear and specified goals for organizational output.

When we enter the realm of controls, even this criterion disappears. An organizational struggle over control becomes purely political. The amount of time and energy taken to exercise control depends on the coalitions involved in the fight and the resources they have available. Where conflict groups are well mobilized on each side, a conflict may go on at very great length with few discernable results for either side. Thus political conflicts within management, or between management and workers, can take up a disproportionate amount of energy, without yielding any output for the organization; but since these are the organizational controllers themselves who are fighting for their own most immediate positions, the battle is sufficiently motivating to absorb their attention. (Takeover battles over corporate management are merely the most visible and highly publicized form of this typical organizational behavior.) For this reason, a purely functional view of organizations cannot capture the main activities on which members spend their time.

Within this situation, what I have called the "sinecure structure," the struggle over "positional property" (Chapter 5) can flourish. It is not "dysfunctional" because all organizations do it, hence there is little competitive pressure from organizations which do not waste their time on organizational politics. This internal struggle within organizations is the most important modern form of the class struggle.

In formal theoretical terms, organizational politics itself is an activity with a high degree of task uncertainty. It generates an informal structure, relying heavily on covert information control. This in turn further serves to complicate the coordination structure at the management level. Higher-level administrators are forced to deal with an increasingly difficult organizational environment just below them, which tends to call forth a structural need for yet more administrators at that level. But adding more administrators adds more personnel to the control game. There is a circular relationship between growth of coordination and control personnel and growth of coordination and control problems. Eventually, sophisticated managers arrive at Barnard's (1938) conclusion: the structure of the organization is indeed a political environment, and efforts to control it in detail must be given up. Only in this way can they bring the tendencies toward administrative expansion to a halt.

DERIVATION OF WOODWARD'S ORGANIZATIONAL TYPES FROM CONTROL THEORY

Woodward's organizational types follow from the application of more fundamental theory of organizational controls, together with Perrow's contingency theory of macro structure of coordination. *Unit production* is characterized by unique or innovative products. Hence workers have a good deal of autonomy on the micro level and much covert power (via information control). Nonalienating normative controls are needed, especially since workers and managers have a good deal of covert power over each other's ability to carry out their tasks. Formal hierarchy and bureaucratic procedures are deemphasized, while mutual consultation is prominent.[11]

Mass production or mass-assembly typically has predictable and standardized products for its separate micro-level activities. Hence controls are by material rewards and efficiency criterion (measuring outcomes), necessitating much record keeping. Record keeping is also called for by coordination needs, since many disparate activities must be assembled. The sheer number of activities to be coordinated tends to make for complexity at Perrow's second level, hence calling for an elaborate administrative hierarchy to do the coordinating. At this level, however, managers have much covert power over each other, due to reciprocal coordination, especially where the structure is loosely coupled (many alternative ways of carrying out sequences). This results in an informal bargaining structure among managers. Formal and informal structures of control are both called for, but conflict with each other.

Process production has a high degree of predictability of micro-level activities as well as of coordination among activities. The machinery itself links processes together, serving as a means of environmental control. Personal methods of control are reduced. Material rewards and record keeping are the principal controls. Since coordination needs are low, these organizations generally are smoothly operating bureaucracies. Perrow (1984) points out, however, when breakdowns occur in such systems, because they are tightly coupled, the whole system is likely to be out of order. Power devolves on the few individuals who repair the bottlenecks in the system, as Crozier (1964) observed in a very routine French factory manufacturing matches.[12]

Pooled production has highly standardized and predictable operations at the micro-activity level and few coordination needs. Material rewards, strict record keeping, and highly bureaucratic procedures will suffice for control at both worker and manager levels. Coordination is similarly bureaucratic, since it consists only of vertical communications between the central pool and local operating units. Such organizations tend to be slow, impersonal, perhaps maddening for individuals who are in a hurry or who have unique requirements, but highly predictable and hence efficient for slow-paced tasks.

---

[11] This explanation concentrates on the first of Perrow's two levels of uncertainty, the micro level of activities. A shallow control structure supposes that the second level of uncertainty, the degree of coordination among diverse activities, is also low. We can envision various possibilities: there may be few separate activities that need to be coordinated, in which case little higher management is called for (for example, a traditional craft like a tailor shop). There may be numerous such activities, but coordination among them is easy, in which case the higher structure can be bureaucratic (for instance, a set of scientific laboratories). Finally, there is the case where many activities have to be coordinated, and the coordination among them is idiosyncratic, resulting in many managers but operating informally (for example, in movie production).

[12] A process-production organization may operate in a very different mode, however, at times when a new production process is being installed, as when an oil refinery is actually building its rigs. In this case, unit production relationships are more likely to prevail, as is typical in the construction industry (Stinchcombe, 1959). Process production firms thus may have a dual structure, depending on how often innovation occurs. Highly traditionalistic process production, such as that observed by Crozier, will have the most extreme form.

ORGANIZATIONAL STRUCTURES AS IDEAL TYPES

Any organization is usually a mixture of different structures. We have already seen that any single control mechanism is rarely used in isolation, and different parts of the same organization (notably the operating personnel and the administrative personnel) tend to be controlled in different ways. Furthermore, an organization may have different task and technology types in different parts. The personnel department of a mass-production firm will nevertheless internally have the structure of pooled production. Unit-production organizations, if they are very large (for instance a movie company, a scientific laboratory) will likely have a bureaucratic, perhaps pooled-production component. A university tends to be a combination of a series of unit-production suborganizations at the level of faculty research, with a routine pooled-production structure at the level of undergraduate teaching. Some highly routinized organizations may have subdivisions which have an idiosyncratic unit-production structure (such as computer divisions within a state bureaucracy: Meyer, 1968). Hospitals often have a structure combining mass production (in which the patients are the raw materials, being moved around through a complex set of technologies), with unit production at the level of the doctors and pooled production in many administrative forms.

In general, any organization is amenable to analysis in terms of theory of control and structure. Organization theory is very powerful in its application, since it gives the specific conditions for people's behavior (the control struggle) and their patterned interrelationships (structure) and in a flexible manner that can do justice to the variety of situations that make up the real social world.

ORGANIZATIONS AND ENVIRONMENTS

In the foregoing, we have attended mainly to the internal structures and control processes of organizations. Organizational environments have entered in principally as seen from the point of view of organizational participants, as posing tasks with varying degrees of uncertainty. In recent years, organizational theorists have focused much of their attention on the environment, either as it affects organizations "from the outside in" or seeing the environment itself as a population made up of organizations.

RESOURCE DEPENDENCY

In order to survive, any organization needs resources, which it may not be able to supply for itself. These include raw materials, people as new recruits, information, and money. Furthermore, organizations are frequently controlled by an outside source, such as owners, a board of investors, banks, or in the case of governmental and nonprofit agencies and organizations, by trustees or higher government authorities. The theory thus emerged that organizations are shaped by the crucial inputs from their environments. The hypothesis of "environmental isomorphism" says that an organization comes to mirror its environment; if the environment is highly differentiated and volatile, the organization must be internally complex in order to interface with these different aspects of the outside world (Lawrence and Lorsch, 1967). From the point of view of neo-rationalist models, it is argued that organizations develop permanent ties with other organizations in order to reduce uncertainty, information costs, and opportunistic behavior by their partners. In general, organizations adapt to changing environments (Pfeffer and Salancik, 1978; Pfeffer, 1982). The question is, how is this relationship best explained?

THE POPULATION ECOLOGY OF ORGANIZATIONS

The ecological model (Hannan and Freeman, 1977; Aldrich, 1979) is a variant of evolutionary biology. It argues that organizations are selected according to their ability to adapt to different environments. We may note that this is a version of the evolutionary model treated in Chapter 1. Variation (generally of an unknown source) results in natural selection as ill-adapted organizations die out and well-adapted ones survive. Why are not all organizations the same? The answer is that the diversity of organizations mirrors the diversity of environments to which they have adapted. That is, organizations exist in various "niches" in the environment.

The principal dimension of organizations examined by this theory is the structural difference between *generalists* and *specialists*. Generalists are organizations which draw upon a variety of resources and which produce a variety of products for exchange with their environmental sources. A business which produces many products for different markets is of this type. It is analogous to "advanced" biological organisms (such as the higher mammals) which are capable of changing their mode of feeding and sheltering themselves as environmental conditions change. A generalist organization has the ability to ride out fluctuations in any particular source of environmental resources, since it can substitute other sources. Specialist organizations, on the other hand, adapt more exactly to a particular environment: a business making a single product, a restaurant appealing to a particular ethnic cuisine. These organizations are more vulnerable to changing resource flows. They are analogous to biological species which developed very precise mechanisms for feeding or reproduction and which survived only as long as certain environmental conditions existed.

Which types of organizations will exist depends on the characteristics of the environment. Where environments are stable, selection favors specialism. Where environments are unstable, there are two further possibilities, depending on the uncertainty and rapidity of the changes. Rapid, short and highly uncertain changes (labelled a "fine-grained" environment) favor specialist organizations, mainly because generalists under these conditions have to carry too much costly overhead. Occasional, long-lasting changes ("coarse-grained" environments) favor generalist organizations. These arguments are derived from mathematical equations borrowed from population biology. Empirical applications have been made, usually to small organizations which exist in large numbers, whose dates of birth and death can be easily charted (for instance, restaurants, newspapers). The empirical curves can usually be fitted fairly well to the theoretical equations.

In a particular example, Carroll (1985) considers the "niche width" of newspapers. Generalist newspapers are those which attempt to appeal to all parts of the audience spectrum; specialists are those which focus on a particular occupational, ethnic, religious, ideological, or local community group. For all newspapers, big organizations have an advantage over smaller ones, because economies of scale in printing and advertising enable big newspapers to bring a much greater economic return for their costs than small newspapers. (Costs of editorial staff and printing remain about the same, whether circulation is small or large.) But newspapers can become big only by being generalists, the major daily newspaper in the area. There is room for few generalists, and their large resources enable them to engage their competitors in circulation wars, which result in the death of most competitors and the survivial of one or a very few generalists. But generalists appeal mainly to the middle of the audience spectrum and ignore the more specialized audiences. Hence specialist newspapers (local subcommunity papers, occupational, ethnic, ideological specialists) of small circulation spring up, benefitting from the death of most of the generalists. The concentration of circulation among the generalists results in a high death rate of generalist organizations and a low death rate of specialist organizations. The image is something like exotic mushrooms spring up on the decaying logs of huge trees squeezed out by a few giants.

Despite its appeal, there are several limitations of the population ecology model of organizations. It has little explicit causality in its theory. It does not tell us much about the conditions under which organizational forms are innovated, but only whether they will survive. Its dependent variable, organizational structure, is a limited typology of generalist and specialist forms, which does not capture much of the structural types that characterize organizations. It deals mainly with small organizations, because it is here that birth and death rates are easiest to observe; yet large organizations, especially states and business corporations, are the major realities of the modern world. Moreover, since these large organizations often dominate and shape their own environments, it is dubious to say that they are responding to environmental conditions. Finally, the population ecology approach shares the weaknesses of evolutionary theory generally (Chapter 1). It implies too easily that organizations are optimally adapted and hence take the best form that they can, on pain of extinction; yet organizations in fact may be highly inefficient, but survive because of their monopoly of control resources. The population ecology model is too much like an idealized laissez-faire view of the capitalist economy, in which small competitors prosper merely because of their ability to adapt to the market. The success of some organizations, however, can destroy the ability of other organizations to form at all. This is not always the case, as Carroll's analysis of newspapers shows; but it cannot be assumed that optimally open capitalist competition always exists. The very conditions for an ecological competition model are themselves variable and need to be explained.

ORGANIZATIONAL BOUNDARIES

Recent concern for organizational environments is to some extent due to the belief that organizations cannot be considered in isolation, that a purely internal focus misses too much of what is important and determinative. Nevertheless, analysis which deals with a population of discrete organizations is itself weak on a crucial aspect of organizations. How do we know exactly what one organization is? Boundaries are often vague, and what is picked out as a separate organization is often done for the convenience of the analyst. For example, government agencies can be regarded as subparts of one large employer, the state; or a single agency or subagency (or in the case of the massive federal bureaucracy, as sub-subagency) can be taken as a separate unit. In the realm of business organizations, too, organizations frequently do not die when they disappear as legal entities, but merely become a subunit in a conglomerate.

This problem is disturbing only if we place a great deal of analytical emphasis on organizations as bounded units. This is particularly likely in a theoretical perspective like functionalism (or organicist analogies generally), which stress the boundary-maintaining and goal-directed quality of social units. But in fact it is highly unlikely that organizations really do have these qualities. Organizational goals, as we have seen, tend to shift as the result of power struggles; and just what is believed to be the goal of the organization depends on which participant one asks. It is sometimes argued that a discrete organization can be defined as one that has a comprehensive list of all members and a clear social identity and purpose. But many voluntary associations lack clear identification of all members, especially those with varying degrees of participation; even in formal, property-based organizations, there can be ambiguity (such as whether outside consultants and network contacts should be regarded as members or not). To define organizations by a visible public identity is too restrictive, since it leaves out "invisible" organizations such as professions or scientific disciplines.

I would argue that *organization theory does not depend on identification of strict organizational boundaries*. Principles of control and structure apply to more complex entities as well as simple and bounded ones. Much of what is most interesting about organizations is in these unbounded areas.

PROFESSIONS AS ORGANIZATIONS   An example is the application of organization theory to the professions. A profession, in the sociological sense of the term, is an occupational group which has acquired an organizational structure of its own, independently of whatever other organizations its members happen to work in. Scientists in a university or in commercial laboratories are not merely employees subject to hierarchic authority; they are also (and usually preeminently) members of their own disciplinary specialty. They are less oriented vertically toward the local organization than horizontally toward their profession: they spend much of their time in horizontal communication with other specialists elsewhere; their careers depend largely on the reputation they get within the specialist group and on the recommendations their peers give for each other, including for hiring and promotion in their local organizations. Medical doctors, and to a lesser degree nurses, cross-cut the hierarchic organization of a hospital with their horizontal professional ties. Lawyers, dentists, architects, and engineers, in varying degrees, all have horizontal ties to peer groups which give referrals and recommendations. The most strongly organized professions are those in which the peer group not only staffs its own training institutes, but has acquired the power as gatekeeper for entry into monopolistic licensing, enforced by the state, for exercise of that occupation (Wilensky, 1964).

Professions are an example of how organizational boundaries are permeated by other organizations. This condition itself is explicable by organization theory. The occupations which are most successful at attaining this horizontal, professional structure are those whose activities involve the highest degree of uncertainty: they deal with areas of creativity (scientific research), or anxiety-charged bodily ailments (medicine), or complex conflicts and negotiations (law). According to the *theory of tasks and control forms,* (pages 462–64) hierarchic controls are difficult in these circumstances; employers of these services need to rely on normative control (as well as, usually, large material rewards) and hence to give considerable autonomy to practitioners. This very high degree of power by practitioners, and uncertainty about their outcomes, creates the potential for considerable distrust among clients and employers. How can they evaluate whether their services in these areas of uncertainty are as good as can be expected? The practitioners put up a united front in the face of this distrust, undertaking collectively to guarantee the validity of individual practitioners. These experts have power over each other, as they are best qualified to judge the extent of the skill applied by any of them. Professionals thus rely on their network of peers for validation of their work. This is how scientific research results and theories become certified as "knowledge" for the outside world, and how doctors and lawyers acquire their reputations and hence referrals for clients.

In organizational theory, then, professions are occupations which have the highest degree of autonomy and power in the exercise of their tasks. In principle, they are merely another kind of worker (some of them, such as surgeons, are actually performing manual labor), and their tasks do not intrinsically involve line authority (coordination and control of others). This is what pushes them toward a horizontal form of organization. In some respects, a strong profession is like a trade union, but going far beyond it, usually, in the degree of control it achieves over work conditions, pay, and monopolization of job entry. This is because the task uncertainty is at an extreme level, making employers and clients concede normative controls as the primary relationship with professionals. This same demand for normative legitimation is what gives the horizontal group such power over individual practitioners.[13]

INTERORGANIZATIONAL RELATIONS AS A SUPERORGANIZATION

It is possible, then, for organizations to permeate other organizations, as well as to be linked together in organizational sets, pyramided into larger units, and connected in other ways. The environment of an organization usually consists, to a large extent, of other organizations. This is particularly true of businesses which are buying and selling (as well as competing and engaging in collusion) with other businesses and of governmental units, whose environment is other agencies, organized political groups, or private organizations that they regulate.

---

[13] The profession which has been most elaborately analyzed as an invisible organzation is science, or rather the variety of different intellectual communities which make up the sciences. In an earlier work (Collins, 1975: 470–523) I proposed that the degree of *task uncertainty* in intellectual research, combined with the degree of *coordination problems* among intellectuals (in getting resources for their research, and for getting recognition for what they produce), and the availability of *communication resources* result in intellectual communities which are similar to informal crafts organizations, personalistic communities, regularized bureaucracies, conflictual bureaucracies, petty intellectual autocracies, or feudal systems. Whitley (1985) gives a more elaborate version of this organizational approach, documented by many studies in the sociology of science.

The question of boundaries turns out to be a trivial one. A linked set of organizations may itself be analyzed as if it were a single organization. Principles of control theory and structure theory work just as well as within a well-bounded unit. We have already seen that a single organization may be the site of conflicts over control, with various resources used by numerous participants interested in their own autonomy, power, and material rewards. The same perspective transfers naturally to units relating to each other externally or quasi-externally.

Perrow (1984) demonstrates this neatly in his theory of organizational structures. Recall that he derives this from the two dimensions of *complex versus linear (predictable) interactions,* and *tight versus loose coupling.* Entire "systems" of organizations can be characterized in the same way: for example, the system of interdependence in marine transport becomes quite tightly coupled when ships are in a narrow river or channel (though with only moderate complexity); an airway system contains many organizations channeled through airports, resulting in similar coupling problems. The very fact that there are numerous organizations operating in such a system is one of the factors contributing to its coordination problems (its complexity). The more elaborate view of structure, given previously, which incorporates various kinds of technologies and techniques of control, should then apply to explaining the shape of relationships among any set of organizations that operate in proximity.

CAPITALISM AND SOCIALISM AS SUPERORGANIZATIONS

As a brief example, let us consider the political economy of capitalism and socialism as superorganizations.

(1) Capitalism decentralizes the economy to the extent of separating governmental from private business organizations. (That is to say, coercive political power and property are independent control resources upon which organizations can be built.) The dominant form of control in the private sector is material rewards. This applies to relations among organizations as well as within them: the profit motive is given prominence as the incentive to deliver goods and services. This has the same effect on interorganizational relations as it does on control of workers: compliance is utilitarian and extrinsic; concern is with material profits rather than quality of products, ideals of safety, comfort, environmental protection and beauty, or ethical principles. Material controls among organizations work only to the extent that they are monitored.

Of course, no organizations can operate entirely by material rewards. Within capitalist organizations, various technological and power conditions force the owners to use other forms of control, making concessions to occupations which control areas of uncertainty and using normative control upon its own managers. But the predominant form of normative control is not egalitarian participation and rituals, but individualistic incentives in the form of exercising power and offering promotion opportunities. The emphasis is still largely upon individualism and competition; although some normative atmosphere emerges among groups of managers, it is simultaneously undermined by the competition among them. Similarly, personal ties are useful for bargaining among business organizations, especially for support from financial institutions. But as long as the system remains capitalist, these normative elements are subservient to the predominant material control, the search for profits.

The structure of capitalist organization as a whole can be analyzed in terms of administrative devices for interorganizational control, and of Perrow's dimensions of complexity and coupling. Because there is no centralized unit dominating the network of business organizations, coordination is not done by formal rules. Environmental control is not generally available between organizations, nor is there much close surveillance. The main forms of administrative connection are via the efficiency criterion, checking outcomes—the main form of capitalist control; all else is forgiven for the profit line. Information control is the main covert source of interorganizational power, primarily as it flows through the financial system of investments.[14]

The relationships among capitalist organizations can no doubt be characterized in terms of the degrees of interdependence, the complexity and predictability of these connections, and the tightness or looseness of the coupling. This has not yet been attempted. It is probably the case that these structural connections vary from one local sector of the economy to another and from one historical period to another over time. One possible theoretical payoff is that the tendency of capitalism to go through business cycles of boom and depression, with points of serious crisis, may eventually be accounted for by organizational theory. Perrow (1984) points out that systems which have both high complexity (multiple, unpredictable linkages) and tight coupling are subject to what he calls "system accidents," accidents which are "normal" for that kind of system, even though they may be catastrophic for persons (and organizations) involved in them. I would suggest that capitalist crises are interorganizational crises of this sort, in which the failure of certain crucially situated organizations (perhaps in the financial sector) can ramify unpredictably through the network of other businesses. Looser coupling of the economic system perhaps would solve or at least localize such disruptions.

Along these lines, we might be able to construct a theory which explained the cyclical nature of capitalism, with its periodic booms and busts. This might look like the process described in Figure 13-3.

The phase of business expansion begins with entrepreneurs, setting up new organizations, putting new products on the market, and increasing output. The increasing number of organizations is a shift toward decentralization in the whole economy—a move toward looser coupling. This constitutes the up-cycle. However, the new products and organzations in the system increase the overall level of complexity, since many more interrelationships are now possible; and the new organizations bring about increased competition, which causes some of them to go bankrupt, while others (the more successful) tend to become the targets of financial takeovers. The number of organizations goes down again, and this consolidation results in a shift toward tighter coupling in the system, which together with the increase in complexity sets the stage for a "system accident"—a business crisis set off by the unforseen ramifications of minor hitches at various points in the network.

---

[14] Notice that I have not characterized capitalism in terms of a *market* for material rewards. The degree to which capitalism is marketlike is a variable. The openly competitive market is restricted precisely by the existence of interorganizational linkages, including oligopoly and various kinds of patterned networks (for example, the noncompetitive niches described by Harrison White's theory in Chapter 12). The theory of material rewards, its causes and consequences, does not require us to drag in the whole apparatus of conventional market economics.

FIGURE 13-3

CAPITALISM AS A SUPERORGANIZATION

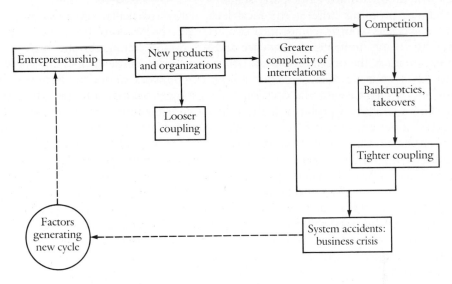

As in most theories of business cycles, it is easier to explain how the upswings give rise to forces which lead to an eventual crisis, than it is to explain how the downswing period eventually bottoms out and starts upward again. This does empirically seem to happen, although I have no mechanism to propose here from organizational theory. This part of the model in Figure 13-3 is obviously incomplete; I recommend it to the attention of future theorists.

(2) Socialism as ideally depicted is one large, coordinated organization, owned and controlled by the entire people who harmoniously plan all economic activities. The ideal is normative control substituting for control by material incentives (property) or by coercion (governmental power). Socialist theorists, however, have given little thought to organizational realities of how such normative control is to be instituted. Of the two major ways of generating normative control, socialism in principle is opposed to the hierarchic method (power participation and promotion opportunities) because these involve inequality and apply to only an elite portion of the populace. Equality and ritual activity are the favored means. But these run into several difficulties. Rituals encompassing the entire population are hard to carry out for large societies, and in any case do not motivate specialized work activities well. Equality tends to be undermined by the Michelsian Iron Law of Oligarchy; although the entire state and economy is supposed to be democratically controlled from below, large size results in delegation of authority to leaders, who in turn are able to exercise power through their control of administrative resources (Michels, 1911/1949).

The problem is particularly acute where the single-party state monopolizes all administrative resources, preventing oppositional movements from mobilizing. Moreover, socialist states which were formed by a revolutionary struggle seem to be organizationally inclined toward just this structure. The revolutionary conflict itself generated a period of emotional solidarity, leading to the belief that the new society could be founded purely on normative control. And the ritual apparatus of maintaining normative solidarity (such as the cult of the leader described in Chapter 12) leads structurally toward a one-party state.

Similar problems arise at the local level within particular organizations. The ideal of workers' control comes into conflict with the necessity for a coordinating hierarchy arising from interdependence and scheduling among various micro tasks. In this situation, the organization can either pay a price for democracy, by allowing decisions to be made collectively but slowly; or else workers' control becomes ritualistic and *pro forma,* with real decision-making power belonging to the administrators. There is again a problem at the level of coordinating various organizations. Workers' control has greatest reality where workers have an economic stake in their own factory or other productive organization. But this control is undermined to the extent that interorganizational relations are determined by a centralized plan. The alternative is collective ownership among workers at a plant, but competitive capitalist relations among organizations.

The reality tends to be that interorganizational coordination in socialist systems is done from above by the power of the state. In its most negative form, this is control by coercive threat, which has been evident in most periods in the Soviet regimes of the twentieth century. In principle, state power need not be organized so dictatorially on the political level. Some mixed socialist-capitalist states exist, such as the Scandinavian democracies; and there is an element of socialist planning in most capitalist states today, although not called by that name. But the difference here is precisely the dispersion of organizational resources for political participation, which prevents government dictatorship by a single faction.

Coercion is the state's easiest resource, and normative control is hard to establish. Perhaps it is a recognition of this pattern that has motivated some Soviet-bloc theorists (for instance, Brucan, 1985) to suggest that the material incentives of the market are the path to workers' democracy, replacing the authoritarian abuses of the state. (In effect, this is workers' capitalism.) But whatever control sanctions the state uses, the centralized form of socialism emphasizes certain administrative control devices. Control is above all by rules and directives, elaborated in the form of plans and production quotas for each organization. There is an effort to foresee the contingencies relating organizations to each other and to plan in advance how these are to be met. The control structure is thus highly bureaucratic. Given that technological linkages may often involve many areas of uncertainties, more decentralized authority would be more efficient in many cases. The high level of bureaucratization, especially when combined with coercive sanctions in Soviet states, leads to considerable alienation, fostering an informal structure which attempts to make up for deficiencies of coordination arising from rigid plans imposed from above. The situation is further complicated by the existence of a dual control hierarchy, with Communist Party members assigned in a parallel structure to watch over administrative line personnel.[15] Overall, the centralized version of socialism tends to resemble the most extreme form of Woodward's mass-production and mass-assembly organiza-

---

[15] This is a concrete embodiment of the analytical distinction made previously, between the organizational hierarchy as coordinating tasks and as controlling the controllers.

tion, where bureaucratic centralization and informal decentralization are locked in continuous conflict.[16]

It would appear, from the detached vantage point of organization theory, that neither capitalism nor socialism approaches very closely to an ideally functioning superorganization. A more realistic conclusion is that very large structures with complex interdependencies are inherently inefficient. There are bound to be conflicts in either one of them, as well as many opportunities for factions to seize disproportionate power, wealth, or honor. Large-scale superorganizations, at least as manifested so far, show no signs of approaching utopia. It remains to be seen if particular variants of technologies and tasks could give rise to structures which are more efficient and/or more democratic. Quite possibly we may have to take our choice between incompatible goals.

SUMMARY

1. Control in organizations can be carried out by three kinds of sanctions: *Coercive control* results in resistance, avoidance, or minimal and alienated compliance. *Control by material rewards* (remunerative control) leads to compliance in only those activities which are directly rewarded and to a struggle over the terms of reward. *Normative or internalized control* results in self-motivated compliance: this can be achieved primarily by giving power or chances of promotion or by ritual participation.

2. Control can be administered by the following devices: (1) *surveillance* results in compliance on tasks which are directly observable and in an atmosphere of petty deference rituals. (2) *Inspecting outcomes* focuses on the most easily measured products or activities and results in a depersonalized, record-keeping orientation. (3) *Rules and written orders* result in impersonality, slowness and low adaptability. This type of bureaucratic control tends to follow from struggles over democratization and other power struggles; it promotes an informal, rule-evading structure alongside the formal structure. (4) *Information control* gives covert power to those who have the resources to define reality to others in the organization, particularly in areas of crucial uncertainties. (5) *Environmental control* confines behavior by the physical setting; when this is available, it can substitute for other forms of control.

3. An organization exists as an enduring structure only as long as there are resources for control. Coercive, remunerative (material rewards), and internalized controls can each be used to generate the other types of control resources. Organizations become relatively permanent to the extent that they acquire property, which can be used as a basis for remunerative control. Organizational managers or "lead-

---

[16] Is there a dynamic mechanism within socialism, comparable to the crisis cycle I have sketched for the capitalist economy? The centralized bureaucratic structure of socialism avoids coordination through the market, and thus attempts to head off any dynamic which would give rise to economic "system accidents." The low level of technological innovation appears to be the price paid for this stability. It is possible, though, that we might substitute political interest groups for entrepreneurs in Figure 13-3. In this case, we would predict a political cycle in which ideological outputs and conflicts are substituted for material upswings and downswings in the business cycle.

ers" do not owe their positions primarily to their greater expertise but to their possession of instruments of control.

4. Tasks with a high degree of initiative and uncertainty tend to be carried out by the "soft" forms: internalized control and information control. Tasks with predictable and standardized outcomes can be carried out by control with material resources, administered by inspecting outcomes. Tasks with low initiative and highly visible outcomes can be carried out by coercion; but this must be administered by surveillance and environmental control and requires a large control staff. Coercive controls were widespread in traditional agrarian societies; in contemporary society, a mixture of bureaucratic and participatory forms are widespread, with no clear tendency for either to displace the other.

5. Organizational structures are related to *task technologies* in the following forms: (1) *unit production* makes a small number of unique products; it has a low hierarchy of command and a predominance of personal relationships, which can be either consultative or dictatorial. (2) *Mass production and assembly* manufactures or procures large numbers of components which must be put together into a complex product. These organizations tend to be pyramid-shaped, conflictual bureaucracies, with a struggle between informal and formal networks. (3) *Process or continuous flow* coordinates production through the production machinery itself, leaving the human organization as a highly formal bureaucracy. (4) *Pooled production* provides a pool of resources for local units, which are not horizontally coordinated; the structure is dominated by record keeping and is impersonal and slow-moving. Any particular organization may have a combination of these structural ideal types resulting from its mixture of activities.

6. Larger organizations are more impersonal and bureaucratic than smaller ones, but only within the same technological type. Beyond a certain limit, large organizations do not become more centralized but devolve into divisional or geographic centers.

7. Organizational hierarchy is a macro coordination of micro activities across time and space. The higher the *uncertainty of tasks* (at the level of micro activities), the more autonomous workers are from bureaucratic control. The higher the *uncertainty in structural connections* between micro activities, the more administrative activities are created to coordinate activities. *Tightly coupled* structures have only one route to achieve a goal, and activities must fit rigidly into a sequence. *Loosley coupled* structures have alternative routes and flexible coordination possibilities. The combination of high complexity in structural connections, and tight coupling, results in "normal accidents": breakdowns with uncontrollable ramifications throughtout the organizational system.

8. The combination of these dimensions (uncertainty and coupling) determines the shape of the organization structure. The types of control used depends on the tasks which are attempted and the control resources available to the persons struggling over control (both controllers and subordinates). Structural shape (summarized in number 5) follows from the administrative hierarchies which arise in the application of control forms to various task problems.

9. Organizational structures develop to control resources in the external environment as well as internally. Population ecology theory proposes that specialist organizations are selected when the environment is "fine-grained" (many rapid and uncertain changes); generalist organizations are selected when the environment is "coarse-grained" (relatively few and long-lasting changes). Large and powerful organizations, however, tend to shape their own environments.

10. The environment of organizations usually consists of other organizations. Boundaries of individual organizations can often be ignored, and theory of organizational control and structure can be applied to networks of organizations as well as within individual organizations. The large-scale systems of capitalism and socialism can be analyzed as "superorganizations." The dynamics of capitalism move through phases of looser and tighter coupling, with business crises as "system accidents." Socialism attempts to replace remunerative with normative sanctions, but takes on massive coordination problems which result in highly bureaucratic forms of organizational politics.

APPENDIX: THEORY AND METHODOLOGY

INTRODUCTION
    Mathematics, Statistics, and Words

A: WHAT IS STATISTICS: METHOD OR THEORY?
    Statistics and Theory Testing
    Must Hypotheses Be Tested Blindly?
    Can General Theory Be Developed if There Are Few Cases?
    Statistics as Substance: The Theory of a World of Chance
    Mathematics Is Embedded in Words

B: DEVELOPING SOCIOLOGICAL THEORY BY COMPUTER SIMULATION
    What Is Learned from Simulating Theories?
    Simulation and Empirical Data
    Additional Payoffs of Computer Simulation
    A Practical Note on How to Work with Simulation Models

INTRODUCTION

MATHEMATICS, STATISTICS, AND WORDS

The field of sociology today is rather badly split between advocates of quantitative methods and those who favor qualitative or purely verbal theory. Members of the former camp tend to dismiss the latter as "nonscientific" or merely "philosophical." Those on the other side attack their opponents as "positivists" following an outmoded vision of science and as practitioners of methods without substance. Before about 1965, the "scientific" side was the prevailing orthodoxy in American sociology, even though its methods were not yet much put into practice but were regarded as the path toward progress in the future. Technical sophistication in mathematics and statistics has greatly increased since that time, but, ironically, the weight of intellectual opinion, especially among theorists, has swung the other way. There has been the revival of Marxism, which typically condemns positivism as a symptom of our alienated capitalist society. Many of the more intellectual sociologists have been attracted to French structuralism, social phenomenology, ethnomethodology, and other sophisticated positions which are openly scornful of traditional science. Historical sociology, which is largely nonquantitative, is in a golden age, and interpretive approaches abound. As a sign of the time, Parsons (1937), whose work was purely qualitative, nevertheless claimed that his theory would eventually become a set of simultaneous differential equations; whereas Alexander (1980–83), in reviving Parsonian theory, has strongly argued that theory is an autonomous level of intellectual activity, irreducible to empirical research of any kind, and apparently immune to mathematical formalization as well.

I do not want to overstate the split, since there are mixed positions in between the extremes. But in general it is true that there is considerable hostility between what is seen as the methodological-quantitative side of the field and the theoretical-qualitative side. Moreover, practitioners of one or another specialty tend to inhabit different intellectual networks, and hence to condemn each other's position *in absentia*, without knowing much about it.

It may well be that the conflict is ineradicable, and that we will have opposing factions of this sort for a long time to come. I will confine myself here to point out several items which may help to adjudicate the conflict for those who are interested in drawing as much strength as possible from the whole range of sociology.

MATHEMATICS OR STATISTICS   What is loosely referred to as the "quantitative" side actually comprises two rather different branches. Statistics is a particular kind of mathematics, concerned with empirical research problems involved in measuring and drawing inferences from data. Statistics (and research methods more generally) is indeed often treated as if it were merely a set of technical problems having no connection to theory. I will attempt to show that this is mistaken, but the fact that statistics is often treated in a dogmatic or "cookbook" manner is one of the reasons why there is such a split between theorists and statistical researchers. Moreover, a

494

narrow application of statistical methods ruled out the qualitative research, whether micro situational or macro historical, which has been favored by many theoretically oriented sociologists.

Mathematical sociology, on the other hand, is actually on the theory side. It attempts to state general principles which model social reality; in other words, it is doing the same thing that substantive theorists do, except that it puts its propositions into symbols and equations which can be manipulated to draw out inferences according to established methods of mathematical reasoning. Qualitative sociologists have sometimes objected to mathematical theories, too, but for different reasons than their criticisms of statistics. Particular mathematical models may be too abstract to capture the nuances and complexities of the real world, or the theories that mathematical sociologists have worked with may not have been very well chosen in the first place. On a less profound level, although an important practical obstacle, is the problem that mathematical models often require a great deal of memorizing of symbolism, or familiarity with the conventions of mathematics, and hence are obscure to the eyes of anyone but an in-group of highly trained practitioners.

These criticisms of mathematical theories are often valid. But this does not mean that mathematical models can be dismissed as "atheoretical" or of no importance. It remains to be seen just what they can contribute (see the summary by Fararo [1984] as well as other papers in that special issue of the *Journal of Mathematical Sociology*). It is still a relevant issue *to what extent* sociology should or will become mathematical, on the theoretical level. On the one hand, it is argued that any substantive theory—that is, one that tells us what sorts of processes are operating in the world, producing what sorts of structures or outcomes—has an underlying form which is ultimately mathematical. Even if the theory is expressed in words, its causal or structural properties are just the framework that mathematics is capable of modeling. I think this is true, up to an point. But there are two limitations: given the complex nature of the social world, it usually does not work well to try to generate a mathematical model right at the outset; our qualitative, verbal formulations are better suited to getting a hold on the main outlines of what we are dealing with. Mathematical refinements come later, in areas which are "past the frontier." The second limitation I believe is intrinsic: mathematics itself is embedded in words, and hence is always dependent upon a larger world of verbal meaning, even while we are using mathematics. For this reason, we will always have verbal theory, although the amount (and success) of mathematical theory may grow.

We have, then, several different points of our spectrum: purely verbal theory, mathematical theory, and statistical research methods. Right now, these are largely separate areas of sociology. But it is possible for them to be brought closer together, or for items to shift between one or the other. Much of verbal theory could become mathematical, although there is a basic level of verbal theory which I believe will always remain crucial. Moreover, the very success of mathematical theory can stimulate verbal theory (Heckathorn, 1984: 307) by fostering further theoretical reflections upon it. I will also argue that statistical methods are really hidden theories: models of what the world is like, against which we test other theories. Finally, I will suggest how computer simulations may provide a middle ground which can combine the strengths and overcome some of the limitations of purely verbal or mathematical theories.

APPENDIX A: WHAT IS STATISTICS:
METHOD OR THEORY?

Statistics is widely regarded as a method, a way of describing relationships and testing theories, not of formulating them. A statistical test compares some given distribution, which a scholar would like to interpret as resulting from some particular cause, against the range of distributions that could be regarded as produced by chance. Only if the null hypothesis is rejected (that is, it is considered highly unlikely that the observed distribution is the result of chance) is the substantive theory accepted. In other instances, a researcher compares the strength of the relationships in various models against each other. For such a test to be valid, the sample must be drawn in such a way as to avoid contamination by some systematic bias in drawing data, by preknowledge on the part of the theorist, and so on. In short, statisticians aim at a kind of untouched-by-human-hands mechanism by which theories can be "neutrally" tested against an objective world.

Such a procedure focuses attention upon the substantive theory that is being tested and makes it seem as if it were the only theory under consideration. But there is also another theory implicitly present: the theory that, in fact, certain distributions are produced by chance.

What, then, is "chance"? Generally we regard chance as merely a negative category, the absence of any determination. Commonly, when we cannot assign a reason for something happening, we describe it as happening by sheer accident, or chance. This is more or less the same thing as "plain dumb luck," which (unless you are a gambler or other superstitious person) we resist any efforts to personify or otherwise reduce to anything beyond a blind nullity.

But a moment's reflection suggests that chance is not indeterminate at all. It is sheer "accident," we would say, if a rock fell off a roof-top and hit you on the head. It could have fallen at any time; it could have hit a thousand other spots on the ground around you, and so forth. Hence we tend to say (somewhat vaguely and picturesquely) "the chances against that happening are about a million to one." But in fact the fall of the rock can be analyzed very easily into casual connections. The path that it described through the air follows quite precisely the law of the acceleration of gravity; where it hit was due to the direction and velocity with which it left the roof, which direction the wind was blowing, and so forth. The fall of the rock onto your head was thus not at all uncaused. It is only an accident from the point of view of the fact that we did not know the inititial conditions under which it fell.

Exactly the same thing can be said about social processes that appear to us as random matters of chance. Social mobility studies which concentrate on the series of variables leading up through completion of formal education can explain only about 40 percent of the variance in occupational attainment. Does that mean the other 60 percent (as Jencks et al. [1972] have suggested) is purely a matter of chance? Only if we mean by this that knowing as much as a conventional survey tells us about what has happened up through school graduation, we can predict occupational outcomes several decades later no more closely than within a certain range. But the other variation is not necessarily mysterious; it is likely determined by other facts (personal friendship networks, on one level; structural changes in the economy, at a larger level; see Chapter 12) that are simply not entered into the individual-level theory.

Chance, then, does not mean the absence of causality. It means the absence of causality that we know about, from the point of view of what we are looking at. More generally, it also means that the different orders of causality are essentially unconnected. The fact that you are walking beneath the building when the rock fell off the roof is also the product of a series of causes: your intention to go to a certain place, to see a certain person, say, which can be further analyzed into such factors as your social class culture which made this person attractive to you as a friend, and so forth. There need be nothing uncaused about any aspect of the situation, either in the social motivation that made you walk by or in the physics which carried the rock down onto your head. But the two causal orders are unconnected. There is no relationship (or if any the most trivially remote one) between your walking that way at that time and the rock falling when it did. *It is this unconnectedness of different causal orders in the universe that gives rise to the phenomenon of chance.*[1]

Chance, in an important sense, is not just a matter of "luck." Chance has its own laws, which are precisely what the discipline of statistics is found upon. These are the laws of *how various distributions arise from the combination of events which are causally independent.* It is not surprising that the mathematical theory of statistics should have arisen from the investigations of Pascal, Bernoulli, and others, into the principles of games of chance. For gambling games are physical situations which have been deliberately devised so that outcomes are independent of each other. A series of rolls of the dice are independent physical acts; further, each die is constructed so that each side reacts the same way to shaking in a hand or cup. The mechanical flipping of a coin, the pulling of black or white balls from an urn, the mixing of numbers in a bingo machine—all of these are mechanical situations in which independent elements are produced in a long series. Counting the distribution of outcomes under these circumstances gave rise to empirical generalizations, to which various mathematical models were then fitted. Later the model was extended to other physical situations (for example, to heated particles, by Poisson; to observational errors of astronomers; to human demographic patterns, by Quetelet; to the characterstics of biological populations, by Fisher and Pearson; and so on). These gave the distributions against which observed hypotheses are tested in order to reject the null hypothesis of causation as "merely" the result of chance.

The interpretation of statistical distributions has been a matter of debate over the years. The traditional "frequency theory of probability" (formulated by Bernoulli, among others), regarded distributions as empirical facts. However, since distributions can be mathematically derived merely by making the assumption that there are certain independent elements, that their combination obeys the additive prop-

---

[1] The type of theory of probability that I am describing falls within the general category of objective theories of probability. Even within this approach, *complete* causal determinism at all levels may be nonexistent. (This is consistent with the discussion of Gödel's theorem, which follows.) There may be *absolute* micro-randomness at the subatomic level, and some theorists argue that macro-randomness is an amplification of this (Gillies, 1973: 133–37). But this residue of randomness does not affect the practical conclusions I am drawing about sociological theories. And even subatomic micro-randomness may be merely another instance of the independence of causal orders, in this case, among subatomic particles or fields. See also Bohm (1971).

erty, and a few other axioms, there has been a tendency to regard statistics as simply the working out of a logical rather than an empirical system. Recently, even the assumpion of independent *elements* has been dropped, and statistical distributions can be shown to be generated merely by having independent *observations*. One tendency has been in the direction of defining statistics subjectively rather than objectively. John Maynard Keynes' *A Treatise on Probability* (1921) began this trend, taking a more extreme position than most subsequent statisticians about the theoretical, nonquantifiable subjective elements involved in any judgment of probability. De Finetti and Savage produced the modern subjective approach to statistics. Kolmogorov and Chaitin have carried along a subjective (but quantitative) approach by defining randomness in terms of the number of bits of information that a computer would need in order to reproduce a given number (see Hacking, 1975; Fine, 1973; Gillies, 1973; Savage, 1954; MacKenzie, 1981).

Nevertheless, I would argue that even though our *use* of statistics can be regarded as a subjective phenomenon, it implies a theoretical model of the external world. That model is what Keynes characterized as the "atomic character of natural law":

> The system of the material universe must consist . . . of bodies which we may term (without any implication as to their size being conveyed thereby) *legal atoms,* such that each of them exercises its own separate, independent, and invariable effect, a change of the total state being compounded of a number of separate changes each of which is solely due to the separate portion of the preceding state. (Keynes, 1921: 249)

Hence (describing Cournot's theory of statistics):

> No one . . . seriously believes that in striking the ground with his foot he puts out the navigator in the Antipodes, or disturbs the system of Jupiter's satellites . . . . Every event is causally connected with previous events belonging to its own series, but it cannot be modified by contact with events belonging to another series. A "chance" event is a complex due to the concurrence in time or place of events belonging to causally independent series." (1921: 283)[2]

We accept this "atomic law" model for practical purposes. Notice this does not endorse the position that the universe consists entirely of atoms, or that there are no "field" or "contextual" effects in subatomic particles, electricity, biological organisms, or human societies. But these are all orders of causality. Each of them implies a certain set of interrelationships, which we may formulate in a theory. The theory then may be tested statistically against an underlying model of independent "atoms" of causality, *at whatever level.* Statistical test theory always implies that there are at least two different causal mechanisms: one of them is the mechanism which produces "random" distributions, wherever certain aspects of the world consist of independent orders of causality; the other is whatever laws we think we discern in the world (that is, our explicit theory).

---

[2] Keynes points out that this model is assumed rather than proven, because it is not clear how we can know that the events are not completely unconnected: "Just as it is likely that we are all cousins if we go back far enough, so there may be, after all, remote relationships between ourselves and Jupiter" (1921: 283).

There are two conclusions which I would draw from the fact that statistics implies a substantive theory of the world. (1) *Statistical testing is less important as a methodological criterion of theoretical validity than we have supposed.*[3] Statistical testing cannot be the ultimate criterion of truth because it itself makes theoretical assumptions; there are more important ways to validate a theory than by exclusive reliance upon statistical tests against an empty null hypothesis. (2) *The greatest value of statistics is as a theory rather than as a method.* Statistics should not be thrown out entirely, although it does need to be put in its place. That place is in understanding the statistical, "bingo-machine" processes of causality which often operate in the social world, especially at the macro-structural level.

STATISTICS AND THEORY TESTING

Whenever we carry out a statistical test of the "significance" of a given pattern of relationships found in the world, we are actually comparing one theory with another: the theory we have in mind versus the theory that some sort of "bingo-game" structure to the universe produce the observed results. If in fact we do not reject the null hypothesis, does that mean that the phenomenon is unexplained? On the contrary, it usually implies that we have extended the range of application of a statistical model of the universe. A major portion of our understanding of the world, then, is assumed on logical grounds, rather than proven by statistical test. There is no way to test a statistical model statistically; we simply demonstrate that the pattern of data are consonant with it. We cannot test the validity of a theory of statistical distributions by comparing it against another statistical distribution; this procedure leads only to a logical regress. As Keynes (1921) pointed out, the theory of probability itself is not based on probability. As long as we assume the theory of probability—and we do this whenever we use it for methdological purposes—we accept it as a structural given, not as something to be tested in itself.

For this reason, statistical tests are not as important for the advancement of scientific truths as they are often taken to be. It requires a considerable number of assumptions before we can decide that statistical tests fit the matter at hand. As Keynes (1921: 21–30) pointed out, the application of a statistical test requires judgments of relevance to the matter at hand. To calculate a probability distribution requires a set of exclusive and exhaustive alternatives of equal probability. But many (or most) instances of scientific evidence for any larger problem cannot be judged strictly against this background. Suppose we have three researchers on the same problem: the first contains the most experiments; the second has varied the control

[3] The dogmatism of many sociological practitioners about statistical tests contrasts sharply with the attitude of professional statisticians regarding their own foundations. A recent overview of the field, for example, concludes: "Reflection upon the many difficulties that beset current theories of probability leads us to wonder whether we can dispense with probability and use alternative methodologies to carry out our tasks. In support of such a position is the observation that probability by itself has not been sufficient for most applications. In practice we most often make inferences, reach conclusions (estimates), or select decision rules only after adjoining an *ad hoc* statistical methodology . . . to a theory of probability. Why not ignore the complicated and hard to justify probability-statistics structure and proceed "directly" to those, perhaps qualitative, assumptions that characterize our source of random phenomena, the means at our disposal, and the task?" (Fine, 1973: 249–50)

conditions most thoroughly and widely; the third produces the widest generalization. Which of the three generalizations is most probable? The answer cannot be stated quantitatively, because there are no grounds for comparison.

How then is scientific evidence actually weighted in developing a theory? In the physical sciences, the three sets of experiments described above might be evaluated and integrated according to how well their various principles fit together logically; special weight would be given to how closely these implications tie in with other principles which have been widely established as basic components of other theories (Lakatos, 1976). (It is here that mathematics plays its principal role in scientific theories.) It is these judgments or relevance that count most, not some arbitrary meeting of, or failure to meet, an arbitrary level of statistical "significance."

Sophisticated users of latent variable measurement models (such as LISREL or EQS) confront this same issue. Typically, we must assume certain relationships between our actual measurements and the variables which they hypothetically represent. If the interrelationships are very complex, we cannot decide whether our model fits the data on purely statistical grounds. It is necessary for us to propose particular models of how we believe the data will behave, introducing limiting assumptions which make it possible to fix certain relationships and thus to calculate others. In practice, the more sure we are on theoretical grounds that certain parts of the model are correct, the better able we are to use statistics to estimate the fit of the parts of the model about which we are less sure. Some critics (for example, Duncan, 1984) have gone so far as to question whether any measurement is really being done at all in these models, since there are unexamined assumptions about the scales, the numbers of distinct variables, and the social process by which measurement was done. Other problems (Lieberson, 1985) arise from models which omit variables or from the possibility of causal relationships which are reversible. All these issues, I would suggest, are really matters of substantive theory introducing into the heart of the statistical inference itself.

How much evidence it takes to prove or disprove a theory, then, varies with the logical relations of that theory to our other knowledge. Some principles are much better founded than others, and need much less evidence for us to accept them. Keynes (1921: 383) illustrates this by commenting that if we only take human experience as a criterion, the odds of the sun's rising tomorrow is something like 1,826,214 to 1, which seems like a very high probability. But the same reasoning concludes that the odds of the sun rising every day for the next 4000 years is only 2/3, which is a good deal less than we would accept. We *know* the sun is going to rise every morning for the next 5 billion years or so, barring certain scientifically forseeable astronomical events whose probability distribution is nevertheless nowhere in the range of 1/3. In short, our knowledge of the principles of astronomy are so well founded, and mesh together from so many different angles of observation and logic, that we do not have to rely on any simple calculation of probabilities based on counting past occurrences.

The conundrum has been raised in the social sciences that if we use the .05 level of probability as our criterion of significance, then 1 out of 20 findings are actually invalid, having arisen solely by chance. But in fact this is a good deal less worrisome if we do not hold such a superstitious veneration for the "level of significance." Findings which fit logically into the larger pattern of scientific explanation are well established thereby; indeed, much more so than a purely isolated finding that may present itself under the guise of some very high level of significance. Choosing .05 or .001, or any other level, is arbitrary. The habit of reporting results as "significant" or not, without giving the actual probability level, simply reduces the range of information by which we might decide, together with all our other theoretical and empirical information, on the usefulness of this particular finding.

MUST HYPOTHESES BE TESTED BLINDLY?

Information is also lost if we take too seriously the orthodox beliefs about the order in which hypotheses are to be tested. It is often taken as a canon of scientific validity that a hypothesis must be proposed before the evidence is examined. If the explanatory principle is induced from the evidence, then it cannot be tested on that evidence. This is often asserted in critiques of historical generalizations in sociology, which necessarily depend upon a very small number of apparently unique cases.

Keynes (1921: 304–306) gives the following example: If we happen to open a biographical dictionary of poets and find that the first five persons listed alphabetically died at ages 48, 76, 84, 48, 45, then we could formulate a mathematical principle which relates the digits of this sequence. But that formula would not be valid for the next poets listed in the dictionary, since it was induced only from the first five.

But, Keynes goes on to argue, if we formulate a principle based on the atomic weights of, say, the first dozen chemical elements, that principle turns out to be valid for succeeding elements in the periodic table. According to the conventional methodological criterion, neither the ages of the poets nor the characteristics of the chemical elements can be established by induction from the first part of the sequence. But in fact the principle so induced does turn out to be true for the chemicals, though it does not for the poets; *and we could have known this in advance.* For if we view the circumstances surrounding the induction, we see that the poets' list is ordered simply by the alphabet (and we see this right away, without having to sample the whole dictionary), and hence we know that the relations among their ages are going to be arbitrary. On the other hand, if we know enough about the chemical structure of a dozen elements, we have a full-fledged theory about how their structural properties relate to each other; hence we have more grounds than a purely statistical probability for expecting that these properties will continue through the remainder of the sequence. Investigation of the later part of the sequence is less a test which proves the theory than a confirmation and extension of a theory in which we can already rest sufficient confidence that it is true.

This runs contrary to our commonly accepted beliefs. We were all told in our elementary methods course that the pattern we find the first time we look at the data may be there just by accident; we need another sample to rule out this possibility. But in fact the second sample (or any number of subsequent samples) hardly overcomes the initial problem. As David Hume pointed out centuries ago, our knowledge of the past is never a strictly logical basis for inferences about the future. The entire universe up til now may be simply one gigantic accidental sample; if we think otherwise, it is because we *impose* a pattern of causality upon it. Statistics does not avoid this; it simply imposes a model of chance distributions, which themselves were induced from past experience. If in fact we feel sufficiently confident to accept *any* theory (including the theory of probability), it is because our theories rest not on a method of blind prediction but on what Keynes calls "general considerations"—that is, on the pattern of theoretical coherence. The reason why, in the above example, it would not be wise to accept a theory that was immediately induced from one sample, is because the pattern was induced in the rawest way, *without* any general theoretical considerations or efforts at larger theoretical coherence. As Keynes puts it:

> The peculiar virtue of prediction or predesignation is altogether imaginary. The number of instances examined and the analogy between them are the essential points, and the question as to whether a particular hypothesis happens to be propounded before or after their examination is quite irrelevant. . . . If a theory is first proposed and is then confirmed by the examination of statistics, we are inclined to attach more weight to it than to a theory which is constructed in order to suit the statistics. But the fact that the theory which precedes the statistics is more likely than the other to be supported by general considerations—for it has not, presumably, been adopted for no reason at all—constitutes the only valid ground for this preference. If it does *not* receive more support than the other from general considerations, then the circumstances of its origin are no argument in its favor. The opposite view, which the unreliability of some statisticians has brought into existence—that it is a positive advantage to approach statistical evidence *without* preconceptions based on general grounds, because the temptation to "cook" the evidence will prove otherwise to be irresistible—has no *logical* basis and need only be considered when the impartiality of an investigator is in doubt." (1921: 305–306; see also Gillies, 1973: 65-66)

CAN GENERAL THEORY BE DEVELOPED IF THERE ARE FEW CASES?

Much of the best work in sociology has been carried out using qualitative methods without statistical tests. This has been true of research areas ranging from organizational and community studies to micro studies of face-to-face interaction and macro studies of the world system. The work of Erving Goffman, for example, or (on an entirely different scale) Immanuel Wallerstein would not have been improved by carrying it out under the rigid program of statistical measurement and hypothesis testing. In all likelihood someone following such methods would not have been able to do it at all.

Historical sociology occupies an especially important place here because of its strategic role in building genuine sociological theory. There are several reasons why it has this significance.

(1) Often only historical evidence can provide the comparisons necessary for the development of explanatory theory. To explain something, we need to know the conditions under which in occurs in one form and when it occurs in another: in short, its variations. For macro structures such as the state, these variations can be seen with a sufficient and full range only if they are treated historically.

(2) The same may also be true of smaller-scale social structures. There are numerous empirical cases of the family in a contemporary society, for example; but

without historical comparisons we fall all too easily into simplified assumptions about the range of family forms and hence about the conditions that produce them. The belief that the nuclear family is to be explained by its functional relationship to modern industrial society was based on a limited historical view which examined only modern societies and took everything else as a residual category. Broader historical evidence (for instance, Macfarlane, 1978) has shown us that the nuclear family has existed more widely, and has spurred the search for more adequate theoretical explanation.

(3) A different line of argument is that local phenomena within particular societies are not explicable by themselves, because they are part of a larger world system. Such arguments have been plausibly applied to economic "development" (Frank, 1967; Wallerstein, 1974), political change (Bendix, 1978), revolution (Skocpol, 1979), and state power as related to external geopolitics (Collins, 1981: 71–106). Such concepts, however, raise a methodological problem: if there is only one world system, how can we test a theory? The number of historical instances reduces to one case, because everything is connected together. Taken to its extreme, this position amounts to the philosophy of historicism, in which history is seen as a constantly changing flow of particulars. In this view, no generalizations are possible, but only interpretations of particular parts of this endless flux.

The problem reduces to this. The essence of the scientific method for producing generalizations is comparison. But how do we compare without an adequate number of cases? If we take the world-system view, or the historical one, there is only one case we can deal with. Even if we take a more limited view—arguments (1) or (2)—usually we find that the number of cases that we can examine are far fewer than the number conventionally used to establish statistical significance. And this limitation may be inalterable. History only presents us with a certain number of instances of revolution, let us say, and there is nothing we can do about it. That is all the data there is.

If these arguments are simultaneously true, sociology as a science is doomed. It cannot be a real explanatory science without history, but history appears not to allow sufficient comparisons.

Nevertheless, I am suspicious of this conclusion. For one thing, there are analogous problems in the natural sciences. The physical world is also a seamless web, yet we have been successful in piecing out various parts of it in abstraction from the others. This is true even in areas such as biology, geology, and astronomy, where the problems of historicism and the small number of instances of large-scale phenomena (such as geological epochs, evolutionary phyla, or cosmological universes) are similar to those in macrosociology.

The part of the conundrum that most easily comes undone is the assumption that generalizations cannot be made without a large random sample of cases. We are often told that historical analysis is invalid science, because the number of variables exceeds the number of cases; or that once we have induced a pattern from a given number of cases, the theory cannot be accepted as true if we do not have another unexamined set of cases left over upon which to test it. But these methodological doctrines are artificial and unnecessary.

Consider the latter principle. It is tantamount to saying that the more we know about history, the less we know of it scientifically. Allegedly we would be better off knowing less, so that we would have materials on which we could test and thereby establish our theories.

Suppose that we had 100 historical cases. If we examined all of them and drew a generalization from it, it would allegedly be worthless because we have produced only a tautological explanation, really a description masquerading as an explanation. But if we made the same generalization based on examining 50 cases, while carefully averting our eyes from the other 50, and then found that if fit the other 50 as well, the generalization would be true. Notice: it is the same generalization, and the same total amount of evidence; only in one case, according to the conventional method, the generalization would be rejected, but in the other case accepted.

Extrapolated, this means that the more we know of history, the more ignorant we are of how to explain it. Someone who knew virtually all of world history (say Max Weber or William McNeill), would know much less than someone (say a highly specialized statistician) who knew virtually none of it.

As we have seen above, the methodological theory in question is invalid. The statistical formalities proposed do not operate to increase our objective knowledge of the world, but only to express our suspicions against theorists who might cheat or who cannot examine their own presuppositions. This is a social criterion and not a logical one.

Fortunately, we do have resources on the logical and the social level for increasing confidence that the theory we have induced from a small number of instances, or that we have exhausted the universe of cases in formulating, is in fact a valid picture of the underlying causal processes which govern our world. On the social level, we can reduce biases by making sure there is mutual criticism among rival theories. On the logical level, the most important techniques involve increasing our precision and our theoretical consistency.

A theory based on a small number of historical instances (or even one) can be accepted with confidence to the extent that we can accumulate more detailed evidence in keeping with our model. Here, mathematics can make it reappearance, but in a nonstatistical guise. It increases our confidence to be able to say that 75 percent of the peasants were becoming impoverished in an area of increasing peripheralization, as compared to 42 percent in a nonperipheral area, instead of merely asserting that the one group is more impoverished than the other. This shows that we have looked more carefully, and also provides a basis upon which mathematical relationships could be built. Thus a theory based on a small number of macro instances would be further validated if it proved fruitful for subsequent elaborations with unforeseen degrees of precision.[4]

The most important way in which the validity of a theory can be established is by showing the coherence of its explanatory principles with other well-grounded

---

[4]The problem of how an established physical science deals with theorizing about a single case is illustrated by theories regarding the origins and overall structure of the universe. An astrophysicist outlines his strategy of a test: "We need to do more detailed quantum mechanical calculations of how bubbles behave in de Sitter space. . . . If it became a nice, self-consistent theoretical framework, that would stand it in good stead. . . . The most important observational test is the large-scale structure of the universe. . . . . This theory might allow us to calculate the initial spectrum of random fluctuations, and see if those fluctuations could grow up into the large-scale structure we see today" J. Richard Gott, quoted in *Science* 215 (26 February 1982): 1083.

theory. This involves raising the explanatory structure of any particular historical theory to a more abstract level, and then showing that the principles invoked are consistent with principles and evidence found elsewhere. A theory about the French Revolution (Moore, 1966), can be validated to the extent that it is shown to be formally related to theories and evidence about peasant revolts (Paige, 1975), or about other revolutions (Skocpol, 1979), and that these theories are consistent with principles induced from the study of geopolitics (see Chapter 5). The process of making theories coherent with one another simultaneously strengthens all of them. Ultimately, theories on highly macro levels can be further strengthened if they can be tied to theories on smaller (for example, organizational, or even micro-interactional) levels of analysis.

Here is a potential place for mathematical formulation of theory. Mathematical statement may not be essential at any particular stage of demonstrating theoretical coherence. But theories which can be formulated in axiomatic and deductive form, which can be shown to produce results consistent with a wide range of empirical applications, will have an especially strong claim to have been shown to be true. The future of mathematics in sociology should be more significant on the theoretical side than in the merely methodological form of statistical tests.

What I have said about historical sociology, moreover, is applicable to every area of sociological research. Qualitative microsociology, for example, or observation-based organizational studies, have not depended upon statistics. Their validity and their contributions to our knowledge—which I would say have been considerable—come from their degree of coherence with all our accumulated theoretical principles. The same is even true of quantitative research itself. The validity of statistical analyses of social mobility data, for example, does not come from whether or not it has met some particular significance test; it comes from whether or not a coherent model has been established that is consistent among various researches and ramifies into other areas of sociology. Social mobility research, in fact, is rather weak on this side, precisely because its practitioners (especially within the "status attainment" tradition) have placed so much reliance upon statistical technique in place of understanding its own theoretical implications.

STATISTICS AS SUBSTANCE: THE THEORY OF A WORLD OF CHANCE

In the physical sciences, a statistical model is not simply a basis against which to test some other theory, but provides the model of the phenomenon itself. Poisson provided a model for the propagation of heat as a process involving the independent interaction of numerous small particles; methodological statisticians with other interests transformed this from a substantive model into a purely procedural one. But such substantive statistical models have had wide application in sociology.

One clear example is in the field of social mobility, when viewed on the structural level. It is well known that the total amount of mobility in any mobility table is partly determined by changes in the occupational distribution. At one time this was referred to as "forced" mobility, although it would be more accurate to say that this is mobility which is *the same thing as* the historical processes which make up occupational change. (That is to say, the changes in the marginal distributions did not cause the mobility observed, because those marginal distributions are not prior to the mobility: they are simply another way of describing it.) Concern with "forced" mobility (I would prefer to say "historical change mobility") has been primarily methodological. It was treated primarily as an artifact which we had to remove with a suitable measure of the "true" amount of mobility. But the search for "pure" mobility has been largely a search for an ideological category, not something that exists to any great degree in the world. As Lipset and Bendix pointed out (1959), much more mobility is "forced" (that is, historical change in occupational distributions) than is "pure." Hence a theory explaining the causes and consequences of mobility should make an especially prominent place for the historical process of occupational change rather than trying to put this aside as a methodological problem. Duncan's (1966) criticism of measures of "forced" mobility ceases to carry weight once we take away the implication that the change in the marginals "forced" the mobility, and instead consider this as mobility produced by the larger processes of historical change which bring about occupational transformations.[5] As long as change in the marginals was considered mere interference in the research, it was controlled by mathematical manipulation and put aside. It constituted a background against which a "pure" mobility effect was to be measured. Notice that in doing so, sociologists assumed the unconditional validity of the underlying substantive theory. They did not test to see whether historical changes in the occupational distribution were associated with mobility; this was simply taken as given.

Here we have an instance in which an important substantive phenomenon was ignored by being made into something merely "methodological." A second instance can be found when we consider the effects upon mobility, not of changes in the marginal distributions, but the beginning-point size of the various occupational categories relative to each other. It is easy to show (Marsh, 1963; Connor, 1979; 106–76) that countries which have a relatively large upper classes are going to have more upward mobility into the elite, and less downward mobility out of it, than countries with a small upper class. Similarly, the amount of mobility across the white-color–blue-collar line is affected by the sheer size of those categories when the process we are measuring begins (see Collins, 1975: 447).

This is a rather pure instance of a "bingo-game" effect on social mobility. It is analogous to take a small jar of white balls and a large jar of black balls, mixing them together, and then filling up the two jars again. A greater proportion of white balls are going to end up in the black jar than vice versa simply because of the size of the jars.[6] A good deal of structural mobility is thus accounted for by the static, relative sizes of different occupational strata. Indeed, there is a good deal more of this sort of mobility than there is of the long-sought "pure" or "circulation" mobility.

[5] Duncan's problem of demographic changes confounding mobility can be dealt with on the structural level, rather than by abandoning that level of analysis entirely.

[6] We could make this model more complex, and more realistic, by having both jars change absolute size over time: this would model population growth. Also we could add the "historical change" dimension discussed above, by changing the *relative* sizes of the two jars between time 1 and time 2. This merely makes the model into a multi-variate one, does not change the basic logic of the argument.

What I would emphasize is that this "bingo-game" mobility is not a statistical artifact. It is not merely something to be controlled away so that "real" mobility can be measured. We should stop worrying about "real" mobility, for all forms of it are equally real. Persons living through an occupational career have no sense of whether the mobility they experience is simply a change in the occupational distribution, a "bingo-game" resulting from living in a country with a large or small white-collar sector, or some sort of "pure" meritocratic movement. On the individual level the question does not make sense; the individual only knows whether she or he has moved up or down or stayed the same, and she or he is just as happy to be carried upward by a historical process of expanding upper occupational brackets as they would be making it upon the superior "openness to merit" of their society. This "openness" in fact may be only a sociologist's myth; it is a residual category of unexplained mobility for which we have an ideological fondness, but which recedes steadily with each advance of explanatory theory.[7]

The propensity to turn substantive causes into methodological artifacts to be held constant mathematically is one of the major obstacles to theoretical advance in such areas as social mobility. A great deal of mobility can be explained on the structural level; much more, I would say, than can be explained by the level of individual careers which is the focus of path analysis. But this means turning statistics into substance, not reducing it to methodology. The probabilistic perspective has potentially many applications. There are numerous aspects of social life in which there are collections of smaller events or units, each of which has its own causal structure upon the micro level, but which are independent with respect to each other. The macro outcomes of such an aggregation can be predicted by an appropriate statistical model. This distribution is produced by chance, if you like; but here "chance" is not just a matter of luck. To speak plainly, chance or random distributions are not uncaused; they are caused by well-known mechanisms. And these mechanisms ought to be given a significant place in sociological theory.[8]

MATHEMATICS IS EMBEDDED IN WORDS

I have argued that sociologists have frequently misconceived the place of mathematics in their field. Its primary application has been taken to be statistical method. In this sphere, I would say, its contributions are considerably exaggerated. The greatest

---

[7] In short, the major causes of mobility appear to be, in descending order of importance: (1) historical changes which produce new occupational positions or eliminate old ones; this implies an entire theory of social change; (2) the bingo-game structure of absolute size relations among occupational categories; this is another result of past history; (3) networks and cultural and emotional capital operating at the level of individual careers. The residual of "meritocracy" beyond these orders of determination is vanishingly small.

[8] Mayhew and Schollaert (1980) provide a good example of a substantive theory, in this case a theory of the distribution of wealth, which shows how chance processes operating under certain constraints produce various patterns of inequality. See also Mayhew and Levinger (1976). Other such applications are likely to be especially valuable in dealing with the micro-macro problem, since this involves the aggregation of many micro events in time and space.

progress in sociological explanation has occurred in precisely those areas which have not become hung up on the rituals of statistical validation. On the other hand, I have pointed out two areas in which mathematics is potentially quite useful for the advancement of sociology. The statistical theory itself can be used as a substantive model for certain macro level processes in society, involving the movement of large numbers of independent individuals. And mathematical formalization may be useful as a means of showing the coherence of theoretical principles involved in particular areas of research, thus serving to validate studies which draw on a very small number of unique instances, as so often in historical sociology. Mathematics, including statistics, is valuable in sociology primarily as theory, rather than as a "neutral" research method.

Mathematics, of course, is not the only way that theories can be systematically stated. A theory can be stated as a set of verbal propositions (for instance, Collins, 1975), which are related to one another as chains of consequences, or wider or narrow applications of similar principles; since different parts of the theoretical system are supported by various kinds of empirical research, the coherence among them passes along this validation to related parts of the system. The whole thing hangs together, including the more purely theoretical parts, the way a spiderweb is mutually supported by the places it touches outside objects. Nearer the mathematical side, there are models (for example, Turner, 1984) which use symbolism to express the shape of relationships, but do not actually derive proofs mathematically.

The stress I have given to coherence among theoretical principles, however, raises the question of whether there are limits to how much coherence can possibly be introduced, especially in mathematical form. The answer, it appears, is that there are certain fundamental limits.

The ideal of producing a completely self-consistent theory by means of mathematical formalization has been attempted in other fields. Leibniz's plan to eliminate all inconsistencies by replacing words with unambiguously defined symbols, was actually carried out by Whitehead and Russell in *Principia Mathematica* (1910) for elementary mathematics and was sketched out as a program for all of physical science by Russell in his *Principles of Mathematics* (1904). The trial, however, proved the impracticability of the enterprise. Not only did Russell turn up a logical paradox at the root of his system, which led to Gödel's proof of the impossibility of a closed and consistent system of the sort Russell envisioned; but even the effort to displace words by mathematics was a failure. For the *Principia Mathematica* itself, despite its avowed intent to replace words with formal symbolism, begins with some 20 pages made up almost entirely of words. And even after this, the bulk of the argument is no more than 50 percent mathematical symbols. Russell's more wide-ranging *Principles of Mathematics* is almost entirely verbal, containing virtually no symbolism at all.

We find the same thing in mathematical journals. Mathematical problems are still introduced in words; discussions are almost always concluded by words; mathematical articles always have verbal titles rather than simply announcing some formula as its heading. Mathematicians in fact frequently use verbal expressions within their technical arguments to summarize some complex formal results known to mathematical readers (for instance, "Banach spaces," "Lesbesgues integrals," and the like).[9] We arrive at the paradoxical conclusion that although mathematics has often advanced by creating new formalisms that clarified the ambiguities of ordinary language, and that allowed the mechanical performance of complex calculations that would otherwise be impossible, nevertheless mathematics keeps re-surfacing back into the world of words from which it starts its plunges. Words seem to be a necessary and inescapable frame within which mathematics is embedded.[10]

Gödel's proof can be interpreted as showing why mathematical symbols depend upon a surrounding structure of less precise but more evocative words. Gödel demonstrated that any formal system is formally incomplete, and that efforts to correct it and to prove its consistency involve adding yet another frame of reference which itself is outside of the system (Kramer, 1970: 447–54). This indeterminacy or incompleteness of the "outermost" frame, in fact, is exactly what we find in mathematical articles: the mathematical formalisms have to be introduced by words (like Whitehead and Russell spending 20 pages explaining how and why their symbolism will work). The intent of mathematical activities is framed in words; it is announced in a verbal title which draws attention to what is being done; and successful mathematical calculations come out the other end as verbal catchwords ("Banach spaces," and so on) which can now enter into other mathematicians' mental universes. For this reason, historians of mathematics write, for the most part, not in formalisms but in words, and not merely for purposes of simplification. The most fundamental developments of mathematical ideas cannot be grasped if one is too closely enmeshed in the formal calculations themselves; words are necessary to establish their significance in relation to other mathematical ideas.

One of the main characteristics of verbal language, of course, is its multi-dimensionally and open-endedness. It is precisely these qualities that motivated mathema-

---

[9] For example, the 1976–77 volumes of two physics journals, *Journal of Low Temperature Physics* and *International Journal of Heat and Mass Transfer,* devote an average of 40–50 percent of their total printed space to abstract symbols, the rest consisting of words. The proportion of symbols is not strikingly higher in pure mathematics. The 1976–77 volumes of two mathematics journals, *Journal of Differential Geometry* and *Duke Mathematical Journal,* contain an average of 50–55 percent symbols in each article. The way in which technical calculations are embedded in verbal discourse may be seen from the following comparisons. In the physics journals, symbols (including numbers) range from 0–3 percent of the total length of titles, 3–8 percent of article abstracts, and 1–10 percent of introductory paragraphs. Concluding paragraphs emerge from the technical symbolism of the mid-sections of these papers back into words, but not to the same degree as their beginnings: concluding paragraphs average 1–27 percent symbols in these physics journals. Mathematics journals show a similar pattern but with proportionately more symbols: 13–23 percent in first paragraphs, 40–45 percent in concluding paragraphs. (These journals include no abstracts.) But mathematics titles contain even fewer symbols than physics titles: only 13 percent of the titles contain any symbols at all, and these are all of the simplest (for example, "2-dimensional" or "*n*-dimensional"; and less than 1 percent of total title space consists of symbols. Mathematicians, in fact, are strikingly fond of verbal designations for the results of technical analyses in their literature.

[10] In the history of mathematics, the relative place of words and symbols has fluctuated several times. Ancient and early modern mathematics was argued out almost entirely in words; this was a major limitation on its capacity for abstraction and for making complex calculations. In the 1600s and again in the 1800s, there were movements, especially in England, toward a total notational system. In the 1700s there was a reaction back toward the tendency to argue entirely in words, like the ancient Greeks. Russell represents another wave of total formalization which has subsequently receded. Most major mathematicians have avoided these extremes; Descartes, Euler, and others have argued in a mixture of words and symbols (Cajori, 1974).

ticians and philosophers like Leibniz and Russell to seek for a perfect symbolic system that would not have these "liabilities." Wittgenstein, whose early work is an attempt to carry the Russellian program into the realm of language itself, later reversed himself and devoted his mature years to analyzing language as a system which is necessarily multi-leveled. To borrow Austin's term, language consists of various kinds of *speech acts* rather than merely of signs with a referential content, and different kinds of speech acts can be embedded within one another (see Goffman, 1974, 1981; Chapter 9). Language thus has precisely the qualities of potentially endlessly expandable frames-around-frames, which Gödel finds at the root of any system of logic. Ethnomethodologists' "indexicality" (Garfinkel, 1967), as well as their critiques of the limitations of mathematics in sociology (Cicourel, 1964), can be seen as hinging upon just this issue.

My conclusion, then, is that words will always be with us. If mathematics itself cannot arrive at total formalizations (or total formal consistency and coherence), how much the less will sociology attain it? Such formalization that may take place in sociological theory will always be dependent upon a larger frame of words which surrounds it and makes sense of it. Formalization is always subservient to the larger purposes of the argument. Words are not only more fundamental *intellectually;* we may also say that they are necessarily superior to mathematics in the *social* structure of the intellectual discipline. For words are a mode of expression with greater open-endedness, more capacity for connecting various realms of argument and experience, and more capacity for reaching intellectual audiences. Even mathematicians must lapse into words to show what are the most important things they are talking about. We might even describe mathematics as a particular form of words, operating within a context specially prepared for it by the use of some other language game. And the open-endedness of words may also reflect the empirical open-endedness of the process of theorizing, which may approach some ideal degree of coherence, without ever reaching it absolutely. Finally, this open-endedness of words is in keeping with the open-endedness of the historical world, continuously unfolding into the future.

Verbal, qualitative theory, then, will always be more fundamental in sociology than mathematics—even if we make progress toward the proper uses of mathematics and statistics that I have outlined above. In fact, in order to produce genuinely valuable mathematical theory, we probably need to be equally adept at words (as Russell was, and as a few of the most mathematically sophisticated sociologists are today). At the same time, theorists and researchers whose work is purely or predominantly verbal are likely to lead our field for a long time to come. As Keynes (1921: 19) put it:

> This question . . . is in my opinion much more a question of style . . . than is generally supposed. There are occasions for very exact methods of statement, such as are employed in Mr. Bertrand Russell's *Principia Mathematica.* But there are advantages also in writing the English of Hume. . . . But those writers, who strain after exaggerated precision without going the whole hog with Mr. Russell, are sometimes merely pedantic. They lose the reader's attention, and the repetitious complication of their phrases eludes his comprehension, without their really attaining, to compensate, a complete precision. Confusion of thought is not always best avoided by technical and unaccustomed expressions, to which the mind has no immediate reaction of understanding; it is possible, under cover of a care-

ful formalism, to make statements, which, if expressed in plain language, the mind would immediately repudiate. There is much to be said, therefore, in favour of understanding the substance of what you are saying *all the time*, and of never reducing the substantives of your argument to the mental status of an *x* or a *y*.

The work of advancing theory can and should go forward on both the verbal and the mathematical fronts. In some respects, similar problems exist on both sides. It is not only mathematics that can be formulated with obscure devices known only to insiders; verbal theories too are often loaded with esoteric terminology and taken-for-granted modes of argumentation. The aim ought to be to produce theories which state what they mean in a fashion that is easiest to communicate, and which say something sufficiently general, powerful, and important enough to make it worth-while.

APPENDIX B: DEVELOPING SOCIOLOGICAL THEORY BY COMPUTER SIMULATION

Computer simulation offers a new possibility for extending existing theory in the direction of greater comprehensiveness and systemization. Simulation as a method is not new. It has been used for a number of years in the physical and biological sciences, especially to model processes (such as astrophysical theories of cosmic evolution) whose time scale cannot be captured naturally or in the laboratory. Simulation has been used in social science, too, especially in economics and political science, most often for projections of the future or scenarios of international conflict. As yet, computer simulation has been little used for the purpose of modeling and developing sociological theories, though it is beginning (Powers and Hanneman, 1983; Hanneman and Collins, 1987; Cook et al., 1983).

Perhaps surprisingly, the special problems in developing general sociological theory make computer simulation especially promising. There are a variety of approaches to sociological theory, and debates among them include the issue of whether it is even possible to have a general theory about the social world, given that that world is historically specific, complex, and self-transforming. According to some perspectives, the prospects are made even dimmer by the existence of human consciousness, and especially its self-reflective capabilities. Compute simulation turns out to occupy a strategic place vis-à-vis these issues. Despite the reputation of computer-using sociology as the epitome of the hard-science, positivistic approach, computer simulation actually offers the possibility of mediating between the more positivist and mathematical end of the field, and the more historicist, humanist, and verbal stances in sociology.

1. THE COMPLEXITY AND HISTORICITY OF THE NATURAL WORLD   Whatever we focus on in the world is always a selection from a larger context that is global and historical. Accordingly, it is sometimes argued, a realistic analysis must always invoke the global context of the world system, even though its "laws" may be historically transitory (Bergesen, 1984; Wallerstein, 1984). A more extreme position, enunciated by French structuralists (Jameson, 1982; and *a fortiori* by post-structur-

alists such as Derrida, 1967/1976) is that the world of changing historical particulars cannot be understood in general terms at all, but that analysis must focus instead on the generating cultural structures of the human mind. It is possible, however, to recognize both the particularity and uniqueness of every historical configuration, *and* to understand this as produced by more general processes.

A computer simulation demonstrates this clearly. Its basic components are a set of general processes, the "laws" of the system. By itself, however, each "law" is merely an analytical device (in the sense stressed by Parsons, 1951, and Alexander, 1983) abstracted from reality. Complexity is introduced by the fact that we simulate a number of processes simultaneously, allowing the results of these processes to flow into or affect one another. In this way, a computer-simulated theory is much closer to historical reality than the analytically abstracted principles which are the object of much empirical research in the positivist mode. Furthermore, a simulation must always specify the particular empirical levels at which processes start, and the actual rates of movement or change over time (for theoretical purposes, these levels and rates might be imaginary). Each run of a simulation is a specific historical scenario, with unique properties.

Computer-simulated theory thus shows us a two-level reality: the set of general processes lying "beyond" empirical realities, and the specific historical instances which are generated by them. Computer simulation bears a resemblance to a structuralist or neo-structuralist position (Poulantzas, 1968; Bhaskar, 1979), in that it focuses attention on the underlying generative "structures," while enabling us to understand the concrete historical mixtures or conjunctures which result from them. In this way, we are able to recognize the force of the historicist position, without being overwhelmed by myriad particularities and giving up all effort at attaining the advantages of general theory. At the same time, we are able to go beyond the merely programmatic statements of structuralism to explore the way theoretical models actually work, and what sorts of empirical realities may be generated by them.

2. DYNAMICS VS. COMPARATIVE STATICS   A major limitation of much of existing sociological theory is that its explanatory principles are static. Principles of the form "X is the cause of Y," or even "the greater the X, the greater the Y," are generally based on cross-sectional comparisons. Even if the principles seem to imply that a change in X will be followed by a change in Y, the process of change itself is not an analytical focus of the theory; time is just another parameter of the analysis (although in fact very few theories spell out how much time is needed for X to affect Y, whether the process occurs abruptly or gradually, and so on). For this reason, among others, some theories which stress the process of change itself (such as symbolic interactionism in its more radical form) deny the relevance of abstract causal principles for capturing what actually occurs in human lives.

This problem exists in my own theoretical work as much as in others. The principles in Collins (1975) assert structural correlations, or causal connections, which are formulated on the basis of comparative statics and take little explicit notice of the process of causality over time. Computer simulation is a way of overcoming this problem. A simulation program necessarily must specify what affects what at various points in time, and it directs attention to just how that process operates: gradually or discretely, and at what rate. Principles formulated as comparative statics are not useless or necessarily invalid; they can be used as components within a simulation model, and thereby dynamicized. In doing so, the theorist is forced to pay attention to the dynamic properties of the theory, and to fill in what are usually missing parts in the theorizing. The resulting dynamic theories are much closer to a full approximation of reality as it actually happens.

3. QUANTITATIVE VS. QUALITATIVE   Another major split within the world of theory, as we have just seen, is between advocates of the formal (especially mathematical) statement of theories and those who argue that verbal statements are more appropriate for the nature of our knowledge and our social world. The language of computer simulation occupies a mediating position in this dispute. A language such as DYNAMO resembles mathematical equations in some respects (Hanneman, 1987). Relationships between particular variables are specified; quantitative levels are calculated for each time point; and graphic representations are available, although discrete, all-or-nothing states may also be part of the system. Simulation thus offers much of the power and precision of mathematical methods. However, simulation is a good deal easier or more "user-friendly" for the nonmathematician. Instead of taxing one's memory with the meaning of arbitrary symbols, DYNAMO allows the variables to be entered in the equations in near-verbal (usually abbreviated) form ("power" may be POWER, "unemployment" is UNEMP). Verbal notes may be interpolated in the program itself to continuously spell out to the reader the meaning of equations. The actual calculations are carried out by the computer; the underlying mathematical formulations are beneath the visible surface, in relation to which the simulation language (in this case, DYNAMO) operates as a higher-order language.

There is another, more important sense in which simulation mediates between quantitative and nonquantitative. The two major branches of quantitative sociology, statistics and mathematical modeling, have their peculiar strengths and weaknesses (Hanneman, 1987). Statistical methods are mainly used for describing the strengths of relationships and for testing whether observed patterns of covariation could have been generated by random mechanisms. The most commonly used statistical models are designed for the analysis of realizations of systems at equilibrium, and hence are appropriate to theories of comparative statics. Statistical models of dynamic processes are not widely utilized in sociology, and are restricted to relatively simple models.

Mathematical modeling is more theoretical than statistics, and mathematical models can be formulated which are dynamic. But the use of mathematics is limited because of set of equations becomes difficult or impossible to solve if they are too complex. If relationships are nonlinear or noncontinuous, and the number of variables exceeds more than a very few, direct solutions of mathematical models may be impossible (see Figure A-1). Even the concept of a "solution" to a system of equations can be inappropriate for dynamic questions, since the "solution" is typically a set of statements expressing unknowns in terms of each other, rather than a depiction of what happens over time.

Verbal statements, on the other hand, are good at expressing subtleties, complexities, and particularities, but they lack precision and (often) generality. The verbal formulation of a theory usually is at a loss to tell us what would be expected to

FIGURE A-1

EASE OF SOLVING MATHEMATICAL PROBLEMS

Equation	Linear Equations			Nonlinear Equations		
	One Equation	Several Equations	Many Equations	One Equation	Several Equations	Many Equations
Algebraic	Trivial	Easy	Essentially impossible	Very difficult	Very difficult	Impossible
Ordinary differential	Easy	Difficult	Essentially impossible	Very difficult	Impossible	Impossible
Partial differential	Difficult	Essentially impossible	Impossible	Impossible	Impossible	Impossible

Source: Ludwig von Bertalanffy, *General System Theory* (New York: George Braziller, 1968) p. 20.

happen in a given occasion where the circumstances are somewhat different than prior known instances. Quantitative approaches so far have not been much better, though for opposite reasons. Statistical methods have been applied mainly to measuring strengths of relationships and to testing the fit between theory and data; these methods have been too tied to particular bodies of data to achieve much generality. Mathematical models have usually sacrificed applicability to complex realities in order to be elegant or technically solvable. Simulation provides a middle way between mathematical oversimplifications and the subtle but weak statements of verbal theories. Processes that are too complex to understand mathematically can be understood by experimenting with the simulation model.

We begin with the verbally formulated theory. Simulation does not require that we reduce the theory to some artificial or extremely limited form, as often happens when we try to make it compatible with a given mathematical method. Generally any verbal statements that express causality, human action, or structural connections can be stated in a language like DYNAMO. Even information, and processes of conscious comparison, goal-direction, or self-reflection can be simulated. Computer simulation has the capacities for capturing many or most of the subtleties of our sophisticated verbal theories and making these into generative models which result in the variety of scenarios of real life. (A model of how everyday social action is produced from generative rules, using techniques of computer Artificial Intelligence, is Fararo and Skvoretz, 1984; compare the Goffman model I proposed at the end of Chapter 9.)

4. THEORETICAL MULTIDIMENSIONALITY AND CUMULATION   Another common complaint about sociology is that its knowledge is fragmentary and noncumulative. I believe that this is an overstatement, as certain areas of work have built up advanced models buttressed by empirical research. It remains true that sociology as a whole is split among various approaches and specialties, which often have one-sided views and polemical stances toward the rest of the field. This situation has inhibited the amount of cumulation that could be possible. Some sociologists have argued that this is a desirable state of affairs, and that sociology ought to remain divided into mutually insulated approaches and world views. I do not agree; without

disputing the right of individuals to pursue whatever approaches they wish, I believe that we equally well have the right to build synthetic models where possible.

Computer simulation of theory contributes to this end as well. Simulation models naturally foster a view of the world as a set of interacting processes. It holds out the prospect of getting all the major processes into a general model. This is of course an ideal, and in practice it is necessary to work with partial models and limited areas of interest. Nevertheless, the method encourages us to theorize systematically and comprehensively; we are not forced in the opposite direction, toward analytical one-sidedness and specialization, by the technical difficulties of dealing with several processes at once. The computer simulation enables us to handle a theoretically complex world instead of a one-sided simplification. In this way, we can provide the multidimensionality which Alexander (1980–83) proposes as the fundamental criterion for a truly adequate general theory. Conflict and order, structure and change, material and ideal conditions are all compatible with a computer simulation; indeed, they are typically entered into the model simultaneously. Simulation is particularly useful for making clear the distinction between the analytical connectedness of a system and any empirical tendencies to equilibrium which it may or may not demonstrate.

The effort to build simulation models of sociological theories should further improve consistency and coherence within them, as well as move toward a larger level of synthesis between various theories. It cannot be assumed in advance, though, that any two theories will prove completely consistent with each other. Even a sociological enterprise in which simulation is widely practiced would not necessarily manage a grand synthesis into a single, all-encompassing theory. But simulation prepares the way for such a synthesis, if it proves feasible; and it will point up the strengths and weaknesses of rival theories, as long as this theoretical plurality remains (which may well be in the foreseeable future.) The feasibility of synthesis, however, is not merely an issue of simulability of theories, but involves empirical matters as well. We turn to this issue shortly.

WHAT IS LEARNED FROM SIMULATING THEORIES?

Some of the advantages of simulating theories have already been mentioned. I will highlight them here, along with other points.

1. Simulation replaces isolated causal or correlational propositions with a system of interacting processes, thus enabling us to model the complexities of the natural, historical world.

2. Simulation shows us the pattern of processes over time; it models dynamics rather than comparative statics. It shifts our attention from outcomes which we mistakenly assume are static, toward ongoing processes.

3. Simulation is a spur to theory construction. Our verbally formulated theories usually turn out to be not completely thought through, especially as they must apply to processes which happen in time.[11] (This is usually true of mathematical theories as well.) Simulation forces us to ask such questions as: How fast do

---

[11] This is what Simon (1957) discovered when he attempted to make a mathematical model out of Homans' basic principle regarding the relationship between interaction and liking (see Chapter 10, p. 340).

processes happen? How smoothly or abruptly? Can processes increase without limit, or do they reach some kind of ceiling? Many processes, which we usually view as isolated because of our comparative-static mode of thought, actually occupy the same universe and thus interact. Simulation encourages (or forces) us to find new theoretical connections among these processes to spell out realistically what is going on.

4. Simulation results in unexpected discoveries of what is latent within the workings of a theory. It makes a big difference in a linked system, for example, if one process happens twice as fast as another; this is one reason why the sheer quantitative specification of a model can drastically change the shape of its outcomes. Interacting processes with feedback loops are especially likely to show patterns of oscillation, as well as (under certain conditions) explosive growth or collapse of certain variables. Understanding the structural relationships among the parts of the system can add crucial information, beyond what we may already know about component processes.

5. Simulation allows experiments with the sensitivity of a system to particular factors. Experimenting with a simulation model under various scenarios reveals whether the system behaves differently when certain variables are changed and which factors turn out not to be sensitive to quantitative differences. The simulation thus helps us put our fingers on particularly crucial points in a causal system.

An example of what may be learned from a simulation is the study by Hanneman and Collins (1987; the main flow-charts are reproduced in Chapter 4) of a Marxian model of capitalist crisis and revolution. This is one of the few examples of a sociological theory that is already cast in dynamic form of a self-propelling system of interacting processes with feedback loops, although of course Marx and Engels did not spell this out so formally. Among the things learned were the following: The logic of the model does indeed result in an economic crisis and socialist revolution; that same logic unexpectedly reveals also that the postrevolutionary situation may continue to have an economic crisis, depending on what kind of postrevolutionary reconstruction is carried out. That is to say, a situation of economic crisis in a socialist society, such as the recent crisis in Poland, is not a theoretical anomaly, but can be derived directly from the structure of Marxian theory itself. Another discovery is that the Marxian model, with a comparatively small modification, can be made to yield a "welfare state" scenario, in which reforms are made that put off economic crisis and prevent socialist revolution. The underlying generative model, in other words, has a variety of latent possibilities; the preferred "Marxian" position, of capitalist crisis and postrevolutionary prosperity, is only a particular realization from this set of possibilities. This is not to say that the generative model here is necessarily valid. The authors produced this simulation of Marxian theory as a formally convenient way of exploring simulation methods, and are sceptical on substantive grounds of some of its key mechanisms (notably the labor theory of value). However, the exercise does show some of the unexpected results that may be turned up by computer simulation. Some other possible models that could be simulated are the Laumann-Knoke model of politics in Chapter 12 or the model of capitalism as a "superorganization" in Chapter 13.

SIMULATION AND EMPIRICAL DATA

How, then, do we judge whether or not to accept a simulation model as realistic? The fact that we can successfully make it work is at least one point of validation in its favor, demonstrating that it is self-consistent and sufficiently rich and specified to produce scenarios unfolding over time. Another point, however, is its relationship to empirical data.

It should be apparent that a computer simulation is not an empirical study. It does not reveal to us anything about the world, but only about the implications of the theory. Nevertheless, the theory can be connected with empirical data in various ways. The component processes, the statements which assert "X causes Y," "X covaries with Y," and so forth, may themselves be grounded in empirical studies. Thus the simulation may work with processes that have already received some empirical validation; it then goes on to show what can be expected from a set of these processes operating together. Things are not always so simple, of course. The component processes may have varying degrees of relationships to empirical data; some parts of a simulation model may be strongly grounded, others weakly, others not at all. Furthermore, given the various levels of abstraction which are possible, and the fact that empirical studies of particular factors usually occur in situations where other conditions have to be disentangled, if may be the case that some of these theoretical processes cannot be directly validated at all. As Quine (1969) and others have pointed out, particular "facts" have meaning only within a larger theoretical context, and there are numerous ways of patching up discrepancies between theory and observation. Thus, when Hanneman and Collins (1987) state that they are sceptical of the reality of the Marxian model (despite the usefulness of its simulation), that is a strategic decision, based on various considerations about the validity of explaining profit by the exploitation of labor. All this underscores the fact that theory building must take place multidimensionally, bringing in a variety of considerations, and trying to establish the most satisfactory system among numerous factors. The empirical evidence in favor of the component parts of a simulation model is one of those considerations, though it is not the only one.

Simulations connect with the empirical world at the other end as well, in the processes over time that they can model. In a very general sense, a simulated theory which can predict (or postdict) future, present, or historical patterns is thereby more validated than one which fails to predict (or postdict) such patterns. Given that there are numerous ways of specifying a simulation model in order to produce various outcomes, this may not turn out to be a very powerful criterion in itself. (For example, we have seen that the Marxian model can be shaped so as to predict a nonrevolutionary welfare state.) The validity of a particular theory is improved if we can constrain it by factual inputs: we require it to start from certain initial conditions which happen to have existed historically, or which are highly plausible on some other grounds, and then see whether the simulated future outcomes are also realistic (or plausible). The theory is also constrained (and hence stands a better chance of validation or disproof) the more that its component processes themselves are well grounded empirically and in terms of other theoretical considerations (such as logical coherence). The methodology of judging the validity of computer simulated theories is not well worked out, although its broad outlines are coming into view.

Everything in sociology moves, at best, by successive approximations. Computer simulation is an effort to connect abstract theory more closely to empirical reality, working from the theory side.

ADDITIONAL PAYOFFS OF A SIMULATION PROGRAM

1. *Theory simulation could be used as a teaching method.* Personal computers have become widely available, in universities as well as in public schools, but useful learning applications as yet are not very common. Computer simulations of theory could be used as a method for teaching sociology. Once some significant theoretical models are available, students could use them to explore the dynamics and consequences of various empirical scenarios. I suspect that this may improve the intellectual motivation for many students, and could also have further consequences of getting students involved not only in applying existing theory but in improving the theory itself.

2. *Theory simulations may prove of use in analyzing social problems and other areas of applied sociology.* Assuming sociological theories will eventually arrive at a satisfactory level of validity and scope, it will be possible for practitioners to start with a given situation (for instance, the prospects of a particular social welfare intervention, or a particular kind of proposed change in a formal organization, or a large-scale change in the world geopolitical situation), and then to run a computer scenario to project future consequences. The feasibility of such practical simulations would depend on availability of sufficient empirical information about real-world starting conditions in the case to be projected and on a sufficiently powerful and valid theoretical model. Such applications may appear to be a remote goal. But I would say that sociological theory even as it now stands gives some grounds for expecting greater practical usefulness in the not-too-distant future.

A PRACTICAL NOTE ON HOW TO WORK WITH SIMULATION MODELS

There are various ways to do simulations. One is to write your own models. This can be done with quite simple languages on personal computers, for example in BASIC (as was done by Powers and Hanneman, 1983). Other programming languages have their particular advantages and disadvantages. Another approach is to use prepackaged programs. A useful one is DYNAMO, developed by Pugh-Roberts, Inc., and distributed by Addison-Wesley Publishing. This is available for various computer operating systems, including IBM and Apple. A third method would be to work with existing models, such as those referred to in the text. These can usually be obtained by writing to the model's creator; hopefully, the custom may grow of publishing the essential part of a simulation program along with the article on its results. Readers interested in working either with existing models or in developing their own may get further information by contacting the author of this text at the Dept. of Sociology, University of California, Riverside, Riverside CA 92521.

REFERENCES

Abercrombie, Nicholas, Stephen Hill, and Bryan S. Turner. 1980. *The Dominant Ideology Thesis*. London: Allen and Unwyn.

Aldrich, Howard. 1979. *Organizations and Environments*. Englewood Cliffs, N.J.: Prentice-Hall.

Alexander, Jeffrey C. 1980–83. *Theoretical Logic in Sociology*. 4 vols. Berkeley: Univ. of California Press.

Althusser, Louis. 1965/1972. *For Marx*. New York: Pantheon.

——. 1971. "Ideology and Ideological Status Apparatuses." In *Lenin and Philosophy*. New York: Monthly Review Press.

Althusser, Louis, and Etienne Balabar. 1968/1970. *Reading Capital*. London: New Left Books.

Alvarez, Luis, et al. 1980. "Extraterrestial Cause for the Cretaceous-Tertiary Extinction." *Science* 208: 1095–1108.

Alves, Wayne, and Peter Rossi. 1978. "Who Should Get What? Fairness Judgments of the Distribution of Earnings." *American Journal of Sociology* 84: 561–64.

Amin, Samir. 1976. *Unequal Development*. New York: Monthly Review Press.

Anderson, Perry. 1974. *Passages from Antiquity to Feudalism*. London: New Left Books.

Anderson, Theodore R., and S. Warkov. 1961. "Organizational Size and Functional Complexity." *American Sociological Review* 31: 497–507.

Andreski, Stanislav. 1968. *Military Organization and Society*. London: Routledge and Kegan Paul.

Ardrey, Robert. 1966. *The Territorial Imperative*. New York: Dell.

Ariès, Phillippe. 1962. *Centuries of Childhood*. New York: Random House.

Arrighi, Giovanni. 1978. *The Geometry of Imperialism*. London: New Left Books.

Atkinson, J. Maxwell, and John Heritage. 1984. *Structures of Social Action: Studies in Conversation Analysis*. New York: Cambridge Univ. Press.

Attewell, Paul. 1984. *Radical Political Economy since the Sixties*. New Brunswick, N.J.: Rutgers Univ. Press.

Austin, John L. 1962. *How to Do Things with Words*. Oxford: Oxford Univ. Press.

Averett, Christine, and David Heise. 1987. "Modified Social Identities: Amalgamations, Attributions, and Emotions." *Journal of Mathematical Sociology* 13. In press.

Baker, Wayne. 1984. "The Structure of a National Securities Market." *American Journal of Sociology* 89: 775–811.

Bales, Robert F. 1959. "Small Group Theory and Research." In Robert K. Merton, ed., *Sociology Today*. New York: Basic Books.

Bales, Robert F., and Philip Slater. 1955. "Role Differentiation in Small Decision Making Groups." In Talcott Parsons and Robert F. Bales, eds., *Family, Socialization and Interaction Process*. New York: Free Press.

Banfield, Edward. 1961. *Political Influence*. New York: Free Press.

Baran, Paul, and Paul M. Sweezy. 1966. *Monopoly Capital*. New York: Monthly Review Press.

Barnard, Chester I. 1938. *The Functions of the Executive*. Cambridge, Mass.: Harvard Univ. Press.

Barthes, Roland. 1964. *Elements of Semiology*. London: Jonathan Cape.

———. 1974. *S/Z*. New York: Hill and Wang.

Baudrillard, Jean. 1981. *For a Critique of the Political Economy of the Sign*. St. Louis: Telos Press.

Becker, Gary S. 1971. *The Economics of Discrimination*. Chicago: Univ. of Chicago Press.

———. 1981. *A Treatise on the Family*. Cambridge, Mass.: Harvard Univ. Press.

Becker, Howard S. 1963. *Outsiders: Studies in the Sociology of Deviance*. New York: Free Press.

Becker, Howard S., Blanche Geer, and Everett C. Hughes. 1968. *Making the Grade*. New York: Wiley.

Beebe, Beatrice, Daniel Stern, and Joseph Jaffe. 1979. "The Kinesic Rhythms of Mother-infant Interactions." In Aaron W. Siegman and S. Feldstein, eds., *Of Speech and Time*. Hillsdale, N.J.: Erlbaum.

Bendix, Reinhard. 1956. *Work and Authority in Industry*. New York: Wiley.

———. 1967. "Tradition and Modernity Reconsidered." *Comparative Studies in Society and History* 9: 292–346.

———. 1978. *Kings or People: Power and the Mandate to Rule*. Berkeley: Univ. of California Press.

Berelson, Bernard, and Gary A. Steiner. 1964. *Human Behavior: An Inventory of Scientific Findings*. New York: Harcourt.

Berg, Ivar. 1970. *Education and Jobs*. New York: Praeger.

Berger, Joseph, Thomas L. Conner, and M. Hamit Fisek. 1974. *Expectations States Theory: A Theoretical Research Program*. Cambridge, Mass.: Winthrop.

Berger, Joseph, Susan J. Rosenholtz, and Morris Zelditch, Jr. 1980. "Status Organizing Processes." *Annual Review of Sociology* 6: 479–508.

Berger, Joseph, David G. Wagner, and Morris Zelditch, Jr. 1983. *Expectation States Theory: The Status of a Research Program*. Stanford Univ. Technical Report No. 90. Stanford.

Berger, Joseph, Cecilia Ridgeway, Susan Rosenholtz, and Murray Webster, Jr. 1984. "Cues, Expectations, and Behaviors." In Edward J. Lawler, ed., *Advances in Group Processes: Theory and Research*. vol. 1. Greenwich, Conn.: JAI Press.

Berger, Peter, and Thomas Luckmann. 1967. *The Social Construction of Reality*. New York: Doubleday.

Bergesen, Albert. 1984. "The Critique of World-System Theory: Class Relations or Division of Labor?" *Sociological Theory 1984*. San Francisco: Jossey-Bass.

———. 1988. *The Ritual Order*. In press.

Bernstein, Basil. 1971–75. *Class, Codes, and Control*. London: Routledge and Kegan Paul.

Bhaskar, Roy. 1978. *A Realist Theory of Science*. Sussex: Harvester Press.

———. 1979. *The Possibility of Naturalism*. New York: Humanities Press.

Blain, Robert R. 1971. "On Homans' Psychological Reductionism." *Sociological Inquiry* 41: 3–25.

Blalock, Hubert M., and Paul M. Wilken. 1979. *Intergroup Processes: A Micro-Macro Perspective*. New York: Free Press.

Blau, Peter M. 1955. *The Dynamics of Bureaucracy*. Chicago: Univ. of Chicago Press.

———. 1964. *Exchange and Power in Social Life*. New York: Wiley.

———. 1977. *Inequality and Heterogeneity: A Primitive Theory of Social Structure*. New York: Free Press.

Blau, Peter M., and O. D. Duncan. 1967. *The American Occupational Structure*. New York: Wiley.

Blau, Peter M., and Richard A. Schoenherr. 1971. *The Structure of Organizations*. New York: Basic Books.

Blau, Peter M., and Joseph E. Schwartz. 1984. *Cross-Cutting Social Circles*. New York: Academic Press.

Blau, Peter M., and W. Richard Scott. 1962. *Formal Organizations*. San Francisco: Chandler.

Block, Fred. 1977. "The Ruling Class Does Not Rule: Notes on the Marxist Theory of the State." *Socialist Revolution* 33: 6–28.

———. 1980. "Beyond Relative Autonomy: State Managers as Historical Subjects." *Socialist Register*: 227–42.

Bloor, David. 1976. *Knowledge and Social Imagery*. London: Routledge and Kegan Paul.

———. 1983. *Wittgenstein: A Social Theory of Knowledge*. New York: Columbia Univ. Press.

———. 1984. "Durkheim and Mauss Revisited: Classification and the Sociology of Knowledge." In Nico Stehr and Volker Meja, eds., *Society and Knowledge: Contemporary Perspectives in the Sociology of Knowledge*. New Brunswick, N.J.: Transaction Books.

Blumberg, Rae Lesser. 1978. *Stratification: Socioeconomic and Sexual Inequality*. Dubuque: William C. Brown.

———. 1984. "A General Theory of Gender Stratification." In *Sociological Theory 1984*. San Francisco: Jossey-Bass.

Blumberg, Rae Lesser, and Robert F. Winch. 1972. "Societal Complexity and Familial Complexity: Evidence for Curvilinear Hypothesis." *American Journal of Sociology* 77: 898–920.

Blumer, Herbert. 1939. *An Appraisal of Thomas and Znaniecki's "The Polish Peasant in Europe and America."* New York: Social Science Research Council.

———. 1969. *Symbolic Interactionism*. Englewood Cliffs, N.J.: Prentice-Hall.

———. 1980. "Mead and Blumer: The Convergent Methodological Perspective of Social Behaviorism and Symbolic Interactionism." *American Sociological Review* 45: 409–19.

Bohm, David L. 1971. *Causality and Chance in Modern Physics.* Philadelphia: Univ. of Pennsylvania Press, 1971.

Bollen, Kenneth A., and Robert W. Jackman. 1985. "Political Democracy and the Size Distribution of Income." *American Sociological Review* 50: 438–57.

Bott, Elizabeth. 1971. *Family and Social Network.* London: Tavistock.

Boudon, Raymond. 1973. *Education, Opportunity, and Social Inequality.* New York: Wiley.

Boulding, Kenneth. 1978. *Ecodynamics: A New Theory of Societal Evolution.* Beverly Hills: Sage.

Bourdieu, Pierre. 1972/1977. *Outline of a Theory of Practice.* Cambridge and New York: Cambridge Univ. Press.

———. 1979/1984. *Distinction: A Social Critique of the Judgement of Taste.* Cambridge, Mass.: Harvard Univ. Press.

Bourdieu, Pierre, and Jean-Claude Passeron. 1970/1977. *Reproduction: In Education, Society, and Culture.* Beverly Hills: Sage.

Braithwaite, Richard B. 1953. *Scientific Explanation.* Cambridge: Cambridge Univ. Press.

Braudel, Fernand. 1949/1972. *The Mediterranean and the Mediterranean World in the Age of Philip II.* New York: Harper and Row.

Braverman, Harry. 1974. *Labor and Monopoly Capital.* New York: Monthly Review Press.

Brenner, Robert. 1977. "The Origins of Capitalist Development: A Critique of Neo-Smithian Marxism." *New Left Review* 104: 25–92.

Brucan, Silviu. 1985. "Market, Socialism, and Revolution." *Review* 9: 155–61.

Burawoy, Michael. 1979. *Manufacturing Consent.* Chicago: Univ. of Chicago Press.

———. 1985. *The Politics of Production.* London: New Left Books.

Burt, Ronald S. 1982. *Toward a Structural Theory of Action.* New York: Academic Press.

———. 1983. *Corporate Profits and Cooperation: Networks of Market Constraints and Directorate Ties in the American Economy.* New York: Academic Press.

Cajori, Florian. 1974/1928. *A History of Mathematical Notations.* La Salle, Ill.: Open Court Publishing.

Calhoun, Craig. 1982. *The Question of Class Struggle.* Chicago: Univ. of Chicago Press.

California State Department of Education. 1986. *Academic Honesty: A Special Study of California Students.* Sacramento.

Capella, F. 1981. "Mutual Influence in Expressive Behavior: Adult-adult and Infant-adult Dyadic Interaction." *Psychological Bulletin* 89: 101–32.

Caplow, Theodore. 1968. *Two Against One: Coalitions in Triads.* Englewood Cliffs, N.J.: Prentice-Hall.

Carey, A. 1967. "The Hawthorne Studies: A Radical Criticism." *American Sociological Review* 32: 403–17.

Carrithers, Michael, Steven Collins, and Steven Lukes, eds. 1985. *The Category of the Person*. Cambridge and New York: Cambridge Univ. Press.

Carroll, Glenn R. 1985. "Concentration and Specialization: Dynamics of Niche Width in Populations of Organizations." *American Journal of Sociology* 90: 1262–83.

Cavanaugh, Michael A. 1986. "Secularization and the Politics of Tradition: The Case of the Right-to-Life Movement." *Sociological Forum* 1: 251–83.

Chafetz, Janet Saltzman. 1984. *Sex and Advantage: A Comparative Macro-Structural Theory of Sexual Stratification*. Totowa, N.J.: Rowman and Allanheld.

Chandler, Alfred D. 1962. *Strategy and Structure*. Cambridge, Mass.: MIT Press.

Chapple, Eliot D. 1981. "Movement and Sound: The Musical Language of Body Rhythms in Interaction." *Teacher's College Record* 82: 635–48.

Chodorow, Nancy. 1978. *The Reproduction of Mothering*. Berkeley: Univ. of California Press.

Chomsky, Noam. 1957. *Syntactic Structures*. The Hague: Mouton.

———. 1965. *Aspects of the Theory of Syntax*. Cambridge, Mass.: MIT Press.

Cicourel, Aaron V. 1964. *Method and Measurement in Sociology*. New York: Wiley.

———. 1973. *Cognitive Sociology*. New York: Free Press.

———. 1974. *Theory and Method in a Study of Argentine Fertility*. New York: Wiley.

———. 1986. "The Reproduction of Objective Knowledge: Common Sense Reasoning in Medical Decision Making." In Gernot Bohme and Nico Stehr, eds., *The Knowledge Society: Sociology of the Sciences Yearbook 1986*. Norwell, Mass.: D. Reidel.

Clegg, Stewart. 1975. *Power, Rule and Domination: A Critical and Empirical Understanding of Power in Sociological Theory and Everyday Life*. London: Routledge and Kegan Paul.

Cole, Robert E. 1971. *Japanese Blue Collar*. Berkeley: Univ. of California Press.

———. 1979. *Work, Mobility and Participation: A Comparative Study of American and Japanese Industry*. Berkeley: Univ. of California Press.

———, ed. 1981. *The Japanese Automobile Industry*. Ann Arbor: Center for Japanese Studies.

Coleman, James S. 1986. "Micro Foundations and Macrosocial Theory." In Siegwart Lindenberg, James S. Coleman, and Stefan Nowak, eds., *Approaches to Social Theory*. New York: Russell Sage Foundation.

Colinvaux, P. A. 1978. *Why Big Fierce Animals Are Rare: An Ecologist's Perspective*. Princeton: Princeton Univ. Press.

Collins, Randall. 1971. "Functional and Conflict Theories of Educational Stratification." *American Sociological Review* 36: 1002–19.

———. 1975. *Conflict Sociology: Toward an Explanatory Science,* New York: Academic Press.

———. 1977. "Some Comparative Principles of Educational Stratification." *Harvard Educational Review* 47: 1–27.

———. 1979. *The Credential Society: An Historical Sociology of Education and Stratification*. New York: Academic Press.

———. 1981. *Sociology Since Midcentury: Essays in Theory Cumulation*. New York: Academic Press.

———. 1981a. "On the Micro-foundations of Macro-sociology." *American Journal of Sociology* 86: 984–1014.

———. 1981b. "Micro-translation as a Theory-building Strategy." In Karin Knorr-Cetina and Aaron V. Cicourel, eds., *Advances in Social Theory and Methodology: Towards an Integration of Micro- and Macro-sociology* London: Routledge and Kegan Paul: 81–108.

———. 1985. *Three Sociological Traditions*. New York: Oxford Univ. Press.

———. 1986. *Weberian Sociological Theory*. Cambridge and New York: Cambridge Univ. Press.

———. 1988. "Sociological Theory, Disaster Research, and War." In Gary A. Kreps, ed., *Social Structure and Disaster: Conception and Measurement*. Newark, Del.: Univ. of Delaware Press.

Comrie, Bernard. 1981. *Language Universals and Linguistic Typology*. Chicago: Univ. of Chicago Press.

Comte, Auguste. 1830–42/1898. *The Course of Positive Philosophy*. London: Bell and Sons.

Condon, William S., and W. D. Ogston. 1971. "Speech and Body Motion Synchrony of the Speaker-hearer." In D. D. Horton and J. J. Jenkins, eds. *Perception of Language*. Columbus, Oh.: Merrill.

Condon, William S., and Louis W. Sander. 1974a. "Synchrony Demonstrated between Movements of the Neonate and Adult Speech." *Child Development* 45: 456–62.

———. 1974b. "Neonate Movement Is Synchronized with Adult Speech: Interactional Participation and Language Acquisition." *Science* 183: 99–101.

Connor, Walter D. 1979. *Socialism, Politics, and Equality*. New York: Columbia Univ. Press.

Contole, Julie, and Ray Over. 1981. "Change in Selectivity of Infant Social Behavior between 15 and 30 Weeks." *Journal of Experimental Child Psychology* 32: 21–35.

Conze, Edward. 1967. *Buddhist Thought in India*. Ann Arbor: Univ. of Michigan Press.

Cook, Karen S. 1975. "Expectations, Evaluations, and Equity." *American Sociological Review* 40: 372–88.

———. 1982. "Network Structures from an Exchange Perspective." In Peter V. Marsden and Nan Lin, eds., *Social Structure and Network Analysis*. Beverly Hills: Sage.

Cook, Karen S., Richard M. Emerson, Mary R. Gillmore, and Toshio Yamagishi. 1983. "The Distribution of Power in Exchange Networks." *American Journal of Sociology* 89: 275–305.

Cooley, Charles Horton. 1902. *Human Nature and the Social Order*. New York: Scribner.

Corning, Peter A. 1983. *The Synergism Hypothesis: A Theory of Progressive Evolution*. New York: McGraw-Hill.

Corsaro, William. 1985. *Friendship and Peer Culture in the Early Years*. Norwood, N.J.: Ablex.

Coser, Lewis A. 1956. *The Functions of Social Conflict*. New York: Free Press.

———. 1975. "Two Methods in Search of a Substance." *American Sociological Review* 40: 691–700.

Crozier, Michel. 1964. *The Bureaucratic Phenomenon*. Chicago: Univ. of Chicago Press.

Curtis, Richard, and Elton F. Jackson. 1977. *Inequality in American Communities*. New York: Academic Press.

Dahrendorf, Ralf. 1959. *Class and Class Conflict in Industrial Society*. Stanford: Stanford Univ. Press.

Davidson, H. R. Ellis. 1981. *Gods and Myths of Northern Europe*. Baltimore: Penguin Books.

Davies, James C. 1962. "Toward a Theory of Revolution." *American Sociological Review* 27: 5–18.

Davis, Kingsley, and Wilbert M. Moore. 1945. "Some Principles of Stratification." *American Sociological Review* 10: 242–49.

DeLamater, John, and Patricia MacCorquodale. 1979. *Premarital Sexuality*. Madison: Univ. of Wisconsin Press.

Derrida, Jacques. 1967/1976. *Of Grammatology*. Baltimore: Johns Hopkins Univ. Press.

Deutsch, Morton. 1985. *Distributive Justice*. New Haven: Yale Univ. Press.

Devine, Joel A. 1983. "Fiscal Policy and Class Income Inequality." *American Sociological Review* 48: 606–22.

Dobash, R. Emerson, and Russell Dobash. 1979. *Violence against Wives*. New York: Free Press.

Domhoff, G. William. 1967. *Who Rules America?* Englewood Cliffs, N.J.: Prentice-Hall.

Douglas, Jack. D. 1967. *The Social Meanings of Suicide*. Princeton: Princeton Univ. Press.

Douglas, Mary. 1966. *Purity and Danger: An Analysis of Concepts of Pollution and Taboo*. London: Routledge and Kegan Paul.

———. 1973. *Natural Symbols*. Baltimore: Penguin Books.

Dreyfus, Hubert, and Stuart Dreyfus. 1986. "Why Computers May Never Think Like People." *Technology Review* 88: 20–30.

Duncan, Otis Dudley. 1966. "Methodological Issues in the Analysis of Social Mobility." In Neil Smelser and S. M. Lipset, eds., *Social Structure and Mobility in Economic Development*. Chicago: Aldine.

———. 1984. *Notes on Social Measurement*. New York: Russell Sage.

Durkheim, Émile. 1893/1964. *The Division of Labor in Society*. New York: Free Press.

———. 1895/1982. *The Rules of Sociological Method*. New York: Free Press.

———. 1897/1951. *Suicide*. New York: Free Press.

———. 1903/1961. *Moral Education*. New York: Free Press.

———. 1906/1974. "The Determination of Moral Facts." In *Sociology and Philosophy*. New York: Free Press.

———. 1912/1954. *The Elementary Forms of the Religious Life*. New York: Free Press.

Eberhard, Wolfram. 1965. *Conquerors and Rulers*. Leiden: Brill.

Eco, Umberto. 1976. *A Theory of Semiotics*. Bloomington: Indiana Univ. Press.

Ekeh, Peter P. 1975. *Social Exchange Theory and the Two Sociological Traditions*. Cambridge, Mass.: Harvard Univ. Press.

Elkin, A. P. 1979. *The Australian Aborigines*. Sydney: Angus and Ferguson.

Emerson, Richard M. 1972. "Exchange Theory, Part I: A Psychological Basis for Exchange. Part II: Exchange Relations and Network Structures." In Joseph Berger, Morris Zelditch, Jr., and Bo Anderson, eds., *Sociological Theories in Progress*. New York: Houghton Mifflin.

Emmanuel, Arghiri. 1972. *Unequal Exchange*. New York: Monthly Review Press.

Engels, Friedrich. 1850/1967. *The Peasant Wars in Germany*. Chicago: Univ. of Chicago Press.

———. 1884/1972. *The Origin of the Family, Private Property and the State*. New York: International Publishers.

Erikson, Kai. 1966. *Wayward Puritans*. New York: Wiley.

Etzioni, Amitai. 1961/1975. *A Comparative Analysis of Complex Organizations*. New York: Free Press.

Fararo, Thomas J. 1984. "Neoclassical Theorizing and Formalization in Sociology." *Journal of Mathematical Sociology* 10: 361–93.

Fararo, Thomas J., and John Skvoretz. 1984. "Institutions as Production Systems." *Journal of Mathematical Sociology* 10: 117–82.

Featherman, David L., and Robert Hauser. 1978. *Opportunity and Change*. New York: Free Press.

Festinger, Leon, Stanley Schachter, and Kurt Back. 1950. *Social Pressures in Informal Groups*. New York: Harper and Row.

Feyerabend, Paul. 1975. *Against Method: Outline of an Anarchistic Theory of Knowledge*. London: New Left Books.

Fine, Terrence L. 1973. *Theories of Probability: An Examination of Foundations*. New York: Academic Press.

Firebaugh, Glenn. 1980. "The Case of the Missing-Values Card, and Other Mysteries: Another Look at the Effect of Government Spending on Income Inequality." *American Sociological Review* 45: 136–46.

Fischer, Claude S. 1982. *To Dwell Among Friends: Personal Networks in Town and City*. Chicago: Univ. of Chicago Press.

Form, William. 1985. *Divided We Stand: Working Class Stratification in America*. Urbana: Univ. of Illinois Press.

Foucault, Michel. 1961/1965. *Madness and Civilization*. New York: Random House.

———. 1963/1973. *The Birth of the Clinic*. New York: Pantheon.

———. 1975/1977. *Discipline and Punish*. New York: Pantheon.

———. 1976/1978. *The History of Sexuality*. New York: Pantheon.

Frank, Andre Gunder. 1967. *Capitalism and Underdevelopment in Latin America*. New York: Monthly Review Press.

———. 1979. *Dependent Accumulation*. New York: Monthly Review Press.

Freeman, Linton C. 1979. "Centrality in Social Networks: I. Conceptual Clarification." *Social Networks* 1: 215–39.

Fuchs, Stephan. 1986. "The Social Organization of Scientific Knowledge." *Sociological Theory* 4: 126–42.

Gabennesch, Howard. 1972. "Authoritarianism as World View." *American Journal of Sociology* 77: 857–75.

Gadamer, Hans-Georg. 1975. *Truth and Method*. New York: Seabury Press.

———. 1976. *Philosophical Hermeneutics*. Berkeley: Univ. of California Press.

Gans, Herbert J. 1962. *The Urban Villagers*. New York: Free Press.

———. 1967. *The Levittowners*. New York: Random House.

———. 1971. *Popular Culture and High Culture*. New York: Basic Books.

Garfinkel, Harold. 1963. "A Conception of and Experiments with 'Trust' as a Condition for Concerted Stable Actions." In O. J. Harvey, ed., *Motivation and Social Interaction*. New York: Ronald Press.

———. 1967. *Studies in Ethnomethodology*. Englewood Cliffs: Prentice-Hall.

Garfinkel, Harold, Michael Lynch, and Eric Livingston. 1981. "The Work of Discovering Science Construed from Materials from the Optically Discovered Pulsar." *Philosophy of the Social Sciences* 11: 131–38.

Giddens, Anthony. 1976. *New Rules of Sociological Method*. New York: Basic Books.

———. 1981. *A Contemporary Critique of Historical Materialism*. Berkeley: Univ. of California Press.

———. 1984. *The Constitution of Society*. Berkeley: Univ. of California Press.

Gillies, D. A. 1973. *An Objective Theory of Probability*. London: Methuen.

Gilligan, Carol. 1982. *In a Different Voice: Psychological Theory and Women's Development*. Cambridge: Harvard Univ. Press.

Gitlin, Todd. 1979. "Prime Time Ideology: The Hegemony Process in Television Entertainment." *Social Problems* 26: 251–66.

Goffman, Erving. 1959. *The Presentation of Self in Everyday Life*. New York: Doubleday.

———. 1961a. *Asylums*. New York: Doubleday.

———. 1961b. *Encounters*. Indianapolis: Bobbs-Merrill.

———. 1967. *Interaction Ritual*. New York: Doubleday.

———. 1969. *Strategic Interaction*. Philadelphia: Univ. of Pennsylvania Press.

———. 1971. *Relations in Public*. New York: Basic Books.

———. 1974. *Frame Analysis*. New York: Harper and Row.

——. 1979. *Gender Advertisements*. Cambridge, Mass.: Harvard Univ. Press.

——. 1981. *Forms of Talk*. Philadelphia: Univ. of Pennsylvania Press.

Goode, William J. 1960. "A Theory of Role Strain." *American Sociological Review* 25: 483–96.

Goodman, Nelson. 1978. *Ways of World-Making*. Indianapolis: Bobbs-Merrill.

Gottdiener, Mark. 1985. "Hegemony and Mass Culture: A Semiotic Approach." *American Journal of Sociology* 90: 979–1001.

Gottfredson, Linda S. 1981. "Circumscription and Compromise: A Developmental Theory of Occupational Aspirations." *Journal of Counseling Psychology Monograph* 28: 545–79.

Gould, Stephen Jay. 1982. "Darwin and the Expansion of Evolutionary Theory." *Science* 216: 380–87.

Gouldner, Alvin W. 1954. *Patterns of Industrial Bureaucracy*. Glencoe, Ill.: Free Press.

——. 1970. *The Coming Crisis of Western Sociology*. New York: Basic Books.

Gramsci, Antonio. 1928/1971. *Selections from the Prison Notebooks*. New York: International Publishers.

Grandjean, Burke D. 1981. "History and Career in a Bureaucratic Labor Market." *American Journal of Sociology* 86: 1057–92.

Granovetter, Mark. 1973. "The Strength of Weak Ties." *American Journal of Sociology* 76: 1360–80.

——. 1983. "The Strength of Weak Ties: A Network Theory Revisited." *Sociological Theory* 1: 201–33.

——. 1985. "Economic Action and Social Structure: The Problem of Embeddedness." *American Journal of Sociology* 91: 481–510.

Gregory, Stanford W., Jr. 1983. "A Quantitative Analysis of Temporal Symmetry in Microsocial Relations." *American Sociological Review* 48: 129–35.

Gusfield, Joseph R. 1963. *Symbolic Crusade: Status Politics and the American Temperance Movement*. Urbana: Univ. of Illinois Press.

——. 1975. *Community*. Oxford: Basil Blackwell.

Guttentag, Marcia, and Paul F. Secord. 1983. *Too Many Women? The Sex Ratio Question*. Beverly Hills: Sage.

Habermas, Jurgen. 1970. "Science and Technology as Ideology." In *Towards a Rational Society*. Boston: Beacon Press.

——. 1975. *Legitimation Crisis*. Boston: Beacon Press.

——. 1979. *Communication and the Evolution of Society*. Boston: Beacon Press.

——. 1981/1984. *The Theory of Communicative Action*. Boston: Beacon Press.

Hacking, Ian. 1975. *The Emergence of Probability*. Cambridge: Cambridge Univ. Press.

Hage, Jerald D. 1980. *Theories of Organizations*. New York: Wiley.

Hall, Richard H. 1982. *Organizations: Structure and Process*. Englewood Cliffs, N.J.: Prentice-Hall.

Halle, David. 1984. *America's Working Man*. Chicago: Univ. of Chicago Press.

Hannan, Michael, and John Freeman. 1977. "The Population Ecology of Organizations." *American Journal of Sociology* 82: 929–40.

Hanneman, Robert A. 1987. *Computer-assisted Theory-building: Modeling Dynamic Social Systems*. Beverly Hills: Sage.

Hanneman, Robert, and Randall Collins. 1987. "A Dynamic Simulation of Marx's Model of Capitalism." In Norbert Wiley, ed., *The Marx-Weber Debate*. Beverly Hills: Sage.

Harris, Marvin. 1974. *Cows, Pigs, Wars and Witches: The Riddle of Culture*. New York: Random House.

Harrod, W. J. 1980. "Expectations from Unequal Rewards." *Social Psychology Quarterly*. 43: 126–30.

Hartmann, Heidi. 1981. "The Family as the Locus of Gender, Class, and Political Struggle: The Example of Housework." *Signs* 6: 366–94.

Heath, Anthony. 1976. *Rational Choice and Social Exchange*. New York: Cambridge Univ. Press.

Hechter, Michael, ed. 1983. *The Microfoundations of Macrosociology*. Philadelphia: Temple Univ. Press.

Heckathorn, Douglas D. 1984. "Mathematical Theory Construction in Sociology: Analytic Power, Scope, and Descriptive Accuracy as Trade-Offs." *Journal of Mathematical Sociology* 10: 295–323.

Heidegger, Martin. 1927/1960. *Being and Time*. New York: Harper.

Heise, David R. 1979. *Understanding Events: Affect and the Construction of Social Action*. New York: Cambridge Univ. Press.

———. 1987. "Affect Control Theory: Concepts and Model." *Journal of Mathematical Sociology* 13. In press.

Herrnstein, Richard. 1973. *I.Q. in the Meritocracy*. Boston: Atlantic-Little, Brown.

Hess, R. D., and J. Torney. 1967. *The Development of Political Attitudes in Children*. Chicago: Aldine.

Hilbert, Richard A. 1987. "Bureaucracy as Belief, Rationalization as Repair: Max Weber in a Post-Functionalist Age." *Sociological Theory* 5: 70–86.

Hirsh, Arthur. 1981. *The French New Left: An Intellectual History from Sartre to Gorz*. Boston: South End Press.

Hirschi, Travis. 1969. *The Causes of Delinquency*. Berkeley: Univ. of California Press.

Homans, George C. 1941. *English Villagers of the Thirteenth Century*. Cambridge, Mass.: Harvard Univ. Press.

———. 1950. *The Human Group*. New York: Harcourt.

———. 1958. "Social Behavior as Exchange." *American Journal of Sociology* 63: 597–606.

———. 1961. *Social Behavior: Its Elementary Forms*. New York: Harcourt. Rev. ed., 1974.

———. 1964. "Bringing Men Back In." *American Sociological Review* 29: 809–18.

———. 1967. *The Nature of Social Science*. New York: Harcourt.

———. 1984. *Coming to My Senses: The Autobiography of a Sociologist*. New Brunswick, N.J.: Transaction Books.

Homans, George C., and David M. Schneider. 1955. *Marriage, Authority, and Final Causes: A Study of Unilateral Cross-Cousin Marriage*. New York: Free Press.

Huber, Joan, and Glenna Spitze. 1983. *Sex Stratification: Children, Housework, and Jobs*. New York: Academic Press.

Jackman, Robert W. 1980. "Keynesian Government Intervention and Income Inequality." *American Sociological Review* 45: 131–36.

Jaffe, Joseph, and Stanley Feldstein. 1970. *Rhythms of Dialogue*. New York: Academic Press.

Jameson, Fredric. 1972. *The Prison-House of Language*. Princeton: Princeton Univ. Press.

Jasso, Guillermina. 1980. "A New Theory of Distributive Justice." *American Sociological Review* 45: 3–32.

Jencks, Christopher, et al. 1972. *Inequality: A Reassessment of the Effect of Family and Schooling in America*. New York: Basic Books.

Jensen, Arthur R. 1969. "How Much Can We Boost IQ and Scholastic Achievement?" *Harvard Educational Review* 39: 1–123.

Johnson, G. David. 1983. "Mead as Positivist." *Theory and Society* 12: 273–77.

Johnson, G. David, and Lewellyn Hendrix. 1982. "A Cross-cultural Test of Collins's Theory of Sexual Stratification." *Journal of Marriage and the Family* 44: 675–89.

Johnston, J. R. 1984. "Personal Attributes and the Structure of Interpersonal Relations." In Joseph Berger and Morris Zelditch, eds., *Studies in Expectation States Theory*. San Francisco: Jossey-Bass.

Kadushin, Charles. 1982. "Social Density and Mental Health." In Peter V. Marsden and Nan Lin, eds., *Social Structure and Network Analysis*. Beverly Hills: Sage.

Kahneman, D., P. Slovic, and A. Tversky, 1982. *Judgment under Uncertainty: Heuristics and Biases*. London: Cambridge Univ. Press.

Kanter, Rosabeth M. 1977. *Men and Women of the Corporation*. New York: Basic Books.

Katz, Daniel, and Robert L. Kahn. 1978. *The Social Psychology of Organizations*. New York: Wiley.

Keegan, John. 1977. *The Face of Battle: A Study of Agincourt, Waterloo, and the Somme*. New York: Random House.

Kemper, Theodore D. 1978. *A Social Interactional Theory of Emotions*. New York: Wiley.

Kempton, Willet. 1980. "The Rhythmic Basis of Interactional Micro-synchrony." In Mary R. Key, ed., *The Relationship of Verbal and Nonverbal Communication*. New York: Mouton.

Kendon, Adam. 1970. "Movement Coordination in Social Interaction." *Acta Psychologica* 32: 1–25.

———. 1980. "Gesticulation and Speech: Two Aspects of the Process of Utterance." In Mary R. Key, ed., *The Relationship of Verbal and Nonverbal Communication*. New York: Mouton.

Keynes, John Maynard, 1921. *A Treatise on Probability*. London: Macmillan.

Knoke, David, and Edward O. Laumann. 1982. "The Social Organization of National Policy Domains: An Exploration of Some Structural Hypotheses." In Peter

V. Marsden and Nan Lin, eds., *Social Structure and Network Analysis*. Beverly Hills: Sage.

Knorr-Cetina, Karin. 1981. *The Manufacture of Knowledge: An Essay on the Constructionist and Contextual Nature of Science*. New York: Pergamon Press.

Knorr-Cetina, Karin, and Michael Mulkay, eds. 1983. *Science Observed: Perspectives on the Social Study of Science*. Beverly Hills: Sage.

Kohlberg, Lawrence. 1976. "Moral Stages and Moralization: The Cognitive-Developmental Approach." In T. Lickona, ed., *Moral Development and Behavior*. New York: Holt.

Kohlberg, Lawrence, and Carol Gilligan. 1971. "The Adolescent as Philosopher." *Daedelus* 100: 1051–86.

Kohn, Melvin L. 1971. "Bureaucratic Man: A Portrait and an Interpretation." *American Sociological Review* 36: 461–74.

———. 1977. *Class and Conformity*. Chicago: Univ. of Chicago Press.

Kohn, Melvin L., and Carmi L. Schooler. 1969. "Class, Occupation, and Orientation." *American Sociological Review* 34: 659–78.

———. 1983. *Work and Personality*. Norwood, N.J.: Ablex.

Korpi, Walter. 1983. *The Democratic Class Struggle*. London: Routledge and Kegan Paul.

Kramer, Edna E. 1970. *The Nature and Growth of Modern Mathematics*. vol. 2. New York: Hawthorn Books.

Kriesberg, Louis. 1982. *Social Conflicts*. Englewood Cliffs, N.J.: Prentice-Hall.

Kroeber, A. L. 1963. *Anthropology: Culture Patterns and Processes*. New York: Harcourt.

Kuhn, Thomas S. 1961. "The Function of Measurement in Modern Physical Science." In Harry Woolf, ed., *Quantification: A History of the Meaning of Measurement in the Natural and Social Sciences*. Indianapolis: Bobbs-Merrill.

———. 1970. *The Structure of Scientific Revolutions*. Chicago: Univ. of Chicago Press.

Kuklick, Bruce. 1977. *The Rise of American Philosophy: Cambridge, Massachusetts, 1860–1930*. New Haven: Yale Univ. Press.

Kurzweil, Edith. 1980. *The Age of Structuralism*. New York: Columbia Univ. Press.

Lacan, Jacques. 1966/1977. *Écrits: A Selection*. New York: Norton.

Lakatos, Imre. 1976. *Proofs and Refutations*. Cambridge: Cambridge Univ. Press.

Langendoen, D. Terence, and Paul M. Postal. 1984. *The Vastness of Natural Languages*. Oxford: Basil Blackwell.

Latour, Bruno, and Steve Woolgar. 1983. *Laboratory Life: The Social Construction of Scientific Facts*. Beverly Hills: Sage.

Laumann, Edward O. 1966. *Prestige and Association in an Urban Community*. Indianapolis: Bobbs-Merrill.

———. 1973. *The Bonds of Pluralism*. New York: Wiley.

Laumann, Edward O., and David Knoke. 1987. *The Organizational State*. Madison: Univ. of Wisconsin Press.

Laumann, Edward O., and Franz U. Pappi. 1976. *Networks of Collective Action: A Perspective on Community Influence Systems*. New York: Academic Press.

Laumann, Edward O., and Richard Senter. 1976. "Subjective Social Distance, Occupational Stratification, and Forms of Status and Class Consciousness." *American Journal of Sociology* 81: 1304–38.

Laumann, Edward O., David Knoke, and Yong-Hak Kim. 1985. "An Organizational Approach to State Policy Formation." *American Sociological Review* 50: 1–19.

Lawrence, Paul R., and Jay W. Worsch. 1967. *Organization and Environment*. Cambridge, Mass.: Harvard Univ. Press.

Lefebvre, Henri. 1971. *Everyday Life in the Modern World*. London: Allen Lane.

Leiter, Kenneth. 1980. *A Primer on Ethnomethodology*. New York: Oxford Univ. Press.

Lemert, Edwin. 1951. *Social Pathology*. New York: McGraw-Hill.

Lenski, Gerhard E. 1966. *Power and Privilege: A Theory of Stratification*. New York: McGraw-Hill.

Lenski, Gerhard E., and Jean Lenski. 1974. *Human Societies: An Introduction to Macrosociology*. New York: McGraw-Hill.

Leontieff, Wassily. 1982. "Academic Economics." *Science* 217: 104–107.

Lévi-Strauss, Claude. 1949/1969. *The Elementary Structures of Kinship*. Boston: Beacon Press.

——. 1958/1963. *Structural Anthropology*. New York: Basic Books.

——. 1962/1966. *The Savage Mind*. Chicago: Univ. of Chicago Press.

——. 1964/1969. *The Raw and the Cooked*. New York: Harper and Row.

——. 1968/1973. *From Honey to Ashes*. New York: Harper and Row.

——. 1968/1978. *The Origin of Table Manners*. New York: Harper and Row.

——. 1971/1981. *The Naked Man*. New York: Harper and Row.

——. 1984. "The Origin of Historical Societies." Public lecture, Univ. of California, Los Angeles.

Lewin, Roger. 1985. "Pattern and Process in Life's History." *Science* 229: 1511–12.

Lewis, J. D., and R. Smith. 1980. *American Sociology and Pragmatism: Mead, Chicago Sociology, and Symbolic Interaction*. Chicago: Univ. of Chicago Press.

Lieberson, Stanley. 1985. *Making It Count: The Improvement of Social Theory and Research*. Berkeley: Univ. of California Press.

Lin, Nan. 1982. "Social Resources and Instrumental Action." In Peter V. Marsden and Nan Lin, eds., *Social Structure and Network Analysis*. Beverly Hills: Sage.

——. 1987. "Social Resources and Social Mobility: A Structural Theory of Status Attainment." In Ronald L. Breiger, ed., *Social Mobility and Social Structure*. Cambridge and New York: Cambridge Univ. Press.

Lind, Joan. 1983. "The Organization of Coercion in History: A Rationalist-Evolutionary Theory." *Sociological Theory* 1: 1–29.

Lindenberg, Siegwart. 1985. "An Assessment of the New Political Economy." *Sociological Theory* 3: 99–113.

Linton, Ralph. 1936. *The Study of Man*. New York: Appleton-Century-Crofts.

Lipset, Seymour Martin. 1950. *Agrarian Socialism*. Berkeley: Univ. of California Press.

———. 1960. *Political Man*. New York: Doubleday.

Lipset, Seymour Martin, and Reinhard Bendix. 1959. *Social Mobility in Industrial Society*. Berkeley: Univ. of California Press.

Luhman, Niklas. 1979. *Trust and Power*. New York: Wiley.

———. 1980. *Gesellschaftsstruktur und Semantik*. Frankfurt: Suhrkamp.

———. 1982. *The Differentiation of Society*. New York: Columbia Univ. Press.

———. 1984. *Soziale Systeme*. Frankfurt: Suhrkamp.

———. 1986. *Love as Passion: The Codification of Intimacy*. Cambridge, Mass.: Harvard Univ. Press.

Lukacs, Georg. 1923/1971. *History and Class Consciousness*. Cambridge, Mass.: MIT Press.

Luker, Kristin. 1983. *Abortion and the Politics of Motherhood*. Berkeley: Univ. of California Press.

Lukes, Steven. 1973. *Émile Durkheim: His Life and Work*. London: Allen Lane.

Lumsden, C. J. and E. O. Wilson. 1981. *Genes, Mind, and Culture*. Cambridge, Mass.: Harvard Univ. Press.

Lynch, Michael, Eric Livingston, and Harold Garfinkel. 1983. "Temporal Order in Laboratory Work." In Karin Knorr-Cetina and Michael Mulkay, eds., *Science Observed: Perspectives on the Social Study of Science*. Beverly Hills: Sage.

Macfarlane, Alan. 1978. *The Origins of English Individualism*. Oxford: Blackwell.

MacKenzie, Donald A. 1981. *Statistics in Britain, 1865–1930: The Social Construction of Scientific Knowledge*. Edinburgh: Edinburgh Univ. Press.

Maine, Henry Sumner. 1861/1963. *Ancient Law*. Boston: Beacon Press.

Malinowski, Bronislaw. 1922. *Argonauts of the Western Pacific*. New York: Dutton.

———. 1948. *Magic, Science and Religion*. New York: Doubleday.

Mann, Michael. 1970. "The Social Cohesion of Liberal Democracy." *American Sociological Review* 35: 423–39.

———. 1986. *The Sources of Social Power*. Vol. 1. New York: Cambridge Univ. Press.

March, James G., and Johan P. Olsen. 1976. *Ambiguity and Choice in Organizations*. Bergen, Norway: Universitesforlaeet.

March, James G., and Herbert A. Simon. 1958. *Organizations*. New York: Wiley.

Marcuse, Herbert. 1941. *Reason and Revolution*. New York: Oxford Univ. Press.

———. 1964. *One-Dimensional Man*. Boston: Beacon Press.

Marsden, Peter V., and Edward O. Laumann. 1984. "Mathematical Ideas in Social Structural Analysis." *Journal of Mathematical Sociology* 10: 271–94.

Marsh, Robert M. 1963. "Values, Demand, and Social Mobility." *American Sociological Review* 28: 567–75.

Marx, Karl. 1842–44/1971. *The Early Texts*. Ed. by David McLellan. Oxford: Blackwell.

———. 1852/1963. *The Eighteenth Brumaire of Louis Bonaparte*. New York: International Publishers.

———. 1867, 1885, 1894/1967. *Capital*. 3 vols. New York: International Publishers.

Marx, Karl, and Friedrich Engels. 1846/1947. *The German Ideology*. New York: International Publishers.

———. 1848/1959. *The Communist Manifesto*. In L. Feuer, ed., *Marx and Engels: Basic Writings on Politics and Philosophy*. New York: Doubleday.

Mauss, Marcel. 1925/1967. *The Gift*. New York: Norton.

———. 1938/1985. "A Category of the Human Mind: The Notion of Person; the Notion of Self." In Michael Carrithers, Steven Collins, and Steven Lukes, eds., *The Category of the Person*. Cambridge and New York: Cambridge Univ. Press.

Mayhew, Bruce H., and Roger Levinger. 1976. "On the Emergence of Oligarchy in Human Interaction." *American Journal of Sociology* 81: 1017–49.

Mayhew, Bruce H., and Paul T. Schollaert. 1980. "The Concentration of Wealth: A Sociological Model." *Sociological Focus* 13: 1–35.

Mazur, Alan. 1973. "A Cross-species Comparison of Status in Small Established Groups." *American Sociological Review* 38: 196–205.

———. 1981. "Biosociology." In James F. Short, ed. *The State of Sociology*. Beverly Hills: Sage.

Mazur, Alan, and Theodore A. Lamb. 1980. "Testosterone, Status, and Mood in Human Males." *Hormones and Behavior* 14: 236–46.

Mazur, Alan, E. Rosa, M. Faupel, J. Heller, R. Leen, and B. Thurman. 1980. "Physiological Aspects of Communication via Mutual Gaze." *American Journal of Sociology* 86: 50–74.

McClelland, Kent. 1985. "On the Social Significance of Interactional Synchrony." Unpublished paper, Dept. of Sociology, Grinnell College.

McPhail, Clark, and Cynthia Rexroat. 1979. "Mead vs. Blumer: The Divergent Methodological Perspectives of Social Behaviorism and Symbolic Interactionism." *American Sociological Review* 44: 449–67.

McPherson, J. Miller, and Lynn Smith-Lovin. 1986. "Sex Segregation in Voluntary Associations." *American Sociological Review* 51: 61–79.

Mead, George Herbert. 1934. *Mind, Self and Society*. Chicago: Univ. of Chicago Press.

———. 1938. *The Philosophy of the Act*. Chicago: Univ. of Chicago Press.

Mehan, Hugh D., and Houston Wood. 1975. *The Reality of Ethnomethodology*. New York: Wiley.

Merton, Robert K. 1949. "The Self-Fulfilling Prophecy." In *Social Theory and Social Structure*. Glencoe, Ill.: Free Press.

———. 1968. *Social Theory and Social Structure*. Glencoe, Ill.: Free Press.

Meyer, John. 1977. "The Effects of Education as an Institution." *American Journal of Sociology* 83: 340–63.

Meyer, Marshall. 1968. "Automation and Bureaucratic Structure." *American Journal of Sociology* 74: 256–64.

Meyer, Marshall, and Lynn Zucker. 1987. *Permanently Failing Organizations*. Unpublished manuscript.

Michels, Robert. 1911/1949. *Political Parties*. Glencoe, Ill.: Free Press.

Miliband, Ralph. 1973. *The State in Capitalist Society*. London: Quartet Books.

Miller, James G. 1978. *Living Systems*. New York: McGraw-Hill.

Mills, C. Wright. 1956. *The Power Elite*. New York: Oxford Univ. Press.

Mitchell, J. Clyde. 1969. *Social Networks in Urban Situations*. Manchester: Manchester Univ. Press.

Mitchell, Juliet. 1971. *Woman's Estate*. New York: Vintage.

Money, John, and Anke Ehrhardt. 1972. *Man and Woman: Boy and Girl*. Baltimore: Johns Hopkins Univ. Press.

Montesquieu, Charles, Baron de. 1748/1949. *The Spirit of the Laws*. New York: Hafner.

Moore, Barrington, Jr. 1966. *Social Origins of Dictatorship and Democracy*. Boston: Beacon Press.

Morgan, David L., and Margaret T. Spanish. 1985. "Symbolic Interactionism and Social Cognition: Two Perspectives on Social Roles and Social Knowledge." Unpublished paper, Univ. of California, Riverside.

Morris, Ivan. 1964. *The World of the Shining Prince: Court Life in Ancient Japan*. Oxford: Oxford Univ. Press.

Murphy, Raymond. 1984. "The Structure of Closure: A Critique and Development of the Theories of Weber, Collins, and Parkin." *British Journal of Sociology* 35: 547–67.

———. 1985. "Exploitation or Exclusion?" *Sociology* 19: 225–43.

Murphy, Robert F. 1959. "Social Structure and Sex Antagonism." *Southwestern Journal of Anthropology* 15: 89–98.

Nagel, Ernst. 1961. *The Structure of Science*. New York: Harcourt.

Needham, Rodney. 1963. "Introduction." In Marcel Mauss and Émile Durkheim, *Primitive Classification*. Chicago: Univ. of Chicago Press.

Nisbet, Robert. 1953. *The Quest for Community*. New York: Oxford Univ. Press.

Oberschall, Anthony. 1973. *Social Conflicts and Social Movements*. Englewood Cliffs, N.J.: Prentice-Hall.

O'Connor, James. 1973. *The Fiscal Crisis of the State*. New York: St. Martin's Press.

Ouichi, William G. 1980. "Markets, Bureaucracies, and Clans." *Administrative Science Quarterly* 25: 129–41.

———. 1981. *Theory Z*. Reading, Mass.: Addison-Wesley.

Paige, Jeffery. 1975. *Agrarian Revolution*. New York: Free Press.

Paige, Karen Ericksen, and Jeffery M. Paige. 1981. *The Politics of Reproductive Ritual*. Berkeley: Univ. of California Press.

Parkin, Frank. 1979. *Marxism and Class Theory: A Bourgeois Critique*. London: Routledge.

Parsons, Talcott. 1937. *The Structure of Social Action*. New York: McGraw-Hill.

——. 1947. "Introduction." In Max Weber, *The Theory of Social and Economic Organization*. Trans. by A. M. Henderson and Talcott Parsons. New York: Oxford Univ. Press.

——. 1949. *Essays in Sociological Theory*. New York: Free Press.

——. 1951. *The Social System*. Glencoe, Ill.: Free Press.

——. 1963. "Introduction." In Max Weber, *The Sociology of Religion*. Trans. by Ephraim Fischoff. Boston: Beacon Press.

——. 1966. *Societies: Comparative and Evolutionary Perspectives*. Englewood Cliffs, N.J.: Prentice-Hall.

——. 1967. *Sociological Theory and Modern Society*. New York: Free Press.

——. 1971. *The System of Modern Societies*. Englewood Cliffs, N.J.: Prentice-Hall.

Parsons, Talcott, and Gerald M. Platt. 1973. *The American University*. Cambridge, Mass.: Harvard Univ. Press.

Parsons, Talcott, and Edward A. Shils, eds. 1951. *Toward a General Theory of Action: Theoretical Foundations for the Social Sciences*. Cambridge, Mass.: Harvard Univ. Press.

Parsons, Talcott, and Neil J. Smelser. 1956. *Economy and Society*. New York: Free Press.

Patterson, Orlando. 1982. *Slavery and Social Death: A Comparative Study*. Cambridge, Mass. Harvard Univ. Press.

Peirce, Charles Sanders. 1868/1955. "Some Consequences of the Four Incapacities." In *Philosophical Writings of Peirce*. New York: Dover.

——. 1897/1955. "Logic as Semiotic: The Theory of Signs." In *Philosophical Writings of Peirce*. New York: Dover.

Perrow, Charles. 1967. "A Framework for the Comparative Analysis of Organizations." *American Sociological Review* 32: 194–208.

——. 1984. *Normal Accidents*. New York: Basic Books.

——. 1986. *Complex Organizations: A Critical Essay*. Glenview, Ill.: Scott, Foresman.

Peters, Thomas J., and Robert H. Waterman. 1982. *In Search of Excellence: Lessons from America's Best-run Corporations*. New York: Harper and Row.

Peterson, I. 1986. "Knowing Little about How Things Work." *Science News* 129: 186.

Pfeffer, Jeffrey. 1982. *Organizations and Organization Theory*. Boston: Pitman.

Pfeffer, Jeffrey, and Gerald Salancik. 1978. *The External Control of Organizations: A Resource Dependence Perspective*. New York: Harper and Row.

Phillips, David P., and Kenneth A. Feldman. 1973. "A Dip in Deaths before Ceremonial Occasions: Some New Relationships between Social Integration and Mortality." *American Sociological Review* 38: 678–96.

Piaget, Jean, and Barbel Inhelder. 1967. *The Psychology of the Child*. New York: Basic Books.

Pilcher, Donald. 1976. *The Sociology of Income Distribution*. Unpublished Ph.D. thesis, Univ. of California, San Diego.

Pollner, Melvin. 1974. "Mundane Reasoning." *Philosophy of the Social Sciences*. 4: 35–54.

Poulantzas, Nicos. 1968. *Political Power and Social Classes*. London: New Left Books.

———. 1974. *Classes in Contemporary Capitalism*. London: New Left Books.

———. 1978. *State, Power, and Socialism*. London: New Left Books.

Powers, Charles, and Robert Hanneman. 1983. "Pareto's Theory of Social and Economic Cycles: A Formal Model and Simulation." *Sociological Theory* 1: 59–89.

Prendergast, Christopher. 1986. "Alfred Schutz and the Austrian School of Economics." *American Journal of Sociology* 92: 1–26.

Pribram, Karl. 1971. *Languages of the Brain*. Englewood Cliffs: Prentice-Hall.

Quine, Willard V. 1969. *Ontological Relativity and Other Essays*. New York: Columbia Univ. Press.

Radcliffe-Brown, A. R. 1922. *The Andaman Islanders*. London: Macmillan.

———. 1952. *Structure and Function in Primitive Society*. New York: Macmillan.

Ramirez, Francisco O., and John Boli-Bennett. 1982. "Global Patterns of Educational Institutionalization." In Philip Altbach, Robert Arnove, and Gail Kelley, eds., *Comparative Education*. New York: Macmillan.

Raup, David M. 1986. "Biological Extinction in Earth History." *Science* 231: 1528–33.

Research Working Group on Cyclical Rhythms and Secular Trends. 1979. "Cyclical Rhythms and Secular Trends of the Capitalist World-Economy: Some Premises, Hypotheses, and Questions." *Review* 2 (Spring): 483–500.

Ridgeway, Cecilia, Joseph Berger, and LeRoy Smith. 1985. "Nonverbal Cues and Status: An Expectation States Approach." *American Journal of Sociology* 90: 955–78.

Rosenberg, Morris. 1979. *Conceiving the Self*. New York: Basic Books.

———. 1981. "The Self-Concept: Social Product and Social Force." In Morris Rosenberg and Ralph H. Turner, eds., *Social Psychology*. New York: Basic Books.

Rubin, Lillian. 1976. *Worlds of Pain: Life in the Working Class Family*. New York: Basic Books.

Rueschemeyer, Dietrich. 1986. *Power and the Division of Labor*. Stanford: Stanford Univ. Press.

Russell, Bertrand. 1904. *The Principles of Mathematics*. Cambridge: Cambridge Univ. Press.

Russell, Diana E. H. 1974. *Rebellion, Revolution and Armed Force*. New York: Academic Press.

Sacks, Harvey. 1972. "An Initial Investigation of the Usability of Conversational Data for Doing Sociology." In David Sudnow, ed., *Studies in Social Interaction*. New York: Free Press.

Sacks, Harvey, Emanuel A. Schegloff, and Gail Jefferson. 1974. "A Simplest Systematics for the Organization of Turn-taking for Conversation." *Language* 50: 696–735.

Sacks, Karen. 1979. *Sisters and Wives: The Past and Future of Sexual Equality*. Westport, Conn.: Greenwood.

Safilios-Rothschild, Constantina. 1977. *Love, Sex, and Sex Roles*. Englewood Cliffs, N.J.: Prentice-Hall.

Sahlins, Marshall. 1972. *Stone Age Economics*. Chicago: Aldine.

Sanday, Peggy Reeves. 1981. *Female Power and Male Dominance: On the Origins of Sexual Inequality*. New York: Cambridge Univ. Press.

Sankoff, Gillian. 1980. *The Social Life of Language*. Philadelphia: Univ. of Pennsylvania Press.

Sapir, Edward. 1921. *Language: An Introduction to the Study of Speech*. New York: Harcourt.

Saussure, Ferdinand de. 1915/1966. *Course in General Linguistics*. New York: McGraw-Hill.

Savage, Leonard J. 1954. *The Foundations of Statistics*. New York: Wiley.

Scheff, Thomas J. 1966. *Being Mentally Ill: A Sociological Theory*. Chicago: Aldine.

Scheff, Thomas, and D. Bushnell. 1985. "A Theory of Catharsis." *Journal of Research in Personality* 18: 238–64.

Schegloff, Emanuel A. 1968. "Sequencing in Conversational Openings." *The American Anthropologist* 70: 1075–95.

——. 1987. "Between Macro and Micro: Contexts and Other Connections." In Jeffrey C. Alexander, ed., *The Micro-Macro Connection*. Berkeley: Univ. of California Press.

Schelling, Thomas C. 1962. *The Strategy of Conflict*. Cambridge, Mass.: Harvard Univ. Press.

Schneider, Herbert W. 1963. *A History of American Philosophy*. New York: Columbia Univ. Press.

Schultz, T. W. 1961. "Investment in Human Capital." *American Economic Review* 51: 1–16.

Schumpeter, Joseph A. 1911/1961. *The Theory of Economic Development*. New York: Oxford Univ. Press.

——. 1942. *Capitalism, Socialism, and Democracy*. New York: Harper.

Schur, Edwin M. 1965. *Crimes Without Victims*. Englewood Cliffs, N.J.: Prentice-Hall.

Schutz, Alfred. 1932/1967. *The Phenomenology of the Social World*. Evanston, Ill.: Northwestern Univ. Press.

——. 1940/1978. "Phenomenology and the Social Sciences." In Thomas Luckmann, ed., *Phenomenology and the Social Sciences*. London: Routledge and Kegan Paul.

——. 1962. *Collected Papers I: The Problem of Social Reality*. The Hague: Martinus Nijhoff.

Scott, Marvin B., and Stanford M. Lyman. 1968. "Accounts." *American Sociological Review* 33: 46–62.

Searle, John. 1970. *Speech Acts*. Cambridge: Cambridge Univ. Press.

Seeman, Melvin. 1959. "On the Meaning of Alienation." *American Sociological Review* 24: 783–91.

Sewell, William H., and Robert Hauser. 1980. "The Wisconsin Longitudinal Study of Social and Psychological Factors in Aspirations and Achievements." *Research in Sociology of Education and Socialization* 1: 59–99.

Shank, Roger C., and Robert P. Abelson. 1977. *Scripts, Plans, Goals, and Understanding.* Hillsdale, N.J.: Erlbaum.

Shubik, Martin. 1984. *A Game-Theoretic Approach to Political Economy.* Vol. 2 of *Game Theory in the Social Sciences.* Cambridge, Mass.: MIT Press.

Simmel, Georg. 1908/1955. *Conflict and The Web of Group-Affiliations.* New York: Free Press.

Simon, Herbert A. 1947. *Administrative Behavior.* New York: Macmillan.

———. 1957. *Models of Man.* New York: Wiley.

Skinner, B. F. 1969. *Contingencies of Reinforcement.* New York: Appleton.

Skocpol, Theda. 1979. *States and Social Revolutions.* New York: Cambridge Univ. Press.

Smelser, Neil J. 1959. *Social Change in the Industrial Revolution.* Chicago: Univ. of Chicago Press.

———. 1962. *Theory of Collective Behavior.* New York: Free Press.

Smith, Anthony D. 1986. *The Ethnic Origins of Nations.* New York: Blackwell.

Snyder, D. and E. L. Kick. 1979. "Structural Position in the World System and Economic Growth 1955–1970: A Multiple Network Analysis of Transnational Interactions." *American Journal of Sociology* 84: 1096–126.

Sokoloff, Natalie J. 1980. *Between Money and Love: The Dialectics of Women's Home and Market Work.* New York: Praeger.

Spencer, Herbert. 1862. *First Principles of a New System of Philosophy.* New York: Appleton.

———. 1874–96. *Principles of Sociology.* New York: Appleton.

Ste. Croix, G. E. M. de, 1981. *The Class Struggle in the Ancient Greek World.* London: Duckworth.

Stack, Steven. 1978a. "The Effects of Direct Government Involvement in the Economy on the Degree of Income Inequality: A Cross-national Study." *American Sociological Review* 43: 880–88.

———. 1978b. "The Effects of Political Participation and Socialist Party Strength on the Degree of Income Inequality." *American Sociological Review* 44: 168–71.

———. 1980. "Direct Government Involvement in the Economy: Theoretical and Empirical Extensions." *American Sociological Review* 45: 146–54.

Stevenson, Harold W., Shin-ying Lee, and James W. Stigler. 1986. "Mathematics Achievement of Chinese, Japanese, and American Children." *Science* 231: 692–99.

Stewman, Shelby, and Suresh L. Konda. 1983. "Careers and Organizational Labor Markets: Demographic Models of Organizational Behavior." *American Journal of Sociology* 88: 637–85.

Stinchcombe, Arthur L. 1959. "Bureaucratic and Craft Administration of Production." *Administrative Science Quarterly* 2: 137–58.

———. 1968. *Constructing Social Theories*. New York: Harcourt.

———. 1983. "Review of Gary Becker, 'A Treatise on the Family.' " *American Journal of Sociology* 89: 468–70.

Stryker, Sheldon. 1980. *Symbolic Interactionism: A Social Structural Version*. Menlo Park, Ca.: Benjamin/Cummings.

Sudnow, David. 1978. *Ways of the Hand: The Organization of Improvised Conduct*. Cambridge, Mass.: Harvard Univ. Press.

———. 1979. *Talk's Body: A Meditation between Two Keyboards*. New York: Knopf.

Swanson, Guy E. 1962. *The Birth of the Gods*. Ann Arbor: Univ. of Michigan Press.

Sweezy, Paul M. 1942. *The Theory of Capitalist Development*. New York: Oxford Univ. Press.

Szymanski, Albert. 1981. *The Logic of Imperialism*. New York: Praeger.

Taylor, Howard. 1980. *The IQ Game*. New Brunswick, N.J.: Rutgers Univ. Press.

Thomas, Keith. 1971. *Religion and the Decline of Magic*. New York: Scribner.

Thomas, William I., and Dorothy Swaine Thomas. 1928. *The Child in America*. New York: Knopf.

Thomas, William I., and Florian Znaniecki. 1918–20. *The Polish Peasant in Europe and America*. 5 vols. Boston: Richard G. Badger. Vols. I and II originally published by the Univ. of Chicago Press, 1918.

Thompson, E. P. 1963. *The Making of the English Working Class*. London: Gollancz.

Thompson, James. D. 1967. *Organizations in Action*. New York: McGraw-Hill.

Thurow, Lester C. 1983. *Dangerous Currents: The State of Economics*. New York: Random House.

Tiger, Lionel, and Robin Fox. 1972. *The Imperial Animal*. New York: Holt.

Tilly, Charles. 1978. *From Mobilization to Revolution*. Reading, Mass.: Addison-Wesley.

Tocqueville, Alex de. 1852/1955. *The Old Regime and the French Revolution*. New York: Doubleday.

Toennies, Ferdinand. 1887/1963. *Community and Society*. New York: Harper and Row.

Treiman, Donald J. 1977. *Occupational Prestige in Comparative Perspective*. New York: Academic Press.

Turner, Jonathan H. 1974. *The Structure of Sociological Theory*. Homewood, Ill.: Dorsey.

———. 1984. *Societal Stratification: A Theoretical Analysis*. New York: Columbia Univ. Press.

———. 1985a. *Herbert Spencer: A Renewed Appreciation*. Beverly Hills: Sage.

———. 1985b. *The Structure of Sociological Theory*. 4th ed. Homewood, Ill.: Dorsey.

———. 1986. "The Mechanics of Social Interaction: Toward a Composite Model of Signaling and Interpreting." *Sociological Theory* 4: 95–105.

Turner, Ralph H. 1968. "Social Roles: Sociological Aspects." *International Encyclopedia of the Social Sciences*. New York: Macmillan.

———. 1976. "The Real Self: From Institution to Impulse." *American Journal of Sociology* 81: 989–1016.

———. 1978. "The Role and the Person." *American Journal of Sociology* 84: 1–23.

———. 1979–80. "A Strategy for Developing an Integrated Role Theory." *Humboldt Journal of Social Relations* 7: 123–39.

Tversky, Amos, and Kahneman, David. 1974. "Judgment under Uncertainty: Heuristics and Biases." *Science* 185: 1124–31.

U.S. Bureau of the Census. 1985. *1980 Census of Population*. PC 802-4C. "Marital Characteristics." Washington, D.C.: GPO.

Useem, Michael. 1986. *The Inner Circle: Large Corporations and the Rise of Business Political Activity in the U.S. and U.K.* New York: Oxford Univ. Press.

van Dijk, Teun A. 1985. *Handbook of Discourse Analysis*. London: Academic Press.

von Bertalanffy, Ludwig. 1968. *General System Theory: Foundations, Development, Applications*. New York: George Braziller.

Wallace, Walter L. 1983. *Principles of Scientific Sociology*. Chicago: Aldine.

Waller, Willard. 1937. "The Rating and Dating Complex." *American Sociological Review* 2: 727–34.

Wallerstein, Immanuel. 1974, 1980. *The Modern World System*. Vols. 1 and 2. New York: Academic Press.

———. 1984. "The Development of the Concept of Development." *Sociological Theory* 2: 102–16.

Walters, Pamela Barnhouse, and Richard Rubinson. 1983. "Educational Expansion and Economic Output in the U.S., 1890–1969." *American Sociological Review* 48: 480–93.

Wanner, Eric, and Lila R. Gleitman, eds. 1982. *Language Acquisition: The State of the Art*. New York: Cambridge Univ. Press.

Warner, Rebecca M. 1979. "Periodic Rhythms in Conversational Speech." *Language and Speech* 22: 381–96.

Warner, Rebecca M., T. B. Waggener, and R. E. Kronauer. 1983. "Synchronization Cycles in Ventilation and Vocal Activity during Spontaneous Conversational Speech." *Journal of Applied Physiology* 54: 1324–34.

Warren, Carol A. B., and John M. Johnson. 1972. "Critique of Labelling Theory from a Phenomenological Perspective." In Robert Scott and Jack D. Douglas, ed., *Theoretical Perspectives on Deviance*. New York: Basic Books.

Weber, Max. 1904–05/1930. *The Protestant Ethic and the Spirit of Capitalism*. New York: Scribner.

———. 1909/1976. *The Agrarian Sociology of Ancient Civilizations*. London: New Left Books.

———. 1916/1951. *The Religion of China*. Glencoe, Ill.: Free Press.

———. 1916–17/1958. *The Religion of India*. Glencoe, Ill.: Free Press.

———. 1917–19/1952. *Ancient Judaism*. Glencoe, Ill.: Free Press.

———. 1922/1947. *The Theory of Social and Economic Organization*. New York: Oxford Univ. Press.

———. 1922/1968. *Economy and Society*. New York: Bedminster Press.

———. 1923/1961. *General Economic History*. New York: Collier-Macmillan.

Webster, Murray, Jr., and James E. Driskell. 1978. "Status Generalization: A Review and Some Data." *American Sociological Review* 43: 220–36.

———. 1983. "Beauty as Status." *American Journal of Sociology* 89: 140–80.

Webster, Murray, Jr., and B. I. Sobieszek. 1974. "Sources of Evaluations and Expectation States." In Joseph Berger, T. L. Conner, and M. Y. Fisek, eds., *Expectation States Theory: A Theoretical Research Program*. Cambridge, Mass.: Winthrop.

Wellman, Barry. 1982. "Studying Personal Communities." In Peter V. Marsden and Nan Lin, eds., *Social Structure and Network Analysis*. Beverly Hills: Sage.

———. 1983. "Network Analysis: Some Basic Principles." *Sociological Theory 1983* 1: 155–200.

White, Harrison C. 1963. *An Anatomy of Kinship*. Englewood Cliffs, N.J.: Prentice-Hall.

———. 1970. *Chains of Opportunity: System Models of Mobility in Organizations*. Cambridge, Mass.: Harvard Univ. Press.

———. 1981. "Where Do Markets Come From?" *American Journal of Sociology* 87: 517–47.

White, Harrison C., Scott Boorman, and Ronald L. Breiger. 1976. "Social Structure from Multiple Networks: I. Blockmodels of Roles and Positions." *American Journal of Sociology* 81: 730–80.

White, Winston. 1961. *Beyond Conformity*. New York: Free Press.

Whitehead, Alfred North, and Bertrand Russell. 1910. *Principia Mathematica*. Cambridge: Cambridge Univ. Press.

Whitley, Richard. 1984. *The Intellectual and Social Organization of the Sciences*. Oxford: Clarendon Press.

Whyte, William F. 1943. *Street Corner Society*. Chicago: Univ. of Chicago Press.

Wilensky, Harold L. 1956. *Intellectuals in Labor Unions*. Glencoe, Ill.: Free Press.

———. 1964. "The Professionalization of Everyone?" *American Journal of Sociology* 70: 137–58.

Wiley, Norbert F. 1967. "America's Unique Class Politics: The Interplay of the Labor, Credit, and Commodity Markets." *American Sociological Review* 32: 529–40.

———. 1986a. "Early American Sociology and the Polish Peasant." *Sociological Theory* 4: 20–40.

———. 1986b. "The Sacred Self: Durkheim's Anomaly." Paper presented at the Annual Meeting of the American Sociological Association, New York.

Willer, David. 1984. "Analysis and Composition as Theoretic Procedures." *Journal of Mathematicala Sociology* 10: 241–68.

———. 1985. "Property and Social Exchange." *Advances in Group Processes* 2: 123–42.

Willer, David, and Bo Anderson, eds. 1981. *Networks, Exchange, and Coercion*. New York: Elsevier/Greenwood.

Williamson, Oliver E. 1975. *Markets and Hierarchies: A Study of the Economics of Internal Organization*. New York: Free Press.

Wilson, E. O. 1975. *Sociobiology: The New Synthesis*. Cambridge, Mass.: Harvard Univ. Press.

Wittgenstein, Ludwig. 1953. *Philosophical Investigations*. New York: Macmillan.

Wohlstein, Ronald T., and Clark McPhail. 1979. "Juding the Presence and Extent of Collective Behavior from Film Records." *Social Psychology Quarterly* 42: 76–81.

Woodward, Joan. 1965. *Industrial Organization*. London: Oxford Univ. Press.

Wright, Erik Olin. 1978. *Class, Crisis, and the State*. London: New Left Books.

———. 1979. *Class Structure and Income Determination*. New York: Academic Press.

Wright, Erik Olin, and Joachim Singleman. 1982. "Proletarianization in the Changing American Class Structure." *American Journal of Sociology, Supplement: Marxist Inquiries* Ed. by Michael Burawoy and Theda Skocpol.

Wylie, R. 1979. *The Self-Concept*, Revised Edition. Lincoln: Univ. of Nebraska Press.

INDEX

Numbers in italics indicate definitions.

Abercrombie, Nicholas, 103
Absolute deprivation, 128, 145
Abstract causal principles, 512
Action theory, 377–78, 398
  and structural theory, 407, 417–18
  multidimensional, 72–74, 76
Adaptation, 57–61, 67, 74–75
Adjacency pairs, 320
Administrative devices and control theory, 449, 455–58
Affect control theory, 341, 370–72
  and interaction ritual chains theory, 337, 368–73
Affectivity vs. affective neutrality, 64–65, 67
Aggression-approval proposition, 350–51
Agrarian society, 15, 18, 31, 38, 42, 155–57, 161, 165, 167, 170–71, 183, 225, 253, 254, 359, 393, 428
Agrarian states and education, 178
Aldrich, Howard, 481
Alexander, Jeffrey, 57, 72–74, 76, 79, 398, 494, 512, 515
Alienation, 80, 87, 91, 101, 102, 104, 279, 452, 455
  and bureaucracy, 456–58
  and capitalism, 101, 102
  and coercive controls, 459, 463
  in everyday life, 77, 103–105, 115
  and interaction, 208
  and organizations, 455–57
  and power, 456, 459
  and powerless, 455
  and species, 450
  and surveillance, 455–56
Alliance theory, 338
  and sexual politics, 168–72
Althusser, Louis, 74, 302–303, 308–309

structuralist Marxism, 105–106, 108–109
Alves, Wayne, 345
Amin, Samir, 93, 99
Anderson, Bo, 442
Anderson, Perry, 20
Anderson, Theodore, 472
Anticipatory socialization, principle of, 213, 218–19, 227, 453
Antiwar movements, 173
Aquinas, Thomas, 34
Archaic societies, 15, 17
Arms race model, 51–53
Arrighi, Giovanni, 93
Artificial intelligence, 6, 181–82, 263, 288–89, 299, 311–12, 332, 335, 514
Ascription vs. achievement, 64–65
Atkinson, J. Maxwell, 385
Austin, John, 318–19, 324, 510
Authoritarian government, 139–40
Averett, Christine, 367
Avoidance rituals, 252

Back, Kurt, 416
Balance of power, 135
Bales, Robert F., 342
Banfield, Edward, 441
Barnard, Chester, 451, 478
Barthes, Roland, 288, 302, 307, 309
Baudrillard, Jean, 307
Becker, Gary, 354
Becker, Howard S., 270–71
Behabitives, 318
Behaviorist model, 312, 376, 393
  propositions, 337, 350–52
Behavioral traits, 240

Bendix, Reinhard, 127, 140, 428, 503, 507
Bentham, Jeremy, 343
Berelson, Bernard, 212
Berger, Joseph, 239–41
Berger, Peter, 264, 276, 377, 383, 385–86
Bergesen, Albert, 99, 197, 511
Berkeley, 267
Bernoulli, 497
Bernstein, Basil, 210, 211, 217, 223
Bhaskar, Roy, 74, 106, 107, 512
Bilateral inheritance, 168
Biological
  analogies, 13
  evolution, 12, 35
  population, 497
"Black box" of the mind, 380
Black ghetto uprising, 151
Blain, Robert, 379
Blalock, Hubert M., 400–401
Blaming the victim, 367, 369
Blau, Peter M., 174, 210
  and control theory, 455
  and exchange model, 340
  and exchange theory, 242, 337–40, 343–50, 352, 356, 359, 365, 366, 370, 415, 418–21
  and exchange theory of power, 435
  and functionalist theory of stratification, 348, 349
  intergroup integration theory, 411, 424–25, 447
  and networks of exchange, 397
  organization model, 347, 450
  organizational size, 472
  power theory, 344, 347, 452
  structural theory of intergroup integration, 416, 424–25, 427
Block, Fred, 110, 115

Blockmodels, 414
Bloor, David, 211, 223
Blumberg, Rae, 165–68, 170, 172, 183
Blumer, Herbert, 377
  attack on macrosociology, 380–81
  creative redefinition theory, 272, 273
  definitional perspective model theory, 271–73
  and functionalism, 380–81, 394
  and "I" sociology, 233
  and micro-macro level, 385, 389, 393
  and roles, 235, 238
  and situational reductionism, 381
  and statistical sociology, 380–82, 388
  and symbolic interactionism, 263, 266–70, 298
  and symbolic interactionism theory, 380–81, 408
  three fundamental premises of meaning, 268, 269
Boli-Bennett, John, 133
Boorman, Scott, 414
Bott, Elizabeth, 416
Boudon, Raymond, 174
Boulding, Kenneth, 39, 53
Bounded rationality, 299, 430
Bourdieu, Pierre, 103, 180, 217, 295
Bourgeoisie, 99, 139–41, 144, 146
Braithwaite, Richard B., 379
Breiger, Ronald L., 414
Brenner, Robert, 99, 100
Brucan, Silviu, 488
Buddhists, 190, 253, 257, 259, 279
Burawoy, Michael, 465
Burden of proof, principle of, 240
Bureaucracy, 139, 146, 467
  and alienation, 456–57
  principle, 456
  and size of organization, 472
Bureaucratic
  frame, 324
  personality, principle of, 213, 214, 228, 454
  state and sexual stratification, 172, 173
Bureaucratization and ethno-methodology, 289, 299, 465
Burt, Ronald S., 407, 413, 416–18, 431–32
Business networks and profits, 432
Business and sociology, 416, 434

Calhoun, Craig, 137
Cannon, Walter, 50
Capella, F., 202
Capitalism, 21, 99–100, 104, 106, 140, 144, 290, 434, 454, 455, 467, 515
  abolishment of, 91
  as alienation and conscious-ness, 101–102
  and bankruptcy, 85–87
  characteristics of, 82, 114
  and class and power, 125, 126
  cyclical nature of, 486–87
  and evolutionary theory, 15, 17, 20, 21, 28, 31, 35, 36, 42
  as Marxian model, 77, 79–92, 430
  origins of, 99–100
  and profit and growth, 82–84
  and superorganizations, 449, 485–89, 491, 516
  and surplus value, 107
  theory, 28, 100, 459
  vs. socialism, 118
  and world system theory, 93, 94, 98, 99, 114–15
Capitalist
  class, 147
  economic system, 81–82, 92
  laissez-faire, 108
  market, 146, 430
  party, 152
  society, 110–13, 115, 125, 152, 345, 399
  system, 165, 450
  world system, 98, 386
Capitalists vs. the state, 110–13
Caplow, Theodore, 452
Carey, A., 340–41
Carroll, Glenn R., 481–82
Caste system, 152
Causality, 67
Cause-and-effect relationships, 157–58
Cave-man stage, 348
Centralized
  empires, 131
  power, 439–40, 448
  structures, 443–45, 448
Ceremonial-cultural exchanges, 416, 447
Chafetz, Janet Saltzman, 165
Chance, phenomenon of, 496–97
Chandler, Alfred D., 472, 476
Charisma, 460, 467
Chodorow, Nancy, 164
Chomsky, Noam, 74
  and frame space, 327
  and generative grammar, 301, 311–17, 319, 335
  and language theory, 330–35
  and linguistics, 307, 315, 319

model of sequencing, 330
model of transformational grammar, 301, 312–14, 316–17, 319–20, 325, 329, 331–32
structuralist model, 314, 335
Christianity, 190
  Medieval, 191
  and self, 253
Cicourel, Aaron, 281, 316, 324, 335
  and mathematics in sociology, 510
  and social mobility, 391
  and studies of demographic re-search, 384
Circulation mobility, 506
Civil rights, 124, 173
Class conflict, 119, 121, 123–25, 142, 151–52, 215, 347
  and control of the state, 89–90, 95, 97, 113–15
  and interests, 465
  and Marxians, 119, 124–25, 142, 151
  and nations, 125
  and organization theory, 449, 464–66
  role-theory version of, 236
  in the United States, 151
Class culture, 210, 211, 217, 390
  horizontal aspects of, 417
  principle of, 453
  theory, 201, 208, 465
  two dimensions, 220–21
Class
  divisions as power divisions, 125–26, 145
  inequality, 431
  interests theory, 130
  model, 151–52, 182
  struggle, 99, 104, 108–109
  theory and community cul-tures, 397
Clegg, Stewart, 393
Closed systems, 51
Closure model, 432
Coalition, 98, 442
Codes
  cultural, 308–10, 315
  polysemic, 308
  ritual, 251
Coercion
  and communications, 437, 439–40
  and control theory, 449, 452, 476, 488
  and enforcement coalitions, 435
  and environmental control, 463
  and exchange theory, 441–42
  model, 436–38
  principle of, 452–53

ritual, 213, 216, 226, 227, 453
and tasks, 463, 490
Coercion and threat, 349, 448
Coercive
coalitions, 437–40, 448
controls, 454, 459, 463–64, 489–90
and exchange theory, 442
organizations, 454, 459, 460, 463, 477
political power, 485
power, 299, 458, 459
and remunerative organizations, 460, 463
sanctions, 488
structures, 436–42, 448
theory, 440
threat, 349, 446, 454, 459–60, 463, 477
Cognition vs. emotion, 263, 271, 283–86, 298–99
Cognitive
construction of reality, 385, 386
radicalism, 263, 276–82
view of reality, 279, 299, 385, 386
Cohesive networks, 411, 416–17, 447
Coleman, James S., 385, 388–89, 393
Colinvaux, P. A., 30
Collective
conscience, 26, 227
reality and rituals, 250
Collectivity vs. individualism, 64, 65
Collins, Randall, 21, 27–28, 100, 168–71, 183, 212–13, 215, 217, 219, 223–26, 228, 254, 265, 298, 338–39, 357–66, 394, 402, 421, 425, 428, 433, 437, 451, 453, 462, 473, 503, 508, 511–12, 516–17
Commodity
exchange, 432
market, 151, 182
symbolism, 434
"Common stock of knowledge," 282
Commonsense
knowledge, 275, 276, 299
rational behavior of society, 343
reasoning, 263, 274, 280, 282, 283, 299
Communications
and coercion, 437, 439–40
diversity of, 395
and education, 217, 228
and enforcement coalitions, 439–41
game, 438–39

network, 89
nonverbal, 241, 246, 247, 260, 321
Communicative signalling, 307–308
Communism in countries, 91, 109
Communist
Party members, 477
society, 15–17, 20–21, 24–25, 41, 56, 80, 91
Community
consciousness, 152
identity, 120–21
and national power structures, 443–47
power structures, 412, 443
retirement, 154
Competitive sector of capitalist society, 111–13, 115
Complementarity of roles, 234–35
Completion ritual, 333
Complex
exchange systems, 348
frames, 335
vs. linear interaction, 473–76, 485–86, 490
Compliance theory, 452–53, 455, 462
Components of signification, 243–44
Compulsory public education system, 133
Computer
and artificial intelligence, 6, 181–82, 263, 288–89, 299, 311–12, 332, 335, 514
language, 513–14, 516
simulation of Marxian system, 81, 90, 92
simulations, 7, 332–35, 493, 495, 511–18
Computers as new technology, 177
Comrie, Bernard, 315
Comte, Auguste, 12, 15–16, 19, 35, 39, 41, 374
Concrete empirical phenomena, 74, 76
Condon, William S., 202
Confederated organizations, 444–45
Conflict
consequences of, 128–30
cross-cutting, 123–124, 130, 145
-domination approach, 458
external, 120–21, 145, 160
internal, 120–21, 145, 160–62
and nationalism, 120, 126
and order, 515
organizations, 459

and property, 124
self-limitation of, 122–23
and social change, 117–47
and social integration, 120–21
and war, 120, 122–23
Conflict theory, 3, 57, 62, 72, 118, 124–30, 137, 145, 259, 338, 346, 446, 450, 458
and education, 179–80
and exchange theory, 338
of inequality, 27, 31, 54, 91, 107, 110, 113
multidimensional, 74, 119, 127
and political change, 130
and quasi-groups, 127–28, 132, 145
and rituals, 199
and self, 259
of social change, 117, 130–44
and stratification theory, 149–50, 150
Conformity, 222
and social density, 215
Conner, Thomas L., 239, 242
Connor, Walter D., 504
Consciousness, 45, 51–53, 52, 102
community, 152
Constant capital, 85
Constructional radicalism, 264
Contingency theory, 468, 478–79
Continuous differentiation and functional upgrading, 25
Contradictory consciousness, 102
Control
and Communist Party, 477
hierarchy of, 45, 61, 64, 75
normative, 463–64, 466, 477–78, 487–89, 491
and rewards, 452, 477, 489
of the state, 77, 85, 88, 89
of the state and class conflict, 89, 90, 95, 97, 113–15
and organizations existence, 449, 458–60
sanctions, 457
structure, 449, 476–78, 490
systems, 47
Control theory, 449–66, 476, 488
and administrative devices, 449, 455–58
and coercion, 449, 452, 476, 488
historical trends in, 449, 454, 455
internalized control, 449, 453
and organizational structure, 449, 478, 479
and property, 449, 460–62
and rewards, 449, 452
who uses and when, 449, 458

Conversation, *332,* 332–34
  computer simulation of, 332–35
  and ethnomethodologist researchers, 335
  and frames, 295, 298, 300
  internalized, 243, 248–50, 260
  rituals, 206–209, 226–27, 321–24, 332, 357–58, 364, 402, 406, 424
  and stage identities, 226
  theory, 243–49
  and turn-taking model, 301, 319–20, 323–24, 335
Conversational
  analysis, 319–22, 388
  motivator, 327
  relationships, 343
  rules, 315, 319–20
Conversations, network of, 405
Cook, Karen S.
  and computer simulation, 509
  and exchange theory, 435–36
  and network analysis, 343
  and performance expectations, 345
Cooley, Charles Horton, 230–32, 235, 237, 377
Core
  self, 258–59, 297
  states and world economy, 95–98, 100, 114–15
Corning, Peter A., 30, 39
Corsaro, William, 329
Coser, Lewis, 119–24, 127, 130, 145, 384
Cosmopolitanism, 395
Cost-push inflation, 112
Counter
  -coalitions, organization of, 439
  norms, 346
Courtship system, 422
Creative redefinition theory, 272–73
Credential
  inflation, 178–83, *179,* 184
  requirements, 175, 178, 183
Credit market, 151, 182
Cretaceous period, 33, 34
Crime, 71
  without victims, 191, 196, 271
Cross-
  classifying power, 228
  cutting conflicts, 123–24, 130, 145
  societal comparisons of societies, 105
Crozier, Michel, 450, 455, 477
Cues, 240–41
Cult
  and ethnomethodology, 273
  of self, 252–55, 261

Cultural
  capital, 103, 337, 358, 360–62, 364, 366, 371, 402, 406–409, 424
  codes, 308–10, 315
  groups, formation of, 161–63
  groups, ranking of, 183
  rules, 398–99
Culture-and-personality school of anthropology, 63
Culture theory, 131
Cumulative
  resource advantage, 135
  turning points, 135
Curtis, Richard, 215, 217, 427
Curvilinear relationship, 158, 160
Cybernetics, 47

Dahrendorf, Ralf, 124–30, 137, 145, 226, 346, 450
Dalton, Melville, 451
Darwin, Charles, 30
Darwinian theory, 13, 266
Davies, James C., 137
De-escalating processes, 122–23, 145
Deadlock war, 137
Decentralized
  domain structure, 443
  power network, 440–41
Decision making and organizational theory, 449, 464, 466–67
Deconstructionism, 301–302, 308–309, 335
Deep structure, 106–107, 335
Deference, 251–52, *252,* 261
Definition of the situation, 263–73, 295, 297
Definitional perspective theory, 271–73, 291
Degradation in society, 105
DeLamater, John, 215
Demeanor, 251–52, *252,* 261
Democracy, 128, 131, 139, 445, 448
  as decentralized power network, 440–41
  dynamics of power in, 445, 448
Democratic
  government, 55–57, 140
  party, 92
  revolutions, 128, 254
  society, 25, 39–41, 56, 65, 68, 73
Demographic research, 384, 497
Dependency theory, 93, 100
Deprivation
  satiation proposition, 350–51
  theory, 128–29, 137, 146

Derrida, Jacques, 74, 302, 308–10, 510
Description vs. explanation, 425
Determinitive principles, 273
Deutsch, Morton, 345
Deviance, 62–64, 75, 450
  and labelling theory, 258, 270–72
  and socialization, 45, 62–64
  theory, 271, 374
Dewey, John, 267
Diachronic, *303*
Dialectic of logical contradictions, 36–37
Dialectical materialist theory, 81
Dialectics, 102
Dictatorship, 56, 109, 131, 403, 436, 440
Differentiation theory, 26–27
Diffuse status characteristics, 240, 242, 260
Diffuseness vs. specificity, 64–65, 67
Dinosaurs and evolutionary theory, 33–34
Discrimination, 232
  against minorities, 162
  and economic theory, 356
Distance vs. closeness, 215
Distribution
  inequality of, 155, 183
  of power, 160–61, 168, 182
  of prestige, 154
  of wealth theory, 3, 155–59
Distributive justice, 338
  norm of, 399
Divide and conquer, 122, 437–38
Dobash, R. Emerson, 197
Dobash, Russell, 197
Domhoff, G. William, 107
Dominant ideology thesis, 102–103
Douglas, Mary
  and class culture theory, 201
  grid and group, 221–23, 226, 228, 254
  group culture theory, 210–11
  and tribal societies, 18
Dramaturgical model of society, 204
Dreyfus, Hubert, 288
Dreyfus, Stuart, 288
Drive-reduction model, 50
Duncan, Otis Dudley, 174, 500, 506
Durkheim, Emile, 1–2, 6, 19, 38, 42, 71–74, 133, 276, 296, 376
  analysis of religious rituals, 250
  and class cultures, 210–11, 217
  collective consciousness, 26

and deviance theory, 376
emotional contagion, 329
evolutionary stage theories, 12, 14–17, 19–20
and exchange, 421
exteriorly constraining social facts, 377
forms of speech, 332
horizontal aspects of class cultures, 417
interaction ritual model, 284, 334, 344
and language, 304, 316
mechanical and organic solidarity, 200–201, 221, 227
micro-macro theory, 450
moral solidarity theory, 187–202, 224
organic differentiation theory, 22–23, 25–27
precontractual solidarity theory, 45, 61–63, 65, 119, 344, 419, 420
and psychological reductionism, 376–77
and religion theory, 376
and religious symbols model, 218, 227–28
ritual density model, 450
and ritual exchange, 418, 420–21
and ritual model, 203–205, 214, 216, 227–28, 294, 310, 326
and ritual theory, 397, 404, 438
self as sacred object, 252, 254, 256
size causes differentiation theory, 26–27
and social control, 376
and social density theory, 417
sociological theory, 302
sociology vs. psychology, 390
soul theory, 250
sui generis, 25–26, 376, 408
symbolism theory, 222, 338
universalization of moral conscience theory, 254
Durkheimian
grounding of interaction rituals, 297
pattern of social density and diversity, 214–20, 226
ritual theory, 357, 365
rituals and interactions, 337, 357–58
theory to the level of situational interactions, 380
version of exchange theory, 305
Dynamic
simulation model, 218
theory, 131

vs. comparative statics, 510–11
DYNAMO computer language, 511–12, 516

Eberhard, Wolfram, 132
Eco, Umberto, 307–308
Ecological model, 481
Economic
conflict theory, 355
crises, 85–86, 89–92, 97
depression, 88
development, 501
market theory, 432
Marxian theory of sexual stratification, 165–68
model, 106–107, 431–32
power, 165–66, 183
rationality, 377
reproduction, 77, 81–82
system labor place, 82–86
structural change, 496
Economic theory, 354, 411, 413, 429–35, 447
crisis in, 411, 430
discrimination of, 354
and network theory, 411, 429–35
Economics, sociological reformulation of, 411, 431–32
Education
as business, 178
and communication, 217, 228
and inequality, 174, 178, 180, 184
purpose of, 178, 180
systems, 178
Educational
credential stratification, 174–82
reform, 179
Efficiency criterion, 456
Egalitarian exchanges, 364
Egalitarianism, 345
Egocentric distortion, 232
Egocentricity, 329
Ego's market, 413–14
Ego's network, 411–14, 426
Ehrhardt, Anke, 234
Eldridge, Niles, 33
Embodied talk, 301, 327–30, 335
Emerson, Richard, 337–38, 343, 346, 349–50, 352, 371, 400–401
Emmanuel, Arghiri, 93
Emotion theory, 210
Emotional
contagion, 296, 329
energy, 337, 358, 361–62, 364, 366, 371, 402, 408–409, 417, 420, 424
solidarity, 487
Emotions of threat, 216, 226–27

Empirical reality microsociology, 375, 391–93, 409
Encounters change, 337, 362–65
Enforcement coalitions
and coercion, 435
communication, 439–41
divide and rule, 437–38
and exchange theory of power, 411, 441–42
and property, 404–406
rankings in, 405–406
theory, 403–407, 409, 411, 436–42, 448
Engels, Friedrich, 15, 165
English revolution, 140–42
Environmental
control, 457–58, 463, 489–90
isomorphism, 480–81
Environments and organizations, 449, 451, 480–91
EPA profile, 367–71
Epistemological rupture, 303
Equality and ritual activity, 487
Equilibrium concept, 45, 50–51, 75
Equitable-reward-for-performance theme, 242
Erikson, Kai, 121
Et cetera assumption, 282, 299
Ethnic
divisions, 123
and gender discriminations, 450
group and status group, 152
party, 153
Ethnobotany, *274*
Ethnomethodologist
and hyper-ethnomethodologist, 279
and power, 393
and symbolic interactionist, 271
Ethnomethodology, 4, 257, 263–64, 271, 273–86, *282*, 288–91, 299, 315–16, 319, 335, 357, 376, 384, 389, 494, 510
and bureaucratization, 289, 299
and conversation, 335
as cult, 273
implications of, 263, 286–91
and symbolic interactionism, 263, 295–97
Ethnomethods, *274*
Etzioni, Amitai, 348, 450, 452–55, 458, 462, 464
Eurocommunism, 109
Everyday interaction as ritual, 206–208
Evolutionary
development, alternative, 17
model of revolutions, 138–39
stage models and explanatory power, 11, 20, 21

Evolutionary (*continued*)
 stages, 12, 14–15, 17–19, 21–
  22, 31, 35, 38–39, 41–42,
  64, 81, 87, 90
Evolutionary stage theory, 12,
  14–17, 19–22, 31, 71
 in China, 15, 17, 20–21, 26,
  31
 in Egypt, 15, 17, 31
 in Germany, 16
 in Greece, 15, 17, 21, 31, 39
 in India, 15, 17, 20, 26, 31
 in Islamic empires, 15, 17, 20,
  31, 35
 in Israel, 15, 17, 21, 31
 in Mesopotamia, 15, 17
 in Rome, 15–17, 20, 31
Evolutionary theories, 2, 19, 33–
  34, 39, 46, 480
 analytical dimension, 20
 and capitalism, 15, 17, 20–21,
  28, 31, 35–36, 42
 and democratic government, 25
 idealist evolution, 13–14
 and integration, 20
 and latent pattern maintenance, 20
 and progress, 11–13, 38–41
 and stage theories, 11, 13–22
 and strains and lags concept,
  24–25, 41
 and two biological analogies, 13
 variety of, 11–14
Evolutionism, 11–43
Exchange
 models, 71, 375, 400, 401,
  409, 436
 networks of, 397
 norm of equal, 397
 or resource dependency, 435
 systems complex, 348
Exchange theory, 6, 242, 305,
  337–40, 343–52, 356, 359,
  365, 366, 370–71, 382, 397,
  400–401, 415–16, 418–21,
  424, 435–36, 442, 446, 465
 and coercion, 441–42
 and conflict theory, 338
 interaction ritual chains, 337,
  365, 366
 and micro-macro issue, 412
 and network theory, 415, 418
 and power, 337, 343–49, 433,
  439, 440
 principles of and network
  models, 413
 profit maximizing structure of,
  441
Exchanges
 balanced and unbalanced, 345–
  46
 ceremonial-cultural, 416, 447

 symbolic-emotional, 418
 and tribal society, 416, 418–19
 of women, 338
Expectation states theory, 239–
  42, 260, 345
Expectations, 240–42
Exploitation of workers, 102
Explosion concept, 45, 50–52
Exponential relationships, 157,
  160, 162
External
 action, 269
 areas and world economy, 95,
  114
 conflict, 120–21, 145, 160
 geopolitics, 503
 threat, 160–62, 182, 444
Eye-contact studies, 387

Face-to-face interactants, 388,
  401, 502
Face work, 251–52, 261
Fair exchange, 344–45, 419
False consciousness, 77, 102
Farraro, Thomas J., 495, 514
Fascism, 25, 139–41, 147
Featherman, David L., 174, 426
Feedback
 and feedforward concepts, 47,
  75
 loops, 26, 45, 50–53, 55–57,
  75, 92, 398
 negative, 50, 51, 75
 positive, 50, 51, 75
Feedback systems, 47–48, 53, 75
 dumb, 47–48, 51, 53
 smart, 45, 49–50, 53–54
Feedforward, 47, 75
Female occupational roles, 238
Females as sexual property, 169,
  171
Feminist movement, 163, 173
Festinger, Leon, 416
Feudal
 -patrimonial household, 171–
  72
 -patrimonial societies, 155
 societies, 15, 17, 20, 99, 108,
  131–32, 152, 290, 440
Feyerabend, Paul, 280
Financial markets, 433
Fine, Terrence L., 498
Finite state grammars, 312
Firth, Raymond, 339
Fiscal crises theory, 77, 110–13,
  115, 459
Fischer, Claude S., 19, 215, 217,
  412, 423
Fisek, M. Harriet, 239, 242

Footings, 258–59, 301, 324–27
Forced mobility, 506
Form, William, 345
Formal
 ceremonies, 332
 Model of Ritual, 192–97, 216,
  332
Forms of speech, 332
Foucault, Michel, 302, 309–10
Fragmentation of consciousness,
  103
Fragmented power, 439–40, 448
Frame
 analysis, 4, 257, 263, 285,
  290–98, 300, 334, 335
 breaks, 263, 293, 326
 of interaction, 335
 space, 295, 324–27, 332, 335
Frames and conversation, 295,
  298, 300
Framing continuum, 294, 296–
  98, 300
Framing and rituals, 294
Frank, Andre Gunder, 93, 99–
  100, 503
Freeman, Linton C., 435–36, 481
French structuralism, 4–6, 288,
  301–11, 397, 494, 511
Frequency theory of probability,
  497
Freud, Sigmund, 37, 62–63, 71,
  105, 308
 and divided self, 257
 and superego, 63
 Oedipus complex, 378
 and unconscious ideas, 249
Freudian theory, 104
Friendship
 markets, 338, 423
 and marriage markets, 416,
  422–24, 447
 networks, 496
Frontstage-backstage ritual model,
  204–206, 209, 211–14,
  223–27, 235, 238, 247,
  252–53, 293, 300, 325–26,
  453
Functional
 analysis, 378
 -teleological approach, 458
 upgrading, 11, 23–25
Functionalism, 2–3, 343, 380–
  81, 394
Functionalist
 action system theory, 45, 56–
  72, 109–10
 feedback loops, 45, 55–57, 75,
  400
 ideology, 357
 stratification theory, 348–49
 theory, 45, 54, 55, 73, 109,
  110, 118

Functionally self-equilibrating system, 46
Fundamental
reality, 276
theory, 3

Gabennesch, Howard, 215
Game theory, 403, 436–37
Games of chance principle, 495
Gans, Herbert J., 210, 212, 217, 427
Garbage-can model, 466–67
Garfinkel, Harold, 1, 247, 327, 384, 389
and alienation, 279
breaching experiments, 283, 296, 299
cognitive radicalism, 263, 276–82
documentary method of interpretation, 288
and ethnomethodology, 264, 273–86, 288–91, 319
indexicality and reflexivity, 276–88, 296–97, 299, 316, 321, 510
and micro-macro level, 385
and social phenomenologists, 377, 383–84
and "what anyone knows," 275
Gemeinschaft, 14–15, 64
Gender
defining by, 230–31, 238, 260
divisions, 123
inequality, 23–24, 28–29, 164, 450
roles, 234–35, 238, 260
stratification theory, 165–68, 170, 172, 183
General systems theory, 45–54, 72
General theory, 301, 330–35
developing, 493, 502–505
of action, 58, 60
of language, 301, 330–35
Generalist newspapers, 481–82
Generalized media of exchange, 348
Generalized Other
theory, 230, 235, 244–48, 257, 260–61, 267, 417
and universal signs, 245–47, 260, 267
Generative grammar, 301, 311–17, 319, 335
Genetic
code, 309–10, 316, 335
determination, 32–33, 174–75
element and religion, 18–19, 31–32

Geopolitical
approach as a world systems model, 136
theory, 117, 131–37, 141–43, 146, 147, 160
Geopolitics, external, 503
Gesellschaft, 14–15, 64
Giddens, Anthony, 106–107
and cultural tradition of society, 398–99
and micro-macro theory, 450
structuralist model, 375, 398–99, 409
structuration theory, 288, 314, 335
Gift exchanges, 411, 415–16, 418–21, 423–24, 447
Gillies, D. A., 498, 502
Gitlin, Todd, 103
Glosses, 276, 281
Goal attainment, 57–61, 67, 74–75
Goffman, Erving, 1, 6, 19, 54, 106, 119, 226, 317, 319, 397, 502
class cultures theory, 208
face work, deference, and demeanor, 251–52, 261
frame analysis, 257, 263, 285, 290–98, 295, 300, 334, 335
frontstage-backstage ritual model, 204–206, 209, 211–14, 223–27, 235, 238, 247, 252–53, 293, 300, 325–26, 453
and information-gathering and trust-assessment games, 430
and interaction ritual, 203–208, 230, 250, 285, 304, 334, 370
and labelling theory of deviance, 258, 270–72
levels of realities, 297
and mental illness, 251, 261
and micro-macro level, 385
and micro theory, 126
multiple levels of reality, 264
organization theory, 450
phenomenology, 327
and problem of reality, 296
and rituals, 188, 198–99, 223, 259, 284, 332
and roles, 327
and self, 250–59, 261, 296, 328
and social action model, 514
social ecology of language, 301, 318, 320–30, 335
and speech acts, 510
and survey research, 382–83, 388, 408
symbolic interactionism and

ethnomethodology, 263, 295–97
and transformation, 329
Goffmanian revolution, 225
Golden rule, 190–91
Goode, William J., 236
Goodman, Nelson, 280
Gottdiener, Mark, 103, 307
Gottfredson, Linda S., 164, 230, 238
Gould, Stephen Jay, 33–34
Gouldner, Alan W., 384, 450
Government, 25, 39
bureaucrats, 139, 146
and power, 265
Grades, 177, 179
Gramsci, Antonio, 102–103
Granovetter, Mark, 426–27, 430, 447
Gregory, Stanford W., 202
Grid and group, 221–23, 226, 228, 254
Grid-lock theory, 123–24, 130, 145
Group
cultures theory, 210–11
leader position, 342
membership and rituals, 357, 358, 454
organization, 208, 218
ritual, 357, 358, 454
solidarity, 401, 409, 415, 454, 465–66
therapy, 37, 42
Groups, formation of, 154
Guerrilla theater, 285
Gusfield, Joseph R., 215, 271

Habermas, Jürgen, 14, 36–38, 42, 57, 101
colonization of the lifeworld, 375, 399–400, 409
and ideal speech community, 288
and impersonal bureaucratic forces, 467
and language theory, 314, 335
and micro-macro theory, 450
Hacking, Ian, 498
Hage, Jerald D., 467
Hall, Richard H., 464
Halle, David, 125
Hannan, Michal, 481
Hanneman, Robert, 48, 511, 513, 516–17
Harrod, W. J., 345
Hartmann, Heidi, 165
Hauser, Robert, 174, 428
Hawthorne effect, 340–41
Heath, Anthony, 356

Hechter, Michael, 401, 409
Heckathorn, Douglas, 495
Hegel, 5, 13, 36–37, 80, 101, 102, 279
Hegelian
    Marxian, 103–105, 115
    philosophy, 78, 80, 87, 92, 101–102
Hegemonic state, 102, 115
Heidegger, Martin, 69, 275
Heise, David, 337, 339, 366–71
Herding societies, 15, 18
Heritage, John, 382
Hermeneutics, 302
Herrnstein, Richard, 174
Hierarchies theories and markets, 30–31
Hill, 103
Hindu
    caste system, 120
    religion, 253
Hirschi, Travis, 215
Historical
    change mobility, 506
    differentiation, 27
    intermediate empires, 15, 31
    sociology, 494
    typology, 223–25, 228, 254
Hitler, Adolph, 439
Hobson, J. A., 93
Homans, George C., 1
    aggression-approval proposition, 350, 351
    attack on macrosociology, 376–79
    behaviorist model, 337, 350–52, 376, 393
    deprivation-satiation proposition, 350–51
    exchange theory, 242, 337–45, 349–52, 356, 365, 370, 371, 382, 397, 400–401, 415, 418–20
    and functionalism, 380, 394
    and micro-macro level, 385, 389, 393
    and psychological reduction, 375, 378–81
    rationality proposition, 351–52, 371
    social exchange theory, 214
    stimulus proposition, 350
    structural sociology, 380
    success proposition, 350
    value proposition, 350
Homeostasis, 50
Homomorphic reduction, 412
Homosexuality and labelling theory, 270–71
Horizontal
    aspects of class cultures, 417
    controls, 465

    relationships, 452
    roles, 236
    status dimension, 209–11, 215, 218
Horticultural societies, 15, 18, 31, 42, 155–56, 166–67, 170, 393
"The house of power," 153
Huber, Joan, 165–66
Human
    cognitive limitations, 263, 286, 299
    relations school of management, 340
    society and transforming frames, 263, 293–95
Hume, David, 257, 267, 501, 510
Hunting and gathering societies, 15, 18, 31, 38, 42, 155–56, 166, 169
Husserl, Edmund, 5, 69
    and phenomenology, 275, 377, 384
Hyperrelativistic consciousness, 297
Hypotheses testing, 493, 501–502

"I" and "me," 235, 268
"I," "me," and the Generalized Other, 230, 232–35, 244–49, 257, 260, 269, 272–73, 298, 329
"I" sociology, 233
"I" vs. "me," 232–34
Ideal speech community, 288
Idealism, 5
    and relativism, 263, 297–98
Idealist
    evolution, 11, 36–38
    theory, 36–38, 41
Ideological
    domination, 77, 102
    hegemony theory, 102–103
Imperialism, 93, 96, 100, 115
Incest taboo, 305
Indexes as objects, *307*
Indexicality, 276–88, 296–97, 299, 316, 321, 510
Individualism vs. collectivity, 64–65
Individualistic sociology, 379
Industrial
    crises, 84–86
    society, 15, 19, 25, 38, 41, 56, 155–57, 161, 166–67, 172, 393
Inequality, 54, 70, 345, 393, 455
    class, 431

    component of rituals, 225
    conflict theory of, 27, 31, 54, 91, 107, 110, 113
    and density, 223–25
    of distribution, 155, 183
    and education, 174, 178, 180, 184
    and expectations states program, 241–42
    explaining, 149, 153–63
    gender, 23–24, 28–29, 164, 450
    of opportunity, 155, 183
    and organic differentiation theory, 28–29
    of sex or gender, 164
    in society, 162, 384
    theory, 3, 183
    variations in, 155
    of wealth and power, 155, 162, 182
Inflation crises, 112
Information control, 457, 463–64, 489–90
Ingroup solidarity, 425
Inhelder, 36
Inside-outside dichotomy, 222
Inspecting outcomes, 456, 489
Institutionalized roles, 349–50
Instrumentalist theory, 107
Intellectual communication and reframing, 295
Intense conflict, 128, 145
Interaction
    alienation from, 208
    complex vs. linear, 473–76, 485–86, 490
    ritual, 62, 203–208, 230, 250, 285, 297, 304, 334, 370, 453
    model, 202–203, 284, 334, 342
    and rankings in enforcement coalitions, 405–406
    and social change, 405
    theory, 6, 187–228, 271, 296, 304, 325, 329, 334
Interaction ritual chain
    and exchange theory, 337, 365–66
    and filmstrips, 402
    and local macro structure, 402
    model, 375, 402–409, 417
    and social ranking, 358
    theory, 250, 258, 273, 286, 337, 339, 357–66, 371, 402, 418, 426, 435, 465
Interactional markets model, 334
Intergenerational mobility, 425
Intergroup integration
    and structural theory, 416, 424–25, 427

theory, 411, 424–25, 447
Internalized
control, 449, 453–55, 458–60, 489–90
conversation, 230, 243, 248–50, 260
International power prestige, 146, 160
Interorganizational relations, 449–50, 484–85
and superorganization, 449, 484–85
Interpersonal
property relationships, 414
rituals, 198
IQ tests, 174–75, 177
Iron cage of bureaucracy, 467
Iron Law of Oligarchy, 129, 460, 487

Jackson, Elton F., 215, 217, 425
Jakobson, Roman, 305
James, William, 267
Jameson, Fredric, 511–12
Japanese
companies, 466
vs. American organization, 451
Jasso, Guillermina, 345
Jencks, Christopher, 496
Jensen, Arthur R., 174
Jews, 121
Job requirements, 175, 179
Johnson, G. David, 268
Johnson, John M., 270
Judeo-Christian societies and capitalism, 20
Juvenile delinquency, 215

Kadushin, Charles, 417
Kahn, Robert L., 49
Kahneman, David, 286
Kant, Immanual, 5, 36, 257, 267, 281
Kanter, Rosabeth M., 212–14, 217, 225, 455
Katz, Daniel, 49
Kemper, Theodore D., 210
Kendon, Adam, 202
Keynes, John Maynard, 498–502, 508–509
Keynesian
methods, 112
unemployment, 180–82
Keys and keyings, 292
Kinship, 18, 20
exchanges, 411, 416, 421, 423, 447
system, 166–67, 169–70, 183,

305–306, 310, 315, 338, 421
theory, 309–11, 315–16, 338
Knoke, David, 443–46, 516
Knorr-Cetina, Karin, 280, 298
Kohlberg, Lawrence, 36
Kohn, Melvin L., 212
Kondratieff waves, 96
Kramer, Edna E., 509
Kriesberg, Louis, 122–23
Kristeva, Julia, 309
Kroeber, A. L., 316
Kuhn, Thomas S., 223, 280
Kuklick, Bruce, 267
Kula ring, 420, 422
Kurzweil, Edith, 308

Labelling, 369
theory, 258, 270–72
Labor
cheap, 100
division of, 24, 27, 38, 40, 42, 62, 64–65, 70
exploitation of, 85
market and class, 150–51
place in economic system, 82–86
saving technology, 77, 84, 85, 107, 114
and unemployment, 85, 96
unions, 129
Lacan, Jacque, 231, 302, 308, 310
Laissez-faire capitalist, 108
Lakatos, Imre, 500
Landowners, 140, 142, 146–47
Language, 304, 316
and general theory, 301, 330–35
and mind, 395
natural, 311–12
reality model, 301–11
social ecology of, 301, 318, 320–30, 335
and sociological theory, 53, 301, 317–20
structure, 310, 313, 316
and surface structure, 335
and symbolism, nature of, 293–94
as a system, 304, 510
theory, 314–15, 330–35
three elements of, 243–44
verbal, 508–10
and world history, 37–38
Latent
conflict, 118
pattern maintenance, 57–61, 67, 75
Latour, Bruno, 280, 468

Laumann, Edward O., 412, 414, 423, 427, 443–46, 516
Lawrence, Paul R., 480–81
Lefebvre, Henri, 103, 104, 106, 115
Legitimacy, 133, 290
as a dynamic process, 133
and military conquest, 136
of power, 134
sentiment and moral of, 402
Leibniz, 508, 510
Leiter, Kenneth, 287, 382
Lemert, Edwin, 270
Lenin, V. I., 93, 139
Lenski, Gerhard E., 106, 149, 153–59, 161, 168, 223, 394
and agrarian systems and inequality, 393
cross-societal comparisons of societies, 105
evolutionary stages, 15, 17, 18, 21–22, 31, 38, 41–42
and variations in inequality, 155
and wealth and power theory, 155–59, 161, 182
Leontieff, Wassily, 430
Lesbesque's integrals, 508
Lévi-Strauss, Claude, 74, 81, 288
and exchange theory, 415–16, 418, 424
and French Structuralism, 301–303, 305–308, 310
and genetic code, 309–310, 316, 335
and kinship theory, 309–11, 315–16, 338
and marriage politics, 421
and short and long cycles, 421, 423, 427
and structural dynamics theory, 421
and tribal kinship as exchange, 411, 416, 421, 423, 447
and tribal societies, 18, 19
Lewin, Roger, 34
Lewis, J. D., 268
Lieberson, Stanley, 500
Limited-cognition
model, 289
strategy, 287
Lin, Nan, 427
Lind, Joan, 38
Lindenberg, Siegwart, 352–54, 356
Line authority, 439
Linear
interaction vs. complex, 473–76, 485–86, 490
relationships, 157–58
Linguistics, 307, 315, 319
theory of, 6, 248, 306–307, 310, 335

Linton, Ralph, 14, 15, 17, 64, 74
Lipset, Seymour Martin, 25, 39, 428, 506
Local frame of reference, 345
Localistic groups, 218
Locke, John, 188
Logarithmic relationship, 157–58, 160, 162
Looking-glass self, 231–32, 237
Luckmann, Thomas, 264, 276, 383, 385–86
Luhman, Niklas, 22, 53, 57, 67, 69–71, 76
Lukacs, Georg, 102
Lumsden, Charles, 32–33
Lynch, Michael, 280
Lynd, Helen, 150

Macfarlane, Alan, 503
MacKenzie, Donald A., 498
Macro-micro levels of analysis, 2
Macro
    outcomes of exchange links, 4
    perspectives of revolutions, 143
    -rituals, 197
    structure, 376, 402
    theories, 2, 2–5, 54
Macrocults, 218
Macroeconomics, 429–30
Macrosociologist, 390
Macrosociology, 79, 299, 316, 392–93
    attack on, 375–76, 378–81
Maine, Henry Sumner, 12, 14–15
Male
    dominated military state, 167
    -female status-group, 164
    military monoply, 168–69
    -stereotyped jobs, 173
Malinowski, Bronislaw, 18, 236, 339, 420, 422
Management
    controls, 465
    styles, 466
Mann, Michael, 132, 386, 442
Mao Zedong, 139, 393, 439
Many-to-one mapping, 412
March, James G., 286, 356
    and control theory, 455
    and garbage-can model, 466–67
    and organization power, 452
    and rationality, bounded, 430
Marchland states, 135–36, 143
Marcuse, Herbert, 101, 103–104, 115
Marginal utility principle, 341, 344

Maritime societies, 15, 18
Market
    dynamics, 447
    economy model, 432–34, 447
    exchange theory, 355, 412
    model, 431–33
    opportunity, 337, 358–60, 362, 365, 371, 402
    theory, 412, 430–35
    utilitarian, 420
Markets
    and hierarchies theory, 411, 429–31
    as interlinkages, 424
    as mutually monitoring producers cliques, 411, 432–35
    and networks, 412
Marriage
    alliances, 305–306
    bargaining, 183
    exchange, 421–23, 447
    and friendship markets, 411, 422–24, 435
    markets, 172–73, 338, 359, 416, 422–24, 447
    politics, 169–73, 183, 421
    rules, 422
Marsden, Peter V., 414
Marsh, Robert M., 506
Marshall, Alfred, 73
Marx, Karl, 3, 72–73, 80
    and alienation of species, 450
    and class conflict, 151–52
    and deterministic model, 80
    mechanical system, 80
    and micro-macro theory, 450
Marx, Karl, and Engels, Friedrich
    and evolutionary stages, 15–17, 38, 41, 81, 87, 90
    and intellectual production, 224
    and macro structure of society, 376
    model of class conflict and control of state, 89–90, 95, 97, 113–15
    model of means of mental production, 103
    model of political mobilization, 128
    and political power of the masses, 439, 450
    primitive communism society, 15–17, 20–21
    theory of class interests, 130
    theory of socialism, 15, 22
Marxian
    alienation theory, 452
    capitalism theory, 459
    class conflict, 119, 124–25, 142, 151
    class relationships, 346

critique of capitalism, 106
definition of class, 125
economic model, 106–107
market model, 431–32
model, basic, 77, 79–93, 114
model and capitalism, 77, 79–92
model of capitalist crises and revolution, 516–17
model, reality of, 517
paradigm, 105
stage model, 17, 22, 36–37, 41, 53
state theory, 77, 107–13, 435
system, computer simulation of, 81, 90, 92
system, criticisms and revisions of, 77, 91–93
tradition in sociology, 78
version of capitalism, 431
world-system theory, 17, 30, 36–37, 99
Marxian theory, 145
    and class and power divisions, 125–26
    and false consciousness, 125
    modification of, 92
    simulation of, 516
    and workers, 465–66
Marxism, 79, 465
    and French Structuralism, 302–303, 307–309
    Hegelian, 103–105, 115
    orthodox, 100
    as philosophy, 77, 101–107
    as political movement, 78
    and profit and growth, 82–84
    revisions in, 3
    revival of, 494
    structuralist, 105–109, 142
Marxists
    and socialism, 126
    theory and fiscal crisis of the state, 459
Mass
    media as ritual procedure, 134
    production and mass-assembly, 469, 471, 479, 488, 490
Material rewards, principle of, 452–53, 489
Mathematical
    formulation of theory, 505
    models, 495, 513–14
    problems, 514
    sociology, 7, 493–95, 510
    symbols, 509
    theories, 494–95, 497
    and words, 493, 507–11
Matrilateral cross-cousin marriage, 421
Matrilineal inheritance, 167
Matrilocal systems, 166–167

Mauss, Marcel, 188, 253, 305
  and alliance theory, 338
  and gift exchange systems, 411,
    415–16, 418–21, 423–24,
    447
Maximal connected subgraphs,
  414
Mayo, Elton, 340
Mazur, Alan, 388
McClelland, Kent, 202
McNeill, William, 504
McPhail, Clark, 268
McPherson, J. Miller, 427
Mead, George Herbert, 1, 6, 317,
  380
  Generalized Other theory, 247–
    48, 261
  "I," "me," and the Generalized
    Other, 230, 232–35, 244–
    49, 257, 260, 268–69, 272–
    73, 298, 329
  and pragmatism, 267
  and shared symbols, 328
  and social self, 230, 235, 237,
    257, 266
  and symbolic interaction, 417
  and theories of social self and
    mind, 377
  thinking as internalized con-
    versation theory, 243–49
Measurement model, 498
Mechanical
  feedback system, 47–48, 53, 75
  solidarity, 14–15, 64, 200–
    201, 221, 227
  system and Marx, 80
Mechanisms of control, 100
Mechanistic or dumb systems, 45,
  47–48
Mehan, Hugh, 382
Membership rituals, 415
Men and exploitative relationships with women, 170
Mental
  health problems, 261
  illness, 251, 255, 270
Merleau-Ponty, Maurice, 275
Merton, Robert K., 57
  and definitional perspective,
    272
  and functional analysis, 378
  and role strain, 236–37
  and self-fulfilling prophecy, 265
Meso theory, 6, 7
  and network analysis, 7
  and organizational analysis, 7
Metacommunication, 333–34
Methodological-quantitative and
  theoretical-qualitative, 494
Meyer, Marshall, 462, 480
Michels, Robert, 129, 290, 450,
  460, 487

Micro
  attack on macrosociology, 373,
    376–78
  attack on symbolic interaction-
    isms and social phenomenol-
    ogy, 373, 378–382
  reduction, 375, 394–97
  theory, 2–7, 126, 446
  translating power and prop-
    erty, 402–407
Micro-based theory of class cultures, 388
Micro-interactional theory, 503
Micro-macro
  connection, 118, 257, 375–
    409, 450
  continuum, 396, 408
  controversy, 6–7
  dispute, 377
  and human agency, 393
  issue, 343, 357, 375, 384–85,
    409, 412
  levels of analysis, 385, 388–89,
    393, 417, 446
  linkages, theories of, 375, 398–
    407
  nature of, 375, 385–97, 449,
    473–76
  phenomena, border between,
    6
  question, history of, 375–85
  relationship between, 6
  theory, 448
Microeconomics and macroeconomics, 429
Microsociology, 3, 366, 505
  and empirical reality, 375, 391–
    93, 409
  and macrosociology ideology
    and reification, 392–93
  and segregation of society,
    232
Middle-aged family neighborhoods, 154
Middletown, Robert, 150
Militaristic
  regimes, 225
  societies, 30, 38–39
Military
  core, 132
  dictatorship, 436
  threat, 182
Miller, James G., 50, 53
Mills, C. Wright, 68
Mind
  and language, 164, 397
  as internalized conversation
    theory, 230
  theory, 377
Minorities and self-esteem, 232
Mirror stage, 231
Mobility, 506

rates theory, 426–29, 447
  theory, 428
Mobilization variables, 92
Modern
  mass armies, 133
  social exchange theory, 422
  status system, 411, 422–24,
    435
  world-system theory, 17
Modes of production, 108
Money, John, 234
Monocephalic organization, 444–
  45
Monopolizing legitimate force,
  132
Monopoly, 86, 88–89, 91–92,
    99, 108–109, 114, 132, 173
  and market models, 431–32
  of occupations, 173
  over ritual attention, 439, 448
  sector of capitalist society, 110–
    13, 115
  unilateral, 346, 347
  and violence, 131–32, 146, 155
Montesquieu, Charles, Baron de,
  139
Moore, Barrington, 138, 146–47,
  386, 394
Moore-Skocpol theory, 153
Moral
  entrepreneurs, 271
  solidarity theory, 19, 187–202,
    224
Morality, principles of, 189–91
Morgan, David L., 287
Morphophonemic rules of grammar, 314
Morris, Ivan, 171, 225
Motivation
  of organizational members,
    465
  and organization theory, 449,
    464, 465
Multidimensional
  action theory, 72–74, 76
  conflict theory, 74, 119, 127
  stratification theory, 149–50,
    153
Multilevelled
  sign theory, 307, 335
  sociology of science, 298
Multiple
  causality and stratification,
    218–21
  realities, 264, 291–93, 298
  status characteristics, 240
Munch, Richard, 57
Murphy, Robert F., 432
Mutually monitoring niche-seekers, 434, 435
Mythologiques, 306
Mythical cliques, 306

Nagel, Ernst, 377
National power structures, 443–47
Nationalism, 88
and conflict, 120
Nationalist sense of legitimacy, 133
Natural
attitude, 279, 283, 285, 289, 291, 296–97, 299
language, 311–12
realities, 382
rituals, 187, 193, 197–99, *198*, 201–204, 214, 216, 226–27, 248, 284, 294, 298, 358, 371
thinking, 279, 283, 291
world complexity and historicity of, 511–12
Natural selection, 26, *29*
models, 13, 42
theories, 11, 13, 29–35, 41, 56
Nazi government, 25, 56
Negative feedback, *50*, 51, 75
Negatively connected network, 435–36
Negotiation, 362
Neo-Durkheimian
class cultures theory, 208
ritual model, 194, 201, 226
Neo-Freudian Theory, 164, 376
Neo-rationalist strategy, 286
Neoclassical economy theory, 50
Neolocal households, *168*
Nepotism, 237
Network
analysis, 7, 343, 411–414, 416, 426, 432, 435, 447
cohesive, 447
communications, 89
conversations, 407
decentralized power, 440–41
dimension social density and diversity, 214–18, 228
ego's 413–14, 426
and exchange, 397, 447
negatively connected, 435–36
positively connected, 435–36, 448
power theory, 444–45
structures, varieties of, 411, 414–15, 443
support, 417
Network theories, 74, 131, 411–48
and cohesion, 411, 416–17, 447
and economic theory, 411, 429–35
effects on action and belief, 411, 416–18

and exchange theory, 415, 418
and market theory, 412
and power, 411, 416, 435–47
and social mobility, 418
and social ties, 411, 418–29
and structural equivalence, 411, 417–18
what it explains, 411, 415–16
Networks of social interaction and inner conversations, 250
New social realism, 77, 101, 106–107
Nisbet, Robert, 412
Nominal power, 439, 448
Non-Marxian theory of conflict, 118, 139
Nonconformity, 216
Nonlocal political, 183
Nonverbal
communication, 321
expressive cues, 241, 260
signs, 246, 247
Norm
of equal exchange, 397
of rationality, 458
of reciprocity, 344, 365, 370, 419, 420
Normative
constraints on interaction, 4
control, 463–64, 466, 477, 478, 487–89, 491
power, 459
solidarity, 488
Nuclear war, 40, 122

Oberschall, Anthony, 137
Objectivity
and relativism, 263, 291–97
and undeceptiveness of appearances, 275, 299
Occupation and self, 230, 237
Occupational
attainment genetic explanation, 174–75
groups, 212–14
monopoly, 173
O'Connor, James, 77, 110–113, 115, 459
Offering accounts and common-sense reasoning, 282–83
Ogston, W. D., 202
Oligopolies, 91, 111
On-the-job training, 176–77, 183
One-dimensional man, 104
OPEC, 151
Open
and closed systems, 45, 47–49
-edness of words, 510
systems theory, 45, 49

Operant conditioning, 400
Opportunity, inequality of, 155, 183
Order-giving rituals, principle of, 211–16, 218–19, 221, 223, 225–28, 259, 362, 435, 453–55, 465–66
Orders of causality, 498
Ordinary reality, 275
Organic
analogy of society, 25, 26
solidarity, 14–15, 64, 200–201, 221, 227
Organic differentiation model, 22, 41
Organic differentiation theory, 11, 13, 22–29, 31, 35, 37, 39, 41–43
causes of, 26–27
criticisms, 11, 25–29
functional upgrading, 11, 23–25
and inequality, 28–29
and integration, 27–28
and natural selection mechanism, 26
and need for integration, 11, 24–25
and sequencing, 27
and size, 26–27
specialization, 11, 23–25, 27–29
and strains and lags, 11, 24–25
and world history, 40
Organization
control theory. *See* Control theory
counter-coalitions, 439
model, 349, 450
monocephalic, 444–45
pooled production, 479
power, 405, 452, 457
process production, 479
size, 472
socialism, 487
specialist, 481–82
unit production, 468–69, 490
and warfare, 168–69
Organization structure theory, 443–46, 451, 468, 473–76, 478–89, 485–86
complex vs. linear interaction, 473–76, 485–86, 490
tight vs. loose coupling, 473–76, 485–86, 490–91
Organization theory, 7, 131, 286, 299, 394, 445–47, 450, 452–53, 505
approaches in, 449, 451
and class conflict, 449, 464–66

and decision making, 449, 464, 466–67
and motivation, 449, 464–65
and resource dependency, 449, 480–81
Organizational
analysis, 451
boundaries, 449, 482–85
coupling, 473–76, 48
culture, 449, 464, 466
environments, 481
framing, 294
group formation and control theory, 452
hierarchy and macro coordination of micro activities, 449, 473–76
members, 465
politics, 175–76, 478
power, 405, 452, 457
research, 450
structure, 444, 449, 467–80, 490–91
studies, observation-based, 505
theory and capitalist and socialist systems, 451
Organizations, 449–91
and alienation, 455, 457
behavior in, 464–67
coercive, 454, 459–60, 463, 477
confederated, 444–45
conflict, 459
and divisionalization, 472–73
and environments, 449, 450, 480–91
existence and control resources, 449, 458–60
functionalist perspective on, 461
generalists and specialists, 481–82
mass production and mass assembly, 469, 471, 479, 488, 490
micro-macro connection, 550
permanently failing, 462
population ecology of, 449, 481–82, 490
professions in, 483–84
rules and written orders, 456–57, 461, 489
and sociological theory, 449–51
women's, 427
Organized crime, 71
Oriental despotism, 15, 17, 21
Ouichi, William G., 466
Out-of-frame activity, 263, 293
Over-reflexive loops and mental health problems, 261

Overcognitive theory, weakness of, 263, 286–88
Overexpansion and disintegration of states, 136
Overproduction, 84–85, 112–13
Overt conflict, 126–28, 145

Paige, Jeffery, 141, 170, 222, 505
Pappi, Franz U., 412, 443
Pareto, Vilfredo, 2, 12, 73, 339, 376–77
Paris Commune of 1871, 129
Parkin, Frank, 431–32
Parsonian
functionalism, 343
theory, reviving, 494, 512
Parsons, Talcott, 1, 2, 380, 494
action theory, 377–78
analytical system, 2
conceptual scheme, 339
criticism of system, 70–72
and democracy, 55
differentiation model, 66–67, 71
evolutionary stages, 12, 15, 17, 20, 71
four-function model, 45, 57–61, 67, 74, 79
functionalist action system, 45, 56–72, 109–10
General Theory of Action, 58, 60
hierarchy of control, 45, 61, 64, 75
law as analytical device, 494, 512
multidimensional model, 78
and organic differentiation theory, 22–27, 31, 35, 37, 39, 41–43
and pattern variables, 64–66
precontractual solidarity theory, 62
social norms, 189
social system theory, 46, 50, 276, 399
socialization and deviance, 62–64
student movements, 25
and structuralism, 398
two theories of social change, 66–67, 73
variables of specificity and diffuseness, 236
Particularism vs. universalism, 64–65
Parties as power groups, 152–54
Pastoral societies, 167
Patriarchal domination, 165

Patrilocal systems, 166–67
Patrilineal inheritance, 167
Patrilineal kinship, 341
Patrimonial societies, 155, 225
Peasants, 139–41, 146–47
and rebellion, 142–43
Peirce, Charles Sanders, 243–44, 248, 267
Performance expectations, 239, 345
Performatives, 318
Periodic economic crises, 84–91, 114
Peripheral
areas and world economy, 95–96, 100–101, 114
states, 135, 146
Perrow, Charles, 446, 451, 464, 468, 473–76, 478–79, 485–86
Personal friendship networks, 496
Peters, Thomas J., 466
Petty deference rituals, 455
Pfeffer, Jeffrey, 464, 481
Phenomenology. See Social phenomenology
Physical reductionist, 321
Piaget, Jean, 36, 329
Platonic philosophy, 5
Platt, Gerald M., 25
Play and entertainment and reframings, 294–95
Pluralist theory, 123–24, 130, 145
Pluralistic ignorance, 439
Polarized structures, 443–44
Political
change, 130, 501
economy, 3, 77–115
groups, 150–54
mobilization, 88–91, 107, 128
parties, charismatic movement in, 467
power, 412, 431, 439, 450, 485
revolutions, 142
scandals, 197
systems, profit and growth, 82–85
tactics and ethnomethodology, 289
Political theory, 117, 131–35, 146, 160, 355, 443
and legitimacy, 131–34
of sexual stratification, 168–71, 183
and territory, 131, 134
and violence, 131–32
Politics
model, 514
organizational, 175–76, 478

Polysemic codes, 308
Pooled production, 470–12, 490
  organization, 479
Population
  ecology theory, 449, 481–82,
    488
  explosion model, 51, 53
Positional property, 478
Population ecology of organizations, 449, 481–82, 490
Positive feedback, 50–51, 75
Positivist philosophy, 318
Positivistic accounts of science,
  102, 380
Possession vs. ownership, 108
Potlatches, 420–22
Poulantzas, Nicos, 106, 108–10,
  115, 302–303
Power, 393, 403
  and alienation, 456, 459
  balances of, 135
  brokers, 411, 435–36, 447
  and class division, 125–26, 145
  coercive, 299, 458–59
  cross-classifying, 228
  dependency, 338
  and dictatorship, 403
  distribution of, 157, 160–61,
    168, 182, 444
  dynamics in democracy, 445,
    448
  and exchange theory, 337,
    343–49, 435, 441–42
  explanatory, 11, 20, 21
  fragmented, 439–40, 448
  groups, 152–54, 182
  hierarchies, 414
  and Mao Zedong, 139, 393,
    439
  and network theory, 411, 416,
    435–47
  nominal, 439, 448
  normative, 459
  and organizations, 405, 452,
    457
  and prestige, 146, 160, 182,
    240, 242
  and property and cultural cap-
    ital, 406, 409
  and revolutions, 403
  and stage theory, 11, 20–21
  and strong centralized, 439–40
  structures, community, 412,
    443
  structures, national, 443–47
  theory, 3, 155–59, 161, 182,
    344, 347, 412, 435, 446,
    452
  vertical dimension, 209–11,
    218
Powerless, alienation of, 455

Powers, Charles, 511–12
Practicality and goal-directed-
  ness, 275, 299
Pragmatism, 267
Prague School of Linguistics, 305
Praxis philosophy, 78–80, 102,
  104
Precalculative solidarity, 189
Precontractual solidarity, 344, 419
  theory of, 45, 61–63, 65, 119,
    188–89, 305, 344, 419–20
Prendergast, Christopher, 377
Presentation of self, 325
Presentational rituals, 252
Prestige
  and status groups, 161–63
  theory, 161, 182
Presumably universal processes of
  everyday reasoning, 280
Primary frameworks, 300
Primitive communism, 16
Principle
  of anticipatory socialization,
    213, 218–19, 227, 453
  burden of proof, 240
  bureaucracy, 456
  bureaucratic personality, 213–
    14, 228, 454
  class culture, 453
  coercion, 452–53
  determinitive, 273
  games of chance, 497
  internalized control, 453, 458,
    489
  marginal utility, 341, 344
  material rewards, 452–53, 489
  morality, 189–91
  of order-giving rituals, 211–16,
    218–19, 221, 223, 225–28,
    259, 362, 435, 453–55, 465,
    466
  of ritual coercion, 213, 216,
    226–27, 453
  social density, 214–17, 219–
    21, 223, 225–26, 228, 397,
    454
  of social diversity, 215–21,
    223–25, 228, 454
  social phenomenology, 69, 275,
    295, 327, 377, 383–84
  surveillance, 455–56, 489
  symbolic interactionist, 366
  task uncertainty, 473
Prior concepts, 281
Privacy, 195, 215, 225, 238,
  252–53
Probability theory, 499–502
Process
  continuous-flow production,
    470–71, 490
  of interpretation, 269

production organization, 479
Professions as organizations, 483–
  84
Profit and growth in political sys-
  tems, 82–85
Progress
  in evolutionary theory, 11–13,
    38–41
  theories, 13
Proletariat, 86–87, 91, 99
  dictatorship of, 109
Promotion possibilities, 453
Property
  conflicts over, 124
  importance of and control the-
    ory, 449, 460–62
  micro-translation of, 404–405
Psychoanalysis, 37, 42, 62
Psychoanalytical symptoms, 310
Psychological reductionism, 375–
  82, 408
Psychology vs. sociology, 390
Public schools, emergence of, 24
Punctuated equilibrium model,
  33–34, 42
Pure mobility, 506

Quasi-groups and conflict theory, 127–28, 132, 145
Quetelet, and demographic patterns, 497

Racial supremicist regimes, 225
Radcliffe-Brown, Arthur R., 179,
  203, 339
Ramirez, Francisco O., 133
Ranking among groups, 163
Rational choice, 337, 350–57
  and exchange models, 375,
    400–401, 409
  theory, 337, 343, 352–57, 361,
    371, 401, 409
Rationality proposition, 351–52,
  371
Real mobility, 507
Reality
  construction models, 233, 397
  of the physical world, 267
  and principles of social phe-
    nomenology, 383
  social construction of, 263–300
Reciprocal obligations, 421, 423
Reciprocity
  norm of, 344, 365, 370, 419–
    20
  of perspectives, 275, 299
Recursive language structure, 313

Reductionism, 375, 389–97, 408
  conclusions on, 396–97
  debate over, 384–85
  and micro processes, 394–97
Reflected self, 231
Reflexive, 266
  consciousness, 273, 299
  frame breaking, 326
  model, 330
Reflexivity and indexicality, 278–88, 296–97, 299, 316, 321, 510
Reframing, 294–95, 298
Reinforce individual resources, 337, 362–65
Relationship
  conversational, 343
  informality in, 225
  rituals, 208
Relative deprivation, 129, 145
Relativism and objectivity, 263, 291–97
Relaxed frame space, 295
Religion, 34, 40, 42, 67, 88, 102, 253
  and genetic element, 18–19, 31–32
  industrial society, 19
  and morality, 190–91
  primitive societies, 18
  as ritual, 188–92, 195, 199, 250
  and sacred objects, 189–93, 196
  theory, 376
  and tribal societies, 216, 423
  and universalism, 66
Religious
  divisions, 123
  group and status group, 152
  party, 153
  societies, 121
  symbol model, 218, 227–28
  taboos, 64
Remunerative control, 460, 463–64, 489–91
Repressive desublimation, 104
Republican party, 109
Resolving the transference, 258
Resource
  dependency and organization theory, 449, 480–81
  mobilization theory, 3, 124, 128, 137–38, 146
Retirement communities, 154
Revolutionary
  challenge, 439–40, 448
  model and geopolitical, 144
  movements and riots, studies of, 25, 129, 137

Revolutions, 117, 138–44, 146–47, 487, 503, 505
  ancient times, 144
  and capitalist crises, 516–17
  Chinese, 141
  democratic, 128, 254
  and distribution of power, 157
  evolutionary model, 138–39
  macro perspective of, 143
  peasant, 142–43
  and power, 403
  sexual, 172
  social, 142
  socialist, 93
  study of, 386
  theory, 3, 5, 138, 146
  types of, 142
  when and how they take place, 5, 34, 78, 86–88, 90–94, 100, 102–103, 105, 109–10, 120, 133
  and world systems, 143
Rewards
  and control theory, 449, 452
  and punishments, 191–92, 380, 408
  types of, 346–47
Rexroat, Cynthia, 268
Rhythmic
  entrainment, 203
  synchronization, evidence of, 201–203, 227
Ridgeway, Cecilia, 241
Riots, violent, 129
Ritual
  attention and monopoly, 439, 448
  avoidance, 252
  code, 251
  coercion, principle of and order-giving rituals, 213, 216, 226–27, 453
  completion, 333
  control, 455
  cooperation, 251
  cultures and historical typology, 223–25, 228, 254
  density, 188, 201, 272–73, 417, 450
  and everyday interaction, 206–208
  exchange, 416, 418–19
  formal model of, 192–97, 216, 332
  interactions, 337, 342, 357–58
  model, 203–205, 214, 216, 227–28, 294, 310, 326
  natural, 187, 193, 197–99, 198, 201–204, 214, 216, 226–27, 248, 284, 294, 298, 358, 371

  order-giving, 211–16, 218–19, 221, 223, 225–28, 259, 362, 435, 453–55, 465–66
  participation, 454
  procedure and school system, 134
  religion as, 189–92
  repair, 322–23, 332–33
  rewards vs. secular rewards, 192
  solidarity, 329, 365, 459
Ritual theory, 357, 365, 397–98, 404, 438
  of class cultures, 208–25
  and the conflict theory of stratification, 188
Ritually based violence, 196–97, 226–27
Rituals, 188, 195, 197–99, 203, 223, 225, 259, 284, 332, 487
  and collective reality, 250
  and conflict theory, 199
  conversational, 206–209, 226–27, 321–24, 332, 357–58, 364, 402, 406, 424
  criminal punishment, 194, 196–97
  elements of, 193–97
  and framing, 294
  gift exchanges, 411, 415–16, 418–20, 423–24, 447
  and group membership, 357–58, 454
  intentional, 187, 197–99, 198, 201
  vs. natural, 198
  interaction, 62, 203–208, 230, 250, 285, 297, 304, 334, 370, 453
  judicial trials, 196–97
  membership, 417
  petty deference, 455
  political speeches, 193, 195, 197, 199
  presentational, 252
  private vs. public, 195
  relationship, 208
  religious ceremonies, 188–92, 195, 199, 250
  sexual, 170
  social, 119
  in tribal societies, 189, 197, 222–23, 253
Ritualization of the collectivity, 225
Robots, and computers, 181–82
Role, 234, 235, 238, 287
  distance, 255–56
  identification, 237–38, 255–56, 281, 287

Role (*continued*)
learning vs. role making, 238–39
sets, 236, 260
socialization, 238
strain model, 236–37, 260
taking, social action as, 235–36, 260
theory, 233–34, 236, 238, 256, 268
Roles, 239, 270, 327
complementarity of, 234–35
conception of, 287
gender, 234–35, 238, 260
horizontally related, 236
institutionalized, 347–48
performance in, 239–40
and selves, 264
and social interaction theory, 235
Rosenbert, Morris, 230–32, 255, 258
Rossi, Peter, 345
Rousseau, 188
Routinization, examples of, 460
Rubin, Lillian, 215
Rueschemeyer, Dietrich, 27, 42
Rules
of grammar, 314
and written orders and organizations, 456–57, 461, 489
Ruling class, 89–90
Russell, Bertrand, 508–10
Russell, Diana, and enforcement coalition, 437

S-shaped curve, 51
Sacks, Harvey, 315, 319–20
Sacks, Nancy, 165
Sacred
object, 189–93, 196, 214, 227, 230, 250–56, 259, 304, 326, 357, 397, 420, 438
and the secular, 189–90
Sahlins, Marshall, 420
Sanday, Peggy Reeves, 165
Sapir, Edward, 310, 313, 316
Sartre, Jean-Paul, 105, 257, 275
Saussure, Ferdinand de, 248, 301–308, 310
Savage, Leonard J., 498
Scapegoats, 121, 197, 222
Schachter, Stanley, 416
Scheff, Thomas, 270, 388
Schegloff, Emanuel A., 287, 319–20, 384, 396–97
Schelling, Thomas C., 36, 386, 403, 436–37, 439
Schneider, Herbert W., 267

School
reforms, 133
system as ritual procedure, 134
Schools of thought, 1
Schumpeter, Joseph A., 431–34, 467
Schur, Edwin M., 271
Schutz, Alfred, 275–76, 279, 283, 291, 299, 377, 383–84
Schott, Marvin B., 247, 282, 453, 455
Searle, John, 318, 324
Seed-bed societies, 15, 17, 21, 31
Self, 230–32, 250, 255–59, 261, 296, 328
and christianity, 253
-conception, 261
and conflict theory, 259
as conventional motivator, 327
divided, 257
-esteem, 232, 260
-expectation, 240
-fulfilling prophecy, 265
-interaction, 269
-limitation of conflict, 122–23
and mental illness studies, 251, 255
multiple or unitary, 255–59
as myth, 230, 256–58
presentation of, 325
-reflection, 258
-referential systems and consciousness, 45, 51–53, *52*, 57, 69, 75
as a sacred object, 230, 250–56
social, 229–35, 237, 257, 266, 377
stage-director, 259
-talk, 322–23
totem, 250
Selves
and gender, 230–31, 238, 260
and occupation, 230, 237
and physical traits, 231, 260
and roles, 264
and social position, 230, 237, 260
Semantics, 243, *314*
Seminal theory, 138
Semiotics, 301–302, 307–309, 335
Semiperiphery areas and world economy, 95–96, 101, 114
Sequencing
model, 330
organic differentiation theory, 27
technologies, 18
Serfdom societies, 21
Sewell, William H., 428

Sex
inequality, 164
-role segregation and capitalist system, 165
stratification, 3, 163–73
Sexual
assault, 166, 170–72
inequality, 23–24, 28–29, 164–65, 450
oppression, 105
politics and alliances, 168–72
politics theory, 168–71
property, 169, 171
revolution, 172
rituals and political alliances, 170
standard, dual, 171
stereotypes, 62, 70
stratification and political theory, 168–71, 183
stratification and the private marriage market, 172–73
stratification theory, *164*–68, 171–73
stratification and tribal societies, 165–67, 169, 173, 183
Shared symbols, 328
Short and long cycles, 421, 423, 427
Shubik, Martin, 430
Sign
theory, 307–308
value, 307
Signs
communicative, 307–308
multileveled theory, 307, 335
system of, 304, 309, 335
universal, 245–47, 260, 267
Simmel, Georg, 12, 119–124, 127, 130, 134, 145
Simmel-Coser pluralist or gridlock theory, 123–24, 130, 145
Simon, Herbert A., 286, 299, 356, 430, 450, 452, 455, 457
Simple societies, 15–16, 20
Simulating theories, 493, 515–16
Simulation
and empirical data, 493, 515–16
model, 218, 493, 518
Sinecure society, 180, 478
Situational
expectations, personality as, 240
interactions, 38
reductionism vs. psychological reductionism, 381–82, 408
Situationalism and social construction of reality, 264
Situationalist theory, 263–73, 298

Size
  causes differential theory, 26–27
  and organizational structures, 449, 472–73
Skill requirements of jobs, 174–78, 183
Skinner, B. F., 342, 347, 379, 380, 400
Skocpol, Theda, 110, 113, 138, 141–44, 147, 437, 503, 505
Slater, Philip, 239
Slavery, 15, 17, 21, 100
Smelser, Neil J., 24–25
Smith, Adam, 343
Smith, Anthony D., 241
Smith, R., 268
Smith-Lovin, Lynn, 427
Social
  action and artificial intelligence, 514
  action theory, 377
  behaviorism and rational choice, 337, 350–57
  change, 117–47, 290–91, 407
  change theory, 66–67, 73, 428, 446
  class, 88–91, 150, 217, 219, 226
  constructionism, 263–300
  control, 374
  density, 214–20, 226, 228, 296, 417
  density, principle of, 214–17, 219–21, 223, 225–26, 228, 397, 454
  density theory, 417
  distance space, 415
  diversity, principle of, 215–21, 223–25, 228, 454
  ecology of language, 301, 318, 320–30, 335
  exchange and related theories, 337–71
  exchange theory, 214, 422
  formation, *108,* 303
  inequality and density, 223–25
  integration, 57–61, 67, 74, 75, 120–21
  integration theory, 424–25
  interaction theory as playing roles, 235
  mentalities, 309
  mobility, 154, 163, 391, 418, 496, 505
  mobility theory, 25, 83, 411, 416, 425–29
  order and change, 263, 289–91
  order, stratified, 299
  phenomenology, 4, 57, 69,

263, 274–76, 295, 299, 327, 375, 377, 380–84, 494
  ranking, 358
  reality and Thomas theorem, 265, 299
  revolution, 142
  rituals, 119
  roles, 270, 397
  self, 230, 235, 237, 257, 266
  self theory, 229–34, 377
  system theory, 46, 50, 276, 399, 446
  ties, 411, 418–29
Socialism, 15, 22, 147, 467
  in China, 91, 98
  and class and power, 125, 126
  in Cuba, 91, 98
  as organization, 487
  and superorganizations, 449, 485–89, 491, 516
  vs. capitalism, 118
Socialist
  capitalist states, mixed, 488
  government, 139–40
  revolution, 93
  societies, 21, 35, 41, 78, 80, 91, 108, 112, 125, 139, 157, 347
  world government, 98
Socialization
  and deviance, 45, 62–64
  and pre-selection, 453
Socially constructed expectations, 240
Socioanalysis, 237
Sociobiology, 12, 32–34, 42
Sociolinguistics, 4, 5
  and structuralism, 301–35
Sociological
  analysis, 386–89, 396, 407, 409
  models, 432
  reformulation of economics, 411, 431–32
Sociological theory, 302, 431–32, 447, 465
  of business, 416, 434
  and computer simulation, 493, 511–18
  of language, 53, 301, 317–20
  organizations in, 449–51
Sociology
  of mind and language, 164, 397
  of thinking, 243–50
  vs. psychology, 390
Sokoloff, Natalie J., 165
Sorel, Georges, 129, 134
Soul theory, 250
Spanish, Margaret T., 287
Specialists organizations, 481–82
Speech act theory, 301, 317–19,

324–26, 331, 334–35, 399, 510
Spencer, Herbert, 29, 41, 47
  evolutionary stages, 12, 15–17, 19, 38
  and macro structure of society, 374
  and organic differentiation theory, 22–23, 27
  and simple societies, 15–16, 20
  synthetic philosophy, 41, 47
Spitze, Glenna, 165–66
Stability and change, 5
Stage
  -director self, 259
  identities and conversation, 226
  models, 11, 18–20
Stage theories, 11, 13–22, 40–41
  and evolutionary theory, 11, 13–22
  and explanatory power, 11, 20–21
  number of stages, 11, 16
  similarity of, 11, 14–15
  single-factor vs. multi-factor patterns, 11, 18–20
  and unilineal development, 11, 16
  and world history, 40
Staging, 334
Stalin, 439
State
  model, 113
  sector of capitalist society, 111–13, 115
  socialism, 147
  structures, kinds of, 131
  theory, Marxian, 77, 107–13, 435
Static-comparative theory, 131
Statistical
  research methods, 494–95
  sociology, 380–82, 388
  test theory, 498
  testing, 500
Statistics, 493, 494, 498, 502
  and mathematical modeling, 513
  and mathematical theory, 497
  and mathematics, 494–95
  method or theory, 493, 496–511
  subjective approach, 498
  as substance, 493, 505–507
  theory, 497
  and theory testing, 493, 499–501
Status
  attainment, 425–26

Status (*continued*)
competition and credential inflation, 178–83
groups, 150, 152–54, 161–63, 182
ranking among groups, 154
system, 3, 394–95, 411, 422–24, 435
Steiner, Gary A., 212
Stewman, Shelby, 429
Stinchcombe, Arthur, 45, 55, 75, 135–37, 400
and geopolitical theory
Stock of commonsense knowledge, 275–76, 299
Strains and lags concept, 11, 24–25, 41
Stratification
educational credential, 174–82
and expectations states, 241–42
and functionalist theory, 348–49
model, 153–55, 162, 168, 182, 226
sex and gender, 163–73
and social change theory, 428
social order, 299
and socialist societies, 125
systems, 5
two dimensions on, 209–10
Stratification theory, 131, 149, *150*–84, 355, 446
and gender, 165–68, 170, 172–73
multidimensional, 149–50
Strength of weak ties theory, 426–27
Strong centralized power, 439–40
Structural
changes in economy, 496
dependence and power brokers, 411, 435–36, 447
dynamics theory, 421
equivalence and network theory, 411, 417–18
exchange theory, 411, 415, 418, 447
mobility, 506
networks, 411, 415–15, 443
organization theory, 449, 468–72, 476, 478–79
sociology, 377, 378
Structural theory
of action, 407, 417–18
of intergroup integration, 416, 424–25, 427
Structuralism, 4–5, 398
and computer-simulated theory, 512
and sociolinguistics, 301–35
See also French Structuralism

Structuralist
exchange theory, 338
Marxism, 105–109, 142
and post-structuralist theory, 301, 309–11
model, 314, 335, 375, 398–99, 409
terminology, 302–303
theorists, 105–10
Structurally equivalent positions, 447
Structuration theory, 288, 314, 335
Structurationism, 106, 115
Structure
centralized, 443–44, 448
and change, 515
coercive, 436–42, 448
and control, 449, 476–78, 490
decentralized domain, 445
polarized, 443–44
of positions, 447
of social action, 2, 12, 73
synchronic, 303, 335
Student movements, 25
Sudnow, David, 301, 327–30, 335
Sui generis, 25–26, 376, 408
Super-feedback loop, 52
Superego, 63, 378
Superorganization, 449, 451, 473, 484–85
and capitalism and socialism, 449, 485–89, 491, 516
and interorganizational relations, 449, 484–85
Supply and demand, 82, 84, 96
Support network, 417
Surface structure of language, 335
Surplus value, 82, 84, 102, 107, 114
Surveillance
and alienation, 455–56
control, 455–56, 463, 489–90
principle of, 455–56, 489
Survey research, 381–82, 384, 388, 408, 413
Survival of fittest, *29*, 42
Swanson, Guy E., 195
Symbolic
-emotional exchanges, 416
ideals, 463, 464
system, 510
Symbolic interactionism, 4–6, 57, 232–33, 235, 255, 263–64, 266–71, 291, 298, 417, 512
Blumer's vs. Mead, 267–70
and ethnomethodology, 263, 295–97
and social phenomenology, 375, 380–84
Symbolic interactionist

principle, 366
role theory, 286–88, 291, 296–97
theory, 271, 377, 380–81, 388–89, 408
Symbolism
commodity, 434
and expressing the shape of relationships, 508
models using, 508
theory, 222, 338
Symbols, 328
mathematical, 509
universalizing, 267
verbal, 334
words, 508–11
Synchronic structures, 303, 335
Synchronization, 202–203
Syntax, 312, *314*, 316
Synthetic philosophy, 47
System
accidents, 446, 473–76, 486–87, 490–91
performance, upgrading of, 23, 24
theory, *2*, 3, 64–65, 107
Systems, *46*, 47
Szymanski, Albert, 100

Tacit coordination, 403
game, 437
Taken-for-granted social life, 299
Taking the role of the other, 235
Tarde's theory of imitation, 304
Task
technology and organizational structure, 468–72, 490
uncertainty principle, 473
Tasks
and coercion, 463, 490
and control forms theory, 449, 462–64, 484, 490
Taxation, 112
Taylor, Howard, 174
Technological innovation, 84–85
Territorial resource advantage, 135, 143
Theoretical
logic in sociology, 73
multidimensionality and cumulation, 514–15
Theory, 1, 7, *8*, 493–518
action, 377–78, 398
alienation, 452
alliance, 338
capitalism, 459
class, 397
class culture, 201, 208, 465
class interests, 130
Theory
coalition, 442

coercive, 442
coercive coalitions, 437–40
compliance, 452–53, 455, 462
computer simulation, 511–18
conflict, *3,* 57, 62, 72, *118,* 124–30, 137, 145, 259, 338, 446, 450, 458. *See also* Conflict theory
contingency, 468, 478–79
control, 449–66, 476, 478–79, 484, 488, 490
conversation, 243–49
creative redefinition, 272–73
culture, 131
dependency, 93, 100
deprivation, 128–29, 137, 146
deviance, 271, 374
dialectical materialist, 81
differentiation, 26–27
distribution of wealth, 3, 155–59
dynamic, 131
economic conflict, 355
economic market, 432
economics, 354, 411, 413, 429–35, 447
emotion, 210
evolutionary, *2,* 20, 33, 34, 46, 482
exchange, 6, 242, 305, 337–40, 343–50, 352, 356, 359, 365–66, 370–71, 400–401, 412–13, 415, 418–21, 435–36, 441–42, 446, 465
expectation states, 239–42, 260, 345
fiscal crises, 77, 110–13, 115
Freudian, 37, 62, 63, 71, 105, 249, 257, 308, 378
functionalists, 45, 54–55, 56–73, 109–10, 118, 348–49
fundamental, 3
game, 403, 436–37
gender stratification, 165–68, 170, 172, 183
general, 301, 330–35, 493, 502–505
general systems, 45–54, 72
General Theory of Action, 58, 60
Generalized Other, 230, 235, 244–48, 257, 260–61, 417
geopolitical, 117, 135–37, 141–43, 146–47
graph, 414
grid-lock, 123–24, 130, 145
group culture, 210–11
hierarchies, 430–31
"I," "me," and the Generalized Other, 230, 232–35, 244–49, 257, 260, 268–69, 272–73, 298, 329

idealist, 36–38, 41
ideological hegemony, 102–103
imitation, 304
inequality, 3, 183
instrumentalist, 107
interaction ritual, 6, 187–28, 271, 296, 304, 325, 329, 334
interaction ritual chains, 250, 258, 273, 286, 337, 339, 357–66, 371, 402, 418, 426, 435, 465
Theory
intergroup integration, 411, 424–25, 447
kinship, 309–11, 315–16, 338
labelling, 258, 270–72
language, 314–15, 330–35
linguistic, 6, 248, 306–307, 310, 335
market, 412, 432–35
market-exchange, 355, 412
markets and hierarchies, 411, 429–31
Marxian, 17, 30, 36–37, 77, 92, 99, 107–13, 125–26, 145, 435, 459, 465–66, 516
mathematical, 493, 495
meso, 6, 7
micro, 2–7, 126, 446
micro-interactional, 505
micro-macro, 3, 375, 398–407, 450
mind, 377
mobility, 426–29, 447
modern world system, 17
moral solidarity, 19, 187–202, 224
multidimensional action, 72–74, 76
multidimensional conflict theory, 74, 119, 127
multidimensional stratification, 149–50
multileveled, of signs, 307, 335
natural selection, 11, 13, 29–35, 40–41, 43, 56
neo-Freudian, 164, 376
neoclassical economy, 50
network, 74, 131, 411–48
non-Marxian of conflict, 118, 139
open systems, 45, 49
organic differentiation, 11, 13, 22–29, 31, 35, 37, 39–43
organization, 7, 131, 286, 299, 392, 445–47, 449–53, 464–67, 505
organization structure, 443–47, 451, 468, 473–76, 478–79, 485–86, 490–91

overcognitive, 263, 286–88
Parsonian, 494, 512
pluralist, 123–24, 130, 145
political, 131–34, 168–71, 183, 355, 443
population ecology, 449, 481–82, 490
post-structuralist, 301, 309–11
power, 3, 155–59, 161, 182, 344, 347, 412, 435, 446, 452
precontractual solidarity, 45, 61–63, 65, 119, 188–89, 305, 344, 419–20
prestige, 161, 182
probability, 497, 499–502
progress, 13
rational choice, 337, 343, 352–57, 361, 371, 401, 409
religion, 376
resource mobilization, 3, 124, 128, 137–38, 146
revolutions, 3, 5, 138, 146
ritual, 188, 208–25, 357, 365, 395–96, 404, 438
ritual density, 272–73
role, 233–34, 236, 238, 256, 268
seminal, 138
sexual politics, 168–71
sexual stratification, *164–68,* 172–73
sign, 307–308
simulating, 493, 515–16
situationalist, 263–73, 298
social action, 375
social change, 66, 67, 73, 428, 446
social density, 417
social exchange, 214
social integration, 424–25
social mobility, 25, 183, 411, 416, 425–29
social role, 397
social self, 229–34, 377
social system, 46, 50, 276, 399, 446
sociological, 53, 301–302, 317–20, 431–32, 434, 447, 449–51, 465, 493, 511–18
soul, 250
speech act, 301, 317–19, 324–26, 331, 334–35, 399, 510
stage, 11–22, 40–41
static-comparative, 131
statistics, 498
stratification, 131, 149, *150–84,* 355, 446
structural, 407, 411, 415–18, 421, 424–25, 427, 447, 449, 468–72, 476
structuration, 288, 314, 335

Theory (*continued*)
  symbolic interactionist, 271, 286–88, 291, 296, 297, 377, 380–81, 388–89, 408
  symbolism, 222, 338
  system, *2*, 3, 64, 65, 107
  Thomas, 265–70, 272, 298–99
  two-dimensional stratification, 209–25, 227
  universalization, 254
  urbanization, 412
  verbal, 7, 335, 494–95, 510–11
  weak ties, 426–27, 447
  wealth and power, 155–59, 161, 182
  world of chance, 493, 505–507
  world system, 17, 30, 36–37, 77–78, 93–101, 107, 113–15, 136, 156, 290, 511
Thinking, sociology of, 243–50
Thomas, Keith, 121
Thomas theorem, 265–70, 272, 298–99
Thomas, William I., 265, 380
Thompson, E. P., 103
Thompson, James D., 449, 458, 468–72, 476
Thought as internalized conversation, 243, 248–50, 260
Threat
  and coercion, 349, 448
  emotions of, 216, 226–27
  external, 160–62, 182, 444
  military, 182
  of punishment, 436
Thurow, Lester C., 430
Tight versus loose coupling and organization structure theory, 473–76, 485–86, 490–91
Tilly, Charles, 129, 137
Time and space, 386–89, 396, 407, 409
Tipping phenomenon, 403, 437
Tocqueville, Alex de, 139
Toennies, Ferdinand, 12, 14, 15, 17, 19, 64, 74, 376
Totalitarian party regimes, 225
Totality concepts, 104
Totemic cult, 191
Totems and self, 250
Trade unions, 88, 90, 138, 140
Traditional
  positivist philosophy, 318
  society, 345
Transcendental idealism, 386
Transformational grammar model, 301, 312–14, 316–17, 319–20, 325, 329, 331–32
Transformation
  of consciousness, 102

and frame analysis, 292, 293, 300
  frames and human society, 263, 293–95
Transfunctionalization, 308
Transmitted class effects, 219
Tribal
  kinship as exchange, 411, 416, 421, 423, 447
  myths, 306, 309–10
  shaman, 308
Tribal societies, 15–21, 23–24, 27, 30, 35, 38, 64, 67, 95, 225, 290, 305, 310, 339, 359, 386, 399, 412, 421, 428, 440, 459
  exchanges in, 416, 418–19
  and marriage alliances, 305–306
  and the occult, 218
  and patrilineal kinship, 341
  religions in, 216, 423
  rituals, 189, 197, 222–23, 253
  and sexual inequality, 165
  and sexual stratification, 165–67, 169, 173, 183
  taboos, 215, 218
  and war, 120, 419
Trotsky, 93
Turn-taking model, 301, 319–20, 323–24, 335
Turner, Jonathan, 54, 237, 287, 349, 377
  and evolutionary stage theories, 16
  and multidimensional stratification theory, 149, 153
  and power distribution theory, 444
Turner, Ralph
  composite model of stratification, 162
  the distribution of prestige theory, 161, 182
  equation for social mobility, 163
  models using symbolism, 508
  propositions, 157, 159–63
  and role identification, 237–38, 255–56, 281, 287
  six-dimensional model of stratification, 153–55, 168, 182
  theory of conditions for macro distribution of power, 435
Tversky, Amos, 286
Twins, studies of, 174
Two-dimensional stratification theory, 209–25, 227
Two dimensions of class cultures, 220–21
Typifications, 275, 299

Under norms of rationality, 458
Underconsumption, 112–113
Unemployment, 84–85, 88–89, 91, 97, 113
Unilateral monopoly, 346–47
Unilineal development, 16
Unit production
  model, 468
  organizations, 468–69, 478, 480, 490
United States
  education studies, 174, 177–78, 182
  population growth, 27
Universal
  code of the human mind, 309
  signs, 245–47, 260, 267
Universalism, 64–67
Universalization theory, 254
Universalizing symbols, 267
Upgrading of system performance, 23–24
Useem, Michael, 107
USSR and education, 178
Utilitarian markets, 420

Vacancy chain model, 426, 428
Validity of statistical analysis, 505
Value integration, 119
Variable capital, 85
Verbal
  formulation of a theory, 513
  formulation vs. statistical and mathematical technique, 7
  interaction theory, 335
  language, 508–10
  statements, 513–14
  symbols, 334
  theory, 7, 494–95, 510–11
Vertical dimension of power, 209–11, 218
Victorian role for women, 171–73
Violence
  as legitimate force, 132, 146
  and monopoly, 131–32, 146, 155
  ritually based, 196–97, 226–27
Violent
  conflict, 128–29, 145
  threat, 216, 226–27, 265
Von Bertalanffy, Ludwig, 47, 50, 52–53
Vrba, Elizabeth, 33

Wagner, 239–40
Waiting for clarification, 282
Wallace, Walter L., 4

Waller, Willard, 338, 422
Wallerstein, Immanuel, 502
    and capitalism, 99
    and economic development,
        503
    study of capitalist world sys-
        tem, 386
    world system theory, 78, 93–
        101, 113–14, 136, 156, 290,
        511
Wanner, Eric, 329
War, 127, 134, 144
    in China, 127
    and conflict, 120, 122–23
    nuclear, 40, 122
    and tribal societies, 120, 417
    See also Revolution
Ward, 12
Warfare
    organization of, 168–69
    and world system, 93–95
Warkov, S., 472
Warner, W. Lloyd, 150, 339
Warren, Carol A. B., 270
Weak ties theory, 426–27, 447
Wealth
    distribution of, 3, 155–59
    and power, 155–59, 161–62,
        166, 182
Weber, Max, 1, 2, 12, 17, 20, 42,
        66–67, 72–73, 108–109,
        223, 276, 394
    capitalism theory, 28, 100
    and charisma, 460
    class model, 151–52, 182
    closure model, 432
    and coercive organizations, 459
    dimensions of power, class and
        status, 452
    examples of routinization, 460
    "house of power," 153
    iron cage of bureaucracy, 467
    market model, 431
    organization theory, 450
    political theory, 117, 131–35,
        146, 160

social action theory, 377
sociological theory, 431–32,
    447
state model, 113
three-dimensional model of
    political groups, 150–54
and world history, 504
Weberian status group organiza-
    tion, 208, 218
Webster, Murray J., 240
Welfare state, 92, 107
Wellman, Barry, 412–13
Western society, 253
White-collar crime, 63
White, Harrison C., 414
    and market economy model,
        432–34, 447
    and market theory, 432–35
    and marriage politics, 421
    and mutually monitoring niche-
        seekers, 434–35
    and network theory, 416
    and vacancy chain model, 426,
        428
White lies, 252
Whitehead, Alfred North, 508–
    509
Whitley, Richard, 298
Whyte, William F., 342, 416
Wilensky, Harald L., 452, 457,
    483–84
Wiley, Norbert F., 151, 254, 266
Wilken, Paul M., 400–401
Willer, David, 442
Williamson, Oliver, 430–31
Wilson, E. O., 32–34
Witch-hunting, 222
Wittgenstein, Ludwig, 4, 5, 317,
    318, 332, 334, 510
Women and sexual assault, 166,
    170–72
Women's
    economic power, 165–66, 183
    movements, 183
    organizations, 427
Wood, Huston, 384

Woodward, Joan, 449, 468–72,
    476, 478–79, 488, 490
Woolgar, Steve, 280, 468
Words, 493–94, 510
    and mathematics, 493, 507–11
    and symbols, 508–11
Work or practical situations, 332
Workers, 139–40
Working-class party, 152
World of chance theory, 493,
    505–507
World economy
    and core states, 95–98, 100,
        114–15
    and periphery areas, 95–96,
        100–101, 114
    and semiperiphery areas, 95–
        96, 101, 114
    and states and areas, 95–96
    vs. world empire, 77, 93–95,
        114
World history, 40, 504
    language, 37–38
    and stages, 16, 40
World system, 98, 386, 511–12
    cycles of, 77, 96–98, 114–15
    model, 136
    and revolutions, 143
    and warfare, 93–95
World system theory, 17, 77, 78,
    93–101, 107, 113–14, 136,
    156, 290, 511
    and capitalism, 93–94, 98–99,
        114–15
    criticism of, 77, 99–101
    Marxian, 17, 30, 36–37, 99
    Wallerstein's, 78, 93–101,
        113–14, 136, 156, 290, 511
World War II, 127
Wright, Erik Olin, 465
Wylie, R., 232

Znaniecki, Florian, 266–67, 378